Advance Praise for *How Wiki...*

"This book was created by Wikip   ter
summary of how Wikipedia work   e of
the Internet should buy this book
—Jimmy "Jimbo" Wales, founder

"To write every day is good advice   ...very day is even better. This
book shows how your casual scholarship and the Wikipedia community work
together so that you can be read tomorrow."
—Ward Cunningham, creator of the wiki

"Frank, helpful, honest, endlessly informative—this book embodies the best of
Wikipedia's values."
—David Weinberger, author of *Everything Is Miscellaneous*, coauthor of *The
Cluetrain Manifesto*

"This wonderful book resolves Wikipedia's paradox: Anyone can edit it, but to
make your edits stick, you need to know what you are doing. Editing Wikipedia
means navigating a minefield of implicit norms, tacit knowledge, secret lore, suggested policies, and enforceable regulations."
—Barry Wellman, director of Netlab, University of Toronto

"As Wikipedia has grown, its processes, policies, systems, and tools have become
inscrutable to many existing and would-be editors. *How Wikipedia Works* provides
an accessible window onto these processes and thoughtful tour through the maze
of Wikipedia policy pages. It's the thoughtful, comprehensive, and freely licensed
manual that I've been waiting years for. Wikipedia would be much improved if
every Wikipedia editor, new and old, were given a copy."
—Benjamin Mako Hill, free software activist, hacker, and scholar

HOW WIKIPEDIA WORKS

And How You Can Be a Part of It

Phoebe Ayers, Charles Matthews, *and* Ben Yates

11 10 09 08   1 2 3 4 5 6 7 8 9

ISBN-13: 978-1-59327-176-3
ISBN-10: 1-59327-176-X

FIBER USED IN THIS PRODUCT LINE MEETS THE SOURCING REQUIREMENTS OF THE SFI PROGRAM
WWW.SFIPROGRAM.ORG

Publisher: William Pollock
Production Editor: Megan Dunchak
Cover and Interior Design: Octopod Studios
Developmental Editor: Tyler Ortman
Copyeditor: LeeAnn Pickrell
Compositor: Riley Hoffman
Proofreader: Rachel Kai

For information on book distributors or translations, please contact No Starch Press, Inc. directly:

No Starch Press, Inc.
555 De Haro Street, Suite 250, San Francisco, CA 94107
phone: 415.863.9900; fax: 415.863.9950; info@nostarch.com; http://www.nostarch.com/

Library of Congress Cataloging-in-Publication Data

Ayers, Phoebe.
  How Wikipedia works : and how you can be a part of it / Phoebe Ayers, Charles Matthews, and Ben Yates.
     p. cm.
  ISBN-13: 978-1-59327-176-3
  ISBN-10: 1-59327-176-X
 1. Wikipedia--Handbooks, manuals, etc. 2. Wikipedia. 3. User-generated content. 4. Electronic
encyclopedias. 5. Social media. I. Matthews, Charles, 1954- II. Yates, Ben. III. Title.
  AE1.5.A98 2008
  030.285--dc22

                              2008023350

Dedication

For John and Sally Ayers, who taught me to always look things up [PSA]

For my wife Clare, in recognition for her support over many years [CRM]

For Susan Shore and Matthew Cobbs [BLY]

Acknowledgments

Special thanks to:

Bill Pollock for supporting a Wikipedia book and a free license, Tyler Ortman for his patience and hundreds of suggestions, Megan Dunchak for her care with the manuscript, Riley Hoffman for layout, and the entire No Starch staff for their support; Samuel Klein for helping develop this book and for teaching Phoebe how Wikipedia (should) work; Benjamin Mako Hill for providing technical support, advice on free culture and licensing, and writing about free software; our reviewers (any mistakes are entirely our own): John Glover, Corprew Reed, Diane Schiano, and Richard Stallman; Eben Moglen for advice on the GFDL; the contributors to *http://en.wikipedia.org/wiki/User:Phoebe/book*: AaronSw, Sj, Clayoquot, Peterblaise, MER-C, Graham87, Jeandré du Toit, Llywrch, BanyanTree, and Kim Bruning; and our many friends who offered advice and support, especially James Forrester, Austin Hair, Lauren Manes, Sasha Wait, and Sarah Wait Zaranek.

And thanks to the thousands of dedicated Wikipedians who make Wikipedia, and this project, possible.

"It is probable that the idea of an encyclopaedia may undergo very considerable extension and elaboration in the near future. Its full possibilities have still to be realized. . . . There is no practical obstacle whatever now to the creation of an efficient index to all human knowledge, ideas and achievements, to the creation, that is, of a complete planetary memory for all mankind."

—H.G. Wells, 1937, *World Brain*

Brief Contents

Contents in Detail

Part III: Community

Part IV: Other Projects

Introduction

Welcome! Wikipedia, the free encyclopedia, is the largest and most popular reference website in the world. Wikipedia is also unique: This encyclopedia is written by everyone and can be read by anyone.

This book is written for readers, current editors, potential contributors, and anyone else interested in Wikipedia. The book describes what kind of writing Wikipedia includes, how Wikipedia works behind the scenes, and how to get involved.

We cover all aspects of participating in Wikipedia, from reading the site to editing articles to navigating the site's community and governance.

Wikipedia is based on a *wiki*, a technology that allows anyone to change pages easily on the site. If you're impatient to work on Wikipedia, go to *http://en.wikipedia.org/* and start improving the encyclopedia right now!

If you learn most quickly by diving right in, or if you already edit Wikipedia, then you can use this book as a reference guide and a source of tips. But if you're just starting out, or if you want to know everything about how Wikipedia works today and how it has developed over time, you should start reading from the beginning.

Inside This Book

This book is divided into four parts, starting with the basics and working through all aspects of Wikipedia.

Part I looks at Wikipedia from the reader's point of view. Chapter 1 describes the type of content Wikipedia contains and the basic policies that determine what content is included. The site's history is explored in Chapter 2; in particular, we look at the way that Wikipedia unites three historical strands: encyclopedias, wikis, and free software. How to search and browse the site (including an explanation of the sidebar and main page) is detailed in Chapter 3, and Chapter 4 covers the structure of an individual article and methods for evaluating article quality.

Part II turns to editing the site. A basic explanation of how to edit a page and an introduction to *wikisyntax* are in Chapter 5; this chapter forms the foundation for the next chapters in this part. Chapter 6 covers how to start a new article and explores encyclopedic writing, research, and collaboration techniques that are useful for working on any article. Formal processes for maintaining content, including collaborative editing drives and cleanup projects, WikiProjects, and article deletion and promotion processes are covered in Chapter 7. Chapter 8 explains how articles are linked together through Wikipedia's category structure, disambiguation pages, and redirects, along with how pages are maintained through merging, splitting, and moving. More advanced syntax, including image formatting, tables, templates, and special characters, is covered in Chapter 9. Chapter 10 steps through the life cycle of a newly created article.

Part III covers Wikipedia's elaborate social side. We begin with how to sign up as an editor, including setting up an account, setting preferences, and using your personal user and talk pages in Chapter 11, in which we also describe Wikipedia's administrator system. Wikipedia's culture and the ways editors communicate (including a list of forums for asking questions and discussing problems) are covered in Chapter 12, and the policies that govern Wikipedia and how these policies are created are described in Chapter 13. Finally, Chapter 14 discusses how the dispute resolution process works—and how to avoid disagreement in the first place.

Part IV steps back from the English-language Wikipedia to cover other Wikimedia Foundation projects, including editions of Wikipedia in other languages in Chapter 15 and Wikipedia's sister projects, including Wikimedia Commons,

Wiktionary, Wikinews, Wikibooks, Wikiquote, Wikisource, Wikispecies, and Wikiversity, in Chapter 16. Finally, we cover the Wikimedia Foundation (Wikipedia's parent organization) and how work at the Foundation level is coordinated in Chapter 17.

Appendix A includes information about reusing Wikipedia's content under the terms of the GNU Free Documentation License and examples of reuse (the GFDL itself, under which this book is licensed, is included starting on page 491). We provide a brief guide for teachers using Wikipedia in the classroom in Appendix B; Appendix C contains a glossary of jargon commonly used in edit summaries; Appendix D has a glossary of jargon frequently used on the site; and, finally, Appendix E is an index of Wikipedia pages quoted in the book.

The basic principles we describe for reading articles, editing pages, and collaborating with others will provide a good foundation for working on any Wikimedia wiki project. But although the Wikimedia projects all share the same general philosophy, any specific policy or custom mentioned here might not apply outside the English-language Wikipedia. If you're interested in exploring another project, remember that each wiki website represents a unique collaborative community, which may have its own rules.

What You Should Know Going In

You don't need any prior experience with wikis or any knowledge of programming to use this book. But you should know how to access web pages on the Internet in the following ways:

▶ Clicking a link with a mouse

▶ Typing a page address (URL) directly into your browser

You should also know how to search the Web using Google or another search engine and have an active email account.

All references in this book to Wikipedia's interface assume that you're using a standard web browser on a personal computer, have logged into the English-language Wikipedia, and are using the default (Monobook) skin without modifications. If you use Wikipedia without logging in, not all tabs and sidebar links will display, but most other functions should be the same.

If you intend to view Wikipedia on a mobile phone or personal digital assistant (PDA), visit *http://en.wap.wikipedia.org/*. This official mobile version was introduced in mid-2007; see [[Wikipedia:WAP access]] for unofficial versions.

Using This Book

Wikipedia is always changing. It's a dynamic collection of web pages in constant motion, so although we've made this book as current as possible, specific details may have changed by the time you read these words. For this reason, we frequently reference pages on Wikipedia.

Within the main text, Wikipedia page names are enclosed in double brackets like this: [[Help:Editing]]. You can go to that page on Wikipedia by typing one of the following:

▶ The title *Help:Editing* into the Wikipedia search box (do not insert a space after the colon)

▶ The URL of the page directly into your browser's address bar, for example, typing *http://en.wikipedia.org/wiki/Help:Editing*

✳ **NOTE:** *All English-language Wikipedia URLs begin with* http://en.wikipedia.org/ wiki/, *and the page name in double brackets always refers to the last part of the URL. So [[The Great Gatsby]] refers to* http://en.wikipedia.org/wiki/The_Great_ Gatsby.

Spaces are automatically translated to underscores in the full URL; you do not need to type them in.

For certain community and policy pages, we provide shortcuts that are prefaced with *WP*. Wikipedia contributors often use these shortcut abbreviations as shorthand in their discussions, for instance:

```
[[Wikipedia:How to edit a page]], shortcut WP:EDIT
```

Type the shortcut into the Wikipedia search box to go the longer page title listed.

At the end of each section, we list the most important pages referred to. Here you can easily access the links on a given topic, which also serves as a reference if you're a more experienced Wikipedian. Every Wikipedia page that we quote directly is listed in Appendix E.

Our Approach to Understanding Wikipedia

Most of the technical information we give is also available on Wikipedia's help and project pages, though these pages are not always neatly organized. In writing this book, we have tried to use our own experience to explain (and condense) a selection of the thousands and thousands of available pages of documentation. We spend time on spelling out unwritten customs and pointing out the implications of the most basic policies for a new editor to give a view of Wikipedia and how it actually works.

Although we attempt to express consensus views about how Wikipedia operates, the views represented in this book are solely those of the authors. They are not necessarily shared by other editors (including those quoted) or the Wikimedia Foundation. Wikipedia is now *enormous*, and every editor's experience on the site will be different. What you encounter as you work on Wikipedia may well vary from what we describe. The authors of this book have a combined 11 years' experience working on Wikipedia and over 150,000 edits, but we have still only directly experienced a portion of the site. In this book, we mostly talk about the common ground: general principles that should apply across the project.

Making absolute, definitive statements about Wikipedia is tricky. Even basic policies may be changed—tomorrow's Wikipedia may be different. Adaptability and change are, in fact, hallmarks of the project. All the same, much of the project setup, on its constitutional and policy side, seems to be relatively settled and understood across the editing community; and after seven years of existence, Wikipedia has a certain maturity. We have tried to be as accurate as possible at the moment of publication, but if you want more definite information, always refer to the live pages on the site itself.

It's Everyone's Encyclopedia: Be Bold!

As you read this book, any time you're curious about a point, we very much encourage you to follow up by exploring and editing the live site at the same time. Wikipedia is open and welcoming to newcomers who make positive contributions, and you should be able to make a good start armed with the information we give.

Be bold is an old saying on the site. Be bold means that Wikipedia editors should update or change the encyclopedia whenever they see a problem and shouldn't feel inhibited by the editing process, which is forgiving. As you learn about Wikipedia, we encourage you to *be bold* in improving the site, and we hope you find it as exciting as we do.

If you want to get started right away and are unfamiliar with wiki editing, here are the basic concepts for how Wikipedia works:

Open and instantaneous editing Wikipedia does not require that you register for an account to edit or create articles. Anyone who has a web browser and an Internet connection can add to or change content on the site. All changes are made instantaneously and are immediately visible online. (See Chapter 5.)

A full record of edits Wikipedia keeps a complete record of all changes that are made to any page. This *page history* is viewable by everyone. Each time a page is changed, a new version is saved, but the old versions are not lost. (See Chapter 4.)

Special editing syntax All content written on Wikipedia is formatted using a markup language, or *wikisyntax*. This special language is considerably easier to learn than HTML, the source language of web pages. (See Chapters 5, 8, and 9.)

Linked pages All pages on Wikipedia are linked to other Wikipedia pages to form a web of *hypertext* or interlinked pages. (See Chapters 3 and 8.)

Multimedia content Wikipedia has hundreds of thousands of images, sounds, and videos. (See Chapters 9 and 16.)

Content standards   Wikipedia doesn't take everything; all articles must be encyclopedic, neutral, and verifiable. (See Chapters 1 and 6.)

Content up for discussion   Each wiki page and article has an associated discussion or talk page. Interested editors can discuss any changes to an article. (See Chapters 4 and 12.)

Incremental improvements to articles   You may see warning or cleanup messages on articles as you browse; these alert you to problems and let other editors know that work needs to be done to that article. Wikipedia is a work in progress. (See Chapters 4 and 7.)

Collaborative decision-making   Decisions are made through discussion and achieving consensus and through processes in which anyone can take part. Disputes are resolved the same way. (See Chapters 7, 12, 13, and 14.)

Community   A dedicated and complex volunteer community is behind Wikipedia, developing content, policies, and practices. Interactions with other editors should be civil and productive. (See Chapters 2, 11, 12, and 13.)

Not just the English-language Wikipedia   Wikipedias exist in many languages, and several other wiki reference projects with different types of content are all part of the Wikimedia Foundation. (See Chapters 15, 16, and 17.)

Totally free   All Wikipedia content is free to use and access; anyone is free to contribute; and all of the site's content is released under a free license, which means anyone may reuse it elsewhere. Wikipedia is a noncommercial project and has no advertisements. (See Chapters 1, 2, and Appendix A.)

Everyone can contribute to Wikipedia. This is possible because Wikipedia is a wiki: Simply click Edit This Page at the top of an article and start writing. Here's a syntax cheatsheet to get you started. Happy editing!

Wikisyntax Cheatsheet

Wiki Syntax	Result
''italic''	*italic*
'''bold'''	**bold**
'''''bold and italic'''''	***bold and italic***
==heading== ===level 2=== ====level 3==== =====level 4=====	Section headings in different sizes
[[article title]]	Internal link to another article on the wiki (links to pages that don't exist will show up in red)
[[article title|*description*]]	Internal link with *description*
[[Wikipedia:Help|Help pages]]	Internal link to Wikipedia namespace page with description
http://www.example.org	External link
[http://www.example.org *description*]	External link with *description*
----	Horizontal line
* one * two * three	Bulleted list: ▶ one ▶ two ▶ three
# one # two # three	Numbered list: 1. one 2. two 3. three
<nowiki>Ignore wiki formatting; displays [[syntax]] as entered </nowiki>	Ignore wiki formatting; displays [[syntax]] as entered
<s>struck text</s>	~~struck text~~
~~	User signature with timestamp (date and time); for use on discussion pages only
<code>computer code</code>	Produces `code formatting`
[[Image:File.jpg|*Text*]]	Image with alternate *Text*
[[Image:File.jpg|thumb|*Caption*]]	Thumbnail image with *Caption*
[[Image:wiki.png|thumb|right|*Caption*]]	Thumbnail image aligned right, with *Caption*

Wiki Syntax	Result
[[Image:wiki.png|thumb|right|300px|*Caption*]]	Thumbnail image aligned right, 300 pixels wide, with *Caption*
[[Media:*File.ogg*]]	Link to audio file named *File.ogg*
{{Cleanup}}	Include Cleanup template in a page (see [[Template:Cleanup]] for template text)
{{Cleanup|date=*June 2008*}}	Cleanup template with date parameter
[[fr:Page en français]]	Interwiki link to the French-language Wikipedia (appears under *Languages* on the left-hand sidebar)
[[Category:*Example*]]	When placed on an article, will add article to category *Example*
[[:Category:*Example*]]	Link directly to *Category:Example* without categorizing the page
#REDIRECT [[*Other article*]]	Redirect one page title to another page
<ref>*Reference goes here*</ref> within the article text	The <ref> tag for producing footnotes
<references/>	Place this tag where you want footnotes to appear, typically under ==References==
√(1−''e''²)	HTML-formatted math: $\sqrt{(1-e^2)}$
$\sqrt{1-e^2}$	TeX-formatted math: $\sqrt{1-e^2}$
<!-- hidden comment in wikitext -->	Produces hidden comment in wikitext, only visible to other editors

## PART I

Content

1 What's in Wikipedia?

Wikipedia is big. You just won't believe how vastly, hugely, mind-bogglingly big it is. Even if you only read the titles of Wikipedia articles, it would take you most of a month, without a break, to scan all of them. If you tried the same with Microsoft Encarta, or any traditional encyclopedia, you could be done in about a day, with time left over to eat, shower, and take yourself to bed. Reading the *full* content of Wikipedia would take you well over two years, if you read continuously—and then you would have to start over, as most of the pages would have changed in the meantime.

There are well over two million articles in Wikipedia. And the site is still growing at an enormous rate, so this total will doubtless be much higher when you read this than it is as we write it (see Figure 1-1). By early 2008, the English-language Wikipedia was estimated to consist of over 960,000,000 words, which is equivalent to over 1,700 copies of *War and Peace* (itself about 560,000 words long in a standard English translation).[1] On average, another 20 to 40 million words were being added each month, or 35 to 70 more copies of *War and Peace*—or one copy every 12 hours, all day, every day, continuously.

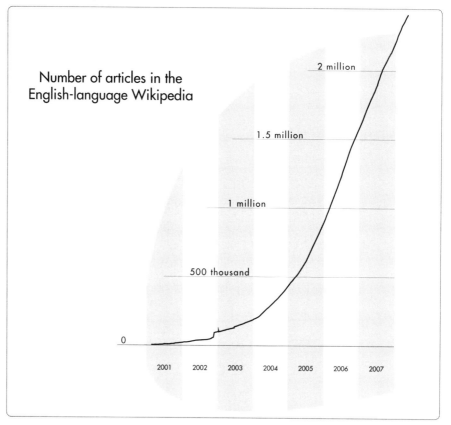

FIGURE 1-1: *Wikipedia's growth over time*

This enormous growth has been occurring since Wikipedia began. Some more statistics show that the site has grown most rapidly since 2005, as Wikipedia's mainstream popularity took off:

▶   The site launched on January 15, 2001.

▶   It ballooned to 250,000 articles by April 2004, on the English-language site alone.

▶   It passed 500,000 English-language articles in March 2005.

---

[1] This figure is based on size estimations at *http://en.wikipedia.org/wiki/Wikipedia:Size_in_volumes*, which also notes that Wikipedia is equivalent to 725 volumes of *Encyclopaedia Britannica*.

- A year later, on March 1, 2006, the English-language Wikipedia surpassed the 1,000,000-article milestone.

- By late 2006, there were over 1.5 million English-language articles, with around 1,700 new articles being added each day.

- The article total surpassed 2,000,000 in September 2007.

- By August 2008, there were over 2,500,000 articles. At this point, articles were being created at a rate of 10,000 articles per week.

During this same period, Wikipedias in other languages were also experiencing tremendous growth; see Chapter 15 for more on these projects.

Wikipedia has never had a target number of articles; any contribution is kept in the encyclopedia as long as it meets Wikipedia's standards. The average Wikipedia article is still quite short, say 500 words, but articles also tend to grow over time.

With well over two million articles in the English-language Wikipedia, topics include almost everything imaginable: from detailed explanations of basic science topics to equally detailed expositions of episodes of popular television shows. There are articles on railway locomotives, programming languages, people of all types, abstract concepts, and cities and towns all around the world. Finding out what's in Wikipedia is one of the great joys of exploring the site.

This first chapter will offer an introduction to the encyclopedia through the following approaches:

- Describing the content found in Wikipedia. (If you're overwhelmed by Wikipedia's labyrinthine setup, Chapter 3 will discuss good ways to navigate around the site and explain how to find content by searching and browsing.)

- Explaining the types of content the encyclopedia aims to include by outlining the criteria for topic inclusion, the style in which topics are covered, and other content policies. Once you understand something about the

---

What Is an Article?

An *article*, in this context, is defined as a Wikipedia page that contains encyclopedic information. Technically, the article count only measures pages of content that are not dead ends (which means they contain at least one internal link leading to another Wikipedia article) and are not *redirects* (pages that simply automatically take you to another article). The article count also ignores a great variety of other types of pages that are not devoted to content (administrative, internal, image description, and community pages, all described in detail in "Non-article Content" on page 25). Counting all these other pages brought the total Wikipedia page count to over 13,000,000 by mid-2008.

policies and guidelines that govern content, you can start to get a feel for Wikipedia's *house style*—the telling details that indicate whether an article has been worked on by good editors. (Chapter 4 will explain in greater detail how to evaluate an article's quality.)

▶ Summarizing the parts of Wikipedia that do not consist of encyclopedia articles and explaining how to tell the difference between articles and other types of pages.

The basic information in this chapter will provide the foundation for understanding how to edit Wikipedia, described in Part II, and how to participate in the site's community, described in Part III.

Wikipedia covers every topic found in general encyclopedias, specialist encyclopedias, and almanacs, along with many topics not covered in any of these traditional references. This is possible in part because Wikipedia is not constrained by the economics of traditional publishing; it does not need to pay writers or spend money on paper. (Wikipedia is instead constrained by the judgment of its volunteers: It does not accept just *any* article. Several inclusion policies are enforced.)

* **NOTE:** *The ultimate purpose of Wikipedia's community is to create and improve articles and to distribute them freely.*

Milestones

There has always been interest in Wikipedia's *milestones*—the moments at which the number of Wikipedia articles surpasses certain round numbers. Friendly betting pools developed around guessing the milestone date for a half-million and then a million articles. At this writing, the five million and ten million article betting pools are open for guessing the exact date when Wikipedia will reach these milestones. (The prize is widespread recognition of your remarkable guessing skills.) See [[Wikipedia:Pools]].

The actual millionth article, created on March 1, 2006, was [[Jordanhill (railway station)]], an article about a railway station in Scotland. Hundreds of people counted down on the IRC channel and the wiki to see which of a flurry of new articles would be the one millionth article. Many editors waited anxiously for the opportunity to post; over one hundred articles were contributed during the same second. There was even major media coverage of the event; see *http://wikimediafoundation.org/wiki/Press_releases/English_ Wikipedia_Publishes_Millionth_Article*. The two millionth article was created on September 9, 2007. Amid some confusion, the article [[El Hormiguero]], about a Spanish TV comedy, was identified as probably being the two millionth article.

Articles vary widely in length, detail, and comprehensiveness. Most of Wikipedia's articles begin their lives as *stubs* (very short summaries) and are gradually built into more comprehensive treatments by several editors. Stubs are incomplete—by definition, they lack something vital—but they are often useful and well written. Approximately 70 percent of Wikipedia articles are still classified as stubs.

The remaining 30 percent of articles (perhaps numbering over half a million) are more in-depth, comprehensive treatments of a subject. These may rival or go beyond the best work in traditional encyclopedias. A high-quality article includes numerous sources and references, pictures or diagrams, and a complete and clear explanation of the topic.

Types of Articles

Are you wondering how Wikipedia found enough topics to fill two million articles? Here are some (but by no means all) of the types of content that are included:

Traditional encyclopedia topics
You can find all the types of content that you might expect from a general encyclopedia such as *Encyclopaedia Britannica*. Articles about science, historical events, geography, the arts, and literature are all included.

People
No occupations or groups are restricted or emphasized, although in order to qualify for an article, the person must be *notable*, that is, well known within his or her major field of endeavor. Once this criterion is met, you may write an article about anyone: artists, musicians, scientists, historical figures, authors, athletes, politicians, monarchs, and on and on. (People are discouraged from writing about themselves, however.) The Wikipedia biography project ([[Wikipedia:WikiProject Biography]]) keeps track of biographical articles; by the end of 2007, there were nearly 400,000 articles listed as biographies, or nearly 20 percent of Wikipedia (see Figure 1-2).

Rambot

Most of the 40,000 articles about American towns were not created by hand; instead, they were created automatically with freely available census data. (The automated user account that created the pages is affectionately called *Rambot*.) For some time after Rambot made its initial efforts in 2002 and 2003, some community members complained that these census-based articles made up too much of the total article count. Now, however, it's not an issue because local residents and others have improved nearly all of the bot's articles, and the increase in other content means these articles now comprise only about 2 percent of the site.

Places

There are articles not just on countries, provinces, and major geographical features but also about cities and towns worldwide. For instance, there is an article about every city or hamlet in the United States (approximately 40,000 are recognized by the US Census Bureau).

There is still plenty to do in these conventional topic areas, but they don't crowd out other topics. Wikipedia includes many nontraditional subjects as well, including the following:

Fictional characters

Want to read up on the personal history of Frodo or Darth Vader? While articles about real people are certainly included on Wikipedia, articles about well-known fictional characters are included as well.

Media—movies, books, albums, songs, television shows (and their episodes), videogames, and more

Work in almost any medium can be considered for its own article.

Companies and organizations

There are factual articles about most well-known corporations. The field of technology is covered particularly well. For example, the articles about Microsoft and Apple, Inc., are both comprehensive; these two articles reference roughly 100 outside sources apiece. Companies can be included in Wikipedia if there is enough reliable information and independent reporting available to support a useful article (simple existence of the company is not enough to qualify, and promotional material is not welcome). As with biographies, writing about your own organization or company is discouraged.

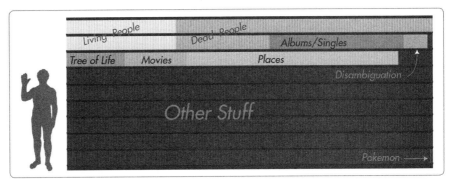

FIGURE 1-2: *A representation of content in Wikipedia from August 2007: 7.2 percent of articles are about places; 3.4 percent about albums and singles; 3.0 percent about tree-of-life zoology; 1.6 percent about films; 10.8 percent about living people; and 8.9 percent about other biographies. Disambiguation (dab) pages comprise 4.2 percent of Wikipedia. Twenty thousand articles represent 1 percent of Wikipedia. These numbers were compiled by Dutch Wikipedian Eugene van der Pijll.*

Computer software and hardware

Considering the way Wikipedia is authored, you might expect a few articles about computers, and you'd be right—there are thousands of articles about programming languages, software, hardware, and computer science theory.

Transport

Wikipedia has been a hit with transportation enthusiasts. There are thousands of articles about railway stations, canals, airports, and other minutiae of transport networks. For instance, the article [[I-35W Mississippi River bridge]], about the interstate highway bridge in Minnesota that collapsed on August 1, 2007, was created well over a year before that event.

Current events

Though the site does not support original reporting, Wikipedia is updated rapidly when major stories break. Current events coverage has had a major profile ever since the up-to-the-minute coverage of the [[2004 Indian Ocean earthquake]] and related tsunami (this article alone had well over 1,000 edits in its first 48 hours). Finding out more about current events on the site is described in Chapter 3.

Some pages are primarily *navigational*. These pages exist to point the way toward other Wikipedia pages. Three types of navigational pages are well worth noting:

Lists

Linked lists are a defining feature of Wikipedia. Want to find a list of songs about Elvis Presley? No problem—it's at [[List of songs about or referencing Elvis Presley]]. Lists can be about nearly about any topic; though like any content, they should ideally be referenced. In fact, [[List of female tennis players]] was one of the earliest pages created on Wikipedia. Lists are browsable; start from [[List of topics]] to find lists of . . . well, nearly anything. (See Chapter 3 for some of our favorites.)

Disambiguation pages

These pages include a whole list of links to possible articles that have similar names. For example, the Wikipedia page [[Orange]] links to articles on the color orange, the fruit, the Orange Bowl, the Dutch royal house of Orange, and numerous other pages (see Figure 1-3). Because it is not possible to anticipate which meaning you may be searching for when different topics share a name, these *disambiguation* pages pull together all the possible options. These pages are especially useful for biographical names: If in the course of some research, you come across a surname only, try the Wikipedia page for that name. It may quickly offer you a range of individuals to choose from.

FIGURE 1-3: *The disambiguation page [[Orange]]*

Redirects

These pages simply push you from one page title to another automatically. You won't actually see these pages directly, but they are used extensively for alternate spellings, variations on names, and any other situation where confusion might exist over the precise article title. Redirects are not included in the official article count, but lists and disambiguation pages certainly are.

Further Reading

http://en.wikipedia.org/wiki/Special:Statistics The auto-generated statistics page that gives the current article count

http://en.wikipedia.org/wiki/Wikipedia:Statistics A page with other statistics and interpretations

http://meta.wikimedia.org/wiki/Milestones A list of historical milestones for the projects

http://en.wikipedia.org/wiki/Wikipedia:What_is_an_article? An FAQ page that describes what an article is

http://en.wikipedia.org/wiki/Wikipedia:Wikipedia's_oldest_articles A list of some of Wikipedia's oldest articles

---

Article and Content Inclusion Policies

When people find out that anyone is allowed to add content to Wikipedia, they often assume that any type of content can be added and in any fashion. But in reality, editing and writing on Wikipedia is constrained by a kaleidoscopic array of rules, or *policies* (these are discussed fully in Chapter 13).

Like a traditional encyclopedia, Wikipedia doesn't accept just anything, although its inclusion policies are clearly much broader than those for most encyclopedias. Articles are only kept on Wikipedia if they meet specific criteria.

Wikipedia has tried to filter out unencyclopedic material by codifying and abiding by general content policies, rather than by creating a list of approved topics ahead of time. What can be added to the encyclopedia is not laid down in advance, but is decided according to some basic principles worked out in the early days.

Policies determine both the kinds of topics that are acceptable and the way in which those topics are treated. If properly applied, the policies are designed to result in a fair treatment, no matter how contentious the topic. If policies cannot be conformed to—for example, if there are no reliable sources about a topic—then an attempt to create a good Wikipedia article for that particular topic may fail. Whether someone likes or dislikes the topic itself, however, should not have any bearing on whether an article is included. In other words, the only limit on what appears in Wikipedia is whether an article can be written that complies with all of the content policies.

No one in particular has the job of deciding whether an article is suitable for Wikipedia. Rather, contributors submit new pages to the site directly, and they go live immediately without intermediaries. Other contributors then review these articles. Large numbers of new articles are deleted every day, but new content that conforms to the content policies is kept. (See Chapter 6 for how to start a new article and Chapter 7 for how articles are deleted.) A new article may also be edited quite savagely to make it more suitable for keeping. An editor who inserts content that falls outside the policies, or removes content that is within them, is not furthering the aims of the project.

Although there is generally broad agreement on these policies, they rely (as with all things on Wikipedia) on editors actually applying them. If you find content that seems to violate these guidelines, it often means that no one has gotten around to fixing it yet.

Core Policies: V, NOR, and NPOV

Three policies are so central to Wikipedia's workings that the encyclopedia would be unrecognizable (or nonexistent) without them. These core policies are Verifiability (V), No Original Research (NOR), and Neutral Point of View (NPOV). In broad strokes, they form the framework in which content is created and edited on a daily basis with no top-down editorial control.

From the outset, Wikipedia was committed to a Neutral Point of View (NPOV). This policy is similar to what journalists mean by *objectivity in reporting*.

As time went by, contributors became more determined to keep out guesswork and rumors, so Wikipedia needed a policy that promoted fact-checking. This principle is now formulated as *verifiability from reliable sources*.

With Wikipedia's growing popularity, there was also a basic need to prevent Wikipedia from being used as a soapbox to spread new ideas that someone had just thought up (euphemistically referred to as *original research*). The No Original Research (NOR) policy says that ideas and facts must be previously published elsewhere by a third party before they are documented in Wikipedia.

Policies Are Important

Most of Wikipedia's policies began as temporary solutions to disputes or other problems. Because they worked well and proved robust in so many contentious areas, they became universal across the encyclopedia. The practical application of these policies is open to some interpretation, but if a Wikipedia contributor has major disagreements with these policies even in theory, that contributor will probably not be happy on Wikipedia.

In outline, each of the major policies is apparently simple enough. The unpacking of their implications is another matter. Imagine, if you can, an article about a rock band that is *neutral* about drug abuse and explicit lyrics, that only reports *published documentation* on trashed hotel rooms and the influence of The Smashing Pumpkins, and that *cites its references* in footnotes as assiduously as any doctoral dissertation. You are coming close to the distinctive Wikipedia voice.

Understanding the Policies

Verifiability ([[Wikipedia:Verifiability]], shortcut WP:V) means that you should always be able to verify that the content of a Wikipedia article is factual, using reliable outside sources that are cited within the article. The Verifiability policy exists to make Wikipedia more accurate. Misremembered facts, casual writing, and gossip should not be included in articles.

In a perfect article, any major statement of fact is attributable to a source outside of Wikipedia, no matter which editor (anonymous or not, expert in the field or not) added the information. References in Wikipedia are explicitly cited, which is different from many traditional encyclopedias. Those works are written by small groups of experts, but because Wikipedia is open to everyone who wants to contribute, even anonymously, it is correspondingly important to be sure that an article's statements can be confirmed by reliable outside sources.

If a topic has never been discussed by any reliable, third-party sources, the Verifiability policy dictates that Wikipedia should not have an article about that topic. Writing the article should be put off until better sources have been published outside Wikipedia. (A lack of published sources might also indicate that the topic is only of interest to a few people; see "Other Guidelines" on page 18.)

In practice, being able to verify information from other sources is very useful, even on apparently minor points. And when an article provides a list of sources, it becomes a convenient jumping-off point for further research.

Aside from benefiting readers, the Verifiability policy also simplifies things for Wikipedia editors by giving them a clear question to ask when evaluating an article's quality: *Is this statement reflected in outside sources?*

Though Verifiability is a core policy, it has yet to be fully implemented, and thousands of articles are tagged as being unreferenced (see Figure 1-4). Verifiability is applied as a general principle. In practice, the ability of editors to verify a statement may depend on, for example, having access to a good library (a major concern in many developing countries). A fact should only be included if checking its accuracy is at least possible in theory; for important true statements, sources can almost always be found with time.

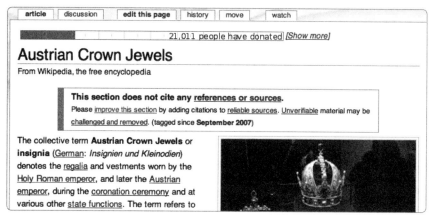

FIGURE 1-4: *This is the template message for articles that don't cite any sources, which is a key part of complying with the Verifiability policy. These messages are meant to warn readers and alert editors that the article is unfinished.*

You will certainly see unreferenced content on Wikipedia. Some of this content remains unsourced simply because sourcing is hard work, and Wikipedia is a work in progress. But some content clearly violates the idea of verifiability (for example, anything that is contentious and badly referenced or that really couldn't be referenced, such as things said in a private conversation). This material may be challenged and ultimately removed. (For more discussion on referencing style and sourcing, see Chapter 6.)

No Original Research ([[Wikipedia:No original research]], shortcut WP:NOR) means that all concepts and theories in Wikipedia articles should be based on previously published accounts and ideas. Wikipedia articles shouldn't contain original ideas, conclusions, descriptions, or interpretations of facts. Nor should they contain editors' personal views, political opinions, or any unpublished analysis of published material.

If you have something innovative to say, Wikipedia is not the right place to present it to the public. In other words, if you have performed an experiment, thought of a philosophical argument, or developed a mathematical proof—good for you! But this content doesn't belong in the encyclopedia unless your work has already been published somewhere else (ideally in a peer-reviewed and scholarly source).

The initial motivation for the No Original Research policy was to prevent people with unconventional personal theories from using Wikipedia to draw attention to their ideas. These days, No Original Research is consistently used against the inclusion of material that is in no sense crackpot but is simply too novel for Wikipedia. Articles may also be tagged as possibly containing original research if it is suspected that material in them comes from an editor's personal experience, rather than verifiable sources (see Figure 1-5).

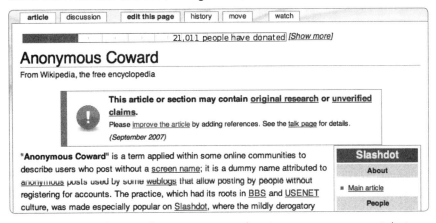

FIGURE 1-5: *Article template message indicating concerns over violations of the No Original Research policy*

NOR also means that editors should not be tempted to provide historical interpretations or draw conclusions, even if they seem self-evident, without citing supporting outside sources giving the same interpretations. One consequence is that historical articles tend not to end with overall summary assessments of people or events. Conclusions from historians can be cited, but if two historians disagree, there should be no authorial attempt to reconcile the views; both sides should be given and the readers left to draw their own conclusions. Some pattern may exist in the facts, but it is not for Wikipedia to break this to the world. If someone else points it out, it can be mentioned and attributed.

Verifiability, Reliable Sources, and No Original Research clearly have something in common. In Wikipedia, both facts and opinions must be based on and referenced to outside information and ideas that have already been published. There is ongoing discussion on whether these principles can be summarized together under the idea of *attribution*.

Neutral Point of View ([[Wikipedia:Neutral point of view]], shortcut WP:NPOV) means that all points of view about a particular topic should be fairly represented. NPOV is one of the oldest, most respected, and most central policies on Wikipedia. A neutral article makes no case and concentrates on informing the reader by providing a good survey of its topic. It is fair-minded and accurate and deals with controversial matters by reporting the main points where there is disagreement.

From the reader's perspective, the effect of neutrality should be this: An article on a contentious topic, such as a historical event that is seen differently by various groups, should not reveal where the article author stands on the matter. In almost all cases, such an article will have been worked over by a group of editors, and their opinions should not come through. Although the example of a rock band was given previously, there are more serious topics where maintaining a neutral point of view is not easy to apply. Consider a neutral treatment of slavery, communism, the history of Ireland, or abortion. Each of these has to be treated on a scrupulous basis, with proper weight given to all sides of the story. The discussion of rival opinions should be in a tone containing no sympathy or bias, regardless of the topic.

Neutral articles should also be comprehensive, though they don't have to be all-inclusive. All significant views should be provided or outlined, however. The reasons why a particular view is popular should be given in fair summary, but the overall expression in an article should not be slanted. NPOV doesn't mean that minority views must be written about with equal coverage to majority views, particularly when there is a wide disparity in their acceptance; points of view should be written up proportionately. Small minority views, such as "the Earth is flat," can be treated briefly, or in some cases omitted as being below Wikipedia's natural threshold of attention. There is no doctrine of *equal time*. In fact, to give all views equal coverage regardless of their outside acceptance is in itself an act of editorializing. The same goes for what facts or incidents are emphasized in an article; a scandal, rumor, or conspiracy theory may be included (if properly sourced), but shouldn't be given unwarranted headline status. Wikipedia is not tabloid journalism.

Using a neutral point of view, all sorts of controversies can be handled. An article should never directly include opinion within the text: "Coke is much better than Pepsi" is the wrong approach. Rather, the statement should be neutral, indirect, accurate, and specific. For example, it is acceptable to write "according to a 2006 Taste Tester's poll published in *Taste Testers Monthly*, 52 percent of taste testers found Coke to be better than Pepsi," with a full citation to the article being referred to. (This is a fabricated quote, by the way. See [[New Coke]] for some real quotes.) Of course, neutrality also rules out all sorts of propaganda tricks based on selective quotation.

NPOV also comes to the rescue where sources differ on the facts. Editors are often faced with contradictions in the historical record or factual matters; for example, whether person *X* was a nephew or a son of person *Y*. Both claims can be included. According to Verifiability and Neutral Point of View, this disputed factual point should appear as "Source *A* says *X* was the nephew of *Y*, whereas *B* says *X* was the son of *Y*," with references. According to the No Original Research policy, the matter should be left there, and if source C publishes some new evidence, this should then be added. Wikipedia is not a court in which verdicts are reached, and editors should not attempt to figure out the "right" answer themselves; an article may simply present the evidence, fairly and at adequate length, for the reader to consider.

Following NPOV means that advertisements, press releases, and other promotional materials aren't welcome on Wikipedia because these are inherently non-neutral. This may sound fairly obvious, but it affects the community's accep-tance of other sources as well. For example, text from promotional websites for companies or schools, which are often used for sources, is often non-neutral and should be considered carefully before being cited.

In addition to making advertising unacceptable, NPOV is also a prime reason why editors are strongly discouraged from working on articles about themselves or their organizations. Except for basic factual corrections, it really is difficult to be neutral about yourself. (Also remember that any statement in an article, even if it's about a subject you know as intimately as your own life, needs to be backed up with a citation to an outside source because of Verifiability and No Original Research. Wikipedia should never be used for promotion.)

Editing Scandals

Some violations of the NPOV policy have been high profile; for instance, it was discovered that staffers for a politician were editing that politician's biog-raphy to be more favorable and removing uncomfortable facts. Naturally, this violated the Neutral Point of View policy. On January 27, 2006, the *Lowell Sun* reported on the Wikipedia article about an American politician, Representa-tive Marty Meehan. It claimed that an anonymous editor, with an IP address traced to the House of Representatives offices, had been at work erasing mention of the congressman's broken term-limit promise. This then became a national news story.

All of the content policies, but particularly NPOV, affect Wikipedia's style and the way its text is worded. Disputes about NPOV often end up on the Talk Page of the article (discussed in Chapter 4); if there is heavy debate about a topic in evidence, an editor may flag the article as being involved in an NPOV dispute (see Figure 1-6).

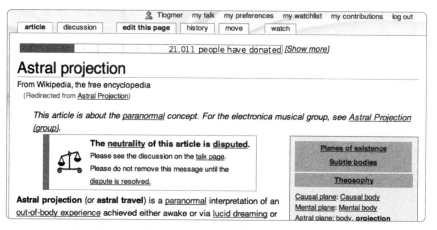

FIGURE 1-6: *Article template message indicating concern that the tagged article does not have a neutral point of view*

Other Guidelines

Along with the three core policies discussed in the previous section, a handful of other guidelines help determine what content is included in Wikipedia.

Notability

Wikipedia should only cover topics considered noteworthy in the outside world, as determined by reliable, independent secondary sources. Notability helps set a baseline level for inclusion to prevent Wikipedia from becoming something other than an encyclopedia. In practice, the lack of notability is the most common reason why a topic is deemed unsuitable for a Wikipedia article.

This concept is distinct from "fame," "importance," or "popularity," but it does mean there shouldn't be articles about topics that are of interest only to a very few people or of such local interest that there are no publications about them. In other words, an article should not be about your pet or your house (unless either of these is particularly well known and has been written about previously).

Notability is easy to think about superficially but difficult to apply or cleanly define in the abstract. A feeling for notability requires a practical sense of the relative significance of topics in a field, and it also requires a scholarly sense of which types of sources determine notability. An encyclopedist has to wrestle with weighing the extent and quality of information available on a topic. To take one example, King Edward V of England, one of the princes in the Tower whose reign was cut short when his uncle, Richard III, took the throne, is clearly notable, even though much that has been written about him and his fate is speculative.

In part because of this ambiguity, Notability is much more controversial and open to debate than Verifiability, No Original Research, and Neutral Point of View, but it is also closely related to these policies. Arguments about it may be tortuous in the abstract, but in practical terms, non-notable articles are deleted from Wikipedia over time.

There are separate notability guidelines that have been set up for various controversial areas, such as actors and actresses, websites, companies, musical groups, videogames, and so on; these guidelines may be found through links on the main notability page. Many of these guidelines are in place to help reinforce the idea that Wikipedia is not a promotional service, and most of them fall back on whether there are any reliable secondary sources to be had and the amount of documentation available on a topic. For example, if Alice has a website that gets thousands of hits a day, but no one has written about it in any sort of publication, Bob will likely not be able to write a successful Wikipedia article about Alice's site that doesn't get deleted by other editors as being non-notable, or with the short dismissive comment *nn*.

Similarly, suppose Carla hopes to write about her favorite band, which is much beloved locally but has no major music press. Not only would writing a neutral article be difficult, but also there are no reliable published sources that Carla can use (even if she knows the band's history first-hand).

As in the previous example, notability is something that should be considered in relation to each individual article, rather than whole classes of topics. Some musical groups are certainly notable, as are some companies and some videogames; others are not. The notability guidelines help sort this out.

On the other hand, there are inherent problems with the idea of notability which have led to many ongoing debates over the years on how to phrase and apply the guidelines. Here are some caveats to keep in mind regarding notability:

▶ Notability may be perishable. Some topics are ephemeral in their interest, such as Internet memes and celebrities in the "famous for being famous" category.

On Notability

Notability is something that is judged by the world at large, not by Wikipedia editors making personal judgments. If multiple people in the world at large who are independent of the subject have gone to the effort of creating and publishing nontrivial works of their own about the subject, then they clearly consider it to be notable. Wikipedia simply reflects this judgment. (Adapted from [[User:Uncle G/On notability]])

- Notability is not the same as having a fan or someone taking time to research a topic in depth; there must be multiple independent sources.

- The availability of accessible literature in English on any given subject can distort perceptions of notability; biographical facts, in particular, are unevenly accessible, leading to systemic bias, which will be discussed in Chapter 12.

- Notability is not distinction. It might arise from scandals or participation in controversies, as well as from recognized work such as writing a book.

- Notability in a field is not the same as reputation. Wikipedia will, for example, include cranks who are now discredited but became famous for some reason, but omit solid scientists who are simply not well known.

On that last point, it is obviously flawed to assume that if there's no Wikipedia article, the subject is not notable. Wikipedia is a work in progress, and many worthwhile potential articles have not yet been written.

To sum up, writing a verifiable article without good sources is a bricks-without-straw exercise, and the presence or absence of sources helps determine notability. Thinking about notability helps to keep the project encyclopedic. The

---

What Not to Write

There are some article topics that are pretty much always bad ideas. For instance, you can safely assume an article about or described by any of the following is among the category of unnecessary articles:

- You or the organization you work for

- Your band, which has only sold 47 copies of its one album (even if you think it will sell 48—or maybe 49!)

- The religion or language that you made up with your friends in school one day

- The street you live on (unless it is on a Monopoly board)

- Any one of the 56 distinct regions in the Pokémon videogame series

- Your apartment building

- A stunt or trick only you have ever attempted, probably unsuccessfully

- Any movie you made yourself that has never been seen by more people at one time than can fit in your basement

From [[Wikipedia:List of really, really, really stupid article ideas that you really, really, really should not create]] (shortcut WP:DUMB). For a more serious version, see [[Wikipedia:List of bad article ideas]] (shortcut WP:BAI).

notability guideline as applied probably still errs in the direction of inclusion, with a bias toward lesser topics that are well documented elsewhere. This is a natural consequence of a policy evolution that has made reliable sources ever more central.

Copyrighted Material

As with other publications and organizations where writing is submitted, plagiarism is not allowed. In addition, any materials submitted to Wikipedia must be specifically licensed under the GNU Free Documentation License (GFDL), which is a "free license" (see Chapter 2) distinct from traditional copyright. This license means that anyone can reuse and redistribute Wikipedia's content for any purpose without asking permission, as long as they meet certain conditions; Wikipedia content can be used on other sites or even republished in print.

For these reasons, materials taken from other places generally shouldn't appear on Wikipedia. You shouldn't take text or photos from the Internet or elsewhere and reproduce them on Wikipedia without explicit permission; copying any work that is not in the public domain or explicitly licensed as being freely available is a copyright violation.

Additionally, material that was not originally written for Wikipedia (such as a term paper) typically doesn't meet the other content guidelines. It is best, in almost all cases, to simply write the article afresh.

Non-encyclopedic Content

Some *non-encyclopedic content* is inappropriate for Wikipedia but may be welcome on other sister Wikimedia projects. For instance, definitions of words (without supporting encyclopedic information) are outside of Wikipedia's scope. The jargon used to describe such articles is *dicdef*, short for *dictionary definition*. A dictionary definition alone isn't sufficient for a Wikipedia article. However, dictionary definitions are very welcome at Wiktionary, Wikimedia's free dictionary project.

Original reporting of events is also not a part of Wikipedia. You may have been an eyewitness to an event, but writing what you know you saw straight into the encyclopedia probably violates the No Original Research or Verifiability policy. Wikipedia must wait for the mainstream media to report the facts, which it can then collate. On the other hand, original reporting is part of the mission of Wikinews, which is a citizen journalism project.

Similarly, a "how-to" article may not be encyclopedic, but would be just fine over at Wikibooks, Wikimedia's project to write free textbooks.

Original source documents (for example, the text of Coleridge's "Rime of the Ancient Mariner") are not welcome on Wikipedia, but that is because primary sources belong on Wikisource.

These sister projects are fully described in Chapter 16.

What Wikipedia Is Not

It's sometimes helpful to think about content inclusion guidelines in negative terms. Here is the basic consensus about what Wikipedia is *not* (adapted from [[Wikipedia:What Wikipedia is not]], shortcut WP:NOT). Taken together, these statements usefully define boundaries applied to Wikipedia's content. They also exist as longer formulations spelled out in policies and guidelines.

Wikipedia is not an indiscriminate collection of information, a directory, or a dictionary.
It's an encyclopedia (and preferably a well-rounded one) in which criteria such as notability are used to weed out entries. For example, an article titled [[List of bands beginning with the word "Lemon"]] was exactly what its title implied: a simple list, without analysis or context, that named the Lemonheads, Lemon Jelly, and a few other bands. It was quickly deleted. Articles on Wikipedia ought to serve some purpose. They should provide something recognizable as "information," concerning something recognizable as a "subject."

On a similar note, Wikipedia doesn't strive to be a *Who's Who* or a catalog of published works. Family trees and other family histories are not stored on Wikipedia, as much family history is considered "indiscriminate": Being related to someone notable doesn't make a person notable (with the exception of royal families and others where the hereditary principle matters).

Wikipedia is not a paper encyclopedia.
In particular, Wikipedia does not need to worry about printing costs or physical unwieldiness. It doesn't need to shorten or triage articles to conserve space. As long as there is money to buy servers and bandwidth, there are no physical restrictions on growth.

The implications for coverage are major: "Not worth including" is a decision that need not be made quite as often. This is another reason Wikipedia's model is a dramatic change from earlier encyclopedias. As long as articles conform to the site's other guidelines, specialized or minor articles can be included. Wikipedia has no set restrictions on what branches of human knowledge should be included.

Wikipedia is not a publisher of original thought, nor a soapbox.
This reiterates the policy of No Original Research: Wikipedia is not interested in personal essays. Indeed, it's a bad platform on which to air personal or political views. If you're looking for a way to get your name and opinions online, many free website and blog providers exist. Reviews of products, companies, and other personal opinions—whether positive or negative—are likewise unwelcome in Wikipedia articles. These are better placed on a website dedicated to reviews.

Wikipedia is not a mirror, repository of files, a blog, webspace provider, or social networking site.

This might seem like a strange point to make as it is directed not at Wikipedia's articles but at its *user pages*, the pages editors create for their own working space. (We will cover user pages in Chapter 11.) Anyone can come along and create a user page, but Wikipedia only supplies this working space to allow editors to identify themselves and collaborate more effectively—not to back up unrelated files, publish a blog, or find a potential mate. Wikipedia is a project with a very specific purpose—to create and distribute an encyclopedia. It is not a helpful web application for storing other unrelated information.

Wikipedia is not a crystal ball.

This is a warning about posting rumor and speculation about future events, such as gossip about films that are currently in production. If it hasn't happened yet, it isn't Wikipedia material (though as with all guidelines, this should be interpreted using common sense: It doesn't mean that the article on the 2012 Summer Olympics should be started only when the opening ceremony gets under way).

Wikipedia is not censored.

Articles aim at a general and educated adult audience, and Wikipedia is neither simplified, nor is it compiled with regard to the needs or protection of children. While content is intended to be factual, it is also frank, and human sexuality is extensively covered. Religion is treated along the same lines as all other content. Some images in the encyclopedia may be disturbing or shocking.

   Thus, some content may be considered offensive or inappropriate for young children. Understandably, this lack of censorship can cause distress—there are many hundreds of articles about topics that many people would prefer not to think about. Considering that the aim is to be a repository of all human information, written by a truly diverse group of people from all over the world, this is unavoidable. And given the policies of Neutral Point of View and Verifiability, Wikipedia is often an excellent source for information on controversial or potentially offensive topics.

✱ **NOTE:** *Wikipedia, however, should certainly not contain anything defamatory toward individuals. [[Wikipedia:Biographies of living persons]] (shortcut WP:BLP) sets down strict conditions of inclusion for articles about people. Verifiability and NPOV apply to all topics and are firmly enforced in cases where real lives may be affected. If, by misfortune, you do feel defamed, turn to "Help, an Article About Me Is Incorrect!" on page 207 for specific complaint advice.*

No Blue Pencil, No Free Speech

"No censorship of topics" does not mean that other inclusion policies and behavioral guidelines for onsite interactions can be ignored. Though broad-mindedness is highly valued on Wikipedia, nowhere in the policies is there anything about free speech. The site is designed as an encyclopedia project, not as a general forum.

Wikipedia is not static.

Articles are never set in stone. The encyclopedia is an open-ended work in progress, and Wikipedia articles are, by definition, always provisional. Even the best articles aren't considered off limits for further improvement. This attitude reflects a shared view of knowledge as something that by its nature is dynamic and expanding, rather than settled.

This final point is often left unspoken, but it is key. Changes can always be made, articles can always be improved, and there is always something else to do.

Further Reading

http://en.wikipedia.org/wiki/Wikipedia:Neutral_point_of_view The NPOV policy

http://en.wikipedia.org/wiki/Wikipedia:No_original_research The NOR policy

http://en.wikipedia.org/wiki/Wikipedia:Verifiability The Verifiability policy

http://en.wikipedia.org/wiki/Wikipedia:Notability The Notability guideline

http://en.wikipedia.org/wiki/Category:Wikipedia_notability_guidelines
Various notability guidelines for specific subjects

http://en.wikipedia.org/wiki/Wikipedia:Reliable_sources Guideline for judging reliable sources

http://en.wikipedia.org/wiki/Wikipedia:What_Wikipedia_is_not The policy on what Wikipedia is not

Non-article Content

All pages on Wikipedia are of two types: About two million articles constitute the encyclopedic content, but ten million project-related pages also exist. What are these pages? Will you see them if you just look something up? If you find them when using a search engine, should you ignore those hits?

Wikipedia's readers should recognize that some Wikipedia pages are not articles, but they do not need to have any particular understanding of the non-article pages and can ignore them freely. On the other hand, involved editors should understand the different types of pages—their purpose and the way they help grease Wikipedia's wheels. The project-related and administrative pages are not as glamorous as articles, but they're of no less importance when it comes to understanding what happens in practice on the site.

Types of Non-article Pages

These extra pages come in several varieties. Non-article pages are devoted to the administration of Wikipedia, discussion of article content, technical infrastructure, descriptions of images, and the Wikipedia community.

Although they are not as widely known as articles, two of these page types—discussion pages and user pages—are actually the easiest places to start participating on Wikipedia.

Talk pages

Every article is coupled with a *talk page* (also called a *discussion page*), which is accessed by clicking the Discussion tab at the top of the screen. Here editors ask questions about the article's content, propose changes, display notices for other editors, and discuss technical matters (like the title of an article and whether an article should be split into pieces or combined with another).

Each discussion page is meant only for discussing the article it is linked to. Despite the name, discussion pages are *not* forums for general discussion of the article's subject.

A discussion page is attached to almost every non-article page as well. (Discussions about Wikipedia policy tend to range more widely than discussions about individual articles, but still remain somewhat tied to the topic of the attached page.)

For more on talk pages, see Chapters 4, 11, and 12.

User pages and user talk pages

User pages are for individual editors (*users*) to describe themselves in whatever detail they see fit. By custom, they are set aside as a private space where editors can work. Often, editors will list projects they're a part of and articles they've worked on.

User talk pages, like article discussion pages, can be reached by clicking a tab at the top of the screen. To communicate with each other, editors leave notes on user talk pages. Whenever someone leaves a note on your user talk page, Wikipedia's software notifies you. (You'll find more on setting up user pages and leaving messages in Chapter 11.)

The other kinds of pages are typically used as references and project coordination pages.

Policy pages and guidelines
These pages provide guidance about editing content and interacting with other volunteers. Policies and guidelines lay out stylistic guidelines for editing, content inclusion policies, procedures to resolve disputes, and much more. Policies will be described further in Chapter 13.

Community discussion, procedural, and project pages
These pages are where the community discusses proposals and coordinates editing projects. Routine procedures, such as deletion discussions, are usually based on policies and are carried out on special procedure pages. These processes will be described more in Chapter 7. On Wikipedia what *the community* means tends to vary according to context—after all, the site is open to all comers—but often enough, it implies those who take part in these open-forum discussions.

Help pages
These pages include documentation of editing syntax, technical procedures, and best practices, and are referenced throughout this book.

Image description pages
Each image is coupled with an image description page. These pages exist to provide the image with a textual description (*metadata*).

MediaWiki-generated special pages and administrative pages
These are pages generated on the fly by the MediaWiki software and serve as utilities rather than editable pages. They are used for special lists and essential pages, such as the account creation pages.

Namespaces

Each type of page is distinguished from every other type (including from articles) by a prefix; for example, discussion pages are prefixed with *Talk:*. This prevents "collisions" between similarly named pages, for example, [[Sorting]], which is an encyclopedia article about *the process of arranging items*, and [[Help:Sorting]], which is not an encyclopedia article but instead offers technical assistance about the sortable tables found on some Wikipedia pages.

Each prefix is actually an indicator that the page is inside a particular namespace. (A *namespace* is a kind of container for different types of content.) For example, in this full Wikipedia URL

```
http://en.wikipedia.org/wiki/Talk:Benjamin_Franklin
```

Talk indicates the namespace where the page exists, whereas *Benjamin Franklin*, separated from the namespace with a colon (:), is the page's name. If you were internally linking to this URL, you'd use the combination of the namespace and page name to properly indicate what page you meant: [[Talk:Benjamin Franklin]].

Articles, which exist in the so-called main or article space namespace, do not have prefixes:

```
http://en.wikipedia.org/wiki/Benjamin_Franklin
```

Benjamin Franklin is the full page name; the absence of a prefix tells you the page is an encyclopedia article.

All other types of content in Wikipedia exist in one of the other namespaces, which are indicated with one of 19 possible prefixes. Seeing a prefix before a title tells you that the page is likely part of the community or administration of the site (and therefore is not subject to the same content guidelines as articles).

The namespace also provides context and indicates the type of content that a page contains. For example, help pages contain technical documentation, rather than (say) encyclopedia articles or policies.

Although two pages in the same namespace cannot share a title, pages can exist under the same "name" in different namespaces. For example, the article [[Phoebe]] is about a personal name and is part of the encyclopedic content of the site. It is not the same thing at all as the page [[User:Phoebe]], which exists in the User namespace and describes an editor who uses this name as a pseudonym.

The lines between encyclopedia content, on the one hand, and the Wikipedia community pages, on the other, are extremely clear and are delineated with the use of namespaces. As implemented on Wikipedia, community namespaces do not always exactly correlate with a single specific type of content. For instance, whereas only user pages are in the User namespace, you may find various pages such as technical documentation, community projects, and policies in the Wikipedia namespace. All of these pages, however, will have something to do with the running of Wikipedia.

All Pages in a Namespace

To scan a list of all of the pages in a namespace, click Special Pages in the Toolbox menu on the left-hand sidebar. At the top of the list that appears is the entry *All pages*. Click that, and a pull-down menu (to select a namespace) and a search box appears. The namespace listing will start at whatever spelling you place in the search box, something very necessary because several namespaces contain millions of pages. (Adapted from [[Wikipedia:Tip of the day/October 25, 2006]])

List of Namespaces

Wikipedia has 20 built-in namespaces. These occur in pairs (for example, User and User_talk); there are nine such pairs, including the main namespace, where page names have no prefix, and two special namespaces, Special and Media. A namespace prefix must be kept when linking to a page. The prefix always comes before the page name and is separated from it with a colon.

MediaWiki

Wikipedia runs using MediaWiki software, so all other wikis running on MediaWiki have these namespaces as well. Wikipedia adds two custom namespaces that do not exist on other wikis (Portal and Portal_talk) and has the Wikipedia and Wikipedia_talk namespaces, which may be appropriately renamed on other wikis.

For reference, the following namespaces exist:

▸ The *main* or article namespace has no special prefix. This namespace is where all regular articles (all the "encyclopedic" pieces of the encyclopedia) exist. Pages in this namespace can be linked to internally with simply their name: [[*pagename*]].

▸ The *Wikipedia* namespace is what could be called the *project page* namespace. It is for pages that are specifically about running Wikipedia and meta-level subjects related to the project. For example, the Community Portal can be found at [[Wikipedia:Community_portal]] and is meant as a place for the Wikipedia community to gather; [[Wikipedia:Statistics]] and its talk page, [[Wikipedia_talk:Statistics]], are meant for describing and discussing the project's statistics. Policies, procedures, guidelines, community projects, and many help pages all exist within the Wikipedia namespace. The Wikipedia namespace may sometimes be abbreviated to WP, enabling shortcuts to be set up. For instance, [[WP:ARB]] redirects to [[Wikipedia:Arbitration_Committee]].

▸ The *User* namespace refers to user pages or pages that have been set up by individual editors to describe themselves, for example, [[User:Jimbo Wales]]. By custom, your user page is available when you register a username.

- ► The *Help* namespace refers to basic documentation and help pages for using and editing Wikipedia. The prefix for these is simply *Help:*. Most of the project documentation pages are here or in the Wikipedia namespace.

- ► The *Category* namespace is a major part of expertly using Wikipedia; we discuss categories at length in Chapter 3 and Chapter 8.

- ► The *Image* namespace is prefaced by *Image:* and is used for describing and attributing images (for example, [[Image:White shark.jpg]]). If you upload any image or other media file to Wikipedia, one of these pages will be created. The *Media* namespace is prefaced by *Media:* and is used for a link directly to a media file, rather than its description page. Details are in Chapter 9.

- ► The *Template* namespace is prefaced by *Template:* and is used exclusively for templates that are transcluded or substituted into an article. You'll find more on templates in Chapter 9.

- ► The *Portal* namespace is for portal pages that collect articles on a particular topic; this is special to Wikipedia and not generally for MediaWiki. For more on portals, see Chapter 3 and Chapter 7.

- ► The *Talk* namespaces contain all the discussion pages. Except for special pages, every namespace has an associated Talk namespace, designated by adding *talk:* after the normal namespace prefix. In this book, we write these compound names with an underscore to be clear, but you can always use a space. The Talk namespace associated with the main article namespace simply uses the prefix *Talk:*, for example, [[Talk:Mathematics]]. The Talk namespace associated with the User namespace, however, has the prefix *User_talk:*. Similarly, Wikipedia namespace discussion pages are in the Wikipedia_talk namespace, so the discussion page for [[Wikipedia:No original research]] is at [[Wikipedia_talk:No original research]]. Generally, pages in the Talk namespaces are used to discuss changes to their corresponding page; however, pages in the User_talk namespace are used to leave messages for a particular user. The User_talk namespace is special in that, whenever a user's talk page is edited, that user (if logged in) will immediately see a message informing them that they have new messages.

- ► The *Special* namespace refers to pages that are autocreated by the site's software on demand. These pages are not editable in the usual way and are generally either tools or automatically generated variable lists, such as a list of all pages on the site. See [[Help:Special page]] for a list.

- ► The *MediaWiki* namespace is used for certain site messages along with a few other areas to define shortcuts and other text strings used around Wikipedia (for example, [[MediaWiki:Disclaimers]]). These pages are not usually editable by users.

Further Reading

http://en.wikipedia.org/wiki/MediaWiki#Namespaces   An article about MediaWiki with a good explanation of namespaces

http://en.wikipedia.org/wiki/Wikipedia:Namespace   The help page on namespaces

http://en.wikipedia.org/wiki/Help:Special_page   A description of each Special namespace page

Summary and What to Read Next

Wikipedia contains a staggering volume and remarkable variety of content, ranging from traditional encyclopedic subjects to articles about popular culture and technical topics.

Even so, every Wikipedia article must meet several criteria related to the site's mission. The most important criteria are the three core policies: Verifiability (V), No Original Research (NOR), and Neutral Point of View (NPOV). A number of further guidelines and corollaries to the major policies, particularly the notability guideline, help define what you should find in Wikipedia and what types of articles are acceptable.

Although there are now over two million articles in the English-language Wikipedia, there are even more pages devoted to the administration and community of the site. These pages, none of which are part of the Wikipedia *encyclopedia*, include discussion (or talk) pages; user and user talk pages; policy, procedure, and help pages; project administration and community discussion pages; image description pages; and MediaWiki-generated special site-related pages. All of these different kinds of pages are differentiated from each other by namespaces, which are indicated with prefixes that are separated from the page's name with a colon. Articles reside in the main or article namespace and have no special prefix.

In the next chapter, we'll discuss the origins of Wikipedia and how three disparate historical strands—wikis, encyclopedias, and free software—came together to influence the site's development. Skip to Chapter 3 to explore the structure of Wikipedia and learn better ways to search and browse the site or to Chapter 4 to learn how to evaluate an individual article.

2 | The World Gets a Free Encyclopedia

The hopeful dreams from the early days of Wikipedia have become reality. There is a free, online encyclopedia, and in Chapter 1, you reviewed its content. But what led to Wikipedia's creation, and what is the philosophy behind the site?

In *Serendipities*, leading Italian academic and intellectual Umberto Eco closed his first essay with this thought:

> After all, the cultivated person's first duty is to be always prepared to rewrite the encyclopedia.[1]

---

[1] See Umberto Eco, "The Force of Falsity," in *Serendipities: Language and Lunacy*, trans. William Weaver (New York: Columbia, 1998), 21.

In 1994, when Eco lectured to the University of Bologna on "The Force of Falsity," he naturally did not mean this statement literally. For him, the encyclopedia is metaphorical; a revision of beliefs is a sign of a civilization that can question itself, and fresh views and discoveries, such as a scientific advance or the exposure of a forgery, prompt new summaries of knowledge. But Wikipedia has allowed this metaphor to spring to life: Daily, thousands of people "rewrite the encyclopedia," and no one checks to see whether these editors have the appropriate degrees or credentials or are even dressed for the occasion.

Wikipedia combines the ideas of the encyclopedia, the wiki website, and free and open content to define how a free encyclopedia can be built by everyone. In this chapter, we'll explore these three ideas and how they have evolved, discuss the motivation behind the project and its early history, and examine the drawbacks to Wikipedia's method by discussing some common criticisms of the site, centered around a few case studies. In the last chapter of this book, we'll return to more recent history and the current organizational side of Wikipedia. In the meantime, as you read and edit articles and participate in community discussions, knowing Wikipedia's philosophical background and influences is key to understanding how it works.

Wikipedia's Mission

What is Wikipedia's role? In the 21st century, distributing information is easier than ever before. A megabyte of data—equivalent to the text of a large book—can be sent to mobile phones in most parts of the world for less than one cent. The Internet's infrastructure is increasingly available to the world's population, and broadcasters and publishers are becoming less-necessary intermediaries.

What *has* been missing is the freely available online information itself. The Web has plenty of other content: news, opinion, virtual shopping, and social networking. What the Web has lacked are hard facts, and quality factual material can change lives.

This is where Wikipedia comes in. Its mission is to make the whole world's information available in all languages. Until now, this has not been possible: Large reference libraries are not spread evenly around the planet. If you believe that good and balanced information is something that everyone needs, you can

---

What Wikipedia Does

"Imagine a world in which every single person on the planet is given free access to the sum of all human knowledge. That's what we're doing."

—Wikipedia founder Jimmy Wales, from an often-quoted 2004 interview on Slashdot

understand why a comprehensive, neutral online encyclopedia is important. And if you believe this information is a tool that everyone should be able to use in their daily work, you can see why a free, accessible encyclopedia is essential. Having quick, easy, everyday access to facts and reference materials matters now and is not merely a science-fiction concept like in Isaac Asimov's *Encyclopedia Galactica* or Douglas Adams's handheld *Hitchhiker's Guide*.

Further Reading

http://en.wikipedia.org/wiki/Serendipities   Wikipedia's article on the Umberto Eco book cited at the beginning of this chapter

http://en.wikiquote.org/wiki/Jimmy_Wales   The Slashdot quote and other Jimmy Wales sayings

---

Wikipedia's Roots

Wikipedia was founded in 2001, but the critical ideas and developments that helped shape the site were developed long before that. These ideas are listed below in chronological order. They show a quickening pace, especially after 1990 when the World Wide Web became a concrete proposal. Throughout the 1990s, technology progressed. New ways of thinking about tools emerged, and thoughtful and innovative developments combined to affect the content and implications of computer technology. These developments have produced ideas that are shaping the world. Wikipedia is part of a long tradition that predates the Internet, however, and some much older ideas feed into Wikipedia's culture—not least of which is the revolutionary concept of the encyclopedia.

Ancient Greece to Today: Encyclopedias

What is an encyclopedia? To most people, an *encyclopedia* is a large book or multivolume work. Comprised of a comprehensive collection of short articles, an encyclopedia divides an area of knowledge into separate topics. Encyclopedias are reference works, designed to orient new readers, summarize details that might have previously been spread over many publications, and provide a summary of available information in comprehensible terms. A good encyclopedia can answer many questions, without replacing the sources from which it was constructed.

Encyclopedias are examples of *tertiary sources*. They are neither primary sources, such as historical documents, nor are they secondary sources, such as textbooks, which usually discuss, report on, or interpret primary sources. Instead, an encyclopedia's compilers have gathered and summarized available secondary sources (often noting primary sources as well) to report on a field of knowledge and current thinking at that particular time.

The encyclopedia has venerable origins. Early examples exist in manuscript form in cultures around the world, and bound encyclopedias have been around almost as long as there have been books at all. Pliny's enormous *Historia naturalis*, written in 77 AD, is often cited as one of the first encyclopedias; this work was influential for at least 1,500 years. Some of the other very first encyclopedias were written in Chinese (the now-lost *Huang lan*, published around 220 AD) and Arabic (the 10-volume *Kitāb 'Uyūn al-Akhbār*, or *Adab al-Kitāb*, compiled around 880 AD). Throughout the medieval era in Europe, other encyclopedic works were developed, many written in Latin and based around philosophical and religious ideas.

The word *encyclopedia* was not used to describe these works until much later, however. So where did this word originate? Wikipedia itself provides this explanation, crediting the 16th-century scholar Joachim Sterck van Ringelbergh (Figure 2-1):

> The word *encyclopedia* comes from the Classical Greek "ἐγκύκλια παιδεία" (pronounced "enkyklia paideia"), literally, a "[well-]rounded education," meaning "a general knowledge." Though the notion of a compendium of knowledge dates back thousands of years, the term was first used in 1541 in the title of a book by Joachimus Fortius Ringelbergius, *Lucubrationes vel potius absolutissima kyklopaideia* (Basel, 1541). The word *encyclopaedia* was first used as a noun by the encyclopedist Pavao Skalic in the title of his book, *Encyclopaedia seu orbis disciplinarum tam sacrarum quam prophanarum epistemon* (Encyclopaedia, or Knowledge of the World of Disciplines, Basel, 1559). (From [[Encyclopedia]], April 2007)

The earliest encyclopedias compiled knowledge about the entire world and were meant to be read straight through as a complete education.[2] This notion eventually evolved into the more modern concept of an encyclopedia as a reference work, more akin to the concept of a dictionary in which words are defined for easy consultation. (Encyclopedic dictionaries, a hybrid form, have existed since at least the second century AD.) An encyclopedia in the contemporary sense may illustrate objects, map places, contain articles about history, geography, science, and biography, and cover the spectrum of factual knowledge.

In the modern age, traditional encyclopedias have worked hard to balance the topics important to their audience with limited space and editorial capacity. Generalist encyclopedias aim to be universal in scope, while being compact enough to be fully updated every

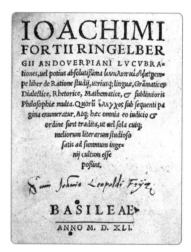

FIGURE 2-1: *Title page from Lucubrationes vel potius absolutissima kyklopaideia, 1541*

---

2 See Robert Collison, *Encyclopedias: Their History Throughout the Ages* (New York: Hafner, 1996), 21.

few decades and to fit on a bookshelf. Specialist encyclopedias can fill a similar amount of space for one field or subfield. A general children's encyclopedia such as *World Book* is written with a different format and goals than a scientific encyclopedia, but both provide clear introductions to topics. This formula has been a successful one, providing publishers with high sales continuing from the 18th century to today.

Today thousands of specialist encyclopedias are in print (Figure 2-2 shows one of these, the *Encyclopedia Lituanica*, an English-language six-volume encyclopedia on Lithuania). General encyclopedias have become household names: *Encyclopaedia Britannica*[3] and *World Book* for English speakers, the German *Brockhaus,* and the French *Larousse.* The *Great Soviet Encyclopedia* grew to 100,000 articles in Russian and produced encyclopedias in other languages of the USSR.

FIGURE 2-2: *The six-volume* Encyclopedia Lituanica, *published from 1970 to 1980 in Boston, Massachusetts*

Late 17th Century:
The Modern Encyclopedia

The encyclopedia as we know it today was strongly influenced by the 18th-century European Enlightenment. Wikipedia shares those roots, which includes the rational impetus to understand and document all areas of the world.

Jonathan Israel[4] cites the *Grand Dictionnaire* of Louis Moréri (Figure 2-3) as being the first modern encyclopedia. Published in 1674, it ran to many editions over half a century. Then, as now, times were changing: The previous decade's Royal Society of London was composed of amateurs, mostly outside the universities, but they were pioneers of learned society and the modern scientific method. The new media of the time were journals, such as the Royal Society's *Philosophical Transactions*, which were used to spread knowledge of scientific discoveries and theories. According to Israel, by the decade after Moreri's compilation appeared, the new institution of the learned journal threatened existing authority.

By the Enlightenment, the Renaissance concept of the polymathic *uomo universale* or *universal man* had been stretched to its limits. Science and exploration had added many facts to the body of knowledge, and no one person could grasp everything significant.

---

[3] For a critique of the *Encyclopaedia Britannica*, see Harvey Einbinder, *The Myth of the Britannica* (New York: Grove Press, 1964). This book by Einbinder, a physicist, is authoritative only for the mid-century editions of *Encyclopaedia Britannica*; it has a hostile bias, but it contains much interesting discussion and research on general tertiary source issues, such as updating, celebrity authors, science coverage, and humanistic approaches.

[4] See Jonathan Israel, *Radical Enlightenment: Philosophy and the Making of Modernity, 1650–1750* (Oxford: Oxford University Press, 2001), 134.

Encyclopedia editors made fields of knowledge available to the reading public by coordinating the efforts of leading scholars and intellectuals and condensing the available information. Israel writes that "these massive works . . . were expressly produced for a broad market." He mentions the "stupendous" 64-volume Zedler *Universal-Lexicon* in German (published 1731–1750); he also comments on the sheer expense of a well-stocked library at that time.[5] Access to general information was now available for the prosperous middle class; it was no longer confined to the rich and those actively involved in the intellectual networks.

FIGURE 2-3: *Louis Moréri (1643–1680), a pioneer of the modern encyclopedia*

The new generation of encyclopedias, of which the best-known is Denis Diderot's provocative French *Encyclopédie, ou dictionnaire raisonné des sciences, des arts et des métiers* (*Encyclopedia, or a systematic dictionary of the sciences, arts and crafts*), were general works. They included all areas of knowledge, from the technical to the esoteric to the theological.

Wikipedia as an Encyclopedia

Wikipedia carries on these encyclopedist traditions but with some radical changes. The most obvious change is technological: Wikipedia stores information online, so its scope is not limited by the economics of printing.

Wiki page structure encourages many short articles rather than a few long ones. This works because pages are *hypertext*: a collection of articles linked back and forth. Earlier encyclopedias used footnotes and indexes as a way to link to other articles, but Wikipedia uses hypertext to its full potential, giving it a very different organizational style compared to the printed page. This extensive linking extends beyond articles in the English-language version: Wikipedias in different languages, from French to Swahili (Figure 2-4), are cross-referenced with tens of millions of links, as described further in Chapter 15.

FIGURE 2-4: *The Wikipedia logo for the Swahili version*

As described in Chapter 1, Wikipedia editors encounter the same issues that the original encyclopedia editors did—what topics to include and how to present them—and address these issues by developing content standards and style

---

[5] Israel, *Radical Enlightenment*, 135.

guidelines. Articles should be concise surveys, not personal essays: complete, accurate, and objective. They should summarize topics quickly in the lead section, as dictionaries do. These stylistic guidelines help Wikipedia fulfill the encyclopedia's traditional function: People consult the site for rapid introductions to a subject, written for the general reader.

Wikipedia's scope is far greater than previous encyclopedic projects, however. Encyclopedias have traditionally been published as comprehensive guides to some defined area of knowledge. Wikipedia is instead a collection of both specialist and generalist encyclopedias, linked together into an integrated work. Its articles can be updated immediately: Articles are dynamic, and their content can change from day to day or even (in the case of current events) from minute to minute. Wikipedia's huge scale and rapid updating is possible in part because the authorship model is completely different from earlier projects: The idea of the famous author or expert-written article has been discarded.

Finally, unlike earlier encyclopedias, Wikipedia is a noncommercial project, and its content is deliberately licensed so others can freely use it. This ease of access alone is surely far beyond what the early encyclopedists hoped for.

The 1960s and 1970s: Unix, Networks, and Personal Computers

Looking ahead several hundred years, we'll now explore the technological part of Wikipedia's heritage: the free software movement, the development and widespread growth of the Internet and the personal computer, and the development of wiki technology.

During the late 1960s, two key developments in computing technology occurred. The first was the beginning of the modern operating system essential to networked computing. In the 1960s, the computers in the public eye were the hugely expensive S/360 series of mainframe computers from IBM, whose twitching tape drives became iconic for speedy electronic brainwork. Meanwhile, comparatively disregarded at the time, the Unix operating system at Bell Labs was created on a humble PDP-7 minicomputer from the Digital Equipment Corporation. (According to legend, the machine had been recycled after having been left in a corridor.) Unix ultimately became one of the most widely used operating systems for the servers that power the Internet, continuing to flourish long after the IBM mainframes became hardware dinosaurs and inspiring a variety of free software projects.

During this same time period, the groundwork for the network that would become the Internet was laid. Called *ARPANET*, the original Internet was a US Department of Defense project first theorized in the 1960s. Along with other networks, ARPANET provided some of the first connections to universities and research institutions. Later, the technology behind this network became available for new networks available to consumers: The first email service was offered by CompuServe in 1979, the same year newsgroup software was developed.

A decade later, Tim Berners-Lee would develop a networked implementation of the idea of hypertext, an idea that would become the World Wide Web. With the development of web browsers in the early 1990s, consumers, who had been buying personal computers since the mid-1970s (a phenomenon that became widespread with the introduction of the Apple II in 1977), could now "go online" and participate in the growing Internet. These developments, occurring over just a few decades, completely reshaped the modern world and made large online projects like Wikipedia possible. The advent of personal networked computing also provided the necessary technical background for the cultural ideas of free software and online communities, which are critical to Wikipedia's development.

The 1980s: The Free Software Movement

In the early 1980s, Richard M. Stallman, a software developer at MIT's Artificial Intelligence Lab, became alarmed at what he saw as a loss of freedom for computer programmers. Stallman had spent two decades working in a collegial environment, where changing or amending software was technically feasible and clear of legal worries. If someone needed someone else's computer program, he just asked for and adapted it.

As explained on Wikipedia:

> In the late 1970s and 1980s, the hacker culture that Stallman thrived in began to fragment. To prevent software from being used on their competitors' computers, most manufacturers stopped distributing source code and began using copyright and restrictive software licenses to limit or prohibit copying and redistribution. Such proprietary software had existed before, and it became apparent that it would become the norm. [...]
>
> In 1980, Stallman and some other hackers at the AI lab were not given the source code of the software for the Xerox 9700 laser printer (code-named Dover), the industry's first. (From [[Richard Stallman]], April 2007)

While Stallman and other hackers had been able to customize another lab printer so that a message was sent to users trying to print when there was a paper jam, they could not do so with Dover—a major inconvenience, as the printer was on a different floor. Stallman asked for the printer software but was refused; this experience and others convinced Stallman of the ethical need for free software.

Software, now produced by companies such as Microsoft, was owned and controlled, and sharing it entailed breaking a license and breaking the law. *Source code*—the version of a program necessary to make changes—was frequently not made available. You couldn't customize software, even after you paid for it.

In 1983, Stallman announced the GNU operating system project and two years later founded the Free Software Foundation. In an essay titled "What is Free Software?" Stallman declared the freedoms essential for free software:

▸ The freedom to run the program for any purpose

▸ The freedom to study how the program works and adapt it to your needs

▸ The freedom to redistribute copies so you can help your neighbor

▸ The freedom to improve the program and release your improvements to the public so the whole community benefits

The GNU project (whose logo, appropriately enough, features a gnu—see Figure 2-5) set out to build a completely free operating system, inspired by Unix. The acronym *GNU* was a programmer's joke that stood for *GNU's Not Unix*. A collaborative project, GNU was largely functional by the early 1990s. In 1991, a young Finnish programmer named Linus Torvalds offered one of the last essential remaining pieces, a kernel.

FIGURE 2-5: *The GNU project logo*

Torvalds called his project *Linux*. The combined system of GNU software run on this kernel is known as *GNU/Linux* and is now widely used by both individuals and corporations. Hundreds of people worldwide have contributed to Linux.[6]

This operating system, which has become the basis of numerous distributions developed for different purposes, has been one of the great successes of the free software movement. Some versions of GNU/Linux are distributed commercially, such as Red Hat Linux. The ideas behind free software have become widespread; other successful examples of free software projects are the Apache software, on which many servers run, and the Mozilla web browser, which millions of people use. Today, freely licensed, collaboratively built software supports work by businesses and individuals worldwide.

GNU developers recognized that new software licenses, which differed from traditional ideas of copyright, needed to be created to preserve the freedom to share these programs legally. Although the rights assigned with copyright have been of concern for a long time—a mention is made of copyright in the US Constitution, which grants Congress the power to "promote the Progress of Science and useful Arts, by securing for limited Times to Authors and Inventors the exclusive Right to their respective Writings and Discoveries"—the advent of the personal computer and the Internet have magnified and broadened copyright issues. Broadly speaking, copyright law assigns the author of a creative work certain exclusive rights to sell and distribute that work, keeping others from copying and profiting from an author's work without permission. Today, copyright is assigned automatically in the United States and in many other countries when a work is created. However, because copying a work, such as a computer file, is now quick, routine, and costs virtually nothing, many questions have been raised about the place and effectiveness of copyright law in an electronic environment.

---

[6] For a discussion of large-scale collaboration sympathetic to Linux, see James Surowiecki, *The Wisdom of Crowds: Why the Many Are Smarter Than the Few and How Collective Wisdom Shapes Business, Economies, Societies and Nations* (New York: Doubleday, 2004). For a history of GNU/Linux, see Glen Moody, *Rebel Code: Inside Linux and the Open Source Revolution* (New York: Basic Books, 2001).

As an alternative to traditional copyright, Stallman created the General Public License (GPL) in 1989; today, this license is widely used for free software. This license is an example of *copyleft*—a movement to protect the freedom of creative works by using new licensing arrangements that incorporate ideas from free software.

As usual, Wikipedia has plenty to say on the matter:

> Copyleft is a play on the word copyright and is the practice of using copyright law to remove restrictions on distributing copies and modified versions of a work for others and requiring that the same freedoms be preserved in modified versions.

> Copyleft is a form of licensing and may be used to modify copyrights for works such as computer software, documents, music, and art. In general, copyright law allows an author to prohibit others from reproducing, adapting, or distributing copies of the author's work. In contrast, an author may, through a copyleft licensing scheme, give every person who receives a copy of a work permission to reproduce, adapt or distribute the work as long as any resulting copies or adaptations are also bound by the same copyleft licensing scheme. (From [[Copyleft]], April 2007)

By the turn of the 21st century, free software ideas had spread well beyond computer code. In 2000, Stallman created the GNU Free Documentation License (GFDL). The GFDL was conceived of as a complementary license to the GPL but was intended for written works such as software documentation rather than code. Wikipedia adopted the GFDL early on as its license for all content created on the site—a move that guarantees the site's content will remain perpetually free for everyone to use and redistribute.

Wikipedia and the Free Perspective

Wikipedia's approach is tied to the ideals of the free software movement. Both the software on which Wikipedia runs (MediaWiki) and the site's content are freely available for use by anyone to adapt and modify, qualified only by the requirements of their respective GPL and GFDL licenses. Wikipedia's slogan is *Wikipedia, the free encyclopedia*. No one has to pay to view Wikipedia articles, but *free* means more than that: Free also means "no strings attached," and this is the consistent goal of the Wikimedia projects. Freedom means free of cost, free of restrictions to change and modify any content, free to redistribute, free for anyone to participate, and free of commercial influences.[7] The GFDL license specifies that any work placed under it may be legally reused and republished by anyone, with the only restriction being that any such republishing must itself also be licensed under the GFDL (and the original authors must be credited). In other words, the license ensures that any GFDL-licensed content is both freely available and open

---

[7] See the Definition of Free Cultural Works (*http://freecontentdefinition.org/*), which the Wikimedia Foundation adopted for its projects in 2007 (*http://wikimediafoundation.org/wiki/Resolution:Licensing_policy*).

to all. Though contributors to Wikipedia *do* retain the copyrights to their work, they lose the right to specify what can be done with it.

Thus another site can repackage and profit from Wikipedia articles, as long as it respects the license. In fact, there are many legitimate sites like this, called *mirror sites*, and anyone using a search engine will come across them often. The only rules are that if a site does copy Wikipedia material, those pages must also be licensed under the GFDL and must acknowledge the content's origin. Because of this clause, the GFDL is sometimes called a *viral license*: It propagates and perpetuates itself.

Any author adding to Wikipedia should know what the license means. If having personal control over your work matters to you, you should not add it to Wikipedia. Once you have saved your contributions to the site, you've conceded that others can modify them and use them in any way they wish under the licensing terms.

Other works using the GFDL include the book you're reading; its text may be reused under the same conditions. The GFDL requires a history of authorship; on Wikipedia, you can look up the full list of original authors of articles (including pseudonyms, automated edits, and IP numbers) on the page histories of every Wikipedia page we cite. You'll find more about the GFDL and reuse compliance in Appendixes A and E.

1995: Ward's Wiki

Tim Berners-Lee, the pioneer of the World Wide Web's technology, has said he always intended for the Web to be interactive. The social and cooperative side of Internet usage is now catching up with that potential, and wiki sites are just one part of a larger pattern.

A *wiki* is a type of website that anyone can edit. Setting up a wiki creates an effective tool for collaborative group authoring. Simply speaking, a wiki is a collection of web pages, located at a common address on the World Wide Web, that link to each other through their page titles and can be edited online by contributors without special permissions. More technically, a wiki is a kind of database, consisting of pages of HTML, the markup language used on the Web, but wiki pages can be edited by contributors using a simpler markup language.

Structurally, a wiki can contain multiple discussions consisting of many topics and is by its very nature dynamic and changing. Most wikis record the changes that are made to them, keep previous versions of pages, and make it very simple to add clickable links from one page to another page on the site. Openness is a key feature of most wikis as well. You don't need much technical knowledge or special permission to edit most wiki pages; instead, you can change them as you see fit. Wiki pages contrast with conventional web pages that have largely static and uneditable content.

The wiki concept and the name come from Howard G. "Ward" Cunningham, an American computer programmer. Instead of calling his idea QuickWeb, his first idea, he chose the Hawaiian term *wiki wiki* when setting up his website, WikiWikiWeb:

> In order to make the exchange of ideas between programmers easier, Ward Cunningham started developing the WikiWikiWeb in 1994 based on the ideas developed in HyperCard stacks that he built in the late 1980s. He installed the WikiWikiWeb on his company Cunningham & Cunningham's website c2.com on March 25, 1995. Cunningham named WikiWikiWeb that way because he remembered a Honolulu International Airport counter employee telling him to take the so-called "Wiki Wiki" Chance RT-52 shuttle bus line that runs between the airport's terminals. "Wiki Wiki" is a reduplication of "wiki," a Hawaiian-language word for *fast*. (From [[WikiWikiWeb]], April 2007)

On this original wiki site, meant for the Portland Pattern Repository (Figure 2-6), programmers exchanged ideas on patterns and approaches to programming, forming a somewhat rambling but fruitful discussion space.

In its original concept, a wiki expresses the views of a community with some common interest and brings people together in a shared space for discussing ideas and building resources. The main point of a wiki website is to make it easy for contributors to collaborate in building its content, whatever that content may be. If the site is wide open, what "the community" is may be nebulous, but a *wiki community* is often simply defined as those people who are editing the site.

A wiki, then, is not simply a technology but a whole approach for a group using a website to collaborate. This approach, which you could call a philosophy, cannot really be expressed by looking at single users or editors: Wikis have a collective aspect. In this, wikis are related to and draw from the culture of other online and open source communities.

1997: Open Source Communities

For software to be freely available is one thing, for many people to contribute to building the software is another. In an influential 1997 essay, "The Cathedral and the Bazaar," Eric S. Raymond drew on the recent history of Linux development and argued that the open nature of free software allowed for widescale collaboration and development. Raymond coined a new term, *open source*, with a definition similar to the idea of *free software*. In the late 1990s, a group of Bay Area computer programmers and Raymond developed an open source movement, which also centered around sharable software but particularly emphasized the pragmatic benefits of collaboratively developed software to companies.

Raymond described how opening up software projects by making source code available and using open development processes could ultimately produce better software by increasing the number of people able to work on it. He coined the aphorism, "Given enough eyeballs, all bugs are shallow," which emphasizes how many different people, all concerned with understanding a program, help to find mistakes and other weaknesses and get them fixed quickly. In the essay, he

Front Page

This site is a ContentCreationWiki whose focus is PeopleProjectsAndPatterns in SoftwareDevelopment.

The ideas of "Wiki" may seem strange at first, but dive in and explore its links. "Wiki" is a composition system; it's a discussion medium; it's a repository; it's a mail system; it's a tool for collaboration. Really, we don't know quite what it is, but it's a fun way of communicating asynchronously across the network.

The name "Wiki" is strange too - what does it mean? The WikiWikiWebFaq answers this and other questions, but the short answer is that "WikiWiki" is Hawaiian for "quick".

You should start with WelcomeVisitors. It describes what we are doing, as well as how to get around, and how to get involved. Watch the pages expand and refine here. Watch the discussions that surround the process. Watch information AutoMagically crystallize!

To find a page on any specific topic, go to FindPage. To see an auto-generated list of pages which have changed recently, try RecentChanges. If you want a short list of randomly-selected pages, try RandomPages. CategoryCategory is the top level of page categorization; you can use it to delve deeper into the site.

Edit pages by using the EditText link at the bottom of the page you wish to edit. Don't worry too much about messing up, as the original text is backed up and can be easily restored (meaning, everyone can see the changes made, and will be able to correct mistakes, erase, and so on, if necessary).

The Text Formatting Rules are quite simple, and the Tips For Beginners will help you learn to apply them gracefully. You'll probably want to start by editing pages that already exist. The WikiWikiSandbox is set aside for editing practice. Go there now to try it. (Please don't edit this page; changes here will likely be reversed within a few minutes).

Once you've made a couple of updates, you'll be ready to participate in discussions on the "Wiki", and before you know it you will be Adding New Pages.

Please read WikiWikiSystemNotice for the latest information regarding the operation of this site.

This site's WikiEngine, WikiBase, has since spawned other WikiEngines, which themselves have become a popular way to document things.

If you want information on the content you can expect to encounter, take a look at OnTopic and OffTopic. WikiInTheNews collects mentions of this site in the wider world.

Note that spam is not allowed on this site. Any spam encountered will be deleted immediately. Spamming this site will not increase your PageRank. See DelayedIndexing.

A history of how this page has evolved over time can be viewed at WikiArchive.

Note: the VisualTour link (at the bottom of every page) no longer works, and is no more. We apologize for any inconvenience.

Navigation Hints:

- StartingPoints
- ReallyValuablePages
- WikiList

EditText of this page (last edited January 16, 2008)
FindPage by searching (or browse LikePages or take a VisualTour)

FIGURE 2-6: *The front page of the original wiki at* http://c2.com/cgi/wiki

also writes about the other benefits of using a self-selected group of collaborators who are only acting out of their own passion for the project:

> . . . contributions [to Linux] are received not from a random sample, but from people who are interested enough to use the software, learn about how it works, attempt to find solutions to problems they encounter, and actually produce an apparently reasonable fix. Anyone who passes all these filters is highly likely to have something useful to contribute. (From Eric S. Raymond, "The Cathedral and the Bazaar," presented at Linux Kongress, 1997)

In a comparable way, Wikipedia urges its many readers to become writers, fact-checkers, and copyeditors, allowing anyone to ask a question or fix incorrect information. In a broad sense, the ideas of shared improvement and collective scrutiny are common to wikis, free software, and the concept of an encyclopedia that anyone can edit.

2000: Online Community Dynamics

Wikipedia is famous for fostering an elaborate, unusual volunteer community, but Wikipedia is far from being the first online community or the first wiki community. Other groups had already explored the ideas that would become the basis of Wikipedia's social principles.

Dedicated virtual communities have been around since the very beginning of computer networks. As the Internet has grown, hundreds of online communities have developed, each with its own mores and traditions. The idea of *community* suggests a focus on the individual people involved and how they interact as being key to understanding how these groups function. Wikipedia suggests a definition of a virtual community as being simply "a social network with a common interest, idea, task or goal that interacts in a virtual society across time, geographical and organizational boundaries and is able to develop personal relationships." For instance, some early notable online communities include the following (adapted from [[Virtual community]]):

▸ Usenet, established in 1980 as a *distributed Internet discussion system*, was one of the first highly developed online communities with volunteer moderators

▸ The WELL, established in 1985, pioneered some aspects of online community culture with many users voluntarily contributing to community building and maintenance (for example, as conference hosts).

▸ AOL offered various forms of chat and gaming from its inception in 1983 and later helped pioneer the contemporary "chatroom." These chatrooms were initially moderated by volunteer community leaders and helped propel AOL to its position as the largest of the online service providers.

The new wiki communities in the late 1990s started with the idea of interacting online, which had been developed by these and many other online communities, and then added the ideas of open mass collaboration articulated by the growing free and open source software movement. But as wikis matured, they had to develop new ideas and principles for how people could collaborate fruitfully on such open, radically different websites.

The people working on the original WikiWikiWeb coined terms and developed ideas that would later become influential in other wiki communities, for instance, that people could take on different roles such as *wiki gnomes*, who beaver around on the site fixing small points of format and style. They also noticed that content could develop on a wiki in various ways (some better than others), for example, as *walled gardens*, dense areas of content that the average editor found hard to access.

The conversation continued on one small but influential wiki, MeatballWiki, which was set up in April 2000 by the Canadian Sunir Shah. This wiki attracted those interested in discussing online communities and their dynamics and typical issues. Much of the conversation on MeatballWiki was about the ways in which individual editors tended to respond to the freedom of editing a wiki. The concepts of *soft security* (security through group dynamics rather than hard-coded limits) and the *right to leave* (someone should be able to both join and leave a wiki community easily and gracefully) were first discussed here. Users also discussed large-scale concepts that affected the whole community, such as *forking* and *interwiki* connections—communities splitting apart or coming together. MeatballWiki continues today, full of essays, discussions, arguments, and musings about what constitutes a healthy, successful online community and what it means to work on a wiki.

Thus, the WikiWikiWeb, MeatballWiki, and other early sites developed the terminology and articulated the principles of structuring community that many wikis, including Wikipedia, operate with today. Wikipedia, in turn, has gone on to apply these ideas in large-scale ways not imagined by these early wikis.

Wikipedia as a Wiki Community

Wikipedia developed in an atmosphere where wikis were already established as a particular kind of online community. The word *wiki* is sometimes interpreted as a *backronym*, a back-formed acronym, as if it stood for *W-I-K-I*. In the style of Internet abbreviations, you could read this as *What I Know Is*, referring to the knowledge contribution, storage, and exchange functions of wikis. A typical wiki is still reminiscent of notes on an extended brainstorming session: The hypertext structure makes it possible to take up any point in its own smaller discussion thread. The early wikis were precursors to Wikipedia, not only in terms of technology, but also because people saw wiki editing, from the start, as a way to share knowledge. Wikipedia, however, changed the model of wikis from being a continuing conversation among peers to being a project for collating information and building a reference resource—and in so doing, showed that you could build a single work with a large, disparate online community spanning language and geography.

Being a wiki site is not intrinsic to Wikipedia's content. The adaptation of wiki technology, however, has been key to Wikipedia's quick success in an area where previous projects have failed. From the point of view of a technology historian, Wikipedia already deserves to be called a *killer app*, the sort of application of a technology that in itself justifies the success of wikis. Wikipedia has used its wiki aspects successfully to collate and develop the world's largest encyclopedia so far.

Embracing the history of encyclopedias, the openness of free software, and the easily accessible, collaborative aspects of online communities and wikis meant that Wikipedia was able to draw on both a large pool of technically aware people who saw the benefits of the free software movement as well as many nontechnical people who were attracted to the encyclopedic mission and community structure. A high level of collaboration has been possible in areas that would have been difficult to foresee. For instance, current events articles are rapidly updated, often with a thousand or more edits from hundreds of people in a single day, demonstrating the extraordinarily responsive power of this collaborative tool.

2001: Wikipedia Goes Live

Wikipedia has been an evolving phenomenon from the start. It has grown rapidly and has steadily attracted more attention.

Wikipedia's immediate predecessor was Nupedia. (This was not the first Internet encyclopedia idea, however; Interpedia, a project from 1993, never got off the drawing board.) Nupedia was started by Jimmy Wales, with Larry Sanger serving as editor-in-chief. The project was supported by Bomis, an Internet portal company founded and run by Wales and Tim Shell. Nupedia sought to provide an online encyclopedia website under a free-content license, built from contributed articles. Its model was more conventional, though; it was not a wiki, and contributors were expected to be experts in their fields. The pieces they submitted would only be published to the site after an extensive peer review process. The momentum of the project became lost in these multiple review stages, and only a few articles were ever completed.

Wikipedia was created on January 15, 2001, as an alternative based on an open wiki site. Initially, the site was presented as a way to attract new contributors and articles to Nupedia. (Both Sanger and Wales participated in developing the site in the early days, and there was later some dispute over whether they were "co-founders" of Wikipedia. Sanger left the project in 2002, while Wales continues to play a leading role in Wikipedia today.) To differentiate the site from Nupedia, the new project was named Wikipedia.

Wikipedia was immediately successful. Its wiki setup lowered the barriers to entry, and its reputation grew by word-of-mouth alone—the site has never advertised directly. A few key mentions on popular websites drew notice to the site; in March 2001, a posting was made on the Slashdot website, and in July of that year, it received a prominent pointer in a story on the community-edited technology and culture website Kuro5hin. These stories brought surges of traffic to Wikipedia, including people with technical savvy. Search engines, especially Google, also brought hundreds of new visitors to the site every day. The first major coverage in the mainstream media was in the *New York Times* on September 20, 2001.

By mid-2001, Wikipedia was beginning to acquire an identity of its own (Figure 2-7). Versions in Catalan, Chinese, German, French, Hebrew, Italian, Spanish, Japanese, Russian, Portuguese, and Esperanto had been created, and technical support had been set up (mostly far from the public gaze, as Jimmy

Wales chatted on IRC and discussed issues on the mailing list). More visitors meant more articles were written and also more edits were made to improve existing articles (just as important, if a little harder to quantify). The Recent Changes page showed increasing activity. The project passed 1,000 articles around February 12, 2001 and 10,000 articles around September 7, 2001 (see Figure 2-8 for how Wikipedia appeared around December 2001). Nupedia, by contrast, only completed some 24 finished articles over its lifespan from 2000 to 2003.

Wikipedia Today

Today, *Wikipedia* is a household word (at least in households with access to the Web). By late 2007, the site had become the #8 most visited website worldwide, as measured by Alexa ratings,[8] and the volunteer-based community organization behind Wikipedia has become highly complex, learning from past mistakes and developing institutions. Wikipedia is not only a piece of hypertext; the site is by far the largest and most inclusive cross-referenced single collection of factual information to ever exist. Due in part to this assiduous cross-linking of content, Wikipedia articles are prominent in search engine results; many (if not most) queries on the Web can be answered with a Wikipedia article. Wikipedia is an *Internet phenomenon*, unlike anything seen before—and it could not have technically existed on a comparable scale until quite recently.

During the early years, Wikipedia was administered (technically, financially, and socially) entirely by volunteers. The hardware and personnel needed to run the site was donated by Bomis. As time passed, however, Wikipedia's needs outstripped the ability of Bomis to meet them. The site's infrastructure (but not its content) is now run by the nonprofit Wikimedia Foundation (WMF), which will be described in depth in Chapter 17.

The WMF, employing a very small staff and governed by a board of directors, has taken on the role of coordinating a very large and disparate group of volunteers from around the world: By 2008, Wikipedias existed in over 250 languages. The Foundation serves as the parent organization for all Wikipedias and sister projects (these other reference projects are described in Chapter 16). Initially based in St. Petersburg, Florida, the WMF moved to San Francisco early in 2008.

FIGURE 2-7: *The Wikipedia logo used from late 2001 until 2003. This logo was designed by a volunteer called The Cunctator and was the winner in an open logo contest. See the progression of the Wikipedia logo over time at* http://meta.wikimedia.org/wiki/Meta:Historical/Logo_history.

---

[8] Alexa is a Web-traffic measuring company that uses data from individuals using the Alexa toolbar (*http://www.alexa.com/*).

HomePage

From Wikipedia

HomePage | Recent changes | View source | Page history | Log in |

Special pages ▾ (Go)

WIKIPEDIA
The Free Encyclopedia

See the current version of this page on Wikipedia

Printable version | Disclaimers | Privacy policy

Welcome to Wikipedia, a collaborative project to produce a complete encyclopedia from scratch. We started in January 2001 and already have **over 19,000 articles**. We want to make over 100,000, so let's get to work--*anyone* can edit any article--copyedit, expand an article, write a little, write a lot. See the Wikipedia FAQ for information on how to edit pages and other questions.

The content of Wikipedia is covered by the GNU Free Documentation License, which means that it is free and will remain so forever. See open content and free content for background.

Current Events and Breaking News
Encyclopedia articles about topics behind the news.
2001 U.S. Attack on Afghanistan - More current events

Philosophy, Mathematics, and Natural Science
Astronomy and Astrophysics - Biology - Chemistry - Earth Sciences - Mathematics - Philosophy - Physics - Statistics

Social Sciences
Anthropology - Archaeology - Economics - Geography - History - History of Science and Technology - Language - Linguistics - Parapsychology - Political Science - Psychology - Sociology

Applied Arts and Sciences
Agriculture - Architecture - Business and Industry - Communication - Computer Science - Education - Engineering - Family and Consumer Science - Health Sciences - Law - Library and Information Science - Public Affairs - Technology - Transport

Culture
Classics - Cooking - Critical Theory - Dance - Entertainment - Film - Games - Hobbies - Literature - Music - Opera - Painting - Recreation - Religion - Sculpture - Sports - Theater - Tourism - Visual Arts and Design

Other Category Schemes
About Wikipedia category schemes - Complete list of encyclopedia topics - Library of Congress catalog scheme - Dewey Decimal System - Wikipedia arranged by topic - Historical timeline - Historical anniversaries - Reference tables - Biographical Listing - Current events

Wikipedias in other languages
About the non-English Wikipedias - Arabic (Araby) - Catalan (Català) - Chinese (Hanyu) - Danish (Dansk) - Dutch (Nederlands) - German (Deutsch) - Esperanto - French (Français) - Hebrew (Ivrit) - Hungarian (Magyar) - Italian (Italiano) - Japanese (Nihongo) - Polish (Polska) - Portuguese (Português) - Russian (Russkiy) - Simplified English - Spanish (Castellano) - Swedish (Svenska)

Wikipedia
About the project: Announcements - How to edit a page - FAQ - Policy - Feature requests - Bug reports - Mailing list - Wikipedia and Nupedia - Wikipedians - Wikipedia Chat
Article pointers: Article news - New topics - Brilliant prose - Receive articles daily by e-mail - Go to a random page - Index of all pages
Content requests: Requested articles - Help desk
Useful resources for us: Wikipedia utilities - Tarballs of Wikipedia data - Public domain resources - Commentary, which is being transferred to meta.wikipedia.com - SandBox
Selected press coverage: *The New York Times -- December 9, 2001* *The New York Times -- September 20, 2001* - MIT's *Technology Review* (and a letter)
Links: Friends of Wikipedia

Today is Thursday, December 20, 2001, servertime (U.S. Pacific Time)

/Talk

Note: Unless you have the administrator password, you cannot currently edit this page. While this is unfortunate, it has turned out to be necessary to prevent vandalism of this page, which has occurred on several occasions.

View source | Discuss this page? | Page history | What links here | Related changes

---

This page was last modified 04:43, 15 January 2005. Content is available under GNU Free Documentation License.
HomePage | About Wikipedia |

[ ] (Go) (Search)

FIGURE 2-8: *Wikipedia as it appeared in late 2001 (from the Nostalgia wiki, http://nostalgia.wikipedia.org, a browsable version of a snapshot of Wikipedia from 2001)*

However, most of the servers that provide Wikipedia's infrastructure are still hosted in Florida, with additional servers in Europe and South Korea.

The Foundation's goals have remained in line with the ideal of volunteers freely creating content and distributing the world's information. Its mission statement is, in part,

> to empower and engage people around the world to collect and develop educational content under a free license or in the public domain, and to disseminate it effectively and globally. . . . The Foundation will make and keep useful information from its projects available on the Internet free of charge, in perpetuity.

The rest of the story of Wikipedia belongs in Part IV. There we'll tell you about the current gamut of projects in many languages and about the Wikimedia Foundation. The key ingredients for these projects and the Foundation were already in place after the first six months: developers to work on the software, open authorship of content, an international and multilingual group of contributors, word-of-mouth publicity, and a loose but effective central control of infrastructure, with community-driven lightweight editorial mechanisms.

Unfinished Business

Wikipedia's growth is still entirely open ended—the project has simplified the problem of where to stop by completely disregarding that question. The number of articles on the English-language Wikipedia might still grow by a factor of three or four, or even more. For instance, information about geography, if added to the same depth for the rest of the world as it has been already for the United States, could swell the English-language Wikipedia to a size between 5 and 10 million articles.

There are better questions to ask, however, than simply concentrating on future growth. How easy is it to find fresh encyclopedic topics? When will the editing community switch to focusing on greater depth and quality for each individual article, rather than on greater breadth of coverage overall? This may well be happening already: Quality of content is becoming just as important as quantity (see Chapter 7 for more on these quality-focused projects and how to get involved).

Enquire Within Upon Everything was a bestselling Victorian reference and how-to book, first published in 1856 (and referenced in the name of Tim Berners-Lee's early web precursor project ENQUIRE). This would perhaps be a better title for Wikipedia, which is gradually becoming a reference about everything. But some caution is still required when using Wikipedia (see Chapter 4), and this is to be expected; the wiki culture has a deep acceptance of imperfection and incompleteness as both inevitable and perhaps even necessary for inspiring a working community.

Further Reading

Encyclopedias

http://en.wikipedia.org/wiki/Encyclopedia#History   A brief history of encyclopedias

http://en.wikipedia.org/wiki/List_of_encyclopedias   A list of encyclopedias

http://en.wikipedia.org/wiki/Internet_encyclopedia_project   Information about projects to build an online encyclopedia

Free Software and Open Source

http://www.fsf.org/   The Free Software Foundation

http://en.wikipedia.org/wiki/Richard_Stallman   A biography of Richard Stallman

http://www.catb.org/~esr/writings/cathedral-bazaar/   The text of Eric Raymond's essay, "The Cathedral and the Bazaar"

Wikis and Communities

http://c2.com/cgi/wiki?WelcomeVisitors   c2.com, the first and original WikiWikiWeb

http://en.wikipedia.org/wiki/Wiki   About wikis, from Wikipedia

http://en.wikipedia.org/wiki/History_of_wikis   The history of wikis

http://meta.wikimedia.org/wiki/Interwiki_map   Meta page on interwiki prefixes

http://en.wikipedia.org/wiki/Virtual_community   Virtual or online communities

http://www.usemod.com/cgi-bin/mb.pl?WikiPediaIsNotTypical   An essay from MeatballWiki, "WikiPediaIsNotTypical"

Wikipedia

http://en.wikipedia.org/wiki/Wikipedia#History   The history of Wikipedia, from Wikipedia

http://wikimediafoundation.org/wiki/Mission_statement   The WMF mission statement

http://www.alexa.com/data/details/traffic_details/wikipedia.org   Alexa traffic details, for the Wikipedia sites

http://reagle.org/joseph/2005/historical/digital-works.html   An essay by Joseph Reagle, "Wikipedia's Heritage: Vision, Pragmatics, and Happenstance," on Wikipedia's influences and early history

The Wikipedia Model Debated

Wikipedia has been extraordinarily successful in its mission of producing a widely used, free-content encyclopedia in many languages. This success is reflected both in the very high use of the site and in the well-developed global community of dedicated volunteers that produce Wikipedia. However, Wikipedia is unfinished and far from being perfect, and this is reflected in the press about the site. Outside news stories about the site are often not "good news" about more free content. The media shows a greater interest in the "bad news" about the site's failings, which means many people first hear about Wikipedia in critical commentaries, usually about inaccuracies.

Over time, Wikipedia has acquired many critics, and hundreds of stories have been published about flaws in Wikipedia's coverage. Some discuss problems with individual articles, while others comment negatively on Wikipedia's overall policies and governance. Some also critique the entire idea behind Wikipedia. This criticism is not limited to outside media: Internally, contributors spend a great deal of time discussing how Wikipedia works and how to improve it.

In this section, we'll highlight some common objections to Wikipedia's working model: the potential for misinformation, academic respectability, and a lack of respect for expert and authoritative opinions and openness to amateur editors. We'll describe a few real-life case studies and critiques and describe Wikipedia's response. None of these objections are settled issues with easy answers; Wikipedia continues to refine its model. We encourage you, as you read through this book and learn more about how Wikipedia works, to consider these and other questions in forming your own opinion.

Misinformation: The Seigenthaler Scandal

In May 2005, a defamatory article slipped past the *New Pages Patrol*, the informal group of Wikipedia editors who check new articles as they are created. An anonymous hoaxer inserted a short fabricated biography, just five sentences, in the article covering John Seigenthaler, Sr., a distinguished American journalist who had served in the Justice Department of the Kennedy White House. The text suggested that Seigenthaler was connected to the Kennedy assassinations. No one noticed for five months—until September 2005 when the prank was revealed and made headlines.

A friend of Seigenthaler's originally discovered the article; he alerted Seigenthaler, who in turn contacted Jimmy Wales to complain. The objectionable content was deleted from the live page almost immediately after being noticed, by September 24, 2005; in early October, the article was then deleted altogether so the objectionable version could not be viewed from the page history (an accurate biography was subsequently re-created). Because Wikipedia content is mirrored on other sites, Seigenthaler also had to request his biography be removed at some of these sites, such as Answers.com and Reference.com.

The matter did not rest there, however. Seigenthaler published a guest editorial in November of that year in *USA Today*.[9] In it, he talks about his "Internet character assassination," damns the "poison-pen intellects" loose on the Internet, and calls Wikipedia a flawed research tool. This sparked off several other articles about the site and interviews with both Seigenthaler and Jimmy Wales.[10]

The whole event was something of a defining moment for the site. The national news story of the vandalized Seigenthaler biography brought home the point that Wikipedia was now prominent enough that the accuracy of an article *mattered*—defamatory or inaccurate content really could harm individuals. Before the Seigenthaler scandal, Wikipedia contributors tended to accept that some incorrect content was on the site and held to the philosophy of "so fix it." This idea, which is still a core part of Wikipedia's basic philosophy, holds that on an open wiki where anyone can contribute, anyone who spots something wrong can—and should—also fix it themselves. The Seigenthaler incident prompted an intense effort to write more accurately sourced articles, to institute a zero-tolerance environment for nonsense, and to recognize that people who have no desire to work on the site themselves may be affected by Wikipedia articles.

Several procedural changes also followed in the wake of this story and the issues attendant with the tremendous growth Wikipedia experienced at the end of 2005. One development was the policy on biographies of living people ([[Wikipedia:Biographies of living persons]], shortcut WP:BLP). This policy holds such biographies to strict compliance with Verifiability and No Original Research and discusses how to maintain the Neutral Point of View policy when dealing with negative and irrelevant information or information that is out of balance with the rest of the article. Violating this policy by inserting gossip or defamatory content is very serious; the article or the revision in question may be deleted, and ongoing violations may lead to an editor being blocked from editing. To deal with article complaints, Wikipedia also set up an email address and answering mechanism staffed by trusted volunteers.

In December 2005, anonymous article creation from IP addresses was stopped. You must now register and log in to create an article (see Chapter 6). This policy helped cut down on the number of nonsense pages being created, pages that site administrators had to delete, which had become a huge amount of work—on the order of thousands of pages a day. Some question whether this measure is effective, and in the future, Wikipedia may experiment with turning anonymous article creation back on to see how much of a difference it makes.

One of the scandal's side-effects has been that people working in the media—and anyone whose name has been in the news—now tend to check whether they have a Wikipedia page, and many request to have the page changed (or in some cases, deleted). Editors treat such requests carefully, however. They consider the issue of neutrality and accurate sourcing and will not change articles simply to meet the wishes of the subject.

---

[9] See John Seigenthaler, "A false Wikipedia 'biography,'" *USA Today* (November 29, 2005), *http://www.usatoday.com/news/opinion/editorials/2005-11-29-wikipedia-edit_x.htm.*

[10] The history of the whole incident is summarized in the article [[Seigenthaler incident]].

John Seigenthaler's sermon about the responsible use of Wikipedia's growing media power has not fallen on deaf ears. The possibility that an article can slip through the cracks is very real. Many increasingly sophisticated mechanisms to watch for and correct bad content have been created (see Chapter 7), but Wikipedia's openness—a key value—means that something incorrect may be submitted and go unnoticed until it causes trouble.

Amateur Contributors, Authority, and Academia

Any Wikipedia contributor can be anonymous, and most are *pseudonymous*. Contributors are under no obligation whatsoever to reveal who they are "in real life," and the majority do not. You can't really know the details of an author's experience with a topic unless he or she volunteers that information. And experience is not supposed to matter: Whether someone is a college professor or a high school student, what matters is whether he or she respects Wikipedia's rules and contributes productively to the encyclopedia. This principle has been of primary importance since the beginning: An author's or editor's background should not affect his or her standing as a Wikipedia contributor.

By the same token, the content policies set out in Chapter 1 (particularly Verifiability) apply to everyone. Wikipedia does not simply accept arguments from authorities. Even widely known experts in a field have to support all claims they make by including appropriate references to published literature (at least in principle).

Given this, many questions arise. If most contributors are semi-anonymous, does it matter if someone lies about who he or she is? Is Wikipedia anti-academic? Does it harm itself by not respecting experts' opinions enough? And is the site credible, given that amateurs have built it?

In this section, we'll look at different aspects of authority and criticisms of the Wikipedia model.

Wikipedia and Academic Authority

Wikipedia has an uneven reputation with educators; some see it as having low quality, and others train students to use Wikipedia appropriately. Many colleges have now made it clear that citations from Wikipedia are not acceptable in term papers.[11] Wikipedia fails some tests of academic respectability for two basic reasons.

One is concern about the quality and accuracy of Wikipedia content, which certainly varies across the site. The other, more fundamental reason is that college-level teaching can properly view encyclopedia articles, of whatever standard, as being for the lazy student. Students should do their own research.

Those who work on Wikipedia would generally agree. Articles are intended to give quick access to information, and Wikipedia's references to scholarly works are meant to facilitate study, not replace it. Students should follow up on the references given in articles and research a topic in other sources too. Writing an essay

---

[11] See Noam Cohen, "A History Department Bans Citing Wikipedia as a Research Source," *The New York Times* (February 21, 2007), *http://www.nytimes.com/2007/02/21/education/21wikipedia.html*.

by paraphrasing Wikipedia is not acceptable, and of course copying Wikipedia directly deserves a grade of *F*. Unfortunately, students can easily use the site in place of other sources. (See Appendix B for specific advice for educators using and concerned about Wikipedia.)

Wikipedia and Experts

The need to find supporting references for statements in articles (enshrined in the Verifiability and No Original Research policies) is connected to the way that controversies are handled on the site, particularly questions of contributor expertise. If you post something at all debatable, whatever your standing in the field, you must allow others to question it. Statements should make clear who said what and where, and neutrality means you include the full range of opinions. You can't just insert your expert knowledge as Wikipedia content, with no references to back up your work.

Wikipedia, therefore, has an egalitarian policy for editors. An expert has the same privileges as any other editor: Expertise must manifest itself through the editing and discussion process. The general argument is that if you're an expert in a topic, you have probably spent some years looking at the literature and should know the relevant publications to cite, so you can follow the policies with ease. The requirement to cite is a concession to the general, skeptical reader and rules out any arguments along the lines of "because I say so, and you should just accept that." If you write extemporaneously, without citing your sources, be prepared for questions along the line of "How do you know?" This challenge will happen to expert and non-expert contributors alike.

Some have argued that this leveling approach to the Wikipedia model is simply wrong. One formulation of this argument is that asking experts and professors for scholarly support for their opinions is disrespectful. Another is that Wikipedia is actively hostile to experts and expert knowledge, forcing even the most knowledgeable in a field to be challenged by extreme skeptics and amateurs.

A mismatch between the encyclopedic tradition of giving conclusions and leaving out some of the reasons why and the emphasis on giving full details and sourcing can occur. Even the reliance on *reliable sources* can be problematic. Reliable sources should be cited, but who determines which sources are reliable? Criticism of sources should be fair-minded, but experts can sound argumentative or too quick in their judgment to outsiders.

The solution Wikipedia offers to these difficulties is the dedicated discussion pages attached to articles. On a discussion page, you can query and clarify steps in arguments that are made in articles, as well as question the source of these statements. If, for example, the status of some book is in question, a hostile review can be brought up on the discussion page, even though it would be misplaced in the article itself. However, discussion alone sometimes can't solve conflicts involving questions of expertise, as shown in the following case studies. If the skeptic feels the expert is dodging the issue, but the expert is just trying to be concise, neither side will be satisfied.

Case Studies in Academic Authority

Wikipedia's interface with academia matters greatly to its progress, but academic authority alone is not sufficient for making one's case on Wikipedia. Wikipedia's approach in this matter has been shaped by real-world experience—including editing disputes, scandals, and matters that have been through the on-site judicial system. When contributors work pseudonymously, their qualifications must be either taken on trust or ignored. In addition, Wikipedia's history shows that even confirmed academic credentials are not a realistic safeguard against editorial clashes on the site. Editing by those holding credentials can be contested.

A contentious and highly visible area of science, the issue of climate change and its possible causes, led to one drama on Wikipedia in 2005. Many articles were involved; at this time, nearly 100 articles on climatologists, over 100 articles on global warming skeptics, and around 100 articles on the science of global warming exist (you can find these in the subcategories under [[Category:Climatology]]).

William M. Connolley, an academic climatologist, edits Wikipedia under his real name. Connolley ran into trouble monitoring and updating climate change pages when confronted with extreme skeptics who were also editing the climate change articles. Sheer disbelief can undermine any attempt to write sensible scientific material in accordance with consensus views, and in this case, the controversy led to edit warring between the two sides.

Due to this dispute, Connolley was sanctioned by the *Arbitration Committee*, the formal body of volunteer editors who help regulate and resolve disputes on the site and have the power to sanction editors if necessary (see Chapter 14).[12] His sanctions consisted of a *revert parole*—he could only undo one change a day made by another editor, a move designed to help prevent edit warring. These sanctions were later reconsidered and dropped. Throughout the case, Connolley's qualifications to write on climate topics were not an issue; the ability to edit productively and in harmony with other editors has little to do with one's knowledge of a subject.

In a later case on *pseudoscience* from late 2006 ([[Wikipedia:Requests for arbitration/Pseudoscience]]), Wikipedia's view of academic authority was further clarified. The underlying issue had to do with neutrality (NPOV) and its implications for representing all major points of view when the matter in question was scientific. This ruling by the Arbitration Committee went more clearly with mainstream science; the scientific consensus is expected to predominate in scientific articles. The relevant principle read, "Wikipedia.Neutral point of view, a fundamental policy, requires fair representation of significant alternatives to scientific orthodoxy. Significant alternatives, in this case, refers to legitimate scientific disagreement, as opposed to pseudoscience."

---

[12] The details of this restriction, from the first case in 2005, are posted at [[Wikipedia:Requests for arbitration/Climate change dispute]]. In the second case on the matter from 2005 ([[Wikipedia:Requests for arbitration/Climate change dispute 2]]), it was found that "William M. Connolley has generally adhered to his revert parole, although isolated instances can be found where compliance is incomplete or questionable," and "The one revert parole placed upon William M. Connolley was an unnecessary move, and is hereby revoked."

A third case along these lines involved Carl Hewitt,[13] an Emeritus Associate Professor at the Massachusetts Institute of Technology, who was banned from editing certain articles on the English-language Wikipedia. Arbitration committee rulings determined that he violated the Neutral Point of View policy and overstated the importance of his own contributions (and those of his students) in theoretical computer science and some other areas such as quantum mechanics and the sociology of science. The issue here is not the demarcation of the academic and non-academic approaches, but rather that Wikipedia articles, as surveys of academic literature, must not give undue weight to one approach. One affected area was logic programming, the basic technology of the "fifth generation computing" project. Here Hewitt overstepped the policy on No Original Research, attempting to impose his own definition of the field in the article.[14]

These cases all illustrate specific difficulties with the Wikipedia model. Academics and other experts are subject to the same policies, on conduct and content, that apply to everyone else on the site. These cases differ, however. Hewitt's approach violated the letter and spirit of Neutral Point of View, clearly causing a conflict of interest. Experts are not immune to human failings and passion. Connolley's problems with troublesome non-experts were short-lived because of his patience with the sanctions and with other editors; his substantiation of his own contributions was never an issue. A neutral point of view is simply not negotiable on Wikipedia, no matter how great your expertise.

Pseudonyms and Claimed Expertise

The role of editors' authority and expertise has also been debated in regards to what editors can say about themselves. The case of User:Essjay, real name Ryan Jordan, came to light in the Spring of 2007 and was prominent in the news for some time.

Essjay was a well-respected and experienced editor on the English-language Wikipedia, holding several trusted administrative positions. He also claimed anonymity, not revealing his real name or identity on the site, but did claim on his user page that he had a theology doctorate and an academic teaching position. He typically worked on the administrative and process side of the site, rather than on content, and became respected as a fair and committed Wikipedian.

In 2006, Essjay was interviewed for a lengthy piece in *The New Yorker*[15] and continued to state that he was an academic. This was later determined to be untrue—Jordan was really a young student without experience in theology—and by misleading the journalist he embarrassed Wikipedia. After the scandal broke, he resigned from the site. Questions remain as to whether he had ever used his claimed expertise to influence content and ultimately whether claimed (but false) topical expertise mattered when considering his well-documented skills as an

[13] See Jenny Kleeman, "Wikipedia Ban for Disruptive Professor," *The Guardian* (December 9, 2007), *http://www.guardian.co.uk/technology/2007/dec/09/wikipedia.internet*.

[14] The details of his case are posted at [[Wikipedia:Requests for arbitration/Carl Hewitt]]. Hewitt did not accept the justice of the rulings and attempted to circumvent the editing restrictions placed on him.

[15] See Stacy Schiff, "Know It All: Can Wikipedia Conquer Expertise?" *The New Yorker* (July 31, 2006), *http://www.newyorker.com/archive/2006/07/31/060731fa_fact*.

editor on Wikipedia. Any attempts to influence the content of articles should have been ignored by anyone aware of Wikipedia's doctrine on not arguing from authority, but whether this was the case or not is open to debate. See Chapter 11 for more on user pages and advice on what to post there.

The Crowd of Amateurs

In these first two chapters, you have seen an outline of Wikipedia's model for content. There have been a few tweaks through the years, but the basic ideas of what material Wikipedia wants to gather, the way it is presented and distributed, and why things are done one way and not another have not changed much over time. That does leave a few questions. Who does the writing and editing? Is the site really an open free-for-all, or is there real project management and bureaucracy behind the scenes? These points are addressed later in this book (see Chapter 12 and Chapter 7, respectively), but the answers, in terms of how Wikipedia works, are complex.

Going hand in hand with the criticism of Wikipedia as being hostile to experts is a related criticism about the community of editors—that Wikipedia relies on amateurs.[16] One common claim is that the only thing behind Wikipedia's success is a group of amateur writers, lacking the necessary expertise to produce a good reference work. Another criticism is that Wikipedia's framing of the issue of expertise is part of a larger problem with Internet culture. (Extensive discussion of Wikipedia's "business model" from this angle has ensued, which may be beside the point, given Wikipedia's status as a nonprofit initiative.)

Is documented contributor expertise necessary to write a great encyclopedia? The answer requires some qualification. Not all Wikipedians are amateurs; many are academics (though they may not write articles in their area of expertise). And when sources are considered, expertise is not rejected at all: Expert-written materials are the most desirable sources for articles on the site. Refer to the mission to clarify what the goal actually is. Wikipedia is building a huge compilation of materials and facts, many of which come from traditional sources, with the content policies simply acting as standards applied to everything submitted. Thinking of Wikipedians as the new encyclopedists makes sense, but, saying it more precisely, they're engaged in creating a *new kind* of tertiary source, for a *networked world*, delivered *free*.

Clearly, though, without widespread and open participation, the world's largest reference work could not have been created in less than a decade.[17] In contrast to the criticism of the site as being created by amateurs, many consider Wikipedia's harnessing of the masses to write a new kind of reference as a brilliant stroke—this new approach simply has a new set of strengths and weaknesses, as

---

[16] See Andrew Keen, *The Cult of the Amateur: How the Democratization of the Digital World is Assaulting Our Economy, Our Culture, and Our Values* (New York: Doubleday, 2007). Keen's perspective is hostile to Wikipedia, emphasizing expertise and the impact on the encyclopedia business.

[17] See Don Tapscott and Anthony D. Williams, *Wikinomics: How Mass Collaboration Changes Everything* (New York: Penguin, 2006). Tapscott and Williams are sympathetic to Wikipedia, discussing it within a business context.

all new media do. For example, very rapid updates are both a strong and a weak point in the model, and this takes some getting used to.

Wikipedia has also succeeded because its arrival was timely. Since 2001, it has accumulated a base of articles—and a community of contributors—that cannot quickly be rivaled. No other multilingual reference sites have been created yet that could compete. Conceivably, criticisms noted in this chapter will lead to changes to the Wikipedia model or procedures and thus improve the encyclopedia, or a new site could improve Wikipedia's basic model. This idea is not impractical: The GFDL license and open ethos of Wikipedia explicitly encourage some kind of sequel to the site. And why shouldn't there be two tertiary sources for the planet, or even more? The future is wide open.

Further Reading

http://en.wikipedia.org/wiki/Seigenthaler_controversy   An article discussing the Seigenthaler controversy

http://www.cs.kuleuven.ac.be/~dtai/projects/ALP/newsletter/may07/content/Articles/kowalski/content.html   An outside view on the Carl Hewitt case by Robert Kowalski

http://en.wikipedia.org/wiki/Wikipedia:Why_Wikipedia_is_so_great
http://en.wikipedia.org/wiki/Wikipedia:Why_Wikipedia_is_not_so_great
   A long-standing pair of essays that address the advantages and problems of Wikipedia's model

---

Summary

On March 15, 2007, a landmark was reached when the word *wiki* entered the Oxford English Dictionary Online, after the technology had existed for just under 12 years. Wikipedia's heritage stretches much further back, though, to the many early encyclopedia and knowledge-gathering projects of the ancient world and the impetus to understand the world during the Enlightenment era. In more recent times, the technological developments of the personal computer and the Internet made both wikis and Wikipedia possible, and the free software movement provided Wikipedia with its philosophical stance. This rich history has helped define Wikipedia's goals to provide free information to everyone in the world in their own language and to do so in a transparent, collaborative, dynamic, and open manner. Free software has also given Wikipedia its content license: the GFDL, which ensures that content will remain open, accessible, and freely reusable by anyone. These goals have been a part of Wikipedia since the site's beginnings in 2001. For all its idealism, however, the site has certainly not been immune to criticism of both the model itself and the implementation; in this chapter, we presented some case studies illustrating these criticisms.

3

Finding Wikipedia's Content

Considering Wikipedia's vastness, finding exactly what you're looking for can be a challenge. Fortunately, search is a powerful technology. This chapter will explain how to search Wikipedia effectively.

But searching for a specific piece of information is not the only way to use Wikipedia. Unlike the sections in a printed book, Wikipedia articles are not in any particular order; instead, they can be bundled together by topic and in many other ways. This grouping makes it great fun to browse Wikipedia casually and facilitates chance discovery: Filling out your understanding of a topic's background is usually painless, and one topic can lead to another in a surprising and enjoyable way.

Whether you're reading Wikipedia for fun or serious study, mastering some key research and navigation skills will help you make the most of your time. Therefore, this chapter will also describe the key structures set up for browsing (portals, categories, and lists) and will explain some basic navigational tools, including the links on the website's left-hand sidebar.

As usual, this chapter will show you where to look up detailed and up-to-date explanations of the topics that are covered here only in brief.

Searching Wikipedia

If you're looking for a particular topic, name, or phrase, searching the site directly is the way to start. Wikipedia's search function is like consulting the index volume of an encyclopedia, minus the tedium. In the best cases, you are only a few seconds away from answering a query.

When you search Wikipedia, you're harnessing a powerful combination of technologies—the organic growth of the encyclopedia itself and the ability to sift instantly through hundreds of millions of words.

The Wikipedia search engine searches not only the titles of all two million articles but also their full text. The search engine also includes alternate article titles (*redirect titles*). (In addition, you can search Wikipedia pages that are not articles, as we'll explain.) The search engine works on the current database, so it will find even the newest articles.

If a search doesn't turn up anything, Wikipedia may not have let you down. Sometimes finding what you're looking for can take persistence. You can make your searches more focused, broad, or powerful. Learning about the structure of the site and the conventions governing how articles are named will also make your searches more worthwhile.

Finally, search doesn't cover all situations. For example, you may suspect that you are using the wrong spelling. You could be looking for a medical term that you would recognize in context but can't remember. Or you might want to know what topics are related to a particular academic field. In those cases, start by browsing categories and portals, as described in "Browsing by Topic" on page 83.

Basic Searching

Searching is simple: First find the search box located in the middle of the left-hand sidebar (see Figure 3-1) or go to [[Special:Search]]. Type your keyword(s) in the search box and then click one of the two buttons: Go or Search.

Clicking Go (or just pressing ENTER) takes you straight to the article with a title that is exactly the same as the words you entered.

If no article with that title exists, a list of articles that contain the search words in their title or text appears. Here you can opt to search again, with either the Wikipedia search engine or an outside search engine. (You'll also see a *redlink* to create a new article with the exact title you searched for; we'll talk about this in Chapter 6.)

FIGURE 3-1: *The Wikipedia search box*

If you click Search instead of Go, a list of articles that contain your search words in their title or text appears. The articles are listed in the following order:

1. Articles whose titles contain your search words
2. Articles whose full texts contain your search words somewhere

Redirects and disambiguation pages might also be listed; these pages can point you to an appropriate article.

The Go button is useful whenever you can guess the title of the article you're looking for. The Search button is a better bet if you're not sure about the exact title or if you're searching for less common terms.

Sometimes Go searches don't end up where you expect—especially when redirects are involved! Plural search terms can be especially problematic, as article titles usually use the singular form. For example, there is no article titled Beatle—if you enter the word *Beatle*, you are taken instead to [[The Beatles]]. But searching for Rolling Stone doesn't take you to [[The Rolling Stones]]; it takes you to [[Rolling Stone]], an article about the magazine. [[Trogg]] has nothing to do with [[The Troggs]] but instead redirects to [[List of characters in Sonic the Comic]]. Who knew? If you've been redirected, a notice will appear under the article's title in parentheses. If you don't get what you expect, a full-text search might help you find the article you're looking for. (And sometimes an article will helpfully point you toward unrelated articles with similar names.)

Varying the Search

If you can't find an article about a topic but you feel sure it must exist in Wikipedia, try a full-text search using different keywords. For instance, the article titled [[Flag of the United States]] could also be titled [[American Flag]], [[The US Flag]], or any of a dozen similar things. You will often be redirected to the proper article— but not always. Redirects will take you to similar articles only in the most popular and developed areas of Wikipedia, so searching for synonyms is also important.

Searching for articles about people can be particularly tricky. The titles of biographical articles are supposed to be standardized (*first name*, *last name*, according to [[Wikipedia:Naming Conventions]], shortcut WP:NAME), but often vary in practice, especially if the name contains a combination of initials. If you're trying to track down John Karl Doe, a nonfiction writer, start by searching for *John Doe*, but also search for *Doe, John* as well as *J.K. Doe*, *J. Doe*, and *Doe, J.* Contributors also bring their own referencing styles to the site, which may invert or shorten names, or mistakes can creep in (like *Carl* for *Karl*). In the end, you might only find the article [[John C. Doe]] with persistence, perhaps as a redirect from *Doe, JK*. For less common names, searching for the last name only may get you what you're looking for and save much time in the end. This technique is particularly true for transliterated names or names with several historical spellings.

Power Variant Searching

An especially organized researcher can compile a list of title variants in a word processor and then copy and paste each variant into Wikipedia's search box. If you're trying to find an article about Willie "The Lion" Smith, you might search for *Willie Smith*, *Willy "The Lion" Smith*, *Willie the lion Smith*, *W. Henry Smith*, *William Henry Joseph Bonaparte Bertholoff Smith*, and whatever else you can come up with. You can also reuse that list in an external search engine.

Search Operators

Using a full-text search, you can search for a complete phrase by placing it in quotes:

```
"in the nick of time"
```

Placing a phrase in quotes only returns results that contain *exactly* what you typed: all of the words in the order you entered them. On the other hand, if you don't use quotation marks, the search will find every article that contains—somewhere in it—each one of those words.

You can add additional words after the phrase search; for instance,

```
"Benjamin Franklin" lightbulb
```

returns all articles that contain both the phrase *Benjamin Franklin* and the word *lightbulb*.

To exclude a word from the search result, put a minus sign in front of it; for instance,

```
benjamin  -franklin
```

returns all the articles that contain *Benjamin* but not *Franklin*.

When searching for lengthy phrases, phrases with wildcards, and phrases with Boolean operators (that is, combining terms or phrases with *and*, *or*, or *not*), use an external search engine, as described in "External Search Engines" on page 65.

Searching Other Namespaces

By default, the search function only searches articles—which means it only searches pages in the main namespace. But you can also search other namespaces (that is, non-article Wikipedia content). Here's how:

1. Perform a full-text search for your terms. A results page appears.
2. At the very bottom of the results page, a list of checkboxes allows you to specify which namespaces to search (for example, you can search user pages or talk pages or both). You can search any combination of namespaces. Check the types of pages you want to search, and then click the Search button.

If you commonly search non-article namespaces, you can automatically include them in your searches by changing your default search options under the Search tab in your User Preferences, in the upper right-hand corner if you are logged in.

Some Special Searches

Wikipedia's search function also has other uses.

Searching for images or other media

Unlike text, images cannot be parsed by search engines. But they can be tagged with text descriptions and other metadata, which itself can be searched.

Wikipedia pulls many of its images from Wikimedia Commons. Searching for images in Commons is easy because images there are comprehensively categorized and indexed with text. The Commons project is described in Chapter 16.

You can also search Wikipedia's Image namespace, though this namespace also contains (counterintuitively) other types of media such as audio files. See the previous section, "Searching Other Namespaces." Again, searching the Image namespace actually searches the text attached to the images, not the images themselves.

Searching for links from Wikipedia to outside websites

You can find any "outgoing" links to other websites that are contained in Wikipedia. Go to [[Special:Linksearch]] and enter the URL you want to search for. (For example, typing *whitehouse.gov* returns all Wikipedia articles that link to the White House website.)

Search Problems and Some Alternatives

Wikipedia's full-text search has a number of limitations, including the following:

Case-sensitivity

Wikipedia article titles are case-sensitive; for example, the article titled [[US]] is not the same as the article titled [[Us]].

This means if you search using the Go button, you might not be taken straight to the article you enter unless you use the exact same capitalization that the article's title uses! (See [[Wikipedia:Naming conventions (capitalization)]], shortcut WP:CAPS, for the full story.)

However, if the Go button doesn't produce any results, the search engine will default to a full-text search, which is not case sensitive, so you should still be able to find the article in question. Additionally, in many cases redirects have been created to get around this problem.

Apostrophes

Words containing apostrophes (such as the name *Mu'ammar*) can be found only if the apostrophe is included in the search. (One exception: Words that end with *'s* can be also found by searching for the word without the apostrophe *and* without the s.)

Special characters

Searching for words that contain special characters such as accents and diacritical marks can be problematic. On Wikipedia, any character with a *diaeresis* over it (for example, the *ë* in *Odiliënberg*) might be stored as one character (in this case, *ë*) or as an HTML entity (*ë*). If a title is encoded with HTML, it may not show up in a simple search—for instance, you might have a hard time searching for *Odilienberg* or *Odiliënberg*. If this is the case, try searching for part of the title, such as just *Odili*.

If these problems seem daunting, remember that with a little cleverness, you can use search engines like Google to replace Wikipedia's built-in search engine (see the next section). Outside search engines don't suffer from the problems plaguing the built-in search engine. Whenever your search comes up empty, try searching using an external engine.

External Search Engines

Wikipedia pages can also be found using ordinary search engines such as Google.

Most search engines allow you to restrict your search results to pages from a particular site. If you restrict your results to pages from Wikipedia, the outside search engine can replace Wikipedia's built-in search engine.

To search Wikipedia using Google, type

```
site:en.wikipedia.org "high and low"
```

into Google's search box.

This search has two components. The first half, *site:en.wikipedia.org,* tells Google to only search pages that begin with *en.wikipedia.org*, which means every page in the English-language Wikipedia. (Use *site:wikipedia.org* to search Wikipedias in every language.) The second half—*"high and low"*—is an ordinary Google phrase search.

Now click the Search button. The results page shows every Wikipedia article that contains the phrase *high and low*, including the Japanese film of that name and the feudal concept of high, middle, and low justice.

You don't have to use Google; you can use any search engine capable of restricting its results to pages from Wikipedia. For example, the search phrase above works equally well in Yahoo! and Google.

Wikipedia also has a drop-down menu next to the search field that allows you to choose, in addition to *MediaWiki Search*, an external search engine to use. As of mid-2008, the available search engines include Google, Yahoo!, Windows Live, Wikiwix, and Exalead. For more information about searching, see [[Wikipedia:Searching]] (shortcut WP:SEARCH), which mentions many other possibilities. For example, other search engines designed for searching Wikipedia include LuMriX, WikiWax (not to be confused with Wikiwix), Qwika, and Wikiseek. LuMriX and WikiWax suggest article titles as you type, in the way an index might. Qwika is a search engine that searches Wikipedia across languages by using machine translation. Wikiseek searches across Wikipedia articles and groups its results into broad categories.

[[Wikipedia:Searching]] also describes plug-ins that let you search Wikipedia using your web browser's interface.

When to Use External Search Engines

There are several cases when using external search engines instead of the onsite search is a good idea:

▶   The onsite search is occasionally disabled when Wikipedia's servers are particularly strained. If you try to use the search engine while it's disabled, you'll be shown a list of links to external search engines.

▶   You might prefer using a familiar search interface instead.

▶   External engines often offer a short preview of each article on the results page.

▶   You may need to perform a complex search that is difficult or impossible to achieve using Wikipedia's built-in engine.

▶   By default, external engines search across all Wikipedia namespaces, making it easier to find relevant policy, category, or image pages.

Using Firefox's Search

If you use the Firefox web browser, you probably know that you can search Google directly from the search box in Firefox's upper-right corner. You can also search Wikipedia with this search box. Click the search engine icon at the left side of the search box (this is a Google *G* by default) to get a drop-down list of available sites, and select the Wikipedia *W*. You can then search the English-language Wikipedia directly from your browser. (If the icon isn't present, click Manage Search Engines at the bottom of the list, and then click the Get More Search Engines link, where you can follow the directions to add a new search engine.)

When Not to Use External Search Engines

Search engines aren't magic. In order to find out what websites say, they send out computer programs called *spiders* that scurry out across the Internet, parse the contents of a web page just as a person might (though, of course, a million times faster), and carry the information back to the search engines.

This means that if a web page has been created recently, Google might not be able to find it. New Wikipedia articles sometimes take days or weeks to appear in external search engines, but Wikipedia's built-in engine can find them minutes after they're created.

Similarly, if a web page has changed recently, Google might "remember" the out-of-date version of the page, not the current version. For example, if the death of Catherine the Great has only just been added to the Wikipedia article [[Toilet-related injury]], a Google search for

`site:en.wikipedia.org "catherine the great" toilet`

might not find that page. Conversely, if the word *breakfast* has just been removed from the [[Youtiao]] article, a Google search for

`site:en.wikipedia.org salted fried chinese breakfast dough`

will return the Youtiao article if Google has not parsed the article since *breakfast* was removed. But once you click Google's link to the article, the word *breakfast* is nowhere to be found. In this event, you might investigate the article's history to discover the circumstances in which your search term was removed.

Further Reading

http://en.wikipedia.org/wiki/Special:Search   Wikipedia's search box

http://en.wikipedia.org/wiki/Wikipedia:Searching   Overview of searching

http://en.wikipedia.org/wiki/Wikipedia:Go_button   About the Go button

http://en.wikipedia.org/wiki/Wikipedia:Tools#Searching   A collection of tools and plug-ins developed to make searching easier

http://en.wikipedia.org/wiki/Wikipedia:Naming_conventions   The policy on naming conventions for articles

Ways into Wikipedia

Wandering aimlessly through Wikipedia is compulsive, addictive, and time-consuming. It's also one of the most enjoyable ways to experience the site. As an editor, you will invariably find just one more thing to add or fix up around every corner.

But goal-directed Wikipedia browsing can also be useful and fun. This section explores some of those more structured methods to explore the site, beginning at Wikipedia's front door.

Welcome to the Main Page

The main page (*http://en.wikipedia.org/wiki/Main_page*) is the first page many visitors to Wikipedia see, and it serves as an entry point to the many neighborhoods within Wikipedia. It is also updated daily with new content. The main page is thus a great place to start a general survey or to start browsing to most areas of the site.

✳ **NOTE:** *If you are at* http://wikipedia.org/, *which is a portal to all of the different language versions of Wikipedia, you are one click from the main page of the English-language Wikipedia. Moreover, the same is true if you are on any page of the English-language Wikipedia; you have only to click the Wikipedia logo in the upper left-hand corner or on the sidebar link called* Main Page.

Navigating the Main Page

The main page is packed so densely with content that it can be overwhelming (Figure 3-2). At the top, a header welcomes you to Wikipedia and offers an automated count of articles—2,428,969 at the time of writing. Clicking this number reveals more statistics about Wikipedia. To the right of the header, you'll find links to broad scholastic topics such as History and Mathematics. (See "Portals into the Encyclopedia," next.)

Below the header, you'll find links to introductory information. *Overview* and *Questions* will give you basic information about the site; *Editing* takes you to the Wikipedia Tutorial, a good walk-through of basic editing techniques. *Help* links to the extensive help pages (this link is the same as the Help link on the left-hand sidebar).

Portals into the Encyclopedia

If you have a broad subject area in mind, notice the group of links on the upper right:

- Arts
- Biography
- Geography
- History
- Mathematics
- Science
- Society
- Technology
- All Portals

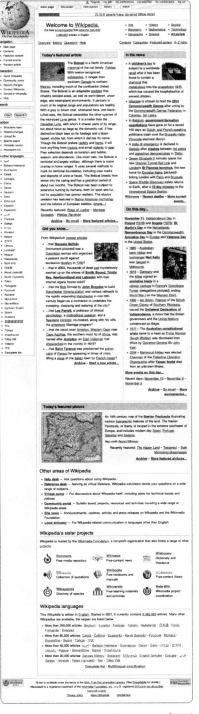

FIGURE 3-2: *The main page of Wikipedia, from September 12, 2007*

Follow any of these links and you will come to a portal. Just as Wikipedia's front page is a gateway to the encyclopedia as a whole, a *portal* is a gateway to a particular topic, offering selected articles, relevant links, and ways of finding editors with an interest in that particular subject.

✱ **NOTE:** *Many more portals exist than are listed here. The final link, All Portals (or [[Portal:List of portals]]), reveals portals on a broad range of topics. [[Category:Portals]] is another, more hierarchical way to explore portals.*

Portals are accessible and user-friendly ways to explore Wikipedia's coverage of a topic. A portal is also a *project*, attracting swarms of wiki editors who help beautify and maintain the articles in that subject area, not to mention the portal page itself. (The articles in the portal are hand-selected and are usually accurate and interesting.) Most portals feature an introduction to the topic; selected articles, biographies, and pictures; and links to any relevant Wiki-Projects and editor collaborations.

✱ **NOTE:** *Portals originated in the Polish- and German-language Wikipedias. In early 2005, the idea was imported to the English-language Wikipedia; later that year, a special Portal namespace was created. Portal pages are, therefore, considered organizational pages, similar to the main page, rather than articles in their own right.*

Some portal topics are broad, others quite specific. For instance, there is a portal for science, [[Portal:Science]], and one for the sport of cricket, [[Portal:Cricket]] (Figure 3-3).

FIGURE 3-3: *Example of a featured portal: The Cricket Portal*

Daily Content

Below the main page's header, you'll find five sections that are updated every day: Today's featured article, In the news, Did you know . . . , On this day . . . , and Today's featured picture. Each provides a taste of the wide variety of content available on Wikipedia.

Today's featured article

Featured articles are a select group representing some of Wikipedia's best content. In order to be called *featured*, an article must pass through a rigorous process that admits only about one article in a thousand. (See "Featured Articles" on page 227.)

Each day, part of a featured article is excerpted here (typically the first paragraph). To read the rest of the article, click its title or the More link at the end of the excerpt.

In the news

This section contains a selection of articles about current affairs. These articles typically concern breaking news stories of international interest.

Articles about current events tend to be updated furiously (Wikipedia's newsroom is a few thousand people worldwide in front of computer monitors). Note, however, that these articles should not contain original reporting; for that, go to the Wikinews project (see Chapter 16).

Where Is the News on Wikipedia?

Wikipedia does not draw a distinction between "news" and "non-news" articles. Current events and new developments are constantly integrated into existing articles or generate new articles linked from older ones. A new article about a major current event is treated no differently from one about a historical figure. To see current news in one place, visit [[Portal:Current events]], where news stories are collated (with appropriate links to the encyclopedia); the sidebar on the right side of the Current Events portal lists Wikipedia articles about breaking events and newsworthy people.

The three remaining items of daily content are less reverent.

On this day . . .
This section contains a selection of noteworthy anniversaries. (For events that happened on other days of the year, follow the More Anniversaries . . . link.)

Did you know . . .
This section highlights random facts from articles that have been created or greatly expanded in the last five days. (Did you know . . . is put together at [[Wikipedia:Did you know]], shortcut WP:DYK, where you can suggest factoids from new articles to include.)

Today's featured picture
This section contains a photograph or image chosen from among Wikipedia's best.

Constructing the Main Page

In some ways, the main page is like any other page on Wikipedia: Delve in and you will find people at work. Like the rest of the site, the main page is maintained by a dedicated group of volunteer editors, who update each section on a regular schedule.

But even when viewed in comparison to other Wikipedia pages, the main page is very unusual:

▶ It receives a constant avalanche of traffic, averaging over 100,000 hits per hour. For this and other reasons, the main page is one of the few pages that are not open for everyone to edit (see "Who Can Edit What?"on page 143).

- Each section of daily content is constructed and updated separately from the rest of the page. The main page then draws these sections together with templates. (See "Templates" on page 270.)

- Because of this, the main page's page history doesn't track its daily changes, unlike most wiki pages (see "Article History" on page 105).

- Most Wikipedia pages are marked with the date and time they were most recently edited, but the main page is not.

If you want to make suggestions about the main page and to learn more about how it is edited and maintained, see the corresponding discussion page [[Talk:Main Page]]. Each section of the main page is linked from the discussion page, and it is here that you can suggest new daily content.

Time Travel

If you have ever wanted to go forward in time, you can always look at tomorrow's main page early at [[Main Page/Tomorrow]]. Miss a day or want to go back in time? Try [[Wikipedia:Main Page alternative (yesterday)]].

Disclaimers, License, and Privacy

Scrolling down the main page, you'll find links to other helpful sections, including links to help and community areas of Wikipedia and to the sister projects. After those, you'll find links to Wikipedias in other languages; these links are only a selection from the total (now over 200) languages available.

At the very bottom of the page, the *page footer*, which is reproduced on every page, has a collection of disclaimers and links to copyright information. The general disclaimer in particular is worth reading. It states that *Wikipedia makes no guarantee of validity*—that is, the site doesn't promise to be correct, factual, or truthful in any way. Use Wikipedia for quick reference only. Double-check any important information—especially legal or medical advice, but information just for homework too. By accepting the disclaimer, you accept responsibility for any possible use you might make of information derived from Wikipedia.

Although this disclaimer sounds dire, it is in fact not so unusual. Many general encyclopedias disclaim all responsibility; Wikipedia simply makes a stronger point of it than most. Using common sense is key, and Wikipedia is great if you can accept its limitations: that the site is a work in progress and individual article quality may vary (more on evaluating individual articles in the next chapter).

In the footer, you'll also find a link to the GNU Free Documentation License, or GFDL, which was described in Chapter 2; this license is the one under which all

Wikipedia content is released. Understanding the GFDL, or at least its most basic implications, matters for a contributor because anything you contribute (from copyedits to whole articles) will be placed under this license. As a reader, you only need to know that you can reuse content if you credit the source in a particular way. [[Wikipedia:Copyrights]], also linked to in the footer, will tell you more about the rights you retain under the GFDL and the copyright status of Wikipedia.

The privacy policy explains your privacy on Wikipedia and what information is collected about you (generally, a session cookie). Personal information about contributors is not collected or sold. However, newcomers to the site frequently misunderstand two key points. First, Wikipedia keeps a *permanent* record of *everything* transacted on the site: Every comment and edit is kept forever. Second, if you edit without being logged in, you are disclosing your IP address publicly and others may be able to trace it. Editing without being logged in is "anonymous" editing only in the sense that your name is not attached. To be more private, you should register an account. Because of Wikipedia's great prominence, you should be in no hurry to disclose any personal details on the site. Using your real name on Wikipedia is fine (the authors of this book do), but you should know the implications; the pros and cons are discussed in Chapter 11.

Finally, the footer contains a link to the Wikimedia Foundation, the parent organization of Wikipedia. The footer also typically shows a date and timestamp telling when the page you are viewing was last edited.

The Omnipresent Sidebar

Every page on Wikipedia is framed by three unchanging elements:

▸ Article tabs at the top (see Chapter 4)

▸ Site information at the bottom

▸ The sidebar on the left (see Figure 3-4)

MediaWiki

These elements are supplied by MediaWiki, the software that runs Wikipedia. You'll see versions of these elements on other websites, too, including on Wikipedia's sister projects and on entirely independent wikis. For more about MediaWiki, see Chapter 17.

This section explores the sidebar. The sidebar presents a handy navigation menu for both readers and editors and provides other essential tools and links.

On the English-language Wikipedia, the sidebar contains five sections: Navigation, Interaction, Search, Toolbox, and Languages (though this last section does not always appear).

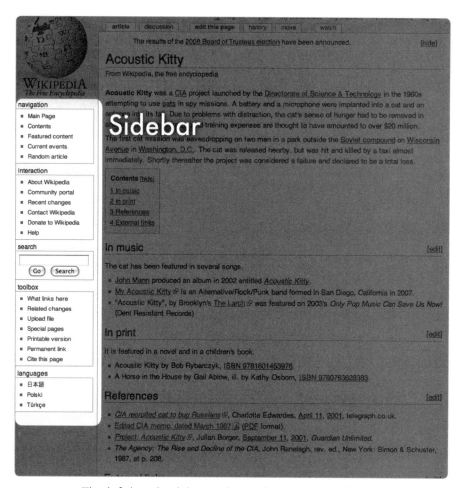

FIGURE 3-4: *The left-hand sidebar includes five sections of links to tools and various navigation pages.*

Navigation

Navigation offers four links to major directory pages and one to a randomly chosen article:

Main Page
As might be expected, this link goes to the main page. (You can also click the Wikipedia logo just above it to get there.)

Contents
A book's table of contents lists its sections in the order they're printed. Wikipedia is not in any particular order, so its contents page provides a wide range of different ways to navigate Wikipedia by topic.

Featured Content

This section showcases articles, images, and other content that Wikipedia's community has deemed particularly good.

Current Events

This section gathers articles related to current news.

Random Article

Clicking this link is like throwing open a book to a random page. The link takes you to a different, randomly selected Wikipedia article each time you click it.

Random browsing can be entertaining for anyone. New readers can grasp the range of content in Wikipedia, and editors can discover neglected articles that need fixing up, though some editors prefer a more methodical approach (see Chapter 7).

Interaction

The links in this section help you find out more about Wikipedia or interact with the site as an editor:

About Wikipedia

This link takes you to a general overview of the project, intended to help newcomers orient themselves. About Wikipedia also links to other FAQ and help pages.

Community Portal

This page helps Wikipedia contributors communicate, collaborate, and mingle. The Community Portal is also a good place to learn more about current onsite happenings. (See Chapter 12.)

Recent Changes

This page shows all edits made to Wikipedia in real time. This page is an important place that's covered in detail in the next section.

Contact Wikipedia

This link may be the least accurately named link in the sidebar. The contact page is devoted mostly to common complaints and their solutions, because, of course, no central authority is in charge of every Wikipedia article. [[Wikipedia:Questions]] (shortcut WP:Q) points to several other places answers might be found. For most questions, it is best to go to the WikiProject that deals with the topic you are interested in or a community forum to track down the active group of editors dealing with the issues you are interested in (see Chapter 12 for how to find community discussion forums).

The contact page does provide a number of email addresses for media inquiries, legal issues, and other concerns. These addresses lead into an email system (the *Open-source Ticket Request System*, or *OTRS*) staffed by a selected number of volunteers. Hundreds of questions from the general public about all aspects of Wikipedia find their way to OTRS every week. Responses are generally quick and courteous, but may be delayed when the volunteers have a large backlog of questions.

Donate to Wikipedia

This page provides a form (and a pitch) encouraging people to donate via credit card, check, or other means to the foundation that runs Wikipedia. (It also advertises Wikipedia-themed merchandise and copies of Wikipedia on DVD.) Wikipedia has no deep-pocketed patron; most of its funding comes from a steady stream of small, private donations. If you like Wikipedia, consider pitching in to help keep it online.

Note that the donation page is not located on the Wikipedia website. To return to Wikipedia from there, use your browser's Back button.

Help

Help takes you to a comprehensive index for Wikipedia readers and editors of every experience level. Many of these basic help pages are worth reading to get an overview of the site, and these pages are also a good place to start if you have a specific question about how to do something.

Take note of the links across the top of the main help page. The glossary and the cheatsheet provide quick answers for editors, whereas the tutorial is a friendly introduction to editing a page. Of course, if you read this book cover to cover, you probably won't need to read it!

Recent Changes

Sandwiched in the middle of the sidebar's Interaction section is a link to one of the most important pages on Wikipedia. Recent Changes is a continuously updated list of every single edit made to Wikipedia, beginning with the most recent (see Figure 3-5).

This list of edits uses the same format as the editing histories of individual articles (see Chapter 4): Each new edit occupies a single line.

Exploring the Recent Changes page can give you a feel for what is happening on Wikipedia at any particular moment. Experienced editors might even get a sense of the site's general mood. But using the Recent Changes page this way is a little like trying to predict a presidential election by looking at a satellite photo of the United States. Hundreds of edits happen each minute, so any given glance at this page offers only the tiniest window into Wikipedia's broader workings.

The *idea* of Recent Changes, however, is a key part of Wikipedia's philosophy of transparent collaboration: Anyone can see any change that has been made to the site. All work in Wikipedia is open; there are no "hidden parts." Every edit made will show up on the Recent Changes page, even if it flashes by in a second.

In practice, the Recent Changes page is primarily used for detecting damaging edits (such as deliberate inaccuracies, wholesale text deletion, and other vandalism) as soon as they occur. Some editors, acting as volunteer security guards, use automated tools that help them sift through recent changes more

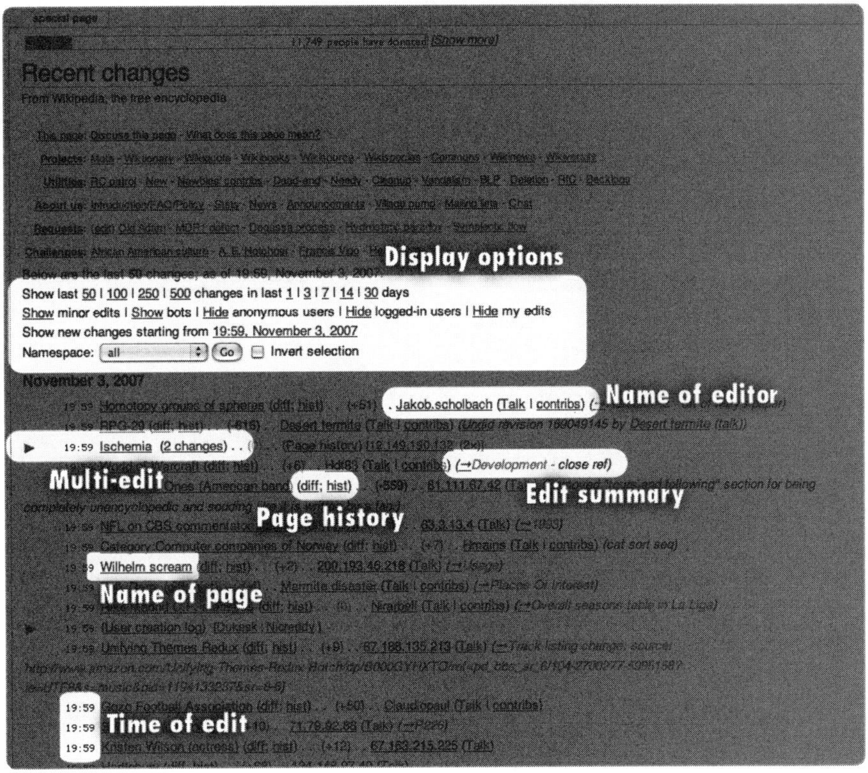

FIGURE 3-5: The Recent Changes display

efficiently in order to find and fix these edits (see Chapter 7). At the top of the page, above the main listing of changes, you'll find two sets of links. The first set (Projects, Utilities, About Us, Requests, and Challenges) are community utilities and help pages that are discussed separately throughout this book.

The second set—beginning with *Below are the last 50 changes*—control how recent changes are displayed. You can change the number of edits listed, hide edits made by anonymous contributors, and so on. By default, minor edits are displayed, though automated edits by bots are not.

You can also watch for entirely new pages as they are created; see [[Special: Newpages]].

The Search Box

Returning to the sidebar, right in the middle you'll find the search box. This is where you enter terms for searching the English-language Wikipedia. Click the Go button to find an article with the exact title you entered; click the Search button to search for any occurrences of the words within the full text of all articles. See "Searching Wikipedia" on page 60.

Toolbox

The Toolbox section of the sidebar (see Figure 3-6) contains several utilities that give you more information about the page you're viewing, allowing you to fit the page into a broader context or letting you see the page in other formats.

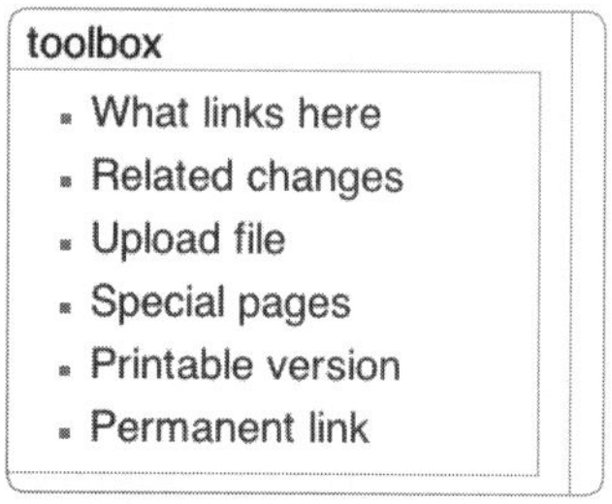

✻ **NOTE:** *Two incongruous links—Upload File and Special Pages—are included with these article-specific utilities. We'll discuss these links at the end of this section.*

> toolbox
> - What links here
> - Related changes
> - Upload file
> - Special pages
> - Printable version
> - Permanent link

FIGURE 3-6: *Close-up of the Toolbox section from the sidebar*

What Links Here lists all the Wikipedia pages that link to the page you're viewing. (For example, [[Central Intelligence Agency]] and [[Acoustic Kitty (album)]] both link to [[Acoustic Kitty]].) You'll come to value this tool if you research less mainstream areas (see Chapter 4).

Related Changes lists every recent edit to any page that links to the page you're viewing. Use this link to track activity in a particular topic area or to check for vandalism occurring across related articles.

Printable Version is a version of the page you are viewing formatted for printing; for example, some wiki formatting is removed, external URLs are spelled out, the sidebar is removed, and the font is different. If your web browser was made within the last couple of years, you'll never need to use this link: Your browser will send this printable version to your printer even if you click Print while viewing the standard page.

Because Wikipedia articles change unpredictably, linking to them can be problematic; someone might follow your link, only to discover a version of the article different from the one you saw. (The problem is especially acute on high-traffic pages that might be edited every few minutes.) When you click Permanent Link, you are taken to a time-stamped snapshot of the article as it currently appears. The text at this URL will never change, so you can link to it or cite it with confidence. (You can also link to any previous version of the article from the page history; every version of every page has a unique ID number.)

Cite This Page provides a handy, appropriate bibliographic citation (with a permanent link) for the article you're viewing, which can then be easily cut and pasted into a list of citations. You can generate citations in various bibliographic styles, including MLA style, APA style, BibTex, and so on.

If you're viewing a user page rather than an article or project page, you'll see two additional links: User Contributions, and, if the editor has enabled email contact, Email This User. User Contributions takes you to a list of all the edits made by that user (or that IP address). Email This User leads to a form where you can send an email to the editor without his or her email address being revealed.

Two last links are for more advanced use. Before images can be displayed on Wikipedia, they must be uploaded to the site. Upload File takes you to a form for adding images and other files to Wikipedia. (See Chapter 9 for a full description.)

Finally, the Special Pages link accesses a list of pages in the Special namespace. Unlike most pages on Wikipedia, these pages are not editable; instead, they are generated automatically each time you visit them. Some, such as My Preferences and My Watchlist, are customized for you and are only valid if you're logged in. (You can locate these two pages more easily, however; they are also available in the top right-hand corner of the page if you're logged in.) Most special pages contain utilities for advanced users and will be discussed throughout this book by topic.

Languages

The last section of the sidebar, if it exists, contains links to versions of the article you're currently viewing in other language Wikipedias. For instance, while viewing the English article [[Astronaut]], if you click the Español link in the Languages section, you'll go to the Spanish-language Wikipedia article [[Astronauta]]. Language links should be alphabetized by the name of the language (Figure 3-7).

An article written by speakers of another language often differs in focus and perspective. But even if you're a monoglot, browsing articles in other languages can be a good way to find images.

These links are sometimes called *interwiki links* (see Chapter 15 for a more thorough discussion). The language links that appear depend on which Wikipedias contain

languages

- Simple English
- العربية
- Bahasa Indonesia
- Bahasa Melayu
- ইমার ঠার/বিষ্ণুপ্রিয়া
  মণিপুরী
- Brezhoneg
- Bosanski
- Български
- Català
- Česky
- Dansk
- Deutsch
- Eesti
- Ελληνικά
- Español
- Esperanto
- Euskara
- فارسی
- Français
- Galego
- हिन्दी
- Hrvatski
- Íslenska
- Italiano
- עברית
- ქართული
- 한국어
- Latina
- Lëtzebuergesch
- Lietuvių
- Magyar
- Nederlands
- 日本語
- Norsk (bokmål)
- Norsk (nynorsk)
- Polski
- Português
- Română
- Русский
- Shqip
- Slovenčina
- Slovenščina
- Српски / Srpski
- Suomi
- Svenska
- ไทย
- Tiếng Việt
- Türkçe
- Українська
- 中文
- **Complete list**

FIGURE 3-7: *The Languages section for the main page: Each of these links takes you to the main page of another language's Wikipedia.*

an article about the topic in question. Even if a matching article exists in another language, an editor must first add an interwiki link to it before it will appear in the languages list.

Further Reading

Browsing

http://en.wikipedia.org/wiki/Main_Page   The front door and main portal into Wikipedia

http://en.wikipedia.org/wiki/Portal:Current_events   The Current Events portal for recent events and news

http://en.wikipedia.org/wiki/Portal:List_of_portals   List of all portals

Finding Out More

http://meta.wikimedia.org/wiki/List_of_Wikipedias   A complete list of Wikipedias in all languages

http://wikimediafoundation.org/wiki/Privacy_policy   The privacy policy

http://en.wikipedia.org/wiki/Wikipedia:General_disclaimer   The general disclaimer

Sidebar Links

http://en.wikipedia.org/wiki/Special:Recentchanges   Recent Changes

http://en.wikipedia.org/wiki/Special:Random   The random article generator

http://en.wikipedia.org/wiki/Wikipedia:Random   Find a random article in another namespace

---

Joys of Hypertext

This section explores the many ways Wikipedia pages are grouped together. For example, pages can be grouped in the following ways:

▸   Informally by topic

▸   By date

▸   Into hierarchical taxonomies (*categories*)

▸   By format (for example, you can browse only high-quality featured articles)

▸   Any way you like! If you follow links from one article to another, you create your own "group" of articles—your own personal story.

A Hypertext Primer

Written language has been around for thousands of years, but its format has changed many times. Stone carvings were expensive and time consuming (and decidedly nonportable) and were, therefore, used mostly for official state purposes. Medieval scholars wrote on valuable animal skins, which they periodically scraped clean and covered with new text. The printing press made written texts easily affordable and accessible.

Writing is circulated today in many formats, and each format has its own way of doing things. For example, newspaper articles are worded tightly to cut down on printing costs, and the most important information is placed at the beginning of the article so that you can conveniently stop reading at any point.

If you're an adult, books are second nature. Certain assumptions, such as the fact that the pages of a novel appear in a particular order or that the millions of extant copies of *Sense and Sensibility* all contain essentially the same text, are so ingrained that they hardly seem worth mentioning.

But Wikipedia violates many of these assumptions. It is a new medium, with its own strengths, weaknesses, and conventions.

The most striking feature of the World Wide Web—and of Wikipedia—is the *link*: text that takes you somewhere else and is traditionally underlined and colored blue. Early information theorists called links *hypertext*, and the term has become a catchall for the ways in which the Internet is different from the printed word.

What does hypertext mean on Wikipedia?

▶ Wikipedia articles can be read in any order.

▶ A Wikipedia article need not be read "cover to cover." In a single browsing session, you can read ten different paragraphs from ten related articles; indeed, this grazing approach is often the *best* way to gather information.

▶ Wikipedia articles can be grouped in many ways, and these groups can overlap.

Hypertext

Wikipedia is not the first hypertext encyclopedia, but its embrace of hypertext is complete and fundamental. A Wikipedia article that is not linked to by any other article is called an *orphan* and placed in a special cleanup category.

Any word, name, or term in an article can be linked to an article about that concept. As a reader, the practical effect of this is that you can jump from one article and into another whenever you like. You are not constrained by the authors' view of the logical flow of the topic or the amount of background information in any particular article. If you're unfamiliar with a concept, you can easily refer to the article about that concept.

More generally, hypertext means that *every page on Wikipedia references (links to) other pages*—and of course, every page is linked *to* by other pages. Understanding how Wikipedia pages are linked to one another is key to browsing Wikipedia.

Because there are so many ways to explore related topics, Wikipedia is great for getting up to speed about subjects you don't know well—even areas in which you don't know what you don't know. (A search might lead you to a particular article, but that article itself can become a jumping-off point to another topic.)

Three Types of Links

There are three types of links on Wikipedia.

Internal links

These links lead from one Wikipedia page to another. Clicking the link will take you to the Wikipedia page being linked to. Internal links (also called *wikilinks*) are blue. You'll see internal links throughout the text of articles and other pages.

When you're editing an article, you can create an internal link by surrounding a word with double brackets. (See Chapter 5.)

∗ NOTE: Wikification *and* wikifying *are terms for adding wikilinks to a page.*

Internal links don't always have the exact title of the page they're linking to; any text can link to any page, which is occasionally confusing. For instance, clicking a bluelink that reads *Samuel Clemens* might take you to the page [[Mark Twain]] (and your reaction might be "Huh?" "I knew that, I suppose," or "Of course!").

Naming

This Twain example illustrates one of Wikipedia's painstakingly negotiated conventions about article titles. Even though Mark Twain is a pseudonym, this name is the most common way to refer to Samuel Clemens, so the article bears that title.

Redlinks

These internal links lead to articles that don't exist yet. They look like ordinary internal links except that they're (unsurprisingly) red.

Clicking a redlink takes you to a page asking if you want to create the new article. Appropriate redlinks are a natural part of the encyclopedia, as they show what topics have yet to be covered.

External links

These are links to other websites. These links are always light blue and marked with a small arrow, but they can take three forms:

▶ A full URL (such as *http://www.google.com/*)

▶ A bracketed number ([3])

▶ Ordinary words or sentences linked to an external site

External links normally appear at the bottom of an article in the External links section, but they can appear throughout article text.

Using Tabbed Browsing

This feature, offered by most contemporary browsers, is a good option for serious study. By opening internal links in new tabs as you read through an article, you can add a new tab for each less-than-familiar term you encounter. After your first pass through some unfamiliar topic, your tabs will constitute a detailed set of Wikipedia notes.

Browsing by Topic

Using the Random Article link is fun, but if you have work to do, you need a way to find specific articles (unless your research area is the dynamics of online encyclopedias). Using search is the best-known way to find Wikipedia articles, but other ways to inform your understanding of a topic exist. For example, you can

▶ Peruse lists of articles

▶ Visit subject portals

▶ Navigate categories

Lists of Articles

Most Wikipedia articles have traditional paragraph structures, but some take the form of lists. Each list item usually links to its own article. Thus, each list becomes a miniature index to its own topic area.

Wikipedia is pieced together collaboratively, bit by bit. It relies on contributors bold enough to slide new information into a complete-looking article. In this context, lists can feel particularly welcoming to new writers: After "This is a list of items" and "This list was written by a bunch of different people," the next logical thought is often "I can add another line item to the end of this list."

Consequently, lists abound throughout Wikipedia, indexing a staggering array of topics. Some are well maintained and quite complete, others more informal and amateurish. Sometimes they define an unexpected topic, such as [[List

FIGURE 3-8: The Lists of Topics page

of songs about or referencing Elvis Presley]]), or provide a new view of a familiar topic, such as [[List of accidents and incidents on commercial airliners grouped by location]]. Smaller lists also exist within ordinary, paragraph-style articles.

✱ **NOTE:** *Lists help Wikipedia expand because they encourage the creation of redlinks—links to articles that haven't been written yet.*

Of course, lists can be grouped. They can be organized chronologically, by theme, or by annotation. Many lists are accessible through the main contents page, which is linked on the global sidebar. Some of the links available from the contents page include the [[List of academic disciplines]], which provides a list of broad overview articles by academic discipline (such as engineering); these articles in turn link to more detailed articles. The [[List of overviews]] has a similar function: It presents a number of articles in a subject area (philosophy, for example) that give a survey of that area. The top-level page for lists is the Lists of Topics page, which is a directory of list articles.

List Policy

What makes for a sensible stand-alone list is supposed to be regulated by policy (see [[Wikipedia:Lists]], shortcut WP:LIST), but Wikipedia policy, like much else on the site, is rarely static. In general, new lists should not advance a thesis, and "frivolous" lists are discouraged, though many have existed in the past (for example, a list of guesstimated IQs, including those of Beethoven and Madonna). Lists are subject to the Verifiability policy: One problem with having a [[List of geniuses]] is the verification of geniusness. See [No original research]] and [[Verifiability]].

One interesting way to proceed from a list is to click Related Changes in the left sidebar. Related Changes is a list of recent changes to any articles that the current page links to, which, in the case of a list article, includes all items in that list. If you're seeking editors working in your field of interest, this is one way to make quick contact.

You do have to filter out some noise: Related Changes shows changes to *all* pages linked to from a given page. If you apply it to [[List of glaciers]], you may find edits to [[Glacier]], [[Sierra Nevada]], or [[Mount Kilimanjaro]], alongside edits to less relevant articles such as [[Argentina]] and [[2007]]. For certain lists, Related Changes is an impractical way to proceed.

List of Our Favorite Lists

- ▶ [[List of encyclopedias]]
- ▶ [[List of unsolved problems]]
- ▶ [[List of glaciers]]
- ▶ [[List of glossaries]]
- ▶ [[Timeline of chemistry]]
- ▶ [[List of English words containing Q not followed by U]]
- ▶ [[List of oldest continuously inhabited cities]]
- ▶ [[List of states of matter]]
- ▶ [[List of comic book superpowers]]
- ▶ [[List of historical elephants]]
- ▶ [[List of trees]]
- ▶ [[List of problems solved by MacGyver]]
- ▶ [[List of unusual units of measurement]]

New lists are created all the time. But some existing lists are being phased out in favor of *categories* (a more rigid, automated classification scheme; see "Browsing by Categories" on page 96).

A great deal of debate has surrounded the relative merits of categories and lists. Lists can be annotated, reverted to older versions, and peppered with references. Categories, on the other hand, are more automated and thus work better with really large collections of pages.

Traditional Classification Schemes

If you're feeling nostalgic, you can browse Wikipedia using traditional library arrangement schemes: the *Dewey Decimal Classification* and the *Library of Congress Classification*. These schemes might seem archaic, but because they were designed to organize broad arrays of human knowledge (and secondarily to sort books), they can be interesting to browse.

See [[Library of Congress Classification]] for the top level of the classification. If you click one of the 21 linked articles, you'll drill down into the next level of classification, with topics linked to the appropriate articles. [[Category:Library of Congress Classification]] also lists the breakdown by letter codes. The article [[List of Dewey Decimal classes]] gives the first three digits of the Dewey class, with some topics linked to those articles.

Further, you can find an outline of *Roget's Thesaurus*, with appropriate articles wikilinked, at [[Wikipedia:Outline of Roget's Thesaurus]].

Date-Related Articles

There are a wide variety of date- and time-related articles that list significant events during a particular date, year, or even century.

Articles exist that summarize the following:

▶ Every year between 1700 BC and the present (see [[List of years]])

▶ Every decade between the 1690s BC and the 2090s AD ([[List of decades]])

▶ Every century between the 40th century BC and the 31st century AD ([[List of centuries]])

▶ Every millennium between the 10th millennium BC and the 10th millennium AD (see [[List of centuries]] again)

▶ Every geological division, epoch, period, and era (see [[List of time periods]] for these and many more)

Simply type a year in the search box or go to one of these lists.

As you might expect, the quality of these articles vary widely, usually in predictable ways. [[Jurassic]], [[December 2004]], and [[1800s]] are detailed; [[1485 BC]] is not. In general, the less-detailed articles are scattershot collections of factoids. If you're unsatisfied with a yearly article, move up to the decade or century level.

For most modern years, such as 1954, dozens of dedicated articles exist—for instance, [[1954 in architecture]] or [[1954 in baseball]]. However, *1954 in cricket* is a category rather than an article, and if you want to learn more about crime in 1954, you might look at [[FBI Ten Most Wanted Fugitives by year, 1954]]. The overall [[Category:1954]] is the right place to start for intensive research, as it collects all these articles in one place and numerous subcategories will point you in the right direction.

✳ **NOTE:** *Year articles take precedence over other articles that might have numeric titles. For example, if you go to the article called [[137]], you get an article about the events occurring in the year 137 AD. As it happens, 137 is an interesting number in physics, but to read about that you should go to the article [[137 (number)]].*

You can also find an article for every date from [[January 1]] to [[December 31]]. These are lists of anniversaries, not articles specific to a given year. They convey the significant events, births, and deaths for any date, such as January 20th—helpful, perhaps, for college students looking for a party theme. These lists populate the On this day . . . section of the main page. (The title convention is simply the month and day number, or April 1; no suffix is required for ordinals.) [[List of historical anniversaries]] is a handily arranged list of all these pages.

✳ **NOTE:** *If you ever find it too tiring to work out 20th century dates in Roman numerals, such as those you might find in old copyright notices, copy the letters (for example, MCMLXVIII) into Wikipedia and let a redirect take the strain.*

Decade articles are in a familiar form: the first year of the decade plus *s* (for example, [[1660s]], no apostrophe). Again, [[List of decades]] is a handy list with coverage stretching from the 17th century BC to the 21st century AD.

Century articles are found in either the form [[18th century]] (for centuries AD, you can leave out the AD) or [[2nd century BC]] (for centuries BC). The Common Era convention of writing BCE and CE, as many scholars do, is also supported and used within Wikipedia, coexisting with BC/AD (refer to [[Common Era]] for background); date links using this convention will redirect to the proper articles. (If you're really clever, type 0 AD into Wikipedia. Go ahead!)

These by-date articles stretch not only into the past (there is a century article for [[40th century BC]], before which Wikipedia only has articles for millennia), but also into the far future. These future year articles record not only future anniversaries and future astronomical events, but also fictional events that are supposed to have happened in these years. (In the [[25th century]] article, for instance, we are reminded that Buck Rogers lived around 2419.)

Timelines provide detailed chronologies for various topics. The [[List of timelines]] lists timelines covering hundreds of topics, offering detailed perspectives for understanding history. If that's not enough, the [[Detailed logarithmic timeline]] and its linked pages could claim to be an education in itself.

Browsing by Categories

Another way to find articles is to browse through categories. *Categories*, like lists, collect related articles. But although Wikipedia's software treats a list the same way it treats any other article, it treats categories differently. In order to place an article in a category, an editor does not edit the category's page. Instead, the editor adds a specialized *tag* to the article itself, and the MediaWiki software automatically populates the category page with every article *tagged* as a member of that category.

Alongside links and templates, categories help provide structure to the wiki. In every topic area, categories are created and used to group related pages together: For example, [[Category:American novelists]] contains thousands of articles about authors, for those interested in exploring American literature. In an area where you already have some expertise, the category system may be your best bet for finding content of interest.

The categories in which an article has been placed are listed at the very bottom of the article page, underneath the article text, in a small shaded box (Figure 3-9). Each category name is a link: Click one to visit the corresponding category page, which lists all the articles in that category.

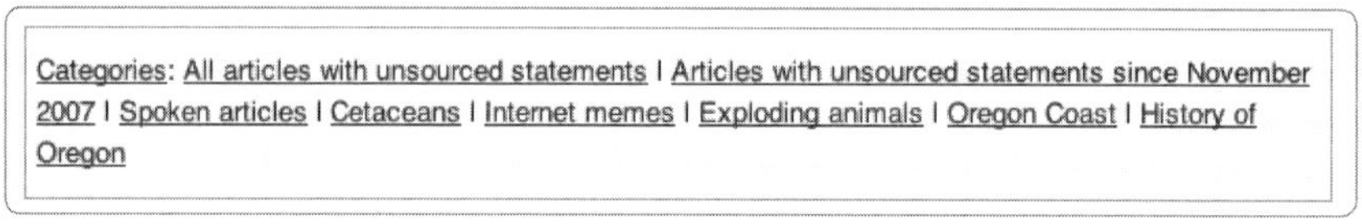

Categories: All articles with unsourced statements | Articles with unsourced statements since November 2007 | Spoken articles | Cetaceans | Internet memes | Exploding animals | Oregon Coast | History of Oregon

FIGURE 3-9: *The category listing at the bottom of an article, showing the categories in which an article appears: These are the categories for the article [[Exploding whale]].*

A page can be placed in any number of categories; indeed, most articles are in more than one. No category excludes any other, and categories can even be placed inside other categories, which can themselves be placed inside other categories! This creates a tree structure (or a *taxonomy*, if you prefer). For example, the article [[Malta]] is in [[Category:Malta]], itself in [[Category:European micro-states]], which is in [[Category:Microstates]], which is in [[Category:Countries by characteristic]]; this is then categorized under the broad category of [[Category: Countries]]. Browsing successive layers of subcategories is a useful way to find content: You can get to a high-level category any way you like and then drill down into a more specific area. Because Category is also a Wikipedia namespace, you can go directly to a category using the search box, for example, [[Category:Poets]].

Categories may be surprisingly specific as well as sweepingly broad. Some are just fun: [[Category:Toys]] has as subcategories [[Category:Toy cars and trucks]] and [[Category:Yo-yos]], whereas [[Category:Teddy bears]] is one subcategory of [[Category:Fictional bears]].

Everyone is welcome to categorize pages as needed, either by placing an article in an existing category or creating an entirely new category (see Chapter 9). As with every type of content, guidelines for creating and placing categories have been established. See, for example, [[Wikipedia:Naming conventions (categories)]] (shortcut WP:NCCAT).

Structure of a Category Page

When you click a category name from the linked categories at the bottom of an article, you are taken to a category page located in the Category namespace. These pages are divided into four main parts (Figure 3-10):

▶ The top part describes the topic. This section is editable and may contain wikilinks to relevant encyclopedia articles. This section is not always present.

▶ The second part lists the immediate subcategories of the category. For example, [[Category:American crime fiction writers]] is a subcategory of [[Category:American novelists]]. This section is only present if the category contains subcategories.

▶ The third part of the page displays an automatically generated, alphabetical list of wikilinks to the articles in the category. This list is the heart of the category page—it is always present and is usually the section that proves most useful. A category can contain any number of pages; some contain thousands. It would be impractical to display such a large number of links on one page; on Wikipedia, a category page will only display as many as 200 links at a time, sorted alphabetically. Click the Next 200 link to jump to the next page of links.

✳ **NOTE:** *Alphabetical order is not always obvious: Articles about people, for example, are normally best sorted alphabetically by surname. However, if the correct sort tag hasn't been added to the biography, it will be alphabetized conventionally (i.e., by the first word in the page title, which is often the first name of the person). Details on sorting are in Chapter 9.*

► The last part of the page shows *supercategories*—the categories that this category belongs to. These categories appear in a shaded box named (somewhat confusingly) *Categories*, just like the categories for articles.

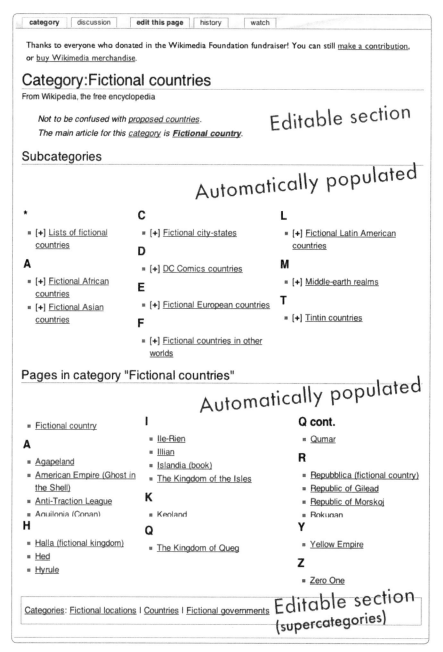

FIGURE 3-10: *Example of a category page (the category of Fictional Countries), showing editable sections*

Navigating Categories

Categories form a kind of parallel Wikipedia universe. If you're lucky, a small cluster of categories will cover just the articles you're seeking. Think of subcategories as being under a category, and you'll appreciate that clicking can take you both "up" (to a more comprehensive category) and "down" (to a more specialized category). You can move to a category of greater scope and generality or (conversely) narrow things down.

Therefore, the other significant part of a category page is the list of categories to which the page belongs, in other words, the *supercategories* for which this category is a subcategory. These are your ways inside the category system.

Up-and-down navigation is a very handy way to move from a related article to the one you really want. For example, you can move from a place in the right state but wrong county to a category of places in the state to a subcategory of places in the right county, where you'll find the title of the article you want. That journey is like going in and up and then down and out of the category system. Most browsing using categories requires a combination of navigating up (to a more comprehensive category) and down (to a subcategory) in search of the category of greatest interest, followed by a systematic search of pages in that category.

A Longer Journey Using Categories

The article about the ocean sunfish (which is also known as the *Mola mola*) might be placed in the Molidae category, for the fish's scientific family name (Figure 3-11). Looking at the category page for Molidae displays the other species in this family (as long as those species have properly categorized articles).

FIGURE 3-11: *The ocean sunfish (Mola mola) or common mola is the heaviest bony fish in the world, with an average weight of 1,000 kilograms. The species is native to tropical and temperate waters around the globe. (From [[Mola mola]], image from NOAA)*

Navigating from this category, you may go up, down, or out to one of the linked pages. [[Category:Molidae]] is a subcategory of [[Category:Tetraodonti-formes]]. If you're interested in the biology of related fish, click that link. Once there, you'll see various families of the order Tetraodontiformes (such as the Puffers) listed as subcategories. This category system follows standard scientific classification.

You can eventually get to [[Category:Water]] from the fish articles. Using a less-than sign (<) to mean "clicking up to the next category," here is the chain of subcategories:

Ray-finned fish < Bony fish < Fish sorted by classification < Fish < Aquatic organisms < Water

---

Tetraodontiformes is one of more than 50 subcategories of [[Category:Ray-finned fish]]. Going from [[Category:Water]],

---

Water < Inorganic compounds < Chemical compounds < Chemical substances < Chemistry

---

to find out where [[Category:Chemistry]] fits in, look at

Chemistry < Physical sciences < Scientific disciplines < Academic disciplines < Academia

---

Is there no end to this? Actually, keep clicking through categories:

Academia < Education < Society < Fundamental

---

and you end up here:

Fundamental < Articles < Contents

The [[Category:Contents]] is the top category of all categories.

This non-serious exploration makes a serious point: Wikipedia not only brings knowledge together, it also classifies it. You can find an exhaustive, unwieldy list of all categories at [[Special:Categories]], or try [[Wikipedia:Cate-gorical index]] for an arrangement by topic.

The highest levels of categorization are so broad that they are usually impractical even as starting points. But they do provide a novel way to sort con-tent from a distance, as Robert Rohde did in some statistics from October 2007.[1] Programmatically tallying the articles in the broadest categories (and their subcat-egories), he was able to estimate the composition of Wikipedia itself: 28.0 percent science, 10.5 percent culture, 16.0 percent geography, 6.3 percent history, 0.8 per-cent religion, 5.5 percent philosophy, 1.8 percent mathematics, 14.3 percent

---

[1] These figures are taken from an October 2007 post to the *WikiEN-l* mailing list: *http://lists.wikimedia. org/pipermail/wikien-l/2007-October/083862.html*

nature, 6.0 percent technology, 1.4 percent fiction, and 9.6 percent general biography. These categories are, of course, fluid and negotiable (for example, the Politics
category is inside the Philosophy category).

Browsing by Page Type

You can also browse by article type rather than by topic.

Finding Excellent or Poor Content

Perhaps you want to read only the very best Wikipedia content. In this case,
browse the Featured Content portal at [[Portal:Featured content]], which includes
all types of content (including articles, images, and portals) deemed to be the best
Wikipedia has to offer.

Featured articles, available directly at [[Wikipedia:Featured articles]] (shortcut WP:FA), have been vetted, reviewed, and voted on by community members.
They meet high standards of completeness, accuracy, and referencing, and represent some of the very best articles available on the site. Try your hand as a critic
at [[Wikipedia:Featured article candidates]] (shortcut WP:FAC). *Good articles* are
articles that may not be as extensive as featured articles but are still excellent
quality; you can browse a collection of these articles at [[Wikipedia:Good articles]]
(shortcut WP:GA).

Featured lists can reveal odd Wikipedia content. Whereas a list page taken
at random from Wikipedia will (at most) have some navigational value, a featured
list such as [[List of Oz books]] will have a good lead section, images, and much
greater credibility. See [[Wikipedia:Featured lists]] (shortcut WP:FL) for several hundred featured lists.

Articles of poor quality or in need of attention are also collected in maintenance categories, such as [[Category:Cleanup by month]]. Another quick way
to find articles with problems is to search for misspelled versions of commonly
misspelled words in order to find errors and typos to correct, or (perhaps more
interesting) search for dead-wood phrases such as "it is important to remember
that," which can be replaced with more precise wording. The project page at
[[Wikipedia:Cleanup]], where you can add articles you find with problems, also
provides a quick way to start getting involved. Finding poor-quality articles and
systemized maintenance work will be covered thoroughly in Chapter 7.

Finding Images

Apart from text, images are the most common and important kind of media used in Wikipedia. They help bring the encyclopedia to life, showing places and people, plants and animals, book covers, and machinery types. They illustrate processes and diagram complicated procedures and systems. They include logos, trademarks, heraldic devices, and flags. You can also find large numbers of maps.

To find some of the very best images on Wikipedia, visit the list of featured images at [[Wikipedia:Featured pictures]] (shortcut WP:FP). There is also a link from this page to a category on the Wikimedia Commons for featured desktop backgrounds, or pictures whose aspect ratios are suitable for wallpapering your computer desktop. You can find some lovely images here.

To browse for other images, go to the Wikimedia Commons, where images are organized by category. The Commons is actually designed as a repository of media and images that all the Wikimedia projects can use and link to. Thus you may find images, for instance, that are described in languages other than English. More on searching the Commons is in Chapter 16.

Finding Media Files

Every media file found on Wikipedia is intended to illustrate an encyclopedia article, not to stand alone. Wikipedia and the Wikimedia Commons offer a range of these files, from short animations to sound recordings. For instance, in the article about Mozart, you'll find a list of a few dozen or so audio files; these are short excerpts of his works for illustrative purposes. All of the media files in Wikipedia should be freely available under the GFDL license.

Like images, finding media files is a bit easier on Wikimedia Commons than on Wikipedia itself; on Commons, you'll find categories for sounds and videos, subcategorized into animations, animal sounds, and so on.

Again, just as for images, each file has a description page. Confusingly at first, these pages are all within the Image namespace; Wikipedia does not separate different media file types into different namespaces.

To play media files, you can try Wikipedia's embedded media player, which will play media files in your web browser. Simply click the Play in Browser link next to the file icon. Alternatively, you can download the file. However, playing it may present some obstacles as you may need to download special software. The major sound file type used on Wikipedia is the audio format Ogg Vorbis, whereas video files use the Ogg Theora format. These formats are broadly similar to others used to play digital audio and video, such as MP3 and MPEG, and can be played on almost all personal computers. Unlike MP3, QuickTime, and many other common formats, however, Ogg formats are completely free, open, and unpatented. Microsoft Windows and Mac OS X computers do not support Ogg formats by default and require additional software to play them. If your computer does not automatically play these files when you click them, you'll need to download and install free software from the Internet to play them. Go to *http://www.vorbis.com* for links to versions of downloadable players or codecs suitable for common systems.

If you already have a media player such as Windows Media Player or RealPlayer, or iTunes for a Mac, you can first download the *.ogg codecs*—small programs that decrypt the format—for these players, which will enable them to play Wikipedia's files. For Linux/Unix users, many recent free Unix systems are able to play Vorbis audio without any new software; however, many media players are available if you don't have any audio software installed. [[Wikipedia:Media help (Ogg)]] has a list of the free players available for all systems and directions for downloading the Ogg codecs for other music players.

Music files may occasionally use the MIDI format (*.mid* or *.midi* extension). MIDI is usually playable without new software. Most computers have a MIDI-enabled player and sound card.

In addition to music files, a small but growing number of articles contain spoken versions of the article recorded in *.ogg* Vorbis format by volunteers. With the right player, you can listen to Wikipedia articles in your car! Go to [[Wikipedia: Spoken articles]], [[Category:Spoken articles]], and [[Wikipedia:WikiProject Spoken Wikipedia]] (shortcut WP:WSW) to find these articles.

Further Reading

Linking

http://en.wikipedia.org/wiki/Wikipedia:Orphan   Information about orphaned articles

http://en.wikipedia.org/wiki/Category:Orphaned_articles   The list of orphaned and unlinked articles

http://en.wikipedia.org/wiki/Wikipedia:Build_the_web   Build the web guidelines and philosophy about internal linking and building hypertext

http://en.wikipedia.org/wiki/Wikipedia:Make_only_links_relevant_to_the_context   Only make links that are relevant to the context guideline; in other words, use judgment when linking

Indexes and Other Ways to Browse

http://en.wikipedia.org/wiki/Wikipedia:Quick_index   An alphabetized, automatically generated index to all Wikipedia articles

http://en.wikipedia.org/wiki/List_of_academic_disciplines   A detailed list of academic disciplines with links to articles

http://en.wikipedia.org/wiki/Portal:Overviews   Overview of basic articles for many fields

http://en.wikipedia.org/wiki/Portal:Lists_of_topics   All sorts of lists arranged by topic

http://en.wikipedia.org/wiki/List_of_Dewey_Decimal_classes   List of Dewey Decimal classes

Further Reading, continued

http://en.wikipedia.org/wiki/Wikipedia:Outline_of_Roget's_Thesaurus The classification used for *Roget's Thesaurus*, with terms linked

http://en.wikipedia.org/wiki/List_of_timelines Timelines about various topics

http://en.wikipedia.org/wiki/List_of_historical_anniversaries A list of what happened on this day in history

http://en.wikipedia.org/wiki/List_of_decades A list of all the decade articles

http://en.wikipedia.org/wiki/List_of_centuries A list of all the century articles

Browsing by Quality

http://en.wikipedia.org/wiki/Wikipedia:Featured_content The Featured Content portal for featured articles and more

Browsing by Categories

http://en.wikipedia.org/wiki/Help:Category Information on how categories work

http://en.wikipedia.org/wiki/Wikipedia:Categorical_index Topic index to all categories

http://en.wikipedia.org/wiki/Wikipedia:Categorization Guidelines for categorization and category use

Finding Images and Sounds

http://en.wikipedia.org/wiki/Wikipedia:Featured_pictures Wikipedia's featured pictures

http://commons.wikimedia.org/ The Wikimedia Commons, where you can find free images, sounds, animations, and videos

http://commons.wikimedia.org/wiki/Category:Commons_featured_desktop_backgrounds The category of pictures on Commons that have aspect ratios suitable for computer desktop backgrounds

http://en.wikipedia.org/wiki/Wikipedia:Media_help Help with playing media files, including downloading instructions for various players

http://en.wikipedia.org/wiki/Wikipedia:Spoken_articles A list of spoken Wikipedia articles by subject

http://en.wikipedia.org/wiki/Category:Spoken_articles Spoken articles by category

http://en.wikipedia.org/wiki/Wikipedia:Sound/list A list of full-length copyleft/public domain musical works available on Wikipedia or the Commons

Summary

Wikipedia as a collection of information is amazing, but its real strength is as a collection of findable information. Searching is useful for finding articles on specific topics, but you may need to search using a variety of names to find the article you're looking for. You can configure Wikipedia's search to search multiple namespaces along with other options; you can also use external search engines. Access the search engine on the left-hand sidebar, which also includes a number of other links and tools. Some of these links and tools are consistent throughout the site, whereas others change depending on the page.

Wikipedia also has intricate and well-developed structures for browsing, including links within articles, editor-constructed portals, the main page, and categories. These structures all use hypertext, where one page leads to another via links, with information split between various pages that reference each other. Categories, which show up as links at the bottom of pages that are categorized, provide a powerful way to browse through related pages, including pages categorized by quality (such as featured articles). Categories set up a classification system, with more specific areas becoming subcategories of broader areas.

In the next chapter, we'll home in on the individual articles, describing their specific parts. We'll cover what you can expect to find, as well as how to evaluate the quality of a given article.

4

Understanding and Evaluating an Article

Once you've found the content you're looking for, the next thing you need to know is what you're looking *at*. With an understanding of namespaces and content types in Wikipedia, you can easily tell whether you're looking at an article, a discussion page, a community page, or a user page; and once you know how to search and browse the site, finding articles on your topic is simple. The next step is assessing an article's quality.

Understanding how to read all the components of an article—from its edit history to its discussion pages—is key for skilled and sensible reading of Wikipedia. Experienced editors and readers use many tricks to quickly evaluate pages and understand their state. It's a matter of knowing where to look and determining which clues are most significant.

In this chapter, we'll identify the different parts of a typical article and discuss what each part can tell you. We'll then list some detailed questions to ask when critically evaluating an article. Throughout this chapter, as we describe how articles are put together, we'll list **Clues**—points to pick up on for quality evaluation. If you're in a hurry, we've summarized our best clues at the end of the chapter.

✳ **NOTE:** *In this discussion of the look and feel of Wikipedia, we'll be talking about viewing pages with the default configuration, the Monobook skin. Skins are customizable, and there are a variety to choose from; for more, see "Setting Your Preferences" on page 308.*

Anatomy of an Article

Every editable page on Wikipedia is made up of three related parts: the text of the page or article, the page history, and a separate discussion page. The tabs that are visible at the top of (almost) any page are your entry points to these components. There are four tabs if you are logged out and six if you are logged in.

Assuming you're logged in, the tabs you'll see are shown in Figure 4-1: Article, Discussion, Edit This Page, History, Move, and Watch.

▸ The Article tab shows you the text of the article you are viewing; this is the default view when you go to a page and the view you'll want to return to after exploring other components. The title of this tab changes across namespaces; for instance, it displays as *Project Page* if you're looking at a page in the Wikipedia namespace, and *User Page* if you're looking at a page in the User namespace.

▸ The Discussion tab shows you the discussion or talk page for that article; this is a separate page dedicated to discussion of the page's content.

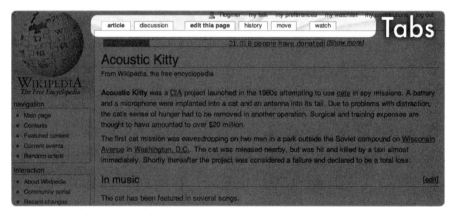

FIGURE 4-1: *The tabs at the top of a Wikipedia page*

∗ **NOTE:** *The terms* talk page *and* discussion page *are used somewhat interchangeably. Although the tab intended for discussion of an article is labeled* Discussion, *it leads to a page located in the Talk namespace. Discussion pages attached to user pages, which are intended for conversation between editors, are called* talk pages *as well—though, to be pedantic, they are user talk pages in the User talk namespace.*

▸ The Edit This Page tab allows you to edit whatever page you are currently viewing. Clicking the tab opens up an edit window, where you can modify the text of the page.

▸ The History tab shows you the edit history of the page you are viewing.

▸ The Move tab moves the page to a new title. Leave this advanced operation alone for now, until you've had a chance to read Chapter 8.

▸ The Watch tab adds the article you're currently viewing to your own personal watchlist. (If you are already watching an article, the tab will display *Unwatch* instead and clicking it will remove an article from your watchlist.)

In this chapter, we'll cover articles as a whole along with talk pages and history pages. Editing is discussed in Part II, from Chapter 5 onward, and then we'll return to watchlists in Chapter 11.

Absent Tabs

There are some exceptions that apply to the tabs you can view on a particular page. Protected pages, for instance, won't display an Edit tab, but will instead display a View Source tab that shows the wikisource of an article but doesn't allow you to edit it. Pages in the Special namespace, which are not editable, don't display any of these tabs. If you aren't logged in, the Move and Watch tabs are not available.

The Article Text

Did you ever wonder what makes Wikipedia articles seem so standardized? The conventional way of writing a Wikipedia article combines a number of recognizable features, which will generally appear as an article matures. In this section, we'll review the different parts that you may encounter in an article. **Clue:** *All articles don't have to have all of these parts, but if you see an article without any of them—or if the text appears unformatted—chances are good the article was added by an inexperienced editor.*

Directly underneath the page tabs, you'll see the title of the page you're viewing in large bold type, followed by a line and the words *From Wikipedia, the free encyclopedia*. This is where the editable portion of the page starts.

Like trailers before a feature film, messages may appear in italics at the beginning of an article. These messages are not part of the article, but are a rubric properly called a hatnote. *Hatnotes* point you toward disambiguation pages or other articles that might be confused with the one you are viewing; for example, *For the medical term see [[rigor (medicine)]]* occurs at the top of [[rigour]].

You may also see one or more warning messages in brightly colored boxes at the beginning of articles; for instance, warning you that *this article requires attention from an expert* or *the neutrality of this article is disputed*. Other messages may simply note that some kind of cleanup needs to happen on the article. These messages serve two purposes: They alert the reader to problems, and they let editors know that "something needs to be done here." They are produced with templates (see a list at [[Wikipedia:Template messages]]), and any editor may add (or remove) any template, so they are not particularly "official." They are, however, useful alerts to many kinds of quality issues, and they tell you that at least one editor has concerns about the article.

Color Coding

Article warning messages are of a standard shape (slim and rectangular) and are color coded: orange for content issues, red for a deletion candidate, and yellow for cleanup. Blue is used for any general informative messages. See [[Wikipedia:Article message boxes]], shortcut WP:AMB, for a full explanation.

Following any messages, the text of the article itself begins. Often the article text is broken up into numerous sections, which should convey a logical structure to the article and break it into manageable pieces. If there are three or more such sections, a Table of Contents (ToC) is automatically displayed. Clicking any of the links in the ToC takes you directly to that section of the article. You can hide a lengthy ToC by clicking the [show/hide] link; if you are logged in, you can also disable all ToCs from showing in your user preferences.

Regardless of how many sections there are, the article should start with a strong introductory paragraph that tells you the topic of the article and why it is important.

The text itself should also be sprinkled throughout with internal links, or wikilinks, to other articles; these links are displayed in blue. **Clue:** *If no wikilinks exist in the text, there's a strong chance the article was written by someone unfamiliar with Wikipedia's conventions, and the article itself may be questionable.*

The text may also contain images (which should have captions) or graphics that summarize information about the topic. To see the full-size image and more information about it, simply click the image; this takes you to the image description page.

You may also see an *infobox* near the beginning of an article, typically on the right-hand side. These boxes are standardized presentations of key facts about the article's topic. Different styles of infoboxes have been developed for articles in many diverse fields, from species of plants to Australian cricketers. They are all based on *templates*, which are described in Chapter 9. **Clue:** *Authors do not sign anywhere in articles, so if you see a signature in article text, it was left by someone unfamiliar with Wikipedia's conventions.*

For references, the article may contain footnotes or inline references. Sometimes external links are embedded in the text; this referencing style is discouraged, however, in favor of footnotes. Footnotes will appear as small superscript numbers at the ends of sentences; clicking the footnote number takes you to the appropriate footnote at the end of the article and vice versa; clicking the caret (^) at the beginning of a footnote takes you back to the text.

At the end of a good article, you'll find several standardized sections: See also, References, and External links. (On a disambiguation page, which serves as a dedicated navigational structure to point you to articles with related names, these aren't used.) The See also section should include a list of other relevant Wikipedia articles. Generally, articles that are already linked in the text are not included in this section. References, sometimes called *sources* or *notes*, include the sources used in writing the article. When present, footnotes are often listed here, or in a Notes section appended to the references. The External links section includes links to other relevant non-Wikimedia websites on the topic. For instance, if the article is about a company or organization that has a homepage on the Web, a link to this site should be included in External links.

There are occasionally Bibliography and Further reading sections included as well; the former may list publications by the subject of the article, whereas Further reading may list other important sources of information that aren't directly cited in the article. There may also be links to other Wikimedia sister projects in this section—for example, links to related media on the Wikimedia Commons or to a dictionary definition of a term on Wiktionary. There may also be messages in this section explaining that material has been imported from a non-copyrighted

Reference and Research

The more critical attention you are giving an article and the more seriously you are researching a topic, the more the article's references are going to interest you. Though this is far from always being the case, references should be a mixture of online and paper sources and of recent works along with standard texts that give broad context. A good References, External links, or Further reading section can be a great place to start doing research, especially if you are new to a topic.

source. **Clue:** *Any material imported from another source, such as an old encyclopedia, may need to be updated.*

At the very bottom of the article, you find any stub messages. A *stub*, as mentioned in Chapter 1, is simply a short or beginning article that may be incomplete. Stub articles are sorted by topic and identified with these short template-based messages that tell you the article is a stub and what broad topic category it falls into. **Clue:** *A stub article will likely be incomplete in terms of the information provided—seeing a stub message is an alert to check other sources as well.*

A small box listing the categories into which the article has been placed follows the body of the article. Clicking any of these category links takes you to the category page, which lists other related articles in the same category. **Clue:** *All articles should be in at least one category. An article that doesn't have any categories listed is likely new or orphaned.*

Backlinks

If you want to place an article in a broader context, or if you're researching a topic in depth, the What Links Here link in the sidebar can be useful. Clicking this link shows you other pages that link to the article you are currently viewing. In other words, this link gives you a list of *backlinks*—places where your article is referenced on other pages. Checking the backlinks is one of the tricks of the trade for getting the most out of Wikipedia.

For an article on a basic topic, there may be a great number of other articles that link to it, and there may be too many backlinks to tell you anything useful. You won't learn a great deal from the backlinks to the article on [[New York]], except that they are very numerous indeed. On the other hand, only a handful of articles may link to a more obscure article. For instance, for a historical figure you are researching, the backlinks may well turn up points of entry to research further: articles about events that occurred during their lifetime or lists of officeholders that include the person of interest. Don't assume the article itself will send you to all those other pages in its See also section—articles are always works in progress. Searching the site for the article's title won't necessarily turn up all the references to it on other pages, either, if the references are hidden in internal wikilinks with different alternate text. Using What Links Here will catch all the references to an article, however, including where it may have been discussed on user or project talk pages. If you're checking the quality of an article, it's always worth checking the backlinks.

No backlinks at all means you have found an orphan, which is considered a debilitating condition. An orphaned article is unfortunate and possibly suspect, alerting the reader to issues of potential concern. It may simply be that the article is new and no other articles have had a chance to link to it yet, or it could be a topic that is not really encyclopedic. If an article claims to be about an important topic, but nothing links to it, it may well be a hoax. Check to see how old the article is, as described in the next section. **Clue:** *No incoming links can also mean the article has a poor choice of title, perhaps not conforming to Wikipedia style. It is also conceivable that an orphaned article has a typo in the title (for instance,* *a subtle error such as the wrong punctuation or* Mc *instead of* Mac*).* If this is the case, it's worth searching for other articles about the same topic, as described in Chapter 3.

Article History

Once you've read an article thoroughly, you want to understand its next important aspect—how to read its history. Every page on Wikipedia, whether an article, a talk page, or any other page (except for the auto-generated special pages), has a record of all changes made to it that is captured in the page history.

Page histories are revealing to those in the know. The goal of reading a page history is often to determine the story of what has happened to an article over time. How old is an article? How many and which editors have worked on it? Has the topic been contentious, the subject of debate between editors? Has the page improved over time, or has any good content been lost? Was a particular edit valuable to the article? Is the current version that you're looking at vandalized? The page history can answer all of these questions and can also give you a good idea of an article's trustworthiness. Experienced Wikipedians glean a great deal about articles from looking over the page history and then following up on some of the individual edits that make up that history. **Clue:** *How contentious the article topic is matters, because a subject that turns into a combat zone often drives off all but highly partisan editors; with careful investigation, the page history can tell you whether this is the case.*

The page history is accessible by clicking the History tab at the top of the page. The History tab always leads to the history of whatever page you're looking at. For instance, if you are viewing the talk page of an article, clicking the History tab will take you to the history of edits to that talk page, rather than the history of the article it's associated with. Go back to viewing the article, and then click the History tab to see the article's history.

Substantial articles usually have a number of contributors. If the page history indicates that the page is entirely or almost entirely the work of one person, you are dealing with a situation more comparable to evaluating an article on someone's private website. **Clue:** *A short history is a warning sign. If only a few people*

You Can't Change Wikipedia

You can't actually change anything in Wikipedia . . . you can only add to it. An article you read today is simply the current draft; every time it is changed, both the new version and a copy of the old version are kept. This allows you to compare different versions and restore older content if necessary. Except for page deletions (discussed in Chapter 7), no content is ever actually removed from Wikipedia. (Adapted from [[Wikipedia:Ten things you may not know about Wikipedia]])

have edited an article, it is likely that only a few people have reviewed the factual content, and the page may represent a limited view of the topic.

Even in a long history, however, some edits should be discounted as being of little significance to the content. A number of editors may have simply made minor formatting changes to an article. Some passing bot may have edited it mindlessly. These contributors may not have verified any of the content but have simply brought the article up to Wikipedia stylistic standards. A common situation is that a single contributor has written the bulk of a short or beginning article, and then a few people will reformat the article but not change the content substantially. In these cases, there is still only one primary author.

Reading a Page History

First and foremost, the page history tells you who has worked on the page, and it allows you to examine the successive versions of the article and the differences between them (see Figure 4-2). You can also see the date and time of each edit and compare versions of edits. Finally, you can see the comments that contributors have left in the Edit summary field regarding their edits.

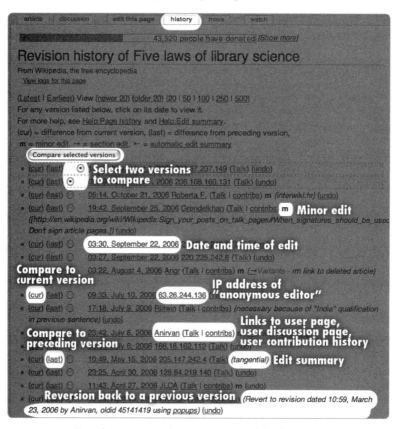

FIGURE 4-2: *Reading a page history, accessible from the History tab*

Each line in the page history represents a single edit. Every time a wiki page is modified and saved, a new version of that page is saved, and a new line is added to the page history. The most recent version is displayed at the top of the history, so reading down is reading back into any page's history.

Every line in a page history has several elements. Reading across, they are as follows:

▶ First are two links, curr and last, along with a radio button. Clicking curr for a particular version compares it to the most recent version of the article (so you can see how that version compares to the version currently displayed on the site), whereas clicking last compares a particular version to the immediately preceding version (so you can see exactly what was changed with that particular edit). The radio buttons allow you to compare any two versions of an article, as described in "Analyzing a Page History" on page 108.

▶ Next, the date and time of the edit are displayed as a blue link. By default, this time is set to display in the UTC time zone. (You can change the time to your local time zone if you are logged in by going to My Preferences, as described in "Setting Your Preferences" on page 308.) Clicking this link will show you that particular version of the page. When you're viewing an old version, a warning message is displayed at the top of the page, and the page URL in your browser will display the version number, or unique ID, of the version you are looking at. You can use this URL to link to this particular revision of the page. (This is also how Permanent Link on the left-hand sidebar works.)

▶ Next, the author of the edit is displayed. This author will be listed by either a username (if the editor was logged in) or an IP (Internet Protocol) address (if they were editing anonymously). Clicking the username will bring you to the editor's user page, if he or she has one; if the username is displayed as a redlink, that means the editor was logged in but has not yet created a user page. If an editor was not logged in, the numeric IP address of the computer he or she was editing from will display instead, and clicking the IP address will bring you to a list of that IP's contributions.

▶ After the editor's name, there are links in parentheses to the editor's user talk page (Talk) and, if the editor is logged in, his or her contributions (contribs). Whether an editor was logged in or not, you can go to his or her talk page to leave a message. **Clue:** *If you suspect vandalism, it can be particularly helpful to go the talk page to see if a particular editor has racked up any warnings from other editors. Again, a redlink means there are no messages yet on an editor's talk page.* Clicking the Contribs link shows you a list of all the edits that particular editor has ever made.

▶ Next, some edits will display a lowercase *m* if the edit was marked as minor by the editor; minor edits are generally small changes, such as spelling or typo corrections. The number in parentheses that follows (for edits made since mid-2007) shows the number of bytes that were changed with that individual edit; a large number is generally reflective of the entire article being edited and saved. (Somewhat more usefully, the net number of bytes changed with a single edit is also displayed in Recent Changes and in personal watchlists).

▶ Finally, any text that follows is part of the *edit summary* provided by the editor. This is (one hopes) an informative comment that is intended to describe what the edit accomplished and why it was made. Sometimes these summaries are created automatically and contain a variety of links; often they contain a kind of shorthand or jargon that has been developed over the years.

Problem IPs

If an edit was made by a user who was not logged in, you can at least get a look at the other contributions made using the same IP address. But remember that the same IP address may represent different people editing, and different IPs may represent the same person, because Internet service providers don't always operate IP allocations in the simple way that telephone numbers are handed out. Many Internet service providers issue temporary IP addresses to their users from a pool of addresses, and when the user disconnects, the address is returned to the pool for allocation to someone else. These are known as *dynamic IPs*. (IP numbers that differ only in the last three places may be the same editor using a dynamic IP.) Furthermore, even if an IP address is fixed, it might be the IP for a computer in a public place, such as a library, an Internet café, or a school. This means, of course, that you may be seeing many people's contributions from the same IP address, and you cannot be sure a message left on the talk page will reach a particular user. IP addresses from public settings can sometimes reveal an extreme and baffling combination of excellent edits and vandalism. However, you still might be able to see that the particular edit occurred in the midst of a series of edits, which can help you gauge the character of whoever was at that machine at that time. If they've been determined to be from public computers, the discussion pages for IP addresses will sometimes have notices to this effect.

Analyzing a Page History

Comparing versions of an article, or *examining diffs*, is the most useful tool an editor has for determining how an article has changed over time. *Diff* is short for the *differences between pages*. The term *diff* is also commonly used as shorthand to refer to a particular old version of a page.

Checking the diffs can tell you not only how the page has changed over time but also if the current version displayed is the best one. If you suspect vandalism in the current version, for instance, flip back a change or two, using the radio buttons or the curr and last links, to see if the information persists. If something in the article seems untrue, it's worth comparing versions until you can determine when it was added and by whom. (After all, if you can ask the person who edited something into the article about the edit, you can perhaps get somewhere with your difficulty.)

Because all versions of a page are kept, any two versions can be compared. To do so, choose the radio button for the version you are interested in looking at. Another radio button will appear for all versions of the page that are newer than the one you chose. Choose this new right-hand radio button for the newer version you are interested in. (To compare to the most current version, choose the top radio button.) Now click the Compare Selected Versions button at the top of the page history.

A split screen will appear with two headers, as shown in Figure 4-3, each of which tells you the version date and time, the edit author, and his or her edit summary. The version on the right is always the newer version of the two you

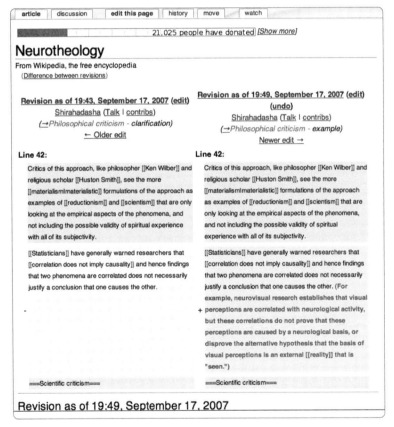

FIGURE 4-3: *A diff is accessible by clicking Compare Versions on the page history. The newest version is shown on the right. Shading indicates a changed paragraph. The editor's name, the date and time of the edit, and the edit summary are listed at the top.*

Undoing Vandalism

Any old version of a page can be edited and resaved to become the most current version, overriding any other edits. When this is done to undo a single edit, it's called *reverting* that edit. Reverting is how mistakes can be easily fixed, as explained in Chapter 5, and how most vandalism is removed, as explained in Chapter 7.

---

have selected. You will then see a line-by-line comparison of the wikisource of the two versions you have selected. On the old version, paragraphs that differ from the new version are highlighted yellow, and on the new version, they are highlighted green. Text removed within a paragraph is shown in red on the old version, whereas new text within a paragraph is shown in red on the new version; if a whole paragraph was removed or added, the text is simply black, whereas the other side is blank (white).

Below this highlighted summary of changes, the entire rendered view of the more recent of the two versions you are comparing is displayed. Note that you can change this view in your user preferences, under Misc.

If no line-by-line differences are displayed, there are no differences between the two versions of the page. If there are also intermediate edits in between the two versions you are comparing, the comparison will tell you this (for example, *5 intermediate edits not shown*). Only differences that occur between the two versions you are comparing are displayed.

If an edit was made by a registered user, you can follow up by going to that user's page to see who he is (or at least who he claims to be). Associated with each user page is the accompanying user talk page, which can give you a flavor of the user's interactions with other users: Is it full of thank-you notes or vitriolic arguments? Clicking the contributions of any particular contributor shows you the edits this particular person has made in Wikipedia. **Clue:** *Is this a new or experienced contributor? What else has he or she been working on?*

You'll sometimes need to find the exact revision in the history when a particular piece of information was added to an article. Perhaps you need to know who added a questionable statement or what the reasoning was behind adding a cleanup tag to the article. You could simply go back from the current revision one diff at a time, comparing each version until you find the one you are looking for. This method works well for articles with very short histories, but quickly becomes tedious for an article with a long edit history. Rather than doing this, then, there are a few tricks for quickly reviewing long page histories:

1. First, at the top of the page history, set the number of changes viewable to 500 rather than 50, so you can see all of the history (or at least more of it) on a single screen.

2. Quickly scan the edit summaries—does anything pop out? If, for instance, you are looking for the addition of a cleanup tag, does anyone mention adding this tag? Using CTRL-F to do a search for a particular term can sometimes be helpful.

3. If you don't find the version you're looking for, skip back a large number of changes and bisect the edit history by picking a revision somewhere in the middle. Review this revision by clicking the linked date or compare it to the current revision using the radio buttons. Is the information you're looking for in this old revision?

4. If so, keep going back several changes at a time until you find a version where it's not present. If not, go *forward* several changes until you find a version where it *is* present.

5. Once you've done this, you'll have located two revisions on either side of when the information you're looking for was added—one before the information was added and one after (the earliest revision you found that included the information). Once you've narrowed down a range in this manner, work your way backward and forward within the range a few revisions at a time, comparing revisions using the radio buttons.

6. Narrowing down the exact diff when something was added is usually quick. You can then follow up by checking the editor's edit summary and other contributions and determining whether it seems like a trustworthy edit.

Edit Summaries and Minor Edits

When reading page histories, you'll see comments and explanations. These are *edit summaries*, short comments provided by editors to help explain their edits. Edit summaries display in the page history, Recent Changes, and in user watchlists. The ideal edit summary briefly explains the nature of the edit and gives some context for it (for instance, not simply saying *rewriting* but *rewrote 2nd paragraph for grammar and clarity*). Edit summaries don't have to be complicated. If you make a test edit yourself, add *test* in the Edit summary box. When you reverse the edit, simply write *undo test* in the box.

Edit summaries are optional (though a very good idea), and even if present, they may be cryptic because a large body of jargon has been developed over the years. For instance, you might not be able to fathom *avoid dab* the first time you see it, but it is shorthand for *avoided a disambiguation page*, which, in turn, means that a link was fixed to point to an appropriate article instead of to a disambiguation page. To *wikify* a page is to add appropriate wikilinks to a page, by linking appropriate words, names, and phrases to other articles; it is one of the most common operations, as editors weave the web of the wiki, and it may also appear in a summary as *wfy*.

There are also some edit summaries that are automatically added by the software. For instance, the title of the section that was edited is automatically added and appears in grayed-out type in edit histories. Occasionally, you will see small conversations between editors as they go back and forth on a point (edit summaries are not indexed or searchable, however, so any really important discussion should always go on the talk page). Edit summaries can contain wikilinks if needed.

Refer to Appendix C or D or [[Wikipedia:Edit summary legend]] (shortcut WP:ESL) for other possible terms that may occur in edit summaries. If you are having trouble figuring out an edit summary, compare the version in question with the immediately preceding version. The diff should make things clear.

In assessing an article, look for edit summaries that indicate reversions of a page to a previous state. These will be denoted by *revert* or abbreviations such as *rv* or *rvt,* and indicate either reversal of vandalism or editors disagreeing on a point. **Clue:** *A patch of edits with many reverts in a page history indicates some sort of editing war. The quality of articles, unfortunately, is likely to degrade sharply in an extended edit war, so be warned.*

Another important warning sign is an editor who never bothers with edit summaries. **Clue:** *Especially if the editor is editing as anonymous, rather than editing with an account, you should treat such uncommented edits with suspicion.*

The lowercase bolded *m* that sometimes appears next to the edit summary refers to a minor edit. This edit is one that the editor deemed small enough that it doesn't have to be reviewed by other editors. Examples of minor edits include spelling and grammar corrections, link fixes, and small formatting changes. Edit summaries for minor edits, if they exist, are often quite short: *typo* or *spp* for a spelling correction. Only logged-in users can mark an edit minor. While logged in, you can also choose to exclude minor edits in your views of the Recent Changes page and your watchlist.

Further Reading

http://en.wikipedia.org/wiki/Help:What_links_here   About backlinks

http://en.wikipedia.org/wiki/Help:Page_history   How to read a page history

http://en.wikipedia.org/wiki/Help:Edit_summary   An introduction to the edit summary and more information about automatic edit summaries

http://en.wikipedia.org/wiki/Wikipedia:Edit_summary_legend   A glossary of commonly used edit summaries; helpful if you come across an abbreviation you don't recognize

http://en.wikipedia.org/wiki/Help:Diff   How to read the difference between two versions of a page

---

Talk Pages

Discussion or talk pages are meant for discussion about articles and other pages. Nearly every page on Wikipedia has an attached, dedicated discussion page. These pages exist in the various Talk namespaces. You access or create a talk page by clicking the Discussion tab; if the type is blue, the page already exists; if it is red, you will be creating it.

Talk pages are important, socially and practically. They help strengthen content, and they're also an integral part of Wikipedia's community. Talk pages are the "grass roots"—they function as a space for conversation between all the readers and editors of an article. Editors can mention possible problems, leave notes about current or ongoing work on the article, and negotiate a way through conflicts on content. Wikipedia's main aim, to build up its editing community and improve the articles that have been started, is played out here. Talk pages play a large part in making Wikipedia work by keeping discussion close to the article's content, rather than on a centralized discussion forum. And anyone may take part, even if they're not logged in.

We mention how talk pages work early on in this book, not because you're necessarily going to post to them immediately, but because talk pages are essential components of articles, and they often carry important information about an article's quality. Examining talk pages is key to evaluating articles properly.

Reading and Contributing to Talk Pages

Talk pages provide a way for people to discuss articles without leaving comments in the actual article itself. They also provide a handy place for WikiProjects and other editing projects (discussed further in Chapter 7) to place evaluations and messages. The beginning of a talk page may have several templated messages, warnings, or ratings, as well as links to archives of older talk page discussions.

Sooner or later, as a reader of Wikipedia you will disagree strongly enough with something in an article to want to do something about it. Or perhaps some point in an article is a mystery, and you'd like a reference to another source. Although you can simply edit the article, the best way to express concerns or get feedback or help from others working on the article is to leave a message on the talk page. If necessary, start a new thread yourself. Simply edit the page by clicking the Discussion tab to go to the talk page, and then the Edit This Page tab or the New Section tab. Add a new section or a new comment, as described here.

A given conversation may be joined by two, three, or dozens of contributors. Talk page discussions usually consist of threaded comments below a topical header; the most recent comment is at the bottom. Replies to a comment are placed underneath it and are indented to help the dialog stand out more clearly. At least that is the theory: Complex discussion often generates branches within one thread or page section. Editors may want to come back to some point made higher up the page; if so, they should use deep indenting to try to keep the side-issue clearly delineated. Unlike contributions to articles, comments are signed by their authors.

By convention, each new topic on a discussion page is set off from the previous topics with a header like this:

```
==sheep foraging habits==
I was just wondering: what is the deal with the foraging habits of sheep? do
the listed references cover this? I think we need some more detail about this
important topic. -- Phoebe 19:11, 13 Jan 2007 (EST)
```

Using the ==*Heading*== formatting will add a heading to your comment, which will create a table of contents automatically. Add a new comment, with a header, to the very bottom of the page, below any other text that appears in the source box; then click Save at the bottom of the page. Alternatively, use the New Section tab, which allows you to start a new section without needing to edit the whole page. The Subject/Heading field will become the section heading for your comment. When you use the Post a Comment feature, shown in Figure 4-4, the section heading will also become the edit summary, so you don't need to create a separate edit summary when you save the page.

FIGURE 4-4: *Post a Comment tab from a talk page*

You can indent comments with a bullet point and space (type an asterisk, followed by a colon); or more commonly, you can simply use a colon. Subsequent replies should be further indented using more colons; the number of colons provides a reference to the discussion level. For example, when you edit a talk page, the page source code may look like this:

```
==sheep foraging habits==
I was just wondering: what is the deal with the foraging habits of sheep? do
the listed references cover this? I think we need some more detail about this
important topic. -- Phoebe 19:11, 13 Jan 2007 (EST)
:* Sheep foraging habits are covered in ''Sheep of the world'', listed in
references. -- Sj 18:24, 10 February 2007 (EST)
```

```
::* There's also some info in ''Sheep Past and Present.'' -- A New Zealander
(talk) 18:55, 10 February 2007 (EST)
:::* ok, thanks everyone! -- Phoebe 12:11, 11 Feb 2007 (EST)
```

and will produce the page shown in Figure 4-5.

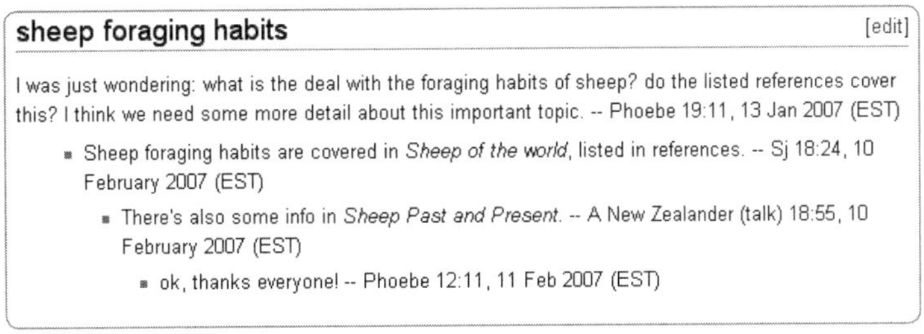

sheep foraging habits	[edit]

I was just wondering: what is the deal with the foraging habits of sheep? do the listed references cover this? I think we need some more detail about this important topic. -- Phoebe 19:11, 13 Jan 2007 (EST)

- Sheep foraging habits are covered in *Sheep of the world*, listed in references. -- Sj 18:24, 10 February 2007 (EST)
  - There's also some info in *Sheep Past and Present*. -- A New Zealander (talk) 18:55, 10 February 2007 (EST)
    - ok, thanks everyone! -- Phoebe 12:11, 11 Feb 2007 (EST)

FIGURE 4-5: *A threaded discussion on a talk page*

This clearly shows the threaded discussion over time. A new topic is added to the bottom of the page with another section heading:

```
==Wool==
The paragraph about wool types is confusing. Could someone who understands the
subject rewrite it?  -- Charles Matthews 21:14, 14 Jan 2007 (EST)
```

You will see various styles of indentation used on Wikipedia.

The editor name and date are produced with automatic signatures. Comments on talk pages, unlike changes made to articles, should always be signed. To produce your signature, type four tildes (~~~~). If you're logged in, this will generate a signature that by default consists of your username with a link to your user page and a timestamp with the date and time of your edit. It looks something like this:

```
Username 19:36, 10 January 2006 (UTC)
```

If you're not logged in, typing four tildes will produce your IP address plus a timestamp. When adding talk page comments, it is certainly an advantage to have an account. It inspires some confidence in other editors to know your username—you are identifying yourself as a member of the Wikipedia community, rather than just a number. With an account comes a user page and a personal user talk page, where people can, in turn, leave messages for you. If you aren't logged in, your IP address will be recorded; this address may be shared with other contributors if you are editing on a public computer, or it may change from edit to edit if it is a dynamic IP. IP addresses also have talk pages where messages can be left for that IP, but there is no guarantee that the message will reach the intended editor.

Making Good Use of Talk Pages

On talk pages, the basic idea is to make a clear point about how the article should be improved or what you'd like to know. For a suggested change, make a brief, calm case for your change (no need to go on at great lengths) backed up by necessary references. Chances are someone will change the article for you. If not, after a few days, you can do it yourself. Posting a preliminary comment on the talk page before making a change acts as a kind of insurance policy, as well as an explanation of your change. If you discuss first and then edit, you should not come under suspicion of high-handed behavior. Any controversial action should always be discussed on the talk page first. You are also welcome to weigh in on other ongoing discussions. In Chapter 12, we'll take up how to use talk pages to communicate with other editors most effectively.

User talk pages are meant for conversation between editors, rather than conversation about a particular article. If you have an account, others may leave you messages on your user talk page by going to [[User_talk:*yourusername*]] and editing the page there. When new messages are left for you on your user talk page, you'll receive a pop-up message when you next log in that notifies you about the messages (see Figure 4-6).

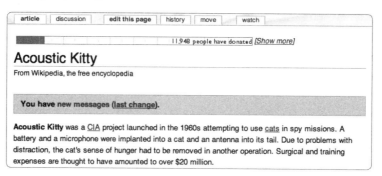

FIGURE 4-6: *A notice alerts you to a new message on your personal talk page.*

This notice makes it easy to know when you have new messages, and the prompt persists until you go to the page. If you're not logged in, you might still find a prompt and messages for your current IP number.

You can reply to any messages left for you on your own talk page, in a threaded discussion, or on the other editor's talk page. For more about how to conduct a good discussion with another editor on a user talk page, see Chapter 11. The basics are to be straightforward and, of course, polite.

Further Reading

http://en.wikipedia.org/wiki/Wikipedia:Talk_page   Discussion page guidelines

http://en.wikipedia.org/wiki/Wikipedia:Signatures   Signing talk pages

---

Evaluating Articles

Wikipedia is in a constant state of development, with contributors adding new articles and improving existing articles every minute. Inevitably, quality varies greatly from article to article. Although most articles in Wikipedia are useful as a basic reference, the majority are still incomplete treatments of their topic. Furthermore, some articles are unreliable, as discussed in this section; spotting these is the first concern of a careful reader. This unreliability does not make Wikipedia useless, but it does imply that you need to exercise a degree of caution.

Evaluating articles is one of the fundamental skills for becoming both a skilled reader and an involved editor of Wikipedia. Whereas any reader should be able to judge the value of the information he or she is looking at quickly, editors must be able to discern what could be improved about an article as they set to work.

With experience, editors can quickly assess articles, even on unfamiliar topics, on the basis of clues and tricks of the trade. Although there are some established Wikipedia rating systems, judging articles remains more like choosing fresh produce rather than pulling processed food off a supermarket shelf—it helps to know what you're looking for and how to judge blemishes.

Misinformation, Missing Information, and Mistakes

Misinformation in an article is a real possibility, given the way that Wikipedia is compiled. The general public is, fortunately, now aware of this point: It is a very bad idea to rely on the uncorroborated testimony of a Wikipedia article. Use articles as stepping stones into a subject, not crutches to lean on. As it says at [[Wikipedia:General disclaimer]], *Wikipedia makes no guarantee of validity.* A surprisingly common misconception is that Wikipedia employs fact-checkers for its articles, but that doesn't represent the situation on the ground. Facts are checked all the time by many active editors, but there is no one class of people on the site whose job is to confirm facts.

In most reference works, facts and other statements of truth are presented as having been vetted by a complex publishing process involving writers, editors, and fact-checkers, so the reader expects them to be correct. In Wikipedia, you cannot be so complacent. Though there are systems for peer review and developing accurate information, there is no guarantee at all that these processes and systems will have been applied to the particular article you're reading; the article might have been created in the past hour or not evaluated at all since it was created years ago. Each article is written by a different group of people with a varying amount of attention paid to it. Because of this, there is no serious way to judge Wikipedia as a whole; saying the site is a "good source" or a "bad source" is not precise enough. Instead, there are good and bad articles and a wide spectrum in between.

There are a few specific kinds of problems that may occur, each with different causes—misinformation, missing information, and simple mistakes. They all lead to inaccurate information being presented to the reader.

Misinformation, or bad information, comes in a few flavors. Wrong information that is purposely added is considered vandalism. Much of the vandalism on Wikipedia is obvious and silly graffiti or removal of article text in favor of graffiti. One of the great successes of Wikipedia is that this kind of vandalism can be easily cleaned up by anyone and is usually cleaned up very quickly; researchers that studied editing histories in 2003 measured the median cleanup time for obvious and vulgar vandalism as being less than three minutes.[1] Low-level vandalism, and its correction, is a constant occurrence in the open world of Wikipedia; a more recent study by University of Minnesota academics analyzed 57,601,644 article revisions and found that although about 5 percent of the revisions were vandalized, 42 percent of these damaged revisions were repaired essentially immediately, within one reader pageview.[2] (See Chapter 7 for more on vandal-fighting efforts).

However, deliberately added misinformation or vandalism can also be quite subtle. Misinformation can be introduced deliberately by people attempting to get a point of view across (which violates Wikipedia's core policy of Neutral Point of View). This might be done by only including a certain side of a debate, adding in and emphasizing controversial views, or relying on sources that only promote a certain point of view. Convincing misinformation can persist for a long time, especially in little-trafficked articles, though a close eye on the article can usually reveal it as suspect when it was added. Much misinformation has a distinctive slanted tone that is out of character with the rest of the article and other properly written Wikipedia articles. The Taner Akçam case involved misinformation that was both *vandalism* (malicious damage to site content) and *defamatory* (targeted at an individual's reputation).

[1] Viégas, Fernanda, et al. "Studying Cooperation and Conflict Between Authors with History Flow Visualizations." (CHI 2004, April 24–29, 2004). The IBM History Flow project: *http://www.research.ibm.com/visual/projects/history_flow/.*

[2] Priedhorsky, Reid, et al. "Creating, Destroying, and Restoring Value in Wikipedia." (GROUP '07, November 4–7, 2007). *http://www-users.cs.umn.edu/~reid/papers/group282-priedhorsky.pdf.*

The Problem with Misinformation

A high-profile example of the problems that can result from not checking for vandalism occurred on February 16, 2007, when the Turkish scholar Taner Akçam of the University of Minnesota was held up when traveling to Canada by border officials. Akçam reported that, when pressed on why he was being detained, immigration officials showed him a copy of his Wikipedia article from December 24, 2006, which had been maliciously altered to claim he was a terrorist. The immigration officials had placed reliance on this misinformation. See [[Taner Akçam]] for some links to the story and background on Akçam's work on highly controversial issues.

Much more common than deliberate misinformation is the simple failure of *missing information*. Articles may be completely correct but missing key aspects of the topic. Further information and a more complete treatment could help put the topic better in context, or perhaps even totally change the meaning of the information in the article. Because Wikipedia is built piecemeal, for an article to be missing some information is extremely common—and even expected. Stub articles, for instance, are known to be missing substantial details, but even longer or untagged articles may be missing parts. The only sure way to know you are getting the complete picture is to compare the article to other sources on the same topic.

Mistakes—misinformation that is not added maliciously—can happen in a wide variety of ways. Editors may add information that they remember to be true, but human memory is fallible. Perhaps they will add facts or ideas that have been discredited or are otherwise outdated. The sources that editors rely on might be wrong or misinterpreted. Copying and pasting information is very easy to do on the Web, so mistakes may be copied from one site to another and then repeated in Wikipedia (and then copied back out to other websites). Even simple typos, such as in numbers and dates, may lead to changes in meaning.

What should you do when Wikipedia gives you wrong information? The important thing, perhaps, is not to rely on the site for crucial information; always check other sources in addition to Wikipedia for important topics. More fundamentally, however, evaluating the content that you find is important.

If a subject is unfamiliar to you, evaluating an article may turn out to be difficult as well as important. Fortunately, the transparency of Wikipedia's development process means there are a variety of places to look for problems. So far we have flagged *clues*—any aspect of an article or its history where problems may be indicated if present. In this section, we'll outline a systematic approach, which should be applied more rigorously the more seriously you are studying a topic. A key theme is to *look for clues to an author or authors' inexperience with Wikipedia*.

D-R-E-W-S

There are five general areas to evaluate for every article.

D: Discussion   Check the talk page of the article for any controversy regarding the article.

R: Rating   Is there a formal rating of the article, or a cleanup notice? WikiProject ratings are on talk pages, not in the article itself.

E: Edit history   The history of an article will tell you how and by whom it has been put together.

W: Writing and format   How does the page read? How does it look?

S: Sources   Are claims in the article well supported by solid references?

Discussion on the Talk Page

A talk page may not yet exist for a given article (in which case it will show up in red), but for controversial topics, there are most likely some notices and discussion already there. A particular point that's bothering you may already have been discussed. Any warning tag appearing on the article referring to a content dispute should (though it doesn't always) also lead you to the appropriate discussion thread on the talk page.

The talk page is, therefore, where to start looking to see if the validity of the article content is disputed or other questions have been raised. Is there a long Table of Contents on the talk page? Are there links to archives of previous discussions? Both of these indicate involved debates in the past.

If you have your own concerns or questions about an article, the talk page is the place to post them. Anyone working on the article should notice these messages.

Ratings

Another aspect to consider is how articles have been rated by other editors. Ratings may be in the form of negative evaluations (such as cleanup tags on the article) or positive ones, as articles are assessed as being among the best in Wikipedia.

There are two formal rating processes to choose excellent articles, both of which involve getting consensus among editors. The lengthy peer review processes that produce featured articles and good articles do guarantee attention to quality. *Featured articles*, which may end up on the main page, represent some of the best content available; however, they make up only about 0.1 percent of the total content of Wikipedia. Once featured, an article will have a small bronze star in the upper-right corner along with a note indicating this on the discussion page. *good articles*, which do not need to be as extensive as featured articles, will only include a note on the talk page. (See [[Wikipedia:Featured articles]] and [[Wikipedia:Good articles]] to browse collections of these articles.)

There have also been several formal rating projects to assess the quality of articles within a certain topic area; these ratings typically don't require consensus but instead reflect an individual editor's opinion of the article, based on set standards. Most rating projects have been organized by WikiProjects that focus on a particular topic area (for instance, [[Wikipedia:WikiProject Chemistry]], which was one of the first to rate articles). If you're using Wikipedia for research on a particular topic, you may be fortunate enough to find that basic article rating is well advanced in your area of interest. Most of the rating systems amount to saying, *On a scale of 1 to 5, where is this article?* Any rating notices will be placed on the article talk page.

One general assessment project is the Wikipedia 1.0 WikiProject, which has taken the idea of rating articles and applied it across topics in a drive to collect high-quality articles on basic topics for release in collections. (The project has already helped issue some CDs of basic Wikipedia content.) Wikipedia 1.0 uses six classifications to rate articles: *stub, start, B, A, good article,* and *featured article* (which is reserved for articles that have gone through the featured article process). This editorial classification is also adopted by some WikiProjects. Again, members of the 1.0 project leave their ratings on article talk pages.

Finally, editors may assess articles as needing work. This is less formal than the processes just described, but is more widespread. As described, you may see warning messages at the tops of articles. These message boxes are produced by templates and may be added by any editor (as described in Chapter 7), and if you see one, it's a clue to look closely to see what the problem is. Sometimes it's obvious: A completely unformatted article or one with terrible spelling and no wikilinks is likely to get a cleanup message. Sometimes it's not obvious, however, especially since templates don't automatically go away: Someone may fix the problem but fail to remove the template. One trick is to go through the page history to see when the message was added and if the edit summary gives any further information.

If you see a message noting that an article is up for deletion, this is a huge red flag that it's probably poor quality. The deletion message should give some short reason for deletion. Deletion decisions are made through one of several processes; often articles will be up for discussion for a period of time before the decision is made, and the message will link to this discussion. See Chapter 7 for more information.

All of these ratings are simply indicative and should be taken with a grain of salt—ratings are approximate and subjective, often reflecting just one editor's assessment and not the current state of the article. However, knowing what other experienced editors think of the article can be extremely helpful in making your own decision about the article's quality.

Edit History

A wiki page, quite unlike most pieces of published writing, carries all its drafts along with it. One of the major benefits of keeping all versions is that investigative work can be carried out; you can track when a piece of information was inserted into an article and by whom. There are also a few bigger-picture things to consider when looking at an article history.

Was the article recently created? When was it last edited?

Though age is certainly no guarantee of quality, older articles have likely been seen and evaluated by more editors.

Have many people contributed to the article, or is it the work of only one or two editors? Were those contributors logged in or editing anonymously?

More people working on an article should mean that more editors have seen, evaluated, and checked the article; however, minor edits such as spelling corrections probably don't indicate a full check of the article. If in doubt about a particular editor's change, check his or her overall contributions by clicking the Contribs link.

Is there evidence of ongoing edit wars or arguments over content (that is, are there continual reversions of changes between two or more people)? Do the same changes keep getting made and undone, whether this is indicated in the edit summaries or not?

This may indicate a controversial topic, one on which there is no consensus, or an unverifiable topic. Verify any key facts with outside references. Serious edit wars tend to cause deterioration of the text, so also look at older versions of the page, which may be better than the current page. Not every edit war is over a serious matter: If the disagreement is niggling back and forth at some small point, does it matter to you?

Is there evidence of heavy or continued vandalism (that is, constant changes and reversions, often between IP addresses and other editors, with edit summaries like *revert* or *rvv vandalism*)?

Although this is not in itself evidence of quality problems—some of the very best and most heavily trafficked articles on Wikipedia receive the most vandalism, simply because they are so visible—it does mean you should make sure the article you are viewing is an unvandalized version. Some vandalism may be subtle, for instance, changing a date or a conclusion, and again it is best to verify important facts in outside sources. It's worth checking the differences between the version you're viewing and some previous versions that were edited by other people to make sure the version you're viewing is complete, not randomly cut by a vandal.

In general, for any article you are assessing, pick a few versions to compare to the current version. Get a sense of the page as dynamic: Has it changed a great deal over time, or was it submitted to the site nearly complete? How fast is the article changing? Was it once much longer than it is now? Although articles will generally get better and longer over time, sometimes they drift. Occasionally you will find that a previous version—sometimes months or even years earlier—was actually clearly better than the current version.

> ## Wikipedia Brown and the Case of the Captured Koala: A Page History Mystery
>
> This exciting online mystery by Adam Cadre hinges on reading a Wikipedia page history! See actual screenshots on page 91 at *http://adamcadre.ac/content/brown/*.

Writing and Formatting

Read an article through, for example, as you would a newspaper article. In evaluating articles, you must, of course, consider the nature of the article text itself. First impressions of quality are significant. Is it properly presented and apparently comprehensive? Does it carry conviction, as to its authority and balance of coverage? These points matter, along with close reading for factual accuracy. However, there are more concrete clues to the level of an article's development, as well.

Is the article well written, well explained, and in proper English? Within the article, is the topic explained in a way that makes sense to a casual reader, with a good explanatory opening paragraph and a clear definition in the first sentence?
If not, then it has likely lacked attention from experienced editors; it also may not have been written by someone really familiar with the topic. Good writing doesn't ensure factual accuracy, but as a piece of circumstantial evidence, it can make it more likely.

Of course, we are not saying that an article written by a non-native speaker of English is necessarily worse than one written by a native speaker: Expertise outranks language skills. But if mistakes in English *persist* in an article, no editor on the site with good English has worked over it. What matters is the neglect, not who the first author was. If an article is well written in a tight factual style and properly organized, it was either originally written that way, or it was subsequently improved by other editors. Either way, the article was likely looked at by someone with a good knowledge of encyclopedic writing and Wikipedia conventions.

Is the article formatted according to the *Manual of Style*? These are the guidelines for making Wikipedia articles look like Wikipedia articles.
Experience shows that this question is also very useful, at least if you are familiar with standard format on Wikipedia pages. Chapter 6 describes the Wikipedia *Manual of Style* in some detail. **Clue:** *Compliance with formatting guidelines means that the original author or subsequent editors were familiar with them. If you read Wikipedia for a while, it won't be hard to recognize a page that has obvious formatting problems.*

For instance, is the page conventionally wikilinked to other Wikipedia articles? Are the See also and External links sections formatted as bulleted lists? Ask yourself, does the article look and read like a respectable article? A page with unconventional formatting or plenty of formatting mistakes probably was not written by an experienced editor, which means, in turn, that the author also may not have followed more fundamental content policies. Probably the article has also been neglected since it was first posted. It may also have been cut and pasted from another site (which is usually a copyright violation). They say you can't judge a book by its cover . . . but if the dust jacket had obvious typos, you might begin to wonder.

Now you can assess the content itself.

Are there sections that explain various parts of the topic in more detail (such as History and Modern Status or Biography and Works)?
Articles without sections tend to be unsorted, sometimes just collections of facts without much logical order. This could indicate work by an editor who is unfamiliar with Wikipedia, or perhaps there has been much editing without a comprehensive overview. If this is the case, expect some factual errors to have crept in. Take a look for gossip and rumor, urban myths, and so forth.

Depending on the topic, do you see the elements that you would expect to be there?
For instance, an article about an author should include a formatted bibliography of works; an article about a historical event should place the event in context and provide some sort of chronology. The lack of these may not mean the article is poor but simply that it is incomplete, and other sources should also be used to get a complete picture.

What tone does it take? Does it read like an encyclopedia article or like a personal essay or advertisement?
If an article clearly violates some of the core content policies, such as NPOV, then it was probably added by someone unfamiliar with Wikipedia, and it may or may not be suitable for the site. If there are outrageous claims in the midst of otherwise fair text, this may indicate vandalism and you should check back a few versions.

Sources

Is the article referenced? This is a fairly simple but fundamental test of an article's quality. If you are troubled by other aspects, this is where you will be led to conclusions on trustworthiness.

Many older encyclopedias do not list references in the text or at the end of an article. Instead, readers are expected to trust that the authors of those articles are experts in their field. The credibility of the work as a whole is an appeal to authority. In Wikipedia, there is really no way of knowing whether an article author is an expert or not. Instead, the references that are used matter greatly, both for verifying information and for giving you as a reader sources for further reading on the topic.

A *reference*, in this context, refers to a citation to an outside work: for example, a printed article, book, or a web page. Other Wikipedia articles do not count as references; although these may be linked in the text or listed in the See also section, using them as sources is circular and misses the point of trying to get *outside* verification. (You might check those other articles to see if they are better sourced.)

Sources and references provide a very tangible way to evaluate an article's accuracy. You can (in principle) always go back and check the original sources yourself to find out what they say. Most people will first try the more indirect approach of quick plausibility checks on the Web. This is where searches excluding results from Wikipedia can be handy, as mentioned in Chapter 3.

The best kind of reference is for a specific piece of information in the article to be footnoted appropriately, with the citation being specific as to where to find the relevant information. This is the *inline* referencing style. More than anything else, a footnoted reference to a page in a scholarly book should confer confidence in the footnoted statement's accuracy. If in doubt, always check what the cited source and other sources say.

In a fully referenced article, all specific facts should be referenced. There have been extensive debates in the Wikipedia community over what this means and how far to go with references. As a reader, you probably have priorities: Check references first for claims that are surprising or likely to prove contentious. That is, good references are most vital for statements that you are unlikely to just take the author's word on.

Many articles are still not referenced inline. At the very least, sources should be clearly listed at the end of an article. Other references that are not used but that are relevant to studying the topic are placed in a Further reading section. Naturally, these references may still help you in verifying something.

Trivia Sections

From the point of view of quality, it is hardest of all to assess isolated facts. A list of such facts with bullet points is a real challenge: How can one infer anything at all about the truth of any given point? This is precisely the state of trivia sections in many articles. If no reliable sources are given, there is no reason to trust them, since trivia may be surprising, obscure, or even bizarre. See [[Wikipedia:Avoid trivia sections in articles]], shortcut WP:TRIVIA.

There are still hundreds of thousands of good, verifiable articles, contributed by experienced editors and about notable topics, that list no references. Referencing content is a slow and ongoing task, and strong emphasis was not placed on it during Wikipedia's early years. On the other hand, no references for a dubious topic may mean it's not suitable for inclusion in Wikipedia. The other evaluative criteria can help you tell which is the case. If it's a topic you know something about, adding good references is one of the key tasks that Wikipedia needs help with. Asking on talk pages is one basic way to request better referencing of a given article. Chapter 6 deals with techniques and syntax for referencing.

Further Reading

http://en.wikipedia.org/wiki/Wikipedia:General_disclaimer   The General disclaimer

http://en.wikipedia.org/wiki/Wikipedia:Version_1.0_Editorial_Team/ Assessment   The criteria used by the Wikipedia 1.0 team

http://en.wikipedia.org/wiki/Wikipedia:Researching_with_Wikipedia   An overview of considerations and techniques for using Wikipedia for research and evaluating individual articles

http://en.wikipedia.org/wiki/Reliability_of_Wikipedia   An overview of the general reliability of Wikipedia

---

Summary

Look over the article text, its associated discussion page, and their histories. The reader aware of Wikipedia's editing process can use these related pages to understand the provenance of an article and evaluate it. This process of evaluation is mostly based on experience with Wikipedia's standards—so if you're daunted by it, keep reading the site. Here is a baker's dozen of our best clues for evaluation, once more:

▶ If no wikilinks exist in the text, there's a strong chance an article was written by someone unfamiliar with Wikipedia's conventions, and it may be questionable. Does the text comply with other content guidelines?

▶ Compliance with Wikipedia formatting and style guidelines is a positive indication that an experienced editor has worked on the article. Are all the usual parts of an article present? Is it categorized in one or more categories?

▶ Is the article a stub? Stubs will likely be incomplete in their information. Are there obvious aspects of the topic missing?

▶ Did the material originally come from another source? Imported material, for example, from an old encyclopedia, may need updating.

- No incoming links (backlinks) is often a sign that an article is new, has not been much scrutinized, or has a poor title. Check for duplicate articles on the topic with different titles. Is the topic verifiable in outside sources?

- Is there evidence of disagreement or serious questions about content on the article discussion page?

- Are there warning or cleanup messages at the top of the article? Has the article been rated by other editors?

- A short page history is a warning sign. Is the article the work of more than one major author?

- A patch of edits with reverts in a page history indicates some sort of editing war going on. The quality of articles is likely to degrade sharply in an extended edit war. Are earlier versions of the article better?

- Are the authors new or experienced? Check their contributions—what else have they been working on?

- Especially for edits from an IP number, rather than an account, readers are entitled to treat edits without an edit summary with suspicion. Does the diff reveal vandalism or possible vandalism?

- If you suspect vandalism, check the editor or IP's talk page; are there any warnings from other editors?

- Are there sources present in the article? Are questionable or controversial statements referenced?

Final Thoughts for Part I

For those who don't know where to begin: The structures set up for browsing help provide in-depth explorations of nearly any topic, in ways that you might not have imagined.

For those with concerns about quality: Wikipedia is remarkably transparent, and it is the first encyclopedia to be so open about its editorial process. While the transparency of edit histories doesn't guarantee correctness, it provides much more opportunity than most reference sources to judge quality for yourself.

For those who think Wikipedia ought to be a one-stop shop: Although Wikipedia in general is excellent as a first source for research, it should hardly ever be the end of your research. As with any encyclopedia, checking with other reference sources and primary sources is a must.

For those who would like to help: The transition from lurker to worker on the site is easy. This book's next part covers what you need to know about editing.

For those who like to have the last word: There is no last word on Wikipedia, a work in progress.

## PART II

Editing

5 Basic Editing

Editing wiki pages is at the heart of all activity on Wikipedia, from working on articles to participating in community discussions. Here's where Wikipedia becomes more than a reference tool. The Edit This Page tab above Wikipedia articles invites everyone to contribute.

Editing a Wikipedia page is not difficult. And whether you're interested in copyediting, research and writing, fact-checking, or fixing vandalism, you shouldn't have any trouble finding articles to improve and expand. This chapter describes the basic mechanics of editing existing pages—opening and understanding the edit window and using wikisyntax to format text. We'll also discuss how to perform both major and minor edits, how to revert edits to fix mistakes, and how pages are protected. The information in this chapter forms the basis for understanding the more advanced editing techniques described in the next five chapters.

Editing a Page

The term *edit* refers to a single change made to a wiki page: the act of modifying and then saving a page. Edits range from fixing a typo to rewriting an entire article from scratch; you can change any amount of text with a single edit to a page. In other words, you have permission to modify any article as you see fit. What you do with this editing permission naturally reflects on you.

By editing, you become a Wikipedia editor. You'll find a whole gamut of editors on the site, from those just trying out the system to those who are effectively on Wikipedia full-time. This free-form editorial process contrasts with the editorial layers found in other forms of publishing. You should be aware, though, that there are some expectations of any editor: Obviously, Wikipedia doesn't want editors to damage the pages or the project. The community of editors has values and norms, embedded in a strong tradition, and editors should also be good colleagues.

To edit an article, simply select the Edit This Page tab at the top of a page, modify the text by typing changes into the source text box (this box is called the *edit window*), add an edit summary in the field provided, and then click the Save Page button to create a new version of the page, which is immediately visible to everyone. The edit is then logged on Recent Changes, and others working on the article can see it immediately.

When you click Save Page, not only is your saved version viewable online right away, but it is also stored in perpetuity as a revision in the page history associated with your name or IP number and visible from the History tab. If someone subsequently makes an additional revision to the page, that new revision will display as the new "live" article, but your version is retained by Wikipedia and is accessible by anyone at any time by reviewing the page history.

Contributors vs. Editors

The terms *contributor* and *editor* are mostly used interchangeably on Wikipedia. Every editor acts as a contributor, and vice versa; the term *editor* can be roughly equated with "someone who uses the Edit This Page tab." The traditional publishing roles of author, illustrator, editor (who makes substantive changes), copyeditor (who fixes grammar and style), and proofreader (who fixes typos) may be filled by any participant. Many contributors become specialists over time and choose to work primarily in one area or within structured projects on the site.

Once edited and saved, pages are immediately and automatically updated. (If this doesn't happen, you are very likely experiencing an artifact of article caching caused by overloaded servers. Clear your browser cache, if necessary, by pressing CTRL-F5 in Firefox, Internet Explorer, and most other browsers.)

Understanding the Edit Window

The display that appears when you select the Edit This Page tab consists of several parts (see Figure 5-1). At the top, an editing toolbar displays buttons for easily adding common syntax and formatting. The edit window is next; this window gives you a single undivided view of the *wikitext*, or source text, of the page you're editing. Here, you can change the text, the formatting, or both. Wikitext is formatted in a special markup language (*wikisyntax*), which is described in the second half of this chapter.

Below the edit window, you'll find the edit summary field and three buttons that allow you to view or save your changes. At the bottom of the page, you'll find several other syntax options along with a menu of special characters. When you edit, you change the article's text in the edit window. First, however, you need to understand a typical article's structure.

Reading Article Wikitext

Take a moment to orient yourself in the edit window. What are the first words of source text? They may not be the actual first words of the article, which sometimes puzzles new editors. Instead, you may see some formatting syntax before the article itself.

To understand what you're seeing, consider the different layers of a typical article, as described in Chapter 4. The actual article content is often between two layers of wikitext. At the beginning of the source text but before the first words of the actual article, you may see some structured information: cleanup templates, hatnotes, image links, or an infobox with data presented in tabular form. Scrolling past this information and past the article text, you'll find another layer of wikitext at the very end of the page; this information includes categories, stub templates, and possibly interwiki links. You can simply ignore this layer for the moment.

The first layer of wiki formatting can be the most confusing. But you can just scroll down until you reach the beginning of the article and the place where you want to make a change. In other words, in basic editing, you can simply ignore the formatting and improve the content.

Naturally, not all articles have these elements; many articles contain the bottom layer of wikitext, but not the top layer. If you're confused about a piece of syntax or formatting, you can always compare the source text to the *rendered page* (that is, the page as it appears on the Article tab). You might find it helpful to open two copies of the article you want to edit in different browser tabs or windows; use one window to edit and the other as a reminder of how the article appeared before you started editing.

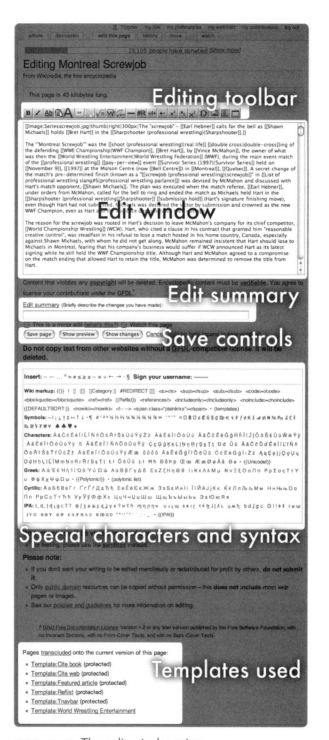

FIGURE 5-1: *The edit window view*

Using the Edit Window Tools

Above the edit window is the *editing toolbar*—a collection of buttons that provide various pieces of wikisyntax (Figure 5-2). Hover your cursor over each button to find out what it does. Like the menu of options in a word processor, these buttons can be extremely helpful, both as timesavers and if you can't remember the exact formatting of a particular piece of wikisyntax. To use the buttons, place your cursor in the edit window where you would like the syntax to appear. Then click the appropriate button, and the syntax will appear on the page. (Each piece of syntax will be described individually throughout the next several chapters.)

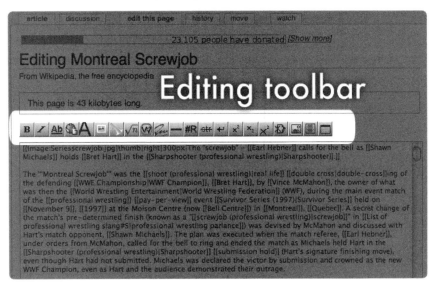

FIGURE 5-2: *The editing toolbar*

Below the edit window, you'll see a warning about the GFDL and the edit summary field. This is for summarizing your changes for the benefit of other editors who are working on the page. Although not mandatory, it's good etiquette to add a short summary after making any edit. Simply type a brief description of what you changed. We describe edit summaries in Chapter 4; see Appendix C for some common terms and Chapter 6 for more on using edit summaries to communicate with other editors.

Next are three buttons: Save Page, Show Preview, and Show Changes:

▶ Save Page saves your work and publishes a new version of the page immediately.

▶ Show Preview allows you to preview the page with your changes before saving them. You can also click Show Preview to experiment and test the effects of a change when you're not sure of the exact syntax to use—but be careful not to save accidentally! Once you've edited a page, we strongly recommend previewing your edits *before* saving, especially if you are new to wiki markup or are doing something unfamiliar with complicated syntax.

▶ Show Changes displays the differences between your unsaved version and the current version in the source code, which is handy if you can't figure out exactly how your changes will affect the page—or if you can't remember what changes you made!

If you decide to do nothing, instead of saving the page, click your browser's back button, or click the Cancel link next to the Show Changes button. No changes will be made to the page or the version history.

If you need editing help, you'll find a link below the edit summary field. Click the Editing Help link to open a help document in another window; until you become more familiar with marking up pages, keep help documents open in a separate browser window or tab. Above and below the edit summary field, you'll find some brief but important messages about verifiability, the GFDL, and violating copyright—this information should be familiar if you've read Part I of this book.

Below the buttons, you'll also see many pieces of wiki markup and special symbols. This display is provided for easy access to common or complicated syntax and characters. To add one of these characters to your text, such as an accented letter, place your cursor at the appropriate spot in the edit window. Then click the character you wish to add, and it will show up in the text.

Below this and the final note on the GFDL, you'll find a list of the templates used (or *transcluded*) on the page you're editing (if any have been used). To view one of these templates by itself, simply click the template name to go to the template page.

If you're a fan of keyboard shortcuts, you can use them to navigate various parts of Wikipedia and to edit pages. For instance, pressing ALT-S-ENTER will save a page in Internet Explorer (or pressing ALT-SHIFT-S in Mozilla Firefox), while pressing ALT-V-ENTER (or ALT-SHIFT-V) is equivalent to clicking the Show Changes button.

Customizing the Edit Window

By default, the edit window displays 25 lines of text, and each line is 80 characters wide. If you have a large monitor, setting the edit window to be wider and longer can be helpful; if you're using a smaller device to edit, you may want to make the window smaller. You can change the edit window settings in your user preferences if you're logged in. Click the My Preferences link in the upper-right corner of the page, select the Editing tab, and enter new numbers of rows and columns in Editbox dimensions. You can also set other editing options here; for instance, you can choose to open an edit window by simply double-clicking a page, which, if you're a fast editor, can save time.

More shortcuts are described at [[Wikipedia:Keyboard shortcuts]]; the shortcuts depend on your browser and on your chosen skin.

Losing your place in the source text when editing very long documents is easy, so work on longer articles one section at a time. To edit within only a single section of an article, click the Edit link that appears to the right of any section heading in an article (Figure 5-3). Only the wikitext of the section you are working on appears in the edit window.

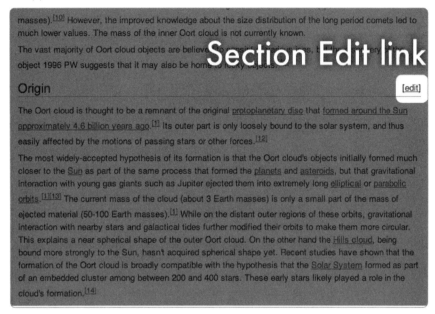

FIGURE 5-3: *Section header with Edit link*

The Sandbox

To gain editing experience, visit [[Wikipedia:Sandbox]]. As its name implies, the sandbox is a dedicated page for playing around without altering a real article. The sandbox is also a good place to go if you want to test your wiki markup and you are not sure what it will look like once saved. The sandbox is regularly cleaned out, so you don't need to worry about your tests lingering. (Because of this, the sandbox is not a good place to start work on something you would like to keep; see "Drafting the Article" on page 169 for how to set up your own personal sandbox.)

Major vs. Minor Edits

A *minor edit* is an edit that the editor believes requires no review by other editors. Typical minor edits are spelling or grammatical corrections, adding a single internal link, fixing punctuation, or making small formatting or presentational changes. Though most minor edits change only a small amount of text, not all small edits are minor. Changing a single date in an article, say 1776 to 1667, is small but not minor. A minor edit should never substantially change the meaning of an article, and it should never be the subject of a debate.

Registered users who are logged in can indicate edits as minor when saving the page by checking the This is a minor edit box. That edit will then show up in the page history marked with a bold lowercase *m*. The purpose of minor edits is to allow others to filter out simple spelling or format fixes from lists of edits such as personal watchlists and Recent Changes. If a minor edit comes up on your own watchlist, you should not have to bother checking it.

Minor edits deserve an edit summary, the same as any other change. In general, if a change requires a long edit summary, the edit is not minor. With experience, you'll get a feel for what others consider minor. Making serious cuts or inserting anything likely to be contentious under cover of a minor edit description is considered heinous (just as full edit summaries are better than too-scanty ones), so err on the safe side in not calling an edit minor. If in doubt about whether an edit qualifies as minor, don't check the box. Logged-in users can choose to mark all of their edits minor by default on the User Preferences Editing tab, but we advise against doing this: Sooner rather than later it could cause you trouble by marking a major edit incorrectly.

Major edits comprise all other edits. Any change that affects the meaning of an article is major (not minor), even if the edit is a single word. Think of it this way: A major edit is a flag to all concerned editors that the modifications ought to be checked.

Handling Major Editing Tasks

Wikipedia's editors are encouraged to *be bold*: [[Wikipedia:Be bold]] is an editing guideline and one of the oldest slogans on the site. Sometimes articles are poorly written, and piecemeal changes are not enough—a complete transformation is called for. In that scenario, boldness is the order of the day. Still, editors can and should take steps to ensure that they perform really major editing jobs smoothly and acceptably.

We strongly recommend breaking large editing jobs into small stages. This is not the same as frantic saving; you shouldn't save every few seconds, unless your Internet connection is really bad. Saving your work every few minutes is reasonable, as leaving an edit window open for a long period of time without saving can cause a session error message. When making major changes, copying the wikitext into a word-processing document as a backup can also protect against saving mishaps.

Before implementing a major edit, you should seriously consider discussing proposed changes on the article talk page first by posing the question "Would

Edit Conflicts

Edit conflicts may occur by accident when two editors try to edit and save the same page at the same time. If this happens, you'll get an edit conflict notice at the top of the page, and you won't be able to save your change. Don't panic! First, copy the text of your change into a word-processing document so you don't lose it. To see the wikisource with your changes, you must scroll down to the lower of the two windows on the page (the upper window contains the other editor's conflicting text). Then you can cancel the edit by clicking the back button in your browser. Next, refresh the page and check the last diff to see what changed in the previous version. Re-edit the page, integrating your change and the previous editor's work; don't simply paste your version on top. Edit conflicts are common only on high-traffic pages. Be warned, though, that if you save a page twice, perhaps thinking the first Save Page click didn't work, you might be in conflict with yourself! Note also that an edit conflict is not the same as an *edit war*, when two editors cannot agree on changes.

anyone mind?" Wait a little while (at least a few days) for any responses. When editing, divide big edits into a series of smaller edits that you explain. Ideally, all major rewrites occur in a number of steps, each of which is clear. Others working on the site are then able to pick out, for example, a more specific point where they don't like or understand what you've done.

We also recommend working section-by-section in longer articles. If no sections exist in a messy or unstructured article or new sections need to be added, add this section structure first. You can follow this edit by sorting material into sections and then copyedit each section and add references.

Once you've completed the editing process, write an overall, final edit summary to document the changes. Including a final summary is good etiquette and will help to ensure that particularly major edits are well received by the other

Work in Progress

A systematic approach may mean working on an article over an extended period of time. If this is how you prefer to edit, type {{inuse}} at the top of the page, which will create a template message stating that the article is *under construction*. Just don't forget to remove it when you're done! You can also leave a note on the talk page detailing your editing plan. Other editors will patiently let you finish.

editors working on the article. Even if they disagree, they'll still see that you're trying to work with others, with the goal of reaching consensus on the article. Put any longer comments on the discussion page. For more advice on structuring articles and making major changes, see Chapter 6.

Fixing Mistakes and Other Reasons to Revert

If you accidentally save a version of a page with a mistake on it, or your edit does not work the way you intended, don't fret! Because all versions of every article are saved, you can always *revert* a page back to a previous version. You can never make an irreparable mistake just by editing. Any page can be reverted to any older version, including the first version—the initial posting. Standard good practice, however, is to revert only when necessary to the *latest good version*: the version of the page before bad changes were made.

To revert an article, choose a previous version from the edit history and then restore that older, saved version, as described here.

Sorting Through Old Versions

You might find it helpful to use the radio buttons and compare version features on the page history to figure out which precise version you want to restore. Keep comparing old versions of the page to the current version until you find the one that you want. In the page history display, the most recent version is always on top. When paging through diffs, the right-hand side is the more recent version. See tips for sorting through page histories on pages 110 and 111.

Once you have found the page version that you want to make the current version, select it: From the page history, click the linked date and time to view that version of the page. If you're comparing two versions, click the header that says *revision as of (date and time)* for the version you'd like to edit. You should get a warning message that you are viewing an old revision of the article (see Figure 5-4).

Next, select the Edit This Page tab at the top of the article. The text of the old version will display in the edit window. You will now see a warning message that you are editing an old version (see Figure 5-5). You are going to ignore these warnings.

To revert a page back to an old version, you don't have to make any changes to the text—you just have to resave the page. After you have retrieved the text of the version you'd like to revert to, scroll down, add an appropriate edit summary ("reverting because . . .") and click Save Page, without making any other changes. The version you were just looking at will become the newest latest version, and you're done!

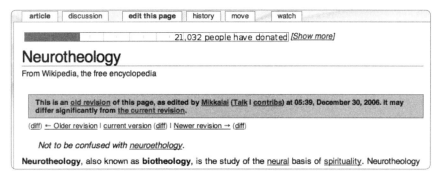

FIGURE 5-4: *A warning message appears when you view an old version of a page.*

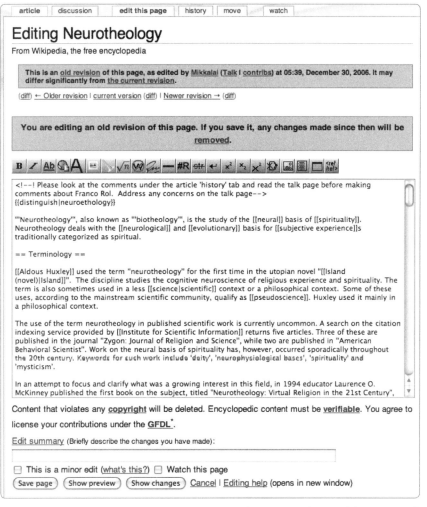

FIGURE 5-5: *A warning message appears when you edit an old version of a page.*

✱ **NOTE:** *Use previews! Most self-reversions and editing accidents can be avoided by pressing the Show Preview button before saving changes.*

Reverting to a previous version is also how most vandalism is undone. If you see a vandalized article, go to the edit history and find the last good version, which is often simply the next-to-latest version, and then revert back to it. Be careful not to lose any "good" information or changes by doing this. Compare a few earlier versions with your latest save to make sure all the vandalism is removed and all the good content is kept. Sometimes vandalism can be spread over two or three edits, often by the same editor. Be sure to add an appropriate edit summary; *rvv vandalism* is common.

If you are logged in, you can *undo* most edits in a similar fashion. Go to the page history and compare two versions. The most recent version of the two pages you are viewing will display an Undo link next to the Edit link on the right-hand side. Clicking the Undo link will automatically remove the inserted text (or replace the removed text) with that version. Click the Save Page button to finish undoing the edit.

The Undo link is most useful for removing obvious vandalism or fixing a mistake in the most recent revision. Be cautious about using this link for anything else; although any change can be undone, making mistakes and inadvertently undoing good changes when reverting to versions in the middle of the page history is easy to do.

Overuse of Reverts

Statistically speaking, as many as 20 percent of edits to Wikipedia are now reverted. Much of this is due to vandalism on popular articles. However, reverts should not be used to try and win arguments or impose your view on articles. To reinforce this, an official *Three-Revert Rule (3RR)* has been created, meaning that three reverts by any one person to a single article in a 24-hour period (except for vandalism control) is quite enough. In practice, editors with differences of opinion should discuss the issue and come to consensus on talk pages instead of reverting each other's changes in an article. A good rule of thumb is to revert only once before going to the talk page and making a rational case for your version. See [[Wikipedia:Three-revert rule]] (shortcut WP:3RR). Trying to get around 3RR is severely frowned upon, and users can be blocked for excessive reverting of the same article. This policy has gone a long way toward preventing *edit wars*, disputes between two or more editors where the same content is continually inserted and removed over a period of time.

Who Can Edit What?

The vast majority of Wikipedia pages can be edited by anyone, whether they're logged in with an account or not. The rare exceptional pages not open to editing include some system-generated pages and a few key pages that are permanently restricted, such as the site's disclaimers at [[Wikipedia:General disclaimer]] and the main page.

Apart from those, a small number of other pages at any given time have been closed to editing with an administrative action called *protection*. This is usually a temporary measure that is generally prompted by a surge in vandalism to a page. Protection comes in two flavors: full protection and semi-protection. Protected pages should be clearly identified with gray-bar template messages at the top of the page. If you ever find that you can't edit a regular article, the page is probably protected; instead of an Edit This Page tab, you'll see a View Source tab.

A *fully protected* page is editable only by site administrators and is effectively out of circulation for a while. Such temporary protection is, these days, almost always a reaction to an intractable edit war over an article's content and is quite rare. For example, [[Burt Reynolds]] was protected after a serious dispute over the actor's birthplace. Here is a sample of the dispute between two editors on the talk page:

> As JSDA added above, Lansing, Michigan is now on his "Official Web Site" as his place of birth. How do you explain this one away??? Are you going to continue the hype? And as I've mentioned before, it's fine that he claims he's from the south, but it is not the truth. Again here's the website link. Burt Reynolds.com Lugnut215 00:47, 6 July 2007 (UTC)

> It is obvious the person doing the page is just regurjitating [sic] facts found on the web and not fact checking. Because here is another "LIE" that is in the personal FAQs .. Bottom line is in his televised interviews when asked his birthplace, he says Waycross, Georgia. He has said it about 10 different interviews, and there isn't one televised interview where he says Michigan. Rogue Gremlin 03:33, 7 July 2007 (UTC)

Only arguments that prove to be very contentious, with much edit-warring between two or more people, will result in protection. Protection allows a time-out for content disputes to be resolved by discussion and fact-checking, rather than changing the article itself back and forth.

Semi-protected pages, on the other hand, are editable by the vast majority of logged-in users. They are not editable by those who are not logged in (*anonymous* editors editing from an IP address) or by editors who have an account that was only created within the last four days. Semi-protection is now quite common for pages on subjects in the news headlines, for example, celebrities that are at the center of a short-lived media storm. Such articles attract bad edits, and semi-protection filters out a high proportion of vandalism.

In these cases, protection is generally removed when media attraction to the topic lessens. Some other pages are semi-protected when they are highly visible or prone to constant vandalism, and these pages may be protected for longer; for instance, the article about the current President of the United States is subject to a constant stream of vandalism. Other articles may also fall under semi-protection because they are often vandalized by school students (some articles about elementary and high schools are particularly vulnerable). Some very visible page components, such as high-use templates, are also protected to prevent vandalism; sometimes this is done automatically through a mechanism called *cascading protection* in which the components that make up a fully protected page, such as the main page, are also protected.

Semi-protection, therefore, compromises the purist wiki principle of *anyone can edit anything*, but protection has been necessary essentially because of Wikipedia's own prominence. Administrators are responsible for protecting pages and for reviewing the protection status of pages. You can find out more at [[Wikipedia:Protection policy]] (shortcut WP:PROT). The [[Wikipedia:List of indefinitely protected pages]] (shortcut WP:PERMPROT) lists pages with long-term protection. You can discuss any case of semi-protection on the talk page of the article, which will not be protected. If you feel an article needs semi-protection—for instance, if it is attracting a few dozen incidents of vandalism a day—add a note to [[Wikipedia:Requests for page protection]] (shortcut WP:RFPP), and an administrator will take a look and decide what to do.

Further Reading

http://en.wikipedia.org/wiki/Wikipedia:How_to_edit_a_page   A summary of basic syntax and instructions on how to edit a page

http://en.wikipedia.org/wiki/Wikipedia:Keyboard_shortcuts   Keyboard shortcuts for editing Wikipedia

http://en.wikipedia.org/wiki/Help:Minor_edit   Information about minor edits

http://en.wikipedia.org/wiki/Wikipedia:Be_bold   The Be Bold guideline for updating pages

http://en.wikipedia.org/wiki/Wikipedia:Protection_policy   The Protection policy

http://en.wikipedia.org/wiki/Wikipedia:Sandbox   The sandbox, for experimenting with editing

---

Syntax

Wikipedia uses a special markup language for formatting pages; this syntax is variously known as *wikisyntax*, *wiki markup*, or simply *wikitext*. It styles wiki pages and determines how text will appear on the screen. This syntax is common to all wikis that use MediaWiki software (though it will not work on wikis that use other software).

A Quick Word About Templates

Over time, Wikipedia has moved toward the presentation of structured information and messages to the reader using *templates*, or special page elements (such as navigation elements or message boxes) that can be included on other pages. You can recognize templates by their appearance in the markup: A template placed in another page appears in the source text as the template name enclosed in double curly brackets, like {{*message*}} or {{*mystatsbox*}}. You can simply edit around these for the moment. Throughout the next several chapters, we'll refer to useful templates for formatting and styling pages. If you want to use one, simply place it on the page by typing in the curly-bracket syntax exactly as it's given, replacing any variable text as necessary (use the Show Preview button to see how it looks before you save the page). To learn more about templates and how to edit them directly, see Chapter 9.

You don't need to know HTML, the standard web page markup language, to become a proficient Wikipedia editor. The fundamental markup is very simple and can be used both for simple formatting tasks—such as whether text will appear indented, italicized, or bold—and for more complicated tasks—such as displaying images or math formulas and coding templates to be reused on many pages. What we cover here is enough to start editing and writing. If you need an additional reference as you work, wikisyntax is documented extensively at [[Help:Editing]] and [[Help:Wikitext examples]].

Fundamentals of Text Markup

Here we introduce the first things you need to know about markup.

Bold and Italic

Text may be rendered **bold** by placing three apostrophes on either side of it, like this:

```
'''bold text goes here'''
```

In standard Wikipedia article style, bold text is always used for highlighting the article topic in the initial paragraph. Bold text for emphasis should be used very sparingly in articles.

Make text *italic* by using two apostrophes:

```
''italic text goes here''
''A Farewell to Arms''
```

Italics are used for the titles of works, as well as for emphasis.

You can combine the two by using five apostrophes to make text **bold-and-italic**:

```
'''''a highlighted title'''''
```

Bold-and-italic text is appropriate for highlighting an article's subject when the article is about a particular work. For example, in the first sentence of the article about *War and Peace*, the book's title would be rendered in bold-and-italic.

Underlined and strikethrough text are not commonly used. Create underlined text by enclosing the text with the <u> and </u> tags. In articles, italics are preferred to underlined text. Strikethrough text is convenient in threaded discussions on talk pages to retract something that was said (simply deleting something can be mystifying if other editors have already replied to it). Enclose the strikethrough text with the <s> and </s> tags.

Indentation, Line, and Paragraph Breaks

Line and paragraph breaks are created on Wikipedia by simple *newlines* (or *carriage returns*, if you are old enough to have used a typewriter). Create a space between paragraphs by leaving an empty line, which will display as entered in the source code.

To produce an indented line, place a colon (:) before the line you wish to indent. Two colons (::) will produce a line that is indented two steps, and so on. For example,

```
:This is a comment
::This is a reply
:::This is another reply
```

produces formatting like that in Figure 5-6.

```
This is a comment
    This is a reply
        This is another reply
```

FIGURE 5-6: *Indentation on Wikipedia*

Indented text is commonly used on discussion pages, when you want to produce a more-readable threaded discussion. Indentation is also used in articles for setting off quotations and mathematics or computer code examples, but you do not need to indent the beginnings of paragraphs.

Numbered and Bulleted Lists

Lists are commonly used on Wikipedia, both by themselves and for sections of articles such as See also and External links. Bullet points are used more often in articles than in ordinary prose; bullet points can improve readability, though at the cost of some typographic elegance.

To create a bulleted list, use an asterisk for every new item:

```
* Example 1
* Example 2
* Example 3
```

To indent an item in a bulleted list, use more asterisks:

```
* each new item starts with a star
** more stars mean
*** deeper levels
* which can be combined
```

This produces a list like the one in Figure 5-7.

- each new item starts with a star
  - more stars mean
    - deeper levels
- which can be combined

FIGURE 5-7: *A bulleted list*

You can also indent text using both asterisks and colons:

```
* Example 1
:* Example 2
::* Example 3
```

This will produce the same effect and is commonly seen on discussion pages.

To make an ordered numbered list, use a hash mark (#). (To ensure sequential numbering, do not use empty lines to separate the list items.) For example,

```
# Example 1
# Example 2
# Example 3
```

produces a list like the one in Figure 5-8.

```
1. Example 1
2. Example 2
3. Example 3
```

FIGURE 5-8: *A numbered list*

For indented levels, use more hash marks. Using more hash marks will start the numbering over for that level, but as long as you don't separate list items, you can continue the numbering for each level. For example,

```
# List item A1
## List item B1
## List item B2
### List item C1
# List item A2
```

produces a list like the one in Figure 5-9.

```
1. List item A1
        1. List item B1
        2. List item B2
                1. List item C1
2. List item A2
```

FIGURE 5-9: *A more complex numbered list*

Internal and External Links

Links were introduced in Chapter 3 as the key to browsing and discovering Wikipedia. Links are very simple to add to articles, and *wikifying* a page by adding appropriate internal links is one of the easiest and most helpful tasks for getting started on Wikipedia. Links build the hypertext web of Wikipedia articles, and they build Wikipedia into the Web. Correspondingly, Wikipedia has two types of links: internal links to other Wikipedia pages and external links to other websites.

Internal Links

Create an internal link (also called a *wikilink*) to another page on Wikipedia by enclosing the name of the page you wish to link to in double square brackets:

```
[[Article name]]
```

When you save the page, the article name will show up as a blue underlined term in the article text; clicking that link will take you to the page you linked to.

The article name that you use to create the link is the part of the page URL after */wiki/*. Therefore, [[*Article name*]] links to *http://en.wikipedia.org/wiki/*Article_name.

Internal links should not contain underscores: [[*Article_name*]] is equivalent to [[*Article name*]], and in article text, the underscore is unwelcome. Only the first letter of an article name is automatically capitalized, so [[wikipedia]] goes to the same place as [[Wikipedia]].

To display linked text that is different from that of the link itself, use the pipe character (|) in between the page name and the text you wish to display:

```
[[Article name|display name]]
```

For instance, if you type this:

```
[[Mickey Mouse|Walt Disney's Mickey]]
```

Walt Disney's Mickey will appear in the text, linked to the Mickey Mouse article.

The pipe character is also known as the *vertical bar* and is usually found on the backslash key on standard (QWERTY) keyboards.

Be sure that any alternate or display text makes sense and doesn't break the flow of the article; use descriptive text rather than "click here" or "this link," which should not appear in articles.

Redlinks

You can also link to a page that doesn't exist yet. To do so, simply enclose the name of the page that you think should exist in double square brackets. A link to a nonexistent page will show up as red instead of blue; consequently, these links are called *redlinks*. Clicking one will take you to a screen where you can create the new page. Redlinks help Wikipedia grow. A redlink may disappoint a reader; but it challenges an editor to create a needed article.

Redlinks can also be piped, just like regular internal links. Occasionally, you will find that two or more article-worthy subjects share a name, but only one is already an actual article. In that case, go ahead and create a redlink for the second subject. For instance, if you're writing an article about Samuel Smith, the Mayor of Brooklyn in 1850, you don't want a link to the already-present article on [[Samuel Smith (chemist)]], co-inventor of Scotchgard, or any of the other dozen Samuel Smiths who have articles. In this case, you might make a redlink to [[Samuel Smith (Brooklyn Mayor)|Samuel Smith]], which is less misleading for the reader than linking to the wrong historical figure and is also more likely to provoke the creation of an article about the politician.

If Wikipedia has no article on a particular topic, creating a redlink asking for one is appropriate if the site ought to have such an article. Create a redlink only if the topic deserves an article itself. For example, fans of an author often wikify all the titles in a bibliography, implying each work is worthy of its own article. Opinions may differ on that. Still, redlinks introduced by others should only be removed if overlinking within the article is evident, or you can make a strong case that an encyclopedic article cannot or should not be written about the topic. Occasionally text will be mistakenly linked, and the link can be removed while keeping the text intact. In general, though, if you start removing redlinks, you're making a statement that the proposed growth would be a negative for the site, and except in some clear-cut cases, others will tend to question your authority to decide that.

Tricks with Internal Links

Text that you type immediately after an internal link without spaces will display as part of the link. This trick is handy for making plural words out of links. For instance, if you want to link to the article [[Horse]] but need the word *horses* in the text, simply type:

```
[[horse]]s
```

✳ ***NOTE:*** *This trick applies only to text characters and doesn't work with apostrophes.*

To link to other namespaces outside of the main article namespace, include the full namespace name: For instance, link to [[User:Phoebe]] to access the user page for the user Phoebe. Use the pipe character and alternate text if you do not want the prefix to display as part of the link. Alternatively, for pages with prefixes, to create a link that produces the name of the page without the prefix (without having to retype the article name), you can use the pipe character at the end of the link, with nothing after it:

```
[[User:Phoebe|]]
```

Typing this will produce a link named simply *Phoebe* in the text. Inserting a space after the pipe character hides the link entirely.

To link to a category page (rather than placing a page in a category), use a colon before the link. For example,

```
[[:Category:Dogs]]
```

will display a link to [[Category:Dogs]] on the page. Without the initial colon, no text will be displayed; instead, the page will be placed in that category and the category name will appear at the bottom of the page.

Internal links work to create links in nearly all situations. You can include them in image captions and template text.

Internal Linking Policy

There is a Goldilocks-style policy for wikilinks in articles: not too many and not too few. Adding too many wikilinks (*overlinking*) is usually caused by novice over-enthusiasm. Here's the basic idea: Link any term once per article, at most, and usually on the first occurrence. This excerpt from a lead section shows the style:

> '''Tom and Jerry''' are an [[Animation|animated]] [[cat]] (''Tom'') and [[mouse]] (''Jerry'') team who formed the basis of a successful series of [[Metro-Goldwyn-Mayer]] theatrical [[short subject]]s created, [[screenwriting|written]] and [[film director|directed]] by animators [[William Hanna]] and [[Joseph Barbera]] (later of [[Hanna-Barbera Productions|Hanna-Barbera]] fame). One hundred and fourteen ''Tom and Jerry'' cartoons were produced by the [[Metro-Goldwyn-Mayer cartoon studio]] in [[Hollywood]] from 1940 until 1957, when the animation unit was closed down. These shorts are notable for having won seven [[Academy Award for Animated Short Film|Academy Awards for Best Short Subject (Cartoons)]], tying it with [[Walt Disney]]'s ''[[Silly Symphonies]]'' as the most-awarded theatrical animated series.

The piped link [[Animation|animated]] is enough about animation: The words *animators*, *animation* (in *animation unit*), and the second use of *animated* do not need links. [[Metro-Goldwyn-Mayer]] and [[Metro-Goldwyn-Mayer cartoon studio]] are different articles ([[Metro-Goldwyn-Mayer cartoon studio]] might have been a redirect, but actually isn't), so they both get links. The words *cat* and *mouse* will not need to be links later in the article.

In a long article with multiple sections, the rule on only linking once is sometimes relaxed. If a reader would have to scroll a long way back to find a wikilink, repeating the link is kinder.

What should be linked? You do not need to link every common noun: *Tree* doesn't always need a link, if there is nothing special about the tree. Every year of modern time has a page, but *1966* does not need to be a wikilink whenever it occurs. A rule of thumb is to reserve links of dates for events having some historic weight. In general, link to the most specific concept you can: Adding a link to London or Paris adds little value to an article when compared to a link for a particular neighborhood or suburb of a major city; readers are almost certain to know something about London, but they may have no idea where [[Kensington]] is in relation to [[Buckingham Palace]].

Avoid splitting up a single concept. It should be [[Roman Catholic Archdiocese of Chicago]], rather than [[Roman Catholic]] [[Archdiocese]] of [[Chicago]]. If a single concept is suitable as a topic in its own right, make it a single internal link, even if the article hasn't been written yet. Sometimes you'll need to change awkward syntax: Wikifying *Professors Bohr and Einstein* as *Professor [[Neils Bohr]] and Professor [[Albert Einstein]]* makes a lot of sense, but then you should wonder why *Professor* is used at all. Does knowing that Einstein was a professor add anything useful? Ending up with *[[Neils Bohr]] and [[Albert Einstein]]* is actually much better.

Don't introduce *self-links*—links that lead back to the same article. These are quite easy to notice if they simply consist of the article title: In that case, the software displays them as bold type rather than as a link. Usually self-links occur when an editor inadvertently links to a page that redirects to the article you are linking from. For instance, in the article [[Romulus and Remus]], the name *Remus* should not be linked because [[Remus]] redirects straight back to [[Romulus and Remus]]. The only exception to this ban is when you link to another section of the same article, as described in "Sections and Headings" on page 155.

> ### Check Wikilinks as You Introduce Them
>
> Sometimes problems with self-links will only show up when you check the links; this is a good habit to develop, anyway, because wikilinks will not always lead where you expect.

External Links

To link to an external website, you can simply paste the URL (with the *http://* prefix) into a wiki page:

```
http://www.google.com
```

and it will appear as a clickable hyperlink.

You can also enclose the link in single square brackets:

```
[http://www.google.com]
```

The URL will show up as a number in square brackets, like this: [1]. The numbers will automatically increase serially as more links are added to the page.

The preferred method for displaying an external link is to label it. To produce alternate text for external links, leave a space in between the URL and the text you wish to display. For example:

```
[http://www.google.com Google's search engine]
```

will display *Google's search engine* as the link in the text. Do not use the pipe characters for external links.

External Linking Policy

Wikipedia articles often include a section called *External links* that is conventionally placed near the end of an article and should include links to web pages outside Wikipedia that are relevant to the article.

> ## Prefer Internal Links
>
> Don't use external links in place of internal links. If Wikipedia doesn't have an article about a concept or entity, create a redlink rather than creating a link to an external site; any external links can be used as references instead.

Wikipedia has several guidelines about which external links to include. Types of sites that are welcome include pages directly relevant to the topic of the article (such as a company homepage for an article about a company), pages from reputable sources that contain further description or research that is accurate and on-topic, pages with information that could not be added to the article because of copyright or density of detail (such as professional athlete statistics or full film credits), or any other relevant content that may add to a reader's understanding of a topic but is not suitable for inclusion in an article (such as an interview). If an external page is used as a source for information in an article, it should be listed as a source and placed in the References section of the article rather than in the Fxternal links section. The sites in External links should provide additional information beyond that provided by source citations.

Though some external links are welcome, Wikipedia is not the place to include a comprehensive list of external links related to each topic—Wikipedia is not a directory. Typically, commercial pages or sites that only exist for selling a product are not included; the article about television should not include a list of links to companies that sell television sets (such link inclusions are generally removed as spam). In general, you should remember that Wikipedia is not meant for self-promotion; webmasters and web authors should not add links going to the websites they work on or for.

Nofollow

Wikipedia uses *nofollow* tags, which means that search engines do not take into account whether a site is linked to from Wikipedia when they calculate rankings. From a search engine optimization standpoint, including a site in a Wikipedia article has no benefit. This decision was made in order to discourage zealous webmasters from trying to use Wikipedia to boost their sites.

If you do remove a link from an article, take care the author didn't use it as a source, whether as an inline link in the text or a link in the External links or References section. If you're trying to decide if a link is useful, check the page history to see who added the link and whether they provided an explanation for adding it. Removing links is a tricky business; if you're unsure, you can always post a quick message to the talk page.

Some whole sites should not be linked to. Wikimedia maintains a *blacklist* of these sites, which is incorporated into MediaWiki software. If a link to one of these sites is included in a page, you'll be unable to save the page; instead, you'll get a message prompting you to remove the offending link(s). (You might occasionally get this message even if you're not the person who added the link originally, for instance, if the link was not removed after blacklisting). The vast majority of blacklisted sites are pornography sites and commercial sites that have been consistently "spammed" on one or more projects (typically by being placed as links, sometimes automatically, on many unrelated articles). As the explanation for the list on Meta wiki says, "The spam blacklist exists primarily to control widespread spamming of Wikimedia Foundation projects. It is intended as a last resort for spam which spreads across multiple projects, and which is pursued by multiple individuals or IP addresses." See [[Wikipedia:Spam blacklist]] to suggest any additions or to appeal a decision. In addition to this restriction, any site that violates another's copyright (such as an illegally posted copy of a work) should not be linked to.

Links to sites in languages other than English are somewhat discouraged, but that does depend on the topic. If a topic is connected with Germany, German speakers, or the German language, a link to a site in German is generally fine. Other instances where you might want to include a link to a non-English site are when the material the site covers is not available in English on the Web, authoritative information on the topic is typically published in that language, or the site is obviously scholarly and important.

One helpful trick is to preface the link with a language icon template such as {{de icon}}, which warns the reader that (in this case) the site is in German. Templates for many languages can be found at [[Category:Language icons]].

Sections and Headings

Sections divide articles into readable pieces. They also have other uses such as dividing conversations on talk pages. A section marks out a subtopic and also serves to define an editable unit on a page. You can create internal links to a specific section by adding a hash mark (#) and the section name; external links to sections also work, though the section name must then use underscores instead of spaces.

You can click and open any section on a page to edit separately, except for the top section (lead section or introduction). By convention, the page does not start with a section heading but with the first words of an article. Editing a page by section is more convenient in several ways: It saves excessive scrolling and produces an automatic prefix in the edit summary.

Sections are produced by using equal signs, like this:

```
--Section--
===Subsection===
====Sub-subsection====
```

Although you can use just one equal sign, using only one produces a title that is the same size as the automatically generated page title and is not recommended for articles. The section headers are in bold, so you don't need to add other formatting (and indeed, this doesn't work). Headings should not use uppercase except when ordinary English does: Fried eggs, not Fried Eggs. You can include wikilinks, or even external links, in headings. This is somewhat ugly, though, and is not recommended in articles. Section headings show up in the table of contents for the article.

If an article has four or more sections, a *table of contents (ToC)* will automatically be generated; this table of contents contains links to the sections that are present. The table of contents provides an easy way for readers to navigate long articles. You can hide the ToC by clicking the Hide link.

Formatting the Table of Contents

You can entirely remove a ToC from an article by including the special syntax __NOTOC__ somewhere on the body of the page. You can also format or modify the ToC (for instance, to display as an alphabetical A–Z list) by using special templates, as described in Chapter 9.

For a clearer writing style, you should introduce sections (as a good first step) in editing a badly organized article. Expanding and varying the existing section structure of an article can also help clarify the text. The {{sections}} template is the cleanup message used to request the introduction of sections; see [[Help: Section]] (shortcut WP:SECT) for some more detailed advice.

Linking into and out of Sections

Sections of pages serve as anchor points and can be linked to. For example,

```
[[Lion#cubs]]
```

is an internal wikilink to the section Cubs in the article [[Lion]]. In an article, you'd certainly pipe such a link:

```
[[Lion#cubs|lion cub]]
```

to end up with a wikilink that reads *lion cub* but that takes you directly to the Cubs section of the [[Lion]] article. The full URL for this link would be:

```
http://en.wikipedia.org/wiki/Lion#cubs
```

which takes you right to the section.

Occasionally, you will want to direct readers to another article from a section, for instance, when a top-level article on a topic, such as [[History of the United States]], provides an overview of a broad topic that is addressed in more detail by several more specialized articles. In this case, the section of [[History of the United States]] that deals with the Civil War era directs the reader to the main article [[History of the United States (1849–1865)]] for more information.

These links are generally produced by templates, such as

```
{{main|page name}}
```

which points the reader toward the main article on a topic with a message saying *Main article: page name.*

Another template is

```
{{details|page name}}
```

which creates a message saying *For more details, see page name.*

A related template,

```
{{see|page name}}
```

renders *For further information: page name.*

Simply place the template at the beginning of the section you want to link from. In each case, replace *page name* with the name of the page to link to.

Linking from sections to other articles plays a major organizational role in building Wikipedia as a piece of hypertext. This structure is widely used to place invitations in high-level articles to explore details in other articles.

Hypertext Is Not Prose

Some criticisms of Wikipedia have appeared based on the incorrect premise that articles are stand-alone prose. The notion is that, for example, [[History of the United States]] really represents what Wikipedia has to offer on the topic—that readers will read through it all, looking at that article in isolation. But that article is also there to give access to other articles. Although long articles in traditional encyclopedias might be assessed in such a fashion, Wikipedia is designed for surfing between many interlinked articles.

Removing Formatting and Hiding Comments

Sometimes you may want to display wikisyntax on a page, without it actually functioning as markup. For instance, you may want to discuss a formatting issue on a talk page or write help pages with examples for other editors.

The easiest way to do this is to use the `<nowiki>` tag, which ignores wiki markup and reformats text by removing newlines and multiple spaces. To use `<nowiki>`, enclose the text you want to display with markup between `<nowiki>` and `</nowiki>`. The syntax you put between these tags will be displayed just as you type it.

The <pre> and </pre> tags are similar, except that they do not reformat newlines or multiple spaces.

You can also produce constant-width text that stops newlines and spaces from being reformatted but still interprets wikisyntax. Simply place a leading single-space indention at the beginning of a line. This creates text with a dotted-line box around it that is not formatted like the rest of the page. You'll only see this occasionally in articles, but it is good, for instance, for displaying snippets of computer code. You will also see this formatting when a space is accidentally left at the beginning of a line of formatted text.

Hidden comments can be left on a page with the *comment* tags: <!-- comment text -->. Replace *comment text* with the comment or remark you wish to leave. Text in between the tags will not display for readers in the rendered page, but it will show up in the wikisource when others edit the page.

Usually, leaving comments in the raw text of a page is inappropriate; anything addressed to readers or editors should be left on the talk page instead. Comments left in the page wikitext can be useful, however, as a note on how a particular template is being used or as a note to yourself for quick drafting. The comment tag is rarely used and should not be confused with comments left on talk pages, separate comments pages that sometimes exist as part of rating pages, or the Request for Comments process.

Further Reading

http://en.wikipedia.org/wiki/Wikipedia:Build_the_web   The guideline on internal linking

http://en.wikipedia.org/wiki/Wikipedia:External_links   The guideline on external linking

http://en.wikipedia.org/wiki/Help:Wikitext_examples#Links   Basic examples of adding links

http://en.wikipedia.org/wiki/Help:Link   The extensive help page about all aspects of how links work

Lists and Sections

http://en.wikipedia.org/wiki/Help:List   Help with list syntax

http://en.wikipedia.org/wiki/Wikipedia:List_guideline   Guidelines for using lists on Wikipedia

http://en.wikipedia.org/wiki/Help:Section   Help using and editing sections and the table of contents

http://en.wikipedia.org/wiki/Wikipedia:Manual_of_Style#Invisible_comments   The guideline on leaving comments in text

Summary

Wikipedia pages are editable by everyone quickly and directly, whether they are logged in to Wikipedia or not. There is no moderation before a new version of a page goes live and replaces the previous version. Only a few pages are protected in any way from editing. You can start editing by clicking the Edit This Page tab to access the edit window. The source code that appears when you edit a page is called the wikitext or wikisource.

Most markup for the wikitext can be learned as you need it. Knowing the basics of formatting text and the layered approach of wikitext will serve you well, making quick edits possible. Understanding lists and headings also helps you organize articles and contribute to discussion pages.

6 Good Writing and Research

This chapter explains how to take part in the main activities on Wikipedia: writing, researching, and improving encyclopedia articles. It covers how to start articles—a simple matter—and how to write them well—a considerably more difficult one. Good writing comes as a result of practice, as well as having a knack with words, and understanding the style, tone, and referencing of encyclopedia articles.

A good writer will always consider a projected article in a wider context. The sheer scale of Wikipedia has an impact on research work. Existing articles and the research that others have already added to Wikipedia will help inform your choice of topics and will likely give you feedback on the research you intend to do. Reviewing the site to find what has already been written in a subject area is a kind of due diligence: You'll avoid duplicating the efforts of others and save time.

Wikipedia has the added complexity of having been developed by tens of thousands of editors. Learning how to work productively in this collaborative environment can mean acquiring some particular skills. In this chapter, we'll discuss how to write a good article using advice accumulated from Wikipedians who have collectively written hundreds of thousands of articles.

Starting New Articles

The Wikipedia community greatly values new articles that fill a gap, are well written, and are well referenced. This really is praise from experts! If you have already eased into editing, perhaps by copyediting the work of others, you can certainly consider starting a fresh article.

Anyone with an account can start new articles easily in a couple of seconds. If you don't have a user account, you can still propose articles, as we'll describe in the next section. Before you start typing, though, keep some things in mind. It's as true for Wikipedians as for Boy Scouts: Be prepared! Consider the preliminaries before investing substantial amounts of time in writing. These are the steps involved in writing a new article:

1. Decide on a topic.
2. Check Wikipedia for existing coverage.
3. Find references and research the topic.
4. Choose a title and start the article.
5. Draft the article.
6. Link it to other articles and categorize it.

The more flexible, thorough, and resourceful you are in carrying out these steps, the simpler you'll find it to make good additions to the encyclopedia. Research hard, and then write well, whether you're adding one long article about a detailed topic, a short stub, or a group of related articles. The same techniques also hold true if you're rewriting an article or expanding an existing stub article; for many topics these days, you're far more likely to find a poor-quality article in need of cleanup and expansion than no article at all. The challenge for the writer is the same, however.

Deciding What to Write About

Is an encyclopedia of two million articles complete? Not at all. If you don't know what to write about, visiting a good library is an easy way to come up with a notable topic. Or, you can investigate some of the many projects that have been set up to gather topics that need to be written about:

Requested articles (shortcut WP:RA)
This page—really a suite of pages by topic—is where anyone can add a request just by creating a redlink. Note that requested articles pages tend to be rather messy, and just because an article is listed here doesn't mean the

topic meets inclusion guidelines. Always double-check to see whether the requested article actually exists in some other form and if it should be written at all.

Articles for creation (shortcut WP:AFC)
This is where new or unregistered users can request an article be created. The page consists of a template form that article requesters fill out; registered users then go through and approve or deny requests. If you're a registered user in good standing, don't use this form for creating new articles; however, you can often find ideas here that deserve to be turned into articles.

Missing encyclopedia articles
This WikiProject is a centralized place to determine what topics might be missing from Wikipedia, based on researching other reference works. The project states that its goal is "to ensure that Wikipedia has a corresponding article for every article in every other general-purpose encyclopedia available."

[[Category:Wikipedia missing topics]] is the umbrella category that collects lists of potential missing articles. Likely topic areas for missing articles include politicians from anywhere that isn't the United States or Europe; biographies from before the 20th century (check any public-domain biographical dictionary, particularly ones not in English); scientists in a prominent national academy; and so on. Some individual editors' compilations of missing articles can be found at [[Category:Red list]], which collects so-called redlink lists that editors set up as working pages.

If you understand copyright and what's in the public domain, you can use imported material from older sources to start your article. For instance, much of the text of the now-public-domain 1911 edition of the *Encyclopaedia Britannica* has been imported into Wikipedia. Other materials from Wikisource, which should be public domain or GFDL, can be reviewed with a view to adapting it. Copy-and-pasting is almost never enough, though; adapting older material requires skilled editorial work to bring both the language and the factual content up to date (for instance, a subpage of the missing encyclopedia articles project works on verifying articles from the 1911 *Britannica* to ensure these articles are accurate and timely).

Before Starting a New Article

Once you've selected a topic, make sure an article about that topic hasn't already been written in Wikipedia. You'll have to search the site thoroughly to avoid creating a duplicate article. This step is important because of the lack of top-down structure on the site: Whereas in a traditional encyclopedia, an editorial committee would assign authors topics, Wikipedia has nothing like this, and authors are responsible for understanding what else exists on their topic and making new articles fit into this structure.

Good Timing

What if your information goes stale? What if it hasn't happened yet at all? As mentioned in Chapter 1, future occurrences—a sporting event, a film under production, or construction work in progress—are usually not suitable article topics if they are just speculative. Wikipedia is not a crystal ball. If you have good verifiable sources and a precise future event, then you can write about it in Wikipedia. Material related, for example, to a new road being built can be in articles, but only when appropriately tagged. Blue-bar informative templates exist for this purpose (in [[Category:Temporal templates]]). If a topic is time sensitive, you should flag the information correctly. For example, as of 2008, no confirmed sightings of a [[Yeti]] have been made. The quick way to indicate that information is valid as of a particular date is to use the {{As of|*year*}} template, replacing *year* with the valid year. See [[Wikipedia:As of]] (shortcut WP:AO) for how this helps maintain the site.

After you search the site for the topic and working article title you have in mind, you'll find one of the following cases is true:

▶ An article on the topic already exists (possibly under a different title than the one you had in mind).

▶ More than one article has been written on the topic, all using different titles.

▶ Some material on the topic exists, but in a more general article that encompasses several topics.

▶ The topic is briefly mentioned in another article, but has not been developed.

▶ The article title you want has been used, but the article is about something else.

▶ No references to the topic are anywhere on the site.

If an article already exists on the topic (but under a different name), simply make your article title into a *redirect* to that page, as described in Chapter 8. Working on the existing article to improve it is a good next step; very few articles on Wikipedia are comprehensive. At this point in the English-language Wikipedia's history, this outcome is the most common one for people looking to write about a particular topic, considering the vast number of existing articles.

If more than one article has been written about the topic and they seem to duplicate each other, they may need to be merged; see Chapter 8 for directions on merging. You can continue to work on improving the articles in the meantime.

If your topic has been developed in an existing, broader article, you'll probably want to work on that article to improve the existing content. If enough material for a separate article on that specific topic has been written, you'll want to split the content into an article with a new title; see Chapter 8. Be sure to add an appropriate introduction, conclusion, references, and See Also links to the new page.

If a topic is mentioned in other articles but not developed, make sure each mention of the topic is wikilinked to the title of the new article you want to write. This will connect your new article to existing content on Wikipedia. Additionally, checking out these topic mentions could give you research leads. Take note of anything interesting and unexpected and any relevant references you find as you come across them.

If the article title has already been used but the article itself is about a different topic, you'll probably need to move that article to a more precise title, create your article with another precise title, and then create a *disambiguation* page to direct readers between the articles, as explained in Chapter 8. For example, *John Gray* is a fairly common name. If you want to write an article on an architect with that name, you may title your article [[John Gray (architect)]] instead of simply [[John Gray]]. If [[John Gray]] already has an article about a physicist, that article could be moved to the title [[John Gray (physicist)]], and the main page [[John Gray]] could be reformatted as a disambiguation page to refer readers to these different articles.

If you don't find any articles or references to your topic on Wikipedia, you should pause before writing. Why is your topic not mentioned anywhere? Is your topic notable (see "Avoiding Treacherous Topics" below)? Have you looked for all the potential alternate names for the article or topic? Perform a thorough search, using all the title variations you can think of. If you decide your topic is notable (and simply missing), make sure you can place it into the context of already-written articles. Generally, you should add redlinks in existing articles to your new proposed article (either in the text or in the See also section) before you begin writing; then when you do create the article, you won't be creating an orphan.

Avoiding Treacherous Topics

If your intended topic hasn't been written about or mentioned, find out why. Revisit the article inclusion guidelines, mentioned in Chapter 1 ("Other Guidelines"), especially the notability guidelines (shortcut WP:NOTE) and the sidebar on classic topics not to write about (shortcut WP:DUMB).

New authors can fall for a handful of common traps. Perhaps the most dangerous are so-called vanity articles and wishful thinking about notability. *Vanity articles* are articles that have been written for promotional purposes (usually by the subject of the article) rather than for their encyclopedic value. If you're considering an article about yourself or your company—please don't. Even with the best of intentions, this can be seen as self-promotion and often leads to the article being deleted. Even if this doesn't happen, writing an article about yourself can be a mixed blessing: You don't control the content once the article is posted, and any relevant negative information will be highlighted just as prominently as the good. (Think of it another way: *Encyclopaedia Britannica* won't publish your résumé, either.)

Wishful thinking about notability can occur in other areas too. Common topics that are often borderline in terms of notability are articles about local bands, living people, and new movies, books, or albums. As mentioned in Chapter 1, Wikipedia has specific notability guidelines for all of these areas. Consider these guidelines and how your article fits in context.

Other treacherous topics are articles that have been deleted in the past. If you begin to write an article on a topic that was been previously created and deleted, you'll get a warning message that reads, *Notice: You are re-creating a page that was deleted.* In other words, one or more editors decided that the topic was not suitable for Wikipedia. If the article was deleted through the community process, Articles for Deletion (see Chapter 7), a link to the discussion about that article will be included in this warning message. Follow that link and figure out why the page was deleted: Is the topic itself unsuitable for Wikipedia, or was the original article simply flawed in a way that's fixable? If in doubt, an administrator (who can view the deleted version) can probably help.

Starting the Article

As a logged-in user, you can choose a title and begin writing. Want to create a new article? Now is the perfect time to choose a Wikipedia username and open an account, as you must be logged in to start a new page. In the meantime, consult [[Wikipedia:Your first article]] (shortcut WP:FIRST) for a concise list of things to do.

Click a Redlink

The best way to initiate an article is to begin from a redlink on an existing page. Let's say your chosen topic is gingerbread cottage architecture, and you want to write a new article with this title. This term may already be used on some existing Wikipedia page (perhaps the general article about cottage architecture or gingerbread houses), and you can turn it into a redlink. Or, an unsuccessful search could bring up a page with a redlink matching your search term.

Redlinks

The What Links Here link works for redlinks as well (the search page also offers this option when a page does not exist: *See all pages within Wikipedia that link to this page*). Checking what backlinks exist before starting an article can point you to related existing content and give you an indication of how popular a redlink is by how many pages link to it already.

You can set also set up a redlink to [[Gingerbread cottage architecture]] on your user page, thus starting your *braglist*. Describing your new articles in this way is perfectly acceptable and will undoubtedly be of interest to Wikipedians checking out what articles you've started.

Clicking the redlink will bring up an empty editing window with the heading *Editing Gingerbread cottage architecture*, as shown in Figure 6-1. Start typing! Or, if you're more prepared, paste in text that you've already written (see "Drafting the Article" on page 169).

Preview your work, correct the formatting, punctuation, and typos, and save the new article. Add a short edit summary indicating that this page is the first version. If you've followed these instructions, the new page will not be an orphan (not quite anyway) because at least the page with the once-redlink now has a bluelink to your article. And clicking What Links Here in the sidebar on [[Gingerbread cottage architecture]] will reveal those unexpected pages that already link to your article (for example, if this article is on another editor's to-do list).

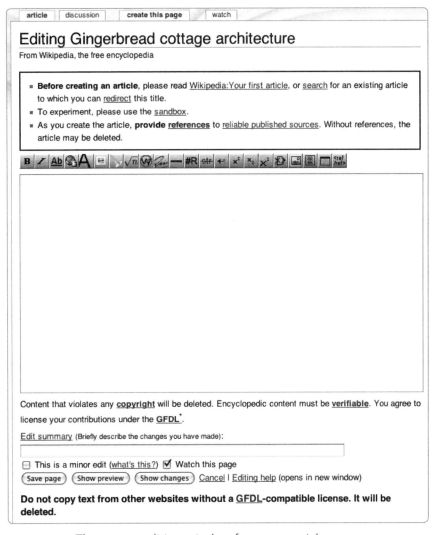

FIGURE 6-1: *The empty editing window for a new article*

Typos in the title require page moves to correct them because titles are not directly editable. One good reason to start with a redlink is that you are less likely to make a mistake in the title itself.

Two More Ways to Start an Article

For maximum user-friendliness, you can visit [[Help:Starting a new page]] for further help in creating a page. Enter your article title in the search box at the top. If it does not already exist, you'll be walked through the process of creating the page.

The most basic (but also the most primitive) way to start an article is simply to type the article's name into the browser as a URL. For instance, you can start your article titled [[Gingerbread cottage architecture]] by sending your browser to *http://en.wikipedia.org/wiki/Gingerbread_cottage_architecture.*

Once you have sent your browser to a nonexistent Wikipedia page, you'll see some text telling you the page doesn't currently exist, which you should already know, along with a link to start the article, which will work if you're logged in. While starting an article this way is very quick, finding a page where you can first create a wikilink to your topic is the best method since you shouldn't ever create orphan articles. Using the browser method also increases the possibility of accidentally creating duplicate articles or articles with misspelled titles or other typos.

Titles Are Tricky

Wikipedia has some title conventions you should respect when starting a new article. When you're searching, these conventions work for you by making it more likely that you can infer the exact title of a topic. This is (naturally) why respect for conventions is more than pedantry; consistent titling is a usability issue. In a given area, the titles of existing articles offer good clues to the conventions in force. The most basic convention is to always use singular forms: [[Siberian Tiger]], not [[Siberian Tigers]]. But exceptions are made for plural nouns; the article about stilts is at [[Stilts]] (as a single stilt is something you'd probably want to trade for a [[Pogo stick]] and, in any case, a [[Stilt]] is a bird).

Titling an article about a person can be particularly confusing. Articles about people should generally be in the form of *first name last name*. This convention can be hard to follow for articles about nobility, ancient Romans, people with multiple surnames, and any other special case. An article about someone called *Raymond, Count of Provence* might be under *Raymond of Provence* because nobility titles are often omitted. What if more than one such historical figure existed—for instance, Raymond II of Provence with Roman numerals (not "Raymond the Second")? But how is the name spelled? Raymond, Raymund, Raimund . . . ? What if *of* should be the French *de*? The article is actually located at [[Ramon Berenguer II, Count of Provence]], using the Catalan spelling for *Ramon*. If redirects have been set up to this article from possible name variations, using Google is probably the quickest method for finding the article by searching for the words *Raymond*, *Count*, and *Provence*. Detailed case studies for naming articles about people are covered in [[Wikipedia:Naming conventions (people)]].

Here are more examples. The article about Saint Francis of Assisi is [[Francis of Assisi]], not [[Saint Francis of Assisi]], although the latter is a redirect. You can find specific advice for naming articles about saints on the Saints WikiProject at [[Wikipedia:WikiProject_Saints]], where editors have developed special style guidelines for these particular articles. Even though the most commonly used and recognized name is preferred, the article on Madame Mao is under [[Jiang Qing]], not [[Madame Mao]], though again the latter name is a redirect. Initial articles are not included in page titles: [[Statue of Liberty]], not [[The Statue of Liberty]]. Only proper names are capitalized: [[Pythagorean theorem]], not [[Pythagorean Theorem]]. If several possible articles could have the same title, Wikipedia has a wide variety of disambiguation schemes depending on the topic. The most common is to add a qualifier in parenthesis to the article name, such as in the previous example of [[John Gray (architect)]]. General guidelines on how to disambiguate page titles are on the main disambiguation page (shortcut WP:DAB#NAME).

Depending on what area interests you, looking at similar articles may save you time in figuring out a good title. These matters are all documented: For ample detail, see [[Wikipedia:Naming conventions]] (shortcut page WP:NAME), which is an official policy and includes information on naming conventions for many specific topic areas. Also see [[Category:Wikipedia naming conventions]].

A few characters are forbidden in page names, including

```
# < > [ ] | { }
```

and some others that are problematic. Full details can be found at WP:NAME.

As we mentioned in Chapter 5, the first letter of a title is always capitalized by the MediaWiki software, but otherwise titles are case sensitive: Capital letters in multiword titles, such as names, must be treated with care. [[Thomas Jefferson]] is not the same as [[Thomas jefferson]]. For titles that really should have a lowercase first letter, like [[iPod]] or [[e (mathematical constant)]], there is a special workaround: the template {{lowercase}}. This template displays the title of the article with a lowercase first letter (though the article name is still automatically capitalized in the URL). As for the famous case of [[E. E. Cummings]], the article explains it, so we don't need to.

Drafting the Article

Once you've selected a topic and picked out a title, you need to actually write the article. Making several drafts is often needed to produce good writing. Drafting a new article somewhere else first before posting it to the site is often best. Drafting allows you to note ideas, gather sources, and leave unfinished sentences and comments to yourself while you figure out what you want to say—without the risk of adding "bad" content to the encyclopedia.

You can draft articles in three possible places. You can draft in the article itself or in your user space. You can also work offline in a text editor. Drafting in live articles is not recommended for newcomers, as an article may be severely edited or nominated for deletion while you are still working on it. For a quieter experience, work in your user space, where other editors are unlikely to edit what you've written; to start out, draft on your user page, and create subpages for drafts when you become more ambitious.

You can create a subpage in your *user space*—your user page and any subpages under it (see Chapter 11). For instance, if your username is Ydobon, your user page will be at [[User:Ydobon]], and you can create a subpage in your user space by simply starting a new page with a forward slash in between your user page name and the new page name, such as [[User:Ydobon/Draft1]]. Simply create the redlink by typing [[/Draft1]] on your user page and then click it to begin writing. Subpages link back automatically to their main page. Constructing subpages with the forward slash works elsewhere but is not allowed in the article namespace. Subpages are widely used in project space, especially on process pages (described in Chapter 7) where every discussion is on a separate page. See [[Wikipedia:Subpages]] for more information.

You can also work entirely offline in a word processor, and then paste the content into the article when you are done. This method has some advantages. Printing the draft article to review it can often reveal inconsistencies and awkward phrasing and flow. Working in a word processor also makes it easy to spellcheck and restructure.

The user space method of drafting has the "what you see is what you get" advantage: You'll see the draft formatted exactly as it will appear in the article. Drafting in user space is thus a good method if you want to test out or perfect the wikisyntax formatting. Perhaps the best method is to start writing offline and then copy the work in progress to your user space when adding wikisyntax. User space is a public space to which you can invite other editors for feedback. But by convention no one else should edit a draft there, unless asked to directly.

Once an article is posted in the main article space, you no longer control it. If you are still doing major drafting while working in article space, you may want to add the anti-hassle template {{inprogress}} at the top. This template will fend off almost all intruders, reduce edit conflicts, show you know what you're doing, and probably deflect any early deletion proposals. Leaving the template up for a long time is not okay (and not a way to keep others from editing your work). In the same way, if you add hidden comments as a way of drafting, remove them when you're done.

Don't Forget

Articles are not signed. When you create a new article, provide a descriptive edit summary, perhaps summarizing the topic in a few words. Finally, once you click Save, you don't control the content. Perfect strangers—out of the hundreds of millions online—can now edit it.

Further Reading

http://en.wikipedia.org/wiki/Wikipedia:Requested_articles   Article requests, sorted by topic

http://en.wikipedia.org/wiki/Wikipedia:WikiProject_Missing_encyclopedic_ articles   Articles found in other encyclopedias but missing from the English-language Wikipedia, sorted by topic

http://en.wikipedia.org/wiki/Wikipedia:Most_wanted_articles   Articles that don't exist and have a high number of incoming links

http://en.wikipedia.org/wiki/Help:Starting_a_new_page   Directions on how to start a new page, with a handy search box where you can check to see if a page is really new

http://en.wikipedia.org/wiki/Wikipedia:Articles_for_creation   The Articles for creation process, where unregistered users can request that an article be created

http://en.wikipedia.org/wiki/Help:Page_name   Technical restrictions on creating page names

http://en.wikipedia.org/wiki/Wikipedia:Naming_conventions   Policy on naming articles

http://en.wikipedia.org/wiki/Wikipedia:Subpages   How to create a subpage, including directions on how to create a user subpage

Writing Well

The perfect Wikipedia article probably doesn't exist, though discussions of good writing on Wikipedia have become catalogs of what this article should be. If you truly think the journey is more interesting than the destination, you may be a natural-born Wikipedia editor, because Wikipedia's reality is constant, incremental improvement. Articles evolve over time.

A good article fulfills a need for information—it informs the reader with broad coverage, relevant context, and deliberate, thoughtful prose. At the very least, a good article is understandable and clearly expressed, for both experts and non-experts. It thoroughly explores and explains the subject in appropriate detail. But the article isn't only its *content*; it's a web page, too. Wikipedians should write with this context in mind and continue to build the web. Good articles contain incoming wikilinks and external links. These external links should take readers to the best sites for following up on the article. Refer to the academic literature, if any applies, by providing references. By doing this, you are building not only Wikipedia but also the Web as a whole. *Nodal pages*—pages that connect you as well as inform you—carry added value for readers. A Wikipedia article is not trying to replace specialist information available elsewhere, but to give access to this material. Good web pages fill niches: The niche in question is an encyclopedia article, but now in a vastly enlarged Web context.

In this section, we'll discuss eight broad areas to consider when writing an article as well as two tips for accomplishing your task—consulting the *Manual of Style* and getting reviews. For more advice, [[Wikipedia:The perfect article]] (short-cut WP:PERFECT) lists about 20 pointers for producing excellent articles. Again, perfection may not be humanly attainable—we mentioned in Chapter 2 that acceptance of imperfection is deeply rooted in wiki culture—so please take our advice as aspirational and complementary to [[Wikipedia:Guide to writing better articles]] (shortcut WP:BETTER).

Consulting the *Manual of Style*

Much of the advice and many of the links in this section come from the *Manual of Style*, which is a style guide developed by the Wikipedia community for the purpose of helping editors write articles consistently and well. The *Manual of Style* is a lengthy document that has been developed over time and represents a tremendous collective body of knowledge about writing encyclopedia articles. Its main page resembles the kind of style guide produced by book publishers and newspaper editors. This conceals other pages that have been developed wiki-style: a complex web of further advisory material on how to write for Wikipedia. These *Manual of Style* pages provide guidance both for global issues (such as tone and organization) and small grammatical details (such as whether to use a serial comma). The term *Manual of Style* is usually understood as including [[Wikipedia:Manual of Style (abbreviations)]] along with other pages in [[Category:Wikipedia style guidelines]].

The *Manual of Style* itself, available at [[Wikipedia:Manual of Style]] (short-cut page WP:MOS), is a Wikipedia guideline, which gives it an official standing. Together with the specialized pages it links to, the *Manual of Style* is essential reference material. Authors and editors should refer to it often (of course, they don't need to read it all before starting to write).

Most likely, a handful of manual pages will be most relevant to your particular topic area. For example, [[Wikipedia:Manual of Style (command-line examples)]] (shortcut WP:MOSCOMM) is of interest to those (and only those) intending to

---

Acronym Overload

The *Manual of Style* is often abbreviated *MOS* or *MoS*, and guidelines within the *Manual* are referred to by shortcuts such as *MOS:FLAGS*. Wikipedia has a list of these shortcuts at [[Special:Prefixindex/MOS:]]. Not everyone will know these or other Wikipedia acronyms. Too many acronyms can make a page hard to decipher (just you wait for Chapter 13), a sentiment expressed nicely by the essay [[Wikipedia:WTF? OMG! TMD TLA. ARG!]] (shortcut WP:OMG).

include examples of computer code in articles they write. Rather than trying to remember where the pages are and what they say, create internal links from your user page to the pages you reference most. For instance, one of the most useful pages is [[Wikipedia:Summary style]] (shortcut WP:SS), which explains how to structure lengthy articles and topics too large to handle in a single article.

Introduction and Topic Sentence

An article should begin with a clear description of the subject. The first sentence should define the topic of the article, using the title or subject of the article, which should be formatted in **bold type**. The rest of the introductory paragraph should explain the subject and its significance clearly and accurately, without going into excessive detail. If you're having trouble with the topic sentence, you might want to think further about the article title.

Although the opening of an article should convey why a topic is interesting, an encyclopedia article is not a book review or personal essay, and you are not trying to entice the reader. The article [[Robinson Crusoe]] should indicate in its first sentence that this is an English novel. References to Daniel Defoe's journalism and historical discussion about sea voyaging in the early 18th century should be postponed until later. If you are submitting an article adapted from research written for other purposes (such as a dissertation or school paper), your original opening will almost certainly need to be recast.

A lead section may be split into three paragraphs, at most, but it shouldn't be longer than this. The opening section should encapsulate the rest of the article. More advice can be found at [[Wikipedia:Lead section]] (shortcut WP:LS).

Some basic insights into the structure of newspaper articles can be useful as a reference point (the article [[inverted pyramid]] describes this style). The lead paragraphs of news stories frequently treat several strands of a story simultaneously, before giving the details. This technique is also very useful on Wikipedia, as a way of placing a good summary ahead of the main part of a longer article.

Let's analyze one introduction from Wikipedia [June 2007]:

> Herbert George Wells (September 21, 1866–August 13, 1946), better known as H. G. Wells, was an English writer best known for such science fiction novels as *The Time Machine*, *The War of the Worlds*, *The Invisible Man*, and *The Island of Doctor Moreau*. He was a prolific writer of both fiction and non-fiction, and produced works in many different genres, including contemporary novels, history, and social commentary. He was also an outspoken socialist. His later works become increasingly political and didactic, and only his early science fiction novels are widely read today. Wells, along with Hugo Gernsback and Jules Verne, is sometimes referred to as "The Father of Science Fiction."

This introduction has a fairly simple A-B-A structure, with A being "science fiction" and B being "political views." (You may notice some possible issues with Verifiability: Who says his later work is not read much, and who gets to award the title "father of" anything? But these might also be covered better later in the article.) According to the Wikipedia guideline, a lead section should ideally have at most three paragraphs, so it could be a little more complicated than the example.

But if an article has three main ideas, A, B, and C, you should introduce only one idea per paragraph. The topic structure could be something like A-BA-BC, with A being the headline and B and C the most significant related points, but that's about as complex as the opening should be.

Comprehensiveness and Appropriate Length

A well-written Wikipedia article acknowledges and explores all aspects of the subject. In other words, it covers every encyclopedic angle. This goal in itself can be a strain on a writer. Cover every angle of William Shakespeare? The Neutral Point of View policy, however, does require *comprehensiveness*, defined as the inclusion of all significant perspectives. Something should be said about Shakespeare's influence on literature other than English and something about authorship theories.

Clearly, ensuring such an article is an appropriate length is difficult. Using *summary style*, mentioned in the *Manual*, is critical. Include sufficient information, depth, and analysis on the subject, but without unnecessary detail. Subarticles developed from the main one, related articles (such as the lengthy [[Shakespeare authorship question]] for the Shakespeare example), or in some cases in wiki sister projects can include this extra information. You'll find that material on major topics moves around from article to article until coverage is more balanced.

Structure

You can't expect your readers to have a clearer view of your article's logic and flow than you do. Divide long sentences, especially if they're loosely linked by conjunctions. Any longer threads of logical argument are somewhat suspect in encyclopedic terms. While avoiding a dense or cryptic style, Wikipedia articles should be tight and concise, rather than verbose. W.S. Gilbert wrote, "Never mind the whys and wherefore" in *H.M.S. Pinafore*; Wikipedians know that a good "why" can be valuable, but they look out for elaborate wherefores: Long arguments should be summarized and well referenced.

A good article is logically arranged and divided into sections. Collect the history of a concept into one section. Whether this comes immediately after the introductory section or at the end of the article depends on the particular idea.

An article such as [[Gas mask]] can place the chemistry before the history, or vice versa. For most readers, separating the two aspects of the topic is most helpful. This issue is typical when dealing with anything technological. The article [[Piano]] (as of March 2008) has a section on early history directly following the introductory section. Then the use of subsections for the grand piano, upright piano, and so on is clearly indicated by the subject matter.

Readability

Everyone on Wikipedia wants to be a good writer. Readability should be your ultimate goal. *Readability* means your writing is clear and easily understood. Encyclopedia article prose should be as transparent as possible so the writing doesn't get in the way of the content.

Readability doesn't exist in a vacuum, and good writing certainly does not mean insipid, tediously dry, or dull writing. Some of the excellent content already on Wikipedia can provide examples of strong prose (while you can also see some of the pitfalls in examples of poor articles). Other editors can also help provide input on style.

For guidance on making prose more elegant and readable, any writing guide may be valuable. Choose one that answers your questions and is itself readable. A classic American guide to good writing is Strunk and White's *The Elements of Style*; other classics are *Fowler's Modern English Usage* and Gowers' *The Complete Plain Words*. Just as helpful as a good style guide is saturation: *Read good writing.* Compare similar articles in different encyclopedias—what's similar, what's different? Reading well-written books will make you a better writer. With practice, you can write an encyclopedia article that is factually accurate and fair and also clear, eloquent, and colorful—or, to use a term from the earliest days of the project, written using *brilliant prose*.

Brilliant Prose

Brilliant Prose was one of the earliest project pages on Wikipedia. Larry Sanger created this project and addressed the subject in one of the very first messages to the *Wikipedia-L* mailing list. Sanger reported on January 22, 2001, that of the 184 articles then on Wikipedia, 14 were listed on the brilliant prose page, leading him to conclude that "Wikipedia does rock." (From *http://lists.wikimedia.org/pipermail/wikipedia-l/2001-January/000000.html*)

Audience

Who is the *general reader*? Who is your *audience*? Who Wikipedia's audience is has always been a subject of discussion. The consensus, if not the universal view, on Wikipedia is that articles should be written for a well-educated adult; this choice is also the traditional one made by *Encyclopaedia Britannica*.

Some specialist topics (such as many mathematics articles) will inevitably contain material that is not understandable to a lay audience. After reading an article, however, you should be able to say you know two things: what the topic is and why it's important. The introduction matters most to a nonspecialist. It should summarize the content of the article and place it in context for a lay reader.

Sometimes readability and accuracy conflict. Especially for highly technical topics, understanding a concept at all may be difficult for general readers. To tackle these expository difficulties, provide an acceptable, generally readable summary in the opening paragraph and then an accurate formal definition in the body of the article.

One person's jargon is another person's correct terminology, of course. It may make sense to put the jargon first. But then you have an obligation to define that jargon with a phrase such as *roughly speaking . . . , in other words . . . , simply put . . .* , or some other phrase indicating that what follows is the layperson's summary. All readers should know what content to expect.

This introduction from [[Blood pressure]] shows the use of both technical and everyday language:

> *Blood pressure* (strictly speaking: vascular pressure) refers to the force exerted by circulating [[blood]] on the walls of [[blood vessel]]s, and constitutes one of the principal [[vital sign]]s. The pressure of the circulating blood decreases as blood moves through [[artery|arteries]], [[arteriole]]s, [[capillary|capillaries]], and [[vein]]s; the term blood pressure generally refers to arterial pressure, i.e., the pressure in the larger arteries, arteries being the blood vessels which take blood away from the heart. *Arterial pressure* is most commonly measured via a [[sphygmomanometer]], which uses the height of a column of mercury to reflect the circulating pressure (see [[#Non-invasive measurement|Non-invasive measurement]]). Although many modern vascular pressure devices no longer use mercury, vascular pressure values are still universally reported in [[torr|millimetres of mercury]] (mmHg).

One great advantage of hypertext, as shown here, is *indirection*. If you provide a wikilink for a technical term, those who follow it for more information will be a self-selected group who really want that information. The link to [[sphygmomanometer]] reduces the need for long explanations in the blood pressure article itself.

Use of Language

Many older encyclopedias err on the side of pomposity, but Wikipedia's tone is direct, crisp, and contemporary. Wikipedia articles are a kind of academic writing, but they do not adopt the formal or specialist tone of a learned journal. They should be interesting—not dry, colorless, or bland. They should not be literary, personal, argumentative, or investigative. In controversial matters articles should aim to be descriptive rather than opinionated. In this, Wikipedic prose is close to the journalism of a newspaper of record, reporting events from above the fray and presenting all notable sides of an issue.

Deaths may be *accidental* but should not be *regrettable* or *premature* or *tragic*. By the same token, though, euphemisms are misplaced: Don't write *passed away* for *died*. A discovery may be called *highly significant* or just *significant*. If you think about it, *significant* can be more impressive. Why? Perhaps because the general reader doesn't want to be bombarded with superlatives but would like to understand the main stages of a development. This point is covered in a general way at [[Wikipedia:Avoid peacock terms]] (shortcut WP:APT). Understatement also helps with neutrality. The historian Lord Acton said that "the best way of doing justice is a little reserve in uttering judgments."

Language should not be colloquial and should conform to usage guides. Follow standard writing conventions: Use complete sentences and correct grammar, punctuation, and spelling. Choppy writing is distracting. To the reader. To put it. Mildly. Abbreviations, however common in a specialist field, should not only be linked to their own article but also generally spelled out for the lay reader's benefit.

Whose English?

American English and Commonwealth English coexist on the English-language Wikipedia. This coexistence is supposed to be peaceful; strife involving Wikipedians with different settings on their spellcheckers is unwelcome. See [[Wikipedia:Manual of Style#National_varieties_of_English]] (shortcut WP:ENGVAR) for the *Manual of Style* section on what is acceptable where. The rule is *when either of two styles is acceptable, an editor should not change from one style to another unless he or she has a substantial reason to do so*. In other words, if an article is already written in British or American English, stick with that existing style when making additions. This was a hard-fought compromise in the early days of Wikipedia!

One special rule for writing in Wikipedia is to *avoid self-references*—that is, avoid references within Wikipedia articles to the Wikipedia project. Unlike in talk and community pages, where discussing Wikipedia is natural, in articles it is distracting. It also makes the content less suitable for *forking* to a new project, one of the goals of Wikipedia's open license. Avoid phrases like "this Wikipedia article discusses" and even "in this encyclopedia." This ban on articles mentioning Wikipedia obviously does not apply in articles about Wikipedia-related topics. For the

Manual of Style page on this issue, see [[Wikipedia:Avoid self-references]] (shortcut WP:SELF).

Graphics

A good article includes informative, relevant images—diagrams and graphs, maps, portraits, photographs, and artwork—that add to a reader's interest in or understanding of the topic. Each image should have an explanatory caption. See "Images and Media Files" on page 262 for the technical details of how to add images to articles.

Graphics should support the text; the images should not be so numerous or so predominant as to detract or distract from the article itself. Don't include pictures just to make the article pretty. Use graphs, infographics (see [[infographics]]), and *tables* (tabular data) where they are the most appropriate format, not in all circumstances. Remember, any data should be referenced but not analyzed—analyzing data can become original research.

Infoboxes (templates displaying key facts) should not be intrusive and should not be *tendentious* (all facts should be verifiable). It should be clear to the general reader where to place the article as one of a related series. For example, [[War of the Austrian Succession]] includes a box listing the combatants of this 18th-century European war in chronological order (Figure 6-2). Thetwo boxes at the bottom, whose

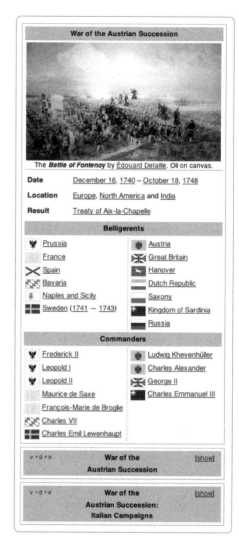

FIGURE 6-2: *Shown is the elaborate infobox from [[War of the Austrian Succession]]. The bottom two sections are additional infoboxes that can be expanded.*

contents are viewable by clicking the Show link in the box corner, are additional infoboxes that list the major battles of the war (a complete list is also at [[Category: Battles of the War of the Austrian Succession]]). Infoboxes are generally only included when Wikipedia has several related articles about a topic.

Applying Basic Content Policies

The reader of an article should, above all, feel that it summarizes the topic responsibly. The way to do this is well understood. An article conforming to content policies is completely unbiased; it has a Neutral Point of View (NPOV), presenting competing views on controversies logically and fairly. Language use is also affected by the basic policies, and we'll give examples here.

Consider the phrase "the notoriously bloodthirsty and keelhauling pirate Blackbeard." To the trained eye of a Wikipedia editor, *bloodthirsty* is probably opinion, but *keelhauling* might be factual. *Pirate* is one of those words that could be used in different ways according to point of view: Was Sir Francis Drake a pirate? You might find a Spanish book that says he was. The response to this particular phrase might be to delete everything except *Blackbeard* and include a link to the fine Wikipedia article on [[Blackbeard]], also known as Edward Tench. After all, you don't need to introduce someone who already has a dedicated article.

Appositive phrases such as *convicted fraudster*, *quack doctor*, *disgraced politician*, and *international terrorist* would most likely be purged. Before crying "Censorship!" be clear that this type of editing is considered housekeeping: The editor is applying Wikipedia's policies. Surprisingly often, people confuse cleaning up language into more encyclopedic style with censorship of facts. Wikipedia's Neutral Point of View may not speak for your point of view. This same reasoning may call for taking out *renowned* or *extraordinary* in front of a name. You may think a scientist deserves *Nobel laureate* with each mention of his or her name, but Wikipedia doesn't. *Legendary* is restricted to things and people in legends.

In any tricky area, be a neutral party. Point out all sides of an argument, without favoring particular viewpoints. Emphasize factual and accepted views. Give minority views a lower prominence, but provide sufficient information and references so readers can learn more about particular views.

Older material often gives clearer examples of editing for neutrality and tone. This extract, imported unchanged from a 1913 encyclopedia, illustrates the problems. It is verbose and slanted. The article is about the French mystic Madame Guyon (from [[Jeanne Marie Bouvier de la Motte Guyon]]):

> Her strange conduct brought upon her severe censures, in which she could see only manifestations of spite. Evidently, she too often fell short of due reserve and prudence; but after all that can be said in this sense, it must be acknowledged that her morality appears to have given no grounds for serious reproach. Bossuet, who was never indulgent in her regard, could say before the full assembly of the French clergy: "As to the abominations which have been held to be the result of her principles, there was never any question of the horror she testified for them." It is remarkable, too, that her disciples at the Court of Louis XIV were always persons of great piety and of exemplary life.

You could cut this back considerably (and it still needs some work):

> Her conduct brought criticism, but her morality gave no grounds for it. Bossuet, one of the critics, said before the French clergy: "As to the

abominations which have been held to be the result of her principles, there was never any question of the horror she testified for them." Her disciples at Versailles were pious people of exemplary life.

The two sentences at the start have been combined, increasing clarity and neutrality. Adjectives used as editorial comment or for unneeded emphasis were removed: *strange* in "strange conduct," *severe* in "severe censures," and *great* in "great piety." This type of editing and tightening should be applied to all writing in draft. The quote, by the way, has to be left as is. Quotes in Wikipedia shouldn't be copyedited. In this instance, you would have to find the original French quote and retranslate it. Although you could probably paraphrase the quote to say, "Bossuet was hard on her but thought her no hypocrite," it sounds like original research, and independently verifying Bossuet's attitude would be a better option.

One hazard of Wikipedia's NPOV policy is that unclear phrasing can seem more neutral, but you can avoid this. See [[Wikipedia:Avoid weasel words]] (shortcut WP:WEASEL). Apparently those weasels can also be blamed for wordiness, passive voice constructions, convoluted syntax, implicit endorsement of faulty logic, and monotonous repetition.

In its early days, you could find too much writing on Wikipedia in the form "some say *X*, while others say *Y*." This form aims at neutrality but fails. Problems with this phasing include lazy writing, as well as those weasel words:

▶ The phrase should be verifiable, reading "*A*, *B*, and *C* say *X*, while *D* and *E* say *Y*," with citations for each claim.

▶ What about those saying *Z*? Aren't they being sidelined unfairly?

▶ Does the whole comment represent the entire debate fairly, including the main reasons for controversy?

Although one side may have to be wrong because the two perspectives are incompatible, a neutral point of view is still about presenting both sides fairly, no more and no less. The temptation to add weasel words can be particularly strong in articles about controversial subjects; for instance, the phrase *nothing was ever proven* occurred in the offending article in the Seigenthaler scandal (see Chapter 2).

Reviews

At any point, you can ask others to look over your work. Review happens naturally on Wikipedia, which is one of the site's strengths. To prompt other people to comment, Wikipedia also has dedicated places to go for help; see [[Wikipedia:Peer review]] (shortcut WP:PR). Here you can nominate an article for others to review and leave comments. Going through peer review is a common step for good articles being nominated for featured status, as described in Chapter 7. Anyone is welcome to give reviews as well, and reviewing other authors' articles can be a good way to learn to think critically about an article's structure. For less formal reviewing, see [[Wikipedia:Requests for feedback]] (shortcut WP:RFF).

Quality and the Good Stub

A writer contributing to Wikipedia may add new long articles that attempt full coverage of a topic, add good stubs that are clearly needed for the encyclopedia, or work on existing articles to improve quality. The end goal is to ensure that any article is a reliable and comprehensive summary of information about a topic and provides an excellent overview. This goal has always been the traditional objective of encyclopedia compilers.

The only question is how to get there. Writing well takes time, but contributing at a low level of quality is not very satisfying after a while. Wikipedia uses intermediate versions as stepping-stones. This is why stubs matter. To say a stub may be "good" means that even articles that aren't comprehensive have a concept of quality. A good stub article—the *ideal stub article* described at [[Wikipedia: Stub]]—constitutes a quick start to a page. It adds value to the encyclopedia, and other editors will not come after you cursing quietly.

To summarize, article quality is comprised of the following:

▶ Compliance with Wikipedia's inclusion standards, particularly NPOV and NOR

▶ References included throughout the text (indicating that individual facts have been checked against or derived from external sources)

▶ Factual accuracy, as verified by the external sources

▶ A list of pertinent reliable external links and sources on the subject

▶ Writing that conforms to a high standard of written English

▶ Appropriate images or diagrams and formatting that conforms to Wikipedia style guidelines, including logical sections and appropriate internal links

▶ A complete and clear explanation of the topic, with a logical flow to the article

---

Further Reading

http://en.wikipedia.org/wiki/Wikipedia:The_perfect_article   A short checklist of what a perfect article includes

http://en.wikipedia.org/wiki/Wikipedia:Guide_to_writing_better_ articles   Advice on writing better articles

http://en.wikipedia.org/wiki/Wikipedia:Manual_of_Style   The *Manual of Style* for writing and formatting Wikipedia articles

http://en.wikipedia.org/wiki/Wikipedia:Stub   The style guideline for stub articles

http://en.wikipedia.org/wiki/User:Tony1/How_to_satisfy_Criterion_1a   An essay on how to meet Criterion 1a of the Featured article guidelines—that article prose is "engaging, even brilliant, and of a professional standard"

In starting an article, even if you can't yet give it the completeness and visual pizzazz mentioned in the last two points, you can ensure all the other aspects of quality listed. If you do this, then you've written the ideal stub.

Researching Articles

Research is important. If you don't cite references at all . . . well, we have to break it to you, others may delete parts of the article they don't find credible, and in some cases, the whole article may be deleted. A good article is well documented, with reputable sources cited for all facts. As an article author, you're responsible for referencing your work; at the very least when writing, include a selection of the sources you used to put the article together. If you can't find a source for a fact, it probably doesn't belong in the encyclopedia.

The research for any substantial article should take at least as long—and probably much longer—than the actual writing. This requirement to research puts limits on how prolific anyone can be as a Wikipedia author; after all, Wikipedia is not a touch-typing test. Thus, although wiki editing is quick and spontaneous, writing a good article depends on a great deal of preparation time spent gathering sources and searching for information, and the skilled Wikipedia editor must also be skilled at these research tasks. Although adding things you know "off the top of your head" is easy and tempting, think about how you actually know that fact. Is it something you learned in school or spent time researching? Have you seen it yourself, or is it something you heard? If you can remember how you learned it, you can probably cite a source. You'll still need to research even if you mainly modify existing articles, rather than beginning new ones. Edits and additions to articles are more easily accepted by other editors if they are accompanied by good supporting citations. And if you enjoy doing research, fact-checking existing articles and adding existing citations is also a major cleanup task, as described in Chapter 7. Finally, good research skills are useful for evaluating information in an article; if you question a particular point on a talk page, for instance, first do a quick search to see if the information is supported elsewhere or not.

In this section, we'll talk about research techniques and the different citation styles for Wikipedia articles. Research, like writing, is a skill that takes some practice to do well, and this is just a brief introduction to the topic. Other resources include guides to doing research (*The Oxford Guide to Library Research* by Thomas Mann is one such guide), libraries and librarians (whose job is to help with research questions), and forums such as Wikipedia's own reference desk (at [[Wikipedia:Reference desk]]), where you can ask questions about any topic. Ideally research will be interesting and natural, rather than burdensome; collating facts is the primary job of the encyclopedist, and research is the process behind that.

Good Wikipedia Research

What is meant by *good* research? On Wikipedia, research makes the site a quality reference work. For an individual editor, doing your research before writing is also thoughtful preparation ahead of exposing your work to criticism and modification in an open forum. Good research can give you confidence in the content you're submitting to Wikipedia, and it fortifies an article against questions from other editors about content—which may be important, because Wikipedia, like online communities in general, can be an argumentative place.

The Verifiability and No Original Research policies are the background to referencing information on Wikipedia. All facts should be verifiable, and theories that are advanced must be based only on what is already published, without novel synthesis. In practice, this means that sources should be cited for facts in accordance with the Reliable Sources guideline. From Wikipedia's point of view, some sources are better than others. What is also true is that, whereas all facts should flow from reliable sources, some facts are more worthy of thorough research before including them in an article than others. Anything contentious, or possibly suspect, should be well documented first. In contentious areas, however, don't expect complete agreement on what a reliable source is. If an article presents two sides of an issue, its editors should find reputable authorities on both sides.

Occasionally information in Wikipedia has turned out to be *urban myth*, something that comes from a friend of a friend. . . . Make sure, in cases like this, that what's been said is actually something that's documented somewhere and not just gossip or lazy journalism. Cite a good, reliable, printed source for the information. If verifying a point is harder than you thought, that's all the more reason to record where you found it for the sake of Wikipedia readers. Remember that Wikipedia doesn't pass judgment on what is true, but the site is responsible for reporting on and gathering reliable information about all topics.

The easiest topics to research well have mostly been added to the encyclopedia. More obscure topics may be more difficult to research, but again, part of learning about a subject well enough to write about it for a lay encyclopedia audience is doing good background research.

Doing Research

Researching is hard work, but like hunting for treasure or solving a crossword puzzle, the act of discovering the unknown through careful steps can be quite satisfying. Regardless of the topic you're interested in, doing research to corroborate information in an article or to find out more about a topic consists of a few basic steps:

1. Determine the question you're trying to answer. The question may regard specific facts in an article that you want to cite or may be more general (for instance, "What year did this scientist receive a Nobel Prize?" or "What basic topics did this scientist work on, and did he or she receive recognition for this work?"). With existing articles, if you need a place to begin asking questions, take a second and skeptical look at the factual content. Which salient facts are most likely to be in doubt?
2. Figure out what kind of sources are likely to have the information you're looking for and where you can find those sources.
3. Use the appropriate type of source. This is a critical (and often overlooked) part of good research: Not all sources are right for all topics. For information on a recent natural disaster, review newspaper or news agency accounts

and governmental bulletins; these news stories can be found either through searching web indexes such as Google News, which is free online, or news indexes such as LexisNexis, which many libraries subscribe to. On the other hand, if you're researching a 19th-century writer, accounts of his or her life may be found in literary encyclopedias, biographical dictionaries, introductions that appear in his or her work, or (if they were quite famous) dedicated biographies, which may be found in library catalogs. Often specific questions are easiest to answer: For the scientist example, a list of Nobel Prize winners may be found easily on the Nobel Prize committee website. For more in-depth information, however, you will need to turn to biographies.

4. Search for appropriate sources. This requires turning your search question into keywords that can be used in a web search engine, library catalog, article database, or similar system. If you can't find anything using one term, try another similar term or name variation. It is at this stage and the previous one that asking for help from people knowledgeable about the topic and librarians can be very helpful.

5. Read and evaluate potential sources. This is the time-consuming part of doing research. Do the sources answer your questions? Where did they get their information? Do they seem trustworthy? What *trustworthy* means can vary depending on what you're looking for; although a scholarly biography published by an academic publisher is usually a reliable source for investigating a scientist's life, an essay about that scientist that was written by a student and posted online on a personal website probably isn't. The Reliable Sources guideline, discussed starting on page 186, talks a good deal about what a reliable source is for most topics on Wikipedia. The point is, however, that statements of fact should be based on the best information available.

6. Document your sources. Once you've found a good, reliable source that answers your question, cite it, either with the inline style described in "Referencing Styles" on page 188 (for specific facts) or in a separate References section (for more general sources).

    Congratulations, you're done! (For that article, anyway.)

* **NOTE:** *File away URLs. If you find likely web pages by searching online, save the URLs, even if you remember exactly how you found a key reference. Searches are not always repeatable experiments because search engines and inbound links update themselves.*

A few particular research resources are worth mentioning:

For academic articles
Google Scholar, available at *http://scholar.google.com/*, indexes citations to research articles in all fields. Note that the articles themselves may not be freely available online, but often the abstract will be. This source is good for finding recent scientific literature, though search results are almost always

something of random assortment of potentially relevant material. Google Scholar is general; the article [[Academic databases and search engines]] covers other databases, which are often available through libraries, for finding articles in many specific fields.

Recent Research and NPOV

Use cautious language regarding announcements of contemporary scientific discoveries. Be careful not to overstate the importance of any particular research you find simply because it's easily available online. For scientific research especially, new findings must be vetted by others; it sometimes takes many years before it becomes clear whether or not new research is truly notable. Additionally, remember that part of NPOV is balance: You are seeking to provide an accurate and broad overview of a topic for a general reader, not catalog all the research that has been done or the most recent discoveries in a subject. Rumors, preprints, and scientific research reported in the news are not reliable sources.

For websites

In addition to using search engines (a long list of which can be found at [[List of search engines]]), try a directory such as the Librarians Internet Index, at *http://lii.org/*. This site, like other web directory building projects, collects websites by topic, but each site is reviewed by librarians to make sure the content seems reasonable before it is posted. Another well-known, volunteer-edited web directory is *http://dmoz.org/*; other directories can be found at [[List of web directories]].

For books

WorldCat, at *http://worldcat.org/*, is a combined catalog for libraries all over the world and is now free online. If you have a particular book in mind, this catalog can point you to libraries nearby that have that book, and books are searchable by subject. Three good sources for online books are Google Books, at *http://books.google.com/*, which scans books held in libraries around the United States and makes their full text searchable (though if the work is under copyright, only a snippet of the book will be viewable); the Internet Archive's Texts project, at *http://www.archive .org/details/texts*, which scans public domain and freely licensed books and makes them available along with other online collections; and Project Gutenberg, *http://www.gutenberg.org/*, which has the full text of 20,000 public domain books available.

For reference works

[[Category:Wikipedia sources]] lists some common sources used in articles, whereas [[Category:Reference works in the public domain]] lists reference works in the public domain, which are often available online and can be reused freely for articles (though often require some cleanup).

Other good sources for finding books and articles are general textbooks or overview sources about a topic, which almost always include a bibliography of core sources that you can then turn to. And as with any research project, local libraries and librarians can also help suggest and locate possible sources.

ISBNs and Book Sources

An International Standard Book Number (ISBN) is a 10- or 13-digit number that is used to uniquely identify books by publishers and libraries worldwide. You may notice on Wikipedia that linked ISBNs are often listed after references to books. Clicking one of these linked ISBNs takes you to a special page, [[Wikipedia:Book sources]], which is a long list of library catalogs from all over the world. If you arrive at this page by clicking an ISBN, clicking any of the library catalog links will search for that book in that catalog automatically. If you have access to one or more of these libraries, this can be a great time-saver. Some online book retailers are also listed. If you have a book's ISBN, you can also search it directly at [[Special:BookSources]]. To insert an ISBN into a reference, simply type ISBN and the number, without punctuation. The number will automatically be linked to the Book Sources page.

Reliable Sources

Some sources are better than others for verifying information. Always use the best possible sources you can find. In addition, Wikipedia has a few general preferences for sources:

▶ Given Wikipedia's global availability as a research tool and the possibility that collaborating researchers will have access only to publicly available sources, try to use sources that are freely available to everyone online (usually in addition to printed or subscription-based sources). Beware, however, that many resources accessible through universities or libraries, such as online magazines, are paid for by subscription and not available to the general public.

▶ Up-to-date sources are preferable, though deeper coverage of a topic may depend on older scholarly sources. New sources can always be added in as they are published.

- ► Use a mixture of sources whenever possible: A combination of external links to websites, references to standard textbooks, and specific references to academic books and journals is ideal.

- ► Don't rely on blogs or any other sources that are led more by opinion than factual reporting; editorials may be good sources for discussing viewpoints about a controversial subject, but they are generally not the best sources for factual information. When researching a very controversial subject, be extremely careful to double-check the origins of sources and present both sides of the story.

- ► For any source, ask about the expertise of the author writing. The idea of who an expert is will clearly vary in context; an expert in current popular musical culture might be a music journalist, not an academic professor. Regardless, be clear on where information is originating from.

- ► Don't randomly cut well-referenced information or reasonable sources. If you find a better source than the one listed, by all means add it, but in most cases, don't remove the old source. If the sources disagree, note this in the article or on the talk page.

Debates are ongoing on Wikipedia about what a reliable source is and what claims need to be sourced within an article. Scholarly sources are, for the most part, going to carry more conviction than (say) what a columnist once wrote. But you should also be reasonable about sources: Reliability is not the same as infallibility.

✳ NOTE: *Don't self reference by using other Wikipedia articles as sources. This kind of self referencing defeats the point of getting information from* outside *reliable sources. Links to other articles should go in the See also section.*

For a detailed discussion, see [[Wikipedia:Reliable sources]] (shortcut WP:RS). This guideline on reliable sources and the concurrent debate around it (unfortunately but maybe inevitably) has been dominated by extreme cases, which are not helpful for most articles. The guidelines for sources tend to deal with areas where it makes the most sense to take a tough line on reliability, such as religion, politics, or biographies of living people.

A related guideline deals with sources for biographies. The following is from [[Wikipedia:Biographies of living persons]] (shortcut WP:BLP), which is official policy (accessed October 3, 2007):

> Material from self-published books, zines, websites, and blogs should never be used as a source about a living person, unless written or published by the subject of the article.

> Editors should avoid repeating gossip. Ask yourself whether the source is reliable; whether the material is being presented as true; and whether, even

if true, it is relevant to an encyclopedia article about the subject. When less-than-reliable publications print material they suspect is untrue, they often include weasel phrases. Look out for these. If the original publication doesn't believe its own story, why should we?

Referencing Styles

Once you have the perfect source in hand, you then need to actually add a citation to it in the article. A variety of referencing styles have been adopted and ultimately rejected over the years on Wikipedia—not to mention the half-dozen styles commonly used in academia being added to the mix and technological solutions such as templates being introduced. What all these referencing styles have in common, however, is they attempt to make it clear where information in an article comes from and what sources were used. Getting the specific style of the reference right is much less important than making sure the reference is present in the first place; other editors can always come along and edit it stylistically.

That said, we recommend the *inline* referencing style, where specific references are noted in the main body of the text using numbered superscript links to footnotes. These footnotes appear at the end of the article (usually grouped in a section called References or Notes) and contain the specific references used for each piece of information that has a footnote. This style is gradually becoming the most common on Wikipedia today, and it has several advantages. In-text links to footnotes means a reader can easily click to the source for any particular piece of information and that you can make very specific citations—each sentence in an article could conceivably have a footnote to a different specific source. The citations for each fact can appear directly next to that fact. This style also means that an article can easily acquire more sources over time; if an editor finds a perfect source for documenting a single fact in an article, he or she can easily insert a footnote to that source, and the list of footnotes and their numbers will automatically update. Additionally, if a footnote is deleted through text being edited or moved, the footnote numbers will automatically update. This makes it a good style for collaborative referencing work.

How Much Should You Reference?

Several long-running debates have occurred over the years on whether everything in an article (including common knowledge) needs to be cited to a source or just the key points. Questions have also been raised over whether having a large number of footnotes in an article detracts from its readability and even its usefulness to the reader, who does not have to query every fact to learn the material. These arguments aside, having a specific source immediately accessible is useful, and footnotes make this possible.

Along with footnotes that only contain a reference, they can also comment on or include asides to the main text, though these are less common in articles. For a comprehensively referenced article, the footnote section (which in this case would be called Notes) can also be combined with a separate References or Further reading section, where works can be listed as general references for the whole article. Figure 6-3 shows this style used for the end sections of the article [[Phineas Gage]] (about a 19th-century man famed for surviving a large iron rod puncturing his skull and brain).

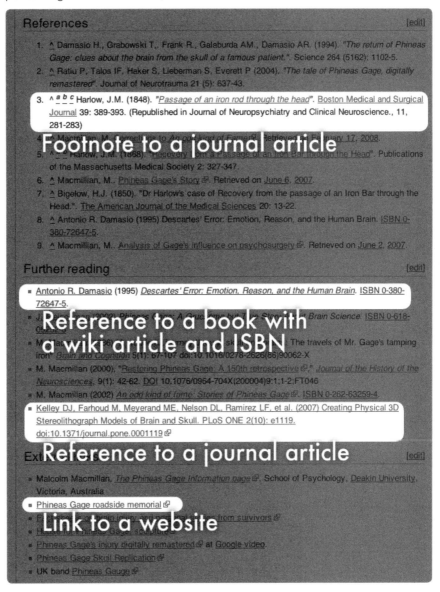

FIGURE 6-3: The References, Further reading, and External links sections of the article [[Phineas Gage]]

Wikipedia has no default style for the citations themselves; several different variations on academic styles are common (see [[Wikipedia:Citations]] for more information). How a work is cited will depend on what it is; a typical Wikipedia article includes sources from web pages, books, and perhaps periodicals and learned journals. Here is some advice for styling citations on Wikipedia:

▸ Remain consistent. If one referencing method or style is already used in the article, stick to that style.

▸ Inverting names is not necessary. Although many academic styles call for putting the last name of an author first in a reference listing, this style is unhelpful for readers who may be searching the site for a specific author.

▸ Wikilinks can be used judiciously; many famous authors and well-known sources have their own articles, and in these cases, names within the citation can be linked for the curious reader.

▸ Include a URL if you can, but make sure the URL is stable and accessible to everyone (not just subscribers to a magazine, for instance). Include the date that you accessed the URL.

▸ Spell it out. Cryptic abbreviations often used in scholarly journals are unhelpful for a reader who may be new to a field of study. Give as much information about the source as you can (the full name of the author, journal name, or ISBN for a book, for instance). Readers from all over the world may ultimately try to find the source.

Reference Sections

There are several standardized sections for references at the end of a typical article: See also, for links to other Wikipedia articles; References, which includes all sources used for the article; and External links, which contains links to external websites. The sections should appear in that order. Occasionally, References will be split into a Notes section (for footnotes), References (for any non-footnoted references), and Further reading (for extra relevant sources not directly cited).

Using Footnotes

The workhorse of the inline style is the <ref> tag. Notes and citations are placed in between a pair of <ref> tags in the text itself, where you want the footnote to appear. For example,

```
According to scientists, the Sun is pretty big<ref> Miller, E: "The Sun", page
23. Academic Press, 2005</ref>, however the moon is not so big.<ref>Smith, R:
"Size of the Moon", ''Scientific American'', 46(78):46</ref>.
```

This example cites two sources: a work by E. Miller published by Academic Press and a work by R. Smith published in *Scientific American*. The references will only display in the text as a numbered link to a footnote, which appears directly where you have placed the first <ref> tag. These numbers automatically update whenever a new footnote is added.

For a reader to actually see the references cited, you must add a second piece—the <references/> tag, which is inserted at the bottom of the article in a section called References or Notes. The text of all footnotes will appear wherever you place this tag (though placing <references/> before <ref> doesn't work). For instance, for the previous example, you would create a section that looks like this:

```
==Notes==
<references/>
```

Don't add anything to the <references/> tag; the linked references from the text will automatically display here:

```
==Notes==
# ^ Miller, E: "The Sun", page 23. Academic Press, 2005
# ^ Smith, R: "Size of the Moon", ''Scientific American'', 46(78):46
```

Each footnote starts with a caret (^), which is automatically linked back to the text where the reference was placed. To edit the reference, you change it directly in the article text rather than in the References section.

Though you don't need to add anything to the <references/> tag, you can list other, non-footnoted references in this section as well. Creating two sections, one called Notes (for footnotes) and one called References (for all other references) is better, however. This form also enables you to use short references in the footnotes (such as "Smith, p. 47"), as long as you spell out the full reference in the References section.

You can use the same footnote (that is, the same citation), and hence the same footnote number, more than once. To do this, insert the **name** variable in the <ref> tag, like this:

```
According to scientists, the Sun is pretty big<ref name="sun"> Miller, E: "The
Sun", page 23. Academic Press, 2005</ref>, however the moon is not so big.<ref
name="moon">Smith, R: "Size of the Moon", ''Scientific American'', 46(78):46</ref>.
```

To refer to each of these citations at a later point, you only need to refer to the abbreviated form of the reference with **ref name**:

```
The sun is also very hot <ref name="sun"/>. The moon, however, is cold <ref
name="moon"/>.
```

Be sure to add that last ending slash, or all the text after the reference won't display when you save the page!

These two references then use the same footnote numbers as the first reference using that name. In the footnotes section, links to each instance of the reference will appear next to the footnote that is used multiple times, labeled alphabetically: a, b, c, and so on.

Using `ref name` is the best way to cite a source multiple times within the text. The old academic convention of *ibid.* (short for *ibidem*, meaning this is the same book as mentioned in the previous note, but on a different page) is not robust enough. Someone could later add a footnote between your successive notes, and the second note wouldn't make sense. The inline system works because if text is edited or moved, the numbers follow automatically. Unfortunately, one limitation of the current footnoting system is that if you want to change any part of the cited reference (such as to cite a different page number) `ref name` doesn't work; you have to type out the entire reference again. If this becomes time consuming in a long article, consider using the short reference style in a Notes section with the full references in a separate References section.

Referencing Templates

Many templates have been developed for formatting citations. You can use templates to ensure that cited references for different types of sources (such as newspapers, books, etc.) are clearly displayed in a standardized way. You can also use citation templates both for formatting citations in footnotes or citations listed separately in a References section.

In a citation template, the editor fills in the template parameters with the source information (such as the author, title of the work, and so on) and the template automatically arranges the citation appropriately, according to the type of source. For instance, here is the wikitext of the citation for an online newspaper story using the {{news}} template:

```
{{cite news |last=Plunkett |first=John |url=http://media.guardian.co.uk/site/
story/0,14173,1601858,00.html |title=Sorrell accuses Murdoch of panic buying
|publisher=The Guardian |date=2005-10-27 |accessdate=2005-10-27}}
```

When you save the page, the reader sees the following citation:

```
Plunkett, John. "Sorrell accuses Murdoch of panic buying", The Guardian,
October 27, 2005. Retrieved on October 27, 2005.
```

with the title of the article linked to the given URL. Templates do the work of making sure citations are correctly formatted. They also help ensure that references include all the necessary information—not just a URL for a website but also a date—so articles can be accessed from an archive if the URL no longer works.

Some templates have been created for specific sources that are commonly cited. In this case, the main source information is already encoded in the template, so the editor only has to add variable information such as author name or article title. The full source citation will appear when the page is saved. For instance, the template {{Fishbase_species}} is for adding a link to FishBase, a scholarly online database of information about fish. In the [[Guppy]] article, the following citation appears:

```
{{FishBase_species|genus=Poecilia|species=reticulata|year=2004|month=April}}
```

The editor only fills in the genus and species information and the date that the site was accessed. The saved page renders this as the following citation:

```
"Poecilia reticulata". FishBase. Ed. Ranier Froese and Daniel Pauly. April 2004
version. N.p.: FishBase, 2004.
```

The title of the database, the editors, and the formatting of the citation are all encoded in the template. This is clearly useful if you're citing the same source multiple times. A list of specific source templates can be found at [[Category:Specific source templates]].

One problem with templates is that they are inflexible; for instance, if you want to wikilink the author name in the news example given, you'll have trouble because the author first and last names are in different fields. There are two solutions for this particular problem: Either don't use the template and write the citation out by hand, or add an extra field that has been developed just for this called *authorlink*, which can be filled out like |authorlink=[[John Plunket]] (for joint authors, you can use authorlink1= and authorlink2=).

As you can see, templates can get complicated. They can also make the wiki markup denser and harder to read, especially if they are used for in-text citations, and they may not add that much to the presentation of references. Templates are certainly optional. They can also be added gradually: Existing references can be converted to templates over time. More information about citation templates can be found at [[Wikipedia:Citation_templates]].

Editing Alongside Others

On Wikipedia, no article stands alone, and no editor works alone. Always consider
your own work both in the context of working with others on the site and taking
their perspectives into account and fitting new content into existing structures.
If you create an article with wikilinks, are you going to be satisfied with all the
pages you find when you click the bluelinks? The site has many articles that need
to be improved, so you'll likely also fix up and expand deficient articles to support
your own articles; you will also most likely come to work edit-by-edit in a piecemeal way. And as an editor you'll find yourself one of a crowd. In the collaborative
environment of Wikipedia, taking into account the input of others is critical. One of
the first questions that newcomers often ask is "What happens when two people
disagree?" The answer is the editors involved try to work toward *consensus*, which
is one of the cornerstones of how Wikipedia works. In Chapter 14, we'll cover the
general idea of getting consensus and resolving disputes in depth; here we'll
give some specific advice on how to work with others productively when editing
articles.

Changing What Others Write

Edit in logical steps rather than in single large edits. If a lot of work needs to be
done on an article, many editing tasks will suggest themselves; if this is the case,
you need a plan of action. For instance, restructuring the logical flow of an article
is more fundamental than rewording and should take priority. Usually, you determine to change certain things about an article but probably not everything, nor
all at once. This is the best way. Making changes in discrete logical steps, using
good edit summaries (and sometimes a note on the talk page) can help others
figure out, and accept, what you're doing to the article. Set yourself limited and
reasonable goals, for instance, choosing a single section to improve content and
wording.

Sometimes, a total rewrite of a page is definitely called for. You then are
effectively pasting a new article on top, and the diff may show just a few words like
and and *the* that were kept. This does pose potential problems. You should aim
to keep anything of value that was already in the article, and the best approach is
for the article to demonstrate a steady improvement, stepwise and sectionwise.

Otherwise, you risk coming under suspicion that you are adopting a high-handed approach. If you hate some format or other minor convention being used, add a note to the talk page before going in and switching it all around. Making wholesale formatting changes across many articles without asking for input from others is likely to cause controversy.

Will Your Own Edits Be Kept?

Added text is not always kept on Wikipedia. Pages can always be rewritten or reverted back to how they were before. Whole articles are subject to deletion if other editors think they fail to meet basic site policies (though decently written, well-researched pieces are much less likely to be deleted). Articles you write will be changed by others, and at some point someone will redo or undo a major change that you have made. While this is a natural part of working on Wikipedia, adding material that is routinely taken out at some later point ultimately becomes fooling around. Will this wholesale rejection happen to you? If you spend any serious amount of time writing for Wikipedia, you'll feel you've wasted it if your edits or articles are not incorporated on the site in some fashion.

Be clear about a few things. The question "Does the encyclopedia need this article?" is quite distinct from the question "Does this addition or change to the article benefit the encyclopedia?" Articles are subject to deletion, but individual edits are also subject to reversion or rewriting. New additions to articles are subject to the same content and style policies as articles overall, but individual edits are discussed in a different way. Articles that have some deficiencies are given the benefit of the doubt and are in time worked on and cleaned up. Only articles that demonstrate a scanty grasp of basic policies should be dealt with harshly. Individual edits, though, may just be reverted as substandard. Try to understand why the edit was undone. Are you simply wrong about a point or inserting opinion as fact? Did you cite a reference?

Suppose your general edits to articles are often rejected by other editors. What can you do? If Wikipedia policies rewarded stubbornness, the site would have overloaded years ago. There are good approaches to editing that are not merely defensive and obstinate. First, you should watch and monitor articles you're interested in, as explained in Chapter 11. Second, consider your choice of topics: Don't always head into controversy, and don't be a stormy petrel, bringing trouble with you. Some topics are certainly more contentious than others; as a new editor, you may want to start working on articles dealing with less controversial topics (starting with articles about politics or historical disputes is never a good idea). Third, be broadminded. Appreciate where other editors are coming from. They may be at least as reasonable and well informed as you, and they probably have a different perspective on the matter. Recognize that others might have a good reason for disagreeing with you: This is a core tenet of *assuming good faith*, which is fundamental for interacting on Wikipedia, as will be described in Chapter 12. Finally, if you can't honestly be neutral on a topic, don't blame the encyclopedia— work on topics you're less invested in.

The best way to make sure your edits are kept is to submit good content in the first place; watch your writing style and incorporate our guide on writing well and other style tips. If you write on Wikipedia in a hurried way, then you can expect your edits to be transformed, if they are kept at all. Use careful, concise English, and place everything in context. This book contains more than enough advice to ensure that a reader who follows it will be a Wikipedian who adds welcome material.

If your submitted articles are deleted, you need to understand the article deletion process and how to contest deletions appropriately (see Chapter 7). You should also make your pieces conform more obviously to content policies. Many newly submitted articles are deleted every day on Wikipedia: approximately one every minute. The reason for deletion is usually self-evident. The articles very clearly don't meet the site's guidelines, which means they often qualify for *speedy deletion*, or deletion without review.

Finally, seek satisfaction in the work you do on Wikipedia. In the end you should find an area where contributing is not too stressful socially and benefits writing and researching or maintaining the site in other ways. *Wikihappiness* is finding the work that best suits you, without preconceptions.

Edit Summaries

We'll now cover edit summaries in more depth; we introduced them briefly in Chapter 4. An *edit summary* is simply a line of text that you supply when editing and saving a page. Edit summaries document the work of upgrading articles. Other editors will use them to check and assess your work and approach, which is only fair since you'll learn to do the same in return. Good edit summaries are a confidence-building measure and are particularly recommended if you're editing in a contentious area. Getting into the habit of adding summaries will help your reputation as an editor and will help others on the site.

Before you save a page, write a summary of what you're doing to the article in the Edit summary box underneath the Edit window. This edit summary is then carried along with your edit (or *diff*) and is displayed in the page history and in lists of changes to articles, such as Recent Changes and watchlists. Edit summaries have a 200-character limit, but you can say a lot in 200 characters. A good edit summary briefly describes the changes you made, and if those changes are not self-evident, why you've made them. Edit summaries are not searched or indexed, so all important information should be added to the discussion page as well.

Standard abbreviations and jargon are commonly used (but are not required). You will notice this right away. Some types of summaries are characteristic of automated (*bot*) edits or other semi-automated tools, and recognizing these edits is useful. For articles you are interested in, you also want to watch for any summaries relating to deletion processes. A list of edit summary jargon is in Appendix C.

Although no one can make you use edit summaries, they matter a great deal in social terms. Edit summaries make Wikipedia work more smoothly. Some standard situations pretty much demand a summary:

▶ Deleting the work of others

▶ Calling attention to talk page threads when a long, detailed explanation is required

▶ Revamping an article in a major way, saving each block of changes with a separate description

▶ Informing others when not everyone will have the background and knowledge about a topic you have, even if the change seems minor

▶ Tagging and untagging and site maintenance

▶ Splitting content out to form a new page, where edit summaries are required in two places to provide an audit trail, so anyone can see where the "new" content came from and where the "old" content went (under the GFDL license requirements, the original authorship should be accessible from the new page's history)

▶ Nominating a page to be deleted

Wikipedia adds an automatic prefix to summaries when you edit a section; in all such cases, you should supplement that with an explanation of what you did.

Edit summaries should answer the question, "Why was this edit made?"—particularly when corrections have been made to an article. For example, in correcting a date for a historical event, consider combining three things: adding an explicit reference in the article itself, writing an edit summary saying "date corrected according to scholarly consensus, see talk page for details," and supplying more backup in a talk page note. Give details at reasonable length. A more detailed explanation (up to a point) is generally better than a vague one: "Rewrote history section for clarity" is better than "rewriting." However, for minor edits, simply noting "spelling" or "typo" is fine.

No Ownership

Remember one thing: However much time you put in to writing or polishing an article, others will still be entitled to edit it. An article is never *yours* alone. The bottom line for authors is that the culture of Wikipedia is *can do*, including *can edit*, meaning that *anyone* is welcome to edit any page. Don't growl, be territorial, or kick up a fuss over this; obstinacy ("You cannot be serious about cutting my work") is not the wiki way.

Never seek to control an article on Wikipedia. Once posted, Wikipedia pages are not only released under an open license, but also they are released into the open and collaborative editing environment, where anyone is both free and encouraged to work on the page. If you disagree with someone's changes to an article you started, work to resolve this dispute on the talk page and come to consensus as you would on any other page. See [[Wikipedia:Ownership of articles]] (shortcut WP:OWN) for a fundamental policy on editorial behavior. And remember the positive benefits of working with others: They will bring a different perspective to the article, may fix mistakes that you never saw, and will add content to the page.

Further Reading

http://en.wikipedia.org/wiki/Wikipedia:Consensus   The fundamental policy on getting consensus and advice on how to get there

http://en.wikipedia.org/wiki/Wikipedia:Edit_summary   All about using edit summaries to communicate

http://en.wikipedia.org/wiki/Wikipedia:Ownership_of_articles   The policy on not assuming "ownership" of what you write

---

Summary

Much of what is needed to become a good contributor to Wikipedia derives from skills that are more generally useful, such as researching and organizing material, writing clearly and logically for a broad audience, and supporting claims with detailed references. Any logged-in user with a registered account can start a new article easily; the best way to begin an article is to start with a redlink on another page. Wikipedia has several style conventions for article titles and how they should be put together. The *Manual of Style*, a collection of style guidelines, provides guidance on how best to style an article. Both good writing and good research skills are critical to producing an excellent article.

A skilled Wikipedia editor must also be patient and consider the work and input of others as he or she edits. Editing is collective, so an editor should comprehend and use the spaces and forums to interact and should treat other editors as colleagues.

7

Cleanup, Projects, and Processes

Please don't say you're at a loss for something to do on Wikipedia today. There is far too much that needs to be fixed for that! Wikipedia's broad concept of cleanup includes most tasks to improve articles once they have been created. Any time you need a break from writing new articles, you'll find plenty of work waiting for you on existing ones.

Work on Wikipedia is self-directed. You can create your own tasks or look into the wide variety of projects and processes for improving and maintaining Wikipedia content in particular areas. You can almost always find someone else who is interested in working in the same areas as you are.

In this chapter, we'll talk about some of the available cleanup tasks and the collaborative projects that have been set up for maintaining articles. We'll also introduce *processes*, the review structures that have been set up to allow interested editors to discuss articles and perform certain formal tasks. Processes are the practical implementation of policies and provide a structure for day-to-day work. We'll discuss two of the biggest processes: deleting articles and promoting good content. The activities described in this chapter are at the heart of the collaborative editing and article improvement that make Wikipedia work.

Cleanup

If you see a message with a yellow bar at the beginning of an article, along with the icon of a broom chasing out the dust, that's a tag indicating the article needs to be cleaned up. Although the majority of articles could be improved—after all, Wikipedia is never finished—some are clearly in more desperate need of help than others. These neglected articles require cleanup.

Cleanup is simply the general term for improving articles. The vast majority of tasks on Wikipedia fall under this broad heading: Sourcing, formatting, rewriting, and linking are all cleanup tasks. Although anyone is free to work on any task at any time, Wikipedia has developed a variety of mechanisms to sort out articles in need of help, so editors can find them and address cleanup issues more easily. In this section, we'll describe the basic mechanism for identifying and flagging articles as needing help, and then we'll discuss the broad categories of issues and how to find articles with these issues.

Spending at least some time on cleanup tasks is helpful for any Wikipedian. Working on articles that need to be cleaned up reveals the kinds of problems that Wikipedia faces, and dealing with similar issues and problems in a number of articles is an excellent way to learn Wikipedia style and develop proficiency at encyclopedic writing (and by extension, any type of writing). Cleanup is also one of the best ways to contribute; Wikipedia always has a tremendous backlog of cleanup needing to be done. Thoroughly improving a poorly written article can also be immensely satisfying: You can always compare the before and after versions of the article from the page history to see just how much you accomplished.

Most people start volunteering by exploring and trying out small cleanup jobs. Try different kinds of editing tasks to see what suits you. The authors of this book have different tasks they like to do on Wikipedia: Phoebe likes merging and fact-checking, whereas Charles prefers creating redirects. Many people end up focusing on one or two tasks—copyediting or referencing, for instance. As described in "Projects: Working to Improve Content" on page 212, many of these tasks have dedicated WikiProjects where groups of interested editors work on them: WikiProject League of Copyeditors (shortcut WP:LoCE) caters to those interested in stylistic editing, whereas WikiProject Fact and Reference Check (shortcut WP:FACT) is for fact-checkers.

Flagging Articles

When editors encounter articles that need to be cleaned up, they have two options: They can immediately fix the problems, or they can flag the article with a message describing the problem for another editor to clean up later. Once articles have been flagged, other editors can then systematically work their way through all the ones tagged as having a particular issue.

These *flags* or *tags* are the cleanup messages you'll see at the top of many articles. They are produced by *templates*, small pieces of code that can be included on pages to produce standardized messages. As noted in Chapter 5, to add a template to a page, you simply enclose the name of the template in double curly brackets and place it on the page where you want it to appear.

For instance, you can find the generic cleanup template at [[Template: Cleanup]]. To flag an article as needing cleanup using this template, insert this code at the very top of the article:

```
{{cleanup}}
```

This will create the message shown in Figure 7-1.

FIGURE 7-1: *The cleanup template message*

If an article has several issues, multiple cleanup templates may be stacked on top of each other. An editor may also replace a general cleanup message with a more specific message as the particular issue becomes clear: For instance, if the article needs to be rewritten for clarity, you would flag it with the {{confusing}} template instead of the more general {{cleanup}} template. Template messages now exist for most conceivable problems. The long list of cleanup messages is available at [[Wikipedia:Template messages/Cleanup]] (shortcut WP:TC); we also list some of these templates in the sections that follow.

If an editor fixes an article so the cleanup message is no longer needed, he or she can remove the template message by simply editing the page and removing the template tag. If the editor only partially addresses the problem, he or she may remove only the appropriate template message if more than one has been added to the article or add a note on the talk page detailing what's been done and what's left to do. Although an editor sometimes forgets to remove a template when cleaning up an article, be careful about removing templates if you aren't sure all the issues have been addressed because content-related templates also serve as warnings to readers.

Most cleanup templates can also be dated, so you can see how long an article has been in need of cleanup. For the general cleanup tag, adding a date looks like this:

```
{{cleanup|date=November 2007}}
```

This tag adds the date to the template message and sorts the article into a cleanup-by-month category.

Although the cleanup process is thus somewhat subjective—no hard and fast rules on when to add any particular template exist, and anyone can add or remove templates—using the template message system allows several different editors (who may otherwise never be in touch) to clean up an article using a loose process and helps readers know when an article has problems.

Cleanup Categories

Adding a cleanup message to an article will automatically place the article in an associated cleanup category. This way editors can easily find all the articles tagged as needing a certain kind of cleanup; they can simply go to the category and get to work. For instance, articles tagged with {{cleanup}} are placed in [[Category:All pages needing cleanup]]. Articles tagged with a dated cleanup tag are automatically sorted into a cleanup-by-month category as well (in the example above, [[Category:Cleanup from November 2007]]), so those with older tags can be worked on first. This also makes the large cleanup category more manageable. If you edit out the template to remove it, the article will automatically be removed from the cleanup category.

Of course, flagging articles is easier than actually cleaning them up. This is reflected in some of the large cleanup categories. These categories have *backlogs*—large numbers of articles awaiting attention. Wikipedia's rapid growth has perhaps made this inevitable. Because there is so much to do, adding a template for every issue isn't really helpful, as this may, in fact, mask an article's worst issues; if a quick edit can resolve the problem, instead of adding a template, go ahead and fix it (the *sofixit* principle described in Chapter 13). Make sure, however, that you flag the biggest issues if you can't fix them right away. As of early 2008, roughly 31,000 articles are in [[Category:All pages needing cleanup]]. Working in this category can be overwhelming; on the other hand, 31,000 represents less than 2 percent of the total number of articles on Wikipedia at this time.

Cleanup Tasks

The most comprehensive place to look for a list of collaborative cleanup projects is [[Wikipedia:Maintenance]] (shortcut WP:MAINT). This page gives an overview of all sorts of cleanup tasks, from the simple to the complex. So many tasks are listed that you might not know where to start. What *is* WikiProject Red Link Recovery?

Well, this project aims to turn redlinks to bluelinks by automating the process of finding close title matches and suggesting redirects.

If you would rather edit by topic, joining a WikiProject may be the best route (see "WikiProjects" on page 213). Alternatively, you can simply scan a list of articles in any topic area to find one that looks interesting and is in need of help. Try [[Category:To do]], which shows articles with *to-do* lists on their talk pages or [[Wikipedia:Cleanup]] for a selected list of articles that need to be cleaned up, along with brief explanations of what needs to be done. If you can clean up one of these articles completely, simply edit the page to remove it from the list.

Cleanup may be basic Wikipedia work, but it still offers challenges and interesting insights. Sometimes articles will require complete restructuring. Some will need to be rewritten: Refer to "Handling Major Editing Tasks" on page 138 for a general approach to handling major edits, and heed the advice in Chapter 6 about keeping the material that can be saved and working so cleanup doesn't leave big breaks and surprise diffs in the page history.

Rewriting

Every article in Wikipedia should aspire to elegant and clear prose that explains a topic gracefully and logically. Unfortunately, this aspiration is far from always being realized.

Poor writing creeps into Wikipedia in different ways:

▶ An article may start with a poorly written draft. The original author may not be a proficient writer or English may be his or her second language.

▶ An article may have gradually become unclear. Articles that have been copyedited in pieces over time, improving the wording but neglecting the logical flow, may still need to be thoroughly rewritten. Perhaps small pieces of information have been added over time, but the article now lacks structure.

▶ Finally, an article may be clearly written but have an inappropriate tone or style for an encyclopedia. An article may lack a neutral point of view, demonstrating an editorial bias toward an event, a product, or a person. An article may also read like a press release, a product announcement, or even an advertisement.

Articles that need language help can be flagged in a variety of ways. Additionally, many of the articles flagged with the generic cleanup tag actually need to be rewritten.

Numerous explicit cleanup tags address the question of poor writing. To see articles flagged with any of these templates, you can go to the template page (such as [[Template:Copyedit]]); generally, the categories articles are placed into will be noted here, or you can click What Links Here from the template page. For instance:

▶ {{copyedit}}   Addresses any problem with grammar, style, cohesion, tone or spelling

▶ {{advert}}, {{fansite}}, {{gameguide}}, {{likeresume}}, {{newsrelease}}, {{obit}}, {{review}}, {{story}}   Address problems with inappropriate tone and style

► `{{abbreviations}}`, `{{buzzword}}`, `{{cleanup-jargon}}`, `{{inappropriate person}}`, `{{quotefarm}}`, `{{toospecialized}}`   Address composition problems

► `{{contradict}}`, `{{misleading}}`, `{{unbalanced}}`, `{{limitedgeographicscope}}`, `{{weasel}}`   Address problems with content and presentation

Depending on the level of problems, many approaches to rewriting articles exist. Guidelines for good articles are given in the *Manual of Style* and a variety of essays on the subject (see Chapter 6), but the most important goal is that information be clearly conveyed to the reader, in line with the content policies. For unclear wording, consider clearer ways to provide explanations without sacrificing facts or ideas. Readers will benefit when you're done. To find other editors interested in writing and copyediting, consider joining the League of Copyeditors WikiProject.

Expanding Stubs

Stub articles are beginning articles that need to be expanded with more information on the topic. Hundreds of thousands of articles have been marked as stubs in all topic areas—so many that stub-sorting by topic is itself a key maintenance task. If you don't want to write an entire article from scratch but enjoy the research and writing process, try expanding one of these articles. Don't forget, however, that new information should be well referenced.

A list of all stub types (which, in turn, links to specific categories for each type) is maintained at [[Wikipedia:WikiProject Stub sorting]]. When working on these articles, review more mature articles in the same topic area. What information is missing? Does an article about an author, for instance, contain a bibliography of the author's work?

Wikipedia has no hard-and-fast rules about how long a stub can get before it is no longer a stub. If an article seems reasonably complete or it seems like a long article, you can probably remove the stub message. If an article seems longer than a stub but still needs to be expanded, flag it with the `{{expand}}` template.

Wikification

Wikification is the changing of any text into wikitext, including marking it with wikisyntax, structuring the article into logical sections, and adding internal links.

Wikification can easily turn into rewriting and fact-checking because, fundamentally, you are converting ordinary prose into Wikipedia hypertext. *Wikification*, in this broader sense, means "formatting according to Wikipedia style." Experienced Wikipedia editors probably wikify before serious rewriting for prose style because wikification brings articles closer to encyclopedic considerations and helps flag related material in other articles.

When you wikify, be alert to other issues:

▶ If the article is a dead-end article with no wikilinks leading from it, check What Links Here to make sure the article isn't also an orphan article without incoming links. These two problems often occur in the same article. Part of wikifying may be adding appropriate links to the article from other pages.

▶ You may need to add sections to the text or rewrite the lead topic sentence to be more encyclopedic. If the whole logical flow of an article is wrong, give that the highest priority of all.

▶ Poorly formatted content should usually also be examined for compliance with notability standards and factual accuracy as well; poor formatting is often a sign that the content was added by someone unfamiliar with Wikipedia.

▶ Wrong tone can be a clue to copyright issues; see "Copyright Violations" on page 208.

Formatting Articles

Sometimes articles in need of stylistic help turn out to not be suitable for the encyclopedia: They may duplicate other older articles, be about non-notable topics, or even be hoaxes. If you see an article with a questionable topic, don't be afraid to ask for a second opinion before spending a great deal of time formatting it. You may also need to add other tags to the article as you edit, such as Citation Needed for questionable statements.

Flag articles that need to be wikified by using the `{{wikify}}` template (Figure 7-2). The article will then be added to [[Category:Articles that need to be wikified]]. The Wikification effort is supported by [[Wikipedia:WikiProject Wikify]] (shortcut WP:WWF). A related cleanup tag is `{{sections}}`, which places articles in [[Category:Articles needing sections]].

Fact-Checking and Referencing

Good sources boost the quality of articles. Sources give the reader a place to find more information when they have finished reading the Wikipedia article, as well helping to ensure stated facts are accurate. Verifiability and Reliable Sources

FIGURE 7-2: *Wikify template message*

(shortcuts WP:V and WP:RS) are key content policies, as discussed in Chapter 1. However, *verifiability*, which means the ability to verify something *in principle*, differs from actually providing verifiable sources. Many Wikipedia articles fall a little short here. Older articles from the more free-wheeling days on Wikipedia may not cite sources at all, whereas other articles may cite sources for only a few of the ideas in the text or not contain footnotes in the text itself.

Sourcing is an ongoing process: Compiling a good bibliography for any topic, even a small one, is a big task. For some topics, you may have trouble finding any reliable sources, and accurate referencing work in these instances is particularly valuable. When original authors do not source their facts, various fact-checking projects perform this work.

Wikipedia has several templates that alert both editors and readers that citations are needed in an article:

▸ {{unreferenced}}   This template places articles in [[Category:Articles lacking sources]]. Use when an article doesn't cite any sources at all.

▸ {{refimprove}}   This template places articles in [[Category:Articles lacking reliable references]]. Use when some sources exist but more are needed.

▸ {{citeneeded}}   The more usual {{citeneeded}} or {{fact}} both place an article in [[Category:All articles with unsourced statements]]. Unlike the first two templates, add these templates inline in the article text wherever the problem occurs (Figure 7-3). For instance, if an article contains a questionable or controversial statement that needs a reference, you can insert the {{fact}} template at the end of the sentence in question.

FIGURE 7-3: *The inline Citation Needed tag*

Sourcing can be time-consuming, but you can add sources to articles gradually. If you can find an outside, reliable source for just one fact mentioned in an article, adding a footnote with this source is quite helpful. If you have a more general source for the article's subject but haven't used it as a source for specific facts in the article, consider starting a Further reading or External links section and listing the source as a place for readers to get more information. For instance, you may want to list definitive biographies for articles on noteworthy people in Further reading or add links to online primary source documents for historical articles in External links. Every article should be as well sourced as possible.

If you are knowledgeable about a particular topic area and want to concentrate on finding sources for that area, joining a WikiProject (as described in "Projects: Working to Improve Content" on page 212) is the easiest way to find articles on that topic that need to be improved.

Help, an Article About Me Is Incorrect!

Wikipedia does not want articles to include mistaken statements, particularly those damaging to people or commercial ventures. On the other hand, Wikipedia content is not determined by outside pressures; neutrality is a key principle, and Wikipedia is not a mechanism for promotion. Therefore, inaccurate information and unfair criticism without a factual basis should not appear in Wikipedia articles; but fair criticism, properly sourced and presented in a balanced way, is not going to be removed from Wikipedia just because the subject or anyone else wants it removed.

If an article about you or your company is factually incorrect, you have several options, but you should first assess the best way to get corrections made.

Discussion

First, remember to take into account the guidelines and policies presented in Chapter 1. All articles must be neutrally presented, factually accurate and verifiable, and about notable, encyclopedic topics. Issues regarding factual inaccuracies can be discussed on the talk page for any article. This is the best first step toward getting a problem resolved. Give a calm account of where the article is factually wrong, and back up your argument with outside references. This should prompt those editing the article to correct it.

Editing

You can also, of course, simply edit the article; but before doing so, please consult [[Wikipedia:Conflict of interest]] (shortcut WP:COI). This guideline distinguishes defamatory comments (which anyone, including you, may remove) from other inaccuracies. Two further relevant pages are [[Wikipedia: Biographies of Living persons]] (shortcut WP:BLP) and [[Wikipedia:Auto-biography]] (shortcut WP:AUTO). Wikipedia has strict guidelines on what can be written about living people, and WP:BLP will help you argue for deletion if someone has posted a hostile piece about you. On the other hand, WP:AUTO (subordinate to the conflict of interest guideline) explains why autobiographical writing is strongly discouraged—under most circumstances, you should not edit an article about yourself.

Email route

If discussing the issue on the talk page does not resolve it, even after you have drawn an administrator's attention to it, do not be tempted to force the issue, make threats, or abuse the editors who are working on the article. Those approaches are likely to be counterproductive. Your best recourse is to send an email, as explained at [[Wikipedia:OTRS]] (shortcut WP:OTRS), detailing the problem. This channel is the official complaint mechanism. If your complaint has any substance, an experienced volunteer will review the article and work to resolve problems.

Copyright Violations

You can often spot copyright violations on Wikipedia simply by their tone. Material from another source usually doesn't read like an encyclopedia article. Most copyright violations are caused by people cutting and pasting material from other sites into an article, which you can detect by searching the Web for the passage. Be sure to search for selected phrases from middle or particular unlikely sounding sentences; editors tend to change introductory and concluding sentences.

If you locate a probable source for some article text, the next question is how much text was copied. If only a sentence or two was copied and the source is simply unattributed, then rewriting and citing the source may solve the problem. If, however, an entire article or most of it has been copied from a single source (as is more common with cut-and-paste violations), then a copyright violation has occurred. Be aware, though, that Wikipedia does include, legitimately, much public domain text and that other sites mirror Wikipedia content—double-check that the other website is not copying Wikipedia, rather than the other way around!

You have a few options for removing copyright violations:

▶ First, the text can be reverted to a good version. Check the page history to see if a clean version exists; if so, simply revert to this good version, adding an appropriate edit summary.

▶ If you're having trouble figuring out if a good version exists, you can always rewrite the text yourself. Be careful that you aren't simply paraphrasing. Strip out most of the detail and start over, citing each fact to a source as you reinsert it. Be sure to add a note to the talk page explaining why you cut article text.

▶ If you are unable to revert or rewrite, flag confirmed copyright violations using the {{copyvio}} tag, which will place the article in a category of possible copyright violations for experienced editors to check.

▶ If you aren't certain that a copyright violation has occurred, use {{copyvio|url=}}, which will trigger a more measured deletion process. After the equal sign, paste in the URL from which you think the material may have been copied. Detailed instructions can be found at [[Wikipedia: Copyright problems]] (shortcut WP:CP).

▶ If you are sure the article violates copyright and that the text or topic doesn't seem to have any redeeming value, you may want to use the speedy delete tag `{{db-copyvio}}`, which will ensure rapid administrator attention (see "Deletion Processes" on page 220).

See [[Wikipedia:Spotting possible copyright violations]] (shortcut WP:SPCP) for more information. If *your* copyright is being infringed in an article, see [[Wikipedia:Contact us/Article problem/Copyright]]; several experienced editors work on resolving copyright issues.

Vandalism Patrolling

Vandalism patrolling, though formally neither a project nor a process, is some of the most important ongoing work on Wikipedia. *Vandalism* is, by definition, a change made to Wikipedia with the malicious intention of having a negative effect on the content. Disputes over content may lead to accusations of vandalism, but no editor should *ever* use the word lightly—always *assume good faith* unless you have very good reason not to. Any good-faith effort to improve the encyclopedia, even if misguided or ill-considered, is *not* vandalism. See [[Wikipedia:Vandalism]] (shortcut WP:VAN) for a general perspective on the topic and [[Wikipedia:Administrator intervention against vandalism]] (shortcut WP:AIV) for a place to file reports against the most problematic editors.

Anyone can just revert obvious vandalism that they see, of course; check the history page and then edit or use the undo version if you're logged in to revert an article to a version before the vandalism occurred, as explained in Chapter 5. (With either method, check the *diff* of the current version with the version you are reverting to make sure you're only undoing vandalism, and then add an edit summary: *rvv vandalism* is common.) Many editors use their watchlists for just this purpose, scanning the list of changes on a regular basis to check for suspect edits that might be vandalism. Others devote substantial time to watching Recent Changes and other logs. Most vandalism is obvious: cutting content for no reason or inserting obscenities, crude humor, or nonsense. If you find a vandalized page, you should spend a couple of minutes reviewing the page history; vandal edits tend to be clustered, and you may have to revert several edits to find the "latest good version" or a version of the page that hasn't been vandalized at all (see "Fixing Mistakes and Other Reasons to Revert" on page 140).

If you can't tell whether an edit is vandalism, check the *diff* of the edit along with the editing history of the user who made the edit to make a final determination. If an edit seems potentially realistic but is unsourced and uncommented, you can always tag it appropriately (with the Citation Needed template, for instance), leave a comment on the talk page, or revert it but copy the text of the edit to the talk page for others to verify one way or the other.

Most vandalism follows a pattern. The *soft security* concept, which will be discussed again in Chapter 12, is worth mentioning here. Wikipedia is open to everyone, so bad edits will happen. As noted in Chapter 4, however, most of these edits are caught quickly. The offenders are often young, and most vandalism is juvenile. Some persistent or more subtle vandals can succeed for a while. But Wikipedia defends in depth, not just with one front line. Wikipedia works by self-healing.

Many tools and systems have been developed to detect (and sometimes automatically correct) vandal edits; the Counter-Vandalism Unit, found at [[Wikipedia:Counter-Vandalism Unit]] (shortcut WP: CVU), is a collection of editors interested in this work (Figure 7-4 shows its logo).

Cleanup Editing Tools

Besides vandalism repair, many cleanup editing tasks (such as correcting spelling or fixing typos) are repetitive, and for these you can use editing tools. These tools help *power editors* get dull tasks done quickly (though editors are always responsible for

FIGURE 7-4: *Counter-Vandalism Unit logo*

the edits they make, regardless of whether they used an automated tool or not).

One popular application is the AutoWiki Browser. Here is a description from its page at [[Wikipedia:AutoWikiBrowser]] (shortcut WP:AWB):

> The AutoWikiBrowser is a semi-automated Wikipedia editor for Microsoft Windows 2000/XP (or newer) designed to make tedious repetitive tasks quicker and easier. It is essentially a browser that automatically opens up a new page when the last is saved. When set to do so, it suggests some changes (typically formatting) that are generally meant to be incidental to the main change.

This tool and other automated tools are meant for experienced editors only; learn the ropes by editing by hand. You can find many other tools, including tools for editing quickly, at [[Wikipedia:Tools]].

Further Reading

General Cleanup Tasks

http://en.wikipedia.org/wiki/Wikipedia:Maintenance   A list of many different maintenance tasks

http://en.wikipedia.org/wiki/Wikipedia:Template_Messages   A reference to the template messages used on Wikipedia, including all the cleanup templates

http://en.wikipedia.org/wiki/Category:Cleanup_by_month   All pages that are tagged as needing "cleanup," arranged by month

http://en.wikipedia.org/wiki/Category:Wikipedia_backlog   A list of various cleanup tasks that have large backlogs of articles needing work

http://en.wikipedia.org/wiki/Category:Wikipedia_cleanup_categories
A category containing all cleanup categories

Further Reading, continued

Rewriting

http://en.wikipedia.org/wiki/Wikipedia:WikiProject_League_of_Copyeditors   A copyediting and rewriting project

http://en.wikipedia.org/wiki/Category:Wikipedia_articles_needing_copy_edit   The category of articles that need copyediting

http://en.wikipedia.org/wiki/Category:Wikipedia_articles_needing_style_editing   The category of articles that need to be edited for style

http://en.wikipedia.org/wiki/Category:Wikipedia_articles_needing_rewrite   Articles that may need to be rewritten completely

Expansion and Stubs

http://en.wikipedia.org/wiki/Wikipedia:WikiProject_Stub_sorting   The WikiProject that organizes stub classification

http://en.wikipedia.org/wiki/Wikipedia:WikiProject_Stub_sorting/Stub_types   All stub articles, sorted by topic

http://en.wikipedia.org/wiki/Category:All_articles_to_be_expanded   Articles that need expansion (may not be stubs)

Wikification

http://en.wikipedia.org/wiki/Wikipedia:WikiProject_Wikify   The WikiProject covering wiki formatting tasks

http://en.wikipedia.org/wiki/Category:Articles_that_need_to_be_wikified   Articles that need to be formatted to conform to Wikipedia's style guidelines

http://en.wikipedia.org/wiki/Wikipedia:Dead-end_pages   Pages that contain no internal links to other pages (and thus need to be wikified)

Copyright Violations

http://en.wikipedia.org/wiki/Wikipedia:Copyright_problems   The page for listing and reviewing possible copyright violations and a good place to ask for a second opinion on an article's copyright status

Further Reading, continued

Fact-Checking

**http://en.wikipedia.org/wiki/Wikipedia:WikiProject_Fact_and_Reference_
Check**   The fact- and reference-check WikiProject

http://en.wikipedia.org/wiki/Category:Articles_lacking_sources   Articles with
no sources, sorted by month

http://en.wikipedia.org/wiki/Category:Articles_with_unsourced_statements
Articles with some unsourced statements, sorted by month

http://en.wikipedia.org/wiki/Wikipedia:Biographies_of_living_persons   The
biographies of living persons policy

http://searchengineland.com/070807-085103.php   An article by a Wikipedia
administrator about the correct way to go about fixing your own or your client's
inaccurate Wikipedia article

Vandalism

http://en.wikipedia.org/wiki/Wikipedia:Vandalism   About different kinds of
vandalism

http://en.wikipedia.org/wiki/Wikipedia:Cleaning_up_vandalism   An introduction to cleaning up vandalism

Cleanup Editing Tools

http://en.wikipedia.org/wiki/Wikipedia:AutoWikiBrowser
The AutoWikiBrowser tool

http://en.wikipedia.org/wiki/Wikipedia:Tools/Editing_tools   Other editing tools

Projects: Working to Improve Content

> The fundamental problem of the Wikipedia method is that massive
> collaboration is *hard*.
>
> —David Gerard, *WikiEN-l* mailing list, 9 October 2007

After being created by individuals, articles are often brought up to a much higher
standard within the broader community of Wikipedia editors. Two types of systems, projects and processes, have developed to work on Wikipedia content
from different directions. *Projects* are loose social groups on the site. In contrast,
processes, discussed later in the chapter, focus on making editorial and other
decisions following specific guidelines. In other words, projects use the more

casual idea of workflow, but processes move articles or decisions from one stage to another, more like a factory.

WikiProjects

A WikiProject is a loose grouping of editors who have banded together. There isn't actually a WikiProject Frogs—but there is a WikiProject Amphibians and Reptiles. WikiProject Philately and WikiProject Skateboarding both exist as well. Some projects are quite specific, whereas others focus on a broad area, such as WikiProject Chemistry, which works on articles related to all areas of chemistry (Figure 7-5). WikiProject Novels "aims to define a standard of consistency for articles about Novels." This aim is typical for a WikiProject: to prescribe certain aspects of structure or format for articles. Such a project takes an interest in developing helpful templates and guidelines for writing about a particular subject area. Projects may also work on rating articles in their area, developing portals and other navigational structures, and determining what articles are missing.

A Note on Naming

WikiProjects are pages that exist within the Wikipedia namespace. The convention for naming them is to use WikiProject (with the *P* capitalized) and then the name of the project. Thus the full internal page name to link to, for instance, WikiProject Chemistry, is [[Wikipedia:WikiProject Chemistry]].

Wikipedia has hundreds of different projects, each addressing a topic area or specific maintenance or cleanup task. The best reason to participate in projects is that they operate on a smaller scale, whereas Wikipedia is enormous. Within the big city of Wikipedia, projects operate more like a small village, where it's easier to to get to know and work with other editors who are interested in the same topics.

There are two types of WikiProjects:

Topical WikiProjects

These projects focus on improving and managing articles in a single topic area. They usually serve as a place for documenting and discussing changes and provide a natural forum (on the talk page for the project's main page) for discussing a topic area. They may provide centralized "to-do" lists for coordinating articles among interested editors.

Maintenance WikiProjects

These projects focus on Wikipedia maintenance and general cleanup tasks by coordinating efforts to clean up needy articles, perhaps using several

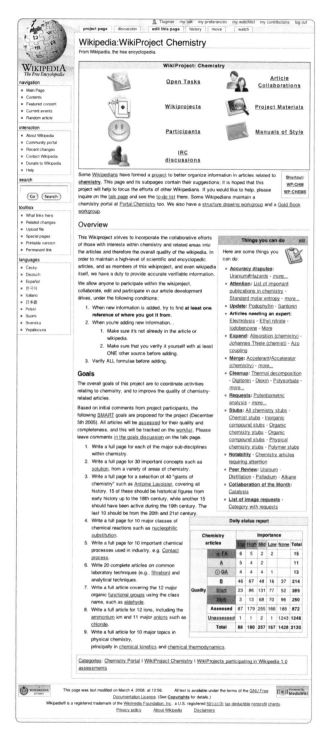

FIGURE 7-5: *The WikiProject Chemistry page*

template types. These projects simply help aggregate the work with formal project pages that describe the tasks needing to be done and techniques for doing them.

A list of both types of projects can be found at [[Wikipedia:WikiProject_Council/Directory]].

To join a WikiProject, simply add your username to the list of interested editors and take on one of the jobs that might be listed. Of course, you don't have to join a project before working on articles in that area! People generally take on tasks on their own initiative. Formal assignments and other kinds of top-down management are pretty much nonexistent. Projects vary in their level of formality and activity; some have editors who provide regular updates about a topic area and active groups who work on tasks or rate articles, whereas other projects simply provide an occasionally updated list of articles that need work.

Any editor who thinks they have a good idea for a project can create a project page, and then other interested editors are free to join the project and get to work. If you see a need for a new WikiProject, you can start one easily. You'll find more information at [[Wikipedia:WikiProject]] (shortcut WP:PROJ) and [[Wikipedia:WikiProject Council/Guide]] (shortcut WP:PROJGUIDE). You don't need special permission before starting a new project, but you might want to ask around—the success of any new project depends on attracting others to help out.

Wikiportals

Portals, those inviting pages with a collection of related articles and projects described in Chapter 3, are not generally under the direct control of WikiProjects. On the other hand, a natural relationship exists between a portal on a topic and a WikiProject on the same topic. WikiProject Poetry announces, "Help is needed in maintaining the Portal:Poetry, including adding quotes, poems, articles, and other material for future weeks." A portal is a natural entry point on the site for a browsing reader, so a WikiProject often aims to sustain and improve a matching portal or to set one up if needed. Portals also often provide a list of articles that need work in their particular subject area, so look here if you're searching for articles to work on. [[Portal:Contents/Portals]] provides a list of portals, organized by topic.

Most portals use a standardized layout that relies heavily on templates and subpages. Setting up a new portal does not require any special permissions, but you'll find that understanding templates before you begin is helpful. Try working on other portals first to get a sense of how they function. See [[Wikipedia:Portal/Instructions]] for a detailed guide on how to create a new portal.

Writing Collaborations

A *writing* or *article collaboration* is simply a drive to improve a particular article. Some people prefer to work on their own, but others enjoy the more focused push that a writing collaboration offers. When several people work on a particular article, it can improve very quickly.

Most of the WikiProjects use collaborations. Some are based on periods of time, such as an article of the week, where the group selects one article for dedicated improvement efforts that week. One long-standing project that is not topic-specific is the Article Collaboration and Improvement Drive, which picks articles to collaborate on that need work. Often the articles, selected by popular vote, are on *core topics* or important articles that have been neglected in favor of more specialized subjects. Broad topics can be surprisingly difficult to write about well! See [[Wikipedia:Article Collaboration and Improvement Drive]] (shortcut WP: ACID).

Another good place to find collaborations is [[Wikipedia:Community Portal]], also accessible from the Community Portal link in the left-hand sidebar. Here, people are free to post collaborations, projects, and cleanup tasks that they want other editors to help with. On the Community Portal page, you can find an entire section devoted to collaborations; many are article collaborations in need of good editors. A further list of writing collaborations can be found at [[Wikipedia:Collaborations]] (shortcut WP:CO).

Further Reading

WikiProjects

http://en.wikipedia.org/wiki/Wikipedia:WikiProject   About WikiProjects

http://en.wikipedia.org/wiki/Wikipedia:WikiProject_Council   A group of Wikipedians who coordinate WikiProjects

http://en.wikipedia.org/wiki/Wikipedia:WikiProject_Chemistry   The chemistry WikiProject

Portals

http://en.wikipedia.org/wiki/Wikipedia:Portal   All about portals and how to find them

Collaborations

http://en.wikipedia.org/wiki/Wikipedia:Collaborations   About article collaborations

http://en.wikipedia.org/wiki/Wikipedia:Article_Collaboration_and_ Improvement_Drive   The weekly article collaboration and improvement drive

---

Processes

Editorial and management decisions have to be made all the time on Wikipedia, yet the site is far too large for a single decision-making center to be an effective solution. Decisions, small and large, are thus made in different forums, where discussions about specific topics are clearly structured. Processes are not formally directed, but they generally follow specific, agreed-on rules for making decisions.

Processes are clearly structured, while projects rarely are, and are more like a conveyor belt for *processing* decisions. Several processes are based on official policy, such as the deletion policy. Anyone can participate in a process; interested editors simply go to the process page to add their views.

Technically, a Wikipedia process is a page, or a suite of pages, normally found in the Wikipedia namespace where editors discuss proposed decisions. Processes are public, open, and transparent. They are also confidence-building mechanisms, as they help ensure that the rules are the same for all editors and topics, and everyone can see (and double-check) that others are playing fair and that the rules do not suddenly change. As the essay [[Wikipedia:Practical process]] says:

> We're here to write an encyclopedia. Process is the temporary scaffolding we put up to help us write an encyclopedia. Having no process or not working to established process leads to chaos. We use process: 1. To give some consistency in similar situations. This helps process feel fair, even though precedent is not binding on Wikipedia. 2. To reduce the redundant effort of making each and every decision from first principles. 3. To encourage institutional learning and lead to a higher overall quality of decision making.

Most processes rely on community consensus as well as policy for making decisions. *Consensus*, as used on Wikipedia, is an unusual and specific term. Within the context of processes, *consensus* means general agreement among participants within a specified time period (almost all processes put time limits on discussion). Sometimes a specific type of voting is used, as in article deletion discussions where editors include their name and whether or not they think the article should be deleted; but even in these situations, everyone understands this is not really a vote—compelling arguments that follow policy are treated with more weight than a simple *yes* or *no*.

Wikipedia's processes are, therefore, systems for getting certain things done. *Process, community,* and *policy*: These are key concepts for *how Wikipedia works*—the real Wikipedia, not a utopian clone. Although Wikipedia has very few committees, it has many processes, each open to anyone who is willing to do the work to understand the issues involved in that particular decision.

Processes should generally be followed, unless very good reasons are given for not doing so; for example, administrators can delete pages *out of process*, but they risk inciting controversy if they do. On the other hand, processes have a tendency to get out of control, and rule-bound processes should not exist for their own sake. The process is important—red tape is not. The anti-bureaucratic nature of Wikipedia is set in context on the official policy page, [[Wikipedia:What Wikipedia is not]]. Searching on WP:BURO takes you directly to the section *Wikipedia is not a bureaucracy*. This section is worth quoting in full (from July 11, 2007):

> Wikipedia is not a moot court, and rules are not the purpose of the community. Instruction creep should be avoided. A perceived procedural error made in posting anything, such as an idea or nomination, is not grounds for invalidating that post. Follow the spirit, not the letter, of any rules, policies and guidelines if

you feel they conflict. Disagreements should be resolved through consensus-based discussion, rather than through tightly sticking to rules and procedures.

In other words, process should not become legalistic. Processes can get out of control and having processes that insist on following their own rules no matter what should be avoided. We'll return to this idea in Chapter 13 (see "Ignore All Rules and Be Bold" on page 364).

What Processes Cover

Wikipedia has numerous processes, dealing with both content and community. These processes include some that implement Wikipedia's official policies, such as the deletion processes, the Featured Article candidate process, the various dispute resolution processes, and the Request for Adminship process for administrator promotion. Other processes focus on making specific maintenance tasks routine, such as renaming categories or approving bots.

One notable exception is resolving disputes over article content. You might believe that an encyclopedic wiki should start with a clear idea of this process. *No such process exists and will not likely ever exist.* This design decision is one of the keys to Wikipedia's model.

Deletion processes deal with the question of whether a topic should be covered at all, and dispute resolution processes help editors who are arguing come to agreement. But Wikipedia has no formal form of adjudication for rival views of suitable article content. Editors are supposed to engage with others about their differing conceptions and deal with disagreements through discussion and common sense and with the assumption that everyone is on the encyclopedia's side. A content decision process would turn into an editorial board for the site, which is against the fundamental ideas of openness and community that are key to Wikipedia. Status on Wikipedia does not allow anyone to dictate content.

In this section, we'll cover the two major content processes that do exist: deleting articles and featuring articles. In later chapters, we'll look at community processes, including dispute resolution.

Deleting Articles

Wikipedia is growing at a tremendous rate, but a great deal of content is also deleted—hundreds or thousands of articles are deleted from Wikipedia every day. Clearly, not all articles that are created belong in the encyclopedia, but what should stay and what should go is not always obvious. The *article deletion* process is used to decide what should be deleted. Primarily used as a housekeeping measure, this process is mainly applied to poorly chosen topics—ones that don't, and can't, lead to proper encyclopedia articles.

Deleting an article is the only way to remove content from the encyclopedia entirely, so readers cannot see the page or the page's history. Deleting is not the same thing as blanking a page by saving an empty revision; in deletion, the history of a deleted article, with access to all revisions, is also deleted. All traces of contributions to that article also disappear from the site—changes to a deleted article won't appear in user contributions, watchlists, Recent Changes, or Related

Changes. The articles do not vanish entirely, however; deleted articles are still visible to administrators, which allows them to review deletions and restore content (*undeleting*) in case a mistake was made. Each deleted article is also logged in a special list, the deletion log, at [[Special:Logs]].

Only Wikipedia's administrators may delete articles, but the deletion process is open for anyone to discuss the fate of articles proposed for deletion. Wikipedia has very specific—and complicated—rules for how pages should be deleted and a large body of past discussion on the subject. Because Wikipedia leans toward including as much as possible, deletion is generally seen as a bad solution if the article can be salvaged. Articles are *not* deleted when the only issue is that they need to be cleaned up or are stubs. Articles are also not deleted based on anyone's personal dislike of the subject matter—Wikipedia has no censorship. How much emphasis to put on deleting content is a long-running philosophical debate on the site; see Chapter 12 for a broad discussion of the "inclusionism versus deletionism" debate.

What does get deleted then? Usually, deletion is for Wikipedia's worst content. Some articles can't possibly be cleaned up. Submitted pages may be nonsense, graffiti, not in English, life stories, advertisements, blatant copyright violations, and spam articles containing nothing but the URL of a website. These examples are not particularly contentious, and many of these types of articles are deleted almost as soon as they are submitted, as part of routine vandalism control (this falls under the speedy deletion process described in the next section).

Deleting articles that were submitted in good faith but that probably violate Wikipedia's content policies is more controversial. Sometimes the violation is clear; plain dictionary definitions or pieces of original research just don't fit within the scope of the encyclopedia. Many articles are deleted because they violate the principle of notability, and this violation is harder to determine. It can also lead to contention—no one likes being told that their company is "not notable." In these deletion discussions, editors discussing the deletion may need to do outside research to find out more about the topic and thoroughly assess the article and whether it belongs in the encyclopedia. Occasionally, editors decide that although the topic doesn't merit its own article, the content should be merged or otherwise incorporated into another article.

Notability can be a problematic notion. If an article's topic violates the principle of notability, then the article will likely be deleted. But turning that around, the best working definition of *notability* comes from which topics are and are not deleted. Applying notability is not an exact science. As discussed in Chapter 1, notability guidelines have been set up for various topics to help guide decisions, but these don't provide exact criteria. Saying that a TV actor is notable because he or she has 421 minutes on screen but not with 419 minutes on screen would be ridiculous, as would be declaring someone notable who has received 76 column inches of industry press but not with 74 inches.

On the other hand, precedent is not binding on Wikipedia—and particularly not in deletion discussions. Many Wikipedians argue that one article's existence does not mean another article on the same topic should be automatically included. For instance, just because an article about one actor is on the site does not mean an article about another actor should also be included by default. Each article should be assessed on its own merits and measured against the basic content policies. Thus deletion discussions are about individual articles, not whole classes of articles.

These complicated issues do help explain why deleting articles is a process—the process helps ensure a timely decision is made one way or another that settles the issue for the time being, if not forever.

Deletion Processes

Anyone can nominate articles for deletion, review the articles that have been nominated, and offer opinions on whether they should be deleted. Nearly every deletion requires some interpretation of Wikipedia policy (which is certainly not always clear-cut). Deletion processes are, however, fairly stable, well regulated, and reasonably consistent.

Of the three main ways to delete an article, Articles for Deletion (AfD) requires community discussion and a dedicated debate, whereas proposed deletions (PRODs; see WP:PROD) and speedy deletions (*speedies*, or sometimes *CSD*, which is short for Criteria for Speedy Deletion, the policy page) do not. Speedy deletions are the most common, due to the sheer volume of nonsense articles submitted. Articles that don't meet speedy deletion guidelines may get deleted though the Articles for Deletion process or the proposed deletion process instead, and contested speedy and proposed deletions are often referred to the AfD process. In other words, when the quicker deletion processes prove contentious, Wikipedia has the more serious AfD as a fallback.

Each deletion process is initiated by an editor tagging the article with a red-bar deletion template. This template adds the page to several lists for review, and in the case of AfD, the editor creates a page explaining why the article should be deleted.

Each specific deletion process covers a different type of problem article:

Speedy deletion

This process is for articles that definitely violate Wikipedia policies. Wikipedia maintains an extensive list of around 20 particular criteria for speedy deletion at [[Wikipedia:Criteria for speedy deletion]] (shortcut WP: CSD), along with the particular deletion templates that can be used. If none of these criteria are met, one of the other deletion processes should be used. *Speedy* does mean quickly, however. *Speedy* can also occasionally mean hasty, and it should never be applied to controversial or unclear cases.

The usual process for speedy deletions is that a new-page or other vandalism patroller will discover a clearly bad article. He or she will tag the page with a speedy deletion template (Figure 7-6) to add it to a list that administrators check routinely. If an administrator agrees that the page should be deleted, he or she will delete the page, citing the appropriate criteria. Speedy deletion can also be requested for non-article working pages that are no longer needed, such as user space subpages; this kind of housekeeping work is rarely contentious.

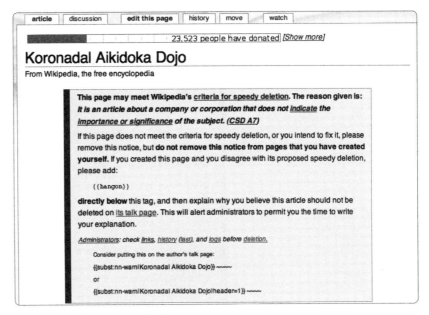

FIGURE 7-6: *Speedy deletion message*

Proposed deletion

Proposed deletions (PRODs) are gentler than speedy deletions and give the community time to review the proposal. PRODs, like speedy deletion, are also designed for deletions that are not likely to be contested, but PRODs can be used for any type of article, not just those falling under the CSD criteria.

When an editor discovers an article that he or she thinks should clearly be deleted, the editor can begin the proposed deletion process by tagging the article with the PROD template (Figure 7-7) and explaining why the article should be deleted. You can find the template at [[Template:Prod]]. The editor should insert the template on the page to be deleted along with this code, {{subst:prod|*reason*}}, replacing *reason* with the specific reason for deletion.

This template remains on the article for five days, during which time the article's talk page is open for discussion. If, at any point during this time, any involved party—the original tagger, the author of the article, or another editor—thinks the article should not in fact be deleted, he or she can simply remove the template and the case is closed. This is called *contesting the PROD*, and at this point, if the nominator wants to pursue it, he or she must submit the article to AfD for discussion in order to delete it. If, at the end of the five days, no one contests the deletion, an administrator will review the article, the reason for deletion, and make a decision. The process is explained at [[Wikipedia:Proposed deletion]].

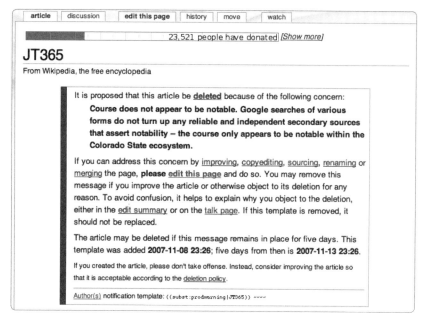

FIGURE 7-7: *PROD deletion message*

Articles for Deletion

This thorough discussion process is for articles flagged for potential deletion; these articles are added to a list, and other editors review them on a dedicated page. Articles for Deletion (AfD) deals with the 5 to 10 percent of seriously contested cases, as well as any deletion case where the nominator wants input from other editors. If, during the course of about a week, consensus emerges, the discussion is closed, and the decision implemented. When no consensus emerges, general practice is to keep the article. Other outcomes are possible (for example, merges or redirections). A small proportion of cases become acrimonious.

Nominating an article for this deletion process requires a few steps. First, an editor adds the AfD template to the article in question (Figure 7-8). Then, the editor creates a dedicated subpage from the main AfD page for discussing the article (this page is created by simply clicking a link in the deletion template). After the editor has created the subpage, he or she explains why the page should be deleted and signs his or her username. (Detailed instructions can be found at [[Wikipedia:Articles for deletion]], shortcut WP:AFD.) Once the page has been nominated, other editors discuss the matter, adding comments that indicate whether or not they think the article should be deleted.

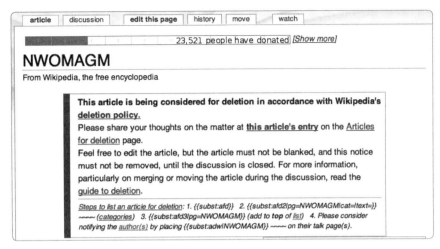

FIGURE 7-8: AfD deletion message

Anyone can discuss AfD nominations by simply going to the main AfD page and adding a signed comment with his or her opinion about whether to keep or delete the article being discussed (page 342 shows a sample comment). Participating in a few debates to see what kinds of discussions crop up can be quite interesting. Some editors routinely review all the current AfD nominations, whereas others just visit the list once in a while to check if any articles they are interested in have shown up there. If you are knowledgeable about a particular subject, giving an opinion on whether a particular article or topic should be kept can be quite valuable to the process, and AfDs are now sorted by topic for those who don't want to search through all of them. Good practice for reviewing AfDs is to read the article in question thoroughly, do any other research necessary (such as looking for information online, checking backlinks, and doing basic fact-checking), and then give a reasoned opinion based on the article's content and Wikipedia's policies. AfD discussions can be lively, but certain ground rules exist: The discussion should always be about the content, not the editor who posted or nominated it, and appeals to personal taste ("I like it; I don't like it") are not helpful.

If an article is no longer relevant, having been superseded by another article, or has a bad title, a deletion discussion is not needed. Instead, turn to Chapter 8 to learn how to move, merge, or redirect an article.

Help, My Article's Being Deleted!

Step one: Don't panic! You can often rescue an article under threat. Wikipedia has different procedures to follow if you want to contest a deletion; getting angry is not one of them.

Sometimes articles will be nominated for deletion immediately after being posted; other times, the article may have been on the site for years before

Deleting Other Kinds of Pages

AfDs, PRODs, and speedies are only for deleting articles or pages in the main namespace. Images and media are dealt with separately; see [[Wikipedia:Images and media for deletion]] (shortcut WP:IFD). Categories and templates also have their own process; see [[Wikipedia:Categories for discussion]] (shortcut WP:CFD) and [[Wikipedia:Templates for deletion]] (shortcut WP:TFD), respectively. For deleting pages in the Wikipedia or User namespace, see [[Wikipedia:Miscellany for deletion]] (shortcut WP:MFD). A handful of debates occur here about unused or inappropriate material that has made its way into the project namespaces. A rare case is administrative blanking, not deleting, of project-space pages. For this, refer to [[Wikipedia:Deletion policy#Courtesy blanking]] (shortcut WP:CBLANK). This page provides a solution for old pages from deletion debates or other discussions that contain very pointed comments, for example, about specific people or companies. As a courtesy, administrators may replace the current page content to ensure that, over time, the old content becomes less prominent on search engines. Because the page itself hasn't been deleted, the content remains in the page history.

someone decides it doesn't belong. Either way, contesting a deletion varies depending on the deletion process being used, but all require discussing and bringing the article up to Wikipedia's standards.

▸ If your article is proposed for *speedy* deletion, don't remove the template. Instead, insert a {{hangon}} template at the top of the article in question, and then go to its talk page immediately to explain why the article is notable and worth keeping. Citing sources will also help a great deal.

▸ You can always remove a *proposed* deletion tag, but then you ought to work on the article to address the issues raised by the nominator. If the article's notability has been questioned, add reliable sources that demonstrate notability. Notable sources depend on context; for instance, for a person, listing publications, awards, and honors helps to prove notability. Putting in enough effort to show the article meets notability and content standards should help prevent a subsequent nomination to AfD.

▸ In an AfD debate, feel free to participate in the discussion. Argue your case clearly, and don't take others' comments personally. During an AfD debate, anyone can clean up the article under discussion, so you can use this opportunity to improve the article according to the critics' points. You can then explain how you've improved the article on the AfD discussion page. Asking people to reconsider based on your own cleanup and extra referencing may have very good results.

If you don't realize the article has been nominated for deletion until it's already been deleted, determine why and how it was deleted. Generally, a reason is given in the deletion log along with the deleting administrator's name. You can view this information by going to the article's title, which will now be a redlink page, displaying the *Wikipedia does not have an article with this exact name* message. Click the Deletion Log link that appears in the middle of the page to see the deletion log entry.

Understand the common reasons for articles being deleted. Remember, you don't need to rush to get an article written and posted. Working on Wikipedia is not a race, and Wikipedia gives out no prizes for speed. Adopt a thoughtful approach, and learn the system rather than rage against it.

The most common reason articles are deleted is because they are judged to be non-notable or *vanity* topics. Articles about local musicians, minor executives, or other people who aren't in the news regularly are likely to be rejected. Remember not to write about yourself either; autobiographies belong on user pages or personal websites.

Here are some other common reasons for deleting articles:

Spam-like postings
Does the article read like an advertisement? Is it all about one project or company? Does it just talk about how great something is, failing to keep to a neutral tone? Content originally written for a company website or a press release is rarely suitable for Wikipedia.

Too specialist
If your article was judged as non-notable but is really part of something larger—for instance, if you're writing about a single college within a university—you may be able to include the information under the broader topic rather than write a new article about it.

Enthusiast
Specialism is a common problem with characters and elements from fiction, such as comic book and video game characters; TV episodes; individual songs; or batches of articles about minuscule parts of a fictional universe. *Fancruft* (sometimes shortened to just *cruft*) is a derogatory term for these types of articles, which are sometimes just barely tolerated. You will win friends by cleaning up the broader articles that already exist on the topic and adding detail to those first, rather than starting new articles. In some cases, the content might really belong on a more specialized wiki (see Chapter 16).

They hate the way you write
Bad writing shouldn't be a valid reason for deletion rather than cleanup, but you can avoid deletion by submitting a well-written article in the first place. Many experienced editors make drafts in userspace, as was discussed in Chapter 6, along with other writing advice.

Finally, if you're sure your article was good and was deleted by mistake, you can start a *deletion review*. For a PROD deletion, getting an administrator to revive the article with no special discussion is usually easy. For a speedy deletion, you'll have to show you can address the reason it was deleted. For AfD deletions, a serious appeal process has been developed (see [[Wikipedia:Deletion review]], shortcut WP:DRV), in which another round of community discussion will take place. This process reviews and checks the procedural side of deletions, and contributors can comment on whether they think deletion was the best option or not. As the Deletion Review page says, however, the first step is to talk to the deleting administrator to see why the page was deleted. If nothing comes from the deletion review, you'll probably have to wait six months before trying to re-create the article.

If you do decide to try again, make sure you address all the criticisms brought up by reviewers and you are confident you can produce an article that meets content policies and guidelines, including Notability, Verifiability, and Neutral Point of View.

Of course, the six-month rule isn't absolute: The notability of a topic can change overnight due to current events or new reliable sources being published. However, repeatedly re-creating an article that was deleted by community consensus without improving it substantially can be considered a form of vandalism. Occasionally, repeated re-creation can lead to an administrator *salting* a page, which means protecting the page and adding a special template that conveys the message that Wikipedia sincerely, truly, hand-on-heart does *not* want an article about this topic (the term comes from the phrase "salting the earth").

A Deletion Case Study

Wikipedia is clearly not a business, but this has not stopped it appearing in a Harvard Business School case study. It was prepared by Andrew P. McAfee of the School, with Karim R. Lakhani.[1] Wikipedia's systems are put under the microscope, as they track a particular deletion debate from August 2006. This was one of the first occasions on which a Wikipedia internal process, AfD in this case, was dignified with such close academic attention. The paper used an analytical and historical approach (all the way back to Ephraim Chambers via Nupedia), amply supported by the case study of the particular deletion debate. The study is interesting for the clear picture drawn of the structures, community, admins, policies, and processes all interacting, focusing on the role of individual editors as a major factor.

The study concerns the fate of the article [[Enterprise 2.0]], a neologism coined by McAfee himself. The topic lies on one of the fringes of Wikipedia's natural content. The classic debate on including new terms has two opposing views:

▶ Wikipedia's mission is factual and has nothing to do with spreading neologisms.

---

[1] The case study is online at *http://courseware.hbs.edu/public/cases/wikipedia/*.

- Many people would like to refer to a discussion of a new phrase making the rounds, in Wikipedia's slightly distanced and neutral style.

These thoughts may be behind deletion debate positions, with "deletionists" (see "Wikiphilosophies" on page 349) aiming to keep Wikipedia out of spreading jargon; but they have to be reconciled with the core content policies of No Original Research and Verifiability. For a neologism, you do have to go by usage in published texts, verifying that new jargon is actually used and used in the way the article claims so that the definition isn't "original research"; sometimes an article on a new phrase really should wait for good sources to appear elsewhere. Wikipedia's content and determinations of notability should never be based solely on a publicity effort.

In the end, this rather slight article survived AfD. The deletion process, decisive as it may seem, is in fact provisional. [[Enterprise 2.0]] actually has had a checkered history since it was kept, suffering redirection to another article, then re-creation. A redirect to [[Enterprise social software]] is its status at the time of this writing.

Clearly, a neologism may flourish or it may not, and Wikipedia can and ought to update to reflect that. From this perspective, Wikipedia's social mechanisms are good, rather than weak, in their flexibility: The conclusions of AfD, or any other process on Wikipedia, are not set in stone.

Featured Articles

Rather than being deleted, some very good articles are promoted in status. *Good articles (GA)* and *featured articles (FA)* are two levels of articles that the community has determined to be some of the best content on Wikipedia. Reviewing and working constructively on articles is one of the key skills of an involved Wikipedian. This skill also applies in formal or informal peer review (as noted in Chapter 6) and on WikiProjects. Gauge content with an eye to improving it. (Working on good articles is also recommended as an antidote to the burnout caused by the other extreme—immersion in deletion debates.)

Finding and browsing featured articles was described in Chapter 3. Wikipedia also has featured review processes for media, images, lists, and portals. Relative to the rest of Wikipedia's content, few articles have been designated good or featured, with only about 1 in 660 articles listed as good and 1 in 1,200 listed as featured. However, many good-quality articles aren't on these lists those that haven't gone through the formal processes. The criteria for good and featured articles are basically those mentioned in Chapter 6, but in the processes, you can experience the criteria in action, as debated through open peer review. For either process, anyone can nominate an article and anyone can review it, though featured articles require a more complex review. If it is difficult for you to receive detailed criticism of your own work, remember the *no ownership* rule. Most articles under review improve greatly, regardless of the eventual outcome.

Candidates for good articles are listed at [[Wikipedia:Good article candidates]] (shortcut WP:GAC). To nominate an article, simply follow the instructions on this page and place the corresponding Good Article Candidate template on the article's talk page. In turn, any editor can choose to review the article (typically, only one person will review the article). The criteria for review are listed at [[Wikipedia:Good article criteria]] (shortcut WP:GA?). The review process is supposed to be fairly informal. Reviewers read through the article and evaluate it based on the criteria, and then they have three options: They may *pass* the article as being a good article, *fail* the article if they feel it doesn't meet the criteria, or make suggestions for improvement by placing the article *on hold*. Often reviewers make detailed constructive comments. Articles that pass are added to the list of good articles at [[Wikipedia:Good articles]] (shortcut WP:GA). Articles that fail need to be improved. An article can be renominated once the criticisms have been addressed.

Featured articles go through a more formal community peer review process, typically with several different editors participating as reviewers. This review is based on [[Wikipedia:Featured article criteria]](shortcut WP:FACR). The criteria include, for example, appropriate use of images. Reviews take place at [[Wikipedia:Featured article candidates]] (shortcut WP:FAC). Here, you can find between 50 and 100 candidates that are under current scrutiny. Reviewer comments are likely to be detailed and extensive, ranging from minor issues, such as formatting, to major issues, such as unclear writing or missing references. Anyone can nominate an article to be featured, but by convention, the nominator is supposed to stick around for the review and help out with fixing up the article. The process is intended as a dialogue, with the nominator responding to the critique by working on the article's issues. Others are also welcome to help, but an article that doesn't improve at all in response to criticism isn't likely to pass. Directions for nominating a new article are on the Featured Article Candidates page (shortcut WP:FAC), along with directions for commenting on nominations. An article should not be nominated for good article status and featured article status at the same time, but a good article can later be nominated for featured article status.

Articles that pass (sometimes only after several rounds of review) are then added to the list at [[Wikipedia:Featured articles]] (shortcut WP:FA). Any featured article may then be listed as Today's featured article on the main page of the site; the current month's selections are listed at [[Wikipedia:Today's featured article]]. Featured articles that degrade in quality may be reviewed through the featured article review process ([[Wikipedia:Featured article review]]), where anyone with concerns can nominate a currently featured article for discussion about whether that status should be removed.

Further Reading

Process

http://en.wikipedia.org/wiki/Wikipedia:Process_is_important (shortcut WP:PI)   An essay about the role of process

http://en.wikipedia.org/wiki/Wikipedia:Practical_process (shortcut WP:PRO)   Another essay about how process works

http://meta.wikimedia.org/wiki/Polls_are_evil   Addresses the genuine need for discussion, not just "yea" and "nay" responses

Deletion Process

http://en.wikipedia.org/wiki/Wikipedia:Deletion   The deletion policy

http://en.wikipedia.org/wiki/Wikipedia:Guide_to_deletion   An overview of the deletion process

http://en.wikipedia.org/wiki/Wikipedia:Articles_for_deletion   Where current articles nominated for deletion are discussed

Good and Featured Articles

http://en.wikipedia.org/wiki/Wikipedia:Featured_articles   The Featured Articles portal

http://en.wikipedia.org/wiki/Wikipedia:Good_articles   The Good Articles portal

http://en.wikipedia.org/wiki/Wikipedia:Featured_article_candidates   Nominations for featured articles

Summary

As part of the overall task of upgrading and updating Wikipedia, a vast range of jobs are accomplished by small teams or through local, open discussions. These collaborations and discussions are how the apparently anarchic Wikipedia works. Behind the scenes, a large and diverse population of supporting projects and processes are at work. What they all have in common is that editors operate within loose frameworks, communicating and pooling efforts to improve the encyclopedia.

8

Make and Mend Wikipedia's Web

In Chapter 3, we described many ways to browse Wikipedia. For instance, readers can explore Wikipedia via the links between pages or through categories of related articles. If an area of Wikipedia has been worked on for long enough, these browsing journeys go smoothly. But Wikipedia's content does not start out perfectly linked or classified, and new articles need to be integrated with existing content. Articles need care and attention to become fully usable in the context of the rest of the site.

This chapter turns to web-building techniques on Wikipedia. You can add to, alter, and mend Wikipedia as a piece of hypertext. We'll cover six concepts for building navigational structures, linking articles, and maintaining article organization. These concepts have been mentioned in previous chapters, but here we'll present them as editorial tools.

First, we'll cover redirecting one page title to another and building disambiguation pages, both of which help readers navigate, avoid duplication, and search the site more productively. We'll then focus on how articles are combined, split apart, or moved to better titles in order to comply with style guidelines and to make them more useful for the reader. In the next section, we'll discuss categories and categorization, which help readers navigate similar topics and editors maintain sets of pages. Finally, we'll review community processes for resolving problems that arise related to these topics.

Redirect and Disambiguate

Redirects and disambiguation pages, first described in Chapter 1, play important roles in internal Wikipedia connections. A *redirect* page directly points the reader from one page title to another and is used when more than one possible page title exists. *Disambiguation* pages clarify the use of a keyword by pointing to all of the articles that are referred to by that term or a similar term.

Redirects

If you go to the article [[Norma Jeane Mortenson]], you'll be automatically taken to the article called [[Marilyn Monroe]] instead.

Although a reader doesn't see it, a page does exist under the title Norma Jeane Mortenson, but not a regular article page. Instead, this page is a special, very short page that only contains a pointer to another target page. This page is a *redirect*, Wikipedia's equivalent of an index entry reading *for Norma Jeane Mortensen, see Marilyn Monroe.*

A redirect can be set from any page to any other page. Redirects are often used for name variants and common misspellings for people, places, or things. Although the article can only exist under one title, redirects automatically take the reader to the actual article from any conceivable title that he or she might search for. Redirects make it easier to find and search for content because they also show up in search results.

Wikipedia has a tremendous number of redirects. As of mid-2007, the site had more redirect pages than article pages, by somewhere between 5 percent to 10 percent. Historical figures, with their varying names, titles, and multiple spellings, are a prolific source of redirects. Other significant sources are Romanizations of names and terms from other languages. For instance, English does not have a standard way for writing Arabic names: *Mohammed*, *Mohammad*, and *Mohamed* are all accepted ways of writing the Prophet's name. All of these possible spellings redirect to the actual article title (currently [[Muhammad]]), saving the reader the trouble of figuring out which spelling variation to use.

As a small part of its mission, Wikipedia has to manage this huge system of redirects and disambiguations. Many reference works face this issue. For instance, an article in *The Economist* in 2007 talked about the problems confronting government intelligence agencies as they reconcile name variations:

> "One of our biggest problems has always been variations of names," says Michael Scheuer, who was the head of the CIA's Osama bin Laden Unit from 1996 to 1999. Mr Scheuer says analysis was "backbreaking," especially for Arabic names, because it involved manually compiling lists of variations deemed worthy of tracing.[1]

Wikipedians know how Mr. Scheuer feels. Names matter to reference works, but names are complex. Previous reference works and printed encyclopedias dealt with the problem by developing *See* references to guide readers from one term to another in an index; Wikipedia, which doesn't have a printed index, has an automatic—and much more comprehensive—solution instead.

Redirects are also helpful when two pages with the same content are merged together, as described later in "Merging Articles" on page 240. When two pages are merged, the result is a composite article at one of the page titles and a redirect from the other one.

Creating and Editing Redirects

You can easily create new redirects. First create a new article using the title you want to become a redirect, as described in Chapter 6. Then type only this text on the page:

```
#REDIRECT [[title of page to redirect to]]
```

For instance, if you want to redirect the page [[Goldfishes]] to the article [[Goldfish]] (although article title convention uses the singular form of nouns, readers may search using the plural), you would create the page [[Goldfishes]] and type this text:

```
#REDIRECT [[goldfish]]
```

Then add an appropriate edit summary (*rdr* is common shorthand for *redirect*) and click Save. Now, if a reader tries to go to the page [[Goldfishes]], he or she will instead end up at [[Goldfish]]. As a bonus, if a link to the page [[Goldfishes]] also appears somewhere in another article, when a reader clicks that link, he or she will be taken to [[Goldfish]].

You don't have to start an entirely new page to create a redirect. If the page [[Goldfishes]] already exists, you can turn it into a redirect by replacing any existing text with the redirect code and clicking Save. Be careful, though; if an article is already on the page, you may want to move it to a better title or merge it with an existing page, as described later in "Merge, Split, and Move" on page 240.

---

[1] See "What's in a Name?" *The Economist*, accessed March 8, 2007 (*http://www.economist.com/search/displaystory.cfm?story_id=8766103*).

If something goes wrong (or you change your mind), you can always edit a redirect. A redirect, like any other change you make to the site, can be reversed. But how?

Suppose [[Erik Weisz]] is a redirect to [[Harry Houdini]], following Wikipedia's practice of titling articles about performers using their most common stage name. If you follow a link to [[Erik Weisz]], you'll be redirected to [[Harry Houdini]]; but don't get frustrated! When you are taken to an article from a redirect, you'll notice the title of the redirected page is displayed below the page title, showing you how you got there (Figure 8-1).

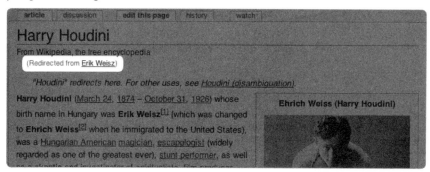

FIGURE 8-1: *A redirect title below a page title—Harry Houdini, redirected from Erik Weisz*

Click the linked page title *(Redirected from Erik Weisz)* to access the redirect page itself (Figure 8-2).

FIGURE 8-2: *A redirect page for Erik Weisz*

When you access an actual redirect page, you'll see a special URL, similar to *http://en.wikipedia.org/wiki/Erik_Weisz?redirect=no*. Adding `?redirect=no` after the page title in the URL prevents the page from automatically redirecting.

You can then edit this redirect page like any other page, either to change the redirect target or to remove the redirect and start an article instead. You can also check the page history for the redirect page to make sure quality content wasn't accidentally lost when the redirect was created.

Here are some reasons for viewing and editing redirects:

▶ Create a full article at the page title to replace the redirect to another page. (This often happens when articles about similar or related items all redirect to one central page; specialty articles may eventually be written about each item.)

▶ Change the redirect to point to a different page (for instance, if the redirect was not quite right or had a typo).

▶ Revert the creation of the redirect if the page contained content before the redirect was created, so you can restore an earlier version (for instance, if the redirect was created accidentally or restoring the original article is important).

▶ Copy content from an earlier version of the article (before the redirect was created) onto some other page (you can find previous versions by browsing the redirect page's history).

Limitations on Redirecting

Redirects are not always called for. For instance, you shouldn't create a redirect to an article that doesn't exist yet unless you plan to write that article immediately. Creating a redirect in this instance is detrimental: It creates a useless dead end, and it turns the redirect page title into a bluelink, whereas a redlink might attract the attention of an author who would want to write the article. For a similar reason, when articles are deleted, redirects to them should also be deleted.

You should also be careful when creating redirects to sections in an article. For example,

```
#REDIRECT [[Ice cream#vanilla]]
```

is the text for a redirect page for [[Vanilla ice cream]]; it takes you to the Vanilla section of the page [[Ice cream]]. Section-specific redirects are useful, but they are not robust. This redirect could be broken easily by an editor retitling the section *Vanilla flavor* (Wikipedia has no way for you to discover What Links Here at the section level). For this reason, the *Manual of Style* recommends leaving a hidden comment, for instance, below the section heading when you redirect to it (see WP:MOS#Section management).

One recurring theory is that you shouldn't pipe links to redirect titles. In other words, some Wikipedians think [[Orville Wright|pilot of the first manned flight]] is worse than [[Wright brothers|pilot of the first manned flight]], given that [[Orville Wright]] redirects to [[Wright brothers]]. If the Wright brothers were given separate articles one day, however, the piped link to Orville would have been a better choice. As long as you don't create double redirects, you can create links to redirects. Some cases are discussed in depth at [[Wikipedia:Redirect]]. The point, generally, is to help readers rather than distract them.

Finally, two technical issues limit redirect creation.

Double redirects

Avoid creating a redirect to a redirect: The database software is unable to forward twice. You can check for double redirects by clicking What Links Here; for instance, if you create a redirect by moving a page, check What Links Here for the old title. As the page mover, you're responsible for updating any redirects to point to the new title.

Redirects across namespaces

Redirecting from one namespace to another is confusing because the whole point of namespaces is to separate different types of content. With a few exceptions, redirects should stay within one namespace. If a list page is replaced by a category, a redirect from the list page (in the main article namespace) to the category (in the Category namespace) could be created. Users may redirect their user pages to their user talk pages (from the User namespace to the User_talk namespace). A Wikipedia: namespace help page may be redirected to an existing help page in the Help namespace. Articles in the main namespace should not redirect to other namespaces, however. For more, see [[Wikipedia:Cross-namespace redirects]] (shortcut WP:CNR).

Disambiguation Pages

Disambiguation pages, colloquially known as *dab pages*, are one of the Wikipedia success stories. Their assigned role is humble enough. Many phrases or single English words are ambiguous because they have multiple meanings. Take, for example, the word *bridge*. Besides being a structure that allows you to cross over a river or other obstacle, *bridge* can be a card game, a piece of dental work, or the command post of a ship. With all these meanings, wikilinks to the article [[Bridge]] could often lead readers to the wrong article. The solution is to create several differently titled articles for each meaning of the ambiguous term along with a dedicated page to link to, or disambiguate, between all of them for readers.

✱ **NOTE:** *Wikipedia coined the term* disambiguation *early on in its history because the site needed a word for pages that served this function.*

If only two or three articles may be confused, a lightweight form of disambiguation are *hatnotes* (see Chapter 4), which point back and forth between two or three articles. For terms with more meanings, a dedicated disambiguation page works better.

In this case, the disambiguation page is located at [[Bridge (disambiguation)]], which lists the possible articles that may be related to the term *bridge*. As of January 2008, this page included links to the following articles:

▸ [[Bridge (dentistry)]], a fixed prosthesis used to replace missing teeth

▸ [[Bridge (ship)]], the area from which a ship is commanded

▸ [[Contract bridge]], the modern card game; see [[Bridge (card game disambiguation)]] for other card games that *bridge* may refer to

- ▶ [[Bridge (music)]], an interlude that connects two parts of a song

- ▶ [[Bridge (structure)]], a structure built so that a transportation route can cross an obstacle

But what article is on the page simply titled *Bridge*? In this case, [[Bridge (structure)]] redirects to the article [[Bridge]]; on Wikipedia, the default meaning of *bridge* is the structure. A hatnote on this default page points readers to the disambiguation page if they're looking for articles using a different meaning of the term. (Figure 8-3 shows the hatnote that appears on the [[Bridge]] article.)

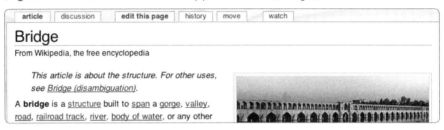

FIGURE 8-3: *The hatnote on the Bridge article, pointing to the related disambiguation page*

Disambiguation pages can be created in more than one way, however. If no clear default meaning for a term exists, the main article may serve as the disambiguation page. For instance, if you go to [[Subway]], you'll find that it is a disambiguation page leading to articles using these meanings for *subway* (among others):

- ▶ [[Subway (rail)]], underground railway, also known as a metro, underground, U-Bahn

- ▶ [[Subway (underpass)]], an underground walkway, usually a tunnel

Descriptions on a disambiguation page do not need to be extensive. They do not serve as summaries of the articles they link to; they simply point to different possible meanings of a term and need only clarify the distinction between those meanings. Keep descriptions succinct: *American film actor* for an actor is probably sufficient; you don't need to include the films he has acted in. For pages that disambiguate between several people, include their profession, nationality, and birth and death dates (providing dates is especially important for an article on someone like George Williams, as half a dozen American politicians have that name).

Disambiguating Articles About People

Wikipedia has hundreds of thousands of biographies (approximately 20 percent of all articles). Because of this, special guidelines have been set up for disambiguating names. Wikipedia handles this complex area in a way that may initially appear unclear if you're creating or updating these types of pages. Note the templates used on pages and don't underestimate the issues involved with biographies.

Tidier Hatnotes

Hatnotes are small text messages at the top of an article. They are useful when only two articles might get confused and for directing readers to disambiguation pages. Wikipedia uses standard templates for hatnotes such as {{for}}, {{otheruses}}, and {{distinguish}}. These templates add standardized messages to a page, which can be easier than writing out your own message (also perfectly acceptable). See [[Wikipedia:Hatnote]] (shortcut WP:HAT) for hatnote templates and common messages. The term *hatnote* is specific to Wikipedia and was created to avoid ambiguity because a *headnote* (the opposite of a *footnote*) is used in legal work.

Many *complete proper names* require disambiguation: John Smith, Thomas Adams, and Juan González are all examples of common names that need disambiguation pages to distinguish between individuals sharing that name. But Wikipedia also lists articles by *surname alone*. For example, [[Category:Irish surnames]] contains around 200 pages, each devoted to a single surname of Irish origin. If you go to [[Nolan]], you'll find an extensive list of articles on Irish, British, American, Canadian, and other Nolans.

Thus, a *surname page* is very much like a disambiguation page: *Nolan* refers to numerous people. Sometimes these surname pages include *(surname)* in the title. For instance, [[Cooper]] is a basic disambiguation page, listing the many places called *Cooper*, a handful of well-known people named *Cooper*, and a pointer to the page [[Cooper (profession)]], which is about the profession of making barrels. Because *Cooper* is a very common English surname, Wikipedia also has a separate page [[Cooper (surname)]], listing articles about people with that name. This page exists in place of [[List of people with surname Cooper]].

Two other kinds of pages about people exist: listings by given names and family history.

Given names are treated differently than surnames. If you search for [[John (first name)]], you'll find this page in [[Category:Given names]]. Listing every article about a person with the first name John would not be useful. Instead you'll discover that *Juan* is the Spanish equivalent—in other words, the article is about the name itself. The basic page [[John]] is a disambiguation page that lists historical figures known just as John, such as the English King who signed the Magna Carta. Use the {{Given name}} template to classify these pages.

These topics are extremely popular on the Web. We mentioned in Chapter 1 that Wikipedia believes that most family history is indiscriminate and only includes it when the family's history meets the standards of notability—and only in articles about specific families (not the general surname), such as [[Bancroft family]], the owners of *The Wall Street Journal* until 2007. Family articles should be placed in [[Category:Families]] and its subcategories. That Bancroft article belongs in the categories [[Category:American families]] and [[Category:Business families]].

Disambiguation Templates

Like other articles, disambiguation pages are tagged with templates that identify them as disambiguation pages and sort them into different categories. Here's how it all breaks down by template:

▶ {{disambig}} is the general disambiguation template. For example, [[Tom Thumb (disambiguation)]] lists articles about the folklore character, a railway locomotive, a feature film with Peter Sellers, a grocer in Dallas, Texas, and some Marvel Comics superheroes. In other words, miscellaneous lists are straightforward disambiguation pages.

▶ {{hndis}} is the template for human names. This template applies, for example, to [[Bill Gates (disambiguation)]], which lists not only Bill Gates of Microsoft but also "Swiftwater" Bill Gates, who took part in the Klondike gold rush, and various people more commonly known by the name William Gates.

▶ {{surname}} is the surname page template. The *Manual of Style* (shortcut WP: MOSDAB, subsection *Given names or surnames*) describes how a surname page differs from a disambiguation page.

▶ {{geodis}} is the template for pages that disambiguate the names of places.

Further Reading

Redirects

http://en.wikipedia.org/wiki/Wikipedia:Redirect   The style guideline for creating redirects

http://en.wikipedia.org/wiki/Help:Redirect   Help page on how to create redirects

Disambiguation Pages

http://en.wikipedia.org/wiki/Wikipedia:Disambiguation   The guideline for creating disambiguation pages, with page naming conventions

http://en.wikipedia.org/wiki/Wikipedia:Manual of Style (disambiguation pages)   The *Manual of Style* page with formatting guidelines for disambiguation pages

http://en.wikipedia.org/wiki/Wikipedia:WikiProject_Disambiguation   WikiProject Disambiguation, for cleaning up disambiguation pages

http://en.wikipedia.org/wiki/Wikipedia:Hatnote   The hatnotes guideline

---

Merge, Split, and Move

Working with and cleaning up individual articles includes determining if each article covers an appropriate scope and does not duplicate other articles. If two articles are very similar, you may need to merge them. On the other hand, if an article grows too long and unwieldy (or covers several topics), you may need to split it into more than one article. And if an article should appear under a more appropriate title, you need to move it. Moves and merges both create redirects from former page titles and copy content and revision history to a new page title.

Merging Articles

Wikipedia has no special process for ensuring that new articles don't duplicate old ones (this is why, in Chapter 6, we suggest checking for other articles on the same topic before starting a new one). Editors who write new articles are responsible for making sure no duplicate articles (perhaps using a slightly different title) exist. If an editor doesn't check, however, and creates a duplicate article, other editors may eventually catch the duplication. In this case, they will most likely flag the two articles as candidates for a *merge*.

The goal of a merge is to end up with one good, coherent article that incorporates all facts, concepts, and references from both articles without duplicating material. The ideal merge results in a better article. No content should be lost in a merge; instead, all of the relevant facts should end up in one article, and the other, alternate title redirects readers to the new combined article.

Another, more complex case is when several small articles need to be consolidated into one more satisfactory and broader article. For instance, an article about a band member may be merged into the article about the band if little independent information about the musician in question is available. Sometimes a noun and antonym, or two similar terms, make more sense in a single article (e.g., [[Supralapsarianism]] and [[Infralapsarianism]]). These cases generally require more discussion and may be controversial.

A good merge is an unhurried, multipass procedure requiring many edits. Because merges require skill, a single editor often performs the merge once all the interested editors have agreed to it. This can vary from article to article; for articles where one title is misspelled or when the two articles are nearly identical, objections are unlikely. ([[William M. Ramsey]] and [[William Mitchell Ramsay]] is an example of this kind of duplication, where two articles were accidentally created about the same person.) Problems may arise, however, if you want to combine two similar concepts and another editor wants to maintain a distinction between the concepts. For instance, in mathematics, fractions and rational numbers are covered in separate articles—[[Fraction (mathematics)]] and [[Rational number]]—even though fractions are, in fact, rational numbers.

How to Merge Articles

Merging is a manual process that can be quite involved for longer articles. Assuming you want to perform the merge yourself, here are the steps to follow:

1. Identify the articles you want to merge. Make sure they are, in fact, duplicate articles or otherwise need to be combined.
2. Tag each of the articles to be merged with a special merge template. Insert the template at the beginning of the article:

{{merge|*otherarticlename*|date=January 2008}}

where *otherarticlename* is the title of the article that you want to merge with the article you're currently tagging, and the current month and year appears after **date=**.

3. Tag the other article to be merged, replacing *otherarticlename* with the title of the first article. These templates alert readers and editors to the possible merge. (Figure 8-4 shows this message at the top of the Bulgarian Education article.)

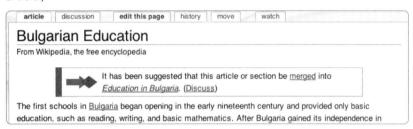

FIGURE 8-4: *The merge message template on the Bulgarian Education article, suggesting a merge to the article called* Education in Bulgaria

In any merge, one article will become the *destination article* (*mergeto* page), where all the content will be combined, and the other will become the *redirected article* (*mergefrom* page), which will become a redirect to the other article. If you already know which article should be which, you can use more specific templates:

▸ {{mergeto|*otherarticlename*|date=January 2008}} on the redirected article

▸ {{mergefrom|*otherarticlename*|date=January 2008}} on the destination article

The merge templates will place the articles into [[Category:Articles to be merged]]; adding the date means they will be sorted into a month-by-month category as well.

4. Add a note to each article's talk page, describing why you think the articles should be merged if the reason is not apparent.

5. After tagging the articles, wait a week (perhaps longer for obscure articles) for editors who have watchlisted the articles to comment on the merge. The idea is to leave sufficient time in case anyone disagrees with the merge. (If you get impatient in the meantime, you can find plenty of other merging work to do on older articles!)

6. Review any comments left regarding the merge; if strong objections have been raised, don't merge the articles.

7. If you have not yet decided, choose the destination article and the redirected article. If you aren't sure, discuss it with other editors on the relevant talk pages to resolve the matter.

8. Edit both articles at once (use two browser windows or two browser tabs). First, copy the text from the mergefrom page to the mergeto page. Make sure to include all references, footnotes, external links, and see alsos (as for editing, you can draft the merged article first and save it later, or you can use subsequent edits to clean up your work). Add an appropriate edit summary when you save the article indicating where the content came from, such as "merging content," and include the title of the article you're merging from.

9. Use several edits to work on the logical order of the new, combined page. Determine the extent of duplication, which sections need to be cut or moved, and if any new sections need to be started. Reducing the duplication in stages is best; sort the material by combining duplicate sections. It is best to determine duplication section by section rather than when you first combine the articles.

10. Polish the text of the new article and work on readability. Try not to delete content, but focus on creating a quality article. Don't lose references and footnotes, and cite any questionable statements.

11. Replace the text on the mergefrom article with a redirect to the new destination (mergeto) article. Save the page, indicating which pages are being merged in the edit summaries.

12. If the two articles disagreed about a fact, include this information in a note on the talk page of the destination article. Also indicate any other changes, such as text cuts or deleted images.

13. Check What Links Here from the redirected article to find double redirects that may have been created by the merge; fix these redirects by editing them to point to the destination article.

14. When you're finished, remove the merge tag from the destination article, and add a note indicating that the merge is complete to your original threads on the talk pages.

15. Congratulate yourself on completing the merge!

For major consolidations with more than one article, you can use the `{{multiplemergefrom|}}` template. Proceed with the merge one article at a time; you will still need to determine a destination article.

Splitting Articles

An article should be split into multiple articles when it has become unwieldy to read and edit. An article should also split into multiple articles if it deals with several diverse topics better suited to individual articles. An article should not be split, however, if the resulting articles would be small stubs. For example, an article about an author should not be split into small articles about each of his or her books; in this case, one long article about the author and his or her work with redirects from the book titles is usually best.

Very long articles are undesirable for a variety of reasons: They are difficult to navigate and read, and in some older browsers and mobile browsers, you can't edit pages with more than 32KB of text. Long articles can also take a long time to load on slow Internet connections. The *Manual of Style* deals with these points at [[Wikipedia:Article size]] (shortcut WP:SIZE).

When a long article includes too much detail on a narrow subtopic, you might want to split it. Splitting is an important aspect of [[Wikipedia:Summary style]], which was mentioned in Chapter 6. Long articles should generally follow summary style. Each section of the article should summarize the major topic points with links to specialized articles that fill in detail. For example, an article about a sports team should not be dominated by material on a famous coach: The coach should be discussed in a separate article and the material sensibly divided between the team's article (which would cover the coach's work with the team) and the coach's article (which would cover mostly biographical information).

Procedurally, a split is similar to a merge. First, post the {{split}} template on the page, perhaps at the beginning of the section you propose splitting into its own article. Add a note to the article's talk page before doing anything drastic. You should normally wait for any comments and discussion among editors.

If a section of text needs to be split into its own article:

1. Give the new article an appropriate title.
2. Edit the old article to obtain the wikitext for cutting and pasting, so any formatting is preserved.
3. Add an appropriate edit summary, indicating that you're splitting the old article and giving the names of the two articles using wikilinks, for instance, *Split [[History of Alaska]] out from [[Alaska]]*.
4. Add a summary to the old article where you cut the text rather than leaving a gap, and add a wikilink to the new article

Using the History of Alaska example, in the main Alaska article just add one or two short paragraphs summarizing the high points of Alaskan history. At the top of the section called ==History of Alaska==, include a link to the new, more specialized article, along with a message such as *Main article: [[History of Alaska]]*. This message tells readers to click the link to go to that article if they want more information on Alaskan history. Use the template {{main|title}} to produce a neat message.

Moving Pages

If an article is located at the wrong title, you can move it to a new title as long as another article isn't already located at that title. Moving is the only way to rename a page.

Moving a page is simple but has several implications. To move a page, you must be logged in and have an account that is more than four days old (as of early 2008). Click the Move tab at the top of the page you want to rename. In the form that appears, type the new title that you want the article to have and the reason you are moving the article to the new title. Keep the Move associated talk page box checked. Check the Watch this page box to add it to your personal watchlist.

A typical move may be as minor as moving [[PT Barnum]] to [[P. T. Barnum]], (adding periods and a space between the initials). Page moves are routinely used to fix title style (correcting punctuation, including the type of apostrophe, or using a hyphen for an en dash are common fixes).

Page moves accomplish three important things:

▶ Change the article title

▶ Move the page history to the new page title

▶ Create a redirect from the old title to the new title

They may also result in three other things:

▶ Turn redirects to the old title into double redirects

▶ Fill in redlinks, if the new title has been linked to on other pages

▶ Prevent future duplication

Creating double redirects is negative, but the other two are positive. If, for example, you move an orphan article with a poorly chosen title to a more reasonable title, you may be rewarded with a stack of new backlinks to the page if others have already linked to that new page title elsewhere. Broken links have suddenly become bluelinks thanks to your observant work.

Limits on Moving Pages

If you're trying to move an article and another article already has the title you've chosen, you won't be able to move your article there. Examine both articles: Should they be merged instead? See "When a Page Move Is Blocked" on page 252 for what to do in that more complicated scenario.

The only time you can move an article on top of an existing page is when that page is a redirect with minimal history.

The move function is the only acceptable way to retitle an article, as moving transfers the version history along with the article itself. Although you can easily copy and paste article content into a new page and then redirect the old page to the new one, doing so is wrong. This results in an article with no history of previous versions, creating a confusing record. These so-called *cut-and-paste moves* can be

> ## Fixing Double Redirects
>
> After you move an article, you're responsible for removing double redirects by checking What Links Here for the old article. After you've moved an article successfully, a message reminds you to check for double redirects and gives you the correct text to use. A good editor will not neglect this task, even though bots on the site may get to it within a few days.

fixed by an administrator through the history merge process; see [[Wikipedia:How to fix cut and paste moves]]. When merging or splitting an article, always provide a good edit summary detailing where the content came from.

Undoing a Move

Page moves can be undone. Immediately after moving an article, you will have the option to revert back if you realize you've made a mistake. Undoing is possible only if the article from which the original move was made has not subsequently been edited. If it has, you can reverse the move function by going back to the original title. If that is not possible, you will need an administrator's help. See [[Wikipedia:How to rename (move) a page#Undoing a move]].

Contentious Title Changes

After you've worked on Wikipedia for a while, you'll get a feel for what is considered contentious and what is not. For article titles, the basic rule is to use the most common expression. Titles should not be changed to make a point—political or otherwise. Obviously, if the new title fails to describe the article's text in a neutral way, problems may arise. In case of doubt, discuss the new title on the article's talk page before moving the article.

For example, consider what type of article might justify including the word *massacre* in its title: Frequent discussions about this type of issue have occurred, and nationalist opinions become involved. For example, the use of the word *massacre* has been contentious in relation to [[Deir Yassin massacre]], which some have wanted renamed [[Battle of Deir Yassin]]. In this instance, Wikipedia engages with contentious history, and sharp debates cannot be avoided.

Wikipedia prefers to be correct rather than populist regarding some exceptions to using the common name or title, such as articles about aristocrats. But take, for example, the article [[J. D. Salinger]]. Moving it to [[Jerome David Salinger]] would cause annoyance because J.D. Salinger is never referred to by his full name. Although full names are often better than initials, in this instance, they aren't; Salinger's initials serve as a sort of pen name. (More examples of this can be found at [[List of people known by initials]].)

Categorize

Each page in the Category namespace represents, lists, and perhaps defines a *category*, or grouping of related pages. Categories place pages on related topics in one "container." A category page on Wikipedia should offer an overview of the coverage of a particular subject. How extensive is the coverage? How are articles organized? Is the particular topic you want there, but under a title that wouldn't be your first choice? Is there a subcategory that's a better fit for the area you want to research?

You learned how to navigate with categories in "Browsing by Categories" on page 88; in this section, you'll learn how to use them as an editorial tool.

All articles should be in at least one category; most articles are in more than one category. Some areas are particularly important to categorize: For instance, work is ongoing to track all Wikipedia's biographies of living persons in [[Wikipedia:Living people]], with the number of articles running well into the six figures.

When an article is in one or more categories, this information appears at the very bottom of the article in an automatically generated section called *Categories*.

Clicking any category link will take you to the main page for that category. As described in Chapter 3 (see Figure 3-10 on page 90), a category page has four parts:

▶ The explanation of the category; this text (along with the category's discussion page) is editable and is what you'll see if you click Edit This Page.

▶ A list of any subcategories within the category; these are listed alphabetically, but if the category is very large, the list may be spread over several pages.

▶ A list of links to articles in the category; this list is automatically populated. If the category is very large, the listing may be spread over several pages; only the first 200 links will appear on the first page. Click Next 200 at the bottom of the page to see the next page of entries.

▶ At the very bottom, you'll find a list of the categories that the category you're viewing is part of. These are editable by editing the category page.

Categorizing Basics

You can assign a page to any category simply by adding

[[Category:*categoryname*]]

---

to the page's wikitext. Substitute the actual name of the category in place of *categoryname*.

For example, to add the article [[Bozo the Clown]] to the Clowns category, you would edit the article and add the text [[Category:Clowns]] at the very bottom of the page.

Placing an article in a category by adding a category tag does two things:

▸ It automatically lists the article on the appropriate category page.

▸ It also provides a link to that category page in the list of categories at the bottom of the article.

Though no connection exists between the location of the category tag in the article source text and where the *Categories* box appears on the page, the general convention is to place categories together at the end of the source text (though before any interwiki links), one per line, so they don't affect the rest of the text and are all in one place. (Figure 8-5 shows the placement of categories in an article's wikitext.) Wikipedia has no standard order for categories.

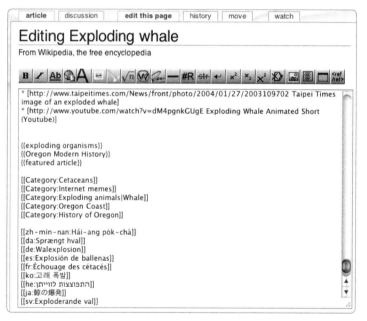

FIGURE 8-5: *Article wikitext with multiple categories listed near the end of a page (after templates and before interwiki links), from the article [[Exploding whale]]*

Articles can be included in more than one category by adding multiple category tags. For example, for a person no longer alive, the standard categories are year of birth, year of death, and occupation. Most articles are naturally in more than one category.

Most Categories

The page in the greatest number of categories can be found at the special page [[Special:Mostcategories]]. As of March 2008, a large number of Fauna categories were added to [[Red Fox]], giving it 96; second as we go to print is [[Black Rat]]. Prior to this, the article in the greatest number of categories was [[Winston Churchill]], with 67; these include [[Category:Knights of the Elephant]], for holders of a Danish decoration, and [[Category:Nobel laureates in Literature]], from 1953, as well as [[Category:Old Harrovians]] and [[Category:Members of the Queen's Privy Council for Canada]].

To link to a category in wikitext without categorizing the page, type

```
[[:Category:Instruction]]
```

Doing this is useful for See also sections in articles. This is also vital if you want to discuss a category on a talk page. If you leave out the first colon, the text of the link won't be displayed, and the page will be categorized in that category.

Categories and Content Policy

Like everything else on Wikipedia, categories are not canonical. Sometimes they are even incorrect or misleading, usually as the result of an honest mistake. Articles should be placed in categories simply to inform, never to make a point or forward a controversial position. Obviously, if an article about a person is in a category damaging to his or her reputation, the classification should be fully supported within the article. No one should just add [[Category:Murderers]], unjustified, to a biography. Wikipedia doesn't allow its category system to be used as a way of commenting on content.

In general, anybody adding categories to an article should follow the same basic policies of Verifiability, No Original Research, and Neutral Point of View that govern the rest of Wikipedia. Categories are part of the informational content of an article and should be treated appropriately: They should be supported by references (or more properly by statements in the article's text that are themselves referenced), especially if the category is contentious. (One disadvantage of categories as opposed to lists: You can add sources to a list to support inclusion, but you can't annotate an article's categories directly.)

Wikipedia has many guidelines for categorizing articles; [[Wikipedia:Catego-rization FAQ]] is one place to find them. [[Wikipedia:Categorization of people]], another guideline, explains the sensitive subject of placing people in categories that might affect their reputation. Especially for biographical articles about living people, use caution when adding categories other than very formal and descriptive ones.

Creating New Categories

You can start a new category easily. If you add a category to an article, but the category doesn't exist yet, it displays as a redlink in the article's list of categories. To turn the redlink blue, simply click it (or visit [[Category:*New category name*]], where *new category name* is the category you want to create) and add some content, such as a brief description of the category and the categories it is a subcategory of, to the category page. Any pages that you or others have already tagged with your new category name will automatically be listed on the new category page.

For example, [[Category:Poisoned apples]] could be created by adding this text to the new page [[Category:Poisoned apples]]:

```
A poisoned apple is an apple that has been poisoned.
[[Category:Apples]]
[[Category:Fairytale objects]]
```

The description will appear at the top of the category page, and adding the categories will instantly make *poisoned apples* a new subcategory of the Apples and Fairytale Objects category.

All new categories should have their broader categories listed, but including a description is optional; in this case, the description isn't very helpful. In some cases, though, a good description (perhaps linking to the main article on the subject) will help the average reader, especially for obscure subjects.

Wikipedia also has naming and structural conventions for creating categories. Use plurals, for example [[Category:Pigs]], for categories. This convention differs from the article title convention of generally preferring the singular form. Proper names such as [[Category:Vermont]], which collects articles about the state, or collective headings such as [[Category:Greek mythology]] are also common category names.

Before creating a new category, make sure the category you want doesn't already exist under a variant name (check articles similar to the one you're trying to categorize). Creating categories that are not obviously needed is considered a nuisance.

Subcategories

Categories can have subcategories. Anyone can create or alter subcategories by simply categorizing the category page. For instance, you could make [[Category:Piglets]] a subcategory of [[Category:Pigs]]; simply tag the [[Category:Piglets]] page with [[Category:Pigs]]. Using the subcategory and supercategory structure is a good way to browse the site and is discussed extensively in Chapter 3.

Here, we'll discuss the issues around classifying articles using detailed subcategories. Are detailed subcategories a good thing or not? Certainly having categories that contain too many articles can be unwieldy; a category with more than 200 articles in it requires multiple pages. Subcategorizing the articles into more distinct categories can help keep categories manageable.

Subcategories are useful on Wikipedia to subclassify when the schematic being followed is fairly natural to the subject matter and the relevance is evident. [[Category:Politicians with blue eyes]] is not helpful—why would anyone be looking for this information? But [[Category:Canadian buskers]] is an acceptable subcategory of [[Category:Buskers]] or of [[Category:Canadian musicians]]. Subcategories should offer the general reader a convenient way to navigate a category and also provide information about the material included in a category.

Following a general but not quite universal convention, articles should not appear in both a category and a subcategory. For instance, [[Category:Beetles]] within [[Category:Insects]] classifies some insects more precisely. According to the convention, the beetle articles should not also be in the more general [[Category:Insects]]. Therefore, in searching [[Category:Insects]] for *all* the Wikipedia articles on insects, you would also have to search [[Category:Beetles]] and, within that, more than a dozen subcategories to find all of the beetle pages. Going through all the subcategories is the only comprehensive way to find all the articles related to a larger category, such as insects; if in this case you went to the page [[List of insects]], you'd discover this list is a redirect to [[Category:Insects]]. While finding all Wikipedia articles about insects is probably unreasonable (as the category is enormous), creating extremely detailed subcategories for smaller topics can make it difficult to see all the related articles at a glance. On the other hand, articles should always placed in the most detailed category that applies: An article about a beetle found in New Zealand should be placed in the Beetles of New Zealand category, not the higher-level category Beetles.

Exploring a Category and Its Subcategories

Wikipedia has a way to show an extended view of the whole structure of a complex category. The special page [[Special:CategoryTree]] will show you all of a category's subcategories arranged in a clickable tree structure. Go to the page and type the name of the category you want to examine in the box provided (JavaScript must be enabled in your browser). This tool makes it easy to see related articles in different subcategories. You can also include an expandable category tree on a wiki page by using the tag <categorytree>*Name of category*</categorytree>. No brackets are needed around the name of the category with this tag.

Categorization Projects

You can find lots of information about projects to improve the use of categories at [[Wikipedia:WikiProject Categories/Current subprojects]]. You can also find an overview at [[Category:Wikipedia categorization]].

One long-standing categorization project that crosses all disciplines is [[Wikipedia:WikiProject Stub sorting]]. This project maintains the article categories for stubs, a list of which can be found at [[Wikipedia:WikiProject Stub sorting/List of stubs]]. These special categories are applied to articles not with standard category tags but with templates, which are discussed in the next chapter.

Further Reading

http://en.wikipedia.org/wiki/Wikipedia:Categorization   The categorization guideline

http://en.wikipedia.org/wiki/Wikipedia:Categorization_FAQ   Frequently asked questions about using categories

http://en.wikipedia.org/wiki/Wikipedia:Categorization_of_people
The guideline about categorizing people

http://en.wikipedia.org/wiki/Wikipedia:WikiProject_Categories
The WikiProject dealing with categorization

http://en.wikipedia.org/wiki/Wikipedia:Categorization_projects_(current)
Current categorization projects

http://en.wikipedia.org/wiki/Category:Wikipedia_categorization
The category of project pages dealing with categorization

Housekeeping

Now that you've seen how the six tools can be used for hypertext editing, we will discuss a few problems that can arise when you try to apply the tools discussed in this chapter and solutions to those problems.

When a Page Move Is Blocked

Suppose you want to move article P to title Q, but the MediaWiki software blocks the move. P and Q might be articles on identical topics; then you will need to merge the articles.

If the other article Q is on a different topic than P but uses the same title that you wanted to use for P, then you need to create a disambiguation page for the main term and move the other articles to appropriate titles, which will then be linked to on the new disambiguation page. For instance, you might want to move [[Jolly Green Giant]] to [[Green Giant]]—but you'd find that [[Green Giant]] is already taken up with a page about the company. You could move the page [[Green Giant]] to [[Green Giant (company)]], and [[Jolly Green Giant]] to [[Green Giant (symbol)]]. Then you could go back to the page [[Green Giant]]—it will be a redirect to [[Green Giant (company)]] from the move—and edit it to be a disambiguation page pointing to the two articles. Any other articles about green giants could also be listed. The page [[Jolly Green Giant]] will be automatically turned into a redirect to [[Green Giant (symbol)]], but you'll need to check for double redirects and add hatnotes to the two articles pointing back to the disambiguation page. This series of actions will help this small corner of Wikipedia make more sense to the reader.

Sometimes the situation is more complicated. Page moves to temporary dummy titles can help. You can tag any unneeded redirects you create for speedy deletion when you're done. See [[Help:Moving a page]] for more guidance and [[Wikipedia:Requested moves]] to request administrator help with moving a page.

Default Meanings

Sometimes an article about a lesser character, say from an anime or comic, will be created before the article about a more important figure with the same name. A disambiguation page should be created in this case. For the good of the encyclopedia, the lesser character shouldn't become the default meaning, however. For example [[Thor]], the Norse god, must have priority over [[Thor (Marvel Comics)]]. Problems of this type have to be sorted out by someone who understands blocked page moves.

Moves are best made from a more general title to a more particular title: from [[John Jones]] to [[John James Jones]], for example. That leaves the way open to making [[John Jones]] a disambiguation page. Moving *uphill*, or removing information from a title, is sometimes more problematic. Removing information can often make a title ambiguous, for example, moving [[George W. Bush]] to [[George Bush]]. If you remove information from a title, you risk deciding on the Wikipedia default meaning: You may be telling the world that John Jones should be read as John James Jones.

In other words, make titles more informative and specialized to the topic. But don't add titles like Dr., honorifics, or post-nominal letters like initials after names; this is against Wikipedia conventions. Moving articles to more general titles should be used mainly for verbose titles, like moving [[List of Japanese Government and Private institutions and Groups (from 1930s to 1945)]] to [[List of Japanese institutions (1930–1945)]].

Avoiding Disambiguation Pages

Wikilinks in articles should generally point to the exact article title meant, not a disambiguation page, since a link with a variety of possible meanings can be confusing to a reader unfamiliar with a topic. The process of changing wikilinks to point to precise articles instead of disambiguation pages is called *avoid disambiguation pages*. Generally, this work is done by checking What Links Here for disambiguation pages.

Here's an example from the article [[Rectangle]]. The initial text in the article was

---

A [[square]] is a special kind of rectangle where all four sides have equal length;

But [[Square]] is a disambiguation page, which includes the meaning [[Square (slang)]] for an un-hip person. To avoid the dab page, change the link to [[Square]] to the following:

A [[square (geometry)|square]] is a special kind of rectangle where all four sides have equal length;

The text now reads the same as before, but the destination of the wikilink is precise and correct. If an article using the precise meaning of a term hasn't been created yet, use a red-and-piped link rather than linking to the disambiguation page (which would be confusing). The redlink may also prompt someone to create the new article.

Finding Disambiguation Work

To find lists of disambiguation pages, including the disambiguation pages that need to be improved, try browsing through [[Category:Disambiguation]]; the subcategories at the top sort disambiguation pages by topic. If you want to work on disambiguation pages that need cleanup help, consider joining the disambiguation WikiProject: [[Wikipedia:WikiProject Disambiguation]]. See [[Wikipedia:Disambiguation pages with links]] (shortcut WP:DPL) for a list of disambiguation pages that have incoming links (which should instead be links to more precise articles).

Controlling Category Sorting

Pages within categories are displayed alphabetically by the first word of the page title, but this order can be modified by *sort keys*.

[[Category:Presidents of France]] may look quite ordinary (Figure 8-6), but a few things are going on here. Under the letter *G*, you'll find the article for Charles de Gaulle. Under *N*, you'll find the article on Napoleon III of France, but under *S* (not *N*), you'll find the article on Nicolas Sarkozy. The case of Sarkozy obviously fits sorting by surname, but what else is happening here? Napoleon III was a president before he was an emperor, but his surname was, of course, Bonaparte. De Gaulle is a surname, but using the appropriate convention for French names, the *de* is not considered here.

FIGURE 8-6: *[[Category:Presidents of France]]*

In a category, you would generally expect the article [[John Smith]] to be sorted under *S* for *Smith* rather than *J* for *John*. Wikipedia has two ways to achieve this result: magic words and sort keys. These two approaches have the same effect—making category listings treat the [[John Smith]] page article as if its title were *Smith John*—but magic words affect every category a page is in, while sort keys only work one category at a time. Each is highly flexible.

The magic word for default sort is used like a template:

```
{{DEFAULTSORT:}}
```

For the page [[John Smith]], it would be filled in like this:

```
{{DEFAULTSORT:Smith, John}}
```

and placed in the wikitext above the list of categories. To classify [[Charles de Gaulle]] under *G*, the template would be filled in this way:

```
{{DEFAULTSORT:Gaulle, Charles de}}
```

The use of this template affects every category page that Charles de Gaulle might be placed in (potentially dozens); the article will always show up sorted under *G*.

To only sort an article in a single category, or to vary sorting according to the category, use a *sort key*, which is added after a pipe character placed in the Category link in the article text:

```
[[Category:1900 births|Smith, John]]
```

If you want to list Napoleon III under *B* for *Bonaparte*, for this particular category, enter

```
[[Category:Presidents of France|Bonaparte, Louis-Napoleon]]
```

on the page [[Napoleon III of France]]; that will affect just how the article is sorted in the category *Presidents of France*. See [[Wikipedia:Categorization#Pipe tricks and sort keys]] for more examples and explanations.

Although titles usually consist of plain text, they may begin with other symbols. The ordering used for category sorting when extended to non-alphanumeric characters is *ASCII order*, a standard used in byte codes for computing. Article titles beginning with numbers come before article titles starting with the letter *A* and article titles starting with symbols are always displayed before these, using a particular order for symbols. The article [[(Like) Linus]], beginning with an opening parenthesis and about a demo by The Deftones, would precede the article about [[@Home Network]], a defunct ISP, beginning with @, if these two articles were ever placed in the same (unlikely) category.

The use of ASCII order explains one more thing about the Presidents of France category page. The listing starts with [[President of the French Republic]], under an asterisk (*). This is because in the article [[President of the French Republic]], the category tag reads

```
[[Category:Presidents of France|*]
```

The asterisk is a device for bringing the article to the top of the listing so it is much more prominent. This method is commonly used for highlighting the main article in a category—the article that will give the reader an overview of the whole topic. A blank space after the pipe character is an extra refinement and has the same effect except no asterisk is included on the category page.

Categories and Templates for Redirects

Certain links on a category page may appear in italics. This is because these are links for redirect pages. If you click the link, you go to the page to which the redirect leads (not to the article with the title you expected).

The probable explanation is this: The redirect is anchored to a section of an article, and the category is right for that section but would be odd for the whole article. For example, the article might be about an author and the section about a film made from one of the author's books: Placing the author's name in a film category wouldn't be correct.

Another example of how to use this device is illustrated by the French Presidents example. [[Charles Louis-Napoléon Bonaparte]] is a redirect to [[Napoleon III of France]]. The category tag [[Category:Presidents of France|Bonaparte]] could be included in the redirect, so the category page would include the correct name for his time as president and be sorted under *Bonaparte*.

Templates on redirects are mostly used to flag redirects that could usefully become articles in their own right. See [[Category:Redirect templates]].

Process-Style Resolutions

Your problem may have a resolution, if you only knew where to go to get an answer.

Category deletion

Annoying and useless categories and categories that need to be renamed (often required to apply conventions consistently) are handled via a process. Go to [[Wikipedia:Categories for discussion]] (shortcut WP:CFD) to apply for deletion, merging, and renaming of categories or to participate in discussions about those issues. The process takes about a week.

Problem redirects

Go to [[Wikipedia:Redirects for discussion]] (shortcut WP:RFD).

Disagreement about default meanings

Editors are supposed to discuss difficulties about default meanings and come to a resolution. Failing that, [[Wikipedia:Requested moves]] (shortcut WP:RM) is the place to discuss any contested title change.

Merges without consensus

Most mergers should be simply tagged and discussed on their respective talk pages, but proposed merges can also be listed on [[Wikipedia:Proposed mergers]] for wider discussion. If there is no consensus, the merge should usually not occur.

Contested title changes

Go to [[Wikipedia:Requested moves]] (shortcut WP:RM) to discuss moves when consensus is not clear. This page is where matters concerning moves can be sorted out if there is real disagreement. Just add the request along with a short justification, and refer back to this page for a few days. Any editor may comment.

Fixing cut-and-paste moves

Go to [[Wikipedia:Cut and paste move repair holding pen]] (shortcut WP: SPLICE) if you need page histories fixed after copy-and-paste moves.

Further Reading

http://en.wikipedia.org/wiki/Help:Moving_a_page#Moving_over_an_existing_ page   How to move over an existing page

http://en.wikipedia.org/wiki/Help:Category#Sort_order   Sort order guideline

http://en.wikipedia.org/wiki/Category:Redirect templates   The category for redirect templates

http://en.wikipedia.org/wiki/Wikipedia:Categories_for_discussion   Category discussion

http://en.wikipedia.org/wiki/Wikipedia:Redirects_for_discussion   Redirect discussions

http://en.wikipedia.org/wiki/Wikipedia:Proposed_mergers   Proposed mergers, sorted by month

http://en.wikipedia.org/wiki/Wikipedia:Requested_moves   Where to request help with moves

http://en.wikipedia.org/wiki/Wikipedia:How_to_fix_cut-and-paste_moves Guidelines for fixing cut and paste moves

---

Summary

Improving Wikipedia can go beyond editing text. The techniques discussed in this chapter complement the more glamorous business of writing articles. They allow you to present the site's content to the readers more clearly by creating navigational structures and sorting existing content.

There are two special types of pages—redirect and disambiguation pages—that are used to help readers navigate Wikipedia. Redirects are a special type of page that take readers from one page title to another when more than one possible title for an article exists. Wikipedia has millions of redirects, all helping readers navigate and search the site. Disambiguation pages, on the other hand, pull together a list of articles with similar titles that could be confused. These pages can be created for any term with multiple meanings, as well as for common personal and family names that may refer to more than one person or family.

Part of editing articles is ensuring that each article's scope is appropriate. If Wikipedia has two or more articles about the same topic or with very similar content, these articles may need to be merged. Any editor can merge two articles by editing them and combining their text on one of the pages and then redirecting the other article to the new combined article. If an article gets too long and unwieldy or deals with multiple disparate topics, the article may need to be split into two or more separate articles. Any editor can do this by creating a new page and copying some of the old article's content to the new page. Finally, an article may be created using the wrong title or a later decision is made to rename an article. In this case, that article needs to be moved to a new title.

Finally, categorizing articles in appropriate categories is a fundamental part of sorting Wikipedia content, making it more accessible to readers and editors. Anyone can help with categorizing pages. Anyone can also create new categories, but understanding how the process works ensures your work is consistent with existing schemes.

For all of these editing techniques, Wikipedia has developed many guidelines detailing how they are done and has created several community processes for dealing with problem cases.

9

Images, Templates, and Special Characters

Articles on Wikipedia can include more than simply text. Images and media files enhance content whereas templates (such as the ubiquitous infoboxes) and tables can help you lay out articles more cleanly. Well-chosen graphics and neat presentations can improve articles significantly. You can also use a number of formatting tricks. For example, you can use some HTML successfully, display special characters, and add mathematical formulas to articles. These tasks all use advanced wikisyntax, which will be covered in this chapter.

Our best advice is to learn the more advanced syntax options when you need them. Much of what is covered in this chapter, particularly information about template syntax, is not usually necessary for basic editing, but you can generally learn how to apply these enhancements quickly if you want to use them to improve an article.

Images and Media Files

Images and media files are a welcome contribution to Wikipedia and complement article text in multiple ways. Images might be illustrations, diagrams, photographs, or maps; they can show the reader what an animal looks like, where a country is, or give a sense of a city's skyline. Media files might include sounds, such as the pronunciation of an unfamiliar word or a short clip of a composer's work, or videos, such as an animation of how a machine works. What all of these files have in common is that they exist to illustrate and clarify article text. Images should not be placed in articles simply for the sake of adding a pretty picture, but a good, clear image of the subject—or an appropriate sound or video file—can greatly enhance any article.

Like all other Wikipedia content, all media and images must be freely licensed. Though today you can find digital images everywhere on the Web, by and large you can't use these images directly in Wikipedia; such use is generally a copyright violation, much like copying someone else's text and uploading it as your own. A better tactic is to take photographs or produce drawings and diagrams yourself, license them freely, and then upload them to Wikipedia for use in articles.

In this section, we'll talk about how to find images on Wikipedia, how to upload your own work for use on the site (and the licensing guidelines to keep in mind when doing so, including whether you can claim a *fair use* rationale), and then how to embed images in pages, using the special image syntax. We'll then discuss media files such as sound and video clips.

Any discussion of images is incomplete without mentioning one of Wikipedia's sister projects, the Wikimedia Commons (*http://common.wikimedia.org/*), which serves as an image and media file repository for all of the Wikimedia projects. These days uploading and working on images on Commons, where images are more easily reusable and searchable, rather than on Wikipedia directly is preferable. A more detailed description of this project can be found in Chapter 16.

Finding and Adding Images

As of early 2008, Wikipedia and the Wikimedia Commons had well over 3,000,000 images. With this many images, you can most likely find existing images to use in your article. If not, anyone is welcome to upload new images to the site, as long as the images can be used in an article and are freely licensed.

Searching for Images to Use

The Wikimedia Commons is probably the best place to start searching for images or media files. The easiest way to search is to use the Mayflower search engine (you'll find a link to it on the front page of Commons); Mayflower searches image description pages on Commons for your keywords and returns a page of thumbnail-size pictures as search results. You can also go to Commons to browse media files and images by subject, as most images have been categorized extensively.

On Wikipedia itself, you can also browse images using categories. The topmost category for images is [[Category:Wikipedia images]]; this category also contains images that are only used as part of the Wikipedia project (rather than in articles), such as images for WikiProject awards. Under this category you'll find [[Category:Wikipedia images by subject]] and [[Category:Wikipedia images by type]], which sorts images based on whether they are drawings, animations, and so on. One image collection especially worth visiting is [[Wikipedia:Featured pictures]], which is a selection of some of the very best images on Wikipedia; here you can find the picture of the day and participate in image judging.

Finally, you can also search image descriptions directly on Wikipedia by searching the Image namespace, as described in Chapter 3. Whether you get any results depends entirely on how well the image has been titled and described.

If you enjoy contributing images and want to help track down needed pictures, there are two places to look for requests for pictures: [[Category:Wikipedia requested images]] on Wikipedia and [[Commons:Picture requests]] on Commons.

Image Licenses and Fair Use

If you can't find an existing image for your article, you can upload a new one. But first make sure the license is acceptable. You shouldn't upload images to Wikipedia without knowing the license restrictions or without permission. All images you upload to Wikipedia must meet one of four criteria:

▶ You (the person who puts the picture on Wikipedia) own the rights to the image (that is, you created it), and you agree to release the image under a free license, such as the GFDL.

▶ If you didn't originally create the image, you can prove that the copyright holder has licensed the image under an acceptable free license, such as the GFDL.

▶ You can prove that the image is in the public domain; this is the case with US government–created work such as photos from NASA, which are automatically placed in the public domain.

▶ You produce a convincing fair-use rationale.

Playing fast and loose with the rules is very unhelpful. *Do not* copy images you find on the Web and call them your own. Although disregarding these points and uploading technically works anyway, many Wikipedians monitor the list of new image uploads, and without a proper license, the image will not remain on the site for long (typically, it will be deleted within a week).

The last of the criteria, fair use, is only accepted on the English-language Wikipedia (*not* on Commons) and is quite controversial, causing much discussion over the years. Under US copyright law, the term *fair use* refers generally to a limited use of a copyrighted work for educational or critical purposes. For instance, when a reviewer quotes a small segment from a book he or she is reviewing, the reviewer can do so because of fair use. On Wikipedia, the so-called fair-use policy documents when it is acceptable to use a non-free image on the site. For example, album covers appear in several articles about albums. Cover art is typically copyrighted, but the fair-use policy may mean that a small scanned image of the cover is acceptable so long as the album artwork *itself* is critically discussed in the article and an image of the artwork is necessary to help clarify this discussion.

Fair use is controversial on Wikipedia because the site aims to include only free content; including any copyrighted material at all is problematic given Wikipedia's license and values, and the legal aspects of what is and isn't fair use can be very difficult to determine. Given this, so-called fair-use images are only used in a very limited range of circumstances. If there is any possibility a *free equivalent* to a copyrighted image could be obtained instead at some point in the future (for instance, if the copyrighted image is of a living actor and another photographer might donate an equivalent photo), then the copyrighted image should not be used.

The full details of fair use on Wikipedia for images and media are something of a mouthful and are explained on [[Wikipedia:Non-free content]] (shortcut WP: NONFREE). Ten points are involved:

1. No free equivalent can exist.
2. Commercial opportunities for the copyright owner must not be affected.
3. Usage on Wikipedia must be minimal. An entire work is not used if a portion or sample would do.
4. The work must have been previously published outside Wikipedia.
5. General Wikipedia content requirements must be met, and the material must be encyclopedic.
6. Other aspects of the media-specific policy ([[Wikipedia:Image use policy]], shortcut WP:IUP) must be met.
7. The content is used in at least one article.
8. The reader must gain significantly from the addition to an article, and the gain could not be achieved by text alone.
9. Non-free content is basically allowed only in articles and not in disambiguation pages.
10. The image description page must be completed properly.

Even so, fair-use images are often culled and deleted from the site.

The best alternative to fair use is to find a free image instead, in line with the site's mission of promoting free culture. For instance, for celebrities or politicians, releasing a single PR photo into the public domain (or under the GFDL) ensures that Wikipedia can use that picture free and clear, and everyone benefits.

Uploading Your Own Images

Images must be *uploaded* before they can be used on the project. You can't link to images on other websites. Images can be uploaded directly to Wikipedia, or alternatively to the Wikimedia Commons, where they may be used by all Wikimedia projects (not just the English-language Wikipedia). The latter option is preferable. A description of how to upload to the Commons, which is quite similar to the process described next, is in Chapter 16.

File Types

The following file types can be uploaded to Wikipedia: PNG, GIF, JPG, JPEG, XCF, SVG, DJVU, PDF, MID, and OGG. The first seven are image file formats, whereas the last three are for documents and media. According to [[Wikipedia:Media]], the preferred file formats are JPEG (*.jpg) for images and Scalable Vector Graphics (SVG; *.svg) for drawings.

To upload an image, you must be logged in to the site. Click Upload File on the left-hand sidebar or visit [[Special:Upload]].

The steps are simple:

1. Save the image or file you wish to upload to your computer.
2. Click Upload File on the left-hand sidebar and indicate how you got the image. Depending on the option selected, you'll be led through a series of licensing questions to answer before you get to the uploading form.

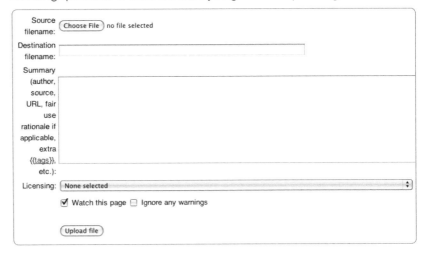

FIGURE 9-1: *The image uploading form*

3. Once you reach the uploading form, scroll down past the warnings on the page to the form itself (Figure 9-1).
4. Fill in the Source filename field; this field is for your original file. Click Browse to access the image on your computer. Once you've found the file, select it and click Open. The filename will then appear in the Source filename field.
5. Select the *destination filename*; this is the name the file will have on Wikipedia or Commons (this name will be prefaced by *Image:* automatically).

The filename for the image on your computer is used by default, but you can edit the name to change it (see the advice on naming files below). Remember that image filenames, unlike article titles, *cannot* be changed once you've named them, so choose carefully.

6. Describe the image in the Summary field. What is the image of? When was the photo taken or the drawing created? Include as much useful information as you can—this is the only way that people searching for images will be able to find yours. This field may be pre-filled in with a template, depending on which option you chose in step 1; if so, you can fill out the appropriate parameters.

7. Choose the appropriate license; if you select *I don't know*, your image will be deleted.

8. Leave Watch this page checked; this way, you'll notice if the image has been tagged for deletion.

9. Click Upload File. You're done!

The image now resides in the Image namespace, using the filename you've given it. Once you've successfully uploaded an image, you'll be taken to its *image description page*; this page is located at *http://en.wikipedia.org/wiki/Image:yourimagename.jpg*, where *yourimagename.jpg* is the filename you entered in the Destination filename field. This page is also where your summary description of the image appears. Once an image is embedded in an article, anyone clicking it will be taken to this page (note that if you click an image from Commons, you will automatically see the description page from Commons instead). The information and description on this page can be edited like any other page. To link to an image description page directly (rather than displaying the image), add a colon (:) before the filename in the wikilink:

```
[[:image:yourimagename.jpg]]
```

Files should be named descriptively; do not use a meaningless string of numbers and letters (such as you might get from a digital camera) or filenames such as *image.jpg*. Image filenames should clearly indicate the subject of the image, and image descriptions should clearly indicate the subject of the image, the photographer or image creator, and the image source. Other information that will also help document the image includes the date the image was taken, location, occasion, and so on. An image is often used in multiple articles, and obviously you have no more say in its use than any other editor does.

Though you cannot change an image filename after uploading it, you can replace an image by uploading a new version of the image with the exact same name; this change will show up in the image history. For an existing image, click the Upload a New Version of This File link, which appears under *File history* on the image description page.

Using Images

Once you've uploaded an image, you can insert it on a Wikipedia page. Use the following syntax to insert an image on a page:

```
[[Image:nameofimage.jpg]]
```

This will display the image on the page, at the same size as the original.

Images may be floated to the left or right of the text. Laying out images on the right is more conventional for articles, though right-left alternation may also make sense, depending on the design of the article and the number of images used. For instance, standard infoboxes tend to be placed in the top-right part of an article, which will affect article layout. For an example of an article using multiple images, see [[Mandelbrot set]], where numerous techniques are used to display and arrange images.

You can set image alignment by adding a parameter using the vertical bar or pipe character (|):

```
[[Image:nameofimage.jpg|left]] or [[Image:nameofimage.jpg|right]]
```

You can also display an image as a thumbnail, which will automatically size the image to 180 pixels with space for a caption at the bottom, using the *thumb* parameter. You do this by adding two parameters:

```
[[Image:nameofimage.jpg|thumb|This is an image caption]]
```

This is an image caption will, in this case, display below the image. Captions should describe an image completely; they can include internal or external links as necessary. You can also combine this with the alignment parameter:

```
[[Image:nameofimage.jpg|right|thumb|This is an image caption]]
```

This aligns the image on the right side of the page in a handy thumbnail size with a caption below it.

Rather than using the default thumbnail sizing, images can also be sized to any dimensions:

```
[[Image:nameofimage.jpg|300px|left|This is an image]]
```

This will display the image at 300 pixels, left-aligned, with *This is an image* displayed as alternative text when a reader hovers the mouse over the image. To add this text as a caption to an image of any size, use the thumb tag with a size parameter:

```
[[Image:nameofimage.jpg|thumb|300px|This is an image]]
```

If you have many small images and you want to display them together, try using the <gallery> tag. Simply list the images you want to include in the gallery between two gallery tags, as follows:

```
<gallery>
Image:Wiki.png|Caption
Image:Wiki.png|Caption
Image:Wiki.png|Caption
Image:Wiki.png|Caption
Image:Wiki.png|Caption
Image:Wiki.png|[[Help:Contents/Links|Links]] can also be put in captions.
</gallery>
```

This will display these six images in a neat table. No double brackets are needed around filenames in an image gallery. Find out more at [[Wikipedia:Gallery tag]].

If you want to include a particularly wide image, such as a panorama of a city skyscape, use the template [[Template:Wide image]]. Full details are included on the template page.

As for which images should be included in an article, Wikipedia's image policies mainly deal with copyright concerns. The guideline at [[Wikipedia:Images]] does define what encyclopedic images are: An encyclopedic image is relevant to the subject at hand, clear, and good quality. Don't overwhelm your articles with images; using the thumbnail feature also ensures that pages will load more quickly for readers. The Featured Pictures project lays out more criteria for good images at [[Wikipedia:Featured picture criteria]]; many of these criteria are related to the technical quality of the image. For help improving images, you can always ask fellow editors interested in images—try the Wikipedia Graphics Lab project at [[Wikipedia:Graphic Lab]].

Using Multimedia Files

Other media files may also be used on Wikipedia. Audio files can be very helpful for some topics; for example, Wikipedia has numerous files designed to help you pronounce Chinese names properly. Chapter 3 covers how to play these files. Sound files must use the free Ogg Vorbis or the MIDI format, and video files must use the Ogg Theora format.

Considering approximately 70,000 articles are devoted to albums and singles, you might expect Wikipedia to have many music files. All music samples from copyright sources, however, have to be specifically tied into the article's description of a song or piece of music. Articles about albums are meant to inform, not to promote.

The fair-use policy also applies. The article on Bob Dylan's "All Along the Watchtower" does include a 14-second sample from the song. This short length conforms to the fair-use policy: The sample has to be minimal and not affect legitimate commercial trade.

Media files, such as sound files, are uploaded in the same way as image files. But when you link to them you replace *Image* with *Media*:

```
[[Media:nameoffile.ogg]]
```

Though you can upload PDF files, they do not generally play a useful role on Wikipedia or the other Wikimedia projects.

To identify a sound link in an article, you can use [[Template:Listen]], which adds a small sound icon and a handy menu for playing the file, as described at [[Wikipedia:Creation and usage of media files]].

Further Reading

Images

http://en.wikipedia.org/wiki/Wikipedia:Images   An overview of using images in pages

http://en.wikipedia.org/wiki/Wikipedia:Picture_tutorial   A tutorial on formatting images

http://en.wikipedia.org/wiki/Wikipedia:Extended_image_syntax   More advanced image syntax

http://en.wikipedia.org/wiki/Help:Images_and_other_uploaded_files
The main help page for images

http://en.wikipedia.org/wiki/Wikipedia:Finding_images_tutorial   A tutorial for finding images to illustrate articles

http://commons.wikimedia.org/wiki/Commons:First_steps/Reuse   Guidelines for using images from Commons

http://en.wikipedia.org/wiki/Wikipedia:Image_use_policy   The image use policy, "including format, content, and copyright issues"

http://en.wikipedia.org/wiki/Wikipedia:10_things_you_did_not_know_about_images_on_Wikipedia   A short list of key points about images on Wikipedia

Media

http://en.wikipedia.org/wiki/Wikipedia:Media_help   A help page for playing media files

http://en.wikipedia.org/wiki/Template:Listen   A template to use with sound files

http://en.wikipedia.org/wiki/Template:Audio   Another template to use with sound and pronunciation files

http://en.wikipedia.org/wiki/Wikipedia:WikiProject_Spoken_Wikipedia
The project to produce recordings of Wikipedia articles

Templates

Templates are generally used on Wikipedia as navigational and formatting aids and to add recurring or boilerplate messages to pages in a consistent way. They are versatile and, when properly used, help with the presentation of information. A *template* is a page—which could contain, for instance, a navigation menu—that you can insert into a wiki page and reuse multiple times.

Each template may be included (technically *transcluded*) in any number of other wiki pages, from just a handful to hundreds of thousands. For programmers, a transcluded template is comparable to an `#include` statement or a macro that is run at page view time. Templates that you are probably familiar with now are the cleanup messages that appear at the top of articles and the stub messages that are placed at the very bottom of articles. Templates can also help incorporate complicated formatting into articles to standardize them, since templates are created once and then reused. A template can provide a consistent, flexible solution for how information displays. Wikipedians, therefore, create templates whenever similar text appears in different places. Some templates that play a major role in the site are protected, but most are editable pages, residing in their own Template namespace.

Some familiarity with templates will help any editor. Although you don't need to learn how to build your own templates in order to be a knowledgeable Wikipedia contributor, knowing the function of templates and what you can expect from them is helpful. You should understand how to use and edit them.

Using Templates

If you want the same style of footer or boxed graphic to show up across all articles on a given topic, then you'll want to create a template. Similarly, if you consistently leave certain messages on user talk pages—greetings or perhaps advice—using a template provides consistency and also saves time.

To add a template to a page, just edit the page where it should go and embed the name of the template (without the Template namespace prefix) in double curly brackets where you want it to appear, like this:

```
{{template name}}
```

A template can be used more than once on a single page. After saving the page, the template will display where you've placed it.

For instance, placing

```
{{cleanup}}
```

at the top of an article will produce the message for readers that was illustrated in Figure 7-1 on page 201. The template message by itself may be viewed by going to the template page at [[Template:Cleanup]]. To see the actual source code of this template, click the Edit This Page tab (which is labeled as *View Source* for this protected page). The complicated-looking piece of formatting you see is actually what's being included in the rendered article when you use the shortcut `{{cleanup}}`.

Using Parameters

As a beginning editor, you'll want to edit around templates, not start changing them right away. In time you may have to edit a template, modifying it to add new text. Many templates require you to input *parameters*, or variables, in a specified form, which then customizes how the template displays on a particular page.

Parameters indicate or allow you to include variables that are going to be different for each template use. For instance, the template `{{WPBooks}}` is used on the talk page of articles about books as an aid to sorting them out. This template is a WikiProject template designed to help editors work on book articles. The template looks like this before it is filled out:

```
{{WPBooks |class = |needs-infobox = }}
```

Each of the choices that are followed by an equal sign is an optional field that can be filled in by the person who inserts the template. For instance, you can fill in the **class** field with a rating reflecting the quality of the article in question at the time that you viewed it. The possible ratings are listed on the main page of the `{{WPBooks}}` template; they are described as "FA, A, GA, B, Start, Stub, Dab, Template, Cat, NA. If blank, this will default as Unassessed." In other words, if you are reviewing an article about a book and wish to rate it as Start class, type **Start** after the **class** parameter.

The **infobox** parameter, on the other hand, is a simple yes/no choice. If the article needs an infobox, which is another kind of template, type **yes** here. If it doesn't need an infobox, you could either type **no** or just leave the parameter blank.

Many templates have optional parameters. For instance, the cleanup template mentioned in the previous section works best with a date parameter like this:

```
{{Cleanup|date=May 2008}}
```

Dating cleanup articles helps ensure that the oldest issues can be addressed first, through the system of cleanup categories by month.

How Templates Work

When just the double curly brackets are used to include a template on a page, the process is referred to as a *transclusion*. Some templates may require you to substitute them instead, through a process called *substitution*. The template directions—generally found in comments on the template page itself—will usually specify when you need to substitute a template rather than transclude it.

Substitution is done by typing

```
{{subst:template name}}
```

Substitution means that the template is expanded and rendered on saving the page, rather than on viewing it. That is, the wikitext that the template produces is saved into the source code of the page where the template is used. This contrasts with transclusion, where you just see the double-bracketed template name when you view the source code.

When a template is substituted, updates to the template page will *not* automatically propagate to the pages where the template has been placed (when a page is transcluded, they will). Substitution can be useful for pages where you want the wikitext to be closer to the rendered view that the reader sees.

Other Transclusions

In fact, any wiki page, not just those in the Template namespace, can be transcluded into any other page. Simply place curly brackets around a colon and the name of the page you want to include: {{:*Yourpagename*}}. Transcluding subpages onto a main page is sometimes done for long pages that are broken up into many parts in the Wikipedia project space (but it is not done for articles). For instance, if you look at [[Wikipedia:Featured article candidates]], each nomination is actually on a subpage, which is transcluded onto the main FAC page with template syntax in order to give a single view of all the nominations. This feature can be helpful when you're designing your own templates—simply work on the template in a subpage of your userspace, where you can experiment at will. To test your template on another page, type {{:User:*yourname*/*yourtemplatename*}}.

Of course, you will move it to the regular Template namespace when you're done.

Templates can—and often do—automatically categorize the pages they are used on, as well. For instance, in the books template, if you include an **infobox** parameter, the discussion page of the article will automatically be added to [[Category:Book articles needing infoboxes]]. Similarly, {{cleanup}} places articles into a large category called [[Category:All articles needing cleanup]]. If you use a **date** parameter of August 2007 in this tag, the article will be categorized into [[Category:Cleanup from August 2007]] as well. Once the template is removed, the article will be removed from the category too.

Varieties of Templates

We don't have space here to discuss all the possible uses for templates and still less space to list all the commonly used ones—Wikipedia has tens of thousands of templates. We'll review a few major types, however. Some should already be familiar to you, such as cleanup templates.

Fact-checking notices are useful for interacting with the Wikipedia site, even if you have no intention of getting heavily involved. These templates raise queries about content. Besides the cleanup templates we already described in Chapters 4 and 7, which can be placed at the very top of an article to produce cleanup message boxes, you can also insert small cleanup and fact-checking templates in the text itself. Apply the templates {{fact}} and {{who}} when the source for a statement isn't clear. Another such template is {{lopsided}}, which adds a query to the article about the neutrality of the treatment. Place these templates directly by the questioned text. For example

```
The Moon is made of old blue cheese, with the dusty surface being a space
fungus that has grown on it{{fact}}.
```

displays an inline message, such as a superscript *citation needed* for {{fact}} (see Figure 7-3 on page 206 for how this tag is used). This template also adds the article to a maintenance category, [[Category:All articles with unsourced statements]].

An *infobox* organizes information to display it cleanly to the reader and at the same time standardizes the presentation of essential facts about an article topic. A variety of infobox, the *taxobox*, is an infobox used for articles on individual species of animals or plants that present taxonomic information about that species. Infoboxes are typically rectangular, right-justified, and placed at the top of the article.

You can go to [[Template:Infobox NBA Player]] to see a basketball player infobox with enough documentation on the page to see how it works (see Figure 9-2 for how this infobox displays in an article). Each piece of information is a parameter that is filled in by the editor placing the infobox.

To set up an infobox, visit [[Help:Infobox]]. Creating and modifying infoboxes is a little more procedural than is standard for Wikipedia. Existing infoboxes may be found on [[Wikipedia:List of infoboxes]] (shortcut WP:IB), though this page may not be consistently maintained, or on [[Category: Infobox templates]] (shortcut WP:INFO), but infoboxes are perhaps most easily found by going to similar articles or the related WikiProject.

Navigation templates are also very common, particularly for article footers. For example, the template

{{Popes}}

is placed near the bottom of pages for any article on a pope, above the listing of categories and interwiki links. This template displays as a box listing links to all the pages about popes of the Catholic Church. As a refinement, because the template contains links to 264 other popes and is thus quite lengthy, the template detail is only displayed when you click the Show link. This kind of *hidden template* is commonly used for large or unwieldy navigation boxes. Hidden templates can be responsible for odd artifacts if you are using your browser search to locate a phrase on a page, however, since the browser can't "see" the text listing all the popes if the template is hidden.

Another navigation aid that is versatile and useful for related articles is the *succession box*, which is also usually displayed at the bottom of the article. Near the bottom of [[Abraham Lincoln]], you'll see a box that could be created by these templates:

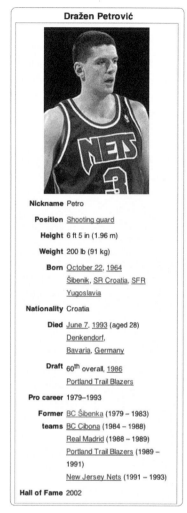

FIGURE 9-2: *The NBA player infobox for Dražen Petrović*

```
{{start box}}
{{succession box
| before = [[James Buchanan]]
| title = [[President of the United States]]
| after = [[Andrew Johnson]]
| years = [[March 4]], [[1861]] – [[April 15]], [[1865]]
}}
{{end box}}
```

This displays a message telling you that Lincoln followed James Buchanan as president of the US and so on (Figure 9-3 shows the many succession boxes used in the Lincoln article). The parameters are filled in with wikilinks. To create a succession box for some other position, edit the box's parameters by replacing, for example, *President of the United States* with *Emperor of Mexico*. In fact, go to [[Maximilian I of Mexico]] to see a stack of such boxes—a useful graphical representation of relationships for which words alone might be clumsy. [[Category: Succession templates]] is full of similar templates, but probably most editors copy and adapt these boxes from other articles.

United States House of Representatives		
Preceded by John Henry	Member from Illinois's 7th congressional district March 4, 1847 – March 3, 1849	Succeeded by Thomas L. Harris
Political offices		
Preceded by James Buchanan	President of the United States March 4, 1861 – April 15, 1865	Succeeded by Andrew Johnson
Party political offices		
Preceded by John C. Frémont	Republican Party presidential candidate 1860, 1864	Succeeded by Ulysses S. Grant
Honorary titles		
Preceded by Henry Clay	Persons who have lain in state or honor in the United States Capitol rotunda April 19, 1865 – April 21, 1865	Succeeded by Thaddeus Stevens

FIGURE 9-3: *The succession boxes at the bottom of the Abraham Lincoln article*

Formatting templates help you with text layout. For example, {{TOCleft}} places the table of contents on the left side of the page. This may be useful if the article also includes a right-justified infobox. Many more complicated templates can also be used for formatting within other templates or for spacing page elements, much as how CSS functions on regular web pages. Wikipedia also has dozens and dozens of templates for projects rather than articles; most of these templates are collected under [[Category:Wikipedia templates]] and [[Category: Wikipedia utility templates]]. See "Formatting Columns" on page 280 for another example of using templates to format text.

How to Build Templates

You might want to postpone reading this section until you need to build your own template. Existing templates are very numerous and can easily be adapted to meet most needs. Editors are welcome to build new templates, however.

We'll use the example of building a template to place on a user talk page to welcome new users. A template already exists for this purpose at [[Template: Welcome]], but you may want to customize it or build your own personal version from scratch. Templates may include variables, which allow the template to display different messages on individual pages depending on which parameters are input at the time the template is placed. This example illustrates how that works.

To start a new template, begin a new page in the Template namespace. For instance, our template example will be called *mywelcometemplate*, and it will include a bold link to Wikipedia's help pages. On the page [[Template: Mywelcometemplate]], you'd type the following:

```
'''[[Help:Contents|click here for handy tips and help]]'''
```

and click Save. So far, so good. Now, when you type {{mywelcometemplate}} on any other page and click Save, you'll see this bold link rendered on the page: **click here for handy tips and help**.

You can then introduce a parameter. In the template definition, the *formal parameter* (the placeholder for the parameter value that is input) is a parameter name with three pairs of braces. So, for example, you would type {{{myVariable-Name}}} for a template parameter that you wanted to call *myVariableName*.

In this example, say you wanted to include a variable article name in your welcome message. You might type this:

```
If you need help with your article called "{{{articlename}}}", '''[[Help:
Contents|click here for handy tips and help]]'''.
```

When you include the template on a page, you'd type this:

```
{{mywelcometemplate|articlename = the article name you want to display}}
```

and when the page is rendered you'd see this:

```
If you need help with your article called "the article name you want to
display", click here for handy tips and help.
```

You can also include unnamed parameters by using sequential numbers: {{{1}}}, {{{2}}}, and so on. In this case, the user could simply place the variable text he wanted to include in between pipe characters with no parameter name. For instance, if your template looks like this,

```
Dear {{{1}}}, if you need help with your article called "{{{2}}}", '''[[Help:
Contents|click here for handy tips and help]]'''.
```

you can fill it out as follows:

```
{{mywelcometemplate|Mary|Truly Tuesday}}
```

And the following will display on page rendering:

```
Dear Mary, if you need help with your article called "Truly Tuesday", click
here for handy tips and help.
```

Templates can become very complex, and it is beyond the scope of this book to give full instructions for coding them. Study existing templates first in order to get an idea of what is possible. Anything that may be included in a regular wiki page may also be included in a template—from ordinary text and images to wikisyntax, CSS, HTML, and even other templates. From the designer's point of view, wikisyntax still behaves as it normally would within templates. With template syntax and *parser functions* (template-like constructs that return a value based on at least one unnamed parameter) you can code extremely complicated templates.

The easiest way to learn how to build a template is to simply look at—and perhaps borrow—the source code of existing templates. If you are attempting to build a new infobox for a specific type of article, for instance, you can simply use existing infoboxes as a model, changing field names and sizes where necessary.

Further Reading

http://www.mediawiki.org/wiki/Help:Templates   A quick, clear guide to using and creating templates with parameters

http://en.wikipedia.org/wiki/Help:A_quick_guide_to_templates   A basic guide to using templates on Wikipedia

http://en.wikipedia.org/wiki/Help:Template   Help with templates—advanced, detailed documentation on template features

http://en.wikipedia.org/wiki/Wikipedia:Template_namespace   An introduction to templates and the Template namespace on Wikipedia

http://en.wikipedia.org/wiki/Wikipedia:Template   A list of standard template messages for articles and project pages, including standard cleanup templates

http://en.wikipedia.org/wiki/Category:Citation_templates   Citation and reference templates

---

Laying Out Articles

Besides sections, paragraphs, and basic wikisyntax, templates and tables are the two primary tools used to lay out and format articles. Special layout templates have now replaced many of the functions that tables were once used for on Wikipedia (for example, infoboxes were once table-driven). However, tables are still very useful for presenting data, such as multicolumn lists. Templates and tables can also be combined; for instance, tables can be included in templates if necessary.

Tables

Tables provide a neat way to organize any information that is best presented in a row-and-column format. Tables should always be used judiciously, however, because they make the wikisyntax less readable. Many dedicated "List of . . ." articles use tables because they can display several data elements compactly (see Figure 9-4). They are not usually necessary in basic articles; generally you can use a simple list instead.

List of best-selling singles in Japan 1968-2006 [edit]

Rank	Year	Sales	Chart Peak	Title	Artist
1	1975	4.547m	1	Oyoge! Taiyaki-kun	Masato Shimon
2	1972	3.256m	1	Onna no michi	Miya Shiro
3	2000	2.934m	1	Tsunami	Southern All Stars
4	1999	2.918m	1	Dango 3 Kyoudai	Kentarou Hayami, Ayumi Shigemori, Himawari Kids, Dango Gasshoudan
5	1992	2.895m	1	Kimi ga Iru Dake de	Kome Kome Club
6	1991	2.822m	1	Say Yes	Chage & Aska
7	1994	2.766m	1	Tomorrow Never Knows	Mr. Children
8	1991	2.587m	1	Oh! Yeah! / Love Story wa Totsuzen ni	Kazumasa Oda
9	2003	2.573m	1	Sekai ni Hitotsu dake no Hana	SMAP
10	1995	2.488m	1	Love Love Love / Arashi ga Kuru	Dreams Come True

FIGURE 9-4: A multirow, multicolumn list that uses a table from [[List of best-selling singles in Japan]]

A table is the easiest way to lay out any kind of data array or multicolumn, multirow list. "When to Use Tables," a guide in the *Manual of Style*, says, "if the information you are editing is not tabular in nature, it probably does not belong in a table." For visual layout (i.e., laying out a page to look pretty, rather than presenting data), tables have been replaced by templates and embedded wiki markup, such as image markup and CSS.

MediaWiki provides an integrated table syntax, special wikicode used for brevity. This code functions much like and is structurally the same as table markup in HTML (which also works in MediaWiki, though it shouldn't generally be used). Table syntax uses the pipe (|) as the main separator element and is thus sometimes called *pipe code*.

This code will now be described in detail. You may also read about pipe code at [[Help:Tables#Pipe syntax tutorial]], which details more elaborate table syntax, including formatting individual rows and cells.

The entire table is encased with curly brackets and a vertical bar (a pipe). So you use {| to begin a table and |} to end it. Each tag needs to be on its own line:

```
{|
table code goes here
|}
```

Table formatting information, such as border width, can be placed on the first line, after {|. An optional table caption is included by inserting a line starting with a vertical bar and plus sign, |+, with the caption after it:

```
{| border=1
|+ The table's caption
table code goes here
|}
```

To start a new table row, type a pipe and a hyphen,|-, on its own line. The codes for the cells in that row will start on the next line.

```
{| border=1
|+ The table's caption
|-
row code goes here
|-
row code goes here
|}
```

Type the codes for each cell in the row on a new line, starting with a pipe:

```
{| border=1
|+ The table's caption
|-
| first cell code in the row goes here
| second cell code in the same row goes here
|-
| first cell code in the next row goes here
...
|}
```

Cells can be separated with either a new line and new pipe or by a double pipe (||) on the same line. Both produce the same output:

```
{| border=1
|+ The table's caption
|-
|Row 1, Cell 1 || Cell 2 || Cell 3
|-
|Row 2, Cell A
|Cell B
|Cell C
|}
```

Finally, column headers may be added with a line beginning with an exclamation point (!) at the beginning of the table. For instance, in Figure 9-5, the column headers are:

```
{|
!Rank
!Year
!Sales
!Chart Peak
!Title
!Artist
|-
 ...
|}
```

Column headers can also be separated by a double exclamation point (!!) on the same line. Column headers will typically display in bold font and be centered at the top of the column. Styling information for the column (such as width, color, etc.) may also be placed in a column heading, using CSS formatting; see [[Help: Table]] for details.

One new development (since 2007) are *sortable tables*, where a reader can sort any column of data in a table by pressing a button at the top of a table column, first in ascending order and then toggling between ascending and descending order. This is achieved by using JavaScript. To make any table sortable, add `class=sortable` in the header of the template, next to {|, where style information and CSS also go. You can find more details at [[Help:Sorting]].

Formatting Columns

If you simply want to format text into columns, rather than order it in table format, you can also use formatting templates. Templates or tables are the only ways to produce true column layout in MediaWiki.

Any list of items can be broken into several columns with the templates {{col-begin}}, {{col-break}}, and {{col-break}}. These templates are a quick way to make a long list of short items take up less space on the page and save readers from excessive scrolling. Place {{col-begin}} to start the column section, {{col-break}} within the list at each column beginning, and {{col-end}} to close the column section. For instance,

```
{{Col-begin}}
{{Col-break}}
Column 1 list items here
{{Col-break}}
Column 2 list items here
{{Col-break}}
Column 3 list items here
{{Col-end}}
```

will produce a three-column layout. More examples can be seen in the template documentation for the [[Template:Col-begin]] template.

To produce a list of references in two or more columns, you need the {{reflist}} template, which can replace the <references/> tag when using foot-noted references. For instance, if you have a long list of footnotes and you want them to display in two columns, use {{reflist|2}} in place of <references/>. Use {{reflist|3}} for a list of references in three columns, and so on. The {{reflist}} template also conveniently makes footnotes display in a smaller font, so they take up less space.

Further Reading

http://en.wikipedia.org/wiki/Help:Tables   Help with tables

http://en.wikipedia.org/wiki/Wikipedia:When_to_use_tables   Guidelines for using tables in articles

http://en.wikipedia.org/wiki/Help:Sorting   Information about sortable tables

http://en.wikipedia.org/wiki/Category:Table_and_column_templates
   Layout templates

Special Syntax

Because MediaWiki serves many purposes, it has many resources for expanding and presenting standard text.

HTML and CSS

Despite the encouraging remark made earlier, that you don't need to know HTML to edit Wikipedia, around 40 HTML tags are permitted. A full list is at [[Help:HTML in wikitext]].

HTML tags that are useful include `<small>` and `<big>` for making text small or large, respectively. In articles, these tags have few uses, but they can be helpful in laying out user pages or templates. Other HTML tags that are useful include `<div>` for making formatting divisions, `<strike>` or `<s>` for strikethrough text, and `<sub>` and `<sup>` for making subscript or superscript characters.

HTML should not generally be used for formatting tables or laying out pages. For most tasks that HTML can do, customized MediaWiki syntax exists instead. Whenever wikisyntax can do the job of HTML, the wikisyntax is preferred. Unnecessary HTML should not be used in articles.

The use of Cascading Style Sheet (CSS) syntax is also widespread, primarily in formatting templates. The look of the site as a whole is styled with CSS *skins* that are individually customizable by any logged-in user; see Chapter 11.

Mathematical Formulas

Science and technology articles may need a sprinkling of mathematical notations or symbols. As of 2008, the treatment of mathematics on Wikipedia is a mixture of two basic styles (and therefore is a potentially confusing work in progress). Definitive Math HTML is not yet in use. This is likely to remain the case until the development time is set aside to find a solution: In other words, it will be a while. The two ways to display mathematics are to use HTML coding or TeX markup, described here.

A minimum requirement for writing basic mathematics is to be able to code exponents and subscripts, for example, to express a simple formula or to write numbers in scientific notation. Superscript text can be displayed with the `<sup>` tag. The text

```
''x''<sup>2</sup>
```

will display as

$$x^2$$

Therefore,

```
10<sup>100</sup>
```

displays as

$$10^{100}$$

(otherwise known as a *googol*).

Subscript text uses the <sub> tags; so

```
H<sub>2</sub>0
```

displays as

H_2O

A number of mathematical symbols have HTML codes, which can be inserted by typing

```
&codename;
```

where *codename* is a Greek letter or an abbreviation for some other symbol. For instance, √ displays as the square root sign ($\sqrt{}$), γ displays as the Greek letter γ, and Γ codes for the capital Greek letter Γ. For a list of supported symbols, see [[Wikipedia:Mathematical symbols]]. How these symbols are displayed depends in some cases on which browser you are using.

If you are interested in mathematics on Wikipedia, you can pick up more symbols as you go along; just consult articles such as [[square root of 2]] and examine the wikitext. Keep in mind, however, that more than one system is being used. In addition to HTML symbols, MediaWiki uses a subset of TeX markup (the standard for mathematical typesetting), including some extensions from LaTeX and AMSLaTeX. A full list of available TeX markup can be found at [[Help:Displaying a formula]].

Math markup in TeX goes inside the special and tags. A TeX formula is recognizable in the wikitext and looks something like this:

```
:<math>\pi = 3.141...</math>
```

Here the colon indents the formula, which is the convention on Wikipedia. This should display as

$\pi = 3.141...$

In TeX, extra spaces and newlines are ignored. The TeX code has to be put literally. MediaWiki templates, predefined templates, and parameters cannot be used within math tags, pairs of double braces are ignored, and # symbols produce error messages.

The Current Compromise

Here's the overall explanation of math symbols: Formulas can be displayed inline (with HTML formatting) or displayed as images, set apart from the text, which is the case if you use TeX formulas with the `<math>` tag. (Figure 9-5 shows the difference between the two styles from the article [[Mass–energy equivalence]].) Unfortunately, TeX renders as PNG images, which can cause strange, disruptive effects in the page formatting. You may not see those effects; this is one of those cases where how a page looks depends on the browser you use. The working agreement, at least in the Wikipedia mathematical community, is a mongrel:

▶ For displayed mathematics, use TeX or HTML.

▶ For inline mathematics, use HTML or wiki markup only.

Because numerous symbols can also be used uncoded in the text, this means that three systems coexist in Wikipedia (rather like written Japanese, in fact, which uses two alphabets and a set of symbols).

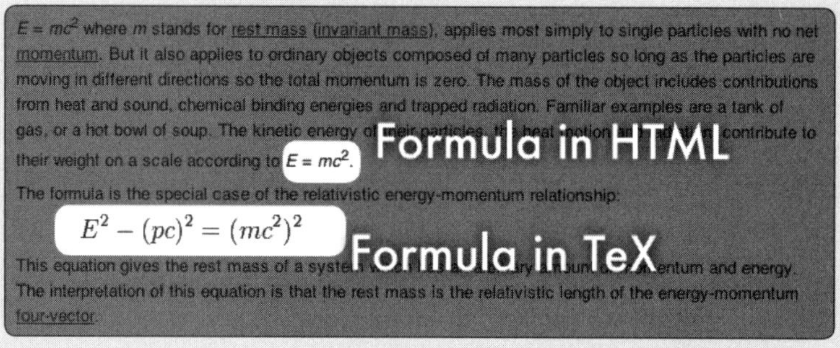

$E = mc^2$ where m stands for rest mass (invariant mass), applies most simply to single particles with no net momentum. But it also applies to ordinary objects composed of many particles so long as the particles are moving in different directions so the total momentum is zero. The mass of the object includes contributions from heat and sound, chemical binding energies and trapped radiation. Familiar examples are a tank of gas, or a hot bowl of soup. The kinetic energy of their particles, the heat motion, [...] contribute to their weight on a scale according to $E = mc^2$.

Formula in HTML

The formula is the special case of the relativistic energy-momentum relationship:

$$E^2 - (pc)^2 = (mc^2)^2$$

Formula in TeX

This equation gives the rest mass of a system [...] momentum and energy. The interpretation of this equation is that the rest mass is the relativistic length of the energy-momentum four-vector.

FIGURE 9-5: *The two math styles from a section of the article on E=mc2*

Variables and Magic Words

To insert the current date in numeric form, insert `{{CURRENTDAY}}` on a page. This is not a template, however, but rather a *variable*. MediaWiki has a wide choice of such variables; a list can be found at [[Help:Variables]]. Enclose them in double curly brackets to use them. They return a new value each time the page is rendered. This value may vary, accounting for the name, and it changes according to circumstances, for example, with the time (`{{CURRENTTIME}}`) or the total number of articles on the site at that moment (`{{NUMBEROFARTICLES}}`).

Variables are just a subset of the larger class of so-called magic words. A list can be found at [[Help:Magic words]]. *Magic words* are symbols recognized by the MediaWiki software. When they are seen in the text of the page, they trigger the

Formatting the Table of Contents

In addition to the magic words listed above, the automatically generated table of contents (ToC) in an article can be formatted or moved with the use of special templates.

To force the ToC to move to the left or right side of the page, add the template {{TOCleft}} or {{TOCright}} at the top of the page. Moving the ToC may improve page layout and image placement (this, like all CSS rendering, is always browser dependent to some extent). If you are developing a long list page, the special template {{compactTOC}} is convenient; it turns the ToC into alphabetical sections A–Z that display on one line rather than 26 separate lines. Several variations on the {{compactToC}} and explanations can be found at [[Wikipedia:Template messages/Compact tables of contents]]. For guidelines on reformatting the table of contents, see [[Help:Section#Floating_the_TOC]].

software to do something specific. For example, when the command __NOTOC__ (note the *two* underscores before and after NOTOC) is placed somewhere on the body of a page, it keeps a table of contents from appearing on a page. Using the magic word __FORCETOC__, on the other hand, will force a ToC to appear when not enough sections appear to automatically generate one. Few other magic words are very commonly used in articles.

Further Reading

http://en.wikipedia.org/wiki/Help:Special_characters   Help with special characters and unicode encoding in wikitext

http://en.wikipedia.org/wiki/Help:Advanced_editing#Special_characters   A table of special characters and how to produce them in wikitext

http://en.wikipedia.org/wiki/Help:HTML_in_wikitext   A list of what HTML tags are permitted in wikitext

http://en.wikipedia.org/wiki/Help:Displaying_a_formula   Information about displaying math in articles

http://en.wikipedia.org/wiki/Wikipedia:WikiProject_Mathematics   All about mathematics articles

http://en.wikipedia.org/wiki/Help:Magic_words   A reference to all the magic words and variables available in MediaWiki

Summary

Images, templates, tables, and special markup can all be used to carefully and accurately format pages and produce visually appealing and engaging layouts. Although every editor should have a passing knowledge of how images and templates work, learning the more complicated aspects of how they function is not necessary for most editing.

Wikipedia's technical resources offer immense possibilities—with some limitations. Learning advanced syntax occurs in three stages: recognizing a construction in wikitext, gaining familiarity with the principles of how it works, and gaining a working knowledge of some possible applications that interest you. Although looking around while working on the site will help, the third stage generally only occurs when developing a project of your own.

10 The Life Cycle of an Article

So far, we've broadly examined Wikipedia from the perspective of readers and editors. Of course, a Wikipedia reader can come and go as he or she pleases, and even the most ardent Wikipedia editor abandons his or her computer from time to time. But a Wikipedia *article* is always on the website, day in and day out.

So, how do things look from that article's perspective?

Let's follow Artie the Article, created by Eddie the Editor. Perhaps Artie's title is [[Gingerbread cottage architecture]], the title used previously in Chapter 6.

Birth of an Article

Eddie types `Gingerbread cottage architecture` into the search field. He discovers the article doesn't yet exist, follows the Start the Page link from the search page, and composes a few sentences. He clicks the Save Page button: Artie is born.

The moment Eddie saves his new article, it goes "live" and can be linked to and discovered through the search function. But, just as importantly, its title is immediately displayed at the top of a list called [[Special:Newpages]]. This page lists the 5,000 most-recently created articles. [[Gingerbread cottage architecture]] will slide down the list for two or three days as other editors—and possibly Wikipedia administrators on patrol—review these new articles.

After this preliminary review, many outcomes are possible.

Deletion

Wikipedia articles are created in a hostile environment, and stub articles—those short compositions of just a few sentences—are in particular peril. They are no more than tadpoles in the Wikipedia pond. New articles that do not seem appropriate for the site are often flagged for deletion as they are reviewed by other editors; this is the fate of hundreds of articles a day, many of them well meaning.

Eddie should therefore keep an eye on his article. If the content is very poor—if it contains graffiti or is un-encyclopedic, or if the topic does not seem adequately referenced for notability—a *red-bar* template might be added to the beginning of the text, nominating the article for deletion. (There are three types of deletion nominations, each using a different template; see Chapter 7.)

Eddie should not remove a deletion template himself, but he can contest the deletion nomination. For example, he can contest a speedy deletion nomination by adding the {{hangon}} template to the article just below the deletion template and then immediately arguing his case on the article's talk page.

If a deletion tag is added to an article and is not contested, Artie's future is bleak, so Eddie needs to find out about any deletion nominations as soon as they happen. Eddie can keep track of changes to his article in a few ways:

▶ Eddie can add the article to his watchlist by checking Watch this page (this is done by default for pages you create). Eddie's watchlist will reveal nominations for deletion and other edits to the article.

▶ Eddie can check his user talk page. Any time an article is nominated for deletion, its creator should be informed via the creator's talk page (in this case, a message should be left on [[User talk:Eddie]]). This is not fail-proof, however, as not all editors may follow this custom.

▶ Eddie can keep a *braglist* in his user space—a list of links to articles he has created. If he puts the braglist on its own page (for example, [[User: Eddie/Articles I created]]), then he can click the Related Changes link from that page for a convenient list of recent edits. This solution is even better than monitoring a watchlist for keeping an eye on just the articles you have created.

If other Wikipedia editors judge the article's content as being good enough, Artie will avoid immediate deletion. Now comes the work of improving the article.

Maintenance Tagging

As they come across articles that need attention, editors tag those articles for maintenance. Many of these *yellow-bar* templates might be added at the beginning of the article. For instance, if the article needs formatting work or rewriting for clarity, the {{cleanup}} tag might be added; if there are no good references, it is likely that the {{unreferenced}} tag will be placed on the article. Other yellow-bar templates may be more technical, for example, {{film-fiction}}: *This film-related article may fail to make a clear distinction between fact and fiction.* Particular criticisms of the writing standard may appear as *orange-bar* templates. For example, {{wikify}} may be added if the article could use more wikilinks. Eddie shouldn't take these templates personally—he's getting feedback on his work and now knows how the article needs to improve. It is a good idea for Eddie to do what he can to fix the article in response to any such messages.

If Artie is still a stub (in other words, just a beginning treatment, lacking something essential), editors may tag him with a {{stub}} template. But since stubs are actively sorted by category (Chapter 8), this general stub template will probably be replaced by a more specific one. For example, {{fairy-tale stub}} denotes all stubs about fairy tales, and this tag would be an appropriate one to add to [[Gingerbread cottage architecture]]. One side effect of this template being added is that [[Gingerbread cottage architecture]] will be placed in a category with similar articles that still need work, such as [[List of mermaid supermodels]] and [[Great Pumpkin appearances in 2008]].

Editing Improvements

As soon as an article is created, other editors may set to work improving and adding to the content. Basic formatting work is often done quickly. If an article is about something in the news or an ongoing event, an editor may add a *blue-bar* template indicating that the article is time critical. Time-critical articles are also likely to be edited a great deal.

If the article is not about a high-profile topic (the vast majority of topics are low-profile), it might not get edited for a while. Editing might also occur in fits and starts; another editor interested in substantively working on the article may not come along for months or even years. WikiProjects generally maintain a list of new articles in their subject area, so Eddie's article may be added to one of those lists and thrive from expert attention. ([[Gingerbread cottage architecture]] might be well received at WikiProject Fairytales, for example.)

Potential Merge

Artie is not out of the woods yet. He might still be merged into an existing article, for instance, [[Building in folklore]]. One editor might feel strongly that material about a common topic has been included in many Wikipedia articles and would be better presented in a single article. Sometimes a duplicate article might not be discovered for months if it is not properly categorized and linked to other articles—did someone else create [[Architecture of gingerbread cottages]], with similar content?

The procedural side of merging was covered in Chapter 8. If an editor proposes a merge, he or she will flag the article with a *purple-bar* template.

If Artie is merged, then the content created by Eddie will be included in a larger article that subsumes the gingerbread cottage architecture material. Artie will not be gone but will have become a humble redirect page. Eddie should dispute any hasty merge or redirect proposals by simply discussing them on the relevant article talk pages.

Discussion and Content Tags

A reader or editor, quite possibly someone visiting Wikipedia who is not a regular, may query what the article says. Is it true? Is it the whole truth? Is it slanted? Can a reference be provided for a specific assertion? These points will likely be added to [[Talk:Gingerbread cottage architecture]]; though in some cases, remarks might be added to [[User talk:Eddie]]—let us hope politely.

This kind of input is a further chance to improve Artie's clarity and accuracy. Comments may also take the form of orange-bar templates. For example, the template {{NPOV}} indicates that someone thinks the article fails to be neutral (does not conform to the Neutral Point of View policy). Whoever added that template should also add comments indicating his or her reason. Templates raising content issues, if not totally self-explanatory, should always be backed up by talk page comments that address the problem or slant in specific terms. Without such a detailed note, Eddie might be mystified as to what needs fixing.

If Eddie is still watching the article, he should respond to all reasonable queries rather than become annoyed. Certainly simply removing a tag requesting some sort of clarification does an article no favors, unless the tag is entirely undeserved. Having a tag on an article for a while does little actual harm, and it is normal for content to be rewritten on Wikipedia, even if the issue raised only relates to cosmetic improvements in writing style.

Categories

Readers can easily find an article about a broad topic (like the United States) but have more difficulty finding an article about a smaller or more specific topic—especially if they don't know the article's exact title. These less prominent articles are often found by editors searching a category.

The chance of an editor finding an article—and correspondingly editing it—improves if the correct category tags have been added. Eddie might do this himself. If you're starting a new article (or undertaking an edit of one), pay attention to the categories that similar articles have been placed in.

It doesn't matter if early categories aren't perfect. Even an approximate category can put an article into a position where an expert can apply the appropriate subcategories.

Bots Arrive

Editors who happen to be programmers can write software for making certain types of procedural edits automatically. These programs are nicknamed *bots*, and Artie may be visited by a slew of them over his life. Some will make spelling corrections or small formatting changes in compliance with *Manual of Style* guidelines, while others analyze the content of a new page—by keywords, for example—and log it to various lists kept as project pages. (The logs can be detected in the backlinks.) Any edits made by bots will be clearly visible in the article's history, just like edits made by human editors; a bot is just another type of account. (A bot's username almost always indicates that it's a bot, not a human, for example, Sinebot, the bot that goes around signing comments on talk pages when editors fail to do so.)

If Artie hasn't been categorized, Artie's first bot edit might be the addition of an {{uncategorized}} tag.

✳ **NOTE:** *See a bot misbehaving? You can normally contact the bot's programmer via the bot's user talk page. So Eddie has some recourse if a bot messes up his article with some automated edit; Eddie should revert the edit but also notify the bot's owner.*

Incoming Wikilinks

In our full review of article creation in Chapter 6, you learned that wikilinks pointing to the new article should be added to related articles (which can themselves be found through the search function). In fact, these links should ideally be added before the new article even exists.

If Eddie is experienced at creating articles, he will consider incoming wikilinks from the outset. How many pages are displayed, as soon as Artie is created, when clicking the What Links Here link on the sidebar? Eddie should check. Being born an orphan would not be so much fun for Artie. If Eddie doesn't add links to his article, someone else might add the {{orphan}} yellow-bar template to it, placing Artie in [[Category:Orphaned articles]].

If there aren't any links to the article, there could be several explanations. For example, the chosen title for Artie the Article, [[Gingerbread cottage architecture]], might be unconventional or spelled incorrectly. It is also possible that the concept or article title is in fact mentioned in other articles but simply has not been wikilinked. After creating the article, Eddie can still create links to Artie.

Creating wikilinks will also (and subtly) draw attention to his article because the wikified pages are likely on the watchlists of editors already working in related areas. Eddie should create redirects to Artie from other possible titles, too.

Artie Is Moved

A Wikipedia *move* is actually a *rename*—something Artie might experience early in life. Particular conventions sometimes govern titles, and articles are often renamed by people familiar with those conventions. (For example, a lowercase title might be capitalized or vice versa.)

A page move, carried out by someone well meaning, might draw more attention to Artie, which might, in turn, draw more incoming links. (Artie will, of course, retain all his old wikilinks even after being renamed.) A move may also create double redirects (see Chapter 8), a technical problem that should be fixed by the article mover.

In Good Times

If all goes well, other editors will develop Artie further. Suppose Fred and Greta like what Eddie has written but think the article could be developed. Fred may standardize the formatting and add wikilinks, external links, and references, improving the article's appearance and its credibility. Greta may divide the article into sections, sorting the different aspects of the topic into some more consistent, logical order. Creating a conventional lead section that tells readers quickly what the content covers always helps an article. Greta will have a better idea about this once she is done with the restructuring. Perhaps, in a whimsical mood, she will even take her camera into the woods and shoot some photos of gingerbread cottage architecture.

Fred's efforts at wikifying will probably leave redlinks in Eddie's article—in other words, suggestions for more articles to write to develop Wikipedia. If these redlinks provoke Harold and Isabel, two more interested editors, to create useful new articles, Artie has really arrived in Wikipedia, and Eddie has contributed to developing the overall coverage of the topic.

In Bad Times

As editors insert additional information, the article might actually get worse, stylistically! When new facts are not integrated properly, they can upend the article's structure and muddy its writing style. (Sometimes this happens when the editors adding those facts aren't familiar with the topic or aren't fluent at editing Wikipedia.) If this continues, Artie could be destined for mere mediocrity. A strong-minded editor could step in and restore an earlier, cleaner version, do a thorough re-write, or take a red pencil to incremental changes that were not, in fact, beneficial.

When adding to articles, keep the article's overall structure in mind. Although adding a new fact onto the end of a convenient paragraph is easy, integrating that fact squarely into the article is much more helpful.

On a more positive note: Articles, on average, tend to improve over time.

Bad Times, and a True Story

Beginning on the day Artie is created, an edit war could erupt over his content, a passing vandal could deface the article, or a user could accidentally delete a chunk of vital content. These risks become more acute as more people read the article. In extreme cases, an article may be protected (or semiprotected), which halts the damage but also may prevent improvement. A *gray-bar* template indicates an article is protected, but full protection should only be temporary.

Another, more serious danger is that Artie may be nominated for Articles for Deletion. If the content really is worthy of an encyclopedia article, this will be a nerve-wracking time for Eddie. Even if Artie should by rights survive, the result can go the wrong way, especially if the writing is poor. That would be the end of Artie, unless a salvage mission during Deletion Review succeeds. (Deleted articles should not be re-created for six months.)

One deletion debate over a new article, which happened on September 17, 2007, has become Wikipedia legend.

During the heat of the debate, the discussion about whether a business was notable enough to have a Wikipedia page seemed typical. (Employees or others associated with a business often start these types of articles, raising questions of notability and conflict of interest.) Indeed, the article's first few hours were filled with the types of wiki perils we've discussed in this chapter. We've reprinted part of the article's edit history here; you can read what happened in reverse chronological order, just as the history would display on the site. At 11:51, less than three hours after creation, the article had been nominated for deletion, and subsequent edits were attempts to improve the article in order to influence the deletion vote.

The punchline, though, is at the bottom of the article history, in the first edit: Despite the typical arc of its debate, this was *not* a business trying to promote itself.

```
Article History:
12:13, September 17, 2007 Wikidemo (Talk | contribs) (2,206 bytes)
(?Description - add material) (undo)
12:00, September 17, 2007 David Eppstein (Talk | contribs) (1,745
bytes) (?External Links - another blog entry, from Jimbo's old
version) (undo)
11:54, September 17, 2007 Carcharoth (Talk | contribs) (1,610 bytes)
(add three more) (undo)
11:51, September 17, 2007 ^demon (Talk | contribs) (1,529 bytes)
(Nominated for deletion; see Wikipedia:Articles for deletion/Mzoli's
Meats.) (undo)
11:50, September 17, 2007 Cobaltbluetony (Talk | contribs) (1,312
bytes) (dunno how the tag got back on...) (undo)
11:49, September 17, 2007 Cobaltbluetony (Talk | contribs) m (moved
Mzoli's to Mzoli's Meats: full name of establishment) (undo)
11:48, September 17, 2007 EVula (Talk | contribs) (1,327 bytes)
(contesting prod; I think if we give this article a bit more than a
couple of hours of existence, we might have something worthwhile) (undo)
11:46, September 17, 2007 Carcharoth (Talk | contribs) (1,695 bytes)
(hmm, we don't have a category on butchers, I'm not surprised) (undo)
11:46, September 17, 2007 Carcharoth (Talk | contribs) (1,717 bytes)
(add categories) (undo)
11:44, September 17, 2007 ^demon (Talk | contribs) (1,645 bytes)
(Proposing deletion) (undo)
11:40, September 17, 2007 Cobaltbluetony (Talk | contribs) (1,277 bytes)
(notability needed according to wiki standards) (undo)
11:36, September 17, 2007 Melsaran (Talk | contribs) (1,262 bytes)
("famous" is a value judgement, and it is not really relevant anyway +
doesn't add anything to the article. the fact that some sources call
it famous doesn't mean that we should.) (undo)
11:34, September 17, 2007 Wikidemo (Talk | contribs) m (1,269 bytes)
(restoring "famous" - source says it is; other coverage suports
claim.) (undo)
11:30, September 17, 2007 Grcampbell (Talk | contribs) (1,262 bytes)
(how is it famous??) (undo)
11:18, September 17, 2007 EVula (Talk | contribs) (1,269 bytes)
(removing G11 tag; just because we have an article on a company
doesn't mean that it is spam) (undo)
```

11:08, September 17, 2007 Cobaltbluetony (Talk | contribs) (1,281 bytes)
(spam) (undo)
11:05, September 17, 2007 Wikidemo (Talk | contribs) m (1,269 bytes)
(Undid revision 158530993 by Deb (talk) rm advertising tag - this is
not written as an ad; it simply reports sourced info) (undo)
11:03, September 17, 2007 Deb (Talk | contribs) m (1,280 bytes) (tag) (undo)
11:01, September 17, 2007 Wikidemo (Talk | contribs) (1,269 bytes)
(write new article; have not seen deleted version but this is new,
sourced content that claims importance/notability of subject) (undo)
09:55, September 17, 2007 ^demon (Talk | contribs) deleted "Mzoli's" ?
(CSD A7 (Corp): Article about a company that doesn't assert significance)
09:37, September 17, 2007 Jimbo Wales (Talk | contribs) (275 bytes)
(just collecting some links as a base for writing more) (undo)
09:33, September 17, 2007 Jimbo Wales (Talk | contribs) (206 bytes)
(just a stub for now, will be adding pictures and more in coming
days... I need help finding reliable sources though)

That final line, at 9:33, reveals the original creator of the article: one Jimmy "Jimbo" Wales, founding father of the Wikipedia site. Jimbo's original stub of a few lines was speedily deleted after around 20 minutes on the site!

During the first few hours that Wales' article about a celebrated South African restaurant existed, it was put through all three deletion processes mentioned in Chapter 7. First, the article was speedily deleted and then re-created by another author. Then it was tagged as advertising and then untagged. It was tagged as spam and nominated for a second speedy deletion. This nomination was contested; the nominator then nominated it again for proposed deletion (PROD).

This proposed deletion was again contested, so the deletion nominator called for the final deletion process at Articles for Deletion (AfD). AfD debates are intended to last five days, so this debate went on at [[Wikipedia:Articles for deletion/Mzoli's Meats]] (note that the content only exists in the page history, as this page was wiped blank and protected, an example of a courtesy blanking). The debate was closed on September 19, 2007, and the article was kept. [[Mzoli's Meats]] eventually grew into a substantial piece, with a photo and a dozen references.

This article went through the entire deletion process and survived. Its story was even featured in the *LA Times*.[1] Other articles are not so lucky; most pieces suspected of being covert promotion—or simply of being about non-notable topics—will face some deletion attempts, and many of these attempts will succeed. The majority of deletion debates are not as controversial as this example, however; this debate garnered extra attention both because the article was begun by Wales and because it became something of a celebrity cause within the community, discussed on the Village Pump (see Chapter 12) and in one of the ongoing mailing-list discussions about how deletions are conducted.

[1] See David Samo, "Wikipedia Wars Erupt," *Los Angeles Times*, September 30, 2007, *http://www.latimes.com/entertainment/news/la-ca-webscout30sep30,0,344107.story?coll=la-home-center.*

Search Engines Find the Article

As soon as an article such as Artie is created, it will be indexed and findable using Wikipedia's built-in search. General-purpose search engines will be able to find Artie within a few weeks or sometimes even sooner—within a day or two for Google. Once registered by search engines, Artie will have much greater prominence on the Web. People searching the Web generally, not specifically looking for a Wikipedia article, will begin to read the article as it shows up in their search results. This can have a good or bad effect on the article's quality. Experts in the topic may contribute to it, but random outsiders could also commit vandalism. For Artie's sake, we hope that he is now on some attentive editors' watchlists.

New Relatives

Over time, Artie's content will propagate outward in two ways: It will be copied verbatim, and it could be translated into other languages.

Within about a month, non-Wikipedia websites will grab Artie's content and reprint it in full. These *mirrors* are perfectly legal as long as they respect the GFDL license. As these copies spread across the Web, Artie's content on Wikipedia can stay more relevant by being continuously updated.

Artie's content might also be translated to provide content for Wikipedias in other languages. These new wiki articles may attract further edits, and their content may begin to diverge from the original article.

One caveat: If Artie contains mistakes, so will Artie's mirrors and translations—and even if the mistake is fixed in Artie, it will remain on the mirror sites (at least until the mirror sites refresh their content from the latest version of Wikipedia) and in translations (until someone corrects it manually).

Getting the Picture

A picture is a worth a thousand words.

Eddie might be tempted to find a relevant image somewhere on the Internet, upload it to Wikipedia, and add it to his article, but unless the image is public domain or GFDL-licensed (and most are not), this addition will lead to nothing but trouble. Non-free images are aggressively deleted from Wikipedia; they live only as long as cut flowers—a few days at most.

Instead, Eddie might take a photograph himself (or create a graphic). Or he might search for relevant images in other Wikipedia articles or on Wikimedia Commons.

Good Article

Assuming Eddie's article avoids the hazards discussed so far, Artie may be developed by skilled editors who know how to improve pages step by step. And apart from regular editing, these editors might send Artie through a number of structured improvement processes, for example, a formal peer review. If Artie is officially recognized as a *good article*, more possibilities open up, including induction into that rarified stratum called *featured articles*. The main page beckons!

Article Quality

Only about 0.1 percent of articles qualify as featured, so this parable is a little on the optimistic side, and a fairy godmother would come in handy. Some dedicated editors aim to produce featured articles from scratch, but most articles obtain this standard of quality gradually.

Other editors produce large numbers of shorter pieces. These approaches are complementary, from the point of view of the encyclopedia, and suit different editor temperaments. What really matters is that articles are in the end written collectively and thoroughly. Wikipedia has no one *correct* way to write an article.

Summary

The whole system for producing Wikipedia's content might seem cockeyed or random. It is certainly fallible. Content emerges from a complex but well-meaning development process, where two steps might be taken forward and then one step taken backward. But Wikipedia offers many layers of review and improvement, even if there is no single set of procedures, and ultimately Wikipedia draws readers because its content is, on balance, very useful. Indeed, Wikipedia's footprint on the World Wide Web is growing steadily.

Conclusion to Part II

Wikipedia needs all types of articles. What should you write about? Many possibilities for new articles exist, but the majority of Wikipedia's two million existing articles still need work as well. If you want to help out with articles, you can always apply basic wikification and formatting (Chapter 5), work on rewriting for clarity and referencing facts (Chapter 6), do cleanup tasks (Chapter 7), sort out hypertext and category issues (Chapter 8), and perhaps even contribute images or expert syntax (Chapter 9).

But our central advice on writing for Wikipedia is that four things matter most to an article:

▶ *Being fairly well written and reliably sourced* from the very first revision helps stave off possible deletion and provides the foundation of a good article.

▶ *Complying with the basic content policies* of Neutrality, Verifiability, and No Original Research.

▶ *Fitting well with existing Wikipedia material* so that incoming wikilinks exist or can be created.

▶ *Being about a topic that is also of interest to others*, perhaps fitting within the scope of a WikiProject, so that others will find and develop it.

Good editors can often find parts of Wikipedia that are currently undeveloped, where new articles might be created. Just as often, many articles exist, but they are in poor shape and require a big structuring and linking effort. When you feel ready to tackle this type of work, you have mastered this part of the book. You can then consider yourself an advanced editor.

## PART III

Community

11 Becoming a Wikipedian

If you have created an account, edited a few articles, and found yourself getting involved in some aspect of Wikipedia—whether rewriting an article, reverting vandalism, or discussing issues with other users—you're well on your way to becoming a Wikipedian. *Wikipedians*, of course, are those individuals who make Wikipedia work—members of the Wikipedia community.

Wikipedians, like any large online community, have a fluid and rich culture; they even have their own mascot, the *Wikipede* (Figure 11-1). You'll get a better sense of this culture as you participate in the project. Many people find themselves with some free time on their hands and decide to do some work on the site, but working on a wiki can be pleasurable, even addictive, and working on encyclopedia articles turns out to be fun. Before they know it, some editors are drawn in and hooked on Wikipedia. And as you edit articles, you'll come to know some of these quirky, wonderful people.

In this chapter, we'll discuss how to create an account (and certain things to consider when you do so), create a user page, personalize your experience on the wiki, and talk with other editors via personal user talk pages. Wikipedia has different classes of editor accounts, as some editors become administrators, and we'll explain this process as well.

FIGURE 11-1: Wikipede, *an unofficial mascot*

On Arrival

Some people start editing, and they know within days that Wikipedia is right for them. Others may drift into it gradually, copyediting anonymously before creating an account and doing more extensive work.

As Phoebe tells it:

> I had read about Wikipedia and spent some time browsing before I got up the courage to actually edit the site the first time, in the summer of 2003. It was browsing, in fact, that convinced me to edit. I carefully read the onsite directions before editing, rather than plunging right in, but it still took a few saves to get the syntax right. I edited [[Jewelry]], which needed some serious fixing up. I felt somewhat qualified to work on this page as I'd been an amateur jeweler for years. Though I had some experience with HTML and creating web pages, I marveled at how easily my wiki edits just appeared.

If you, too, find yourself working on Wikipedia regularly, the next logical steps are to create an account (if you have not already done so) and customize your site preferences.

Registering an Account

You don't have to have an account to edit Wikipedia, but creating an account is recommended for all contributors. Editors have two options: They can either register an account and edit under that username or edit without logging in, as an *anonymous* or *IP editor* (referring to the way that edits show up by IP number when an editor is not logged in). Because by now Wikipedia is a very visible and public place, editing anonymously versus choosing a username has some implications, which we will review in this chapter. If you do decide to register, you'll follow three steps to create an account: Choose an appropriate username, make sure it is available, and fill out a short form.

Creating an account is a good idea for several reasons. The first is that it gives you an *identity* on the site that is distinct from your IP address. You will be able to sign comments and discussion posts with a name that people will remember, not a string of numbers. An account helps you become a trusted editor because other contributors see a username as a commitment to doing productive work on the site. Others will be more likely to remember you and will more readily assume that your changes are good ones.

Second, having a username also makes it easier to communicate with others and participate in the Wikipedia community. If you have an account, people will also be able to send you email, without your having to reveal your email address to them, through the Email This User feature.

Third, registered users also gain some editing privileges. After registering your username, you'll be able to create new pages, move pages to new titles, and upload images. You will also be able to edit *semiprotected* pages (see Chapter 5 for an explanation of these). Finally, having an account gives you access to the site's user-specific features, such as choosing display options and preferences and maintaining an automated watchlist of pages you're interested in.

Autoconfirm

When you first register your account, you'll be able to create new articles, but you'll still have some restrictions: You won't be able to move pages or work on semiprotected articles. After a period of four days and ten edits, these restrictions are automatically lifted. This is known as *autoconfirmation* and was implemented in 2005 as an antivandalism measure, in part because *page move vandalism* (where a good article is moved to an inappropriate title) was rife.

Privacy

The matter of privacy is significant to anyone using the Internet. A variety of views exist on whether editing without revealing your real identity or not is better. You should know, however, that Wikipedia usernames are much more public than usernames in most Internet forums. Wikipedia content—including user pages and article histories with usernames—is mirrored and archived by hundreds of other websites. If you're concerned about privacy, realize that whatever username you choose will definitely show up in search engine results and be associated with you if you reveal your real name on your user page or otherwise.

If you wish to be absolutely anonymous on the site, your privacy is best protected by creating an account under a pseudonym and never editing the site when logged out. So-called anonymous editing without being logged in is not, in fact, the most anonymous way to edit; in many cases, editing from an IP number is no safeguard that your identity will remain completely unknown. For the most privacy, choose a fresh pseudonym, not one you have used online before.

Maintaining contributor privacy is an important issue on Wikipedia. The official privacy policy was already mentioned in Chapter 3, but here we cover what everyone should know when participating on the site. The basic points are these:

▸ Wikipedia respects the right of anyone to contribute either anonymously (not logged in) or pseudonymously (through an account).

▸ Wikipedia does not advise one way or the other on the use of real names on the site.

▸ The IP numbers of those editing anonymously are displayed.

▸ Disclosure of personal details on user pages is neither advised, nor advised against, for adults. Minors, however, are advised *not* to post identifying details about themselves.

▸ Accidental disclosures of personal details by users and of IP numbers when accidentally logged out may be removed from page histories using the *oversight* process. This is a process where particular edits to a page may be semipermanently removed and is only done in special cases. Requests for oversights are made to the small group of editors with oversight privileges. Find out more at [[Wikipedia:Oversight]].

▸ Disclosing personal details of other users goes against Wikipedia's norms and values and is seen as harassment (see WP:HARASS). In other words, don't ever post personal details about other people, even if you are sure those details are already public knowledge.

▸ The IP numbers of logged-in users may be used, in a small proportion of cases, in the investigation of problem users. These investigations are conducted via the CheckUser tool, which is restricted to a small group of trusted editors, and the results are never made public. Find out more at [[Wikipedia: Checkuser]] and under "Users and Administrators" on page 325.

To reiterate, if you are concerned about your privacy, the first step is to create an account, and if you are concerned about anonymity, use a pseudonym.

"Anonymous" Edits

Anytime you edit Wikipedia without being logged in to an account, your IP address will be displayed in the page history and in Recent Changes. An *IP address* is the address that your computer uses to identify itself to the network. Since an IP number's owner can often be traced quite easily by *whois* searches and other more advanced methods, IP editing is not anonymous. How much information is revealed through anonymous editing varies, however. IP addresses do not always identify individual computers; *dynamic* IP addresses, such as those used by many

Internet service providers and wireless hotspots, may only reveal the Internet provider being used.

If you edit when logged out, you may disclose an IP number near other edits from your account; on a little-trafficked article, others may put two and two together. If you're concerned about this, you can use a skin other than the default Monobook solely as an alert to this possibility; the logged-out view of the site will then be very different from what you see when logged in (see "Customizing Skins and Installing Extensions" on page 313 for information on how to do this).

There are other reasons to log in as well: Not only is an IP address less private than having an account name (if anonymity is important to you), but shared IP addresses such as school and company networks or proxy servers are frequently blocked for vandalism, often affecting many innocent editors on the same network. If, however, you have an account and are in good standing and you are affected by such a block, you can request that the block be modified to apply only to anonymous editors.

Wikipedia Scanner

A public tool was created that correlates IP number edits going back over the years (more than 30 million, from 2002) with the IP ranges of corporations and institutions. The tool, called WikiScanner, was built by Virgil Griffith of CalTech; you can find it at *http://wikiscanner.virgil.gr/*. Thus you can discover anonymous edits and match them to their origins. This means, as several newspaper articles gleefully pointed out in 2007, that the IP range used by a politician's office, for instance, can be checked to see if people editing from there have changed the article on that politician in a way that violates NPOV—which was happening occasionally.

Usernames and Real Names

When you create an account, you must choose a username. This username may be your real name or a pseudonym. Don't make this choice casually. You can use your real name, initials, or first or last name as a professional way to present yourself. Many people do use their real names when editing the site (including the authors of this book). Depending on how common the person's name is, contributions can then be traced more readily back to an individual, which can, for instance, provide a way of corroborating claimed expertise. The benefit of choosing a pseudonym, on the other hand, is that it offers a degree of real anonymity. Pseudonyms are perfectly acceptable and widely used on the site. Whatever you choose for your name, you'll become known by it if you make substantial contributions. Choose a username that you are comfortable signing in serious discussion and debate.

Wikipedia has a handful of commonsense guidelines for usernames designed to minimize disruption in collaborative work. Usernames cannot be harassing, misleading, confusing, promotional, or offensive. What constitutes these qualities is ultimately determined by administrators who review new accounts; if a name violates these guidelines, an administrator will ban it, and the editor will be expected to pick something else. *Harassing* is a username that is aimed at disturbing others, such as one that incorporates an attack on a specific user. *Misleading* means imitating another well-known person or Wikipedian, whereas *confusing* means visually confusing (such as nothing but ones and zeros). A *promotional* username is one that seeks to promote, or is the same as, a business or a group; so don't use the name of your company as a username. Finally, *offensive* usernames are those that others might find so offensive as to make positive collaborative editing impossible; any derogatory statements or names using obscenities are generally ruled out.

Additionally, a username for the English-language Wikipedia shouldn't contain non-western characters, which can be difficult for English-speakers to read and recognize. Finally, a username can't be a full email address.

Note that usernames follow the same rules as article page names. They are case sensitive—user:Thomas jefferson is not the same as user:Thomas Jefferson—and the first letter of the name is always capitalized, though you can make it display as lowercase by customizing your signature, as described later in "Setting Your Signature" on page 312. Spaces in usernames are fine.

Deleting, Renaming, and Having Multiple Accounts

You cannot delete an account that has made contributions to the site because of technical reasons and the GFDL license that Wikipedia uses. This is another reason to be wise in starting and naming an account. The closest that you can come to removing yourself from the site completely, once you have contributed, is to request that any user pages be deleted; this is part of the wiki-philosophy that users have the *right to vanish* if they wish to leave the project. Your other edits, except for those to pages that are deleted entirely, will persist and will be permanently attributed to your account.

You can change your username from one name to another. You can request changes at [[Wikipedia:Changing username]]. Your request won't be granted immediately, as a bureaucrat must approve and make the change, which will then be reflected in the attribution for all your previous edits. In certain circumstances, established contributors can request to *usurp* a registered but unused username. These completely unused usernames—names that were registered but never used to make a contribution—account, surprisingly, for millions of registered accounts. To usurp a username, make a request and justify it on the Usurpations subpage of the Changing username page.

An easier solution is to change how your username displays when you sign comments on discussion pages. You can modify how your signature appears, as described in [[Wikipedia:Signatures]] (shortcut WP:SIG) and in detail under "Setting Your Signature" on page 312.

If you are thinking about creating a second account to edit with while maintaining your original account—don't. Although it is not quite against the site rules to have two accounts, the chances of violating the rules against sockpuppetry are quite high.

A *sockpuppet* is a second username employed by a Wikipedian who already has an account. Wikipedia's policy prohibits the use of multiple accounts to mislead others; for instance, creating another account to support your own position in an argument or voting more than once in a poll. Wikipedia accounts should not be used as masks, and those who do this are usually deprived of the right to edit.

You should also not ask other people to create accounts for you; accounts controlled by another editor are known as *meatpuppets*. Using several accounts to manipulate or deceive others on the site is unacceptable. Potential sockpuppets are kept track of through [[Wikipedia:Suspected sock puppets]] (shortcut WP:SSP) or [[Wikipedia:Requests for checkuser]] (shortcut WP:RFCU). These two processes are for determining when sockpuppets are being used. Under certain circumstances, running an extra account for innocent reasons is acceptable; these circumstances are outlined under [[Wikipedia:Sock puppetry]] (shortcut WP:SOCK).

Another pitfall to avoid is sharing a password. Don't let other people use your account. Accounts with multiple users are likely to be blocked, and "role" accounts, such as accounts for businesses or groups, are forbidden.

Is a Username Taken?

You don't have to make sure that a username is available before you try to register it: The system will tell you if a username is already taken. Therefore this section on browsing for usernames is optional, but reading it could save you some frustration or might be useful at a later point, such as when making a renaming request. If you're curious whether a particular name is taken, Wikipedia offers a few ways to find out besides trying to register the name.

Start, perhaps, by seeing if the user has set up a user page at [[User:Nameofuser]]. This method is by no means fail proof, since registered users are not obligated to set up a user page, and many don't. Alternatively, if the name you're looking for is distinctive, you could search the whole site for it using a search engine, which is quick to do.

A better, more systematic way to check if a name has been registered is to visit the [[Special:Contributions]] page. Enter the username you want to find in the IP address or username field. If that username has made any contributions, they will be listed on this page. Registered names are commonly never used, however, so not finding a contribution history doesn't mean the name is not taken. But you can find out if a name is registered: After you enter the username you are interested in on the [[Special:Contributions]] page, look at the link for the name directly under *From Wikipedia, the free encyclopedia*. If the name has been registered, it will display as a blue- or a redlink. A bluelink will take you to the user page. A redlink means a user page hasn't been set up yet, but the name has been registered. If the name is grayed out, the name is not registered.

Finally, if you'd rather browse through a list of usernames, you can go to [[Special:Listusers]], which is a long list of all registered usernames. Most of these are throwaway accounts, registered by vandals or registered and never used. One way this list is useful, however, is you can enter a username in the Display users starting at text box and see all the users registered with names starting with the letters you entered.

Creating the Account

Once you've selected the name you want to register, creating the account is easy. Simply click Log In/Create Account in the upper-right corner of the screen, then click the Create One link next to the words *Don't have an account?*. Follow the instructions to fill out the form that appears (Figure 11-2). Type the words in the CAPTCHA box (just above the Username field) as they appear, without spaces; then enter your chosen username and password.

Entering a valid email address when you register is *highly* recommended. Along with allowing other users to contact you while still keeping your email address private, giving an email address means your password can be sent to you if you lose it. A valid email address is the *only* way to recover a lost password; if you don't have an email address on file and you are unable to log in to your account, you can't do anything. If you do give an email address when you register, you'll receive a confirmation email from *wiki@wikimedia.org*; clicking the link in the email is necessary to be able to use your email address.

Once you've completed these steps, you're done! Now you can edit under your new username, create new pages, create a user page, and set up your preferences and watchlist (all described in this chapter). If you're editing from your own computer, you can check the Remember me box when you log in, so you don't have to log in again every time you want to edit.

Setting Your Preferences

You can set a number of preferences as a registered, logged-in user. Once you are logged in, simply click the My Preferences link in the upper-right corner of the page to set and reset any option. These include settings such as what you see when you click Recent Changes, how the date and time displays, your search preferences, how the editing window works, and even how images display. You can also customize your *skin*, which will change the visual appearance of the site.

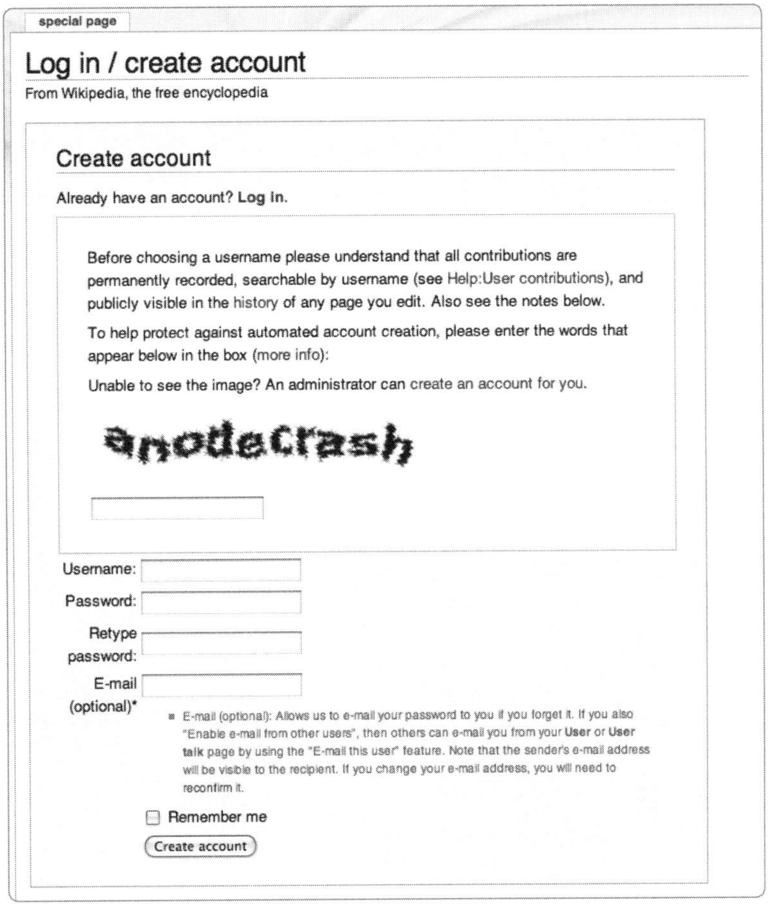

Log in / create account

From Wikipedia, the free encyclopedia

Create account

Already have an account? **Log in**.

Before choosing a username please understand that all contributions are permanently recorded, searchable by username (see Help:User contributions), and publicly visible in the history of any page you edit. Also see the notes below.

To help protect against automated account creation, please enter the words that appear below in the box (more info):

Unable to see the image? An administrator can create an account for you.

anodeCrash

Username:	
Password:	
Retype password:	
E-mail (optional)*	

- E-mail (optional): Allows us to e-mail your password to you if you forget it. If you also "Enable e-mail from other users", then others can e-mail you from your **User** or **User talk** page by using the "E-mail this user" feature. Note that the sender's e-mail address will be visible to the recipient. If you change your e-mail address, you will need to reconfirm it.

☐ Remember me

(Create account)

FIGURE 11-2: *The Create account form*

A Note on Passwords

Secure passwords include both letters and numbers and avoid dictionary words. Nowadays, passwords should generally be chosen with this degree of security. Although choosing a secure password isn't *required*, Wikipedia strongly recommends it. Passwords for Wikipedia may be as short as three characters, but they should generally be longer for security.

If you have been active on the site for a long time or become a prominent editor, change your password occasionally. Administrator passwords make for tempting targets for password crackers, and cases of emergency de-adminning occurred in early 2007 when a couple of accounts were hacked into. This is uncommon but certainly preventable with secure passwords!

Clicking My Preferences takes you to [[Special:Preferences]], where a menu of options is displayed (Figure 11-3). Each tab leads to a set of options that you can customize.

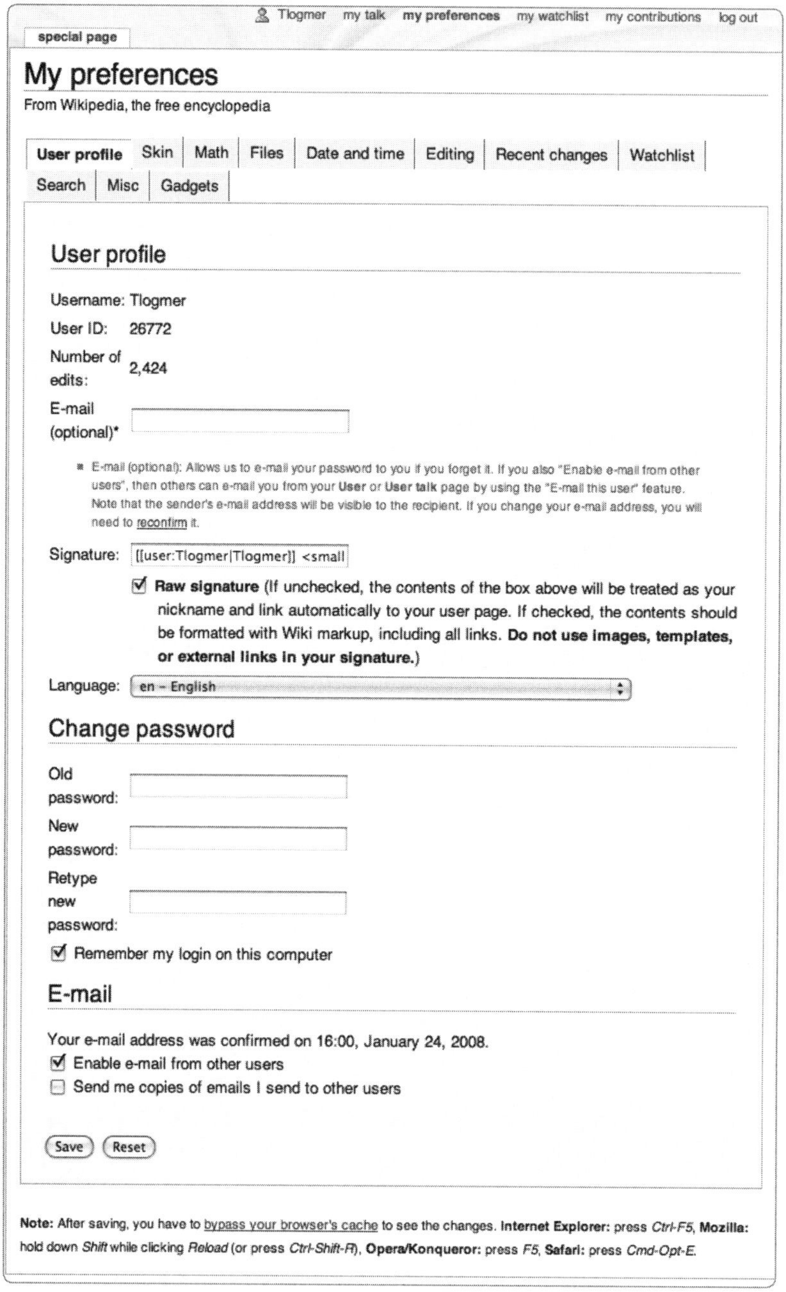

     ⁂ Tlogmer   my talk   **my preferences**   my watchlist   my contributions   log out

special page

My preferences

From Wikipedia, the free encyclopedia

| **User profile** | Skin | Math | Files | Date and time | Editing | Recent changes | Watchlist |
| Search | Misc | Gadgets |

User profile

Username: Tlogmer

User ID: 26772

Number of edits: 2,424

E-mail (optional)*

    * E-mail (optional): Allows us to e-mail your password to you if you forget it. If you also "Enable e-mail from other users", then others can e-mail you from your **User** or **User talk** page by using the "E-mail this user" feature. Note that the sender's e-mail address will be visible to the recipient. If you change your e-mail address, you will need to reconfirm it.

Signature: [[user:Tlogmer|Tlogmer]] <small

    ☑ **Raw signature** (If unchecked, the contents of the box above will be treated as your nickname and link automatically to your user page. If checked, the contents should be formatted with Wiki markup, including all links. **Do not use images, templates, or external links in your signature.**)

Language: en – English

Change password

Old password:

New password:

Retype new password:

☑ Remember my login on this computer

E-mail

Your e-mail address was confirmed on 16:00, January 24, 2008.

☑ Enable e-mail from other users

☐ Send me copies of emails I send to other users

(Save) (Reset)

Note: After saving, you have to bypass your browser's cache to see the changes. **Internet Explorer:** press *Ctrl-F5*, **Mozilla:** hold down *Shift* while clicking *Reload* (or press *Ctrl-Shift-R*), **Opera/Konqueror:** press *F5*, **Safari:** press *Cmd-Opt-E*.

FIGURE 11-3: The My Preferences window

Some preference settings, like the following, should have high priority:

Enabling email

If you didn't provide an email address when you registered for the site, you can provide one on the first tab (User Profile) of the My Preferences page. (You will have to respond to a confirmation email.) If you give an email address and check the Enable other users box, anyone will be able to email you from the site through the Email This User link on the left-hand sidebar, but your email address will not be disclosed, and those mailing you will not see it. Giving an email address should not lead to spam problems. Though most discussions about content are best posted on talk pages, offsite confidential communications are best done by email, as any message left on a talk page is there for the world to see. Still, administrators don't always enable this option, so it is certainly not essential. You can change your email address under the User Profile tab as well; if you do so, you'll get an email each time asking you to verify your account. Simply click the link in the email to do so.

Passwords and verification

We have already mentioned that giving a valid email address is the *only* way to retrieve your password if you forget it. You can also reset your password under the User Profile tab anytime.

Resetting the clock

Precise timestamps show up everywhere on Wikipedia—in editing histories, in signatures on talk pages, and so on. To change the time to your local time zone, go to My Preferences and click the Date and Time tab. There, you can fill in the time from your browser or set a specific time zone. You can also choose how dates appear. By default, timestamps refer to the UTC time zone. For all practical purposes, UTC is Greenwich Mean Time, which is probably confusing as an option. Setting your time zone preference means that all timestamps will display relative to your local time.

Other settings, like these, are not as crucial, and you can modify them when you get around to it:

Setting the size of the editing window

The Editing tab in My Preferences lets you customize the size of the editing window when you click Edit This Page. For instance, if you edit on a large wide-screen monitor, you will probably want to adjust the editing window dimensions from the default 25 rows and 80 columns of text to something larger. To do so, simply type new numbers here and click Save. Conversely, if you are editing with a small laptop or handheld device, you'll almost certainly want to make the editing window smaller.

Further options on this page can help you find tools that suit your preferences as an editor. For instance, if you often find yourself editing pages as you browse Wikipedia, try turning on Edit Pages on Double-click, which will open an edit window whenever you double-click an editable

Wikipedia page. If you are new to editing (or trying to train yourself), try turning on the Prompt me when entering a blank edit summary option.

Special searches
Customizing which namespaces you want to search by default, under the Search tab, can be helpful if you find yourself often searching for material in the project namespaces. Although you can always change which namespaces you want to search each time, as described in Chapter 3, you can save yourself some time by customizing this here.

Displays
You can also set how certain elements display: Choose how you see images on the Files tab and mathematical equations on the Math tab. For instance, if you're reading Wikipedia from a handheld device, you'll probably want to set the default thumbnail image size to be as small as possible.

Setting Your Signature

You can modify the standard way your signature appears when you produce it on a discussion page by signing with four tildes. The standard signature consists of your username, wikilinked to your user page, and a link to your talk page, with the time and date of the edit:

```
Phoebe (talk) 01:47, 30 September 2007 (EDT)
```

You can customize your signature using wikisyntax and HTML. On the User Profile tab of My Preferences, type the code you want in the Signature box and then check the Raw signature box. For instance, placing the following code in the Signature box, checking the Raw signature box and then saving:

```
[[user:myname|myname the great]] -- [[user_talk:myname|talk to me!]]
```

means that you will insert the following whenever you sign a page with ~~~~:

```
myname the great -- talk to me! 01:47, 30 September 2007
```

If you browse on talk and project pages, you'll see many such signatures, some simply customized with links to talk pages or contributions added and some with different fonts and colors from the default. The code that produces these signatures is visible in the page wikitext.

Although becoming a colorful character in this way is perhaps attractive, rainbow signatures and unusual scripts are not really such original ideas, and signatures produced with a great deal of extra code are actually counterproductive for other editors. Who wants to navigate extra wikisyntax on a discussion page that has been signed a dozen times? A fancy signature is not a way to be taken seriously—better to keep customizations to a minimum. Stick to text, don't use images, and remember that overly intrusive signatures will just annoy other people—don't even think about using the blink tag! The page

[[Wikipedia:Signatures]] (shortcut WP:SIG) discusses guidelines for using and customizing signatures.

Customizing Skins and Installing Extensions

The overall appearance, layout, and style of MediaWiki pages is dictated by *skins*, or CSS files that style the website. Users can choose and change skins. The *Monobook* skin is used by default on Wikipedia, and this is what you will see if you're not logged in. This skin is what most of the world assumes is the look-and-feel of Wikipedia. This default skin is also packaged with every MediaWiki installation, so you'll see it all over the Web. If you have no firm preference as to the site's appearance, continuing to use Monobook is generally a good idea, as Monobook is reflected in help page descriptions and is also kept up to date with the new site features.

* **NOTE:** *If the text on the screen is too small, most browsers allow you to change the text size or zoom the view for readability. Pressing CTRL-+ in Firefox makes all the text in the window larger.*

In writing this book, we have been referencing tabs and links on pages as they appear in the Monobook skin. Other skins that you can choose from render pages slightly differently; not all links are visible in all skins, and their placement may be different. To change to another skin, simply log in, click My Preferences, and choose the skin you'd like from the Skin tab. You can always change back if you don't like it!

Skins are customizable in other ways as well, and many people develop their own skins. You can see some of them at the showcase display, Gallery of User Styles on Meta (see "Further Reading" on page 314).

You can also modify your experience on Wikipedia by customizing your own personal JavaScript or CSS files. Among other things, this allows you to install many of the extensions and other modifications, or *user scripts*, that have

Popups

One popular extension is called *popups*. This allows you to see a preview of an article (including the first paragraph or so of text and the first image on the page) when you hover with your mouse over an internal link. The popup window also gives you a menu with a range of quick options, such as viewing the history of the article or the last diff—handy for vandalism patrol. Popups were originally developed by User:Lupin. You can install popups easily by going to the Gadgets tab in My Preferences and checking the box to enable them. You can also install them by customizing your *monobook.js* file, available at username/monobook.js. Find out more at [[Wikipedia:Popups]].

been developed. Each skin's JavaScript file lives at nameofskin.*js* in your user space; so you can locate the JavaScript file for Monobook, the default skin, at yourusername/*monobook.js*. You must have an account and be logged in to take advantage of scripts and modifications.

Scripts range from a way to add your own custom links to the sidebar, [[Wikipedia:Tools/Navigation shortcuts]], to a way to add extra custom tabs across the top of the page. You can find a list of scripts and more information about installing them at [[Wikipedia:WikiProject User scripts/Scripts]]. Other custom tools can be found at [[Wikipedia:Tools]]. Some common tools and gadgets can also be found on the Gadgets tab in My Preferences.

Further Reading

Creating an Account

http://en.wikipedia.org/wiki/Wikipedia:Why_create_an_account   An overview of the benefits to creating a user account, with a link to the form to create an account

http://en.wikipedia.org/wiki/Wikipedia:Username   The official username policy and an overview of guidelines and how to work with usernames

http://en.wikipedia.org/wiki/Wikipedia:Changing_username   The page to request a change in username

http://en.wikipedia.org/wiki/Special:Listusers   The automatically generated list of all registered accounts on Wikipedia

http://meta.wikimedia.org/wiki/Right_to_vanish   Information about the qualified right to vanish

Setting Preferences

http://meta.wikimedia.org/wiki/Help:Preferences   About user preferences, including skins

http://en.wikipedia.org/wiki/Wikipedia:Signatures#Customizing_your_ signature   About customizing your signature

http://en.wikipedia.org/wiki/Wikipedia:Tools   Various tools for using Wikipedia

http://meta.wikimedia.org/wiki/Gallery_of_user_styles   A gallery of skins that MediaWiki users have developed (both for using Wikipedia and for using MediaWiki on other sites)

http://meta.wikimedia.org/wiki/Help:User_style   Various customizations you can make to your CSS and Javascript (for advanced users)

http://meta.wikimedia.org/wiki/Skins   Directions for creating your own skins

User Pages, Watchlists, and Edit Count

If you have a username, you have a user page in the form of [[User:*Yourusername*]]. Here you can post information about yourself for the benefit of other editors, as well as notes for yourself (for example, a list of the project pages that you often use). Note that a user page is not meant to be a personal web page: Wikipedia is not MySpace. Wikipedia has a few commonsense guidelines for user pages, as noted here; otherwise, you are free to post whatever you wish.

If you never edit your user page, it will show up as a redlink. Although this is respected (to an extent), not editing your user page will not inspire confidence in your commitment to Wikipedia. Adding at least some information to your user page is recommended. For users who really don't want a user page, one option is to redirect their user page to their user talk page (at [[user_talk:*yourusername*]]). This means when you sign messages on talk pages your username will show up as a bluelink, but people clicking it will be directed to your talk page to leave a message instead.

The content you add to your user page is up to you. Listing your interests and areas of expertise is certainly helpful—or at least what you're interested in working on in Wikipedia. Inform other editors, for instance, if your edits are in an area that you are knowledgeable about or just consider a hobby. This will help other like-minded editors find you. You can also list what you've done on the site on your user page: articles you've written or worked on, for instance. This kind of brag sheet not only helps you keep track of what you've done but also shows others what you've accomplished and where your main editing interests lie. Pride in your work as shown on your user page is not misplaced!

Many editors also list the languages they speak—a courteous gesture for an international project. If you are multilingual, your help with translations may be requested. Wikipedia has a series of standardized language templates for just this purpose. They contain the language code (such as *en* or *fr*) and a number from 1 to 4 and then *native*. The numbers indicate proficiency: *1* means you're a beginning learner, whereas *native* indicates that this language is your mother tongue. These language templates can be found at [[Wikipedia:Babel]] (shortcut WP:BABEL).

User Page Content

The way of the Wikipedian is to value spontaneity on the site, not formality. When you post any serious amount of information on your user page, though, you should adopt a thoughtful approach. Keep these three concepts in mind: privacy, which we've already mentioned; authority, which we discussed at length in Chapter 2; and neutrality.

The authors of this book happily use their real names on Wikipedia—and you can immediately discover this from Google. Anything posted on Wikipedia may become *very* public, and if you use your real name, your user page may start to climb up the Google hits on your name. Keep this in mind if you add a photo, your location, or any other identifiable information about yourself, particularly if you don't want your identity on Wikipedia linked to other online presences or public roles you may have. Just to drive this point home, a search for *Charles*

Matthews—a fairly common name—now leads directly to one author's very own user page in the top few search engine hits. Furthermore, if you're interested in getting involved in the administrative side of the site, that may involve controversy. Any disclosure may attract online stalkers; in a few cases, the antagonists of administrators have tracked down real-life information such as phone numbers. This is unlikely to happen unless you're engaged in controversial actions; however, as with any online forum, this possibility is a genuine concern. Wikipedia itself can do very little in such cases.

Qualifications in academic areas add to an editor's reputation. Should you mention this qualification on your user page? Listing a doctorate in art history will not make you immediately identifiable. It also should not buttress your art history edits against those who think they have identified mistakes; however, those who don't trust your edits to art articles will probably be more likely to check their own facts before inserting their corrections. Many editors view editing Wikipedia as a professional activity, no less important than working on another encyclopedia or scholarly work that merits the respect of others. If you're known in your field or recognized as an expert, about the only way to prove it is to use your real name as a username, and use a professional tone on your user page. You can use a pseudonym to reduce your real name's prominence, but make no secret of your real name on your user page.

A different set of considerations comes into play when you consider posting your affiliations, say political or religious, the company you work for, or any activism you pursue. This can be seen as *declaring an interest* before editing in some of the more contentious areas. If you do this, your edits will be under more intense scrutiny by other editors for strict neutrality. Self-knowledge helps here. If despite having a commitment to a political party, you really can be neutral in editing political articles, then your reputation as a good editor will grow. If, however, you really cannot be neutral about the company you work for (and many people would find that hard), then if you do edit the article about this company, your declaration may make matters worse. However, fair-minded folk will always give you some credit for honesty, even if you're a declared partisan.

Guidelines

Wikipedia has some limitations on what you can post to your user page. The guideline is at [[Wikipedia:User page]] (shortcut WP:UP). You can't, for example, use your user page for blogging, for an activist campaign, or in other ways that simply treat it as free web space. User pages are meant to help the community of Wikipedia editors, and using them in a combative fashion (a blacklist of users you dislike, for example) is a mistake.

Your user page is also not the right place to raise grievances, for the good reason that others are not entitled to reply to you there (though they may leave messages on your user talk page). By convention, no one else should edit your user page without your invitation, though obvious vandalism to it may be reverted by others.

Userboxes and the Boxen War

One of the less-distinguished episodes in the history of the English-language Wikipedia occurred early in 2006, in a huge controversy over an apparently minor matter of onsite policy. *Userboxes* (*boxen*, to some of those unconvinced on their centrality to the project) are small rectangular templates designed to be placed on a user page to help with various types of self-identification. "This user is a Scorpio" is a harmless example. But what about "This user enjoys pornography" or "This user supports Senator John McCain for president in 2008?" What about the spoof language box, "This person does not understand Bullshit (or understands it with considerable difficulties)"? Or "This user is a Wiccan?" These are all real examples. The question was over whether these were helpful to the site or, in some cases, inflammatory and whether they should allowed.

The first userboxes were the language templates mentioned previously, but the userbox fad came to prominence shortly after a rapid influx of new editors in late 2005. Once the fad caught on, userboxes addressing all issues of religion and politics, profanity and sexuality, were being created. These userboxes became the focus of a fervid argument, essentially about free speech; the question was whether Wikipedia was a free forum for its users or a working environment that needed some regulation.

Thousands of userboxes having been created, deleting those clearly created only to test how far Wikipedia was committed to allowing free expression and self-identification took a while, and a great deal of argument (including one notable case of administrator edit-warring) took place regarding some of the boxes. The debate was ultimately settled by some decisions on namespaces; box templates held in the User namespace (rather than the Template namespace) are now less "official." Some arguments do still persist, however, about what a user page may contain (whether boxed up or not). However, Wikipedia is not a dedicated discussion forum, and the general consensus was that self-identification on the site should help the project, not be seen as an end in itself. See [[Wikipedia:Userboxes]] (shortcut WP:BOX) for a deceptively calm account of the controversy and a list of userboxes, most related to general interests and professions or education, that you might want to use. [[Wikipedia:WikiProject Userboxes]] has taken over this once-contentious area.

These guidelines apply to the user space in general, including subpages. In commonsense terms, these guidelines mean that anything for the benefit of the project can be posted; nothing else should be.

User Talk Pages

With a user page comes a user talk page. This is where other people can leave you messages about your work, articles that you are working on, and so on. A typical user talk page accumulates notes and questions from other editors about article content, ongoing projects, and contributions; notifications from WikiProjects the user belongs to; and occasional complaints and holiday greetings. Early messages on your user talk page may well be automated or created by templates. Please don't take this as typical of Wikipedia: Human interaction is valued. General interaction on talk pages, which are a very important part of social life on Wikipedia, will be described further in Chapter 12, but the basic rule *play nice* applies here as elsewhere.

* **NOTE:** *If you have a specific problem but don't yet know where to go on the site to get an answer, you can add the {{helpme}} template to your user talk page. You should get a response on your talk page from an active editor.*

Most user talk pages use a conventional simple structure, where each message is left as a new section (with two equal signs, ==, around the message title to produce the section header). New messages are added at the bottom. If a conversation produces several back-and-forth replies, any further comments should be indented for readability to produce a threaded discussion, as on article talk pages. Finally, all messages should be signed with four tildes (~~~~) to insert the commenter's username and the date. As described in "Talk Pages" on page 113, whenever you receive a message on your talk page, the next time you log in an orange notification box (see Figure 4-6) will automatically pop up to let you know (this goes away when you "check your messages" by going to your talk page).

You are entitled to keep your user talk page tidy: If you get lots of messages, archive the page periodically to a subpage (see the description of user subpages in "Drafting the Article" on page 169 and directions at [[Wikipedia:User page]]). While ignoring any annoying messages left on your talk page is best, you can also remove them, though removing legitimate discussions about content is generally not a good idea.

If you have a question or comment for another user, feel free to go to his or her user talk page to leave a message. You should be polite (obviously), but you don't have to be ingratiating. A good starting point is to assume that Wikipedia is a working environment—so say what has to be said, and be fairly businesslike. For certain discussions, you might consider requesting an email exchange. The user whom you are contacting is free to delete your message after reading it (or even before). This is not something to make an issue about.

What happens when you begin a discussion on another user talk page depends on the user you have contacted. Logically, a thread started on [[User talk:BeanStalkJack]] would continue there, with [[user:BeanStalkJack]] replying to messages left for him. You can also request that the conversation proceed on your own user talk page: Just finish with "Please respond on my user talk page" before signing the post. If not, you will have to monitor [[User talk:BeanStalkJack]] for any answers. You might click the Watch tab before moving on; then all you have to remember is to consult your watchlist. Some users will respond on your user page anyway.

You often have a choice of where to take up a discussion arising from edits to an article. Should you write something on the article's talk page, or would it be better to go to the editor's user talk page? On the article's discussion page, everyone concerned can chip in, so if you have general concerns about an article, post them here. If you want to address a particular editor on some aspect of his or her work or ask a question about a particular edit, then post on the editor's user talk page.

Watchlists

Your *watchlist* defines your own personal corner of the huge Wikipedia site. It displays a set of recent changes for the subset of pages that you have specifically selected to watch. Using your watchlist means you can easily scan a list of the edits made to the pages or articles you are interested in, without having to go to each of those pages individually. By maintaining a watchlist, you can help defeat vandalism and keep the site tidy while monitoring topics of greatest interest to you. Your watchlist is private—only you can access it.

When you're logged in, you can access your watchlist by clicking My Watchlist, next to the My Preferences link in the upper-right corner.

The watchlist display (Figure 11-4) is similar to Recent Changes. Any changes made to the pages you are watching are listed here, one change per line, with the date of the change, the username of the editor who made the change, and a link to the diff.

One special feature of watchlists and Recent Changes, which is different from reading an individual page history, is the small colored number that appears after the page name and timestamp, but before the editor's name or IP address (Figure 11-5). This number refers to the amount of text, in bytes, that was changed during an individual edit. A green number with a plus sign means text was added; a red number with a minus sign means text was removed. A very large red number, for instance, may indicate that a page was blanked or significant content was removed, and you should check it out; similarly, a large green number with a single edit indicates that a great deal of text was added all at once. Note that the number refers to *net change*, so major edits may still result in a small number being displayed. A zero will display when a word is replaced by a word with the same number of letters (say four); this could still be a vandal!

Any page, whether it's an article or a project page, can be *watched*, or added to your watchlist. To watch a page, make sure you're logged in, and then click the Watch tab at the top of the article in question (Figure 11-6). Now any changes made to the page will show up on your watchlist. To unwatch a page, you can simply revisit the page; you'll notice the tab now says *Unwatch*. Click the tab again to remove the page.

You can also remove pages from your watchlist by clicking the View and Edit Watchlist link at the top of your watchlist; you'll be taken to a list of all the page titles you're watching. On the Recent Changes tab in My Preferences, you can customize the number of changes and the number of days that you wish to display.

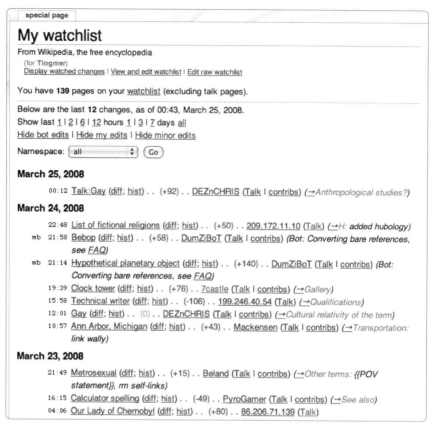

FIGURE 11-4: *A watchlist for a logged-in user*

✳ **NOTE:** *When you watch a page you are also watching its associated talk page; so if you watch an article, any changes made to the article or to its talk page will be listed.*

Watchlists are not limited in terms of size , but the list tends to grow over time, and your interest in a page may only be temporary. For example, in a user talk page discussion, you might watch the page on which an active debate is happening. But when it concludes, you may have no further reason to be alerted to all changes, so you may want to remove the page from your watchlist. By default, any page you create is added to your watchlist; you can select other options from the Watchlist tab under My Preferences.

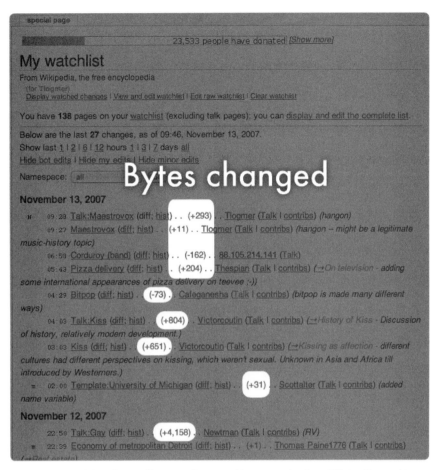

FIGURE 11-5: Number of bytes changed in a particular diff, indicated in a watchlist

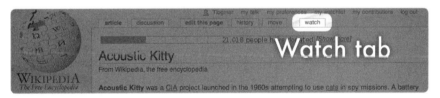

FIGURE 11-6: The Watch tab at the top of an article

Watchlists and Related Changes

Watchlists are easy to use, but they are entirely private. If you'd like to create a tidy shared watchlist for a joint project or a public to-do list, or if you want to watch a related group of pages together, you can use the Related Changes feature instead. Create a subpage in your user space with a list of links to the articles you're interested in. Clicking Related Changes from this page (on the left-hand sidebar under Toolbox) will show you any changes to these pages (though not to their talk pages). If you'd like to include links that won't display publicly, add a link like [[Talk:*topic*]] beside [[*topic*]]; the link won't show up on the page since it isn't piped to any replacement text, but Related Changes will register the change.

RSS Notification

You can also create other types of notifications or alerts about edits to a particular page. This is helpful if you are only interested in a few pages.

To create an RSS feed or Atom feed (which is an alternative to RSS) of changes made to any page, follow these steps:

1. Go to the page you're interested in and click the History tab at the top of the article.
2. Now look under Toolbox on the left-hand sidebar menu.
3. You'll see two links for feed options (under Related Changes): RSS and Atom. You can add the links for these to a feed reader as with any other feed.

The feed will display as a page of diffs (Figure 11-7 shows a feed of changes to the page [[List of trees]] being displayed in NetNewsReader). This option could be handy if you're in the habit of checking your RSS feed reader but not Wikipedia, for instance, if you wanted to keep an eye on a particular page such as your own user talk page.

Contribution History and Counting Edits

If you participate much in discussions about other editors (such as on the Requests for Adminship page), you'll likely hear references to *edit count*. This means the total number of page changes that a user has made, usually counting edits in all namespaces. Any contributor's history of edits and total edit count is publicly accessible; a record of all changes made by any account or IP address is kept. For any registered account, the user's editing history can be found from [[Special:Contributions/*Nameofuser*]], where *Nameofuser* is replaced by the user account name. If you want to see your own contributions, you can just click My Contributions in the upper-right corner, next to My Watchlist. Checking your

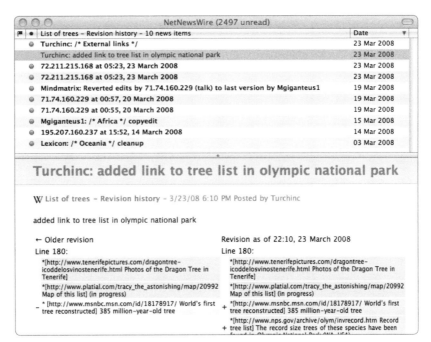

FIGURE 11-7: *An RSS feed of changes made to the page [[List of trees]]*

own contributions can be a quick way to click back to a page that you have been working on or to follow up on a discussion that you have been contributing to.

Checking out an editor's contribution history tells you what he or she has been working on recently. But this display is inconvenient for determining someone's total edit count, especially if that editor has made more than a few thousand edits. You can monitor your own edit count by checking at My Preferences; the count is posted just below your username. To check another contributor's edit count, in addition to [[Special:Contributions]] (which gives you a list of edits but doesn't provide a total number), you can use several automated tools that count edits for a given username. These tools can be found at [[Wikipedia:WikiProject edit counters]]. One caveat is these edit counters are provided as fun utilities, not as crucial project tools, and they tend to go offline or be unpredictably withdrawn. To see the top contributors, Wikipedia has a list, which is updated but not always regularly, at [[Wikipedia:List of Wikipedians by number of edits]] (shortcut WP: WBE). This list currently gives you an idea of the edit counts for the top 3,000 or so editors; as of 2008, you need at least 5,000 edits to appear on the list.

Edit count is important because this measure is the typical one used to enfranchise editors in elections (for instance, in previous years voters for Wiki-media Foundation board members had to have at least 400 edits on a single Wikimedia wiki), so having a certain edit count may bring suffrage in elections where only community members may participate. Additionally, the edit counts and patterns for administrator candidates are also debated (though no particular number is asked for, a count in the low thousands of edits or more is generally required to pass in Requests for Adminship, described in "Administrators" on page 327). In other words, edit count is a measure of how experienced someone is as a Wikipedia editor.

Edit count is only somewhat useful though. Although edit count is correlated with experience editing Wikipedia, this correlation is rough. Don't think better of someone just because he is poor at finding the preview button. The raw edit count is crude and undiscriminating—counting typo fixes and vandalism reverts is the same as adding thoughtful content or references, though anyone who is truly interested can, of course, sample an account's contributions and draw better conclusions about the quality of an editor's work. Historically, the most committed individual editors, editing normally, have contributed at a peak rate of around 3,000 edits a month, or 100 a day. This rate requires full use of free time and not having a life outside Wikipedia and is not necessarily sustainable.

The author of the original tool for counting edits noted that *editcountitis*, or an unhealthy obsession with the notion of edit count, can be fatal. Editcountitis

---

Further Reading

http://en.wikipedia.org/wiki/Wikipedia:User_page The user page guideline

http://en.wikipedia.org/wiki/Wikipedia:Userboxes The guideline on userboxes

http://en.wikipedia.org/wiki/Wikipedia:Talk_page An introduction to reading discussion pages (including user talk pages)

http://en.wikipedia.org/wiki/Wikipedia:Talk_page_guidelines Basic principles and guidelines for working on talk pages (including user talk pages)

http://en.wikipedia.org/wiki/Help:Watching_pages Help with using watchlists and different watchlist options

http://en.wikipedia.org/wiki/Wikipedia:RSS Instructions for getting RSS feeds from Wikipedia and what areas of the site you can get RSS feeds of

http://en.wikipedia.org/wiki/Wikipedia:WikiProject_edit_counters The place to get an edit counter that will count another contributor's total edits

http://en.wikipedia.org/wiki/Special:Contributions A page where you can get a list of the contributions made by any IP address or username

http://en.wikipedia.org/wiki/Wikipedia:List_of_Wikipedians_by_number_of_edits List of Wikipedians with the top edit counts (only lists the top 3,000 individuals or so)

http://en.wikipedia.org/wiki/Wikipedia:Editcountitis A description of the dread disease of editcountitis

http://en.wikipedia.org/wiki/Wikipedia:Wikipediholic A description of how to diagnose Wikipediholism

is often a symptom of *Wikipediholism*, which is an even worse disease. The only sure treatment is worrying more about the quality of your edits than the quantity. You have been warned; head over to [[Wikipedia:Wikipediholism test]] (shortcut WP:WHT) for a humorous diagnosis.

Users and Administrators

If you're editing and aren't logged in, you're in some sense a second-class citizen on the site. Expect less tolerance of minor infractions of policy and guidelines. That being said, everyone editing from an account should be treated equally, *as an editor*. Although editors hold different titles on the site, no one has any actual added authority when it comes to saying what should and should not be in an article.

In particular, the site administrators (or *sysops*) are not supposed to use their greater technical capabilities to exert influence on content. This is a basic point but one that is easily and often misunderstood. Administrators are usually experienced editors, who will naturally know the system better and will probably be more adept at managing discussions about policy and its application. This doesn't mean that what an experienced editor has to say trumps what a complete newcomer has to offer. From its outset Wikipedia has tried to get by with a very flat user structure, without a hierarchy of editors, and in contributions to articles that ideal persists. Wikipedia does have, however, a small variety of account types with different technical privileges, which are detailed next.

User Levels

The majority of tasks on Wikipedia can be performed by anyone, whether that person is logged in or not. A handful of user access levels are defined, with progressively broader privileges; these are detailed in full at [[Wikipedia:User access levels]]. Note that these are *functional* distinctions, not an indication of the editor's importance on the site or the role he or she takes in contributing to content. [[Category:Wikipedia functionaries]] provides some categorization of individuals with particular roles on the site, which may not be related to Wikipedia access level.

IP addresses
Visitors who have not created an account or signed in to an existing account can still do most things, including the most important tasks: editing articles and helping with Wikipedia maintenance.

Signed-in users
Signed-up users can do everything IP addresses can do. They can also upload files, start new articles, and once they reach the *autoconfirm* threshold (after having the account for four days), they can move pages and edit semiprotected pages. The vast majority of Wikipedia contributors, both dedicated and casual, fall into this category.

Administrators

The English-language Wikipedia has over 1,500 administrators (known as *admins* or *sysops*). The main page about them, [[Wikipedia:Administrators]] (shortcut WP:ADMIN), lists their quite varied powers and responsibilities. We say more about these later in this chapter. Admins are generally expected to know more about the site and to be much better informed about the workings of Wikipedia than the average user. They are usually good, helpful people to ask about procedures and for help in editing disputes. Admins represent the community of Wikipedia editors in the sense that they are, in almost all cases, elected volunteers who give time to patrolling the site. They also bear the brunt of much bad behavior from those who don't know or don't care about the site, how it works, and its mission.

Bots

A bot is an automated program or script that can do some routine tasks. *Bot* is also the status of an account that is only used to enable mass automated edits. The edits of approved accounts with bot status turned on do not show up in Recent Changes. Although this status, like all statuses other than regular user, can only be given by a bureaucrat, bots are approved by an informal *Bot Approvals Group*, which consists of interested bot programmers. More information and a list of all currently active and approved bots can be found at [[Wikipedia:Bots]].

The other status classes are listed below for reference. Very few editors, relatively speaking, fall into these classes.

Bureaucrats

Users with *bureaucrat* status can turn other users into administrators (but not remove admin status), change usernames, and flag and unflag bot accounts. All of these changes are recorded in [[Special:Log/rights]] (or [[Wikipedia:Bureaucrat log]] before December 24, 2004). Bureaucrats are created by a process called *Request for Bureaucratship (RfB)*, which is similar to the Request for Adminship process. Bureaucrats are created by other bureaucrats (or by stewards on projects who do not yet have one). Wikipedia has far fewer bureaucrats than admins (and requests on RfB are rare); less than 30 editors are bureaucrats. Thus bureaucrats, like people in the other categories discussed next, make up a small, trusted group of users.

Oversight and CheckUser

These two special technical permissions for tools are generally used only in atypical situations. Users with the *Oversight* permission can hide revisions of pages from all users (rather than delete the entire page). These revisions can temporarily be accessed and reviewed only by other users with the Oversight permission. A log of oversight actions is visible to all Oversighters, who usually are members of the Arbitration Committee (described in Chapter 14). Users with the *CheckUser* permission can retrieve the IP addresses used by a username and can also retrieve all edits by users using a certain

IP or IP range; this helps fight highly disruptive vandalism and sockpuppet abuse.

A log of CheckUser actions is visible to all Checkusers. Checkusers are generally appointed by the Arbitration Committee; stewards and a few other global project people can also serve as Checkusers. The policies and more information can be found at [[Wikipedia:Oversight]] and [[Wikipedia:CheckUser]], respectively; requests for use of CheckUser can be made at [[Wikipedia:Requests for checkuser]].

Stewards

Stewards have cross-project powers; they can act as an administrator or bureaucrat on any Wikimedia Foundation wiki. They are not commonly active on the English-language Wikipedia. Stewards exist especially to help out with smaller Wikimedia wikis that may not yet have their own administrators; see Chapter 17.

Developers

Developers have the highest degree of technical access (actually at various levels, but these levels are not really visible to users). They can make direct changes to the MediaWiki software and the Wikimedia wiki farm and databases. These people, by and large, do not carry out administrative functions on Wikipedia; they are a handful of trusted users who participate in MediaWiki development and technical administration.

Administrators

Administrators, often known as *sysops* (for *system operator*) or just *admins* and sometimes referred to as *janitors*, are editors whose editing privileges have been increased. Ambitious to become one? You'd better know what's involved. The *janitor* nickname is in place for a reason. Administrators have little extra formal power in making editorial or policy decisions. Instead, they tend to do very messy cleanup work, revert vandalism, keep an eye on Recent Changes, watch out for disruptive users, and delete junk pages.

Administrator powers are given to editors who have proven themselves to be experienced and trustworthy though a process called Requests for Adminship (RfA). Adminship was originally designed as a temporary measure to reduce vandalism on the main page; as the community grew, it became a useful way to grant extra privileges to experienced users so they could do needed work.

So what are their superpowers? Admins can block disruptive editors or IP addresses from editing. This not done lightly, and doing it to gain editing advantages would cause a scandal. This power requires a proper understanding of site policies and customs.

Furthermore, admins are able to delete pages from public view, and they can view the histories of deleted pages. They are also able to delete uploaded files, edit protected pages (such as the main page) and protect and unprotect pages. They can protect pages from being moved (or move a protected page) and edit pages in the MediaWiki namespace, which changes the look and feel of the site. There are formal processes for doing most of these things, including blocking, deletions, and making interface changes, which admins are expected to follow. Admins are accountable for their actions and should respond reasonably when their use of power is calmly questioned.

Adminship is a duty, not a prize. The only reason to become an administrator is if you want to help with tasks that need these particular powers. Wikipedia has plenty of very valuable and respected contributors who are not and do not intend to be administrators. Becoming an administrator also exposes you to a certain level of visibility and controversy that might not be desirable; often administrative tasks involve doing things that other people won't want you to do, such as deleting an article that they wrote. In general, becoming a possible administrator candidate is something that you should expect only after extensive work on the wiki, and not something you should strive for in particular. Admins have no fixed term of service, and particular duties are not assigned. Rarely, admins can lose their administrator status, though generally only if serious concerns have been raised and the Arbitration Committee has ruled on it.

It's No Big Deal

One oft-repeated thing you'll hear about adminship is that it's *no big deal*. This means that people shouldn't worry about the fine distinctions of who gets to be an admin and who doesn't; any trusted user with some experience who wants to help out should be able to become an admin. This quote comes from an email from Jimmy Wales, sent when the community was quite a bit smaller in 2003:

> I just wanted to say that becoming a sysop is *not a big deal*. I think perhaps I'll go through semi-willy-nilly and make a bunch of people who have been around for awhile sysops. I want to dispel the aura of "authority" around the position. It's merely a technical matter that the powers given to sysops are not given out to everyone. I don't like that there's the apparent feeling here that being granted sysop status is a really special thing.

A few years later, adminship is a bigger deal (the bar has been raised for becoming an admin), but still several admins are added every week.

Requesting Help from an Administrator

Anyone can legitimately request help from an admin, whether on policy, technical matters, or when troubled by another editor. You can find a full list of administrators at [[Wikipedia:List of administrators]] (shortcut WP:LA). Checking this out is actually a farsighted thing to do. Early in working on the site, note those administrators who are active in your areas of interest. If a difficult issue comes up in a hurry, you can check whether a particular user is currently online by reading their contribution history (bearing in mind possible time-coding differences) and then leave a message on his or her user talk page. Or you can send an email to an admin who has enabled mail from his or her user page. Finally, you can go to [[Wikipedia:Requests for administrator attention]], which has a long list of the various places to ask for help with various problems, or to the [[Wikipedia:Administrators' noticeboard]], which is a discussion page just for requests and notices to administrators. This has the advantage that whichever administrators are active at that particular time will see your request.

You are obviously going to be polite in asking for help, so the next key point is simple enough: Be coherent and give the context. When asking for intervention, you must describe the contentious issue clearly enough so that someone else can grasp the problem at hand.

Becoming an Administrator

Requests for Adminship (shortcut WP:RFA) is the formal process of requesting adminship privileges, and it goes on in an open forum. Anyone with an account may request adminship; simply go to the RfA page and nominate yourself or (better) have someone else nominate you. Other people will comment on your application and ask you questions for a period of a week. Many criteria are discussed, mainly relating to the applicant's knowledge of administrator policy, but none have any official status. You obviously need to be a user of the site in good standing, but that rules out few serious candidates. Probably the best way to get a sense of the process is to review some recent debates; you can find archives at [[Wikipedia:Successful adminship candidacies]]. Once you have an account, you can leave comments on other applicants yourself.

Help, I'm Blocked While Learning About the Site!

Sometimes new editors on Wikipedia find themselves blocked from editing because they are working their way up a learning curve on the site and are making some mistakes. If this happens to you, you are certainly not alone. Such blocks should be short (most likely lasting 24 hours), and the point is to learn from them and rise above it. Your reputation will not suffer. For example, if you infringe the Three-Revert Rule, you might be blocked, though you might feel a warning would have been more helpful and no less likely to make you obey it in future.

But don't waste too much time making that point. This is the golden rule: If you have been given a temporary block, you can more easily make the situation worse than you can improve it. "Come back tomorrow" is the best advice. Wikipedia's system is quite forgiving to those who move on quickly from mishaps. For more about how blocking works, see Chapter 14.

After your nomination closes, a bureaucrat will evaluate the comments and decide whether to promote you; a 75 percent margin of support is generally required. Before trying to become an administrator, you should have at least a few months of experience editing the site and perhaps a few thousand edits across various namespaces. Experience in the areas that administrators work in, such as deleting vandalism, participating in Articles for Deletion, or particularly with helping smooth over controversial articles, is also recommended. Others will be assessing your grasp of major policies but also your coolness under trying conditions. Having a thick skin is useful and a level head even more so.

RfA became formalized as a separate area of Wikipedia in June 2003; until then, adminship requests were made on the mailing list. Before becoming an administrator was formalized even to that degree, administrator privileges were handed out fairly freely by Jimmy Wales to anyone who was a "regular" and known on the site.

Further Reading

http://en.wikipedia.org/wiki/Wikipedia:User_access_levels   The different types of user access levels

http://en.wikipedia.org/wiki/Wikipedia:Bots   Information about bots

http://lists.wikimedia.org/pipermail/wikipedia-l/2001-October/000625.html   The October 2001 message from Jimmy Wales announcing that the main page would be locked and temporary admin privileges would be granted

http://en.wikipedia.org/wiki/Wikipedia:Administrators   Information about being an administrator and the official policy on administrators

http://en.wikipedia.org/wiki/Wikipedia:Requests_for_administrator_attention   A place to post requests for help to administrators

http://en.wikipedia.org/wiki/Wikipedia:Requests_for_adminship   Requests for Adminship, where prospective administrators are confirmed

---

Summary

Arrivals at Wikipedia are usually a little casual. These are the basics: Get an account, choose a couple of options in My Preferences, and then start your user page. You can take care of the rest during breaks between actual editing.

Proceed slowly with getting more deeply involved, either in the system or (by bad fortune) in battling against it. The site is administered by the community, for the community. In the next chapter, we'll talk about the culture of this community and Wikipedian motivations, the public discussion forums where you can talk to other editors, and some of the ins and outs of participating in the community aspects of the site.

12

Community and Communication

A large, diverse, and thriving group of volunteers produces encyclopedia articles and administers Wikipedia. Over time, members of the Wikipedia community have developed conventions for interacting with each other, processes for managing content, and policies for minimizing disruptions and maximizing useful work.

In this chapter, we'll discuss where to find other contributors and how to ask for help with any topic. We'll also explain ways in which community members interact with each other. Though most discussion occurs on talk pages, Wikipedia has some central community forums for debate about the site's larger policies and more specific issues. We'll also talk about the make-up of the community. First, however, we'll outline aspects of Wikipedia's shared culture, from key philosophies about how contributors should interact with each other to some long-running points of debate to some friendly practices that have arisen over time. Although explicit site policies cover content guidelines and social norms, informal philosophies and practices help keep the Wikipedia community of contributors together.

Wikipedia's Culture

Wikipedia's community has grown spontaneously and organically—a recipe for a baffling culture rich with in-jokes and insider references. But core tenets of the *wiki way*, like Assume Good Faith and Please Don't Bite the Newcomers, have been with the community since the beginning.

Assumptions on Arrival

Wikipedians try to treat new editors well. Assume Good Faith (AGF) is a fundamental philosophy, as well as an official guideline (shortcut WP:AGF) on Wikipedia. It can be summarized as: Unless you have strong evidence to the contrary, you should always *assume that people who work on the project are trying to help it*, not hurt it.

Assuming good faith means that if someone doesn't seem to be following policy, assume that he or she simply made a mistake rather than deliberately disrupted the encyclopedia; always give an editor the benefit of the doubt. The assumption that everyone involved simply wants to make the encyclopedia better leads to more constructive debates and helps foster harmony on the site. As part of this attitude, a user's reputation on another Web forum or project should not be used against him or her.

Assume Good Faith is a good place to begin, but practicing it can be difficult. If an editor starts by apparently creating an article about him- or herself or his or her company, assuming this editor is primarily interested in general encyclopedia work is difficult; a tension exists between Assume Good Faith and Conflict of Interest. If an account is *single purpose*—that is, the editor only makes partisan edits in a small topic area—then assuming good faith is harder because promotional and activist editing is unwelcome. Vandalism is a fairly clear demonstration of bad faith and will usually result in short blocks. What Assume Good Faith means, however, is that you should first try to figure out an editor's intentions by engaging in discussion and informing him or her about policies. A single-purpose or disruptive editor might always broaden his or her contributions to the project.

Please Don't Bite the Newcomers is the name of another guideline (shortcut WP:BITE) that focuses on the importance of being welcoming to newcomers. Obviously this guideline is compatible with Assume Good Faith. It encourages you to be gentle with newbies if you see them making mistakes. Encourage newcomers—you want them to keep contributing—and teach them about Wikipedia. We were all new once! A new editor's ignorance of some policy details is not surprising—what would be surprising would be to find someone new who has already mastered them all.

Agree to Disagree

If you disagree with someone's edit or action, but you can see that the edit or action followed from a reasonable position, consider refraining from reverting the edit. Does it matter that much? Different edits might be just as good for the encyclopedia, and not every decision should be treated as a point of principle. This aspect of the site may be one of the harder ones for the newcomer to appreciate. Because no one really directs Wikipedia, you should take a peaceful approach and assume that the community's good sense as a whole will prevail; reasonable people can agree to disagree.

Random Acts of Kindness

Wikipedia has some friendly customs. One of these is welcoming new editors on their talk page. Simply saying, "Hello, good work!" when you notice a helpful edit from a new contributor is encouraging. Many welcomers leave a more involved initial message, with links to help pages and more information about Wikipedia. The `{{welcome}}` template, if left on a talk page, is one example of such a message; editors may also code their own welcome messages, as we did in Chapter 9. A personal greeting is irreplaceable. A welcoming committee works on coordinating messages for new editors, but everyone can help out with this task; see [[Wikipedia:Welcoming committee]] (shortcut WP:WC) for more.

Informal mentoring of new users happens all the time, but a formal mentoring program also exists, known as [[Wikipedia:Adopt-a-User]] (shortcut WP: ADOPT), involving hundreds of Wikipedians. To adopt a new user, you need an edit count of 500; to sign up for adoption, simply follow the directions on that page.

Wikipedians are also in the habit of giving each other awards for work well done. The original and most popular award is the Barnstar (Figure 12-1). The barnstar is a template you can add to any editor's user talk page if you feel he or she deserves the award; Wikipedia has many variations on this award, such as the *Anti-Vandalism Barnstar, The Tireless Contributor Barnstar,* or *The Random Acts of Kindness Barnstar.* See [[Wikipedia:Barnstars]] (shortcut WP:BARN).

The Original Barnstar
In recognition of the incredible work you've done in bringing Wikipedia's lung transplantation article (and countless other articles) to fruition and bringing your knowledge to the wikipedia community I present to you this barnstar. --ImmortalGoddezz 19:28, 1 November 2006 (UTC)

FIGURE 12-1: *The original Wikipedia barnstar*

You can see other awards at [[Wikipedia:A nice cup of tea and a sit down]] (shortcut WP:TEA). In fact [[Wikipedia:Other awards]] runs to wiffle bats, a Zen garden (for Infinite Patience), a medal for Janitorial Services, and the Exceptional Newcomer Award. (Charles has also been given virtual jellybeans and a virtual bicycle as well as a Random Chocolate Chip Smiley—a cross between a cookie and a smiley face.)

Other aspects of recognition and motivation are not quite as well established. *WikiMoney* was a system of incentives operational in 2003–2004, but this system has fallen into disuse. Article writing competitions, such as [[Wikipedia:The Core Contest]], are sometimes held.

The Open Door

People come and go on Wikipedia all the time. As many as 10,000 new accounts are created every day, and over 7 million accounts have been registered. These numbers are a little misleading, however, since most accounts remain unused or are hardly used at all to edit. But this freedom to join up and participate casually helps ensure that Wikipedia is an open community. Now open editing is not quite the same as easy editing, even with a friendly wikitext editing system. Wikipedia itself has become much more complex, as a first encounter might convince you. And yet, beneath all the technical, social, and administrative complications that editors can sometimes run into, the site's radical and open nature is still recognizable.

Compared to other online communities, Wikipedia is unusual. Conventional wisdom holds that online communities tend to grow to a certain natural scale. They wax and wane, with people being closely involved for perhaps six months. They attract a nomadic populace, aside from a few hardcore supporters, and leave memories rather than marks. Wikipedia is an example that contradicts each one of these statements. It has grown much beyond village scale, and many people have been involved for years.

The drive to keep the community as open as possible (*anyone online can edit*) has shaped the whole debate about how Wikipedia should be operated. The 2001 statement [[User:Jimbo Wales/Statement of principles]], now perhaps rarely read, put forth eight points about the community and the project. The first three are:

1. Wikipedia's success to date is entirely a function of our open community.
2. Newcomers are always to be welcomed.
3. "You can edit this page right now" is a core guiding check on everything that we do.

Seven years later, this manifesto has largely been delivered. The autoconfirm restrictions introduced in late 2005 and described in "Registering an Account" on page 302 have been the only big restrictions on accounts.

These principles have many continuing implications. For instance, although many people over the years have suggested restricting editing to registered users, this is still unlikely to happen. (What may happen instead is a version of *stable versions*, where some edited versions will only go live after review; this technical development is still being debated.)

Soft Security

You might not completely believe it, especially if you've had an early encounter with an administrator, but Wikipedia's security system—the measures taken to protect the site—mostly stays in the background. Wikipedia's security is *soft*, meaning security is largely reactionary. Bad contributions cannot be completely excluded from the site, so those cleaning up afterward rely instead on checking contributions and reverting bad changes.

One of the paradoxes of Wikipedia is that this system seems like it could never work. In a completely open system run by volunteers, why aren't more limits required? One answer is that Wikipedia uses the principle of soft security in the broadest way. Security is guided by the community, rather than by restricting community actions ahead of time. Everyone active on the site is responsible for security and quality. You, your watchlist, and your alertness to strange actions and odd defects in articles are part of the security system.

Further Reading

http://en.wikipedia.org/wiki/Wikipedia:Assume_good_faith   The guideline concerning Assume Good Faith

http://en.wikipedia.org/wiki/Wikipedia:Please_do_not_bite_the_ newcomers   The guideline about being nice to newcomers

http://en.wikipedia.org/wiki/Wikipedia:Barnstars   Information about barnstars with links to other award pages

http://en.wikipedia.org/wiki/User:Jimbo_Wales/Statement_of_principles   A statement of community principles

---

Another Take on Soft Security

The idea of soft security on a wiki comes from MeatballWiki (described in Chapter 2). At *http://www.usemod.com/cgi-bin/mb.pl?SoftSecurity*, an essay on the topic says:

> Soft Security is like water. It bends under attack, only to rush in from all directions to fill the gaps. It's strong over time yet adaptable to any shape. It seeks to influence and encourage, not control and enforce. [. . .]

Soft Security follows from the principles of

▶ **Assume Good Faith**   People are almost always trying to be helpful; so, we apply the Principle of First Trust, confident that occasional bad will be overwhelmed by the good.

▶ **Peer Review**   Your peers can ensure that you don't damage the system.

▶ **Forgive and Forget**   Even well-intentioned people make mistakes. They don't need to be permanent.

▶ **Limit Damage**   When unpreventable mistakes are made, keep the damage within tolerable limits.

▶ **Fair Process**   Kim and Mauborgne's theory that being transparent and giving everyone a voice are essential management skills.

▶ **Non-Violence**   Do no violence lest violence seek you.

Communicating with Other Editors

All of these core community principles rely in practice on editors making an effort to communicate with one another. Wikipedia has multiple channels for communication and more forums than any one person can sensibly track. Here we'll guide you through some of the complexities of *where* and *how* you can communicate with other editors to draw attention to a problem, get feedback, ask a question, or even just chat socially.

Wikipedia has several types of pages where editors communicate with one another:

▶ Article talk pages for discussing article content

▶ User talk pages for leaving another contributor personal messages

▶ Project page and policy page talk pages, where individual policies or processes are discussed

336 | Chapter 12

- ▶ Project-wide forums for discussing Wikipedia, asking questions, or offering general proposals

- ▶ Noticeboards for raising alerts to problems or items of interest about a particular topic

- ▶ Process pages for getting feedback or taking polls on a particular kind of issue (such as deletion debates)

Outside of Wikipedia itself, or *off-wiki*, discussions happen on IRC, via email lists, on the Meta site (described in Chapter 17), and during in-person meetups. Many Wikipedians also blog, adding to the hundreds of outside media stories that are published about Wikipedia every year. This is a big, ongoing conversation, and any contributor can join it at any time.

Faced with this full range of possibilities, the best thing is not to be daunted but to reach out steadily. Chat with those you have some contact with on the site. Don't jump from "steady" to "spam": Pasting similar messages to many pages at once is discouraged. Stay generally on-topic, maintain a pleasant and respectful tone, and assume good faith.

Talk Page Guidelines

Talk pages for articles, introduced in Chapters 4 and 6, and user talk pages, introduced in Chapter 11, are the primary way that editors connect with one another. Talk page conventions have been developed over time; in other words, Wikipedia has plenty of experience with discussions, helpful and otherwise. When you are writing on a talk page, certain approaches are counterproductive, whereas others make for good editing and create a friendly atmosphere. Staying on topic is important. While on Wikipedia, you are addressing a sophisticated audience that appreciates focus and relevance. At all times, ask yourself whether your contributions are making the encyclopedia better (*before* you click Save, rather than after). If they're not, it might be time to take a break.

✱ **NOTE:** *Staying with these conventions in all types of discussions and debates, whether on talk pages or other forums, is a good idea. Remember that your Wikipedian persona is something you construct largely through communicating with others.*

Notice the general structure of an article talk page (Figure 12-2). Templates and messages appear right at the top. Also somewhere near the top you'll find a list of any archives. Very long talk pages are archived as subpages of the original page (usually divided by date); ongoing, live discussions should not be archived. Then you'll find a list of discussion topics by section. These sections are not normally divided up into subsections; instead, each discussion within the section is threaded, as shown in "Reading and Contributing to Talk Pages" on page 113. Older topics are higher on the page, and new topics should be started with new sections at the bottom of the talk page. For existing topics, the order of postings within the threaded discussion should be chronological, and you should normally join an existing discussion by adding your comment or reply at the bottom of the section.

| article | discussion | | edit this page | new section | history | move | watch |

Talk:Firefly

From Wikipedia, the free encyclopedia

This article is within the scope of **WikiProject Arthropods**, a collaborative effort to improve and expand Wikipedia's coverage of arthropods. If you would like to participate, visit the project page where you can join the project and/or contribute to discussion.

B — This article has been rated as **B-class** on the quality scale.

Mid — This article has been rated as **Mid-importance** on the importance scale.

Article Grading:
The following comments were left by the quality and importance raters: (edit · refresh)

think this article just makes A class. Has a good amount of info but would be better if it was ordered into more subsections with small rewrites for clarity. Would benefit from a small section on the molecular biology of light production. Otherwise good though. Goldfinger620 22:29, 21 November 2006 (UTC)

Contents [hide]

Regional Note   [edit]

Should there be some mention of lightning bug v. firefly as the common name for these insects, based on regional influences?

Life Span   [edit]

What is the life span of a firefly ranging from? In novels/movies (Chinese/Asian), it has been depicted that Fireflies have really short life spans and would usually die soon after "glowing"

Request for sources...   [edit]

The following facts have been added:

- "Unlike a light bulb, all of a firefly's light is used as light, none as heat. A light bulb is only 50% light and 50% heat."

This is done via a chemical reaction, but it will still generate some heat, I think.

FIGURE 12-2: A talk page

The prime values of talk pages are the three Cs: communicativeness, civility, and considered answers. These principles, after all, are likely what you yourself hope for in discussions. Be wary of the most contentious topics, such as religion and politics, where conversations are likely to be complex. For these topics, review past discussions and get a feel for the tone before joining the discussion. For most articles you can simply start participating.

Now for some detailed advice.

Stick to discussing the article, and save self-expression for your own user page.

Stay on topic, focusing on how to fix the article. Article talk pages are not provided as a place for general discussion about the article's subject, and they shouldn't be used by editors as platforms for their personal views or experiences. Discussion about other articles should note duplications, possible imports or exports of content, or merges with the article in question. Avoid unrelated conversations.

Use the talk pages for discussing facts and sources.

The talk page is the ideal place for raising verification-related issues. If you believe an article is misleading or plain wrong about a claim, go to its talk page and present your case. Ask for help to find some better sources, compare contradictory facts from different sources, and examine critically the reliability of references. Requesting a verifiable reference to support a suspect statement is often better than merely arguing against it ("Can you tell me who else supports that statement?" rather than "I think you're wrong"). And offering a reliable, contradicting reference won't hurt your case either.

Be brief but not abrupt. Be specific about changes you'd like to see.

Amplify your edit summaries with fuller discussions. In some cases you may be editing the talk page but not the article deliberately (for example, if you are personally involved in the topic). You can expect to be heard if you're reasonable; remember being shrill is probably counterproductive, whereas being patient will gain sympathy from other editors. Explain what you see as the problem with an edit or section, and offer suggestions as to how fix it. Help matters along, even if you're in an argument, by offering new drafts.

Talk pages have a warehousing function.

You can post material removed from an article to the talk page. This is commonly done for verification purposes (to ask other editors if they have any references to support a claim, for instance) or to comment in detail on some problems. This technique is less in-your-face and aggressive than simply discarding someone else's work: The implication is not as strong as a permanent cut. You're also acknowledging that the material may be useful if rewritten or incorporated elsewhere. But you can't move copyrighted materials onto a discussion page. If copyright problems have necessitated a heavy pruning of the article, add a talk page note explaining the issue and referencing a source for the apparent violation.

Be civil, and make no personal attacks.

This is absolutely fundamental. Be reasonable and treat other people with respect; after all, you're having a polite and professional conversation with them. Carry yourself as a colleague, not an adversary. Assume good faith by starting with the attitude that others are trying to do the right thing. No insults: Don't make *ad hominem* attacks, such as calling someone an idiot or a fascist. Discussing an editor rather than the article is going down the wrong path. Bear in mind that *level-headed*, *fair-minded*, *constructive*, *consensus-seeking*, and other similar descriptions (from others) are pure gold in terms of developing your Wikipedia reputation; try to epitomize these qualities when discussion becomes heated.

Avoid the absolute no-nos.

Don't threaten people. For example, promising bans for disagreeing with you is not going to help matters. Bringing up the "administrators you know" is not a great topic to raise. Never make legal threats: Threatening a lawsuit is highly disruptive to Wikipedia and almost never has the intended result. (And you'll likely get banned yourself.) Dispute resolution is more effective, so see Chapter 14 for more on the proper channels. Never post personal details or insinuations about others or threaten anyone with anything off the site. Indefinite blocks await those who do these things.

Don't delete comments, and refactor discussion only as a last resort.

Everyone is entitled to their opinion on a discussion page. Do not delete or rewrite comments, including your own. The convention is to leave other people's comments completely alone: Don't even correct the spelling. If you wish to take something back, delete it and insert a quick apology in its place. But if it is too late and removing the offending comment would make other editors' comments look strange, strike out your comment with the <s> and </s> tags. In principle, talk pages can be *refactored*, or summarized, to make discussion clearer. This is relatively rare and requires skill. The better, and definitely easier, course is to add some summaries of your own.

Don't exclude newcomers.

One statement that is frowned on is "We've already decided that point." A newcomer can reasonably reopen any issue about article content. Wikipedia pages are supposed to improve over time. Learn patience. If a point has been discussed previously and then archived, be courteous and point the newcomer to the discussion. If consensus has been reached, take a moment to explain it or gently refer to the archived discussion.

Problem users show themselves over time.

When you first answer a comment, whether reasonable or not, you really don't know whether a teenager or a tenured professor left it. Part of assuming good faith is not judging other editors based on just one or two comments; good manners are never wasted. Avoid accusations: Say "I disagree" rather than "you're obviously biased on this issue."

After a while you may conclude that the editor is a time-waster, someone who knows little about the subject, or an autodidact who has book knowledge but is mightily confused. Or worse: You might be dealing with a true crank, a malicious user (*vandal*), or a provocateur (*troll*)—and he or she may have more time on his or her hands than you do. The basic tips are to keep cool and be polite; don't outwardly assume bad faith, but do become more guarded; taper off your responses, and don't get dragged into escalating futile, repetitive debates.

Don't Feed the Trolls

Some people are simply attention seeking and argumentative, to the point of being disruptive. The saying *Don't feed the trolls* encourages you to ignore this behavior and not be provoked into an unncessary argument. See *http://meta.wikimedia.org/wiki/What_is_a_troll?*.

To round off this discussion: At worst, the three Cs may have to turn into the three *P*s—politeness, patience, and policy. Policy matters especially when dealing with hostility and aggressive, biased editing. Learn the appropriate policies and guidelines in sufficient detail, so you can fend off bad behavior without being drawn in yourself.

Those Tilde Signatures

Unlike article contributions, discussion contributions should be signed. Using four tildes to sign (~~~~) is standard and produces your username and a timestamp. Signing with three tildes produces your username but no timestamp. Five tildes, on the other hand, produce a timestamp but no name.

Voting and Discussing

> Having everybody vote on everything is cluelessocracy. (User:Eclecticology, April 10, 2007, *wiki-en* mailing list)

Wikipedia is not a democracy, though calling it undemocratic would also be rather misleading. Compared to many other online projects, Wikipedia has few majority votes, but instead uses discussions on talk pages and project pages to gather participant consensus. (Though the scale of Wikipedia seems to justify a move to representative democracy rather than direct one-person one-vote polling, this is not happening at all—individual participants are still expected to weigh in.)

The structure at [[Wikipedia:Requests for comment]] (shortcut WP:RfC) is typical. In Wikipedia terms, an RfC is a tightly defined but open forum discussion, addressing an issue in one of three areas: content, editor behavior, or policy. Other editors are invited to contribute to the discussion and offer their opinions on the right solution. In addition to being used on RfCs, polling occurs commonly during deletion debates and administrator promotion discussions.

These polls are not simple votes, however. In almost all discussions on Wikipedia, the reasoning behind each comment is taken into more consideration than the number of people indicating support for a particular position. To add to any discussion, support your comment with public facts. Suppose you participate in a debate on a binary decision: yes/no or keep/delete. Don't simply say, "I like it/hate it," but instead offer a reasoned opinion as to why you feel the way you do. Indicate clearly what site policies and other factors inform your opinion to arrive at your conclusions; if you agree with something already said by another contributor, make that clear.

Here's a full comment, logged in a deletion debate for a highly controversial article, [[Allegations of state terrorism committed by the United States]]. The debate here is whether to keep the article or delete it, and the comment is from someone who thinks the article should be kept:

> **Strong Keep** - what has changed since the six previous Afds? Well, take a good look and you will find that the references are now vastly improved, and the content has been significantly expanded upon and improved since the last afd. The content references what is now a considerable body of academic and human rights literature consisting of either references to descriptions of U.S. state terrorism or in-depth examinations supporting the hypothesis. See the references section which includes contributions from professors from Yale, Princeton, MIT, Columbia and Hong Kong University, among others. If you require more evidence that this is a serious scholarly concern, constituting a significant alternative discourse, albeit not representative of the mainstream, then I would be happy to provide a long long long list of academic references. BernardL (talk) 00:13, 18 December 2007 (UTC)

Not everyone contributes at such length, naturally. But notice how the comment focuses, quite properly, on reliable referencing as a way to support notability and verifiability. The framework the commenter uses is basic content policy, not the topic the article discusses, and the points made are targeted, correctly, toward the existing material available to support such an article.

On-Wiki Forums

The Village Pump ([[Wikipedia:Village pump]], shortcut WP:PUMP) is the primary community discussion place on Wikipedia—water cooler and town meeting rolled into one. The postings are divided up into five sections: Policy, Technical, Proposals, Assistance, and Miscellaneous. Active discussion threads take place here; you'll also find pointers to pages such as [[Wikipedia:Department directory]] (shortcut WP:DEPT), which offers you a view of Wikipedia by Department.

The Community Portal is another entry point into the social life of Wikipedia. Found at [[Wikipedia:Community Portal]], it offers a Community Bulletin Board for announcements. This offers a different way to interface with Wikipedia activity; for example, it links directly to [[Template:RFCsci list]], an updated list of discussions on science articles that asks for community input (in other words, yours). This is a place to post new proposals, requests for help with a topic, and new project announcements.

Further discussion is widely distributed, attached to project talk pages in the Wikipedia Talk namespace and on talk pages (for instance, those for particular templates or categories). Forums about aspects of site management that are not dedicated to particular processes are, by custom, called *noticeboards*; the best known is the Administrators' noticeboard at [[Wikipedia:Administrators' noticeboard]] (shortcut WP:AN). You can post notices there about problems that administrators can help out with.

Asking Questions and Resolving Problems

How do you get help? Here are a few pointers on where to ask questions or raise concerns.

First, go to the Help desk ([[Wikipedia:Help desk]], shortcut WP:HD), the perfect place to ask questions about using Wikipedia. The Help desk deals with a few dozen queries daily—anyone who is knowledgeable about the site can help out. You will need to check back to see if your question has been answered.

You might also find Wikipedia's Frequently Asked Questions page helpful; see [[Wikipedia:FAQ]] (shortcut WP:FAQ). You'll also find other helpful links there, for example, a link to a basic tutorial.

Wikipedia also has a Reference desk ([[Wikipedia:Reference desk]], shortcut WP:RD). This, as the name indicates, functions like a library reference desk. Here you can pose factual questions about any topic, and Wikipedians will try to respond. The service is broken down by broad subject area; for example, the Humanities desk answers about ten questions a day. Again, anyone can help out, and if you are knowledgeable about a topic, feel free to answer a question.

Finally, Wikipedia has a central page, [[Wikipedia:Questions]] (shortcut WP:Q), that links to these pages and a number of others dedicated to fielding questions. For example, from here you can link to [[Help:Contents]], which is the central portal for help pages and documentation.

＊ **NOTE:** *You can read about some of the unusual requests that have been made over the years at [[Wikipedia:Unusual requests]].*

If you have a problem, rather than a question, consider starting at [[Wikipedia:Problems FAQ]]. Is your problem with reading or editing Wikipedia pages? [[Wikipedia:Troubleshooting]] may help. These pages deal with technical issues.

For problems in specific areas, Wikipedia has some specialized places where you can seek help. If your copyright has been infringed by something posted to

Wikipedia, [[Wikipedia:Contact us/Article problem/Copyright]] lists your options. To make a formal complaint, go to [[Wikipedia:Designated agent]]. If you consider that a biography or other article on Wikipedia defames you, go to [[Wikipedia: Biographies of living persons/Noticeboard]], where you can leave a comment for editors who will work to resolve the problem, and/or [[Wikipedia:Libel]], which has an email contact address.

For other content-related problems, join the discussion on the article's talk page, and contribute to the debate in a reasonable, non-adversarial tone. You have a perfect right to be there, but remember others will also have their own views.

Problems with another editor? Leave a civil note on his or her user talk page. In cases where the problem escalates, you can try the Administrators' noticeboard and chose the link that best fits the problem, like vandalism or page protection requests.

If you've been blocked, in particular, you should note that Wikipedia will think of the situation in terms of a *block review*, also called *appealing a block*, rather than being a problem about Wikipedia itself. Go to *http://lists.wikimedia .org/mailman/listinfo/unblock-en-l* for unblock discussions if you feel that you've been incorrectly or unreasonably blocked by an administrator. You'll find more details on what to do (and what *not* to do, more importantly) in Chapter 14.

For more complex issues, or if you're uncertain whether what you've encountered is okay, you can post a comment on [[Wikipedia:Village pump (assistance)]] (shortcut WP:VPA), which is a general forum in which to ask for help. You can also use a mailing list or IRC channel, as described in "Mailing Lists and Internet Relay Chat" on page 346. Try to find a list or channel that matches the issue.

Further Reading

Communicating with Others

http://en.wikipedia.org/wiki/Wikipedia:Talk_page_guidelines   Guidelines on using talk pages effectively

Getting Help

http://en.wikipedia.org/wiki/Wikipedia:Help_desk   A page where you can ask questions about Wikipedia

http://en.wikipedia.org/wiki/Wikipedia:Reference_desk   A page where you can ask questions about any subject

http://en.wikipedia.org/wiki/Wikipedia:Questions   A page where you can ask questions or make comments

---

Getting News

You may want to find out what is currently happening on Wikipedia. [[Category:
Wikipedia news]] is your first source for Wikipedia pages with news content. For
example [[Wikipedia:Announcements]] (shortcut WP:ANN) deals with milestones
and Foundation matters.

Wikipedia has a few projects that bring a broader spectrum of news to the
community. One of the established news services on the English-language Wikipedia is the *Wikipedia Signpost* (Figure 12-3). The *Signpost* is a weekly newsletter
produced on-site at [[Wikipedia:Signpost]] (shortcut WP:POST).

Since 2005, the *Signpost* has carried stories of interest to the Wikipedia
community. You can view all of the archives; this is a quick way to catch up on Wikipedia history. Each newsletter contains a few recurring sections, such as a review
of that week's technical developments and a quick summary of current arbitration
cases. The newsletter was started by User:Michael Snow and is now edited by
User:Ral315, with contributions from a wide variety of editors. Anyone can participate by editing at WP:POST/TIPS, where you can also learn how to document
media coverage of Wikipedia.

WikiProject WikipediaWeekly (shortcut WP:WEEKLY), active since late 2006,
concentrates on producing a podcast about Wikipedia. As is also the case for the
Signpost, you can have WikipediaWeekly delivered to your user page or user talk
page. If you like RSS feeds, the Weekly has one. An alternative is the aptly named
NotTheWikipediaWeekly ([[Wikipedia:NotTheWikipediaWeekly]]), which also produces a podcast show about Wikipedia.

Another such project is *Wikizine*, started in 2006 and edited by user:Walter
from the Dutch and English-language Wikipedias. This newsletter is delivered by
email to subscribers. It covers news about international projects and community,
with a focus on technical issues and Foundation-level discussion. Sign up or read
the current issue at *http://en.wikizine.org/*.

FIGURE 12-3: *The* Wikipedia Signpost, *a weekly on-site newsletter*

Mailing Lists and Internet Relay Chat

A wide variety of mailing lists are used to discuss Wikipedia projects. The *wiki-en* list, which is for general discussion about the English-language Wikipedia, is a very high-traffic list; if you have a specific query, a more specialized forum on-wiki is probably more appropriate. See [[Wikipedia:Mailing lists]] (shortcut WP:MAIL) for more complete information; the lists are generally archived in several places. Lists are typically lightly moderated and publicly archived, so anything you say on them will be accessible through an Internet search.

Wikipedia also uses a number of IRC channels. *Internet Relay Chat*, or *IRC*, is a type of real-time Internet chat, designed for group communication but also allowing for one-on-one chats or private messaging. To access IRC, you need an IRC client. These programs are available for virtually every PC platform. The Chatzilla client for the Mozilla Firefox browser, which runs as a browser extension and does not require additional software, is easy to use and install.[1]

---

[1] If you already have Firefox, you can download and install Chatzilla at *https://addons.mozilla.org/en-US/firefox/addon/16.*

See [[Wikipedia:IRC channels]] (shortcut WP:IRC) for more technical information, a complete list of Wikipedia-related channels, and a link to those classified under Wikimedia. The Wikimedia projects use the Freenode network, which is a network specifically for open-source projects.

The channels most relevant to the English-language Wikipedia include:

▸ *#wikipedia*, the general Wikipedia discussion channel, is notoriously nearly always off-topic. This is a decent place to socialize but not for the faint of heart.

▸ *#wikipedia-en* has fewer people and is more focused on the English-language Wikipedia.

▸ *#wikipedia-en-help* is a help channel.

▸ *#wikimedia* discusses issues related to the Wikimedia Foundation as a whole.

Meetups and Conferences

All it takes to have an offline meetup is to announce it on the wiki and then get a group of local editors together for coffee, drinks, or a meal. The first meetup was in London in 2004 when Jimmy Wales and an international group of editors got together for the afternoon. Remarkably, apart from Larry Sanger, Wales had not met any editors who worked on the site in person during the first three-and-a-half years of its existence. A true child of the Internet era, Wikipedia had been put together almost entirely by people who only knew each other through mailing lists, wiki talk pages, and IRC.

Since 2004, however, hundreds of meetups in dozens of cities from Shanghai to Seattle have taken place. They are usually informal but have ranged in format from picnics in New York's Central Park to formal talks. Meetups are a great way to meet other dedicated wiki editors in a personable forum.

The Meetups page (shortcut WP:MEET) lists current and past meetups; if one doesn't already exist in your area, you can create a subpage for your city from the Meetups page and then recruit others in your area by leaving notes on their user talk pages. Browsing [[Category:Wikipedians by location]] and its subcategories will help you find people who self-identify as being in a particular area. Jimmy Wales has continued to travel to meet Wikipedians; a documentary film, *Truth In Numbers: The Wikipedia Story*, will be released in 2009 and includes footage of his travels.

The first annual Wikimedia Foundation conference, called Wikimania, was organized by volunteers from several Wikimedia projects and held in 2005 in Frankfurt, Germany. This was a major international event, attracting over 300 people from over 50 countries, with a great deal of press coverage. Frankfurt set a trend, featuring research papers about wikis and Wikimedia projects, reports from various communities about the success of the different sister projects, and proposals and community discussions about future work.

Wikimania is now established as an annual event (Figure 12-4 shows the conference logo). Wikimania 2006 was held on the Harvard Law School campus, in Cambridge, Massachusetts, in the United States. In 2007, the conference was in Taipei, Taiwan, where the local community hosted the conference at a youth center; both conferences again attracted hundreds of people from all around the world.

These conferences (2008 in Alexandria, Egypt, at the New Library of Alexandria and 2009 in Buenos Aires), like most things Wikimedia, are organized by a team of volunteers from all around the world. Local communities bid for the opportunity to host the conference, submitting a proposal including location and possible sponsorship to a Foundation-based judging team. Most of the organization work takes place online, on IRC and special wiki pages on the Meta site, and combines efforts of the Wikimedia Foundation and local volunteers who lead the planning process.

FIGURE 12-4: *The Wikimania logo (designed by Ben Yates)*

Further Reading

Getting News

http://en.wikipedia.org/wiki/Wikipedia:Wikipedia_Signpost   The *Wikipedia Signpost* weekly community newspaper

http://en.wikipedia.org/wiki/Wikipedia:WikipediaWeekly   The Wikipedia Weekly podcast

http://www.wikizine.org/   The *Wikizine* newsletter (in English, Spanish, and German)

Mailing Lists and IRC

http://meta.wikimedia.org/wiki/Mailing_lists   Information about mailing lists and links to their archives

http://meta.wikimedia.org/wiki/IRC   Information about Wikimedia's IRC channels

http://www.nabble.com/Wikipedia-f14018.html   Email archives of lists at Nabble (provides a forum-like view that is easier to read for high-traffic lists)

Meetups

http://en.wikipedia.org/wiki/Wikipedia:Meetup   The page for coordinating meetups, including a list of past meetups along with pictures

http://wikimania.org/   Information about the annual Wikimania conference (will redirect to the current year's website)

http://meta.wikimedia.org/wiki/Wikimania   The Meta page where conference planning is coordinated

Wikiphilosophies

Search for *wikiphilosophy* and you'll get a couple hundred hits from individual users who have written about their personal Wikipedia approaches. Topics include how to work collaboratively on a wiki, how to work productively on Wikipedia, and why you should contribute. Some of these philosophies, like Assume Good Faith, have grown to become guidelines and core parts of the culture; others, like inclusionism versus deletionism, have become long-standing philosophical debates.

The most contentious issues on Wikipedia, in the longer term, have turned out to relate to content policy. This is fortunate because debating the principles of encyclopedic content relates directly to the site's mission. We have already seen two major aspects of this debate: Academic authority and the status of mainstream science was covered in Chapter 2, and conflict of interest in the deletion debate around [[Mzoli's Meats]] was discussed in Chapter 10. Although the core content policies have not been expanded by new major principles, avid discussion continues about how to apply those principles to individual articles, with debates that sometimes get picked up by the media.[2]

The debate on what articles should be included has proved to be one of the most basic and long-standing debates. *Inclusionism* is the philosophy that as much of the material submitted to the site should be kept as possible. The basic inclusionist position is this: *Wikipedia is not paper*, which implies that Wikipedia can afford to keep articles, even if, in their current state, they need to be improved or verified, so editors should strive to help the site grow as large as possible. The opposition to the inclusionists are labeled the *deletionists*, and they feel that an article should be in reasonable shape and about a clearly notable topic before being included; questionable material should be deleted more rigorously. Both sides agree, of course, that some new articles and content will need to be deleted; the question is over which articles and under what circumstances. As Chapter 7 showed, some deletion debates prove controversial, especially for new terms or ideas.

Closely related is a methodological question—*eventualism* versus *immediatism*. *Eventualism*, the idea that things will eventually improve if you leave them around long enough, seems most to encapsulate the wiki spirit, where things are done as people get around to doing them. Many have argued that this approach needs to be modified for certain topics, however, such as for biographies of living people, where any needed action should be regarded as urgent and carried out immediately as an ethical matter.

The debate between inclusionism and deletionism and eventualism and immediatism has flared up many times over the years in various forms. The debate has implications not only for what Wikipedia contains but also for how that content is created and worked on. Initially, the debate presented itself as the way in which Wikipedia differentiated itself from the older wiki tradition. Whereas wikis in general simply gathered opinions, Wikipedia aimed to build a factual reference

---

[2] For instance, novelist Nicholson Baker has come out as an inclusionist, interested in trying to save from deletion an article about an individual notable for his face turning blue from drinking colloidal silver. See "How I Fell in Love with Wikipedia," in *The Guardian*, April 10, 2008, *http://www.guardian.co.uk/technology/2008/apr/10/wikipedia.internet.*

resource, using notions of what was and wasn't encyclopedic. The concept of Verifiability became increasingly important, first as a criterion and then as a policy, and the community now accepts that unverifiable material may be deleted.

Attention then shifted for some years to the implications of Verifiability, such as the debate over the guideline on Reliable sources. Over time, the middle way of eventualism has won this debate, at least in practice—articles always need to be cleaned up, and deleting material that really cannot be verified is simply one aspect of the push for quality.

In 2007, attention turned back to deletionism because the net growth of articles seemed to have peaked (though outsiders were increasingly using Wikipedia for promotional ends by writing about themselves and their ventures). Although deletionism favors clear and relatively rigorous standards for accepting new articles, which are increasingly being adopted, inclusionism and the view that new articles should be given a chance have also continued to be major forces. Regardless, the inclusionist view that all processes are supposed to operate case by case rather than determining whether broad topic areas should be included continues to prevail, though this view is subject to great debate, especially in areas of popular culture.

Endless variants and positions have claimed the middle ground. See [[Category:Wikipedians by Wikipedia philosophy]] with around 30 such classes. Wikipedia has some significant hybrid positions, too. For instance, the eventualist-deletionist position is that deleting articles that really don't improve over time is not a great loss, and if a startup company or new idea prospers, an article on it will be accepted in due course. The immediatist-inclusionist position is that Wikipedia's coverage suffers if an article on a new topic is deleted when it didn't have to be.[3] As Wikipedia now tries to be both a reference site and a go-to place for current new information, the debate will continue.

Funny Business

Silliness, bad jokes, and shared humor have a place in Wikipedia culture. You'll find (allegedly) humorous material on many project pages, and some of these memes spill over into supposedly serious debates.

[[Category:Wikipedia humor]] (shortcut WP:HUMOR) is a collection of some of these funny ha-ha pages. The template {{humor}} is also used on funny project pages, so you can use the backlink trick of seeing what links to [[Template:Humor]] to find more pages, dating from all eras of Wikipedia's history. Many humorous project pages poke fun at Wikipedians going overboard. For instance, the collection of "Lamest edit wars" (shortcut WP:LAME) commemorates the epic battles that have occurred over what are often tiny details. Though humorous, this page also serves as an excellent introduction to Wikipedia history, cultural references, and the kinds of details that may provoke controversies.

---

[3] This was argued convincingly by Andrew Lih, a journalist and Wikipedian, who focused on the case of Pownce, an Internet startup whose article was deleted. See "Wikipedia: an Online Encyclopedia Torn Apart," in the *Daily Telegraph*, October 11, 2007, *http://www.telegraph.co.uk/connected/main.jhtml?xml=/connected/2007/10/11/dlwiki11.xml*, which overstates Lih's position; see *http://www.andrewlih.com/blog/2007/10/10/telegraph-uk-on-wikipedia-inclusionismdeletionism/* for Lih's further comments.

Two of the classic funny memes are BJAODN, meaning "Bad Jokes & Other Deleted Nonsense," a collection of humorous vandalism that was finally deleted with much controversy in 2007 (and is now memorialized at WP:SILLY), and TINC. TINC stands for *There Is No Cabal*—a long-running joke carried over from UseNet culture. The joke really is on those who believe a secretive, small, dedicated group controls Wikipedia.

Wikipedia is a diverse enough place that if a joke relies on a shared cultural reference or technical specialty, the witticism may fall flat. Most slang phrases and Internet dialects will confuse *somebody*. Many contributors are not native English speakers, and certainly, even among those who are, not everyone shares a similar background.

Irony, sarcasm, and deadpan humor are especially difficult to convey online and can cause offense. Although adding a smiley face can help people see that you're joking, you may want to consider how funny the joke really is if you have to flag humor with emoticons to get it across. By the same token, though, if you're confused by something that seems preposterous, ask yourself whether the other person is making a joke before getting indignant. The point of using humor is always to make working together more fun. The [[Wikipedia:Department of fun]] is a long-running Wikiproject to help do just that.

Other fun poked at Wikipedia from outside sources, including Stephen Colbert's not unfriendly joshing, can be tracked at [[Wikipedia in culture]], which also includes additional pop culture references to Wikipedia.

Although avowedly humorous material should only be found in the project namespaces, some articles are funny and factual: [[Tarquin Fin-tim-lin-bin-whin-bim-lim-bus-stop-F'tang-F'tang-Olé-Biscuitbarrel]], for example, was the assumed name of a political candidate in a United Kingdom district election in 1981; he was registered with the [[Official Monster Raving Loony Party]]. Wikipedia has a collection of some of these more oddball (nay, eccentric) articles at [[Wikipedia:Unusual articles]] (shortcut WP:ODD).

Further Reading

Wikiphilosophies

http://meta.wikimedia.org/wiki/Deletionism   An explanation of deletionism

http://meta.wikimedia.org/wiki/Inclusionism   An explanation of inclusionism

**http://meta.wikimedia.org/wiki/Conflicting_Wikipedia_
    philosophies**   Information on more wiki philosophies

Humor

http://en.wikipedia.org/wiki/Wikipedia:Silly_things   A collection of silly vandalism (previously called Bad Jokes and Other Deleted Nonsense)

http://en.wikipedia.org/wiki/Category:Wikipedia_humor   A collection of humorous or parody project pages

http://uncyclopedia.org/   The Uncyclopedia site

The classic odd Wikipedia article is [[Exploding whale]]. Also check out [[Undecimber]], the thirteenth month of the year; [[ETAOIN SHRDLU]]; [[colors of noise]]; and many others. A few such articles are selected every year to appear on the main page for April Fool's Day. This is a carefully weighted joke, at the expense of those who assume Wikipedia would deliberately hoax them.

Who Writes This Thing Anyway?

Who writes Wikipedia? Who are the members of the Wikipedia community? No one knows the exact answer to this question, and Wikipedia has no single point of reference for its social side.

One simple but of course inadequate approach is to ask how much work is actually connected with the English-language Wikipedia. Well, the amount of work is equivalent to 1,000 full-time people. Or it's probably more like 5,000 people working one day a week and even more like those 5,000 people devoting 8 hours a week of spare time. Wikipedia has a division of labor, because people gravitate to work they enjoy, but little hierarchy.

Believing that Wikipedia has one community is a mistake, and referring to "the community" is somewhat confusing. Who is the community? After all, the work on the project includes developing software, writing articles, and tending to the practicalities of managing a publicly editable website. Is the community those few people who actively contribute to the general mailing list or hang out on IRC? The people who care about and watch policy pages or post their thoughts at the Village Pump? Are you thinking of the contributors you encounter at a particular WikiProject? Those people who enjoy going to meetups and conferences and meeting other Wikipedians? Or the handful of people who talk to the press and give presentations? Is it those people who spend hours daily contributing and fighting vandalism, or the majority of people who are silent and occasional contributors? What about those involved with governance on the Foundation level, who may help run the sites as a whole but no longer edit articles?

The answer, of course, is that these people are all part of the Wikipedia community. The degree of social complexity, coupled with the site's large scale, probably undermines all assumptions based on previous discussions of online groups.

Demographics

> Wikipedia—also known as Unemployed Ph.D. Deathmatch (User:Finlay McWalter)

Wikipedia's editors are any recruits who can show that they have the talent to write and upgrade encyclopedia articles. Nothing else counts for much. Contributor anonymity is acceptable, in large part because who you are or what prior background you have is not supposed to have any effect on your contributions being accepted, as long as you respect the content policies. Whether you're a teenager or a tenured Ph.D. doesn't matter: On Wikipedia, no one needs to know you're a Doc.

Godwin's Nine Points

1. Use software that promotes good discussions.
2. Don't impose a length limitation on postings.
3. Front-load your system with talkative, diverse people.
4. Let the users resolve their own disputes.
5. Provide institutional memory.
6. Promote continuity.
7. Be host to a particular interest group.
8. Provide places for children.
9. Most Important: Confront the users with a crisis.

These nine points on promoting a successful online community were published in June 1994 in *Wired* magazine, by Mike Godwin. Godwin is a celebrated name on the Internet, for [[Godwin's law]] and other much more substantial achievements with the Electronic Frontier Foundation. In 2007, he became legal counsel to the Wikimedia Foundation.

Seeing where Wikipedia actually fails any of these points is difficult. On point 7, Wikipedia has played host to thousands of people who are intensely interested in a subject. Young contributors are welcome in Wikipedia: They are, for example, enfranchised in elections because voting doesn't have an age requirement. No one can be sure of the median age of Wikipedians, but for Wikipedia's readers, it probably corresponds to the age of the average college student.

Point 9 about a crisis may raise a wry smile from those who read the mailing lists. When has Wikipedia not had a crisis? When have discussion threads not spoken about imminent disaster? In a sense, the morphing of Nupedia into Wikipedia, with the destruction of mechanisms for approving content, was a founding crisis with constant repercussions.

Because no personal data is collected during the registration process, assumptions and information about contributor demographics are largely anecdotal. Although many editors chose to reveal parts of their identity publicly, either on their user page or in another forum (such as what they do for a living or their real name), many others do not. Meetups provide some information, but this is a self-selected group. The German-language Wikipedia, which is distinctly more academic in tone, has given some survey results suggesting a median age in the late 20s for editors.

One thing that is clear from the English-language Wikipedia is that native English speakers do not necessarily predominate. Wikipedia has many editors for whom English is a second language, and they have historically played a large part in building the site. Some edit Wikipedias in two or more languages. See Chapter 15 for more.

Systemic Bias

If you think of Wikipedia purely as an encyclopedia, its coverage of current affairs and popular culture might seem disproportionate. For instance, around half the biographies are about living people: Much effort is devoted to upgrading those 200,000 articles because real lives can be affected by the content available on Wikipedia. But what about the antiquarian, the obscure but scholarly, and topics not so well known in the English-speaking world?

Systemic bias is a term used on Wikipedia to describe the concept that notions of notability and breadth of article coverage both reflect the community of editors and their demographic. And indeed, Wikipedia's coverage is skewed toward subjects relating to Anglophone countries. For example, articles about people and places in the developing world are often missing or incomplete compared to articles about North American and European geography and personalities. Topics related to women (such as biographies of famous women or articles about feminism) are underrepresented, along with articles about blue-collar trades. This is a known problem but not one easy to address with policy. (The term *systemic bias* is not to be confused with *systematic bias*, which is one kind of violation of Neutral Point of View, where a given article or group of articles is one-sided.)

The articles that prosper on Wikipedia, generally speaking, are those that when created can immediately be linked to from existing articles and that attract editors (other than the initial author) who are active in the same general area. These positive factors can also be read the other way: If an area is somewhat neglected in Wikipedia, a new article's life cycle (Chapter 10) is initiated in a less favorable environment.

These issues are more easily understood than remedied. Volunteer editors will choose the areas they want to work on, and Wikipedia can't legislate its way into being more representative. The community must also work through the *founder effect*, a concept from evolution that the system will, for some time, remember or be influenced by characteristics of the founding group, rather than the larger population. See [[Wikipedia:WikiProject Countering systemic bias]] (shortcut WP:BIAS) for a dedicated forum on this topic.

Dress Sense

WikiProject Fashion was started in March 2007 to address a known weakness. Alexandra Shulman, editor of the British edition of *Vogue*, had awarded the [[Haute couture]] article a lowly 0 marks out of 10 in an October 24, 2005, survey in London's *The Guardian*.*

....
* *See "Can You Trust Wikipedia?"* The Guardian. *Monday, October 24, 2005,* http://www.guardian.co.uk/technology/2005/oct/24/comment.newmedia.

Women and Wikimedia

Are more men than women involved in Wikipedia? Evidence from in-person meetups, mailing lists, and other community forums does suggest that more Wikipedia contributors are men than women, though knowing for sure is impossible. This bias is not unusual on the Internet and in computing generally, but it is definitely not ideal for a project that aims to be welcoming to everyone.

Though discrimination based on personal characteristics (including gender) is certainly against Wikipedia's principles, some feel the site's culture is overly aggressive, a criticism that does depend on where you look for evidence. Does Wikipedia do enough to control misogynistic editors who take gender into account in debates and potentially in more harmful ways such as by harassing female editors? Others feel that given Wikipedia's practices and essential values regarding inclusiveness, no particular issue with gender exists on the projects. The topic remains controversial, and no one editor's experience is likely to be exactly the same as another's, always a difficulty in defining systemic problems.

This debate around the treatment of women on Wikipedia (and how to improve it) led to the creation of the WikiChix project in 2007 (*http://wikichix .org/*). *WikiChix*, which is modeled after the similar LinuxChix group, offers a female-only environment to discuss wikis and the Wikimedia projects and explore ways to make the projects more accessible and friendly toward women. On a Foundation level, several women have won elections to the Board of Directors of the Wikimedia Foundation. These include (as of early 2008) the current chair of the organization, Florence Devouard.

All is not gloom, though, since Wikipedia does gradually overcome some of these limitations. Individual WikiProjects are created for weaker areas that need work (such as [[Wikipedia:WikiProject Gender Studies]]), and Wikipedia attracts some academic experts and others who do steady work filling in gaps in coverage. Working on a neglected area can be rewarding as well, as there is more opportunity to create new articles.

Wikipedians on Wikipedia

Wikipedians love to write about Wikipedia. This is revealed in the large number of essays about the site, posted both on user talk pages and project pages. Happy, sad, critical, and usually interesting, these essays are a mosaic of opinions about the site, its people, and its governance. An essay may aim to influence site policies or the way people behave or may simply be self-expression, one small addition to the site's culture. Many end up being cited by other editors in discussions, and some even end up as guideline or policy.

Here is a selection of extracts from a small handful of our favorite essays. Some of them connect to points that are made elsewhere in this book, whereas others concern thought-provoking aspects of Wikipedia that we don't follow up.

A high proportion of Wikipedians are people with issues with authority. That's why many people are attracted to Wikipedia in the first place. Keep this in mind if you become an administrator, for you may have just become, unwittingly, what these people most resent; and no matter how good a job you do, they'll find your one mistake and beat you up with it. It's best just to accept this demographic for the reality it is. They are often the best editors, and as long as Wikipedia remains open to all, this situation will remain. (From [[User: Antandrus/observations on Wikipedia behavior]], shortcut WP:OWB)

Wikipedia is space age Corningware, not ceramic, and it's not going to shatter if you drop it. Don't let your fear of messing things up keep you from editing. (From [[Wikipedia:Can't break it]])

Wikipedia, in many senses, can be a byzantine mess of policies, guidelines, style conventions, formatting tricks, and essays. It is essentially impossible for a new editor to know or anticipate most of them and even experienced editors accidentally run afoul of policies and guidelines occasionally. When this happens, it's not necessarily an indication that the editor is acting badly or has lost the community's trust. Usually, it just means they made a minor mistake and someone else corrected it. That's the way wikis like Wikipedia work: mistakes are constantly found and corrected. What is important to the functioning of any wiki, and especially large, complex ones like the English Wikipedia, is not that people become paranoid about avoiding mistakes. Mistakes are inevitable. What is important is that editors learn from errors, read the relevant policy, guideline, or whatever, and try to follow it in the future. Mistakes will happen; don't let them get you down. (From [[User:Chaser/Make mistakes, then learn from them]], shortcut WP:BOOBOOS)

If a debate, discussion, or general exchange of views has come to a natural end through one party having "won" or (more likely) the community having lost interest in the entire thing, then no matter which side you were on, you should walk away. (From [[Wikipedia:Drop the stick and back slowly away from the horse carcass]], shortcut WP:DEADHORSE)

Writing for the enemy is the process of explaining another person's point of view as clearly and fairly as you can, similar to devil's advocate. The intent is to satisfy the adherents and advocates of that perspective that you understand their claims and arguments. (From [[Wikipedia:Writing for the enemy]], shortcut WP:WFTE)

The fight-or-flight response developed by our pre-human ancestors may have helped them escape from angry mastodons, but it isn't constructive in an online encyclopedia. (From [[Wikipedia:No angry mastodons]], shortcut WP:KEEPCOOL)

A coatrack article is a Wikipedia article that ostensibly discusses the nominal subject, but in reality is a cover for a tangentially related bias subject. The nominal subject is used as an empty coatrack, which ends up being mostly obscured by the "coats." (From [[Wikipedia:Coatrack]], shortcut WP:COAT)

Wikipedia's articles are no place for strong views. Or rather, we feel about strong views the way that a natural history museum feels about tigers. We admire them and want our visitors to see how fierce and clever they are, so we stuff them and mount them for close inspection. We put up all sorts of carefully worded signs to get people to appreciate them as much as we do. But however much we adore tigers, a live tiger loose in the museum is seen as an urgent problem. (From [[Wikipedia:Beware of the tigers]], shortcut WP:TIGER)

A young novice asked, "Is Wikipedia a community, or an encyclopedia?" Alkivar answered "Yes."; later, another novice asked Alkivar the same question, to which he answered "No." (From [[Wikipedia:The Zen of Wikipedia]], shortcut WP:KOAN)

Wikipedia is just an encyclopedia. The Wikipedia community is at its core just a community made up of a bunch of people who think writing a free, complete, and accurate encyclopedia is a good idea (and a lot of fun, too). The Wikipedia community isn't too happy about people trying to use Wikipedia to promote causes other than having a good online encyclopedia. This includes contributions meant to promote websites and products, political causes, religions, and other beliefs, and of course one's personal view of what's really funny. (From [[Wikipedia:Don't hand out panda sandwiches at a PETA convention]], shortcut WP:PANDA)

It is particularly important to get the last word where you are in some doubts as to the merits of your case. The last word will serve as a clinching argument that will make up for any deficiencies in your logic. (From [[Wikipedia:The Last Word]], shortcut WP:TLW)

Before you make yourself and others unhappy, remember this: you have the Right To Leave. (From [[Wikipedia:Right to leave]], shortcut WP:RTL)

You can find many other such essays collected in [[Category:Wikipedia essays]]. Many Wikipedians also blog about Wikipedia and related Wikimedia issues. You can find a list of self-identified bloggers on Meta, but for easier and more focused reading, you can find a collection of blogs about Wikimedia topics at the Planet Wikimedia site, where they are conveniently aggregated; see *http:// en.planet.wikimedia.org/*. An RSS feed is also available.

Operational Analysis: Raul's Laws

One essay in particular, known as "Raul's laws" (shortcut WP:RAUL), contains a collection of observations on how Wikipedia works and how Wikipedians work together. The essay was started by User:Raul654, an experienced contributor, but has been built by dozens of contributors. The page gives what is very much an insider's view of how Wikipedia works, though the later laws that have been added vary greatly in interest.

We've taken 6 "laws" from the original 15. Two bits of jargon are [[Astro-turfing]], a public relations term for an orchestrated campaign meant to look like spontaneous grassroots activity and [[Metcalfe's law]], which points to the square of the number of users in a network as a measure of its value.

▶ Much of Wikipedia's content and all of the day-to-day functions are overseen by a small core of the most dedicated contributors.

▶ Content brings visitors—this is as true for wikis as it is for networks, as dictated by Metcalfe's law. Of those visitors, a certain number will stay and become contributors. Of those contributors, a certain number will stay long enough to become dedicated users.

▶ You cannot motivate people on a large scale to write about something they don't want to write about.

▶ Over time, contentious articles will grow from edit-war inspiring to eventually reach a compromise that is agreed upon by all the editors who have not departed in exasperation. This equilibrium will inevitably be disturbed by new users who accuse the article of being absurdly one sided and who attempt to rewrite the entire article.

▶ Wikipedia's steadily increasing popularity means that within the next year or two, we will begin to see organized corporate astroturfing campaigns.[4]

▶ As time goes on, the rules and informal policies on Wikipedia tend to become less and less plastic and harder and harder to change.

Practical Values, Process, and Policy

Wikipedia has no centralized control, yet the site progresses and is successful. The administration of Wikipedia as a whole has scaled up much better than its critics predicted. Something clearly does work. But what is it that works?

Discussion alone may not achieve much. If no meeting of minds occurs, a productive debate can become an unresolvable dispute. A common theme in interviews with editors turns out to be this: Wikipedians clearly feel they share values with others who are editing.

---

[4] Prediction confirmed, August 28, 2005 (nine months after the prediction was made): One anonymous reader contacted Boing Boing to say that he worked at a marketing company that uses Wikipedia for its online marketing strategies. See *http://www.smh.com.au/news/icon/wikipedia-worries/2005/08/23/1124562860192.html*.

These values include the following:

▶ The worth of open information that is outside copyright barriers (and, therefore, probably support for free software too)

▶ A commitment to sharing knowledge worldwide

▶ Multiculturalism, diversity, and multilingualism

▶ Fairness in representing diverse points of view

Wikis attract people who can live with freeform structures. But shared and practical values mean that Wikipedians will admit that some structure is necessary and some idea of how the encyclopedia should be built has to be present. Wikipedia's structures, such as how editing permissions are provided, must match up with these core values.

The key way Wikipedia gets through its project-related work is its characteristic structure: Processes consist of decentralized discussions about separable issues. That's how decisions are actually made and how site administration moves forward. Backlogs are avoided by limiting discussion time. These processes are, in turn, governed by policy documents that have general consent. (Chapter 13 picks up from here and will explain how you can have wiki-style *editable* policy.)

Policy and process, then, are closely related on Wikipedia, providing a structure for editors to work together through discussion. So much needs to be done that the sensible approach that has evolved is to have all those differentiated processes, not a single executive body. Processes and policies, despite their imperfections, evolve to meet changing circumstances. See an overview essay [[Wikipedia:Product, process, policy]] (shortcut WP:3P) for more on this idea.

More Research Required

At this point, we still simply don't know some things.

▶ Will the English-language Wikipedia have to evolve different social processes in the long term?

▶ Will every language version of Wikipedia go through the same stages of developing content and community?

▶ Will time bring the English-language Wikipedia's community into a stable demographic composed of people with a broad-based interest in encyclopedic knowledge? How can more people, including experts, be involved in editing?

▶ Can quality be sustained in an open encyclopedia with millions of articles?

See [[Wikipedia:Researching Wikipedia]] (shortcut WP:RW) for some ideas for studies. [[Wikipedia:Wikipedia in academic studies]] showcases some work that has already been done.

Further Reading

Community

http://en.wikipedia.org/wiki/User:Raul654/Raul's laws Raul's laws, a collaboratively written collection of thoughts about the community

http://www.wired.com/wired/archive/2.06/vc.principles_pr.html Mike Godwin's nine points

Demographics and Systemic Bias

http://en.wikipedia.org/wiki/Wikipedia:Wikipedians Who are Wikipedians?

http://en.wikipedia.org/wiki/Wikipedia:WikiProject_Countering_systemic_bias WikiProject countering systemic bias

http://wikichix.org/ The WikiChix group, open to any woman interested in wikis

Essays

http://en.wikipedia.org/wiki/Category:Wikipedia_essays Essays about Wikipedia by Wikipedians; these essays in the Wikipedia namespace are often referenced by other users.

http://en.wikipedia.org/wiki/Category:User_essays More essays about Wikipedia by Wikipedians; these essays are in user space and may be less widely referenced or only represent the view of one person.

http://meta.wikimedia.org/wiki/Category:Essays Essays on the Meta site; these are older essays written by Wikipedians about Wikipedia, Wikimedia, and wiki philosophies.

http://en.planet.wikimedia.org Planet Wikimedia is an aggregator of blogs about Wikimedia by Wikimedians.

Researching Wikipedia

http://en.wikipedia.org/wiki/Wikipedia:Wikipedia_in_academic_studies A list of studies that have focused on Wikipedia

http://meta.wikimedia.org/wiki/Research The Wikimedia research network, a page for Wikimedia researchers from around the world to share their work

http://en.wikipedia.org/wiki/Wikipedia:Researching_Wikipedia Some research questions

Summary

Though loose and somewhat ill-defined, the notion of *community* is absolutely fundamental to Wikipedia; without it, the site could not succeed. The way Wikipedia is set up has led to a community that doesn't rely on central authority or a central forum. Instead, Wikipedia's editors communicate largely, but not exclusively, by editing pages for others to read—both article talk pages and central discussion forums. Those pages run quickly into tens of thousands of separate discussions, where issues are separated out and dealt with individually. Each debate will bring together a small, probably diverse group of people interested in any topic. Wikipedia has no true center and no easy overview of all these interactions. Wikipedia's success relies on the way that the overarching philosophies mesh with the intricate, small-scale actions on the site.

13 Policy and Your Input

Wikipedia's official policies apply to everyone—if you're editing Wikipedia at all, rather than just reading it, then you have to accept that site policies apply to you too. Policies determine what types of articles are acceptable, what styles of writing are appropriate, and generally how editors should behave.

These policies are not dictated from on high. Like Wikipedia's articles, they've been developed collaboratively by community members. In principle, anyone on the site can write and edit policy, and this chapter will brief you about how to participate. It will provide background on Wikipedia tradition and customs, which will help you understand the terms in which a debate is usually posed and give you a feel for how change is actually implemented.

This chapter will also give you a working knowledge of the existing policies and some of the core principles behind them.

All aspects of policy are explicitly documented on *project* pages. These pages, just like Wikipedia articles, are editable and supported by discussion pages on which community members work out details and changes.

The Spirit of Wikipedia

You won't master Wikipedia's policies just by poring over policy pages. People new to the site need an introduction to Wikipedia's culture, not just a rule book. Much of what happens on Wikipedia is not strictly governed by written rules.

For example, Wikipedia is a working environment in which a huge encyclopedia is written by a diverse group. This isn't official policy. But this is why serious Wikipedians are on the site. Wikipedia certainly has policies against disrupting the site, but defining disruption is like drawing a line between distracting someone at the desk next to you for a good reason and actually preventing him or her from working. Don't expect disruption to be completely spelled out, any more than in real life.

In that way, common sense is the first aspect of policy to master. You can't expect policies to be summed up completely by any one slogan, but this section will cover what many contributors see as Wikipedia's central principles.

The Five Pillars

We'll start with the *five pillars of Wikipedia*, a harmonious summary of the principles that guide the site.

▶ Wikipedia is an encyclopedia (not anything else).

▶ Wikipedia has a neutral point of view (the NPOV policy).

▶ Wikipedia is free content that anyone may edit. (All Wikipedia content is freely licensed and free of charge, and content is freely editable.)

▶ Wikipedia has a code of conduct. (Editors should behave civilly toward each other.)

▶ Wikipedia does not have firm rules. (The editing community can change the rules.)

The five pillars summarize Wikipedia as a website, a mission, and a community. We don't need to say more about the first three points since they were covered in Chapters 1, 2, and 5. In this chapter, we'll focus on detailing the fourth and fifth pillars and associated behavior policies. In the next two sections, we'll talk about three philosophies—one policy and two guidelines—that are at the core of how Wikipedia operates.

Ignore All Rules and Be Bold

Wikipedia has a degree of organization, but no one could accuse it of precision. The site organizes itself and is not managed by a top-down structure. Some of the consequences may seem contrarian, lax, or possibly a little rude. The principle of no firm rules can seem contrary but is deeply rooted in Wikipedia culture.

The fifth pillar leads to a basic policy: *Ignore All Rules (IAR)*. The policy reads, in its entirety,

> If the rules prevent you from improving or maintaining Wikipedia, ignore them.

This policy appears at [[Wikipedia:Ignore all rules]] (shortcut WP:IAR).

Policies and guidelines, in other words, exist to create the best site possible. They are not ends in themselves; they can be changed, and they may be ignored when common sense dictates. Wikipedia is not, however, an anarchy (see WP: ANARCHY), so most rules are not under threat of being disregarded; Ignore all rules simply serves to release pressure when needed. Rules should be ignored when necessary or for a good reason, and most of the *rules*, or policies and guidelines, help Wikipedia function more smoothly.

Ignore All Rules has been around from the beginning of Wikipedia—it expresses a core value of the project. The earliest version of the policy expresses the intended sentiment well:

> If rules make you nervous and depressed, and not desirous of participating in the Wiki, then ignore them and go about your business.

Closely related is the guideline (and site philosophy): *Be Bold*. Be Bold exhorts contributors to *be bold in editing pages*! This philosophy is fundamental to Wikipedia. With no top-down structure, work gets done, not because it was assigned as a task but because someone decided to be bold and do it. Although Be Bold is not an excuse to contradict standard policies and procedures, don't be shy about improving the site.

In the spirit of being bold, newcomers shouldn't worry about whether their ideas conform completely to custom. Wikipedia has no set demarcations of who can work on what. But newcomers should be polite in presenting their ideas, another core principle. Be bold!—but be civil, too. Edits can be reverted; uncivil exchanges with other editors cannot be unsaid.

This whole attitude of no demarcations is, in turn, related to the idea of *so fix it*, which, though not a policy or guideline, is a core part of wiki culture. Almost everything is freely editable—and thus fixable—by anyone, and volunteers do virtually all the work. The response to complaining is likely to be "so fix it." This is enshrined in a template that can be used to answer complaints about content or other problems. The {{sofixit}} template starts off, *Thank you for your suggestion. When you feel an article needs improvement, please feel free to make those changes.*

This concept helps explain a Wikipedian lightbulb joke:

> Q: How many Wikipedians does it take to change a lightbulb?
> A: Zero. Just tag the light bulb as {{unscrewed}} and let someone else worry about it.

A little cynical perhaps, but the point is true about voluntary projects. You can find more of the same at [[User:Bibliomaniac15/How many Wikipedians does it take to screw in a lightbulb?]].

This doesn't mean constructive criticism isn't welcomed. The point is that wiki sites are designed to allow critics to intervene: If you feel sidelined about making some remarks, those "sidelines" are in your imagination; they aren't coming from Wikipedia.

The essay [[Wikipedia:BOLD, revert, discuss cycle]] (shortcut WP:BRD) makes some interesting points. The essay is couched in the language of dispute resolution and concedes that being bold may be provocative. Someone interested and confident enough can make a sweeping change that may be reverted. This change may still be helpful, though; it may break a logjam or a consensus that has become too entrenched. Be opportunist about new changes: You don't have to revert to a previous, safer version.

Don't Stuff Beans up Your Nose

A modern fable about contrarianism is popular on Wikipedia: the small boy who wouldn't have thought of putting beans up his nose until it was forbidden. Online, contrarians often claim to be the loyal opposition to *groupthink* (discussed further in Chapter 14). See WP:BEANS and the summary, *If they haven't done it already, don't tell a user not to do a specific stupid thing. It may encourage them to do it.* In other words, a contrarian can easily become counter-suggestible, so simply having more and more rules is worse than light regulation that makes good sense to almost everyone.

Assume Good Faith

The fourth pillar deals with conduct on the site. Inevitably, Wikipedia has some problem users, but most users don't cause problems at all. *Assume Good Faith* (often abbreviated as *AGF*) is a key part of understanding how to deal with others on the site. Assume Good Faith was introduced in Chapter 12 as an aspiration. But Assume Good Faith is also a basic guideline because it helps preserve Wikipedia's good working environment. Wikipedia's culture is to assume that mistakes are generally good-faith errors. The Internet has become a place where people are often assumed to bring their own agenda to any discussion. Wikipedia cannot change this assumption directly, but Assume Good Faith helps reduce the tendency to suspect others' motives. In other words, leave your baggage at the door! Assuming good faith is a choice *you* make that reduces friction.

Editors should assume all other editors are sincerely trying to improve the project. This means treating all other editors' contributions in a professional, fair-minded fashion. Someone who ignores a formatting guideline may simply be making an honest mistake. Someone infringing on a policy may be unaware of it. Bias may be unintentional. Discuss your differences with other editors on talk pages *before* jumping to conclusions about their motives.

This is not to say that Wikipedia doesn't have true trolls, vandals, and other scalawags editing articles. Dispute resolution (covered in depth in Chapter 14) provides processes for dealing with a difficult editor when the evidence shows that he or she is not acting in good faith. By and large, however, most people edit Wikipedia because they want to contribute and help. Believing that is best—until you have firm evidence otherwise. Most likely, this is how you would want to be treated in an unfamiliar place; dispute resolution is not for vague suspicions.

Further Reading

http://en.wikipedia.org/wiki/Wikipedia:Five_pillars   Explanations of the five pillars of Wikipedia

http://en.wikipedia.org/wiki/Wikipedia:Assume_good_gaith   The guideline to assume good faith

http://en.wikipedia.org/wiki/Wikipedia:Be_bold   The guideline to be bold when editing pages

http://en.wikipedia.org/wiki/Wikipedia:Ignore_all_rules   Ignore all rules, the first rule on Wikipedia and now a policy

---

What Is Policy?

Policy on Wikipedia refers to the large collection of documents that have been developed over time by the editing community. An important working distinction is made between *official policy* and *guidelines*. Similar to the familiar distinction between what is *mandatory* (regulations you are required to follow) and what is only *advisory*, policies are meant to be followed by all contributors in their work on the site, whereas guidelines are like a manual of standard practices. Policies and guidelines are sometimes first developed in *essays*, which are position papers posted on the site by an individual editor in his or her user space or the Wikipedia namespace for others to work on; though many essays are quite popular and are often cited in discussions, they typically do not have the same level of consensus as policies and guidelines and are not mandatory.

Ignoring official policy or guidelines doesn't benefit you. Policies have a clear status and generally represent more fundamental principles that have broad consensus among editors. Guidelines should at least have wide consensus, though, and reflect common sense or good practice as applied to the production of Wikipedia. A guideline may only be advice about some stylistic detail, but the advice will generally be good.

Official Policy

Official policy is a category. See [[Category:Wikipedia official policy]]. Simply said, project pages belonging to this category are official policy pages. At the time of this writing, Wikipedia has 46 policy pages in this category.

Wikipedia has no body that can make a policy *official*; this declaration is based on consensus. A few policies have been adopted at the Wikimedia Foundation level, which are non-negotiable at the project level, but these deal primarily with the content license and privacy practices (see Chapter 17 for the Wikimedia Foundation's policies). Everyday matters of policy on the English-language Wikipedia are not really affected by the Foundation.

Most policies are, therefore, a matter of consensus within the editing community. Here are two significant comments from the Official policy category page:

> There are only a few key policies that might be regarded as "official"—that is, considered by the founders and the vast majority of contributors as being particularly important to the running of Wikipedia. [. . .] They have either withstood the test of time or have been adopted by consensus or acclamation.

and

> Very often, there is no "bright line" distinction between proposed policy, guidelines, and "actual" policy. Policy at Wikipedia is a matter of consensus, tradition, and practice. While the principles of the policies in this category are mostly well established, the details are often still evolving, so not everything in these pages represent hard and fast rules.

Though this is true, over time policy becomes firmer and less subject to change.

Policies and Guidelines

Policies and guidelines on Wikipedia have a wide scope: They include article style issues, contributor behavior standards, and content inclusion rules. All policies and guidelines exist on pages in the Wikipedia namespace. The policy pages found at [[Category:Wikipedia official policy]] are by no means all equally important. Later in this chapter, we'll analyze these pages to give you a concise, readable introduction.

Policy documents typically have much context and history behind their creation and wording. Both the spirit and the letter of the policy are important; editors should comply with the principles expressed. The most important point will be the expression of some reasonable expectation of how editors should act under normal conditions. The drafting of the policy reflects this: The main thrust of a policy is to convey one idea, and this idea should make good sense to someone familiar with the site. For instance, the ordinary editor doesn't need to read the fine print on the policy page outlining the value of consensus. But administrators making decisions based on discussions will require more information about what consensus means.

Principles of policy are different from specific processes or procedures but are often interrelated. Take, for example, the Article Deletion policy. The policy refers to the various deletion processes; it doesn't discuss the details of how the specific processes work. Rather, it authorizes them.

How Policies Are Created and Developed

Wikipedia does not have a special area just for drafting legislation. The starting point for a new policy may be a new project page in the Wikipedia namespace or possibly an essay that makes sense to other editors and begins to be referenced in discussions. Policies and guidelines, like other content on Wikipedia, are then developed over time by interested editors through a consensus-based process. Policies and guidelines are typically altered to reflect changing practice on the site or to solve a problem that has arisen. If consensus for a new proposed policy can't be reached, the proposal will be dropped.

If a change to policy sticks, in the sense that it has been on the policy page for some weeks without being removed and discussion seems to support the change, the new or amended policy has been widely accepted. The expectation is then that all editors will begin to follow the new policy when someone points it out. Keeping informed about changing policies and guidelines is a real issue for editors; beyond the core content and behavioral policies, many editors may not know about all the policies and guidelines. This is where Assume Good Faith applies: If User:Alice sees that User:Bob isn't following a new guideline, Alice should let Bob know that the guideline changed last month rather than scold him.

Policy and guideline creation, in practice, starts and ends in the Wikipedia namespace. The fact that policy pages are editable is one of the radical, counterintuitive Wikipedia concepts. Minor changes to policy formulations can occur at any time if the community agrees the changes are needed; major changes and new policies are also slowly developed to meet new needs and changing circumstances.

Of course, the practical process for changing policy is not so simple as just making an edit. Policies can and do change; however, the process is often very slow. On pages in the Wikipedia Talk namespace discussions are always ongoing, proposing and criticizing changes to policy. Most policy page changes are reverted if they are substantive and have not been discussed previously on the attached talk page and perhaps on other community forums. Always seek a high level of consensus before making a change to a key policy page. Given a policy's role in regulating the site, more discussion is required than elsewhere. For basic guidance on participating in policymaking, go to [[Wikipedia:How to contribute to Wikipedia guidance]].

For example, on May 11, 2007, a new section was added to [[Wikipedia: Disambiguation]], the guideline regulating 70,000 disambiguation pages on Wikipedia. The material had already been discussed at [[Wikipedia talk:Manual of Style (disambiguation pages)]]; the guideline called for adding a new section, so-called

Set index articles, to recognized page types. In this somewhat notorious area (the ambiguities of ambiguity, you could say), the following case was made:

> A set index article describes a single set of concepts. For example, [[Dodge Charger]] describes a set of cars, [[List of peaks named Signal Mountain]] describes a set of mountain peaks, or [[USS Enterprise]] describes a set of ships. A set index article is both for information and for navigation: just like a normal list article, it can have metadata and extra information about each entry. A set index article can be entertaining and informative by itself, can help editors find redlinks to create articles on notable entries, and finally can also help readers navigate between articles that have similar names. (From *http://en.wikipedia.org/w/index.php?title=Wikipedia:Disambiguation&diff=130088375&oldid=129966757*)

So an exception to the general guideline was made for a small group of articles. This incremental change by User:Hike395 was accepted, replacing what previously only applied to lists of ships with the same name. You can reasonably assume that the amendment, by being vetted through discussion, has been accepted through consensus by the editors interested in disambiguation pages; for other contributors not involved in the discussion who may happen to work in this area, the guideline now provides more detailed information that they should reasonably follow in most cases. If a future contributor comes along and has a serious problem with this or any other part of the guideline, the contributor may state his or her case on the guideline's talk page, beginning the cycle again.

This example is a relatively simple case, affecting a particular stylistic guideline for a certain type of article. On the other hand, proposed changes to the Notability guideline or Verifiability policy—policies that affect every Wikipedia article and indeed, the nature of the site itself—should be debated for weeks or months on the policy's talk page and on other forums. Changes to these policies may be difficult to make unless very compelling reasons are given. This difficulty does not necessarily reflect the proposal's validity, but simply how difficult getting consensus is among the very wide group of editors—potentially, the entire community—who may be interested in site-wide policy changes.

Essays written by individual Wikipedians are not at all official, but they may eventually serve as the basis for policies or guidelines. You can find hundreds of essays at [[Category:Wikipedia essays]]; anyone, naturally, may add to these. Essays are policy development as pamphlet writing; you should expect to present your ideas first before proposing a big policy change. Essays are also a useful platform for expressing an opinion on applying policies. Some of the most-cited essays, however, are humorous expositions on basic Wikipedia ideals and ways to behave; [[Wikipedia:No climbing the Reichstag dressed as Spider-Man]] is an example, pointing out that you shouldn't take debates so seriously you go to extreme measures to make a fuss about them.

Many proposals for future policy are made and then abandoned due to lack of interest or consensus. You can read many of these at [[Category:Wikipedia rejected proposals]], with the template {{rejected}} applied; for example, [[Wikipedia:Changing policies and guidelines]] was an attempt to clarify that certain policy changes require consensus before being made; somewhat ironically, this policy didn't make the cut. You can get some good insights into the shaping of policy from reading rejected proposals.

How Policies Evolve

If you want to change something about how Wikipedia works, you'll have to make an effort and accept that it will only happen piecemeal. Preparing for policy changes matters greatly. You can't always expect to change a guideline with which you disagree on some minor point of style or format and then proceed directly to edit the whole site to change that point wherever you can find it—this behavior is rightly viewed as disruptive. If you encounter some resistance, you have to respect the objections people raise. If they didn't know the guideline was being changed, they weren't part of the consensus you claimed. If too many people disagree with some aspect of policy, the policy will likely be modified.

For example, a controversial change to the *Spoiler warnings* guideline caused a furor in May 2007. The template {{spoiler}} had traditionally been used on the site in a Plot section of a film or book article, as a warning to those unfamiliar with the work being discussed that the text they were about to read would give the story away. These warnings had been an accepted feature of Wikipedia for years. But some pent-up feelings against them existed: Some argued that they interfered with the encyclopedia function, or in other words, serious reference works don't need spoiler warnings. The wide use of spoiler warnings concealed the fact that their presence in articles annoyed many editors.

The page [[Wikipedia:Spoiler]] was edited: What it currently says (as of April 2008) includes this new text:

> Spoilers on the Internet are sometimes preceded by a spoiler warning. In Wikipedia, however, it is generally expected that the subjects of our articles will be covered in detail. Therefore, Wikipedia carries no spoiler warnings except for the Content disclaimer.

Once a tipping point had been reached, with those against spoiler warnings gaining control of that guideline page, over 45,000 spoiler warnings were rapidly deleted from Wikipedia. This change caused tension and many back and forth arguments at the time. Though still controversial, the change has (so far) stuck.

How to Interpret Policies and Guidelines

Don't be legalistic about reading policy pages—a practice known unfavorably as *wikilawyering*. Policies are not drafted like legal documents, so don't push their meaning beyond the basic point or intention. The correct approach is usually this: Read the policy first to see what is required and respect the intent and spirit of the policy.

Assuming that policies can settle arguments is only human. Policies are actually there to help Wikipedia work, defining more closely what should be done and preserving a good atmosphere. They are not primarily tools for resolving disputes over content. Although such disputes may well come down to a discussion of

We Got Here from Where?

Sometimes you need to understand how policies evolved to see what they are really saying and what weight you should give them. Discussions leading up to the development of policies, like all discussions, are kept on the site, though reviewing the archives is not always an easy or clear process. Policies can appear path-dependent, and if you suspect a policy has been widened over time, you might be right. This is also a part of policy evolution.

For instance, the No Original Research (NOR) policy, for example, was first formulated to keep original theories in physics from Wikipedia. Its application has since expanded to include other topics. On the *wiki-en* mailing list (6 December 2004), Jimmy Wales wrote:

> Some who completely understand why Wikipedia ought not create novel theories of physics by citing the results of experiments and so on and synthesizing them into something new, may fail to see how the same thing applies to history.

> By now the NOR policy very much applies to history: Wikipedia wants neither theories about how Einstein had it all wrong about relativity, nor historical theories that have no serious scholarly support, for example, about the Ten Lost Tribes, if these theories are presented as original research and argument.

policies and how they should be applied, be reasonable, collegiate, and open-minded in bringing policy into edit wars. A narrow view of a policy or guideline is not likely to resolve matters.

Further Reading

http://en.wikipedia.org/wiki/Wikipedia:Policies_and_guidelines   The policy on policies and guidelines; a good overview of policies, guidelines, and proposals

http://en.wikipedia.org/wiki/Wikipedia:How_to_contribute_to_Wikipedia_guidance   Advice on changing policies

http://en.wikipedia.org/wiki/Category:Wikipedia_proposals   The category of proposed new policies

http://en.wikipedia.org/wiki/Category:Wikipedia_rejected_proposals
The category of rejected policies

http://en.wikipedia.org/wiki/Wikipedia:Simplified_Ruleset   Basic rules to work by

Letter of the Law

To understand policy details, you first have to find the relevant pages, next get the basic gist of a policy, and only then look at the more specific points. The precise wording of a policy may well change over time while the general idea remains the same.

For many policies, Wikipedia has handy *nutshell* summaries, which we've imported (current as of August 2007). For others, we've written our own summary. The uppercase abbreviated title is the page shortcut, less WP; so, for example, you can find Attack Page (ATP) at WP:ATP.

List of Policies

Policies fall into a few classes. Some deal with article content, and others deal with editor interactions. We've broken them down into four types for convenience.

Content Policies

Content policies deal with article content, both what articles should be and what you can do with them.

Attack Page (ATP)
Aggressive, hostile, biased articles will be summarily deleted.

Biographies of Living Persons (BLP)
From Wikipedia: Wikipedia articles can affect real people's lives. This gives us an ethical and legal responsibility. Biographical material must be written with the greatest care and attention to verifiability, neutrality, and avoiding original research, particularly if it is contentious.

Copyrights (COPY)
Wikipedia operates under a copyleft approach to its content, with the copyright to contributions remaining with those who created them. (See Chapter 2 for more on copyleft.)

Copyright Violations (COPYVIO)
Wikipedia actively removes copyrighted material.

Editing Policy (EP)
From Wikipedia: Improve pages wherever you can, and do not worry about leaving them imperfect.

Libel (LIBEL)
Wikipedia removes any defamatory material it finds, responds to email requests to do so, and regards editors adding libelous material as being responsible for that content.

Naming Conventions (NAME)
From Wikipedia: Generally, article naming should prefer what the majority of English speakers would most easily recognize, with a reasonable minimum of

ambiguity, while at the same time making linking to those articles easy and second nature.

Neutral Point of View (NPOV), Neutral Point of View/FAQ (NPOVFAQ)

From Wikipedia: All Wikipedia articles and other encyclopedic content must be written from a neutral point of view, representing views fairly, proportionately, and without bias.

Non-Free Content Criteria (NFCC)

This policy attempts to delimit the use of non-free content (such as fair-use images) on Wikipedia.

No Original Research (NOR)

From Wikipedia: Wikipedia is not a publisher of original thought. Articles should only contain verifiable content from reliable sources without further analysis. Content should not be synthesized to advance a position.

Ownership of Articles (OWN)

From Wikipedia: If you create or edit an article, know that others will edit it, and within reason, you should not prevent them from doing so.

Reusing Wikipedia Content (REUSE)

Wikipedia material may be re-used by anyone, within the terms of the GFDL.

Verifiability (V)

From Wikipedia: Material that is challenged or likely to be challenged, and all quotations, must be attributed to a reliable, published source.

Social Policies

Social policies deal with how editors should behave and interact with one another on the site.

Civility (CIVIL)

From Wikipedia: Participate in a respectful and civil way. Do not ignore the positions and conclusions of others. Try to discourage others from being uncivil, and be careful to avoid offending people unintentionally.

Edit War (EW)

From Wikipedia: If someone challenges your edits, discuss it with them and seek a compromise, or seek dispute resolution. Don't just fight over competing views and versions.

No Legal Threats (LEGAL)

From Wikipedia: Do not make threats or claims of legal action against users or Wikipedia itself on Wikipedia. If you have a dispute with the Community or its members, use dispute resolution. A polite report of a legal problem such as defamation or copyright infringement is not threatening and will be acted on quickly. If you do choose to take legal action, please refrain from editing until it is resolved and note that your user account may be blocked.

No Personal Attacks (NPA)
From Wikipedia: Comment on content, not on the contributor.

Dispute Resolution (DR)
Try to avoid arguments; if in a dispute, talk it over calmly and consider your words first.

Sock Puppetry (SOCK)
From Wikipedia: Do not use multiple accounts to create the illusion of greater support for an issue, to mislead others, or to circumvent a block. Do not ask your friends to create accounts to support you or anyone else.

Three-Revert Rule (3RR)
From Wikipedia: Edit warring is harmful. Wikipedians who revert a page in whole or in part more than three times in 24 hours, except in certain special circumstances, are likely to be blocked from editing.

Vandalism (VANDAL)
From Wikipedia: Intentionally making repeated non-constructive edits to Wikipedia will result in a block or permanent ban.

Wheel War (WHEEL)
Applies only to administrators. Repeatedly reversing actions of other administrators is considered harmful.

Enabling Policies

These are basic documents on which various processes and administrator actions rely. For example, under the Username policy (UN), accounts with unsuitable usernames will be blocked. These policies are often intended for specific situations.

Arbitration Policy (AP)
See Chapter 14 for details on Arbitration, which is a high-level dispute resolution process.

Appealing a Block (APPEAL)
This policy mentions all the correct appeal routes available to a user blocked by an administrator.

Banning Policy (BAN)
This policy explains why and how editors are excluded from the site.

Blocking Policy (BP), Appealing a Block (APB)
From Wikipedia: Users may be blocked from editing by an administrator to protect Wikipedia and its editors from harm.

Bot Policy (BOT)
This is a procedural guide to automated editing.

Category Deletion Policy (CDP)

This is a policy for the named process.

Criteria for Speedy Deletion (CSD)

This is a very detailed list of the criteria used by administrators to delete articles quickly.

Deletion Policy (DEL)

From Wikipedia: Deletion and undeletion are performed by administrators based on policy and guidelines, not personal likes and dislikes. There are four processes for deleting items and one post-deletion review process. Pages that can be improved should be edited or tagged, not nominated for deletion.

Image Use Policy (IUP)

From Wikipedia: Be very careful when uploading copyrighted images, fully describe images' sources and copyright details on their description pages, and try to make images as useful and reusable as possible.

Open Proxies (PROXY)

Administrators may block open or anonymizing proxy servers that allow you to edit while hiding your IP address.

Office Actions (OFFICE)

From Wikipedia: Sometimes the Wikimedia Foundation may have to delete, protect, or blank a page without going through the normal site/community process(es) to do so. These edits are temporary measures to prevent legal trouble or personal harm and should not be undone by any user.

Open Ticket Request System (OTRS)

This document describes the operation of the Open Ticket Request System, which handles email complaints to Wikipedia.

Oversight (OVER)

This is actually a Foundation-level policy. It describes the Oversight system for removing edits from page histories, with scope to deal with personal information, defamation, and copyright only.

Proposed Deletion (PROD)

From Wikipedia: As a shortcut around AfD [i.e., Articles for Deletion] for uncontroversial deletions; an article can be proposed for deletion, though once only. If no one contests the proposal within five days, the article may be deleted by an administrator.

Protection Policy (PROT)

This policy covers administrator use of the power to protect pages by locking editing.

Username Policy (UN)

From Wikipedia: When choosing an account name, be careful to avoid names which may be offensive, confusing, or promotional. You are encouraged to use only one account.

General Policies

These core policies apply across the site, to both content and social situations.

Consensus (CON)

From Wikipedia: Consensus is Wikipedia's fundamental model for editorial decision-making. Policies and guidelines document communal consensus rather than creating it.

GNU Free Documentation License (GFDL)

This is the license under which Wikipedia is released. The general outline is covered in Chapter 2, but material on secondary and invariant sections and cover texts, although not so relevant to Wikipedia, may have an effect on imported GFDL material.

Ignore All Rules (IAR)

Wikipedia is not a rule-bound place, and the rules should serve the mission. Occasionally, editors can operate outside policy, if they are acting within common sense.

What Wikipedia Is Not (NOT)

This policy defines Wikipedia's mission by describing what it isn't; this is a key reference.

It Used to Be So Much Simpler

The earliest version of [[Wikipedia:Policies and guidelines]] dates back to April 17, 2002 (though an earlier version, just called Wikipedia policy, dates back to 2001; the very earliest history was lost due to technical glitches). Much of the original content is now considered part of the style guide and doesn't relate to policy as such. [[Wikipedia:Most common Wikipedia faux pas]] is still available and useful to know about; it is now under the title [[Wikipedia: Avoiding common mistakes]] (shortcut WP:ACM). [[Wikipedia:Always leave something undone]] was renamed [[Wikipedia:Make omissions explicit]], but this is no longer policy. [[Wikipedia:Look for an existing article before you start one]] was emphasized earlier in the book; this policy was merged into [[Wikipedia:How to start a page]] about a year later. [[Wikipedia:Contribute what you know or are willing to learn more about]] has the nostalgic feel of older wikis; this page also didn't turn into policy. If depressed by the comparison, try [[Wikipedia:What Wikipedia is not/Outtakes]].

List of Guidelines

This is a selective list of some guidelines we consider particularly important. There are over a hundred guidelines total, many of which are part of the *Manual of Style* (you can find a complete collection of guidelines at [[Category:Wikipedia guidelines]]). Summaries for interesting guidelines tend to be significantly longer than for official policies. They are often saying something important but more diffuse. They are certainly more rewarding to read casually.

Assume Good Faith (AGF)
From Wikipedia: Unless there is strong evidence to the contrary, assume that people who work on the project are trying to help it, not hurt it. If criticism is needed, discuss editors' actions, but it is not ever necessary nor productive to accuse others of harmful motives.

Attribution
This policy is not current, but it is of particular interest as an attempt to unify NOR and V (ATT). From Wikipedia: All material in Wikipedia must be attributable to a reliable, published source.

Autobiography (AUTO)
From Wikipedia: Avoid writing or editing an article about yourself, other than to correct unambiguous errors of fact.

Be Bold (BOLD)
From Wikipedia: If you see something that can be improved, do not hesitate to do so yourself.

Conflict of Interest (COI)
From Wikipedia: When an editor disregards the aims of Wikipedia to advance outside interests, they have a conflict of interest. Conflict of interest editing is strongly discouraged, but editors with a potential conflict of interest may edit with appropriate care and discussion.

Do Not Disrupt Wikipedia to Illustrate a Point (POINT)
From Wikipedia: If you think you have a valid point, causing disruption is probably the least effective way of presenting that point—and it may get you blocked.

This applies particularly to those with a grievance or burning issue to raise. Attention-seeking tactics that have a negative impact on others are not acceptable as a campaigning measure. Such disruption is generally considered actionable and can lead to a ban.

Etiquette (EQ)
This is a general guide to expected etiquette on the site.

Harassment (HARASS)

From Wikipedia: Do not stop other editors from enjoying Wikipedia by making threats, nitpicking good-faith edits to different articles, repeated personal attacks, or posting personal information.

Manual of Style (MOS)

This is the *Manual of Style* for articles, with all its many subpages that detail specific style guide issues.

Notability (N)

From Wikipedia: A topic is presumed to be notable if it has received significant coverage in reliable secondary sources that are independent of the subject.

* NOTE: *Despite its daily use in discussions, Notability has not received recognition as official policy. Many people clearly feel that the definition, by means of sources, is flawed and thus still controversial.*

No Disclaimers in Articles (NDA)

From Wikipedia: Disclaimers should not be used in articles. All articles are covered by the five official disclaimer pages.

Please Do Not Bite the Newcomers (BITE)

From Wikipedia: Do not be hostile toward newcomers. Remember to assume good faith first and approach them in a polite manner.

This guideline gives a code of conduct for dealing with inexperienced editors. Although they may come across as *clueless newbies*, they should be treated with understanding and should certainly not be addressed in those terms. The correct approach is to be tactful and helpful, drawing the attention of such editors to any general matters of policy, custom, and convention which they are apparently unaware of.

Polling Is Not a Substitute for Discussion (VOTE)

From Wikipedia: Wikipedia decisions are not made by popular vote, but rather through discussions by reasonable people working toward consensus. Polling is only meant to facilitate discussion and should be used with care.

Reliable Sources (RS)

From Wikipedia: Articles should be based on reliable, third-party, published sources with a reputation for fact-checking and accuracy.

SPAM

This is the guideline against promotional articles, *linkspam* (external links placed to benefit other websites), and excessive internal posting of messages on user talk pages.

Seven Policies to Study

The five pillars are a good place to begin to familiarize yourself with Wikipedia principles. Perhaps they will live up to the resonant name and serve as a time-less description of Wikipedia, or perhaps they'll just be eternal by Internet-time standards. Policy does evolve, and Wikipedia evolves, too. Before you say you understand the site policies, you might want another perspective. Everyday life on the site will convince you that participating is not quite so simple.

Here is our selection, based on sheer utility, of the major policies to familiar-ize yourself with first:

▸ Neutrality (NPOV) from the content policies

▸ Three-Revert Rule (3RR) and Civility (CIVIL) from the social policies

▸ Criteria for Speedy Deletion (CSD) from the enabling policies

▸ What Wikipedia Is Not (NOT) from the general policies

Together, these policies convey the same ideas as the five pillars but are a little more current in their emphasis. Criteria for Speedy Deletion (CSD) is now used in an aggressive fashion to clean up newly created articles that don't meet Wikipedia's standards at all. Therefore, a new editor should know about this policy.

To summarize, be a neutral, civil editor who doesn't rely on reverting pages excessively. Understand that Wikipedia provides space online for its mission to write an encyclopedia and for no other reason, and understand that many submis-sions of new pages will be deleted summarily from the site because they don't fit the content policies.

That's five policies. Two guidelines may also affect you as soon as you start editing: Conflict of Interest (COI) and Reliable Sources (RS). For obvious reasons, not every guideline can be covered in detail, but these two are very important.

Conflict of Interest

This guideline, at [[Wikipedia:Conflict of interest]], matters because Wikipedia articles should not be hijacked by outside interests. Editors acting for corporations or religious groups are not welcome to edit articles about those companies or groups in such a way as to control the content. No article should be marred by long edit wars involving partisan editors with a definite stake in the topic. The COI guideline is relatively new but has become important because many people would like to exploit Wikipedia's pages. The guideline says simply that editors of Wikipedia should not put their outside interests ahead of those of the encyclopedia. The best way to ensure that is to edit as little as possible in areas too close to your own interests. That includes self-promotion, ensuring favorable coverage of a company that has hired you, and certain types of activism. The guideline is not intended to prevent academics from editing in their field, members of major political parties from editing about related political affairs, or believers editing about their religion, as long as these edits respect the Neutral Point of View policy.

Reliable Sources

[[Wikipedia:Reliable sources]] addresses sources and citations on three fronts: the *piece of work* being cited, its *author*, and how it is *published*. First, all sources cited must certainly be published, so an unpublished conversation or email—what academics call a *private communication*—should not be used as a source. Second, published work has limitations: A self-published book is not a reliable source for factual information in general. Furthermore, websites vary widely in reliability. For the most part, blogs are not acceptable sources. Content on other wikis cannot be taken as authoritative. Online copies of newspaper articles are as good as the hard copy, but newspapers are reliable sources only if they are part of the mainstream press. In practice, high standards of source reliability have to be met if you want to write about controversial matters or (particularly) about living people.

Further Reading

http://en.wikipedia.org/wiki/Wikipedia:List_of_policies   List of all official policies

http://en.wikipedia.org/wiki/Category:Wikipedia_guidelines   Category for Wikipedia guidelines

---

Summary

Wikipedia's policies have evolved from being simple principles to being a large group of pages. You can probably count the ones on the site that matter most in daily life on the fingers of two hands. Understanding the basic point of a given policy or guideline, as it affects you, and in combination with Wikipedia's customs, is more important than worrying about the details or how others should comply. Bring policy into arguments only when you have to, and if you become involved in developing or modifying policy pages, make sure you can take the lead in getting consensus among the community.

14

Disputes, Blocks, and Bans

No account of Wikipedia would be complete without discussing conflicts and how they are resolved. That Wikipedia works, considering its open-door policy for editors, is not a minor miracle. Wikipedia has to cope with pettiness and strange behavior, as well as predictable amounts of editing by people with agendas and those bored children whose immediate reaction to a freely editable encyclopedia is to scribble on it. Because of Wikipedia's success in compiling a large, free, open encyclopedia, some might be surprised that the site also experiences various kinds of serious internal strife. Disputes on Wikipedia cannot be wished away ("Can't we all just get along?"). Allowing anyone to edit just about anything has a price.

This chapter will discuss onsite disputes and the procedures for their resolution. Disputes vary from teacup tempests about minor points of formatting or nomenclature to deep-rooted issues about the coverage of controversial current affairs. Without reasonably effective mechanisms for dispute resolution, the Wikipedia model of open editing could never have come as far as it has.

Reading through a realistic description of dispute resolution on Wikipedia is probably somewhat forbidding. Most readers will understandably think that they don't intend to become involved in conflict and acrimony, and this is a good goal to have. If you go far enough into the editing process, however, some disagreements are almost inevitable. Fortunately, Wikipedia has ways to resolve disputes.

Content Disputes and Edit Wars

A *content dispute* is any disagreement about the content of a Wikipedia article. An *edit war* is a content dispute in which two or more editors have decided to try to impose their view on an article by repeatedly changing the article to a version in line with their opinion. This conflict over content is the most common kind and typically takes the form of a *revert war*, with editors going back and forth about what to include. Other content disputes, such as disputed merges and title issues, also arise, and these are handled by the mechanisms mentioned in Chapter 8. Edit wars are common in contentious topic areas, which is no coincidence. But they are otherwise rare, as most articles contain nothing to provoke heated arguments, and if you stay away from editing contentious topics, you may never encounter one.

Keeping Calm

Wikipedians tend to become most involved in heated discussions in areas where they're passionate about the subject matter. [[Wikipedia:Staying cool when the editing gets hot]] (shortcut WP:COOL) is an essay on the vital topic of subduing emotion and aggression during an edit war. Don't underestimate how difficult this can be.

Wikipedia has *no formal process* dedicated to resolving disagreements about content. Instead, most edit wars are resolved over time through discussion and finding consensus, discussed next. Wikipedia does not formally ask another person or group to judge which content version is more correct. Here are three major reasons why:

▸ Socially speaking, if the editors involved can come to consensus, this is better for everyone.

▸ Compromise is more likely to reflect a neutral point of view than choosing the better of two rival versions.

- Creating a group of so called super-editors who could argue with authority on content matters would undermine the egalitarian spirit of Wikipedia. And even if Wikipedia could find people to fill the role of super-editors, these editors would find it impossible to expertly judge the multitude of content on Wikipedia. This solution would not scale well.

A real advantage of the consensus-based approach, when it works, is that the parties feel better about themselves and the ultimate article content. A well-drafted compromise reflects well on those who contribute to it.

The Three-Revert Rule

The *Three-Revert Rule* is a policy (WP:3RR) that says, "Wikipedians who revert a page in whole or in part more than three times in 24 hours, except in certain special circumstances, are likely to be blocked from editing." Chapter 5 warned against overusing reverts. If you find yourself arguing about content with other editors, back off and discuss the issue on the talk page, rather than get carried away re-editing. (Note that the Three-Revert Rule does not apply to simple vandalism removal.) To report violations of this rule, go to [[Wikipedia:Administrators's noticeboard/3RR]].

Coming to Consensus

Wikipedia, therefore, operates by *consensus*. Although the site is dynamic, consensus prevails in most articles, the majority of which are not disputed. A few topics are in rapid flux, but most topic areas are at least temporarily settled because most of the interested editors consider the content good enough. Because of this, a sensible solution to a dispute can sometimes be restoring a disputed article to an older version that had consensus—but that version may be less than ideal, as well. Wikipedia is not static by nature.

As the policy on consensus says (as of April 2008):

> Consensus is an inherent part of the wiki process. Consensus is typically reached as a natural product of the editing process; generally someone makes a change or addition to a page, and then everyone who reads the page has an opportunity to either leave the page as it is or change it. In essence, silence implies consent if there is adequate exposure to the community. (From [[Wikipedia:Consensus]], shortcut WP:CON)

Thus, consensus is reached by the editors involved with a particular article; the *community* for any particular article consists of those people who take an active interest in the page. Other uninvolved editors are welcome to become involved at any point. Generally, consensus occurs through everyday editing of an article, with any disputed points or disagreements discussed on the talk page. In dispute resolution, consensus does not mean everyone *agrees* with the outcome; instead, it means everyone agrees to abide by it.

Good editors on Wikipedia detect problems with existing consensus early on through discussion on an article's talk page (and through noticing controversial edits). Reaching a new consensus on an improved version is a process. Figure 14-1 shows a flowchart taken from [[Wikipedia:Consensus]]. This chart shows an idealized and schematic editing process that may bring about consensus if the editors involved persist and learn the root causes of their disagreements.

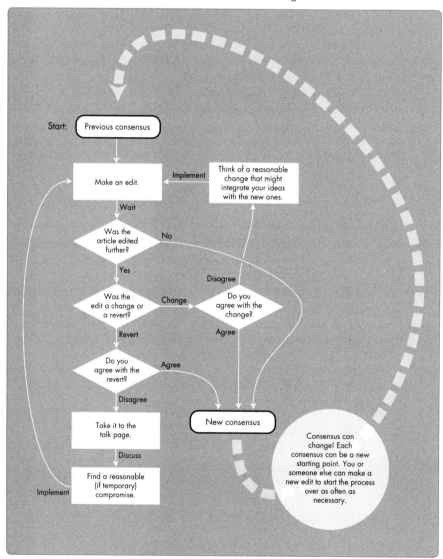

FIGURE 14-1: *Finding consensus in a dispute*

How you handle yourself as an editor can help in the consensus process. To avoid edit wars and interact tactfully with problematic content, try this self-imposed rule: Only revert a change you disagree with *once* before discussing it on the talk page. When disputing something, ask yourself, "What is the problem with this *actual* version?" Address that specific point. You can't always find agreement through rational discussion, but you can narrow the gap by negotiating, as long as you keep the discussion concrete.

Resolving a Dispute: Discussion

The first step in resolving any disputed edit is to post a note on the article's talk page (or other page under discussion) explaining the problem specifically. Ideally, the editors involved will see that note and respond. If you're responding to a particular editor's actions or you want to make sure he or she sees your comment, leave a quick note on that editor's talk page, alerting him or her to the new discussion; though in general, if you wish to discuss an article's content, you should keep the conversation close to the article itself. As noted in Chapter 5, if you have made a change that others may find controversial—or any major change, particularly to a contentious topic—explain the change and your reasoning in a quick, polite note on the talk page, and add helpful edit summaries. This sets the tone for the discussion and gives other editors a reasonable place to comment.

How do you have a civil discussion about a contentious topic? Two fundamentals are

▶ Remember that Wikimedia is a global project. Discussions are about working out the kinks.

▶ Remember that others may have very different perspectives from your own.

Keep in mind the basic guidelines for any talk page discussion, as outlined in "Talk Page Guidelines" on page 337. Maintaining good behavior is crucial, no matter the source of the dispute. There is a huge difference between saying, "I disagree with you and here's why," and "You are obviously a partisan editor and your views will not be tolerated in the article."

Good Sense Should Prevail, So De-escalate

Even though Wikipedia cannot change the real-world situations that drive some disputes, you certainly can change the tone of such a dispute if you're ever involved in one. The basic guideline is to *stick very close to the talk page rules*. By discussing a dispute calmly and resisting being provoked into personal attacks, you can reduce tensions. You will also be helping your case if matters move into more formal processes, making it easier rather than harder for third-party mediation to be effective.

Obviously, participants who are convinced they are right or are unwilling to work under the basic content policies can cause problems. These types would be better off contributing to one of the many online discussion forums that exist or blogging about their opinions. Wikipedia requires a willingness to work toward consensus, with the goal of achieving a good article that meets the content policies. Fortunately, the self-selection of active editors on the site works toward open mindedness. In line with the overall idea of Assume Good Faith, everyone involved should be pleasant and attentive to the other side of an argument. In this context, arguments aren't the same thing as debates—no one should be trying to win a debating-society-style victory—and trying to score points is not constructive.

Remember as well that the discussion process can take a long time: Editors aren't (ideally) online 24/7. Debates may take weeks or even longer to be settled happily. Editing on Wikipedia isn't a race; for most topics, debates don't need to be settled immediately. Compromise a little and work toward being an eventualist rather than being impatient for issues to be dealt with quickly. Stay out of any debates that aren't central to your editing. We introduced *eventualism* in Chapter 12 as the wikiphilosophy that in the long term things will work out. Waiting and returning to an issue a month later is not a bad idea: A reasonable talk page approach is "I still think . . .". The proportion of content issues that should be settled within 24 hours is low.

Once discussion has run its course, two possible extreme outcomes may be reached:

▶   The warring parties agree on a compromise version, and the edit war ceases for the time being.

▶   An unproductive edit war results as editors change the page back and forth between two incompatible versions, without troubling to engage each other in discussion.

Edit wars may not affect an entire article; often only one section is particularly controversial and subject to edit warring. Editors may compromise about other sections of the article more easily.

When reasoned discussion fails to resolve an edit war, you should think further about its underlying causes and possibly turn to others for mediation or temporary cooling-off measures.

More Steps for Resolving a Content Dispute

As discussed, the parties in an edit war should talk to each other on the talk page of the article in question or on the user talk pages of those involved in the dispute. If these exchanges of views are carried out in a cooperative and reasonable way, the edit war will probably be resolved.

But if compromise isn't reached, what happens next? Some basic options are:

▶   Page protection (short term) by an administrator

▶   Mediation (informal) by any Wikipedian

▶   Recourse to a formal process, most usually a Request for Comment (see "Resolving Disputes Between Editors" on page 397) on editor behavior

WikiLove

WikiLove doesn't say more than this: The letter of the law does not overrule the basic need to treat others as you wish to be treated. You may think this sounds as dated as kaftans and wearing a flower in your hair, but these feel-good beliefs really exist on Wikipedia, even though its huge scale means WikiLove is a philosophical influence, rather than a specific policy. Appeals to WikiLove are usually meant to be an antidote to excessive reliance on policy. As such, WikiLove is the natural counterpart of Be Bold! and Ignore All Rules! This trio of ideas (a quartet, with Assume Good Faith) are the result of time-honored wiki thinking.

Although it sounds rather utopian, the desire for WikiLove is consistent with other approaches: soft security rather than eliminating all bad edits before they happen, trying to appreciate the value in different points of view, tolerance and respect of other editors, and allowing an article to have an unfinished feel.

Page protection stops an edit war in its tracks. The administrator applying the protection should not be editing the article (i.e., he or she should be neutral), and the protected version should be the current one—in effect a random choice (this process is humorously skewered on a Meta page called The Wrong Version). The point of the protection should be to give all parties a time-out from the warring during which negotiations take place.

Of course, administrator intervention may occur earlier in an edit war with the application of 24-hour blocks for editors who violate the Three-Revert Rule. In a broader perspective, leaving an article unedited for 24 hours isn't anything major. Edit warriors, however, are more often than not myopic in their view of Wikipedia, believing that a "wrong" version should not be allowed to stand on Wikipedia—even for a day!

Outside intervention, or *mediation* by a third party, has a definite place in the process as soon as bilateral discussion breaks down. Effective mediation can often be simple in its approach: A clear explanation of the fundamental policies on content and conduct can alter the atmosphere. When an article is within the scope of a WikiProject, others involved in the project have an excellent chance of successfully mediating the dispute.

For example, arguing editors may need to be reminded that their opinions cannot stand alone: Reliable sources should be cited. Similarly, cutting reliably sourced material is typically not acceptable; where two points of view exist, set them side by side using the style "*A* says *X* (reference), but is contradicted by *B* who says *Y* (reference)" to convey a neutral point of view. Most incivility can be curbed by pointing to policy: You really shouldn't call other editors names, nor use aggressive language, nor attack their good faith. Since many edit wars are fueled by an editor's attitude, discussing the issue with an outsider can be easier for the parties than making direct concessions.

The first outside intervention may be when an administrator gets involved. Administrators often end up in the middle of a dispute. If you ever come into conflict with an administrator, remember that Assume Good Faith works both ways. From WP:ADMIN:

> If a user thinks an administrator has acted improperly against them or another editor, they should express their concerns directly to the administrator responsible and try to come to a resolution in an orderly and civil manner. However, if the matter is not resolved between the two parties, users can take further action according to [[Wikipedia:Resolving disputes]].

Handling an Unwanted or Unexpected Dispute

Informal mediation is the ideal solution to edit wars: It is humane, largely face-saving, and provides good documentation detailing how compromise is reached. If informal mediation fails or doesn't take place, the conflict will probably lead to more formal dispute resolution. Therefore, if you fall into some dispute without intending to be in conflict with anyone, keep these two basic things in mind:

▶   Stay calm. A polite approach is not weakness and is likely to help you.

▶   Find someone else to involve (an administrator you have encountered, someone editing in the same area or from its WikiProject, or any experienced Wikipedian).

For more on how to use third parties to defuse difficult situations, see [[Wikipedia:Third opinion]] (shortcut WP:THIRD). Although this page is not part of official policy or process, you can list a problem here and seek help with it.

Ineffective Solutions

Certain solutions to edit wars are against basic policies and so will not be applied. This doesn't prevent them from being proposed, usually by outsiders.

Permanent page protection
The theory is that the messy business and raw edits that go live in a disputed Wikipedia article should be kept under wraps. Some theories on *stable versions* of articles amount to the same thing. This solution goes against the general idea that articles should always be open to improvement.

Leave it to the experts

This is a fairly straight recourse to appeal to authority and, as such, is unacceptable on Wikipedia for reasons explained in Chapter 2. Of course, experts in a field editing under their own names deserve every respect. But content is not going to be accepted simply because an expert vouches for it, and nonexperts are not going to be excluded from the discussion.

POV fork

A *POV fork* is an offshoot of a wiki page that is no longer constrained to conform to a neutral point of view. It may adopt a sympathetic point of view or critical point of view. The creation of a POV fork page is typically suggested in a debate over content on a page with too much negative, critical commentary on the topic. See [[Wikipedia:Content forking]] (shortcut WP: CFORK) for why POV forks aren't allowed on Wikipedia.

Wikinfo

Wikinfo is a wiki site set up by Fred Bauder in July 2003. Fred is a Wikipedian who is still active on the English-language Wikipedia. The idea behind Wikinfo is to encourage the writing of articles that are or resemble POV forks. In other words, Wikinfo is something like Wikipedia, but without the central NPOV policy. It also permits original research, another major difference from Wikipedia. Wikinfo contains over 40,000 articles.

Causes of Content Disputes

Disputes caused by poor wording or misunderstandings can usually be cleared up quickly. For more complicated disputes, you should consider various possible underlying causes for the disagreement. These can potentially undermine the dispute resolution model based on everyone being pleasant and fair-minded.

Disputes over factual content, style, and sourcing may stem from the following things.

Factual correction and absent sources

Someone is trying to correct a fact, or at least change it, when the most accessible reference works and/or media coverage do not support the change. "But I know" is not an acceptable reason, and disputes can arise because of this.

Conflict of interest

Someone wants to change an article because it has a direct impact on his or her person, company, or something else of special interest. This causes trouble with non-neutral editing. Such an issue is likely to persist as long as editors are unwilling to follow Neutral Point of View strictly.

Prominence

Although the Neutral Point of View policy cautions against giving undue weight to material in articles (such as minor scandals in the life of a public figure), the policy does not specify exactly how much prominence should be given. Sometimes edit wars are about the content of an article's lead section; if a politician is charged with fraud, does that overshadow his or her other accomplishments?

Unreliable sources

Disputes over particular sources are not uncommon, especially for controversial topics. For instance, in some cases newspapers can be claimed as reliable sources, but they are not infallible. They contain editorial as well as straight reporting; and particular reporters may be known for partisan views. All this means that some editors will not accept major parts of newspapers and other media as sources. This is usually incorrect: If *The New York Times* has portrayed a story incorrectly, and you are sure of this, you should be able to also use your better source. Set source A and source B side by side, and let the reader judge; articles are improved when alternate views are included. Those who disagree with you would have to see whether the *Times* was the only source or whether other sources back up the original claim. Not relying too much on one source is especially important when citing rumors, blogs, and other marginal sources. Accusations of media bias tend to be unhelpful and to exacerbate content disputes.

Disputes can also occur based on the editing *style* in an article:

Alleged groupthink

A compromise, once reached, should not exclude a newcomer from reopening a discussion: That would be *groupthink* (explained in "Consensus vs. Groupthink" on page 393). The question is, how often should the newcomer change an article against the existing consensus? Repeatedly making such changes is a kind of edit warring, even if accompanied with the correct observation that consensus can always be challenged on Wikipedia.

Low-intensity warring

Articles that an editor dislikes are often subject to extended campaigns of relatively minor edits, which over time degrade the content.

Single-purpose accounts

When an editor creates an account and then only edits one article (or a small group of related articles), he or she may be some kind of *activist* with a narrow focus, rather than an *encyclopedist* who views the Wikipedia

Consensus vs. Groupthink

Groupthink is a social psychology term that means an outcome that claims consensus, but only by sidelining minority views and ignoring drawbacks. The primary meaning of this term concerns bad decisions and how they are made. See [[Groupthink]] for general background. The term *groupthink* is used quite often in Internet forum discussions, as the pejorative form of *consensus*. From the perspective of Wikipedia's content policies, consensus versus groupthink looks like this: Neutral Point of View must not exclude minority significant views that are supported by good sources. On the other hand, articles can exclude any views that are *Original Research* (ideas that people develop themselves), that fail *Verifiability* (don't check out against any mainstream literature), or are otherwise on the fringe. Consensus regarding content should, therefore, be based on broadminded, fair discussion that is also critical about contribution quality. It is not "groupthink" to say that views held by only a few people don't deserve prominent coverage in an article.

project in the larger sense. Such editors may be stubborn. See [[Wikipedia: Single-purpose account]] (shortcut WP:SPA), which has no official status but indicates some considerations important in dispute resolution, where the limited range of edits from such an account usually counts against an editor.

Sockpuppetry

Sockpuppets are secondary accounts, and using them manipulatively to edit causes problems. *Sockpuppetry*—the suspicion that an account is being used to further an edit war, evade blocks, create a false impression of consensus, or other abusive tricks—completely undermines assumptions of good faith. *Meatpuppets* can have the same effect: Getting your brother to edit from another account is meatpuppetry of an obvious kind if he just does what you say.

Finally, some topics are inherently more prone to controversy than others:

Fandom

Pop culture topics can cause problems, as it can be difficult to find reputable source material to substantiate claims. For example, which comic books belong in the Batman canon (if such a thing exists) can never really be determined. And sectarian strife in the heavy metal world has fired up many fans who might otherwise have never contributed to Wikipedia. While some of these matters could be handled by insisting on a neutral point of view, it can be difficult to get fans who are passionate about their point of view to agree.

Imported Internet quarrels

Occasionally, disputes that originated elsewhere will spill into Wikipedia. For instance, in late 2006, an arbitration case opened on Wikipedia concerning [[Derek Smart]], the article about the game author known for *Battlecruiser 3000AD* and other videogames.[1] An intractable controversy that was already long established in other Internet forums about Smart's games migrated to Wikipedia. In these circumstances, influencing the editors involved is almost impossible as they will have mostly made up their mind on the issue and will treat others who disagree in an adversarial fashion.

Controversial topics in the real world

Some conflicts on Wikipedia reflect military, political, religious, ethnic, and nationalist conflicts in our world. This situation has a certain inevitability about it. Wikipedia's policies, particularly No Original Research (WP:NOR), mean that Wikipedia articles should only create a record of the conflicts, not pass judgment on them in any way. Partisans may well want to take control of Wikipedia's articles. But the fundamental exclusions of non-neutral editing and original research, like the drawing of historical conclusions ahead of the historians, should block their ambitions. Because the world has no shortage of those who would like to use Wikipedia as a propaganda place, Wikipedia can only do a limited amount by identifying and banning problem editors in these areas. Real-world conflicts can be very contentious; edit any topic that you know to be generally controversial carefully.

Case Study: Gdańsk

What happens when a dispute rooted in real-world issues occurs on a global project that strives to be neutral and fair toward all points of view without cultural bias? Even disputes with a small locus can have wide implications. A particularly salient example is one that arose during the early days of the site concerning nomenclature for the Polish city of Gdańsk, formerly known as Danzig. To explain the issue, Danzig is an *exonym* (placename in another language, in this case German) and is the historically accurate name for the city during certain periods.

The normal Wikipedia approach to historical writing about places whose names have changed is to use the "P in Q (now R in S)" style. For example, writing "New Amsterdam in New Netherland (now New York City, USA)" is helpful to the general reader and appropriate for an article dealing with the first half of the 17th century when the future city of New York was a Dutch settlement. This is an example of an English exonym: Nieuw Amsterdam and Nieuw-Nederland were the Dutch names.

Eastern Europe experienced numerous boundary and language changes during the 20th century. Real-world tensions arising from nationalist and ethnic feeling cannot be discounted in Wikipedia. On the other hand, the project's aim

---

[1] See *http://en.wikipedia.org/wiki/Wikipedia:Requests_for_arbitration/Derek_Smart*.

is to compile a useful reference work. Therefore, editors should use *historical exonyms* to aid reader comprehension wherever possible. The common usage in standard textbooks and scholarly works is at least relevant.

Another example is that of Burma, which renamed itself Myanmar in 1989; the Wikipedia article was under the title *Myanmar* and searches for *Burma* redirected to the Myanmar article. This reflected the usage in many typical English-language news organizations, but in late 2007 a different view prevailed on the site after greater media coverage, and now Burma is used. For Côte d'Ivoire, the official name as of 1985, you'll find greater uncertainty since news organizations sometimes use Ivory Coast, the older English name that has not died ut. At one point this caused a dispute. In this case Wikipedia's basic policy of using the most common English name is tempered by the wish to be reasonably correct, though not pedantic (République de Côte d'Ivoire would be more correct, but encyclopedias don't need to use this full title). In the case of Mumbai, formerly Bombay, the name changed officially in 1995 and has been adopted on Wikipedia. In reporting on current affairs, therefore, the trend in English has been to drop exonyms, but not always. The general acceptance of present-day changes, however, doesn't address the proper conventions for historical exonyms.

In the case of Gdańsk/Danzig, the particular problem of referring to places now in Poland, but which were in Germany before 1945, dogged the English-language Wikipedia almost from the outset. Danzig had a particular and unusual status as a free city between 1918 and 1939. Given its complex history before that, rival proposals arose for a naming convention. Over a period of years, a dispute over the article title festered, and no consensus was reached. As is usual in such situations, editors tended to try to establish "facts on the ground" rather than to engage in patient discussions. The dispute was long-running and contentious, as you can see in the 11 pages of talk page archives for the article, most of which deal with the naming controversy.

Unusually, the dispute over Gdańsk/Danzig was put to a general vote, with multiple questions. This was used as a clarifying measure and a way to end the intractable dispute by sorting out the many potential options and gathering consensus in the community and among interested editors. The vote closed in March 2005 and produced a complicated solution. From [[Talk:Gdańsk/Vote]]:

* For Gdańsk, use the name Danzig between 1308 and 1945.

* For Gdansk, use the name Gdańsk before 1300 and after 1945.

* In biographies of clearly German persons, the name should be used in the form Danzig (Gdańsk) and later Danzig exclusively.

* In biographies of clearly Polish persons, the name should be used in the form Gdańsk (Danzig) and later Gdańsk exclusively.

* For Gdańsk and other locations that share a history between Germany and Poland, the first reference of one name in an article should also include a reference to other names, e.g., Danzig (now Gdańsk, Poland) or Gdańsk (Danzig). An English language reference that primarily uses this name should be provided on the talk page if a dispute arises.

The voting produced clear results, except for the period from 1466 to 1793: The majority voting for Danzig was not very substantial, so you can't say a consensus was reached.

Votes do not serve to create consensus: A vote may, however, happily confirm that a minority objection is only narrowly supported. A vote also cannot close down an issue entirely, since latecomers may rightly feel they had no chance to express a view. This particular instance of polling to deal with a complex issue about which feelings are strong and which connect to wider themes was considered a success for this unusual technique, which worked to resolve an unusually contentious dispute—at the time, a *Signpost* article referred to the Gdańsk dispute as "arguably the largest and longest-running article content dispute on Wikipedia."[2] Most disputes do not use explicit votes, however, relying more on editors judging the strength and quality of the particular arguments being made.

Further Reading

http://en.wikipedia.org/wiki/Wikipedia:Consensus   The policy on building consensus

http://en.wikipedia.org/wiki/Wikipedia:Edit_war   The policy against edit warring

http://en.wikipedia.org/wiki/Wikipedia:Three-revert_rule   The Three-Revert Rule on edit warring

http://en.wikipedia.org/wiki/Wikipedia:Staying_cool_when_the_editing_gets_hot   Essay on keeping your cool during editing disputes

http://meta.wikimedia.org/wiki/The_Wrong_Version   An essay about the wrong version always being the one protected

http://wikinfo.org/   Wikinfo

http://en.wikipedia.org/wiki/Talk:Gdansk/Vote   The final outcome of the long Gdańsk/Danzig debate

http://en.wikipedia.org/wiki/Wikipedia:Naming_conventions_%28geographic_names%29   The conventions for naming places, generally

---

[2] See *http://en.wikipedia.org/wiki/Wikipedia:Wikipedia_Signpost/2005-03-07/Gdansk_or_Danzig*.

Resolving Disputes Between Editors

In the worst disputes, Wikipedia employs *formal dispute resolution*. These formal processes reverse normal discussion conventions: Instead of discussing the article content, formal processes provide pages to discuss the behavior of the editors involved in a dispute to try to resolve problems. In other words, the *content is not judged*, but *editor behavior is scrutinized closely*. This is a last resort. Disputes between editors should be resolved without formal processes whenever possible since informal, civil discussions offer the best results—on Wikipedia, try to stay out of court.

Despite this good advice implicit in the Wikipedia ethos from the start, some disputes are hard to resolve or can escalate over time. Wikipedia has a progression of processes, ending in arbitration. Currently about 100 cases go to arbitration each year; these cases can be tracked at the Wikipedia Signpost (shortcut WP: POST), which gives a weekly summary of each case.

Dispute Resolution Processes

The vast majority of disputes are resolved through regular discussion and consensus building. Occasionally, a third party, such as an administrator, may step in to try and mediate a public dispute. If this process does not resolve the dispute, you can try one of the following remedies.

Request for Comment

The *Request for Comment (RfC)* process creates a page on which the community at large can contribute views regarding a specific complaint, which may be about editor conduct, articles, content types, or policies. For an RfC on an editor's conduct, the idea is that general grumbling about an editor can be focused and clarified. The RfC is mostly evidence-led: Discussion should center on specific versions that illustrate the alleged problem. The RfC process allows the issue to be discussed and results in no judicial conclusion. After the RfC, everyone, including the editor about whom a complaint is being made, should understand the reason for the difficulty, which can then hopefully be resolved.

Mediation

Mediation is a somewhat different approach, though it also clarifies the cause of a dispute. Involved parties have to consent to the mediation process. In mediation, experienced Wikipedians try to delineate the issue more closely and through formal discussion with the involved parties (on a dedicated subpage of the mediation project page) reach some compromise that has a chance of working in practice.

Arbitration

Arbitration is a last resort. Here, an elected, formal body of editors will look at both sides of a dispute, sometimes imposing remedies (sanctions) on an editor about whom a complaint is being made or the editor bringing a complaint. Settling your differences with another editor before a case is brought to arbitration is best. Most cases accepted for arbitration have already been through the RfC or mediation processes. Arbitration rulings are binding and enforced by administrative actions if needed.

The Nature of Formal Evidence

The approach in all of the formal dispute-resolution processes listed above relies on other editors reviewing *evidence*: What actually happened? Most evidence, in turn, is based on the *diff*—individual edits and the differences between versions of a page. Since all edits are kept and traceable to their authors (even edits to deleted articles are visible to administrators), the site is extremely transparent when it comes to tracking editor behavior even months later, creating a great incentive to follow Wikipedia's policies and guidelines, even when involved in a controversial dispute—*especially* when involved in a controversial dispute!

Often an editor will say or imply, "That editor is behaving badly and those edits make Wikipedia look bad, so I'm going to behave badly too." This attitude is wrong, dead wrong. Excess reverts are just one common aspect of editor behavior discussed in content disputes. All individuals are expected to behave civilly and are judged on their own edits. Any time you behave badly, the diffs may be used against you later.

Policies like the requirement to interact civilly (WP:CIVIL) are most important during quarrels: Use civil language and be level-headed and reasonable when discussing disagreements. Editors using a bull-headed approach, who may make allegations of bad faith and accuse their opponents of conspiracy, are seen as self-righteous and aggressive and often end up violating basic policies. Passionate views that don't respect those who might think otherwise lead to editors betraying the norms of the Wikipedia community.

Arbitration Committee

The worst onsite disputes may end with the *Arbitration Committee (ArbCom)*, an elected body of up to 15 editors who review cases of editor disputes in a formal process. The arbitration decision on a case is nearly the final step in dispute resolution on the English-language Wikipedia. Cases are presented by the editors involved or by other interested parties; the Arbitration Committee reviews them and chooses whether to accept the case. Article content is not judged in arbitration cases, only editor behavior.

The decisions are intended to serve Wikipedia's mission. The ArbCom is the highest court on Wikipedia and, in fact, close to being the only real court because the lower levels of formal dispute resolution are still ways to gather community opinion, not strictly to evaluate evidence. The English-language Wikipedia ArbCom only deals with issues on the English-language Wikipedia; problems on any other project must be resolved on that project.

An arbitration decision relies on evidence presented, takes several weeks to prepare, and consists of three parts. These decisions may be appealed to Jimmy Wales, but few appeals are successful. The three parts of the decision are Principles, Findings of Fact, and Remedies.

The *Principles* are of potential interest to anyone closely involved in the management of Wikipedia. They are good indications on how existing policy may be implemented because they select ideas by considering policies broadly (the whole stock of policies and guidelines along with other writings) to explain how a decision is made and how the decision fits into a larger picture of editor conduct, good and bad. The principles are not policy or legislation since the community as a whole decides on policy using the guidelines explained in Chapter 13, and they are not binding precedents for future decisions because Wikipedia itself changes.

The *Findings of Fact*, in comparison, are largely a transparent set of judgments based on how editors behaved on the site backed up by the different versions. These findings generally do not take into account editor conduct elsewhere (in other Internet forums, for instance); editors who can reliably be identified in other contexts, however, will be cited if they, for example, blog about Wikipedia or invite others to edit.

The *Remedies* are the effective judicial outcome of the case. They consist of the application of a now-standard collection of sanctions; Figure 14-2 shows the remedies section from the "Derek Smart" arbitration case. Remedies range from bans from the site for periods of up to one year; topic bans, disallowing the editing of all articles in some definite area; various kinds of paroles for civility and reverting; and the loss of privileges (notably administrative powers). Administrators enforce the Remedies.

Arbitration decisions may, in complex cases, run to as many as 50 points (in other words, the total number of Principles, Findings, and Remedies), each of them voted on separately by the Arbitration Committee. The decisions are pragmatic rather than punitive and, despite all the judicial trappings, do not treat Wikipedia policy as a strictly defined body of law.

Anyone may bring an arbitration case; though, as previously mentioned, most cases must go through other dispute resolution processes before being accepted. Anyone may also comment on arbitration cases in progress. Find out more at [[Wikipedia:Arbitration]].

The site is policed by administrators and ordinary editors, and the Arbitration Committee considers only cases brought to it; more cases are rejected than accepted. Fortunately, most editors don't need to pay close attention to

Remedies   [edit]

Note: All remedies that refer to a period of time, for example to a ban of X months or a revert parole of Y months, are to run concurrently unless otherwise stated.

Limitation on reverts by single-purpose accounts   [edit]

1) For a period of six months, no single-purpose account may revert any edit made to the Derek Smart article. Any single-purpose account which performs such a revert may be kindly informed of this restriction and given the opportunity either to lay out their concerns on the article's discussion page or to e-mail the volunteers who deal with requests from article subjects. Any editor so informed who continues to revert the article may be blocked at the discretion of any administrator. All blocks to be logged at Wikipedia:Requests for arbitration/Derek Smart#Log of blocks and bans.

Editors are encouraged to use judgment and discretion in enforcement of this remedy, rather than implementing it in a mechanical fashion. The Committee would prefer that Wikipedians who have already had significant involvement in the development of the article leave enforcement of this remedy to their peers.

Passed 8 to 0, 23:25, 2 March 2007 (UTC)

Referred for cleanup   [edit]

2) The article is urgently referred to the Wikipedia editing community at large for cleanup, evaluation of sources, and adherence to NPOV. This request should be publicized on such noticeboards, mailing lists, and IRC channels as are necessary until the article receives due attention.

Passed 4 to 0, with 4 abstentions, 23:25, 2 March 2007 (UTC)

Supreme Cmdr   [edit]

3.1) For personal attacks and edit warring, Supreme Cmdr (talk · contribs · deleted contribs · logs · block user · block log) is banned for one year.

Passed 6 to 1, 23:25, 2 March 2007 (UTC)

Supreme Cmdr and other surrogates   [edit]

7) Supreme Cmdr and other surrogates of Derek Smart are banned from editing Derek Smart. They may edit the talk page.

Passed 6 to 0, 23:25, 2 March 2007 (UTC)

Derek Smart   [edit]

8) Any user may fully apply the principles and practices of Wikipedia:Biographies of living persons to Derek Smart. This may include deletion of the article and its history as well as its talk pages and archives and the project pages and talk pages of this Arbitration proceeding.

Passed 5 to 1, 23:25, 2 March 2007 (UTC)

FIGURE 14-2: *The Remedies section from the Derek Smart arbitration case*

arbitration proceedings. Arbitration rules only directly impact highly intractable disputes, and those are usually within small topic areas.

Arbitration cases do provide a more complete view of the seamy side of the English-language Wikipedia than you can find anywhere else. The Arbitration Committee gradually removes the most problematic editors from the site or endorses bans made by administrators. Arbitration reporting is transparent, and you can find links to the diffs showing who did what. This information is not only public to editors but also to the whole online world (including Wikipedia's critics and media folk interested in Wikipedia stories, two groups that overlap significantly).

Further Reading

http://en.wikipedia.org/wiki/Wikipedia:Dispute_resolution   The policy on and formal steps of dispute resolution

http://en.wikipedia.org/wiki/Wikipedia:Request_for_comment   The Request for Comment process

http://en.wikipedia.org/wiki/Wikipedia:Mediation   The policy on formal mediation

http://en.wikipedia.org/wiki/Wikipedia:Requests_for_mediation   Where to request formal mediation

http://en.wikipedia.org/wiki/Wikipedia:Arbitration_Committee   The Wikipedia Arbitration Committee

http://en.wikipedia.org/wiki/Wikipedia:Requests_for_arbitration   Making arbitration requests

Blocks and Bans

Blocking of user accounts, IP numbers, and IP ranges may be carried out by any administrator. A *block* simply means that an account or IP number cannot edit the site except for its own user talk page. Because a block has no effect on reading Wikipedia's article and project pages, it represents a temporary administrative suspension of the right to participate in the project. Blocks are most often used to stop ongoing vandalism and to provide a "cooling-off" period for editors who are behaving badly.

This matter should not be treated lightly, though. The Blocking policy is a formal policy document. All blocks are logged, and the blocking administrator must give a reason for the block. Any administrator blocking a user is accountable for the block and should be responsive to queries about it. Administrator discretion, for example, in policing various conduct paroles imposed by the Arbitration Committee (such as an injunction to not edit certain topics), is quite broad, and administrators are constantly making judgment calls in blocking matters. Therefore blocked users may lodge appeals against blocks.

Short blocks indicate that an editor is transgressing site policy. A first offense is normally—at most—a 24-hour block. For the first instance, a block will not be total, so the editor can still edit his or her user talk page (even if editing from an IP number). The editor can also email people through his or her user page. If you receive a short block, use these privileges to communicate wisely. Blocks are not generally given without warning; several standardized series of user talk page templates exist (at [[Wikipedia:Template message/User talk namespace]]) to warn against inappropriate behavior. These are supposed to be placed before a block is issued by those monitoring vandalism.

The reason for a block is entered into the block log by the administrator issuing the block, when setting the block period. Block logs accumulate information over time. To inspect block logs, either for accounts or for IP numbers, go to [[Special:Log/block]] and fill in the form with the account name you are interested in. You can check for IP numbers whether or not you are editing from that IP yourself. For example, most vandalism on Wikipedia arises from the use of shared school computers. School IT staff can use the logs to monitor problem editing from their machines and find out who to contact on Wikipedia in case editing is blocked.

How to (Oops) Block a Whole Country from Wikipedia

The entire Gulf state of Qatar was blocked briefly in early 2007. This only happened because Qatar connects to the Web through a single IP address. (See a story from *USA Today* about the blocking of Qatar at *http://www.usatoday.com/tech/news/2007-01-04-wikipedia-qatar_x.htm*.)

Short Blocks

Remember that while Wikipedia maintains an open-door policy, that door gets closed to troublesome contributors. Editing rights are a privilege, not an entitlement. Blocked editors can still read the site while a *time out* has been imposed on their editing. They can, for example, research in depth for future additions to an article of interest. Perhaps that's expecting too much, but if you're blocked for a day or so, you can make a favorable impression by returning to work with something to offer the project.

Here's a list of what you might do with your time away from the site:

▸ Take a long walk outside.

▸ Spend time with your family or friends.

▸ Find a new article to improve.

▸ Send polite emails or apologies to the administrator or editors involved with your dispute.

▸ Go to your local library and find better sources to substantiate your claims.

The need for patience and perspective should not have to be pointed out, but often people simply can't accept a short break from editing. When blocked for a short period, *don't* do these things:

▸ Personalize the issue by vowing that the blocking administrator will pay for it.

▸ Send rude emails.

▸ Obsess about a particular article and how you'll impose your view on it.

- ▶ Decide that the first thing you'll do when getting back on the site is exactly what got you blocked.
- ▶ Create a sockpuppet account or otherwise get around the block to start editing.

Longer Blocks

Longer blocks and permanent bans are not Wikipedia's first line of defense but may be imposed due to destructive or disruptive behavior. A month-long block might be applied in the case of a returning vandal, for example, an account or IP number with an accumulated history of malicious edits. Blocks are not punitive (a misconception) but implemented to protect the project.

For blocks longer than a few days, the blocked editor may want to request a review. The procedure is explained at [[Wikipedia:Appealing a block]] (shortcut WP:APB). A blocked editor initiates the review by placing the template {{unblock|*give reason here*}} at the bottom of his or her user talk page. This will trigger a review by a different administrator.

Ahead of an appeal, the blocked editor should think through his or her position. The difference between edit warring as disruptive behavior and as an attempt to straighten out what an article says may depend on who is considering the issue. The blocked editor should try to separate out policy matters, for example, on reverting and civility, from content matters.

In some cases [[Wikipedia:Autoblock]] is relevant. This mechanism for blocking IP ranges can affect an account even after it is unblocked according to the block log.

Bans

Bans are more serious than blocks because they signify that a formal decision has been made to exclude an editor from the site. A ban may be for period of time, or it may be indefinite. Wikipedia has two kinds of bans.

A ban handed down by the Arbitration Committee is for a time period of at most one year. A *community ban* means an indefinite block has been imposed such that no other administrator is willing to lift it based on the facts of the case. Community bans are typically blocks that occur after a series of other blocks have been made that have not been successfully appealed by the editor in question.

An ultimate appeal against either kind of ban may be made to the Arbitration Committee. Making an immediate appeal to the ArbCom is not usually worthwhile, however; the banned editor and the blocking administrator should discuss the ban first to clarify the issue. The Arbitration Committee judges cases by considering the facts in addition to the editor's previous contributions to the site. An editor with few meaningful contributions to articles is unlikely to be successful in appealing a community ban.

If a block is imposed to enforce a ban after an arbitration ruling, trying to get the blocking administrator to lift it is pointless. The ban can in this case be reviewed by the Arbitration Committee.

Further Reading

http://en.wikipedia.org/wiki/Wikipedia:Blocking_policy   The official blocking policy

http://en.wikipedia.org/wiki/Wikipedia:Appealing_a_block   Information on how to appeal a block

http://en.wikipedia.org/wiki/Wikipedia:Banning_policy   The official banning policy

Summary

This chapter should make it clear that most disputes are settled in informal ways. That's how it should be. Good editors are only on the site because they think Wikipedia's project is important and worthwhile. Disputes should not take up too much time, and proportion and perspective are needed to keep them from doing so. The few formal dispute resolution mechanisms should be entered into with good faith and reserved for only the most intractable arguments. If you have a quarrel with another editor, take a resourceful approach to sorting out your mutual difficulties—this will probably pay off in terms of time saved.

Conclusion to Part III

You are encouraged to be bold as a contributor and to become an involved and communicative Wikipedian. To do this, you will eventually need to understand site policies as well as site culture.

Wikipedia should not be judged by its most difficult content quarrels; these affect only a tiny proportion of articles. Most difficulties are solved through good sense and good will.

WP is a standard abbreviation for *Wikipedia*, but it also can stand for *Work in Progress*, *We're the People*, *Wide Perspective*, or *Worldwide Project*. We're writing this book with the simple hope that as an informed editor, you can move Wikipedia forward more effectively.

## PART IV

Other Projects

15 200 Languages and Counting

So far we've concentrated on the English-language version of Wikipedia, but Wikipedias have been created in over 250 languages, each representing its own individual community and unique collection of content. A common assumption is that articles in the other Wikipedias are basically translated from English, but this couldn't be more misleading: These sites all create their own content with translations only playing a minor role. Taken as a whole, the Wikimedia projects count as one of the most comprehensively multilingual and global projects on the Internet today.[1]

---

[1] Byte Level Research publishes an annual globalization report card that regularly ranks Wikipedia second in the world after Google for "how successfully companies developed web sites for international markets." See *http://bytelevel.com/news/reportcard2008.html*.

The English-language Wikipedia is the largest site, but other Wikipedias are also impressively large: Fifteen of the other-language editions of Wikipedia have over 100,000 articles. These very active sites often have high growth rates and are technically innovative. If you visit *http://wikipedia.org/* (Figure 15-1), you'll see that it serves as the gateway to the other language editions of Wikipedia.

In this chapter, we'll explore what being global means for Wikipedia, by now a truly international and connected project. What are other-language Wikipedias like, and how can you get involved in them? We'll also talk about language issues as they relate to the English-language Wikipedia, including displaying foreign-language characters, writing about topics from a global perspective, and adding links to other-language versions of Wikipedia.

Languages and Scripts

A very early goal of the project was to make Wikipedia multilingual; Jimmy Wales first proposed a German-language version of Wikipedia in early 2001. By May 2001, within months of the English-language Wikipedia's founding, Wikipedias had been started in Catalan, Chinese, German, French, Hebrew, Italian, Spanish, Japanese, Russian, Portuguese, and Esperanto.

New language editions continue to be added, as described in "The Long Tail of Languages" below. As of mid-2008, the largest Wikipedias were in English (2.3 million articles), German (755,000 articles), French (665,000 articles), Polish (505,000 articles), and Japanese (494,000 articles). Size alone should not be taken as the only criterion of prominence, however. For instance, the Chinese-language Wikipedia has often attracted media attention, in part because the Chinese government continues to partially limit access to the site within China (as part of the so-called Great Firewall of China). Despite this, the Chinese-language Wikipedia has more than 178,000 articles, written in large part by the many Chinese editors in Taiwan, Hong Kong, and outside East Asia.

Wikipedia has at least 77 language editions with over 10,000 articles and 155 with over 1,000. By the time a Wikipedia reaches 1,000 articles, it usually has a consistent approach, a self-regenerating community, and a basic policy structure in place. The remaining sites are just getting started, with a handful of articles and active contributors, as the next section explains.

The Long Tail of Languages

In the generally optimistic Wikipedia way, many language versions of Wikipedia have been started but, at this time, have only a few hundred articles. What function do these sites serve? No one could call them a comprehensive encyclopedic resource yet. The truth is that they are just beginning wikis—much like the English-language Wikipedia in 2001 or 2002. If you do speak one of these languages fluently enough to contribute, working on a smaller Wikipedia can be a great deal of fun. You'll find the culture of a small site with few users is very different from the giant English-language Wikipedia, which has so many customs, rules, and (obviously) so many more articles already written. Even on the small

WIKIPEDIA

English
The Free Encyclopedia
2 341 000+ articles

Deutsch
Die freie Enzyklopädie
739 000+ Artikel

Français
L'encyclopédie libre
649 000+ articles

Polski
Wolna encyklopedia
492 000+ haseł

日本語
フリー百科事典
485 000+ 記事

Italiano
L'enciclopedia libera
442 000+ voci

Nederlands
De vrije encyclopedie
431 000+ artikelen

Português
A enciclopédia livre
372 000+ artigos

Español
La enciclopedia libre
353 000+ artículos

Svenska
Den fria encyklopedin
281 000+ artiklar

search · suche · rechercher · szukaj · 検索 · ricerca · zoeken · busca · buscar
sök · поиск · 搜索 · søk · haku · suk · cerca · căutare · ara · пошук

English

100 000+

Català · Deutsch · English · Español · Français · Italiano · Nederlands · 日本語 · Norsk (bokmål) · Polski · Português · Русский · Română · Suomi · Svenska · Türkçe · Українська · Volapük · 中文

10 000+

العربية · Asturianu · Kreyòl Ayisyen · Azərbaycan / آذربایجان دیلی · বাংলা · Беларуская (Акадэмічная) · বিষ্ণুপ্রিয়া মণিপুরী · Bosanski · Brezhoneg · Български · Česky · Cymraeg · Dansk · Eesti · Ελληνικά · Esperanto · Euskara · فارسی · Galego · 한국어 · हिन्दी · Hrvatski · Ido · Bahasa Indonesia · Íslenska · עברית · Basa Jawa · ქართული · Kurdî / كوردی · Latina · Lumbaart · Latviešu · Lëtzebuergesch · Lietuvių · Magyar · Македонски · मराठी · Bahasa Melayu · नेपाल भाषा · Norsk (nynorsk) · Nnapulitano · Occitan · Piemontèis · Plattdüütsch · Shqip · Sicilianu · Simple English · Sinugboanon · Slovenčina · Slovenščina · Српски · Srpskohrvatski / Српскохрватски · Basa Sunda · Tagalog · தமிழ் · తెలుగు · ไทย · Tiếng Việt · Walon

1 000+

Afrikaans · Alemannisch · ܐܪܡܝܐ · Aragonés · Armãneashce · Arpitan · Bân-lâm-gú · Basa Banyumasan · Беларуская (Тарашкевіца) · भोजपुरी · Boarisch · Corsu · Чӑваш · Deitsch · ديور · Eald Englisc · Føroyskt · Frysk · Furlan · Gaeilge · Gaelg · Gàidhlig · 古文 / 文言文 · 'Ōlelo Hawai'i · Հայերեն · Hornjoserbsce · Ilokano · Interlingua · Ирон æвзаг · ಕನ್ನಡ · Kapampangan · Kaszëbsczi · Kernewek · ភាសាខ្មែរ · Ladino / לאדינו · Ligure · Limburgs · Lingála · മലയാളം · Malti · Māori · Монгол · Nāhuatlahtōlli · Nedersaksisch · नेपाली · Nouormand · Novial · O'zbek · پاکتو · Pangasinán · پښتو · Қазақша · Ripoarisch · Rumantsch · Runa Simi · संस्कृतम् · Sámegiella · Scots · Kiswahili · Tarandíne · Tatarça · Точикй · Lea faka-Tonga · Türkmen · اردو · Vèneto · Võro · West-Vlams · Winaray · 吳語 · ייִדיש · 粵語 · Yorùbá · Zazaki · Žemaitėška

100+

ᏣᎳᎩ · Avañe'ẽ · Авар · Aymara · Bamanankan · Башкорт · Bikol Central · བོད་ཡིག · Chavacano de Zamboanga · Diné Bizaad · Dolnoserbski · Emigliàn-Rumagnòl · Eʋegbe · ગુજરાતી · كليبي · ਪੰਜਾਬੀ · 客家語 · Igbo · ᐃᓄᒃᑎᑐᑦ / Inuktitut · Interlingue · कश्मीरी · کشمیری · Kongo · Кыргызча · ᐊᓂᔑᓈᐯᒧᐎᓐ · lojban · Malagasy · Māzərūni / مازرونی · Ming-dĕng-ngṳ̄ · Молдовеняскэ · ᐅᒃᒃ · Ekakairũ Naoero · Nēhiyawēwin / ᓀᐦᐃᔭᐍᐏᐣ · Norfuk / Pitkern · Нохчийн · ଓଡ଼ିଆ · Afaan Oromoo · অসমীয়া · ਪੰਜਾਬੀ · پنجابی · Papiamentu · Qırımtatarca · Romani · रोमानी · Kinyarwanda · Gagana Sāmoa · Sardu · Seeltersk · سنڌي · سنڌي · Словѣньскъ · Af Soomaali · SiSwati · Reo Tahiti · Taqbaylit · Tetun · ትግርኛ · Tok Pisin · ᏣᏫ · Удмурт · تۇيغۇرچە · Uyghur · Tshivenḓa · Wollof · isiXhosa · Zeêuws · isiZulu

Other languages · Weitere Sprachen · 他の言語 · Kompletna lista języków · 其他语言 · Другие языки · Aliaj lingvoj · 다른 언어 · Ngôn ngữ khác

FIGURE 15-1: Wikipedia.org portal page, showing all the languages

Wikipedias, articles are, for the most part, not translations but instead newly written pieces in that particular language.

Sometimes other-language Wikipedias are small because they are very new or because not many people speak the language, and thus, the potential contributor base is small. Alternatively, Wikipedias may exist in widely spoken languages that do not have a strong presence on the Internet, such as Telugu, the third-most spoken language on the Indian subcontinent and one of the top fifteen spoken languages in the world (Figure 15-2 shows the front page of the Telugu Wikipedia). These languages may not have a strong written tradition, or perhaps Internet access is limited in the areas where most native speakers live. Some of these Wikipedias quite possibly constitute the largest online corpus for their language; in any case, they represent the language online in a place where others can easily find it.

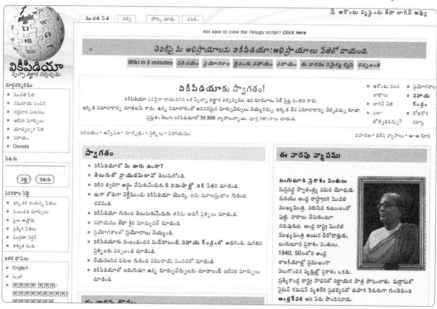

FIGURE 15-2: *The front page of the Telugu edition of Wikipedia at* http://te.wikipedia.org, *from April 2008*

The range of languages represented by Wikipedia is very large. Wikipedias exist in constructed languages (*Esperanto* [eo] and *Volapük* [vo] with their internationalist aim) and significant dead languages (*Latin* [la] and *Old Church Slavonic* [cu]), which have no native speakers.[2] (The two-letter codes are language identifier codes, explained in "Links Between Languages" on page 414). The issue of language preservation, when few native speakers of a smaller language are living, is not an explicit Wikimedia Foundation goal. But, on the other hand, providing free information to all people in the world, regardless of their language, certainly

_____

2 "Veni, Vidi, Wiki: Latin Isn't Dead On 'Vicipaedia'" (*Wall Street Journal*, September 29, 2007); see *http://online.wsj.com/public/article/SB119103413731143589.html.*

is, and many of the smaller Wikipedias represent the *only* online reference works in that language. In some cases, Wikipedia may be the *only encyclopedia* in a particular language! Despite this diversity, the 250+ languages already supported by Wikimedia come nowhere close to representing all of the world's active languages. SIL, creators of the *Ethnologue*, a standard reference work for languages and one of the maintainers of the ISO standard for identifying languages, suggests the total count of world languages is closer to 5,000.

Therefore, new language editions are still being proposed and started. How does this work? The key requirement is that you can provide evidence of a potential active user base. Active volunteers for the new Wikipedia will be needed to provide the content and watch the wiki for spam and vandalism. Wikipedia has a procedure for beginning a new language project, and all new requests must be approved by the site developers, who can create the project. Meta, the Wikimedia wiki discussed in Chapter 17, has a special page for making these requests. Once a request has been submitted, a committee on new language editions, or *langcom*, reviews the request. Someone fluent in the language must commit to translating the Mediawiki interface (including the text of tabs, buttons, and key pages) for the new project. You can see (and participate in) some new projects in the translation process at *http://incubator.wikimedia.org/*.

The Klingon Wars

A Wikipedia existed in Klingon, the language used by the Klingon race in the fictional Star Trek universe, from 2004 to 2005. After some debate, Jimmy Wales decided to close the site, and the decision was implemented on-the-spot at Wikimania 2005. As the History of the Klingon Wikipedia page on Meta tells it, "The existence of the Klingon project was divisive and led to entrenched debates over fairness and parity with other languages, and particularly with other constructed languages [. . .] Work was limited by the fact that the Klingon vocabulary is closed and incomplete." The content was ultimately moved to a new site hosted by Wikia at *http://klingon.wikia.com* in December 2006, and it had 161 articles as of July 2008.

Getting Involved in Other Languages

The challenge of editing on another language Wikipedia can be interesting and worthwhile, even if you only have a minimal knowledge of the language in question. All the Wikipedias use the same MediaWiki engine, so buttons, navigation links, and icons have familiar functions, regardless of the labels on them.

One way to help out is to watch content on a small wiki. Simply remember to check Recent Changes every so often on a slow-growing wiki, and you can help keep spam and poor contributions to a minimum. To adopt a wiki, you really need only be familiar enough with Wikipedia's standards to recognize definitely unhelpful changes. Seeing the fresh edits will help you to direct new editors to multilingual meta-pages and to identify good new editors. The *wikipedia-L* mailing list is for discussions of general Wikipedia-related issues in any language.

At this time, you must create an account for each new language project you wish to work on. This is changing with the introduction in mid-2008 of *single-user login*, sometimes called *unified login*, which users can use to link their existing accounts across all Wikimedia projects (see "Project Accounts and Single-User Login" on page 420 for more). All Wikipedias should allow anonymous editing, however, which may be easier if you just want to make a few changes. If you edit when not logged in, watch out for *compulsory previews* when you try to save: Click what you suspect must be the Show Preview button.

What about adding an edit summary in another language? Projects may vary on this. For instance, an edit summary is compulsory on the Polish Wikipedia; otherwise, you won't be able to save unless you're logged in. On the Portuguese Wikipedia, if you're not logged in you must fill in a CAPTCHA box before saving your edit. If you're prepared for these occasional extra formalities, editing Wikipedias in other languages is actually very easy.

Remember that policies, guidelines, and community practices may vary a great deal between different language communities. Although some basic principles—NPOV, civility, and the GFDL license, for instance—are fundamental to all Wikimedia projects, how procedures are carried out is decided by the project community. You'll often find that a smaller project has fewer rules and guidelines and debate tends to be more thoughtful than on larger projects that receive more outside attention.

Script Support

With a full range of languages comes a full range of writing systems: Greek, Cyrillic, Arabic, Hebrew, ideograms, and other less-familiar ones. Even languages

Embassies

You can find a list of people who speak various languages and participate in the English-language Wikipedia and are willing to help with questions in those other languages at [[Wikipedia:Local Embassy]]. This page forms part of the *Embassy system*, a special place on each Wikipedia for visitors speaking other languages. The particular language Wikipedia is described, and visitors can ask questions or request help. You can find a list of all Embassies at *http://meta.wikimedia.org/wiki/Wikimedia_Embassy*. This list contains links to each embassy, along with the names of contributors on that wiki who speak other languages and are willing to help out.

that use the basic Roman alphabet may use accents and other diacritics. Scripts of all kinds are also used and integrated into the English-language version of Wikipedia, for instance, to give original forms of proper names. Figure 15-3 shows an example in the article [[Mohandas Karamchand Gandhi]], which uses Gujarati and Sanskrit scripts in the lead section as well as IPA pronunciation symbols.

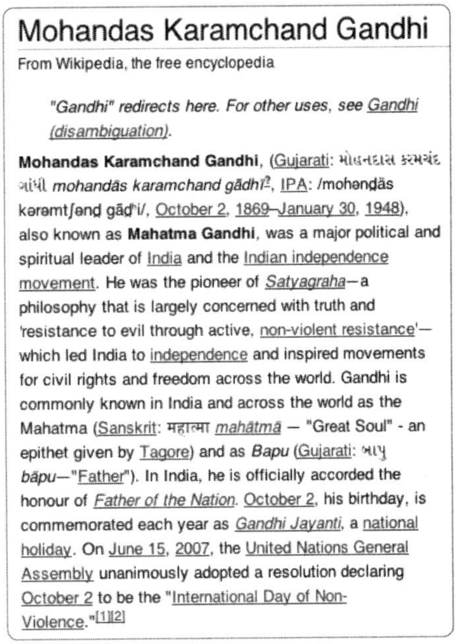

Any one of these scripts may fail to display properly in your web browser if you don't have the necessary fonts installed. If you're viewing text that you don't have font support for, you may see small boxes or question marks instead of the correct characters. If this is the case, you need to download and install the proper font. [[Help:Multilingual support]] collects information and some advice about font support. This page has a chart where you can compare images of some of the common problematic fonts (such as East Asian character sets) to what you see

Mohandas Karamchand Gandhi

From Wikipedia, the free encyclopedia

> *"Gandhi" redirects here. For other uses, see Gandhi (disambiguation).*

Mohandas Karamchand Gandhi, (Gujarati: મોહનદાસ કરમચંદ ગાંધી *mohandās karamchand gādhī*, IPA: /mohənɖəs kərəmtʃənɖ gɑ̃d̪ʱi/, October 2, 1869–January 30, 1948), also known as **Mahatma Gandhi**, was a major political and spiritual leader of India and the Indian independence movement. He was the pioneer of *Satyagraha*—a philosophy that is largely concerned with truth and 'resistance to evil through active, non-violent resistance'— which led India to independence and inspired movements for civil rights and freedom across the world. Gandhi is commonly known in India and across the world as the Mahatma (Sanskrit: महात्मा *mahātmā* — "Great Soul" - an epithet given by Tagore) and as *Bapu* (Gujarati: બાપુ *bāpu*—"Father"). In India, he is officially accorded the honour of *Father of the Nation*. October 2, his birthday, is commemorated each year as *Gandhi Jayanti*, a national holiday. On June 15, 2007, the United Nations General Assembly unanimously adopted a resolution declaring October 2 to be the "International Day of Non-Violence."[1][2]

FIGURE 15-3: *The first paragraph of the English-language Wikipedia article on Mahatma Ghandi, which uses three languages with different scripts (English, Sanskrit, and Gujarati), as well as IPA symbols*

on your computer. The Firefox web browser provides relatively good multilingual support, as do most newer operating systems, including Windows Vista.

Language support for operating systems is certainly still driven by demand in the developed world, and this means that many of less widely used scripts, such as those for some Indic languages, will not typically be supported natively by your browser or operating system. Character sets that usually need to be downloaded include those for native languages. To find these fonts, the Wikipedia edition in that language can be a good resource; Wikipedias that use non-Latin scripts often have a help page about where to get the necessary fonts for viewing them linked from their main page. For instance, to see the proper rendering of Cherokee in native script in the [[Cherokee]] article, you must download a special font; the help pages on the Cherokee-language Wikipedia at *http://chr.wikipedia.org/* give details on how to find the appropriate fonts.

When composing articles, if you don't have a keyboard with the characters you need, you'll find that many types of scripts, for example, Cyrillic and Chinese characters, can be copied and saved successfully onto Wikipedia pages from other documents. (This works because of *Unicode character encoding*, or [[UTF-8]].) Most operating systems, including Windows, Mac OS X, and many Linux distributions, also allow you to change your keyboard layout virtually so you can type directly in another language. In Windows XP, for example, you can do this via the Control Panel under Regional and Language options. The [[Help:Multilingual support (Indic)]] page gives complete directions for inputting characters in Indic languages for several operating systems; these directions are also appropriate for other character sets.

Finally, the editing box below the main editing window (described in "Understanding the Edit Window" on page 133) gives easy access to many characters with accents and diacritics, as well as the Greek, Cyrillic, and IPA alphabets. Just click one of these characters to insert it in an article.

Further Reading

http://wikipedia.org The portal to all language versions of Wikipedia

http://stats.wikimedia.org/ The statistics site gives information on number of articles and users for each language for all the projects

http://meta.wikimedia.org/wiki/Wikimedia_Embassy The Embassy system between languages

http://incubator.wikimedia.org Where new language Wikipedias are started

http://meta.wikimedia.org/wiki/Requests_for_new_languages The page for requesting new language editions

http://www.ethnologue.com/ Encyclopedic resource for the world's languages

http://en.wikipedia.org/wiki/Help:Multilingual_support Help with multilingual script support

Links Between Languages

Interwiki links or *interlanguage links* are links to an article on the same topic in another language version of Wikipedia. These special links display in the left-hand sidebar under Languages, as first mentioned in Chapter 3 ("The Omnipresent Sidebar" on page 73). These links to other-language Wikipedias appear under the native spelling of the language (such as *Français*) and are ordered by the two- or three-letter code for that language (such as *fr* or *ja*). Clicking the link takes you to the appropriate article in the other-language Wikipedia.

Any page, not just articles, can be *interwikied*. For instance, if you have a user page in Russian as well as English, you can add an interwiki link to the Russian version of your page on your English-language user page, and vice versa. Many help and community pages exist in multiple languages and are linked to one another in this way. These links can be very helpful if you want to find an equivalent project or policy in another language; for instance, if you want to find spoken articles in German, simply go to the English Spoken Wikipedia project, which has an interwiki link to the German-language Wikipedia page, WikiProjekt Gesprochene Wikipedia.

Editors must add links to other languages, article by article, for them to show up. The links are created using special language codes. These codes are mostly two letters (a few are three letters) and are based on the international standard [[ISO 639]], which catalogs languages. If no ISO code exists, a special code is developed and used; for instance, the Simple English Wikipedia (a Wikipedia written in simpler English) uses the prefix *simple* (according to [[Wikipedia:Multilingual coordination]]). These prefixes also appear in the Wikipedia URL for each edition: So *http://en.wikipedia.org/* is the English-language Wikipedia. A table of all existing Wikipedia languages with their corresponding code may be found on the Meta site at [[meta:List of Wikipedias]]. These codes are also used informally on the projects to refer to the various language Wikipedias; you may see *en:WP* or *enWP* used to mean the English-language Wikipedia, *de:WP* to mean the German-language Wikipedia, *ru:WP* to mean the Russian-language Wikipedia, and so on.

Once you have found the two articles you wish to link and know their respective title and language code, creating the links is simple. Edit one article, and scroll to the end of the text. Interwiki links are placed at the very bottom of the article, underneath all article text.

The link takes this form: [[*language code:article name in native language*]]. For instance, if you're working on the article [[Cat]] in English, and you want to link to the article [[Chat]] in French, you would add the link

```
[[fr:chat]]
```

at the end of the English-language article. After saving the page, a link with the text Français will show up on the left hand sidebar; if you click it, you'll be taken to the French article at *http://fr.wikipedia.org/wiki/Chat*. Similarly, to link to the article in German you would type

```
[[de:Hauskatze]]
```

which will give you a link to *http://de.wikipedia.org/wiki/Hauskatze* under Deutsch in the sidebar.

By convention, interwiki links are placed below category tags on pages, each on its own line. The most popular arrangement for ordering interwiki links on a page is alphabetically by code.

Broken Interwiki Links

Make sure you have the right article when linking. Especially for concepts with more than one meaning, finding an exact equivalency can sometimes be difficult—take care to not link to the wrong concept. Also be careful about linking to disambiguation pages, which may exist in one Wikipedia but not another. Obviously, not all articles exist in all languages; since the English-language Wikipedia is the largest, it often has articles that other languages do not, but you may be surprised at the coverage of smaller Wikipedias. If you have created an interwiki link that appears to lead nowhere, check to make sure you haven't entered the title incorrectly.

To be complete, you should also go to the articles in the other languages to add an interwiki link back to the first article (for instance, the page [[Hauskatze]] should also link to the English [[Cat]]). When creating interwiki links, add a simple *+en:* or *interwiki* as an edit summary. You may also find more interwiki links to that article to add to the original article you were working on. Today bots do much of this missing interwiki linking automatically.

To link to another language page without having it display as an interwiki link, use the same syntax but place a colon in front of the language prefix, as if you were linking to a category name. Typing [[:fr:chat]] on an English-language Wikipedia page will display as a light-blue link just as you write it that links to *http://fr.wikipedia.org/wiki/Chat*, but the link doesn't appear on the left-hand sidebar. Some important general principles still apply: *Prefer the internal link* means don't use links to another-language Wikipedia to replace a redlink to an English article and *Seek outside references* means you shouldn't rely on another Wikipedia to source important facts in an article. Translation isn't by itself sufficient verification, and other Wikipedia pages—no matter the language—are not acceptable as sources.

Further Reading

http://en.wikipedia.org/wiki/Wikipedia:Multilingual_coordination Multilingual coordination, an introduction to multilingual projects

http://meta.wikimedia.org/wiki/List_of_Wikipedias List of all Wikipedias, including language codes (in the Wiki column). Language codes are the same no matter which project (Wikipedia, Wiktionary, and so on) you're linking to.

http://en.wikipedia.org/wiki/Wikipedia:Interlanguage_links Help with interwiki links between languages

English in Global Focus

The English-language Wikipedia has a global community of editors, and as an editor, you'll regularly collaborate with people from many time zones. A typical contributor to the English-language Wikipedia may well be a native speaker in an Anglophone country—the United States, Canada, the United Kingdom, Australia, and others—but many editors are neither native speakers nor in one of those places. Getting to know people from all over the world is one of the benefits of getting involved in Wikipedia. Because editors are relatively anonymous, you'll often have no idea where your on-wiki friends are from or even their nationality. To get around cultural differences, remember the guidelines on interacting politely with others online, and don't rely too heavily on regional slang or Internet jargon, which not everyone will understand.

The diversity of contributors is also reflected in the global breadth of subjects on Wikipedia. Notability is not culture- or language-specific; geographical features, important individuals, and other notable regional topics should clearly be included in Wikipedia, no matter where they are or relate to in the world.

Simple English Wikipedia

The *Simple English* Wikipedia is a separate project from the English-language Wikipedia. This Wikipedia aims to provide articles in simplified English and is designed for people learning English and children. The whole interface has been rewritten to use simpler language, so that, for example, the Random Page link is the Show Any Page link. Most articles are "translated" from the English-language Wikipedia version into shorter, simpler articles. These articles, in turn, can be a resource for people working in other languages. Simple English is an ideal project for those interested in teaching or learning English as a second language. Simple English lives at *http://simple.wikipedia.org/*, and as of mid-2008, had around 33,000 articles.

Several WikiProjects also focus on specific areas of the world. An example is WikiProject India, which focuses on writing articles about India, reviewing the existing articles about India, and supporting a community portal for editors interested in India-related topics. A list of WikiProjects that deal with geographical topics can be found at [[Wikipedia:WikiProject Council/Directory/Geographical]].

Other WikiProjects focus on translating useful or interesting articles from other Wikipedias into English (other-language Wikipedias have similar projects that focus on translating articles into their local language). The place to coordinate translations in English is [[Wikipedia:Translation]]. Translation offers a double challenge: writing good English that is also good Wikipedia content.

Stylistic issues often appear in articles written in English by non-English speakers. Cleanup work on these articles helps make worthwhile material available. When evaluating an article according to the criteria laid out in Chapter 4, or in a deletion debate, take into account that the article may have been written by a non-native speaker with expertise in the topic.

When writing articles in English about topics from non-English speaking parts of the world, sources can be problematic. Finding source material in English can be much more difficult, for instance. Checking interwiki links to find the relevant article on other-language Wikipedias can be helpful for finding sources and more information.

Although citing non-English sources is not ideal, you can do this. You can use special templates to identify sources in other languages; for instance, placing the optional template {{it icon}} before a link to an Italian website alerts the reader that the source is in Italian (the language codes are the same standard ISO codes already mentioned). Citing a source that is not in a Wikipedia's native language is better than not citing a source at all. Try to locate English-language sources as well, so readers can verify your facts more easily. (If sources in different languages disagree, this can be useful information to note and include.)

Further Reading

http://en.wikipedia.org/wiki/Wikipedia:WikiProject_Council/Directory/ Geographical   WikiProjects about geographical regions and places

http://en.wikipedia.org/wiki/Wikipedia:Translation   The place to request and coordinate translations from foreign-language Wikipedias into English

---

Summary

While English remains the largest single Wikipedia community, less than a quarter of the total number of articles across all language Wikipedias are written in English. Other languages, taken together, are growing twice as fast as the English-language Wikipedia.

Each language Wikipedia includes many original articles and its own unique topics. The various sites attract communities, develop their own procedures and customs, and sustain themselves over time. The cross-linking (interwiki linking) of corresponding articles draws every Wikipedia into a larger network. To truly get a feel for the global Wikipedia, spend time in a number of these communities.

16

Wikimedia Commons and Other Sister Projects

In addition to Wikipedia, the Wikimedia Foundation runs several other projects to produce free-content reference material. Commonly known within Wikimedia as *sister projects*, *sibling projects*, or simply *the projects*, the nine current Wikimedia projects are Wikipedia, Wiktionary, Wikinews, Wikibooks, Wikisource, Wikiquote, Wikispecies, Wikiversity, and the Wikimedia Commons. Each project handles a different type of material, from textbooks to images, and each has a separate group of volunteers working on a dedicated wiki, usually with many language versions. The Wikimedia Foundation also coordinates the MediaWiki software that all of the projects run on. Often thought of as the tenth sister project, the MediaWiki software development process will be described more in the next chapter. The Meta-Wiki site, also described in the next chapter, serves as a coordination site for all of the projects and languages. Volunteers produce the content for all Wikimedia projects using a wiki model similar to Wikipedia's, and all of the projects license their content under the GFDL or another free license.

These different wiki projects all complement each other. The intention is to separate out *types* of content, such as dictionary definitions, encyclopedia articles, and archival material, while allowing *crosslinking* between the projects topic by topic. For instance, you would add quotations related to Abraham Lincoln to Wikiquote, and the Wikipedia article [[Abraham Lincoln]] can link to that store of quotations, rather than trying to include them all. With over 500 sites involved— nine sister projects, each with a large number of language versions—a systematic naming system to enable linking is obviously needed. We'll explain how this works in "Linking Between Projects and Copying Content," on page 439.

All of these projects use the MediaWiki wiki software, so you don't have to learn new editing processes to contribute to them; all you need to learn are some different namespace and page structure conventions. Don't expect every project to have the full development seen now on Wikipedia, however, because the projects were started at different times and develop at their own (sometimes leisurely) pace. Additionally, you shouldn't assume that Wikipedia culture (particularly English-language Wikipedia culture) transfers automatically to these other projects. Each project, and each language version of each project, can and should be thought of as a community in its own right. Each has its own policies and variations in how processes, such as deletion debates and promotion of administrators, are handled. Watch for and learn the norms of each new project when you start to participate. But each project has some familiar features: help pages and some variation on a community portal and a village pump for discussing and coordinating the project. Just as on Wikipedia, these are good places to begin learning

Project Accounts and Single-User Login

In the past, it has been necessary to create a new account on each Wikimedia project you edited, which occasionally led to different people having the same name on different projects. As of mid-2008, single-user login is being implemented, making it possible to register your account "globally" across all Wikimedia accounts. Simply register your name on your home project. Then to "claim" it for other projects, go to [[Special:MergeAccount]] on your home project, or click Manage Your Global Account under your preferences when logged in. Once you merge your accounts, your chosen username will be reserved for your use on any Wikimedia project, enabling you to log in and out of all Wikimedia projects at once. To avoid naming conflict with others on other wikis, you may need to pick a distinctive username or use your full name.

more. Wikimedia projects all share some key values, too. Civility and assuming good faith are always important when interacting with other editors, and copyright violations are *never* acceptable on any of the projects. And naturally, all projects are open for editing by anyone. Just find a task you want to work on and start editing, either anonymously or logged in with a user account.

In this chapter, we'll describe each of the sister projects in turn. The default license is the GFDL; however, we'll note when another license may apply. Following that, we'll describe how to link all of these projects together (and link to them from the English-language Wikipedia) and how to move content between them. Finally, we'll briefly discuss non-Wikimedia wikis.

Wikimedia Commons

Founded: September 7, 2004

Scope: Free images and other media

URL: *http://commons.wikimedia.org/*

Short prefix: commons

Languages: Cross-language project, many languages having a welcome page

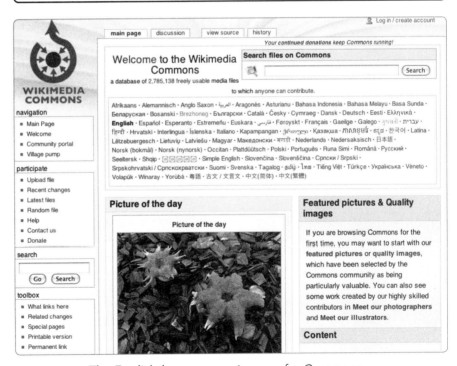

FIGURE 16-1: The English-language main page for Commons

Of all the sister projects, we highlight the Wikimedia Commons first (Figure 16-1) because the Commons is considered an integral part of Wikipedia operations these days, as well as a worthwhile and popular site in its own right, ranking among the top 300 websites worldwide. The Commons is a repository of free media, including images (both photographs and illustrations), sound files, animations, and video clips. If you produce images for the encyclopedia, you are strongly encouraged to create an account for uploading your images directly to Commons. Like other Wikimedia content, all Commons media are both free and freely licensed, but the *free license* guidelines are stricter on Commons than on the English-language Wikipedia, as fair-use materials are excluded completely.

You can link directly to images and other content on Commons from any language version of any Wikimedia project, without having to upload that media separately to each project. For instance, you can easily insert a picture in a Wikipedia article that is actually hosted on Commons (rather than on the English-language Wikipedia itself). By comparison, when you upload an image to the English-language Wikipedia, you can only link to it from within the English-language Wikipedia. Wikimedia Commons was founded in 2004 in order to remove some obvious redundancy among the other Wikimedia projects, such as having multiple images of the same thing on different Wikipedias. Commons can be thought of as a kind of stock photography archive of free materials, designed for the other Wikimedia projects and for anyone searching for free media. The other advantages of using Commons are apparent when you want to sort and search for media. Commons is also useful for consolidating media efforts, such as projects to take pictures or make sound files.

Because all the language projects may use it, Commons is multilingual; image descriptions may be in any language, and the Commons main page interface and welcome page has been translated into a few dozen languages (links appear at the top of the main page). Commons has been so successful that nearly 3,000,000 files had been uploaded by mid-2008.

Searching and Browsing Commons

Searching Commons for images and media files is easier than searching Wikipedia. To begin searching on Commons, use the left sidebar search box or the search box in the upper-right corner of the main page (Figure 16-1). This searches through filenames, file descriptions, gallery pages, and category names. As with Wikipedia's search, you can choose to search specific namespaces by checking the boxes for those namespaces at the bottom of your search results.

The main namespace on Commons, equivalent to the Article namespace on Wikipedia, is often called the *Gallery* namespace; use this namespace for producing *galleries*, or collections of images. The Gallery namespace does not have a special prefix. Galleries provide a way to group related images together, making them similar to Wikipedia's lists. If a gallery page with a name matching your search terms exists, this page will be displayed first in the search results.

From your search page results, you will also see a link to the external Mayflower search engine, a special tool developed for image searching. If you use

Mayflower, your search results will be displayed as a thumbnail gallery of images, which can be helpful if you are searching for just the right picture for a Wikipedia article.

You can browse Commons in a number of ways. If you start at the Commons main page and scroll down, you'll see a wide variety of categories to browse by, including topic, location, content type, and categories of files arranged by license or source. One good way to start browsing is in the Featured images and Quality images categories, which are Common's equivalent of featured and good articles.

Using Commons Material in Wikipedia

To link to a file on Commons from Wikipedia, use the same image syntax as described in Chapter 9. The image will appear just like an image you uploaded directly to Wikipedia. For instance, in a Wikipedia article, if you want to display an image with this URL:

```
http://commons.wikimedia.org/wiki/Image:file123.jpg
```

you can simply use this syntax in the Wikipedia article:

```
[[Image:file123.jpg|thumb|descriptive text]]
```

Use the filename from Commons with the `image` prefix, but nothing else. When a reader clicks the image to view its description, the text from Commons will be displayed.

Participating in Commons

Anyone can participate in Commons by uploading media or by helping to organize and describe existing images. You have to create an account or log in with a global Wikimedia account (see "Project Accounts and Single-User Login" on page 420) to upload a file. If you create a new account, the procedure is similar to creating an account on Wikipedia (described in Chapter 11).

Maps

Maps are a critical part of any reference resource. One way Commons organizes maps is with the Commons Atlas, *http://commons.wikimedia.org/ wiki/Atlas*, which manages a wide variety of maps for various countries and areas of the world (scroll down to the bottom of the Atlas page to see a listing of all the places maps have been collected for). This is a tremendous resource in its own right. On the English-language Wikipedia, WikiProject Maps, at *http://en.wikipedia.org/wiki/Wikipedia:WikiProject_Maps*, coordinates the use of maps.

Inclusion Guidelines

All images and other media uploaded to Commons must fall within the inclusion guidelines of one of the other Wikimedia projects. Media files that are not potentially useful for any Wikimedia project are, therefore, beyond the scope of Commons. Note that the site isn't a personal image hosting service; your birthday party snaps don't belong here!

Additionally, all content on Commons must be completely freely licensed; *fair-use* images, such as you'll sometimes find on the English-language Wikipedia, are not acceptable. All content must be reusable by anyone for any purpose, including commercial uses. The licenses that Commons will accept include the following:

▶   Public domain images, which are released without any restriction. Certain works produced by the US government and others are automatically placed in the public domain, but any individual may also release work into the public domain.

▶   The Creative Commons free licenses, CC-BY and CC-BY-SA, both of which require attribution of the original author but allow commercial reuse. The Creative Commons licenses are also "copyleft" licenses, with similar features to the GFDL; find out more at [[Commons:Choosing a license]] and *http://creativecommons.org/*. The Creative Commons licenses CC-NC and CC-ND are not accepted by Commons; if you're not prepared to allow commercial reuse, then Commons is not for you.

▶   The GFDL, which probably discourages commercial reuse because the entire GFDL license must be reprinted with the image.

Commons will not accept a number of image types, including screenshots of copyrighted software, scans of copyrighted works (such as book or album covers), or screen captures of television programs. Of course, any other copyrighted work that is not your own is also unacceptable. [[Commons:Licensing]] gives the full story, including legal information for a number of other non-US jurisdictions.

Commons accepts a variety of file types. Preferred file types include JPEG for photography, SVG for illustrations, and Ogg for audio and video; [[Commons:File types]] gives more information. For audio and video, MP3, WAV, and so on, are not free formats and are therefore not acceptable.

Uploading Images

Uploading an image or media file to Commons is similar to uploading files on Wikipedia (see Chapter 9). You can access the upload form via a link on the left-hand sidebar. A series of several steps will guide you through the process, or you can jump directly to the upload form from the first page.

1.   Choose the image's origins; if you created the image, simply say so.
2.   Choose the appropriate license, as discussed in the previous section.
3.   Choose an appropriate descriptive filename. Do *not* simply use the filename from your digital camera; choose a helpful name. Images and files cannot be

renamed after they've been uploaded, though you can upload new versions of the image. If you happen to choose the same name as an existing file, a warning appears, and you'll be asked to double-check that you really want to upload a new version.

4.   Add an appropriate description. If you created the image, what is it a picture of? Where and when was it taken? What is your name or username? Remember that this text will help other users find your image.

For bulk uploading, see [[Commons:Tools]], which lists a number of tools for uploading multiple files quickly, as well as other helpful tools such as experimental search engines.

If you'd like to contribute media but don't know how to get started, try [[Commons:Picture requests]]. If you are looking for that perfect picture for a Wikipedia article, you can also make a request here. Requests are often for images of particular places, so you can look to see if any requests are for images of places near you before going to shoot photos.

✱ **NOTE:** *You can read profiles of a few of the talented photographers on Commons at [[Commons:Meet our photographers]].*

Categorizing

Once you've uploaded an image, you need to categorize it. Good categorization makes finding images easy on Commons. Anyone can help out with this sorting process; you don't have to have an account. [[Commons:First steps/Sorting]] has more information on the sorting and categorizing process.

If you have a new image, have described it specifically, and uploaded it, the next step is to place it in an appropriate category. In general, place images in the most narrow category possible. For instance, an image of a paperclip belongs under [[Category:Paperclips]], which is better than [[Category:Fasteners]] or [[Category:Office equipment]]. Categorize all images by topic and by other meta-level categories, for instance, by the license that applies to them.

[[Category:Topics]] is the topmost category for topics on Commons; as on Wikipedia, you can drill down into subcategories from here (this process is described fully in Chapters 3 and 8). An alternative way to find the appropriate category is to check images similar to your own and see how they're categorized. For instance, try searching for your image's topic to see if Commons already has a gallery page; then study how the images on this page are categorized.

You can add images both to a category and to the appropriate gallery page (Figure 16-2). To add your image to a gallery page, simply go to the gallery page and edit it. You'll see images placed in between <gallery> tags, like this:

```
<gallery>
Image:Mars Valles Marineris.jpeg|Valles Marineris on Mars
Image:Mars Hubble.jpg|Mars seen by the Hubble Space Telescope, Realistic Colors
</gallery>
```

You can add your image between those two gallery-tags (one opening and one closing tag) in the following way:

```
Image:Your photo name.jpg|A brief description
```

After saving your edit to the gallery page, you'll see your image as a thumbnail in the gallery. Unlike incorporating a single image in a Wikipedia article, you don't use the [[and]] brackets around the image. You can also categorize sound and video files and add them to a gallery page the same way, except that media files display a sound file icon in the gallery instead of an image.

Along with categorizing images, other projects you can get involved with include identifying and describing unknown images (at [[Category: Unidentified subject]]) and, for those with graphics experience, cleaning up images in the Graphics Lab (at [[Commons: Graphic Lab]]). Commons also has two projects that anyone can get involved with to review and pick out the highest-quality images: *featured pictures*, which chooses outstanding work (much like featured articles on Wikipedia); and *quality images*, which reviews and identifies images that meet certain technical criteria that are useful for Wikimedia projects. Anyone can nominate his or her own work for quality images at [[Commons:Quality images candidates]].

FIGURE 16-2: *A photo gallery*

Other Sister Projects

Besides Wikimedia Commons, Wikipedia has seven additional sister projects. From a Wikipedian perspective, these projects are less close to the work of the encyclopedia. These projects serve as reference sites licensed under the GFDL, covering different types of content. The exception is Wikinews, which is a citizen journalism site now using a Creative Commons license. Six of the projects have versions in many languages, as Wikipedia does, with the exception of Wikispecies, which maintains a single site. You could think of MediaWiki software development as yet another sister project, with the obvious difference being that it exists to develop and distribute a program, not content.

Wiktionary

Founded: December 12, 2002

Scope: Dictionary definitions

URL: http://wiktionary.org/

Short prefix: wikt

Languages: As of early 2008, 9 (fr, en, vi, tr, ru, io [which is the code for ido, a constructed language], zh, el, ta) with over 100,000 entries; 23 more with over 10,000 entries; 172 languages total

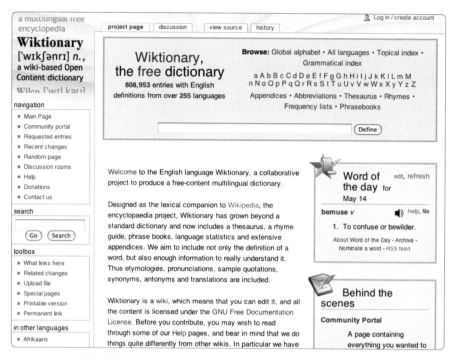

FIGURE 16-3: *The English-language Wiktionary main page*

If your interests are more lexicographic than encyclopedic, you should visit *Wiktionary* (Figure 16-3), a free wiki-based dictionary. Instead of full articles about a topic, Wiktionary provides concise word definitions. Wiktionary's scope overlaps with Wikipedia: A term with an article in Wikipedia may also be defined in Wiktionary. For instance, whereas the Wikipedia fish article discusses types of fish, where they can be found, fishing methods, and so on, the Wiktionary definition will tell you that *fish* in English can be a noun or a verb, that a fish is a cold-blooded animal that lives in water, how to pronounce it, and so on. The English-language Wiktionary had over 878,000 entries as of mid-2008, though many of those had been imported from public-domain dictionaries by bots.

For Wikipedians, Wiktionary provides both a resource to link to for further information about terms that appear in both projects and a place to move articles that are simply short dictionary definitions and therefore unsuitable for Wikipedia articles.

Wiktionary is a multilingual dictionary (also thesaurus and phrase-book) and has distinctive content policies. Words must be *attested* and *idiomatic* (that is, words should be in use, and phrases should be commonly used idioms), and submissions should be neutral and verifiable. Although definitions and descriptions in the English-language Wiktionary are in English only, words from any and all languages can be included: Wiktionary not only defines English words but also serves as a French-English dictionary, a Spanish-English dictionary, and so on. Thus the site can be an excellent place to look up unfamiliar foreign words; as of

2008, words in 104 languages were included in the English-language Wiktionary. Additionally, when viewing an entry, the In Other Languages links on the left-hand sidebar will take you to definitions in other languages of the same English word (similarly to Wikipedia), and generally these entries will also link to the local equivalent of the word. Translations in other languages may also appear at the bottom of the entry.

Wiktionary, unlike most other dictionaries, includes supplementary data in definitions, including sound files of pronunciations, images, links to the other projects (often Wikipedia), translations, and other information such as usage notes and references (Figure 16-4 shows these elements in the entry for *incunabulum*). Compound words, idioms, and abbreviations are all acceptable; neologisms that

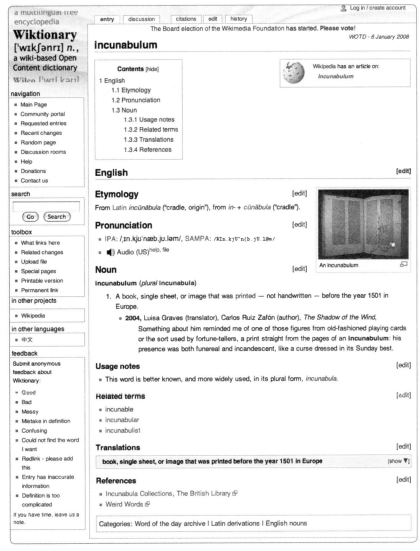

FIGURE 16-4: *A good Wiktionary entry for the word* incunabulum

have references to current use may be included (naturally, made-up words will be deleted). Featured entries are highlighted as the Word of the Day on the main page; for the English-language Wiktionary, an RSS feed of these interesting words is available.

Wiktionary was proposed on the *Wikipedia-L* mailing list in April 2001 by Larry Sanger, just three months after Wikipedia was launched.[1] The site was brought online in English on December 12, 2002; on March 29, 2004, the first non-English Wiktionaries were initiated in French and Polish. Wiktionaries in over 200 languages now exist, and more than 100 have more than 100 definitions. An outside project called *Omegawiki*, started by a handful of Wiktionarians, is working on a grand combination of data from Wiktionary into a single dictionary for all languages.

Further Reading

http://wiktionary.org/   The portal to all Wiktionaries

http://en.wiktionary.org/wiki/Wiktionary:Welcome,_newcomers   An introduction to the English-language Wiktionary, linking to the Community Portal and other help pages

http://en.wiktionary.org/wiki/Wiktionary:Criteria_for_inclusion   The criteria for inclusion in Wiktionary

http://en.wiktionary.org/wiki/Category:Phrasebook   Phrases in many languages, defined in Wiktionary

http://en.wiktionary.org/wiki/Wiktionary:Word_of_the_day   The Word of the day page, highlighting Wiktionary's best content—the word of the day can also be delivered to you via email

http://www.omegawiki.org/   The OmegaWiki project

Wikinews

Founded: December 3, 2004   **Short prefix:** n

Scope: News stories   **Languages:** 23 total

URL: *http://wikinews.org/*

---

[1] See *http://lists.wikimedia.org/pipermail/wikipedia-l/2001-April/000076.html* for the original proposal for a Wiktionary site.

article | collaboration | view source | history

See what donors say

Welcome to **Wikinews**
The free news source *you can write!*

Wednesday, May 14, 2008, 12:41 (UTC)

Crime and law · Culture and entertainment · Disasters and accidents · Economy and business · Education · Environment · Health · Obituaries · Politics and conflicts · Science and technology · Sports · Wackynews · Weather

Africa · Asia · Central America · Europe · Middle East · North America · Oceania · South America · World

Browse articles · Wikinews RSS · Get involved · Report Breaking News · Audio Edition · Print Edition · Best of Wikinews · Help · IRC

WIKINEWS

navigation
- Main Page
- Archives
- Newsroom
- Recent changes
- Random article
- Upload free media

wikinews
- Water cooler
- Style guide
- Live chat
- World News Quiz
- Help
- Donate
- Contact us

regions
- Africa
- Asia
- Central America
- Europe
- Middle East
- North America
- Oceania

image credit

Five of six accused over 9/11 to be tried; charges against '20th hijacker' dropped

Five men out of six accused of involvement in the September 11 attacks have been referred to trial by the Guantanamo military commission. The war crimes tribunal also dropped charges

Bomb destroys Spanish police barracks and kills policeman in Basque Country

A car bomb car exploded in the Basque town of Legutiano, near the barracks of the Spanish paramilitary police Guardia Civil. A policeman died and 4 more were injured. Authorieties have blamed Basque separatist group ETA for this attack.

» Full story   [edit lead]

Pakistan's coalition government faces split

FIGURE 16-5: The English-language Wikinews main page

Wikinews is a wiki site devoted to news and citizen journalism (Figure 16-5). The project aims to report and summarize news on all subjects from a neutral point of view, providing a free-content alternative to proprietary news agencies. Anyone can contribute, either from direct experience or by summarizing from elsewhere. In terms of content policy, Neutral Point of View (NPOV) and Verifiability (V) apply to content on Wikinews, but Wikinews differs from Wikipedia in that original reporting is welcomed. The site aims to provide a stable news source, so after articles have been drafted, they are published, with the expectation that major changes will not be made to the article once they have been published for 36 hours. After a week, articles are archived and "frozen" (protected against further editing).

Also unlike Wikipedia, original articles may be signed with the reporter's byline. Wikinews has developed several features over the years to make original reporting easier, including a 1-800 number tipline and a process for accrediting reporters. To become accredited, a contributor must be established and submit to a process with a community vote; his or her identity may be verified by other trusted Wikinews reporters.

Wikinews stories may link (sparingly) to Wikipedia articles for definitions and further information; in turn, Wikipedia articles about a current topic should link to the appropriate Wikinews story, if one exists. Wikinews articles may be cited in Wikipedia articles. Breaking news is better suited to Wikinews, but you will often see stories about current events developing in both places simultaneously.

Wikinews is better for some topics, however; a person may be briefly "in the news" as reported on Wikinews, without meriting a biography in Wikipedia. Also unlike Wikipedia (and the rest of the Wikimedia projects), Wikinews uses the Creative Commons Attribution 2.5 license, which is also a free license. This means that content from Wikipedia generally cannot be copied directly to Wikinews, however.

The idea of a Wikinews site was first proposed in 2003; after much discussion, a demonstration wiki was established in November 2004 to show how such a collaborative news site might work. In December 2004, the site was moved out of the demo stage and into the beta stage. A German-language edition was launched at the same time. Soon editions in Dutch, French, Spanish, Swedish, Bulgarian, Polish, Portuguese, Romanian, Ukrainian, Italian, Serbian, Japanese, Russian, Hebrew, Arabic, Thai, Norwegian, and Chinese (in that chronological order) were set up; currently Wikinews has sites in 23 languages altogether.

Further Reading

http://wikinews.org/ The Wikinews portal

http://meta.wikimedia.org/wiki/Wikinews Statistics for all Wikinews editions

http://en.wikinews.org/wiki/Wikinews:Introduction An introduction to the English-language Wikinews

---

Wikibooks

Founded: July 10, 2003

Scope: Free textbooks

URL: *http://wikibooks.org/*

Short prefix: b

Languages: 121 total, with 14 (en, de, fr, pt, hu, es, it, jp, pl, sq [Albanian], nl, he, fi, and vi) having over 1,000 book modules

---

Wikibooks is a wiki for the creation of free-content textbooks and manuals (Figure 16-6 shows its logo). The books range from how-tos to textbooks for learning subjects such as math, computer science, or languages, to cookbooks of recipes from around the world. Wikibooks is only for instructional works such as textbooks, annotated texts, instructional guides, and manuals; fiction and many types of non-fiction are not included. Original research is also not acceptable; Wikibooks is not the place for publishing primary research or results. Out-of-copyright source texts are better placed at Wikisource, with

FIGURE 16-6: *Wikibooks logo*

the exception of annotated texts designed for study. Like all the projects, all Wikibooks materials should have a neutral point of view; but unlike Wikipedia, writing extensive descriptions of how to do something or the best way to learn a process is perfectly acceptable.

Wikibooks has no fixed audience, unlike Wikipedia, which aims to appeal to a broad base. Though many books are designed for adult learners, books may be for any audience, including children. One special project hosted on Wikibooks is called *Wikijunior*, which is a collection of nonfiction books for children. Wikijunior projects have been created in 8 languages, with 25 Wikijunior books in English completed or underway. This project was originally started with a special grant in 2004 from the Beck Foundation to help support development of children's books. Other Wikibooks may be technical, specialist works.

Wikibooks uses *modules*, or short sections of the book (akin to a short chapter), as the main structure for the site. Each book has a single main page on the wiki, and each module is built as a subpage of that page. A special visual grading system with small squares (Figure 16-7) indicates how finished the works are; see *http://en.wikibooks.org/wiki/Help:Development_stages*.

FIGURE 16-7: *The set of Wikibook development stages*

Extended topic discussions or instructions on how to do something may be moved to Wikibooks from Wikipedia. In turn, books on Wikibooks can link back to the relevant Wikipedia articles for background information, and images from Commons may be used for illustrating Wikibooks when needed.

Wikibooks sites exist in over 100 languages, and 47 of these sites have more than 100 modules. The project was first begun in 2003 in response to a request for a place to create textbooks; in 2006, Wikiversity (described on page 438) was spun off as a separate project.

Further Reading

http://wikibooks.org/   The Wikibooks portal

http://en.wikibooks.org/wiki/Wikibooks:Departments   Wikibooks in English sorted by content

http://en.wikibooks.org/wiki/Wikibooks:Featured_books   The best content of English Wikibooks

http://en.wikibooks.org/wiki/Wikijunior   Wikijunior, books for children

http://meta.wikimedia.org/wiki/List_of_Wikibooks   List of all Wikibooks editions

---

Wikiquote

Founded: July 10, 2003

Scope: Quotations

URL: *http://wikiquote.org/*

Short prefix: q

Languages: 89 languages total, 48 of which have over 100 articles and 7 of which (en, de, it, pl, sk, pt, and ru) have over 10,000 articles

Wikiquote aims to compile a collection of quotations from notable people and works (Figure 16-8 shows its logo). Quotations can come from published works, such as books and films, but can also include proverbs, epigrams, and sayings. For instance, at [[Category:Proverbs]] on *http://en.wikiquote.org/*, you can find proverbs from many languages, both literally translated and rendered as the English equivalent. Quotes and sayings are arranged by theme or by author; for instance, Wikiquote has a page called Love, which has quotes relating to the theme of love, and a page collecting Samuel Beckett quotations.

FIGURE 16-8:
Wikiquote logo

Quotes should be sourced to the work they origi- nally appeared in whenever possible, and they should only come from notable people or works. As with all the Wikimedia wikis, links to the appropriate articles on Wikipedia and elsewhere should be included. Many Wiki- pedia articles for well-known works and authors also include a few quotes, but if many notable quotes come from one person, they should primarily be included on the Wikiquote page, with an appropriate interwiki link from the Wikipedia article.

Wikiquote was started in 2003. At the end of 2007, Wikiquotes editions had been created in 89 languages, with 46 of them having more than 100 articles. The English-language Wikiquote has over 14,000 pages. The English Wikiquote also has a Quote of the Day feature that displays a new notable quote each day; you can even receive this by email.

Further Reading

http://wikiquote.org/   The portal for all Wikiquotes

http://meta.wikimedia.org/wiki/Wikiquote#List_of_Wikiquotes   A list of all Wikiquote editions

http://en.wikiquote.org/wiki/Category:Proverbs   Proverbs in many languages

http://en.wikiquote.org/wiki/Wikiquote:Quote_of_the_day   The English Wikiquote Quote of the day page

Wikisource

Founded: November 24, 2003

Scope: Primary sources

URL: *http://wikisource.org/*

Short prefix: s

Languages: 55 languages total, 10 of which (en, fr, es, zh, de, it, pt, ru, pl, th) have more than 10,000 pages

Wikisource is a collection of source documents and primary texts that are in the public domain (and thus not covered by copyright) or released under the GFDL. (Figure 16-9 shows its logo.) The project serves as a free library of important works. Texts may include (but are not limited to) novels, nonfiction, letters, speeches, historical documents, constitutional documents, and laws. Translations are also welcome, though texts in original languages should go to the appropriate language Wikisource. Texts must be previously published to be included here; Wikisource does not host *vanity press* books or documents produced by its contributors. Spoken or audio versions can be included; you can browse these at [[s:Category:Spoken works]].

FIGURE 16-9: *Wikisource logo*

Usually texts are in the public domain in the United States because they are old enough that they are no longer covered by copyright. The texts may have also been released into the public domain in the first place, such as US government–produced materials (for instance, federal court opinions and military journalism). Many texts on Wikisource come from existing digital libraries and scanning

How Do You Collaborate on Texts?

Even though Wikisource consists of previously published texts that participants do not write, plenty of work needs to be done. Tasks include proofreading uploaded texts, wikifying texts into MediaWiki format, categorizing, and uploading incomplete texts (because transcribing a long document onto the wiki can be a big job). Other possibilities include finding public domain texts, checking copyright status of submissions, and working on producing audio versions (such as audiobooks) of texts; you can find directions for creating audiobooks at [[s:Help:Audio]] and more open tasks at [[s:Community Portal]].

projects, such as Project Gutenberg. Digitizing free texts from scratch is also certainly acceptable. Texts may be scanned and then converted to an editable digital format with Optical Character Recognition (OCR) software. Texts produced with OCR do need to be proofread.

Wikisource was originally conceived of as a way to store useful historical or otherwise important public domain texts, both as a supplement to Wikipedia and as an archive in its own right. For instance, the Wikipedia article on the US Constitution may link to the full text of the Constitution at Wikisource. This provides a valuable addition to the article for readers who want to learn more about the topic. Wikisource does have things in common with other free-text projects like Project Gutenberg, but the emphasis of Wikisource is on historical and culturally important material.

The project was originally begun in 2003 under the name *Project Sourceberg*, a play on the name *Project Gutenberg* (which is why the logo is a large iceberg lying in the water). Wikisources exist in 55 languages, 50 of which have over 100 source texts.

Further Reading

http://wikisource.org/   The Wikisource portal

http://en.wikisource.org/wiki/Wikisource:Community_Portal   The English-language Wikisource community portal

http://meta.wikimedia.org/wiki/Wikisource#List_of_Wikisources_by_size
A list of all Wikisources

Wikispecies

Founded: September 13, 2004

Scope: Systematic biological database of species

URL: *http://species.wikimedia.org/*

Short prefix: wikispecies

Languages: Background language is English with Latin species names, some support pages, and vernacular naming multilingual

Wikispecies is a collection of information about living species. (Figure 16-10 shows its logo.) It aims to create a comprehensive free-content catalog of all species (including animalia, plantae, fungi, bacteria, archaea, and protista) and is geared to scientists rather than the general public. Pages consist of the scientific names and classification of organisms, aligned along the *Linnaean taxonomy*, or standard hierarchical biological classification.

FIGURE 16-10:
Wikispecies logo

Wikispecies is not designed to compete with Wikipedia (where articles may exist about many of the species noted) but rather to complement it by providing taxonomic information. The need for a comprehensive taxonomic database that scientists and others could edit was cited as a reason for creating the site in 2004. As with the other projects, Wikipedia, Commons, and Wikispecies can link to one another in order to provide a comprehensive reference to a species with encyclopedic information, images, and a complete taxonomic listing. To contribute, editors can (among other tasks) search for pictures to add to species listings, add references, and fill in missing species.

Only one Wikispecies site exists, but the site has several dozen portal pages for various languages. In addition, each species name is translated into the local vernacular (including English, which makes Wikispecies a useful place to look up an unfamiliar Latin name).

Further Reading

http://species.wikimedia.org/   The Wikispecies site

http://species.wikimedia.org/wiki/Help:Contents   The help page for Wikispecies

http://meta.wikimedia.org/wiki/Wikispecies   About Wikispecies and why it was created

http://en.wikipedia.org/wiki/Wikispecies   The Wikispecies article from Wikipedia, which also includes links to other related projects

Wikiversity

Founded: August 15, 2006

Scope: Educational materials

URL: *http://wikiversity.org/*

Short prefix: v

Languages: 9 (en, fr, de, es, it, pt, cs, el, ja), plus one multilingual site

FIGURE 16-11: *The English-language Wikiversity main page*

Wikiversity is a community for creating and using free learning materials and activities and is geared toward developing communities dedicated to learning, teaching, research, and service (see Figure 16-11). Its primary goals are to create and host free content, multimedia learning materials, resources, and curricula for all age groups in all languages and develop collaborative learning projects and communities around these materials.

Resources on Wikiversity include teaching aids, lesson plans, curricula, links to off-site resources, and reading lists, which can all be combined to create a web of resources about a topic. Learning groups on Wikiversity discuss and do activities using these materials, and educators outside of Wikiversity can use them for their own purposes under the terms of the GFDL. Wikiversity participants can also express their individual learning goals, and the Wikiversity community collaborates to develop learning activities and projects to accommodate those goals; projects that encourage learning through editing Wikiversity pages are also welcome.

Wikiversity organizes its content with Portal and School namespaces; *Portals* provide a way to browse a range of related topics, whereas *Schools* (such as the School of Chemistry) provide lessons related to a particular topic. Connections to other projects—such as further reading on Wikipedia or Wikibooks—are welcome.

Wikiversity is the newest formal Wikimedia project. Although it was originally started at Wikibooks in 2003, a formal proposal to create Wikiversity as an independent project wasn't voted on by the Wikimedia Foundation Board until 2005. Wikiversity officially began as an independent project (in a beta phase) on August 15, 2006, with the English-language Wikiversity. As of mid-2008, 10 language Wikiversities had been created.

Further Reading

http://wikiversity.org/   The portal page for Wikiversity

http://en.wikiversity.org/wiki/Wikiversity:Welcome,_newcomers   About Wikiversity's goals

---

Linking Between Projects and Copying Content

Linking between sister projects is very much encouraged where it is appropriate. For instance, if Wikipedia has an article about a term that is also defined on Wiktionary, links to the other should be included in both. Quotes from a famous figure who is also the subject of a Wikipedia article may appear on Wikiquote, or a how-to book about an article topic may be on Wikibooks. Article topics may also first appear on another project besides Wikipedia: A current event covered on Wikinews might well evolve into a Wikipedia article. Like interlanguage links, these interwiki links should only be made to existing articles on an equivalent topic.

Also, like links between different-language versions of the same project, interwiki links between projects use special codes to identify the project. These codes were given in the boxes included in the previous section describing the individual projects; they are *commons*, *wikt*, *b*, *s*, *q*, *wikispecies*, and *v*. These prefixes can be combined with language codes to produce a double prefix using a consistent naming scheme: For example, *de:wikt:* is the double prefix referring to the German-language Wiktionary.

How to Link

You can link between Wikimedia projects in two ways. The first is to use regular in-text links, with full or abbreviated names, similar to interlanguage links.

These standard links may simply take the form

```
[[nameofproject:nameofpage]]
```

where *nameofproject* is the name of the Wikimedia project you wish to link to (Wikipedia, Wikiversity, Commons, and so on) and *nameofpage* is the page title that you wish to link to on that page. This is simple and intuitive enough: [[Wiki-quote:Lord Byron]] is the page for quotes relating to Lord Byron. Notice that no indicator is included about which language version of Wikiquote you are linking to; if you don't specify a language, the link will go to the equivalent project in the same language you're linking from. For instance, if you include the Lord Byron link on the English-language Wikipedia, clicking it will take you to the English-language Wikiquote page for Lord Byron. After all, most of the time that would be what you wanted to achieve.

The name of the project may also be abbreviated in a shortcut form, as mentioned previously. Because the shortcut form for Wikipedia is simply w, you can link to a page on Wikipedia from another project with a link that looks like this:

```
[[w:nameofpage]]
```

If you want to link to another language edition of another project, use the double prefix—the project code with the language code, with a colon in front of it. For instance,

```
[[:es:wikt:fish]]
```

will take you from any project to the Spanish-language Wiktionary entry called *fish*, which in this case contains a Spanish explanation of the English word and a link to the Spanish equivalent—*pez*. The colon convention is required for the same reasons we explained in Chapter 15: No colon means a link is moved onto the sidebar as an interlanguage link.

These links may be piped as for conventional wikilinks, so for instance, you could set the link to read like this:

```
[[w:nameofpage|read more about this on Wikipedia]]
```

Defined shortcuts, which we have listed project by project, are also detailed with those for some other sites on [[Wikipedia:Interwikimedia links]].

The second way to link to a sister project is to use one of the special templates that have been set up for this purpose. On Wikipedia, this is the preferred way to provide such links. The advantage of using a template is that the resulting link is set apart in a box with the logo of the project being linked to and some explanatory text. You will generally see these templates at the bottom of articles when they are included, in the Further reading or External links section, though they can appear anywhere throughout an article; for instance, a template linking to Wikiquote may appear in the Quotes section of a Wikipedia article.

These templates are detailed at [[Wikipedia:Sister projects]]. Except for a few special ones, they link to a search for the parameter name (usually an article name) that you type, rather than to the page with that exact title directly; that way, if no title matches are found on the sister project, full-text matches will be displayed instead.

Wikipedia has individual templates to link to all of the sister projects. A separate template for linking to all of the projects at once is also available and can be used for a very common topic that may have an article on Wikipedia, a definition on Wiktionary, media on Commons, a text referring to it on Wikibooks or Wikiversity, and so on. This template is located at [[Template:Sisterlinks]]. To use it, place it on a page with a single parameter that is the page name you want to search on (typically the same as the article name):

```
{{sisterlinks|energy}}
```

This results in an infobox (Figure 16-12) with links to search for the term *energy* in Wiktionary, Wikibooks, Commons, Wikinews, Wikiquote, and Wikiversity.

FIGURE 16-12: *Sisterlinks template*

The individual templates for linking between projects are fairly intuitive. All should be used with the name of the page being linked to as a parameter. The templates are as follows:

```
{{Wikipedia}}
{{Wiktionary}}
{{Wikinews}}
{{Wikibooks}}
{{Wikiquote}}
{{Wikisource}}
```

```
{{Wikispecies}}
{{Wikiversity}}
{{Commons}}
```

You can use

```
{{MediaWiki}}
{{Meta}}
```

for linking to the MediaWiki wiki and Meta-Wiki. These last two are primarily help-ful for linking cross-project help pages and documentation.

　　Note that the Wikipedia template is not necessary (and, in fact, just won't work) when linking from one language version Wikipedia to another; using the language code is sufficient. Many variations of these templates exist for linking to categories on other projects; you can find all of the templates at [[Category:Inter-wiki link templates]].

Moving Content Between Projects

Occasionally, a page will be added to Wikipedia that doesn't belong but would be appropriate for one of the sister projects. For instance, a dictionary definition doesn't belong on Wikipedia—but would be great at Wiktionary. These pages are candidates for being copied to another project. The jargon *transwiki* applies to moves of material from one wiki to another. The term is appropriate for pages from any namespace that need to be moved to another Wikimedia project; for instance, technical help pages might need to be transwikied to MediaWiki, whereas Foundation-wide pages might need to be moved to the Meta site.

　　Pages that need to be moved can be marked with *transwiki templates*; these work like other templates and can be found at [[Category:Transwiki templates]]. These templates mark the pages for automatic moving to other projects.

Further Reading

http://en.wikipedia.org/wiki/Wikipedia:Interwikimedia_links　Provides a chart of interwiki prefixes, shortcuts, and templates

http://en.wikipedia.org/wiki/Wikipedia:Sister_projects　Detailed information on the sister project templates

http://en.wikipedia.org/wiki/Wikipedia:Template_messages/Moving#Copying_to_other_projects　A list of commonly used transwiki templates, for placing on articles that would be better in other projects

---

Other Wikis

Since their original development in the mid-1990s, wikis have become commonly used for all sorts of applications, both private and public, and many interesting wiki communities that aren't affiliated with the Wikimedia Foundation have been created. These wikis may explore a topic area in more depth than Wikipedia does or provide a place for reviews and commentary that would violate Wikipedia's content policies. If what you want to work on doesn't seem like a good match with Wikipedia or any of the sister projects, try looking for another non-Wikimedia wiki instead. Most of these public wiki sites encourage reader participation, and you may find a culture and style that suits you.

✳ **NOTE:** *Though* wiki *is often used as an abbreviation to refer to Wikipedia, this is actually incorrect;* wiki *is simply a generic term for the particular type of website. Though Wikipedia is one of the most famous wikis, it is certainly not the only one!*

For instance, many fan communities for television shows and videogames have built wikis. Some wikis have a particular political orientation or are meant to document a particular project or piece of software. Large wikis exist that aim to build worldwide travel guides (such as *http://wikitravel.org/*) or collect comprehensive how-to guides for every topic area (such as *http://wikihow.org/*). A movement is growing to start wikis for individual towns and communities and collect useful information about that place for residents and visitors. Some wikis even provide variations on the idea of building an encyclopedia. Many of these sites are commercial, while others may be nonprofit; many use an open content license. A directory of wiki sites can be found at *http://www.wikindex.com/*. Wikipedia itself comes through with the [[List of wikis]], which is sorted by type. Other wiki sites

---

Wikia

Wikia is a commercial wiki hosting service (*wiki farm*) based in San Mateo, California, which hosts wikis about a wide variety of topics, including fan communities. Jimmy Wales, the founder of Wikipedia, and Angela Beesley, who has served on the Wikimedia Foundation Board, founded Wikia in 2004. Wikia, Inc., is independent from the Wikimedia Foundation. Wikia does share with Wikimedia a reliance on the MediaWiki software and the GFDL license (except for Memory Alpha, a Star Trek wiki, which uses a Creative Commons license). Wikia sites are generally supported with ads. See *http://wikia.com/* for more information.

---

may be very different both technically and socially from Wikimedia sites and Wikipedia, but the basic ideas we've presented in this book, of editing and interacting respectfully, should apply to every wiki.

Starting Your Own Wiki

For many interests, a wiki community may already exist. If you have an idea for a new Wikimedia project, see the next chapter for how to make a proposal. New Wikimedia projects are started slowly, however, and for most specific wiki ideas, either finding an existing project to join or starting your own is best. Are you interested in starting a wiki for your own purposes? You should keep a few factors in mind. For instance, are you willing and able to take on the technical maintenance yourself? How much are you willing to pay for software and hosting? Most importantly, for what purpose are you building a wiki? Consider whether the wiki is intended for a few collaborators on a particular project or as a larger community site. Who are your potential audience and editors?

Building a wiki community requires more than simply installing the software. Even the simplest online community needs some structure and goals. If you have only a few editors, keeping up with spam and vandalism may present a problem. You can find much advice on how to start a viable wiki community online; the Wikibooks article at *http://en.wikibooks.org/wiki/Wiki_Science/How_to_start_a_Wiki* is a good place to start.

The New Project Creation Process

New language versions of the Wikipedia, Wikinews, Wikiquote, or Wiktionary projects are tested at the *Wikimedia Incubator* (*http://incubator.wikimedia.org/*). Here a proposed new version can be tried out and key pages can be translated before the project goes live. Anyone can help out with this initial process.

Wiki Software

MediaWiki is available for free download, as described in the next chapter, but other wiki software packages, as well as companies that host wikis for a fee, are available. Wikipedia has, naturally, a list of the many wiki software packages at [[List of wiki software]]. A comparison of these packages can be found at [[Comparison of wiki software]] or at the useful Wikimatrix site, *http://wikimatrix.org/*.

Further Reading

Finding Other Wikis

http://en.wikipedia.org/wiki/Wikipedia:Alternative_outlets   A list of alternative outlets for material not appropriate for Wikipedia

http://en.wikipedia.org/wiki/List_of_wikis   A list of wiki sites arranged by topic

http://www.wikindex.com/   A huge index of wikis on the Web, from large to tiny, that shows the relative level of activity on each

Starting Your Own Wiki

http://en.wikibooks.org/wiki/Wiki_Science:How_to_start_a_Wiki   "How to start a Wiki," from Wikibooks

http://en.wikipedia.org/wiki/Comparison_of_wiki_software   A chart comparing various wiki software packages

http://wikimatrix.org/   Provides information on and offers comparisons between dozens of wiki software packages

Summary

In this chapter, we've covered the eight Wikimedia projects besides Wikipedia that aim to produce free-content, wiki-based reference materials: Wiktionary, Wikinews, Wikibooks, Wikiquote, Wikisource, Wikispecies, Wikiversity, and the Wikimedia Commons. These projects offer complementary content, and you can link pages between the different projects, providing a comprehensive reference resource about a topic.

This survey of the sister projects run by Wikimedia sets the scene for our last chapter. With so much diverse activity enabled by so many editable sites, the projects need a central supporting structure, which is provided by the Wikimedia Foundation.

17

The Foundation and Project Coordination

Who is actually in charge of Wikipedia and its sister projects? The Wikimedia Foundation (WMF), first introduced to you in Chapter 2, has taken on this role. The Foundation does not oversee any project content but instead owns the projects legally and provides a central resource to keep the projects' infrastructure, such as the web servers, up and running.

Because the Foundation staff is small for such an ambitious venture, most day-to-day decisions are still made by the community that has developed around each project. The wiki spirit of volunteering does not stop at the individual project level, however. Daily work on Foundation-level tasks is carried out by hundreds of people, from running elections to talking to the press to helping out with fundraising. Foundation volunteers generally come from individual wiki projects and use that background knowledge in their work. Perhaps they first contributed to Wikipedia, then fanned out to another project such as Wiktionary, and discovered they were interested in cross-project or cross-language issues. Much of the discussion between community members on Wikimedia's different projects occurs on the *Meta-Wiki*, which we'll describe later in this chapter. Its pages are referenced in the style [[m:Help]], where the interwiki symbol *m* stands for *http://meta.wikimedia.org/wiki/*. This is distinct from the Foundation's own wiki, at *http://wikimediafoundation.org/*; the interwiki code for the Foundation is *wmf*. We'll refer to pages on both of these wikis throughout this chapter.

This chapter describes the governance structure for the projects as a whole, how operational work gets done, and how to get involved. Wikipedia, Wiktionary, Wikibooks, Wikinews, Wikisource, Wikiquote, and Wikiversity in all their language versions together represent thousands of varied, individual wiki communities. A few broad policies apply to all the projects, but central control is mostly *ad hoc*; the Foundation is really a federation of projects and activities, bringing together everyone who wishes to help with cross-project work.

The Foundation: Mission and Structure

The Wikimedia Foundation was first proposed in June 2003 by Jimmy Wales. With the Foundation's announcement, Wales transferred ownership of all Wikipedia, Wiktionary, and Nupedia domain names to Wikimedia along with the copyrights for all materials related to these projects that were created by Bomis employees or

Wales himself. Wales also donated the computer equipment used to run all the Wikimedia projects to the Foundation. The domain names *wikimedia.org* and *wikimediafoundation.org* were secured for the Foundation by Wikipedia contributor Daniel Mayer. The Foundation logo (Figure 17-1) was designed in 2003 by user:Neolux; this logo came in second in an international contest to choose a new Wikipedia logo. (The first-place choice, designed by user:Nohat, became the current Wikipedia logo, while the third-place choice became the current MediaWiki logo.)

FIGURE 17-1: *The Wikimedia Foundation logo*

Since those early days, the WMF has taken on multiple roles. The main areas in which the Foundation operates, both with volunteers and paid staff, are the following:

▶ Maintaining the technical infrastructure for all of the projects, including hardware expansion and server maintenance in three countries

▶ Starting new projects, overseeing existing projects, and encouraging translation among them

▶ Providing a central wiki forum for discussion, the Meta-Wiki

▶ Supporting and directing the development of the MediaWiki software

- ► Fundraising and finance

- ► Handling legal matters, including organizational trademarks and domain names

- ► Developing chapters and coordinating volunteers

- ► Coordinating publicity work, including outreach and the Wikimania annual conference

- ► Participating in free culture and free license discussions and initiatives

The Wikimedia Foundation is a nonprofit charitable organization under US law. From 2003 to 2007 the Foundation was based in St. Petersburg, Florida; in January 2008, the organization moved to San Francisco, California. Most people working on Foundation matters, including members of the Board of Trustees, are volunteers. The Foundation now has about 15 paid employees, including an executive director, chief technical officer, and technical and administrative support staff.

As of August 2007, the Foundation's mission statement is:

> The mission of the Wikimedia Foundation is to empower and engage people around the world to collect and develop educational content under a free license or in the public domain, and to disseminate it effectively and globally.

> In collaboration with a network of chapters, the Foundation provides the essential infrastructure and an organizational framework for the support and development of multilingual wiki projects and other endeavors which serve this mission. The Foundation will make and keep useful information from its projects available on the Internet free of charge, in perpetuity.

Wikimedia also has a clear role in promoting free culture and free content—not just text, but also images and other media files. In addition to adopting free licenses for all of the projects, the Foundation has adopted the Free Cultural Works Definition, which is similar to the free software definition, for all of its projects (see *http://freedomdefined.org/Definition*).

Infrastructure and the Board

The Foundation is governed by a Board of Trustees. Currently (mid-2008) the Board has eight members: three members directly elected by the Wikimedia community and five appointed members. In Spring 2008, the Foundation announced that the Board would be expanded to ten seats, with the addition of two seats appointed by the local chapters of the Wikimedia Foundation, which are community-based organizations operating within a specific geographic region. The Board is generally responsible for the Wikimedia Foundation, including supervising the finances and legal and technical infrastructure.

The Foundation as a whole tends not to become involved in internal debates on Wikipedia or any of the other projects, and the Foundation Board members and staff are not responsible for project content, editorial policies, or resolving disputes. Instead the Foundation provides broad guidance for the projects, such as advocating for free content. Foundation-level volunteers like stewards (described in "Project Coordination" on page 454) may deal with issues on smaller projects, especially ones that are just getting started and having troubles. Overall, however, the Foundation model assumes very loose central control.

Although the general public might still assume that Jimmy Wales runs Wikipedia, that is far from being the case. Wales still sits on the Board of Trustees but stepped down from being Board chair in 2006. He still retains an informal leadership position on the projects but is, for the most part, continually on the move as a goodwill ambassador for the Foundation and the projects.

An advisory board, currently consisting of 20 appointed members who are experts in many areas, including free software, law, technology, outreach, and nonprofit organization, provides advice to the Board and staff as needed.

Elections

Elections for community representative Board members have been held periodically since 2004. In the past, to vote you needed to have a registered account with at least 400 edits on a single Wikimedia project. Each candidate for the Board posts a short campaign statement on Meta, which is then translated into many languages; secure voting takes place over a set period of time. Any community member is welcome to ask the candidates questions. Details, including the results of previous elections and previous candidate platforms, may be found at [[m:Elections]].

Foundation-Level Policy

Of all the WMF official policies found at [[wmf:Policies]], here are the most important ones for members of the public, readers, and editors:

▶ [[wmf:Resolution:Licensing policy]] indicates that projects are expected to host only content that is under a Free Content License.

▶ [[wmf:Non discrimination policy]] prohibits any type of discrimination against current or prospective users and employees.

▶ [[wmf:Privacy policy]] indicates that if you only read the Wikimedia project websites, no more information is collected than is typically collected in server logs by websites in general; but if you write something, assume the project will retain it forever.

▶ [[wmf:Access to nonpublic data policy]] allows only persons whose identity is known to the WMF be permitted to access any nonpublic data held by the WMF.

- ► [[wmf:Code of Conduct Policy]] includes the need for those acting on the WMF's behalf to respect confidentiality of sensitive information.
- ► [[wmf:Gift Policies]] relates to gifts to the WMF and the role of the Grants Coordinator.

Fundraisers and Donations

Project users expect continuous service with few outages, yet traffic keeps increasing exponentially. This requires more bandwidth, the annual budget for which is already in the high hundreds of thousands of dollars. These costs, and the other expenses of running the projects, must be met in order to provide a stable platform for the voluntary effort of content creation.

Project costs, from staff salaries to new servers, are funded almost entirely with private donations. Typical donations to the Foundation are from individuals who give on the order of $20 to $40. The money goes entirely to the costs of running Wikimedia projects. Although you can donate at any time of the year, the Foundation also sponsors periodic fundraising drives; these are generally announced in project-wide site notices. You can dismiss these site notices if you're logged in.

Why Not Have Ads on Wikipedia?

Advertisements on Wikipedia? This is an old idea that is constantly brought up, though more often these days by "helpful" outsiders.* Wikipedia has a large share of Internet traffic, the reasoning runs, and so is prime real estate for ads. And yet, the status quo in the WMF is that the projects have no ads, nor are they ever likely to. To sum up the reasons why, ads would be (1) inconsistent with the tradition and culture of free culture and an affront to many community members who would likely leave over the issue, (2) difficult to reconcile with the Neutrality policy, (3) ugly, and (4) the wrong way of forking because anyone can always fork out a commercial version.

*See, for example, Alana Semuels, "Wikipedia's Tin-Cup Approach Wears Thin," Los Angeles Times (March 10, 2008): http://www.latimes.com/business/la-fi-wikipedia10mar 10,0,7404443.story?page=1.

Wikimedia Chapters and Outreach

The WMF has 17 *chapters* (as of 2008), which are independent organizations created by Wikimedians around the world to support and promote the Wikimedia projects within their particular country or area. Chapters have no particular tie to any particular project in any language. Though they are clearly related to the WMF, they are each independent organizations, not subsidiaries. The Foundation enters into separate agreements with the individual chapters regarding use of the Wikimedia name and logos.

In order of their formal founding and recognition, the chapters are

- 2004: Wikimedia Deutschland (Germany) and Wikimédia France

- 2005: Wikimedia Italia, Wikimedia Polska, and Wikimedia Србије (Serbia)

- 2006: Wikimedia UK, Wikimedia Nederland, and Wikimedia CH (Switzerland)

- 2007: Wikimedia Taiwan, Wikimedia Israel, Wikimedia Sverige (Sweden), Wikimedia Argentina, and Wikimedia Hong Kong

- 2008: Wikimedia Österreich (Austria), Wikimedia Australia, Wikimedia Česká republika (Czech Republic), and Викимедиа Ру (Russia)

You can find a current list at [[m:Wikimedia chapters]].

Chapters are geographical-based, rather than language-based entities; for instance, Wikimedia Deutschland supports activities in Germany, rather than the German-language projects specifically (which cater to German speakers all around the world).

Chapter creation is centrally coordinated by the Wikimedia Foundation, under the auspices of the Chapters Committee. Any experienced contributor who is interested in forming a chapter should get in touch with this group and visit [[m: Chapters committee]]. Chapters may run promotional activities, fundraise for the projects within their countries, and pursue other Wikimedia-related projects.

✳ NOTE: *You can begin activities in your area, such as local meetups, without forming a chapter—and, in fact, this is good preliminary activity. You need a group of interested people who can work together before beginning a formal organization.*

Other Foundation outreach comes in the form of conferences and special events. *Wikimania*, the annual international conference of the WMF, was already profiled in Chapter 12; this event is run by project volunteers. Other events related to Wikimedia have included Wikimedia Academies, which are designed as small conferences focused toward academics and teaching about Wikimedia projects, and regional conferences, such as the Wikimedia Conference Netherlands. You can find a list of such events past and present at [[m:Events]].

MediaWiki

MediaWiki, the free program used to run the Foundation sites, is available as open-source software for anyone to use and customize for his or her own wiki site. Download it from *http://www.mediawiki.org/wiki/Download*. To run the software, you need a web server (such as Apache), a database server (such as MySQL), and PHP. To install the software, you must have access to your web server. You can find installation instructions on the MediaWiki site, *http://mediawiki.org/*, which also lists documentation pages and many user-developed extensions.

Development of MediaWiki is now directed by the Foundation, handled by a small team of paid developers, and supported by many volunteers. Brion Vibber, long-time head of MediaWiki development, serves as the current CTO.

Further Reading

The Wikimedia Foundation and Chapters

http://wikimediafoundation.org/   The Wikimedia Foundation site

http://wikimediafoundation.org/wiki/Mission_statement   The Wikimedia
   Foundation mission statement

http://wikimediafoundation.org/wiki/Donate   The Foundation donation page

http://meta.wikimedia.org/wiki/Wikimedia_chapters   Information on Wikimedia
   local chapters

http://meta.wikimedia.org/wiki/Events   Information about Wikimedia events

MediaWiki

http://mediawiki.org/   The MediaWiki site, including links to install the software
   and documentation

http://www.mediawiki.org/wiki/Manual:Installation   Instructions for installing
   MediaWiki software

http://bugzilla.mediawiki.org/   Bugzilla for MediaWiki, to report software bugs

Wikipedia was first written on the UseMod wiki engine developed by Clifford Adams. Early wikis still used *CamelCase*, a convention for forming wikilinks automatically by using uppercase in the middle of a word and now an occasion for *WikiNostalgia*. CamelCase was phased out in January 2002 when Wikipedia migrated from the UseMod engine to its own software. This software was originally developed for Wikipedia as a PHP script by Magnus Manske, a German computer science student, rewritten by Lee Daniel Crocker, and later worked on by dozens of developers. The *MediaWiki* name, with its intentional play on Wikimedia, was not coined until 2003.

To report a bug in MediaWiki, go to the Bugzilla installation, accessible at *http://bugzilla.mediawiki.org/*. Here you can report problems with MediaWiki and some other selected Wikimedia software tools or search for information about currently open bugs.

The Meta-Wiki

Meta is the central wiki for coordination and discussion of all Wikimedia projects. Located at *http://meta.wikimedia.org/*, Meta is one of the extraordinary "hidden" parts of Wikimedia and showcases the projects' diversity. Meta is also where announcements are made that affect all of the projects.

The Meta site includes project proposals, discussions about existing projects, translation and language coordination, and day-to-day community development work for all of Wikimedia's wikis. General discussion happens at the [[m:metapub]]. Wikimedia-wide announcements are collected on the [[m:Goings-on]] page, while a list of historical milestones for all the projects can be found at [[m:Milestones]]. Although much of Meta is written in English, some pages are written in other languages; for example, [[m:Aide:Manuel de MediaWiki]] gives access to manual pages for French speakers. The normal rules of civility and professionalism apply, and remembering that you are working with people from all over the world is helpful. Related email lists, IRC channels, and in-person meetups provide ways for the thousands of people who work on Wikimedia projects all around the world to meet, plan, and talk.

Links to Meta may be found on Wikipedia, usually on documentation and proposal pages, and occasionally such pages may be *transwikied* from Wikipedia over to Meta. Meta, therefore, serves to collect general help pages and as a repository of documentation relevant to all of the projects. Meta is *not* a place for article development or idle discussion unrelated to the projects.

Project Coordination

Anything that requires cross-project coordination may be discussed on Meta. For instance, Meta is where new projects and new languages are proposed as well as set up.

Stewards are a special class of users who can assign bureaucrat or system administrator (sysop) privileges on any of Wikimedia's wikis (these users were discussed in Chapter 11). Typically, they help with small projects or new languages that might not yet have any system administrators. To see a list of stewards, you can go to [[m:Stewards]]. Normally, they will not perform actions that local bureaucrats or administrators can carry out. Stewards are elected in regular elections on Meta; they are trusted users who may be from any language or project but are generally multilingual. Steward actions are recorded at [[m:Special:Log/rights]] on Meta; specific requests for their assistance can be made at [[m:Steward requests]].

Translation

Meta is also where translations are coordinated across the projects. Some texts related to all the projects, such as fundraiser and project-wide election notices, need to be widely translated into many or all of the languages used in Wikimedia projects. The Meta page where such requests are posted is [[m:Translation requests]]. Questions and discussions regarding translations and translating can be posted at the *Babylon* noticeboard; see [[m:Babylon]].

If you are fluent in another language and wish to help with translation, you can join a translation team. Especially if you speak a language that is not widely spoken or that lacks current translators, you can also volunteer to be a *translation coordinator*, someone who keeps an eye on Foundation announcements and other material that needs to be translated and helps recruit volunteers for translations.

New Projects

Periodically, new sister projects are suggested. These projects should be discussed first on Meta at [[m:Proposals for new projects]]. Any new project must align with the values of the Foundation, particularly with its educational goals. Any new project also requires a large community of interested editors, so Meta is the place to recruit other people for your idea.

Starting a new project is a substantial commitment for the Wikimedia Foundation, so the vast majority of suggestions never come to fruition as Wikimedia projects. If this happens to your project, remember that finding other wiki projects and starting your own wiki are easy. The Meta page also serves as a way to locate other editors who might be interested in the same topic; if you find a number of potential supporters, you will probably be encouraged to start your project independently.

Requests for new language editions of existing Wikimedia projects are handled at [[m:Requests for new languages]].

Communication

There are a number of mailing lists and IRC channels related to Foundation work (rather than related to individual projects). The two main places to look are the *Foundation-L* mailing list, which has open subscription and open archives, and the *#Wikimedia* IRC channel.

Additionally, nearly all of the projects and many individual language projects (such as the English-language Wikipedia) have their own mailing lists; some of them are more active than others. If you're thinking about getting involved in another project, or a Wikipedia in another language, try browsing the relevant list's archives. You can find a full listing of mailing lists on Meta at [[m:Mailing lists]].

Further Reading

http://meta.wikimedia.org/   The Meta site

http://meta.wikimedia.org/wiki/Proposals_for_new_projects   The page to request new projects

http://meta.wikimedia.org/wiki/Requests_for_new_languages   The page to request new languages

http://meta.wikimedia.org/wiki/Mailing_lists   A list of all Wikimedia mailing lists

http://meta.wikimedia.org/wiki/Metapub   The Meta community portal

http://meta.wikimedia.org/wiki/Translation_requests   The place where translations are coordinated

http://meta.wikimedia.org/wiki/Stewards   Information about stewards

---

Looking Back and Going Forward

Part IV showed you the rest of the picture: the hundreds of Wikimedia wikis that are not the English-language Wikipedia. Maybe the English-language Wikipedia's role as flagship project will persist, but internationalism is clearly a component of all the projects as a whole. The proportion of English content over all the Wikimedia sites is still dropping: Today, three out of four Wikipedia pages are not in English.

As noted in Chapter 2, most of the ingredients for how Wikipedia (and indeed, all of the Wikimedia projects) works were in place by early 2001: a working site with an encyclopedic mission, a strong community, and core wiki philosophies. After all we've said in Parts III and IV about the current Wikipedia and Wikimedia communities, reviewing some features of early Wikipedia history is worthwhile, so we'll pick up where we left off in Chapter 2.

Early Days

Constant growth has always been a defining feature of Wikipedia. In Wikipedia's first year, over 1,500 articles per month were created; now that number of articles is created in a *single day* on the English-language Wikipedia. On August 30, 2002, the article count reached 40,000; a year later; the article count was 150,000; and a year after that, in August 2004, the total count was over 300,000 articles. In broad terms, the rate of growth has increased steadily from the project's inception, discounting a few technical slowdowns. (Growth may be slowing, however, for the English-language Wikipedia, if not for the other projects; early 2007 saw continued growth but some flattening of the trend.)

This growth has been technical as well; the initially fairly basic technology behind the site, both MediaWiki and the server infrastructure, has required constant upgrades to keep up with Wikipedia's phenomenal popularity. The number of servers nearly tripled in 2005 alone (the year of the first Wikimania conference, heavy news coverage, and the Seigenthaler scandal), from 39 to over 100. Oldtimers on the site still remember the glitches. How slow the site could be! Early on, the onsite search was often switched off to improve performance, but edits were still commonly lost, in contrast to today's reliability. The number of technical staff has always been small compared to the size of the projects; as of early 2008, all of Wikimedia's projects on hundreds of servers worldwide are run by just four paid technical staff with the help of a few volunteers.

As Wikipedia and the software powering it grew and changed, basic article structure and the style governing articles also changed, and the initial, somewhat primitive look-and-feel was incrementally improved. Big advances in editing came with the use of sections in articles. The category system was delayed, and lists proliferated in Wikipedia's first three years. In the end, categories were enabled somewhat casually in 2004, and three haphazard months of category creation ensued, which annoyed many people (but this settled down in time).

Another theme has been the slow evolution of the Wikimedia community. Wikipedia's social structure has defined itself over time. A preference for very flat hierarchies, which still prevails, didn't stop various classes of Wikipedians from emerging: developers and sysops (administrators), which were first defined as classes of editors in 2001. These classes remain limited, however; today, just as in 2001, any editor who has worked on the site for a few days has the same content privileges as any other editor. Certain community structures also evolved in the first few years as the site grew: The process for requests for administratorship, for instance, was not set up until 2003. This community growth was also reflected in the first in-person meetups in 2004. At the same time, the Foundation began fundraising to try to keep up with the site's growth.

Late 2005 initiated a new era for Wikipedia, as the media generally started to take a much greater interest in the project, its critics, and its internal affairs—a trend that continues to the present. By 2005, the site had arrived.

Continued Values

Some early key policy and technical decisions helped shape the success of Wikipedia and the other Wikimedia projects. One of these is the license: Since the content of Wikipedia is released under the GFDL, anyone can reuse Wikipedia content. The emphasis on open content and open source remain absolutely fundamental to the project.

Another innovation from the early days of Wikipedia's development was originally technical—the development of the article talk page. The very first versions of the wiki software had no talk page; comments were left at the bottom of the article. In retrospect, separating out the talk page seems like a simple idea: You have the article page, for instance [[Goldfish]], and [[Talk:Goldfish]] is the separate forum in which to discuss the content of the Goldfish article. The clear division of content (always unsigned) versus editorial comment (signed), was actually a huge step forward. Separating content debates from the articles themselves led to a strong belief that such discussions should be conducted gracefully and certainly not in the *flame war* style rampant on most Internet forums. Using discussion to work out content and community problems has proved to be a critical part of how Wikipedia deals with contentious issues.

Finally, the key values mentioned in previous chapters—some of which are enshrined as policy, whereas others are simply part of the philosophy behind the site—have made Wikipedia what it is today. On the content side, the ideas of free content, neutrality, and verifiability have been present since the project's first days. On the community side, the ideals of civility, assuming good faith, and being bold have encouraged large-scale participation in a project with shared and interlocking ideals.

Summary

Wikipedia has come a long way. Its first seven years have seen the development of many millions of articles and the building of a worldwide community of hundreds of thousands of active editors. At the same time, Wikipedia has become part of the larger Wikimedia Foundation, with hundreds of sister projects and communities, each running the volunteer-developed MediaWiki software. The Wikimedia Foundation is both a crowd of volunteers doing varied work from locations around the globe and in a broad range of languages and an effective, distinctive voice for globally distributed, reusable free content, available to anyone.

Conclusion to Part IV

On March 27, 2008, a few minutes after midnight GMT, Wikimedia announced that 10 million articles across all language editions of Wikipedia had been created. This announcement made a media splash, while another significant milestone a few days later, that 100 Wikipedias now have at least 5,000 articles, slipped by without fanfare. Wikipedia watchers won't be surprised at the details. Article number 10,000,000 was on the Hungarian Wikipedia and about Nicholas Hilliard, a painter of miniatures during the reign of Elizabeth I. The 100th language to reach 5,000 articles was Kapampangan, a major language in the Philippines. According to the Wikipedia *Signpost* from April 7, 2008, 40 percent of new articles are now coming from languages outside the top 10 (by size) language editions of Wikipedia—the leading group including most of the languages dominating global communications (though not Arabic). Wikipedia as a global project, encompassing both the topics and the languages of the world, has become a reality.

Scope exists for another book—or many books—on different models for user-contributed content: Other models are gaining prominence on the Web. A fitting place to end is with the thought that Wikipedia's model, which has become Wikimedia's model, may be one of the hardest to make work. Wikipedia took from earlier wikis the post-moderation concept: Allow people to contribute freely and deal with problematic content later. That this approach could succeed at all is counterintuitive, and even more debatable is whether the approach is feasible as a way to produce quality reference material. But surprisingly to many, Wikipedia has succeeded beyond anyone's hopes, perhaps leading to the truth of the oft-repeated saying that *Wikipedia only works in practice, not in theory.*[1]

We have written at length about the technical and social means that make this collaboration possible, that underpin the work on the Wikimedia projects, and how you can easily be a part of it all. We hope we have also made clear that technology is not in itself enough to build an editing community. *Community* is an essential part of Wikipedia's jargon. For each of the hundreds of new Wikimedia Foundation projects, the first and most important milestone is the day an editing community assembles to collaborate on a new reference project.

----

[1] See, for instance, the user essay *http://en.wikipedia.org/wiki/User:CatherineMunro/Why_am_I_here%3F.*

A Reusing Wikimedia Content

Wikimedia site content is freely licensed. This means anyone can reuse Wikimedia content in any number of ways, for commercial or non-commercial purposes. Under the site's license, you have the freedom to reuse and remix content, provided that the same license is retained for your new creations—a radical departure from traditional notions of copyright. Not only can you become an editor and rewrite Wikipedia articles, but you are also free to use the material elsewhere, as long as you follow some specific and fairly simple guidelines. Reuse is part of the WMF's fundamental aim to distribute knowledge and content as widely as possible. The conditions of reuse come with the license chosen for the Wikimedia sites, which is, in most cases, the GNU Free Documentation License (GFDL), printed at the back of this book. Here we'll briefly discuss reusing Wikipedia content.

Guidelines for Reuse

The general policy that outlines reuse of Wikipedia content is at [[Wikipedia:Reusing Wikipedia content]], but the legal requirements for reuse come from the text of the GFDL license. The Wikimedia sites can be forked or *mirrored* (copied) in their entirety, or individual pages can be copied or reprinted. Under the GFDL, direct copying is referred to as *verbatim copying*, whereas creating new versions of works by changing or adding to Wikipedia content is referred to as making a *modified version* or producing a *derivative work*.

If you want to post either a full or partial copy of a Wikipedia article on your own website, reprint the article in a book or magazine, or reprint images, these conditions apply:

▶ New works that use GFDL-licensed content have to be licensed, in turn, under the GFDL: The license cannot be changed. (Because of this clause, the GFDL is often referred to as a *viral* license.)

▶ You must include a full copy of the GFDL license text with any GFDL-licensed work, to be reproduced in all copies of that work (for websites, this copy of the license should be locally hosted). The license can be found at *http://www.gnu.org/copyleft/fdl.html*.

▶ You must acknowledge the authorship of the article(s) you reuse; this can mean including either a prominent link to the original article history on Wikipedia or a list of all the authors from the article's history along with crediting text such as, "This page uses material from the Wikipedia article *<name of article>*."

▶ You must provide access to the *transparent copy* (in other words, a machine-readable copy) of the article you're using. (The transparent copy for a Wikipedia article can be any of a number of formats available from Wikipedia, including the wiki text, the HTML web pages, the XML feed, and so on.)

You may be able to fulfill the latter two obligations partially by providing a conspicuous direct link to the article hosted on Wikipedia. Moreover, for the purposes of creating derivative works of individual Wikipedia articles, a direct link to the particular Wikipedia article used is generally considered to be in compliance with the GFDL (provided your derivative work is also licensed under the GFDL).

As set out at [[Wikipedia:Copyrights#Definitions and trademarks]], Wikipedia considers each Wikipedia article to be an individual document. Wikipedia does not use invariant sections or cover texts. *Fair-use* content, such as fair-use images, does not fall under the GFDL license as such, but under the fair-use (or similar) regulations of the country where the media are retrieved; any such images should be credited to their original sources rather than Wikipedia. You can find more information about the copyright policy at [[Wikipedia:Copyrights]]. Content that is also in the public domain, such as older texts or photos from government agencies, can be copied without restriction; but if the text or photo has been modified on Wikipedia, the terms of the GFDL must be followed.

Examples of Reuse

Examples of reuse include printing Wikipedia articles in a book or magazine, hosting them on another reference website, or issuing a collection of articles on CD. Several selections of Wikipedia content have been released on a CD or DVD. The first was a German version published by Directmedia Publishing in October 2004. It was followed by a DVD-ROM of articles in April 2005. The DVD was wildly popular, selling out all 10,000 copies within 10 days.

In April 2006, a Wikipedia CD Selection was put together by the charity SOS Children. This CD was the first English-language CD version of Wikipedia and featured around 2,000 articles of particular interest to schools and children. The articles were selected by volunteers working for SOS Children, checked for suitability, and cleaned up. This CD was followed up in 2007 with a DVD selection called the "Wikipedia Selection for Schools," which SOS Children UK launched in coordination with the Wikimedia Foundation. This release was significantly larger, with 4,625 articles (or the equivalent of 15 printed encyclopedia volumes). A 2008 release is also planned.

In July 2007, the Polish Wikipedia was released on DVD by the Wikimedia Polska chapter, in cooperation with Helion SA. This DVD edition contained around 239,000 articles (and 59,000 images) and was put together by a combination of volunteers and paid editors who checked over the articles.

Also in 2007, the Wikipedia 1.0 WikiProject released its first DVD ("Version 0.5") with Linterweb, containing approximately 2,000 high-quality articles from the English-language Wikipedia. These articles were selected through the WikiProject, which assesses articles for quality specifically in preparation for releases in print or CD/DVD, as well as gathering collections of *core articles*, selections of important topics that every encyclopedia should have.

Printing Wikipedia has often been discussed but has proved trickier as a practical proposition than selecting articles for a disk. The German Wikipedia has led the way with printed selections of articles called *Wikireaders*, which were published by a company called WikiPress, an offshoot of Directmedia. In 2008, Bertelsmann, a German publisher, announced that it would work with the German Wikimedia chapter to produce *The Wikipedia Encyclopaedia in one volume*, a selection of the opening paragraphs of some 50,000 articles.

Finally, dozens of other websites mirror Wikipedia content, often combining Wikipedia articles with other reference sources; *http://www.answers.com/* and *http://www.reference.com/* are just two such sites.

Further Reading

http://en.wikipedia.org/wiki/Wikipedia:Text_of_the_GNU_Free_Documentation_License   Wikipedia's local copy of the GFDL (shortcut WP: GFDL)

http://en.wikipedia.org/wiki/Wikipedia:Copyrights   The Copyright policy and information on the GFDL and reuse

http://en.wikipedia.org/wiki/Wikipedia:Reusing_Wikipedia_content   The policy on reusing Wikipedia content

http://commons.wikimedia.org/wiki/Commons:Reusing_content_outside_Wikimedia   A guide to reusing images from Commons

http://en.wikipedia.org/wiki/Wikipedia:Database_download   Discusses the available downloads from the Wikipedia database, which are regularly produced for copying purposes

http://en.wikipedia.org/wiki/Wikipedia:Forking_FAQ   Information about forking Wikipedia

http://en.wikipedia.org/wiki/Wikipedia:Mirrors_and_forks   A list of Wikipedia forks and mirrors, including information about what to do if you find a mirror site that is not in compliance with the GFDL or has remote-loading pages

http://en.wikipedia.org/wiki/Wikipedia:Wikipedia_CD_Selection   Project page for the 1.0 project CD selections

http://schools-wikipedia.org/   A browsable collection of the articles chosen for the SOS Children's CD for schools

http://blog.wikimedia.org/2008/04/22/wikipedia-in-german-book-form/   Information about Bertelsmann's plan to publish *The Wikipedia Encyclopaedia in one volume*

B Wikipedia for Teachers

Student use of Wikipedia is very widespread—and understandably so! Wikipedia is readily available, easy to use, and covers an immense amount of information about subjects that students at all levels study.

In addition to reading the site, students may even contribute. Recognizing this, some teachers have incorporated editing and analyzing Wikipedia articles into their syllabi. On the other hand, many teachers and schools have profound concerns about using Wikipedia. In this section, we'll talk about using Wikipedia in two educational contexts: as a reference resource used by students, both in and out of the classroom, and as a possible source of teaching material for classroom editing projects.

Wikipedia as a Classroom Reference Resource

Wikipedia makes a natural reference resource: It's free, easily accessible, and has a much greater breadth of coverage than most reference sources. The downsides of using Wikipedia in a classroom setting include, of course, the potential for inaccurate, incomplete, or vandalized material and, for young children, possibly inappropriate material.

One possible solution to these problems is to use Wikipedia article selections on CD or DVD, as summarized in Appendix A. Two of these selections were designed specifically for schools, one particularly geared toward the UK National Curriculum. You can browse the articles on the DVD, which were edited and checked for suitability, at *http://schools-wikipedia.org/*.

For children or English-language learners, the Simple English Wikipedia may also be appropriate. Available at *http://simple.wikipedia.org/*, this site aims to cover the same topics as the English-language Wikipedia, but in a simpler version of English. The breadth of the site is not nearly as large as that of the English-language Wikipedia, however, and many articles are still stubs.

Guiding Student Use of Wikipedia

Some school districts have banned the use of Wikipedia, an action which has made news.[1] The question is, of course, whether banning Wikipedia as a source will actually prevent students from using the site—or simply encourage students to avoid citing it. Our feeling is that students will use Wikipedia regardless; simply requiring students to go beyond Wikipedia (as with any encyclopedia) in their assignments may be a better solution. Students should cite additional sources for their projects, and often good Wikipedia articles can point students to some of those additional sources, though teachers should make sure these aren't the only references students use. Make your expectations regarding using Wikipedia for assignments clear. Discussing Wikipedia and its policies in detail can also be a good introduction to thinking critically about bias and authorship of any information source, online or off. Just figuring out what a neutral point of view might be for a controversial topic is a lesson in itself! Teaching students to assess each article separately, using the criteria mentioned in Chapter 4, is also important; Wikipedia is not a monolithic source and it should be clear that it is not of uniformly good or poor quality.

Whenever students use Wikipedia as a source, citing it accurately is important. Citations to Wikipedia should always include the (accurate) name of the article and a link to the particular version of the article that was accessed. You

---

[1] See, for instance, Lynn Olanoff, "School officials unite in banning Wikipedia," November 21, 2007, *http://seattletimes.nwsource.com/html/living/2004025648_wikipedia21.html*, an earlier discussion on Slashdot at *http://ask.slashdot.org/askslashdot/07/04/13/2018210.shtml*, and a Wikinews story from March 22, 2007, "Several US universities ban Wikipedia as primary source," *http://en.wikinews.org/wiki/Several_US_universities_ban_Wikipedia_as_primary_source. This topic was discussed at Wikimania 2008; see* http://wm08reg.wikimedia.org/scheule/events/37.en.html.

can get this by clicking either the Permanent link or the Cite This Page link on the left-hand sidebar when you are viewing an article. Cite This Page, in particular, provides an easy way to get citations for the article formatted using a number of academic styles. For instance, an American Psychological Association–style, or *APA-style*, citation generated by the Cite This Page feature for the article [[domestic sheep]] looks like this:

Domestic sheep. (2007, February 4). In *Wikipedia, The Free Encyclopedia*.
Retrieved 17:59, February 8, 2007, from http://en.wikipedia.org/w/index.
php?title=Domestic_sheep&oldid=105635704

Assigning Wikipedia Editing

Several projects have been developed that incorporate editing Wikipedia articles into classroom activities. Some teachers (primarily at the university level) have even made contributing good Wikipedia articles a requirement in place of term papers. A list of current and ongoing projects can be found at [[Wikipedia:School and university projects]], which also collects other resources for those trying to start a classroom project. [[Wikipedia:WikiProject Classroom coordination]] (shortcut WP:WPCC) also has a list of Wikipedia volunteers who are willing to help teachers work with Wikipedia at any level. If you start a classroom project, listing it on these pages and making other active editors aware of the articles your students are working on can be helpful; other editors are usually glad to help answer questions and help students navigate Wikipedia.

In general, assignments for student writing on Wikipedia should take into account the realities of the core policies and the fact that unwanted contributions will be quickly removed or changed. Make sure that students are familiar with Wikipedia and content policies and have time to experiment with editing and learn basic syntax. Having the students create logins (and having them edit while logged in) is also recommended, as this gives you a way to keep track of their contributions if they share their usernames with you. Keeping track of your students' contributions also helps you make sure things are going smoothly. Students can work individually or as a team, but it's important to reinforce that Wikipedia is generally a collaborative project. They will be working with other editors who are outside the school environment and who will not give them any special consideration for being students.

Assigning an article for cleanup or expansion is probably a better route to take than asking students to create brand-new articles. As noted in Chapter 5, finding a new article topic that meets notability standards can be difficult; much of the "low-hanging fruit" is already taken. Wikipedia has hundreds of thousands of existing articles that could use a thorough reworking, however. (If you're working with advanced-level students in a topic area that needs to be expanded, requiring that students start new articles may be a good idea.) Be creative: If the class is focusing on a particular subject area, have students research new information to add to articles that need expanding or fact-check poorly cited articles. If you are teaching composition or editing, you might have students copyedit or rewrite poor-quality articles for practice. If you're teaching upper-level students, you might have them rate articles in their topic area or have students work on the article version in the Simple English Wikipedia as a way to practice explaining information clearly using simpler language. For students at any level, working on adding reliable references and sources to articles provides an ideal opportunity to learn research skills.

Finally, though it may be tempting, don't encourage students to add work written for another project, such as a term paper, directly to Wikipedia. Often such work is cast in a tone and style that is inappropriate for a general encyclopedia (see Chapter 6). If you require students to edit Wikipedia articles, make this a separate writing project from other work.

Further Reading

Using Wikipedia in the Classroom

http://en.wikipedia.org/wiki/Wikipedia:FAQ/Schools An FAQ page for teachers and school administrators

http://en.wikipedia.org/wiki/Wikipedia:Researching_with_Wikipedia
Guidelines on using Wikipedia as a source for doing research, helpful for students

Editing Wikipedia in the Classroom

http://en.wikipedia.org/wiki/Wikipedia:School_and_university_projects A list of school projects that focus on editing Wikipedia, along with many links to other resources

http://en.wikipedia.org/wiki/Wikipedia:WikiProject_Classroom_coordination
A list of Wikipedians who are willing to help out with and "mentor" classroom projects

http://en.wikipedia.org/wiki/Wikipedia:Wikipedia_Signpost/2006-12-26/Wikipedia_and_academia A *Signpost* story on various Wikipedia classroom editing projects

http://en.wikipedia.org/wiki/Wikipedia:Wikipedia_in_academic_studies A list of papers that have studied Wikipedia and links to other research resources

C

Edit Summaries Jargon

Every time a person edits a Wikipedia article, he or she can add a line of text that summarizes the edit in the Edit summary box that is provided underneath the edit window. Wikipedia has no formal etiquette governing the content of edit summaries, but a vast body of jargon has developed over the years. This jargon is useful because it makes describing common types of edits easy, but the jargon can also be daunting to readers who are unfamiliar with it. This cheat sheet lists common edit summary terms and explains their meanings.

See [[Wikipedia:Edit summary legend]] for more terms used in edit summaries. See "Edit Summaries and Minor Edits" on page 111 for a full explanation of edit summaries and "Major vs. Minor Edits" on page 138 for an explanation of minor edits.

Common Edit Summaries

- **cat, +cat, fix cats** Categories have been added or altered.

- **cp or copyedit** A minor rewrite occurred that doesn't affect the article's basic meaning.

- **copyvio** Response to a copyright violation occurred. The editor may have removed the part of the article that violated copyright or just tagged the article as being a copyright violation. In extreme cases, the entire page might have been wiped blank.

- **lnk, lk, wfy, wikify, wik, wk** The text was wikified by adding links to other articles and sometimes by formatting according to Wikipedia style.

- **merge** The article was melded with another (see "Merge, Split, and Move" on page 240). This summary usually appears alongside other supporting information, such as the names of the articles merged.

- **mv or move** The page is being renamed by moving the entire contents and edit history to another (previously unused) page title. See Chapter 8.

- **NPOV or POV** The article did not have a Neutral Point of View and the edit corrects this (or adds a tag pointing out this flaw).

- **rdr, redirect** The page was turned into a redirect, taking readers to another wiki page automatically. See Chapter 8.

- **rv, rvv, rvt, or revert** The page was *reverted*, which means restoring it to a previous version. Reverts are often used to reverse acts of vandalism. They can be carried out using automatic software or "by hand."

- **Spam or linkspam** Spam or an unnecessary commercial link that had been placed in an article was removed.

- **Sp or spp, typo** A spelling mistake or typographical error was corrected.

- **Tighten** Inessential material was cut out or verbose wording was tightened.

- **+ro, +fr, +de:, and so on** These *language codes* signify that interwiki links have been created to versions of this article written in other languages—in this case, versions on the Romanian-, French-, and German-language Wikipedias, respectively. See Chapter 15 for more.

Deletion and Maintenance Summaries

- **Db (as in "db-nonsense" or "db-nn")** This means "delete because" or "delete because non-notable." It is more often seen in deletion discussions than in edit summaries and is sometimes used with speedy delete tags.

- **PROD, prod, or prodding; AfD**   This refers to the proposed deletion and deletion processes. The editor has probably just inserted a {{prod}} tag on the article, which, if not removed within five days, will lead to the article being deleted; see "Deleting Articles" on page 218.

- **{{cleanup}}, {{wikify}}, {{npov}}, or a variety of others**   Any term that is quoted in double curly brackets likely refers to the associated template (such as [[Template:Cleanup]]), which the editor has probably just placed on the article in question.

- **{{A7}}, {{G3}} or A7, G3, and so on**   These and similar codes refer to speedy delete tags; the cryptic codes refer to various reasons why a page may be speedily deleted. More on speedy deletion in Chapter 7. The template that is placed on the article should also contain further information.

Automatically Added Edit Summaries

Wikipedia has various editing mechanisms that don't involve clicking the Edit This Page tab directly. These edits are treated just the same as any other edit and show up normally in the article's revision history. When edits are made using nonstandard means, however, the edit summary is often filled in automatically by the MediaWiki software.

Editing a section
When you follow an Edit This Section link next to an article's subheading, the software automatically fills in the summary field with the name of the section you are editing. In the Edit summary field, the name appears between asterisks and slashes, like this: /*Further Reading*/. In the article history, the edited section title appears in grayed-out type next to a right-pointing arrow (→), which is a clickable link to that section of the article.

Using rollback or undo
The Undo button displays on the history page and lets you reverse a particular edit. The Rollback button is similar but can only be used by administrators. When these buttons are used, the summary of the resulting edit contains the term *rollback* (as in "rollback version to X") or *undo* (as in "version X undid by phoebe to version Y") with links.

Bots and editing tools
An edit summary that contains the text *AWB* refers to an edit that was completed with the help of the AutoWiki Browser, an automated tool (see Chapter 7). This and other tools help editors make repetitive edits (such as correcting spelling) or quickly revert vandalism. An edit summary that refers to a *bot* was made by an automatic program that performs even more highly repetitive tasks.

Other circumstances

Any edit summary with a left-pointing arrow (←) was added automatically by the software when no edit summary is provided by the editor. This only occurs when a page is blanked, when the page content is completely replaced (often vandalism), or when a new page or redirect is created. See [[Wikipedia:Automatic edit summaries]] (shortcut WP:AES).

Further Reading

http://en.wikipedia.org/wiki/Wikipedia:Edit_summary_legend   A longer list of common edit summaries, arranged by type of action

http://en.wikipedia.org/wiki/Wikipedia:Automatic_edit_summaries   About automatically added edit summaries

---

D

Glossary

Wikipedia's glossary, which contains many terms not found here, can be found at *http://en.wikipedia.org/wiki/Wikipedia:Glossary*.

admin   A Wikipedia administrator; administrators are users with extra technical privileges to delete and restore articles and block accounts and IP numbers

AfD   Articles for Deletion; an open forum for discussing article deletion on a case-by-case basis

AGF   Assume Good Faith; a guideline requesting civility and mutual trust among editors

ANI   The Administrators' noticeboard for incidents, where Wikipedia administrators discuss and can be alerted to current problems with vandalism, edit wars, or other issues that require administrator attention

anon   An anonymous or IP user who is not logged in when editing

ArbCom   The Arbitration committee; a body that resolves on-site disputes

arbitration   The top-level, formal, and lengthy dispute resolution procedure performed by the ArbCom

backlinks   The wikilinks that link to a page, displayed by clicking What Links Here on the left-hand sidebar

BOLD   Short for the slogan, "Be bold in updating articles," which means if you see an article that needs work, don't hesitate to improve it

bot   An automated editing program operating on the site

bureaucrat   An administrator with power to promote other editors to administrator status

COI   Conflict of interest, which occurs when the editor of an article is somehow personally invested in the topic

Commons   *See* Wikimedia Commons

contribs   The list of contributions, or edits, made by an editor

copyvio   Short for *copyright violation,* such as an article or image that contains copyrighted material from another source

CSD   Criteria for speedy deletion; the policy detailing when articles may be deleted without going through a review process. *See also* speedy

disambiguation page   A page that links to alternate articles with similar titles. For example, the Boston disambiguation page lists at least 20 places named Boston, as well as the rock band and WWII-era aircraft

dead-end page   A Wikipedia page with no outbound wikilinks. *See also* orphan article

diff   The display showing the differences between two versions of a wiki page

DRV   Deletion review; the appeals system for deleted articles

edit   Any saved change made to a wiki page

edit conflict   A conflict that occurs when two editors try to save versions of a page at the same time

edit count   The total number of edits made by a user's account

edit war   An extended dispute between two or more editors over article content; during an edit war, changes to an article are reverted multiple times and no consensus emerges about the article's content

external link   A hyperlink leading to a site outside Wikipedia

featured article   An esteemed category of peer-reviewed Wikipedia articles; each day a different featured article is spotlighted on the main page

Featured Content   A category of Wikipedia content including featured articles, images, lists, and portals

fork   (verb) To split a wiki into two editing communities, with the intent to develop the existing content in different ways; (noun) the end product of such a split

GFDL   The GNU Free Documentation License under which Wikipedia content is released

IAR   Ignore All Rules; a traditional slogan suggesting Wikipedians should rise above formalities in unusual situations

internal link   A hyperlink on a wiki leading to another location on the same wiki; an internal link is implemented in wikitext using special syntax rather than a URL

interwiki   To link different wikis by extending internal link syntax; on Wikipedia, to link corresponding articles in different language versions of Wikipedia

lead section   The introductory section of an article, which appears before the first heading

main namespace   The main or article namespace is the namespace that articles appear in; this namespace does not have a prefix

Manual of Style   The collection of Wikipedia writing guidelines (WP:MOS)

meatpuppet   An account operated by someone who is acting for the benefit of another partisan editor. *See also* sockpuppet

mediation   A dispute resolution procedure, where a member of the mediation committee attempts to resolve a dispute between two or more editors through formal negotiation to reach consensus (WP:M)

MediaWiki   The open-source, free software used to run the Wikipedia sites and many others

Meta, Meta-Wiki   The site at *http://meta.wikimedia.org/,* for coordinating Wikimedia Foundation projects

mirror site   A website posting content from Wikipedia (legitimately, if GFDL conditions are fulfilled)

monobook   The default skin or template on Wikipedia; this is how pages appear to anyone who has not logged in and changed his or her user preferences. *See also* skin

namespace   A virtual container for different types of content on the wiki; namespaces are defined by different prefixes, such as *talk:* or *Wikipedia:,* which appear before page names; articles are in the main namespace

Notability   The criteria that article topics should be notable to an outside observer, as determined through outside sources

NPOV   Neutral Point of View; the Wikipedia policy that article content should be presented in an objective, neutral, and substantiated manner

orphan article   An article that has no incoming wikilinks from other articles

OWN   A shortcut for Wikipedia's policy on no ownership of articles (WP: OWN); in conversation, the term *OWN* may serve as a warning not to take control of an article's content

page history   The list of edits that have been made to a wiki page, displaying in reverse chronological order and viewable from the History tab

permalink   A link to a specific version of a Wikipedia page

portal   A project page that collects articles, images, and facts about a particular topic

PROD   Proposed deletion; the deletion process for article deletions expected to be uncontroversial

redirect   (noun) A page serving solely to send a reader to an article with another title; (verb) to redirect from one page to another

revert   To return an article to a previous version; often abbreviated as *rvv* or *rv* in edit summaries

RfC   Request for Comment; a part of the dispute resolution procedure in which editors can discuss issues such as the conduct of other users

sandbox   The sandbox is a page set aside for test edits [[Wikipedia: Sandbox]]

sister project   A Wikipedia sister project (for example, Wiktionary) is a multilingual collection of wikis set up by the Wikimedia Foundation to pursue a generally reference-related goal

skin   The appearance of Wikipedia pages; logged-in users can select how Wikipedia pages appear in their user preferences

sockpuppet   A second account operated covertly by an editor with an existing account. *See also* meatpuppet

speedy   A speedy page deletion by an administrator, in line with the criteria for the speedy deletion policy and criteria for speedy deletion

steward   An administrator who can change any user's status on any Wikimedia project

subpage   A page constructed with a forward slash (/), as in [[User:Abelard/ Letter to Heloise]]; subpages are not allowed in the main article namespace

sysop   Short for *system operator*; a synonym for administrator

Three-Revert Rule (3RR)   The prohibition on reverting an article more than three times in 24 hours, except for reverting vandalism

transclusion   To include content stored on one page within another page, for example, by adding a template to a page

transwiki   To move an article to another wiki (usually deleting the original article)

user page   A registered user's personal page, usually containing information about the editor and his or her interests

userfy   To move an article into the User namespace as a subpage

watchlist   A personal list of articles that can be maintained by any logged-in user that lists all recent edits to the articles on the list

wiki   An online database of freely editable web pages, forming an evolving hypertext; Wikipedia is just one example of a wiki

wiki engine   The software underlying a wiki. *See also* MediaWiki

wiki markup language   The special simplified syntax for wiki page editing and formatting; also called *wiki syntax*

wikify   To add appropriate *internal links* to existing text and to impose standard format and other house style

wikilawyer   A pedantic, over-literal interpreter of Wikipedia policy and custom

wikilink   A synonym for an internal link. *See also* internal link

Wikimedia Commons   A project of the Wikimedia Foundation to collect free media (images and video); Wikipedia articles can contain links to files on Commons

Wikimedia Foundation (WMF)   The nonprofit organization that has overall responsibility for running the Wikipedia sites and sister projects

wikitext   The text of a wiki page visible when editing (as opposed to what readers see)

E History

This book is dependent on thousands of pages of documentation for Wikipedia, MediaWiki, and Wikimedia Foundation operations that have been written by members of the Wikimedia community over the years. In this appendix, per the terms of the GFDL that both Wikipedia and this book are licensed under, we list the Wikipedia pages that we have quoted or paraphrased and the images from Wikipedia that we have used. These do not reflect all of the ideas in this work, many of which are our interpretation of Wikipedia policies and practices, or all of the links given in the "Further Reading" sections in this book.

The citations below list a link to the Wikipedia page, permanent link to the version used, and the top five contributors to the page (not including bots or IP addresses), as measured by a tool designed by User:Aka and available at *http://vs.aka-online.de/cgi-bin/wppagehiststat.pl.*

Part I

p. 4: *http://en.wikipedia.org/wiki/Wikipedia:Size in volumes*
Version: *http://en.wikipedia.org/w/index.php?title=Wikipedia:Size_in_volumes&oldid=170841967*
By: Blofeld of SPECTRE, Александр Сигачёв, Vlsergey, Tompw, Conte0, and 5 other editors of Wikipedia

p. 19: *http://en.wikipedia.org/wiki/User:Uncle G/On notability*
Version: *http://en.wikipedia.org/w/index.php?title=User:Uncle_G/On_notability&oldid=175040125*
By: Uncle G, Cryptic, Seraphimblade, Ingolfson, Jehochman, and 16 other editors of Wikipedia

p. 20: *http://en.wikipedia.org/wiki/Wikipedia:List of really, really, really stupid article ideas that you really, really, really should not create*
Version: *http://en.wikipedia.org/w/index.php?title=Wikipedia:List_of_really%2C_really%2C_really_stupid_article_ideas_that_you_really%2C_really%2C_really_should_not_create&oldid=139147895*
By: Lubaf, Patstuart, SPUI, Thivierr, Cyrius, and 198 other editors of Wikipedia

p. 22 and 217: *http://en.wikipedia.org/wiki/Wikipedia:What_Wikipedia_is_not*
Version: *http://en.wikipedia.org/w/index.php?title=Wikipedia:What_Wikipedia_is_not&oldid=137533965*
By: Rossami, Radiant!, Kosebamse, Anthony, Tony Sidaway, and 1,263 other editors of Wikipedia

p. 28: *http://en.wikipedia.org/wiki/Wikipedia:Namespace*
Version: *http://en.wikipedia.org/w/index.php?title=Wikipedia:Namespace&oldid=116696709*
By: Patrick, Angela, Bensaccount, Francis Schonken, Mac, and 171 other editors of Wikipedia

p. 34: *http://en.wikipedia.org/wiki/Encyclopedia*
http://en.wikipedia.org/w/index.php?title=Encyclopedia&oldid=123699237
By: Flux.books, Stbalbach, E Pluribus Anthony, ClueBot, Apwoolrich, and 1,727 other editors of Wikipedia

p. 35: *http://commons.wikimedia.org/wiki/Image:EL_cover.jpg*
Uploaded by Renata3

p. 36: *http://commons.wikimedia.org/wiki/Image:Louis Moréri (1643-1680), engraving by Gérard Edelinck.jpg*
Uploaded by I.R. Annie IP

p. 38: *http://en.wikipedia.org/wiki/Richard Stallman*
Version: *http://en.wikipedia.org/w/index.php?title=Richard_Stallman&oldid=160960086*

By: Gronky, Lentower, Marudubshinki, Nandesuka, Chocolateboy, and 1,092 other editors of Wikipedia

p. 40: *http://en.wikipedia.org/wiki/Copyleft*
Version: *http://en.wikipedia.org/w/index.php?title=Copyleft&oldid=128028746*
By: Francis Schonken, MrDemeanour, Gronky, RossPatterson, Marudubshinki, and 523 other editors of Wikipedia

p. 42: *http://en.wikipedia.org/wiki/WikiWikiWeb*
Version: *http://en.wikipedia.org/w/index.php?title=WikiWikiWeb&oldid=123964514*
By: Earle Martin, 2004-12-29T22:45Z, Redeyed Treefrog, Ronaldomundo, Comet-styles, and 213 other editors of Wikipedia

p. 44: *http://en.wikipedia.org/wiki/Virtual community*
Version: *http://en.wikipedia.org/w/index.php?title=Virtual_community&oldid=189720908*
By: Bellagio99, DXBari, Sunray, Leuko, JRR Trollkien, and 547 other editors of Wikipedia

p. 64: *http://en.wikipedia.org/wiki/Wikipedia:Searching*
Version: *http://en.wikipedia.org/w/index.php?title=Wikipedia:Searching&oldid=110837327*
By: Quiddity, Patrick, Rick Block, Aude, AxelBoldt, and 960 other editors of Wikipedia

p. 69: *http://en.wikipedia.org/wiki/Wikipedia:Portal*
Version: *http://en.wikipedia.org/w/index.php?title=Wikipedia:Portal&oldid=110838967*
By: Trevor MacInnis, CJ, LatinoMuslim, Ausir, FayssalF, and 404 other editors of Wikipedia

p. 91: *http://en.wikipedia.org/wiki/Ocean sunfish*
Adapted
By: Fred Hsu, Moose15, PaladinWhite, GrahamBould, Mgiganteus1, and 425 other editors of Wikipedia

p. 94: *http://en.wikipedia.org/wiki/Wikipedia:Media help*
Version: *http://en.wikipedia.org/w/index.php?title=Wikipedia:Media_help&oldid=118165825*
By: Raul654, Pile0nades, Brian0918, Demi, Keenan Pepper, and 106 other editors of Wikipedia

p. 105: *http://en.wikipedia.org/wiki/Wikipedia:Ten things you may not know about Wikipedia*
Version: *http://en.wikipedia.org/w/index.php?title=Wikipedia:Ten_things_you_may_not_know_about_Wikipedia&oldid=170805889*
By: Eloquence, Mets501, Melsaran, Omegatron, Jeandré du Toit, and 101 other editors of Wikipedia

p. 106: *http://en.wikipedia.org/wiki/Wikipedia:How to read an article history*
Version: *http://en.wikipedia.org/w/index.php?title=Wikipedia:How_to_read_an_article_history&oldid=85822968*
By: Jmabel, Alan Canon, Quiddity, Bcasterline, JesseW, and 5 other editors of Wikipedia

Part II

p. 173: *http://en.wikipedia.org/wiki/H. G. Wells*
Version: *http://en.wikipedia.org/w/index.php?title=H._G._Wells&oldid=133292677*
By: Bruce1ee, Old Moonraker, Nick Cooper, Stbalbach, Stephen Burnett, and 1,064 other editors of Wikipedia

p. 174 and p. 204: *http://en.wikipedia.org/wiki/user:David Gerard*
Adapted from: *http://en.wikipedia.org/w/index.php?title=User:David_Gerard&oldid=193516061*
By: David Gerard and 73 other editors of Wikipedia

p. 176: *http://en.wikipedia.org/wiki/Blood pressure*
Version: *http://en.wikipedia.org/w/index.php?title=Blood_pressure&oldid=162374628*
By: DMacks, Pol098, Jfdwolff, Davidruben, Ocdcntx, and 702 other editors of Wikipedia

p. 178: *http://en.wikipedia.org/wiki/Template:Infobox Military Conflict*, as used in [[War of the Austrian Succession]]
Version: *http://en.wikipedia.org/w/index.php?title=War_of_the_Austrian_Succession&oldid=224301200*
By: Kirill Lokshin, La goutte de pluie, David Kernow, Tariqabjotu, Kevin Myers, and 45 other editors of Wikipedia

p. 179: *http://en.wikipedia.org/wiki/Jeanne Marie Bouvier de la Motte Guyon*
Version: *http://en.wikipedia.org/w/index.php?title=Jeanne_Marie_Bouvier_de_la_Motte_Guyon&oldid=158692263* and *http://en.wikipedia.org/w/index.php?title=Jeanne_Marie_Bouvier_de_la_Motte_Guyon&oldid=162551146*
By: CConnla77, Erkin2008, Charles Matthews, Alfredie, Blainster, and 63 other editors of Wikipedia

p. 187: *http://en.wikipedia.org/wiki/Wikipedia:Biographies of living persons*
Version: *http://en.wikipedia.org/w/index.php?title=Wikipedia:Biographies_of_living_persons&oldid=161551724*
By: SlimVirgin, Jossi, Black Falcon, NYScholar, WAS 4.250, and 450 other editors of Wikipedia

p. 189: *http://en.wikipedia.org/wiki/Phineas Gage*
Version: *http://en.wikipedia.org/w/index.php?title=Phineas_Gage&oldid=224632089*

By: DrFlo1, Garrondo, Malkinann, EEng, Vaughan, and 285 other editors of Wikipedia

p. 191: *http://en.wikipedia.org/wiki/Wikipedia:Citing sources*
Version: *http://en.wikipedia.org/w/index.php?title=Wikipedia:Citing_sources*
&oldid=111600726
By: SlimVirgin, Stevenj, SallyScot, SEWilco, Francis Schonken, and 1,555 other editors of Wikipedia

p. 217: *http://en.wikipedia.org/wiki/Wikipedia:Practical process*
http://en.wikipedia.org/w/index.php?title=Wikipedia:Practical_process&oldid
=185488562
By: David Gerard, Ummit, Radiant!, Tom harrison, Phil Sandifer, and 50 other editors of Wikipedia

p. 278: *http://en.wikipedia.org/wiki/List of best-selling singles in Japan*
Version: *http://en.wikipedia.org/w/index.php?title=List_of_best-selling_singles_in_*
Japan&oldid=198410846
By: Katsuya, Garion96, K-ohman, ReyBrujo, ACSE, and 35 other editors of Wikipedia

p. 279: *http://en.wikipedia.org/wiki/Help:Tables*
Version: *http://en.wikipedia.org/w/index.php?title=Help:Table&oldid=123499358*
By: Patrick, Omegatron, Omniplex, Eequor, Tarikash

p. 294: *http://en.wikipedia.org/wiki/Mzoli's*
Version: *http://en.wikipedia.org/w/index.php?title=Mzoli%27s&oldid=158544644*
By: Carcharoth, Zagalejo, Wikidemo, Melsaran, SqueakBox, and 85 other editors of Wikipedia

Part III

p. 357: *http://en.wikipedia.org/wiki/Wikipedia:Can't break it*
Version: *http://en.wikipedia.org/w/index.php?title=Wikipedia:Can%27t_break_*
it&oldid=145417595
By: Nneonneo, Thespian, Gregbard, Санта Клаус, Calgary, and 1 other editor of Wikipedia

p. 357: *http://en.wikipedia.org/wiki/User:Chaser/Make mistakes, then learn from them*
Version: *http://en.wikipedia.org/w/index.php?title=User:Chaser/Make_mistakes*
%2C_then_learn_from_them&oldid=154217958
By: Chaser, Flyguy649, SMcCandlish, Charles Matthews, and Rdsmith4

p. 357: *http://en.wikipedia.org/wiki/Wikipedia:Drop the stick and back slowly away from the horse carcass*
Version: *http://en.wikipedia.org/w/index.php?title=Wikipedia:Drop_the_stick_and_*
back_slowly_away_from_the_horse_carcass&oldid=153217258

By: Redvers, Picaroon, Jimp, Tkgd2007, Mathwhiz 29, and 18 other editors of Wikipedia

p. 357: *http://en.wikipedia.org/wiki/Wikipedia:Writing for the enemy*
Version: *http://en.wikipedia.org/w/index.php?title=Wikipedia:Writing_for_the_enemy&oldid=94101557*
By: Alfadog, Jossi, Shanes, Ed Poor, FT2, and 17 other editors of Wikipedia

p. 357: *http://en.wikipedia.org/wiki/Wikipedia:No angry mastodons*
Version: *http://en.wikipedia.org/w/index.php?title=Wikipedia:No_angry_mastodons&oldid=220477256*
By: Durova, GeorgeLouis, Omicronpersei8, Power Of Delusion, Akiyama, and 65 other editors of Wikipedia

p. 358: *http://en.wikipedia.org/wiki/Wikipedia:Coatrack*
Version: *http://en.wikipedia.org/w/index.php?title=Wikipedia:Coatrack&oldid=185942320*
By: Dhaluza, Gordonofcartoon, Moreschi, Risker, Face, and 22 other editors of Wikipedia

p. 358: *http://en.wikipedia.org/wiki/Wikipedia:Beware of the tigers*
Version: *http://en.wikipedia.org/w/index.php?title=Wikipedia:Beware_of_the_tigers&oldid=182395468*
By: Mil Falcon, JzG, William Pietri, Circeus, The prophet wizard of the crayon cake, and 28 other editors of Wikipedia

p. 358: *http://en.wikipedia.org/wiki/Wikipedia:The Zen of Wikipedia*
Version: *http://en.wikipedia.org/w/index.php?title=Wikipedia:The_Zen_of_Wikipedia&oldid=154081712*
By: Lubaf, Gwern, Pomte, Kim Bruning, Reinis, and 16 other editors of Wikipedia

p. 358: *http://en.wikipedia.org/wiki/User:SB Johnny/Don't hand out panda sandwiches at a PETA convention*
Version: *http://en.wikipedia.org/w/index.php?title=User:SB_Johnny/Don%27t_hand_out_panda_sandwiches_at_a_PETA_convention&oldid=128429572*
By: SB Johnny, Radiant!, Pascal.Tesson, Flyguy649, Tagishsimon, and 2 other editors of Wikipedia

p. 358: *http://en.wikipedia.org/wiki/Wikipedia:The Last Word*
Version: *http://en.wikipedia.org/w/index.php?title=Wikipedia:The_Last_Word&oldid=152693638*
By: Doc glasgow, Dorftrottel, Scoutersig, Abu badali, BenAveling, and 17 other editors of Wikipedia

p. 358: *http://en.wikipedia.org/wiki/Wikipedia:Right to leave*; accessed August 28, 2007

p. 359: *http://en.wikipedia.org/wiki/User:Raul654/Raul's laws*
Version: *http://en.wikipedia.org/w/index.php?title=User:Raul654/Raul%27s_laws&oldid=151328753*
By: Raul654, HereToHelp, Kizor, Deckiller, Durova, and 196 other editors of Wikipedia

p. 364: *http://en.wikipedia.org/wiki/Wikipedia:Five Pillars*
Version: *http://en.wikipedia.org/w/index.php?title=Wikipedia:Five_pillars&oldid=151411706*
By: Neutrality, Centrx, Jc37, Ryan Delaney, Quiddity, and 408 other editors of Wikipedia

p. 365: *http://en.wikipedia.org/wiki/Wikipedia:Ignore all rules*
Version: *http://en.wikipedia.org/w/index.php?title=Wikipedia:Ignore_all_rules&oldid=140690017*
By: David Levy, Kim Bruning, Chardish, Rockstar915, Haukurth, and 389 other editors of Wikipedia

p. 368: *http://en.wikipedia.org/wiki/Category:Wikipedia official policy*
Version: *http://en.wikipedia.org/w/index.php?title=Category:Wikipedia_official_policy&oldid=158702116*
By: UninvitedCompany, Enchanter, Radiant!, Phoebe, Mindmatrix, and 53 other editors of Wikipedia

p. 371: *http://en.wikipedia.org/wiki/Wikipedia:Spoiler*
Version: *http://en.wikipedia.org/w/index.php?title=Wikipedia:Spoiler&oldid=205006052*
By: Tony Sidaway, Ned Scott, Phil Sandifer, David Gerard, David Levy, and 266 other editors of Wikipedia

* **NOTE:** *Some of the earliest history of policy pages that were begun prior to late 2001 has been lost due to technical problems. Many of the ideas behind the core content and behavioral policies were developed by early community members not cited here.*

p. 373: *http://en.wikipedia.org/wiki/Wikipedia:Attack_page*
http://en.wikipedia.org/w/index.php?title=Wikipedia:Attack_page&oldid=149789509
By: Melsaran, HisSpaceResearch, Radiant!, Blaxthos, Ais523, and 72 other editors of Wikipedia

p. 373: *http://en.wikipedia.org/wiki/Wikipedia:Biographies_of_living_persons*
Version: *http://en.wikipedia.org/w/index.php?title=Wikipedia:Biographies_of_living_persons&oldid=167897975*
By: SlimVirgin, Jossi, Black Falcon, NYScholar, WAS 4.250, and 450 other editors of Wikipedia

p. 373: *http://en.wikipedia.org/wiki/Wikipedia:Copyrights*
http://en.wikipedia.org/w/index.php?title=Wikipedia:Copyrights&oldid=149693166
By: Mav, Angela, Superm401, Francis Schonken, MartinHarper, and 241 other editors of Wikipedia

p. 373: *http://en.wikipedia.org/wiki/Wikipedia:Copyright_violations*
http://en.wikipedia.org/w/index.php?title=Wikipedia:Copyright_violations&oldid=114158640
By: Gurch, Jeepday, Kingturtle, Garion96, R'n'B, and 14 other editors of Wikipedia

p. 373: *http://en.wikipedia.org/wiki/Wikipedia:Editing policy*
Version: *http://en.wikipedia.org/w/index.php?title=Wikipedia:Editing_policy&oldid=160847843*
By: Viajero, Atlant, 168..., Centrx, MartinHarper, and 183 other editors of Wikipedia

p. 373: *http://en.wikipedia.org/wiki/Wikipedia:Libel*
Version: *http://en.wikipedia.org/w/index.php?title=Wikipedia:Libel&oldid=137250226*
By: Hiding, Masssiveego, UninvitedCompany, Maurreen, Radiant!, and 64 other editors of Wikipedia

p. 373: *http://en.wikipedia.org/wiki/Wikipedia:Naming conventions*
Version: *http://en.wikipedia.org/w/index.php?title=Wikipedia:Naming_conventions&oldid=167419746*
By: Francis Schonken, Mav, Pmanderson, Philip Baird Shearer, Hyacinth, and 463 other editors of Wikipedia

p. 374: *http://en.wikipedia.org/wiki/Wikipedia:Neutral point of view*
Version: *http://en.wikipedia.org/w/index.php?title=Wikipedia:Neutral_point_of_view&oldid=167579325*
By: Francis Schonken, Bensaccount, Jossi, Dreftymac, FT2, and 1,370 other editors of Wikipedia

p. 374: *http://en.wikipedia.org/wiki/Wikipedia:Non-free content criteria*
http://en.wikipedia.org/w/index.php?title=Wikipedia:Non-free_content_criteria&oldid=150608777
By: Tony1, Ned Scott, Gmaxwell, Wikidemo, DCGeist, and 141 other editors of Wikipedia

p. 374: *http://en.wikipedia.org/wiki/Wikipedia:No original research*
Version: *http://en.wikipedia.org/w/index.php?title=Wikipedia:No_original_research&oldid=152747020*
By: SlimVirgin, Slrubenstein, COGDEN, Jossi, Vassyana, and 588 other editors of Wikipedia

p. 374: *http://en.wikipedia.org/wiki/Wikipedia:Ownership_of_articles*
Version: *http://en.wikipedia.org/w/index.php?title=Wikipedia:Ownership_of_articles&oldid=167401562*

By: Viriditas, Richard001, Gscshoyru, Kransky, Apostle12, and 162 other editors of Wikipedia

p. 374: *http://en.wikipedia.org/wiki/Wikipedia:Verifiability*
Version: *http://en.wikipedia.org/w/index.php?title=Wikipedia:Vervifiability&oldid =166913408*
By: SlimVirgin, Crum375, Jossi, Francis Schonken, Brimba, and 1,157 other editors of Wikipedia

p. 374: *http://en.wikipedia.org/wiki/Wikipedia:Civility*
Version: *http://en.wikipedia.org/w/index.php?title=Wikipedia:Civility&oldid =168100248*
By: Newbyguesses, Shoemaker's Holiday, Littleolive oil, Crum375, Rhanyeia, and 344 other editors of Wikipedia

p. 374: *http://en.wikipedia.org/wiki/Wikipedia:Edit war*
Version: *http://en.wikipedia.org/w/index.php?title=Wikipedia:Edit_war&oldid =176614185*
By: Jossi, Radiant!, Light current, Heimstern, Wikidemo, and 298 other editors of Wikipedia

p. 374: *http://en.wikipedia.org/wiki/Wikipedia:No legal threats*
Version: *http://en.wikipedia.org/w/index.php?title=Wikipedia:No_legal_threats &oldid=151227322*
By: MartinHarper, Ottava Rima, Mangojuice, Ned Scott, Mr Senseless, and 153 other editors of Wikipedia

p. 375: *http://en.wikipedia.org/wiki/Wikipedia:No personal attacks*
Version: *http://en.wikipedia.org/w/index.php?title=Wikipedia:No_personal_ attacks&oldid=149788493*
By: SlimVirgin, MONGO, Risker, Mantanmoreland, Jossi and 531 other editors of Wikipedia

p. 375: *http://en.wikipedia.org/wiki/Wikipedia:Dispute resolution*
By: Centrx, Mav, Michael Snow, Radiant!, Netscott, and 326 other editors of Wikipedia

p. 375: *http://en.wikipedia.org/wiki/Wikipedia:Sock puppetry*
Version: *http://en.wikipedia.org/w/index.php?title=Wikipedia:Sock_puppetry &oldid=150434904*
By: FT2, SlimVirgin, Zzuuzz, Jossi, Dijxtra, and 584 other editors of Wikipedia

p. 375: *http://en.wikipedia.org/wiki/Wikipedia:Three-revert rule*
Version: *http://en.wikipedia.org/w/index.php?title=Wikipedia:Three-revert_rule &oldid=149669250*
By: Neutrality, Netoholic, SlimVirgin, JzG, William M. Connolley, and 354 other editors of Wikipedia

p. 375: *http://en.wikipedia.org/wiki/Wikipedia:Vandalism*
Version: *http://en.wikipedia.org/w/index.php?title=Wikipedia:Vandalism&oldid=151541085*
By: Hellno2, John254, Dan100, Azer Red, Crum375, and 1,764 other editors of Wikipedia

p. 375: *http://en.wikipedia.org/wiki/Wikipedia:Wheel war*
Version: *http://en.wikipedia.org/w/index.php?title=Wikipedia:Wheel_war&oldid=150014030*
By: Radiant!, FT2, Centrx, SlimVirgin, Jehochman, and 94 other editors of Wikipedia

p. 375: *http://en.wikipedia.org/wiki/Wikipedia:Arbitration policy*
Version: *http://en.wikipedia.org/w/index.php?title=Wikipedia:Arbitration_policy&oldid=150070174*
By: MartinHarper, Jdforrester, Grunt, Camembert, Picaroon, and 101 other editors of Wikipedia

p. 375: *http://en.wikipedia.org/wiki/Wikipedia:Appealing a block*
Version: *http://en.wikipedia.org/w/index.php?title=Wikipedia:Appealing_a_block&oldid=150160242*
By: Netsnipe, FT2, King of Hearts, Zzuuzz, Radiant!, and 85 other editors of Wikipedia

p. 375: *http://en.wikipedia.org/wiki/Wikipedia:Banning policy*
Version: *http://en.wikipedia.org/w/index.php?title=Wikipedia:Banning_policy&oldid=151142124*
By: FT2, MartinHarper, Szyslak, Mercury, Jehochman, and 254 other editors of Wikipedia

p. 375: *http://en.wikipedia.org/wiki/Wikipedia:Blocking policy*
Version: *http://en.wikipedia.org/w/index.php?title=Wikipedia:Blocking_policy&oldid=150535074*
By: MartinHarper, SlimVirgin, Jossi, Radiant!, Guanaco, and 860 other editors of Wikipedia

p. 375: *http://en.wikipedia.org/wiki/Wikipedia:Bot policy*
Version: *http://en.wikipedia.org/w/index.php?title=Wikipedia:Bot_policy&oldid=147459199*
By: Ram-Man, FT2, AllyUnion, Pathoschild, Locke Cole, and 518 other editors of Wikipedia

p. 376: *http://en.wikipedia.org/wiki/Wikipedia:Category deletion policy*
Version: *http://en.wikipedia.org/w/index.php?title=Wikipedia:Category_deletion_policy&oldid=14262360*
By: Radiant!, Xdamr, Tim!, Hiding, Beland, and 41 other editors of Wikipedia

p. 376: *http://en.wikipedia.org/wiki/Wikipedia:Criteria for speedy deletion*
Version: *http://en.wikipedia.org/w/index.php?title=Wikipedia:Criteria_for_speedy_deletion&oldid=151113674*
By: Radiant!, Netoholic, Black Falcon, Centrx, Tony Sidaway, and 1,111 other editors of Wikipedia

p. 376: *http://en.wikipedia.org/wiki/Wikipedia:Deletion policy*
Version: *http://en.wikipedia.org/w/index.php?title=Wikipedia:Deletion_policy&oldid=151382127*
By: MartinHarper, Radiant!, Rossami, Angela, Black Falcon, and 655 other editors of Wikipedia

p. 376: *http://en.wikipedia.org/wiki/Wikipedia:Image use policy*
Version: *http://en.wikipedia.org/w/index.php?title=Wikipedia:Image_use_policy&oldid=148010515*
By: MartinHarper, Gmaxwell, Lee Daniel Crocker, Patrick, Omegatron, and 297 other editors of Wikipedia

p. 376: *http://en.wikipedia.org/wiki/Wikipedia:Open proxies*
Version: *http://en.wikipedia.org/w/index.php?title=Wikipedia:Open_proxies&oldid=176793817*
By: Gurch, Pathoschild, Crum375, EngineerScotty, Thesocialistesq, and 76 other editors of Wikipedia

p. 376: *http://en.wikipedia.org/wiki/Wikipedia:Office actions*
Version: *http://en.wikipedia.org/w/index.php?title=Wikipedia:Office_actions&oldid=147957627*
By: CesarB, Bastique, Prodego, Cbrown1023, Pathoschild, and 145 other editors of Wikipedia

p. 376: *http://en.wikipedia.org/wiki/Wikipedia:OTRS*
Version: *http://en.wikipedia.org/w/index.php?title=Wikipedia:OTRS&oldid=147630563*
By: Daniel, FCYTravis, Tony Sidaway, Centrx, Jeandré du Toit, and 59 other editors of Wikipedia

p. 376: *http://en.wikipedia.org/wiki/Wikipedia:Oversight*
Version: *http://en.wikipedia.org/w/index.php?title=Wikipedia:Oversight&oldid=150184987*
By: Voice of All, Kylu, FT2, AGK, WJBscribe, and 83 other editors of Wikipedia

p. 376: *http://en.wikipedia.org/wiki/Wikipedia:Proposed deletion*
Version: *http://en.wikipedia.org/w/index.php?title=Wikipedia:Proposed_deletion&oldid=140973398*
By: Radiant!, Splash, NickelShoe, Sandstein, Ruud Koot, and 251 other editors of Wikipedia

p. 376: *http://en.wikipedia.org/wiki/Wikipedia:Protection policy*
Version: *http://en.wikipedia.org/w/index.php?title=Wikipedia:Protection_policy&oldid=151123994*
By: Zzuuzz, Gurch, Steel, Ryan Delaney, Happy-melon, and 582 other editors of Wikipedia

p. 377: *http://en.wikipedia.org/wiki/Wikipedia:Username policy*
Version: *http://en.wikipedia.org/w/index.php?title=Wikipedia:Username_policy&oldid=151773953*
By: MartinHarper, H, Gurch, Radiant!, Ryan Postlethwaite, and 559 other editors of Wikipedia

p. 377 and 385: *http://en.wikipedia.org/wiki/Wikipedia:Consensus*
Version: *http://en.wikipedia.org/w/index.php?title=Wikipedia:Consensus&oldid=205341400*
By: Newbyguesses, Kim Bruning, Kevin Murray, Philip Baird Shearer, Rhanyeia, and 349 other editors of Wikipedia

p. 378: *http://en.wikipedia.org/wiki/Wikipedia:Assume good faith*
Version: *http://en.wikipedia.org/w/index.php?title=Wikipedia:Assume_good_faith&oldid=149634828*
By: Isomorphic, Kenosis, Xavexgoem, Paolo.dL, David Levy, and 359 other editors of Wikipedia

p. 378: *http://en.wikipedia.org/wiki/Wikipedia:Attribution*
Version: *http://en.wikipedia.org/w/index.php?title=Wikipedia:Attribution&oldid=163062819*
By: SlimVirgin, Jossi, JulesH, Robert A West, EngineerScotty, and 247 other editors of Wikipedia

p. 378: *http://en.wikipedia.org/wiki/Wikipedia:Autobiography*
Version: *http://en.wikipedia.org/w/index.php?title=Wikipedia:Autobiography&oldid=151262695*
By: Jitse Niesen, MartinHarper, Democritus, Mike4ty4, BrianH123, and 414 other editors of Wikipedia

p. 378: *http://en.wikipedia.org/wiki/Wikipedia:Be bold*
Version: *http://en.wikipedia.org/w/index.php?title=Wikipedia:Be_bold&oldid=151560372*
By: JDG, Matt Yeager, Monicasdude, Grutness, Irpen, and 1,130 other editors of Wikipedia

p. 378: *http://en.wikipedia.org/wiki/Wikipedia:Conflict of interest*
Version: *http://en.wikipedia.org/w/index.php?title=Wikipedia:Conflict_of_interest&oldid=150864297*
By: Charles Matthews, Jehochman, Jossi, SlimVirgin, Scottperry, and 422 other editors of Wikipedia

p. 378: *http://en.wikipedia.org/wiki/Wikipedia:Do not disrupt Wikipedia to illustrate a point*
Version: *http://en.wikipedia.org/w/index.php?title=Wikipedia:Do_not_disrupt_Wikipedia_to_illustrate_a_point&oldid=151577674*
By: Chocolateboy, Anthony, Phil Sandifer, David Gerard, SMcCandlish, and 282 other editors of Wikipedia

p. 378: *http://en.wikipedia.org/wiki/Wikipedia:Etiquette*
Version: *http://en.wikipedia.org/w/index.php?title=Wikipedia:Etiquette&oldid=149647447*
By: 168..., Kingturtle, NCdave, Moreschi, Stevertigo, and 288 other editors of Wikipedia

p. 379: *http://en.wikipedia.org/wiki/Wikipedia:Harassment*
Version: *http://en.wikipedia.org/w/index.php?title=Wikipedia:Harassment&oldid=151162517*
By: Lubaf, FT2, ChoobWriter, Newbyguesses, Radiant!, and 117 other editors of Wikipedia

p. 379: *http://en.wikipedia.org/wiki/Wikipedia:Manual of Style*
Version: *http://en.wikipedia.org/w/index.php?title=Wikipedia:Manual_of_Style&oldid=206995737*
By: Tony1, Noetica, SMcCandlish, Pmanderson, T00h00, and 1,522 other editors

p. 379: *http://en.wikipedia.org/wiki/Wikipedia:Notability*
Version: *http://en.wikipedia.org/w/index.php?title=Wikipedia:Notability&oldid=151660631*
By: Kevin Murray, Centrx, Dhaluza, Radiant!, SMcCandlish, and 354 other editors of Wikipedia

p. 379: *http://en.wikipedia.org/wiki/Wikipedia:No disclaimers in articles*
Version: *http://en.wikipedia.org/w/index.php?title=Wikipedia:No_disclaimers_in_articles&oldid=151593981*
By: CesarB, Tony Sidaway, Dbachmann, Kizor, Radiant!, and 66 other editors of Wikipedia

p. 379: *http://en.wikipedia.org/wiki/Wikipedia:Please do not bite the newcomers*
Version: *http://en.wikipedia.org/w/index.php?title=Wikipedia:Please do not bite the_newcomers&oldid=149671115*
By: Paolo.dL, Cerejota, BrittonLaRoche, Kaspazes, Chocolateboy, and 325 other editors of Wikipedia

p. 379: *http://en.wikipedia.org/wiki/Wikipedia:Polling is not a substitute for discussion*
Version: *http://en.wikipedia.org/w/index.php?title=Wikipedia:Polling_is_not_a_substitute_for_discussion&oldid=138851338*
By: Radiant!, Netscott, 6SJ7, Sam, David Levy, and 101 other editors of Wikipedia

p. 379: *http://en.wikipedia.org/wiki/Wikipedia:Reliable sources*
Version: *http://en.wikipedia.org/w/index.php?title=Wikipedia:Reliable_sources
&oldid=167891837*
By: SlimVirgin, Jossi, Blueboar, Francis Schonken, Fahrenheit451, and 676 other
editors of Wikipedia

p. 379: *http://en.wikipedia.org/wiki/Wikipedia:Spam*
Version: *http://en.wikipedia.org/w/index.php?title=Wikipedia:Spam&oldid
=149268041*
By: Morton devonshire, DepartedUser, Jc37, Leuko, Trialsanderrors, and 325 other
editors of Wikipedia

p. 386: based on *http://en.wikipedia.org/wiki/Image:CCC_Flowchart_5.jpg*
By: Kevin Murray

p. 390: *http://en.wikipedia.org/wiki/Wikipedia:Administrators*
Version: *http://en.wikipedia.org/w/index.php?title=Wikipedia:Administrators
&oldid=176061066*
By: FT2, Angela, Eloquence, Ed Poor, Centrx, and 843 other editors of Wikipedia

p. 395: *http://en.wikipedia.org/wiki/Talk:Gdansk/Vote*
Version: *http://en.wikipedia.org/w/index.php?title=Talk:Gdansk/Vote&oldid
=92886003*
By: Chris 73, John Kenney, Curps, VicFromTheBlock, Szopen, and 145 other editors
of Wikipedia

p. 398: *http://en.wikipedia.org/wiki/user:Geni/Disputes*
Version: *http://en.wikipedia.org/w/index.php?title=User:Geni/Disputes&oldid
=27898918*
By: Geni and 1 other editor of Wikipedia

Part IV

p. 413: *http://en.wikipedia.org/wiki/Mohandas Karamchand Gandhi*
Version: *http://en.wikipedia.org/w/index.php?title=Mohandas_Karamchand_
Gandhi&oldid=209059248*
By: Classicfilms, Rama's Arrow, Nirvana2013, Lostintherush, Gurubrahma, and
3,450 other editors of Wikipedia

p. 429: *http://en.wiktionary.org/wiki/incunabulum*
Version: *http://en.wiktionary.org/w/index.php?title=incunabulum&oldid=3517999*
By: EncycloPetey, KYPark, Ruakh, Dcljr, Widsith, and 8 other editors of Wiktionary

p. 460: *http://en.wikipedia.org/wiki/Wikipedia:Reusing Wikipedia content*
Version: *http://en.wikipedia.org/w/index.php?title=Wikipedia:Reusing_Wikipedia_
content&oldid=166606332*
By: Lupo, Momusufan, Stevage, Martial75, MER-C, and 16 other editors of
Wikipedia

GNU Free Documentation License

Version 1.2, November 2002
http://www.gnu.org/copyleft/fdl.html

0. PREAMBLE

The purpose of this License is to make a manual, textbook, or other functional and useful document "free" in the sense of freedom: to assure everyone the effective freedom to copy and redistribute it, with or without modifying it, either commercially or noncommercially. Secondarily, this License preserves for the author and publisher a way to get credit for their work, while not being considered responsible for modifications made by others.

This License is a kind of "copyleft", which means that derivative works of the document must themselves be free in the same sense. It complements the GNU General Public License, which is a copyleft license designed for free software.

We have designed this License in order to use it for manuals for free software, because free software needs free documentation: a free program should come with manuals providing the same freedoms that the software does. But this License is not limited to software manuals; it can be used for any textual work, regardless of subject matter or whether it is published as a printed book. We recommend this License principally for works whose purpose is instruction or reference.

1. APPLICABILITY AND DEFINITIONS

This License applies to any manual or other work, in any medium, that contains a notice placed by the copyright holder saying it can be distributed under the terms of this License. Such a notice grants a world-wide, royalty-free license, unlimited in duration, to use that work under the conditions stated herein. The "Document", below, refers to any such manual or work. Any member of the public is a licensee, and is addressed as "you". You accept the license if you copy, modify or distribute the work in a way requiring permission under copyright law.

A "Modified Version" of the Document means any work containing the Document or a portion of it, either copied verbatim, or with modifications and/or translated into another language.

A "Secondary Section" is a named appendix or a front-matter section of the Document that deals exclusively with the relationship of the publishers or authors of the Document to the Document's overall subject (or to related matters) and contains nothing that could fall directly within that overall subject. (Thus, if the Document is in part a textbook of mathematics, a Secondary Section may not explain any mathematics.) The relationship could be a matter of historical connection with the subject or with related matters, or of legal, commercial, philosophical, ethical or political position regarding them.

The "Invariant Sections" are certain Secondary Sections whose titles are designated, as being those of Invariant Sections, in the notice that says that the Document is released under this License. If a section does not fit the above definition of Secondary then it is not allowed to be designated as Invariant. The Document may contain zero Invariant Sections. If the Document does not identify any Invariant Sections then there are none.

The "Cover Texts" are certain short passages of text that are listed, as Front-Cover Texts or Back-Cover Texts, in the notice that says that the Document is released under this License. A Front-Cover Text may be at most 5 words, and a Back-Cover Text may be at most 25 words.

A "Transparent" copy of the Document means a machine-readable copy, represented in a format whose specification is available to the general public, that is suitable for revising the document straightforwardly with generic text editors or (for images composed of pixels) generic paint programs or (for drawings) some widely available drawing editor, and that is suitable for input to text formatters or for automatic translation to a variety of formats suitable for input to text formatters. A copy made in an otherwise Transparent file format whose markup, or absence of markup, has been arranged to thwart or discourage subsequent modification by readers is not Transparent. An image format is not Transparent if used for any substantial amount of text. A copy that is not "Transparent" is called "Opaque".

Examples of suitable formats for Transparent copies include plain ASCII without markup, Texinfo input format, LaTeX input format, SGML or XML using a publicly available DTD, and standard-conforming simple HTML, PostScript or PDF designed for human modification. Examples of transparent image formats include PNG, XCF and JPG. Opaque formats include proprietary formats that can be read and edited only by proprietary word processors, SGML or XML for which the DTD and/or processing tools are not generally available, and the machine-generated HTML, PostScript or PDF produced by some word processors for output purposes only.

The "Title Page" means, for a printed book, the title page itself, plus such following pages as are needed to hold, legibly, the material this License requires to appear in the title page. For works in formats which do not have any title page as such, "Title Page" means the text near the most prominent appearance of the work's title, preceding the beginning of the body of the text.

A section "Entitled XYZ" means a named subunit of the Document whose title either is precisely XYZ or contains XYZ in parentheses following text that translates XYZ in another language. (Here XYZ stands for a specific section name mentioned below, such as "Acknowledgements", "Dedications", "Endorsements", or "History".) To "Preserve the Title" of such a section when you modify the Document means that it remains a section "Entitled XYZ" according to this definition.

The Document may include Warranty Disclaimers next to the notice which states that this License applies to the Document. These Warranty Disclaimers are considered to be included by reference in this License, but only as regards disclaiming warranties: any other implication that these Warranty Disclaimers may have is void and has no effect on the meaning of this License.

2. VERBATIM COPYING

You may copy and distribute the Document in any medium, either commercially or noncommercially, provided that this License, the copyright notices, and the license notice saying this License applies to the Document are reproduced in all copies, and that you add no other conditions whatsoever to those of this License. You may not use technical measures to obstruct or control the reading or further copying of the copies you make or distribute. However, you may accept compensation in exchange for copies. If you distribute a large enough number of copies you must also follow the conditions in section 3.

You may also lend copies, under the same conditions stated above, and you may publicly display copies.

3. COPYING IN QUANTITY

If you publish printed copies (or copies in media that commonly have printed covers) of the Document, numbering more than 100, and the Document's license notice requires Cover Texts, you must enclose the copies in covers that carry, clearly and legibly, all these Cover Texts: Front-Cover Texts on the front cover, and Back-Cover Texts on the back cover. Both covers must also clearly and legibly identify you as the publisher of these copies. The front cover must present the full title with all words of the title equally prominent and visible. You may add other material on the covers in addition. Copying with changes limited to the covers, as long as they preserve the title of the Document and satisfy these conditions, can be treated as verbatim copying in other respects.

If the required texts for either cover are too voluminous to fit legibly, you should put the first ones listed (as many as fit reasonably) on the actual cover, and continue the rest onto adjacent pages.

If you publish or distribute Opaque copies of the Document numbering more than 100, you must either include a machine-readable Transparent copy along with each Opaque copy, or state in or with each Opaque copy a computer-network location from which the general network-using public has access to download using public-standard network protocols a complete Transparent copy of the Document, free of added material. If you use the latter option, you must take reasonably prudent steps, when you begin distribution of Opaque copies in quantity, to ensure that this Transparent copy will remain thus accessible at the stated location until at least one year after the last time you distribute an Opaque copy (directly or through your agents or retailers) of that edition to the public.

It is requested, but not required, that you contact the authors of the Document well before redistributing any large number of copies, to give them a chance to provide you with an updated version of the Document.

4. MODIFICATIONS

You may copy and distribute a Modified Version of the Document under the conditions of sections 2 and 3 above, provided that you release the Modified Version under precisely this License, with the Modified Version filling the role of the Document, thus licensing distribution and modification of the Modified Version to whoever possesses a copy of it. In addition, you must do these things in the Modified Version:

A. Use in the Title Page (and on the covers, if any) a title distinct from that of the Document, and from those of previous versions (which should, if there were any, be listed in the History section of the Document). You may use the same title as a previous version if the original publisher of that version gives permission.

B. List on the Title Page, as authors, one or more persons or entities responsible for authorship of the modifications in the Modified Version, together with at least five of the principal authors of the Document (all of its principal authors, if it has fewer than five), unless they release you from this requirement.

C. State on the Title page the name of the publisher of the Modified Version, as the publisher.

D. Preserve all the copyright notices of the Document.

E. Add an appropriate copyright notice for your modifications adjacent to the other copyright notices.

F. Include, immediately after the copyright notices, a license notice giving the public permission to use the Modified Version under the terms of this License, in the form shown in the Addendum below.

G. Preserve in that license notice the full lists of Invariant Sections and required Cover Texts given in the Document's license notice.

H. Include an unaltered copy of this License.

I. Preserve the section Entitled "History", Preserve its Title, and add to it an item stating at least the title, year, new authors, and publisher of the Modified Version as given on the Title Page. If there is no section Entitled "History" in the Document, create one stating the title, year, authors, and publisher of the Document as given on its Title Page, then add an item describing the Modified Version as stated in the previous sentence.

J.   Preserve the network location, if any, given in the Document for public access to a Transparent copy of the Document, and likewise the network locations given in the Document for previous versions it was based on. These may be placed in the "History" section. You may omit a network location for a work that was published at least four years before the Document itself, or if the original publisher of the version it refers to gives permission.

K.   For any section Entitled "Acknowledgements" or "Dedications", Preserve the Title of the section, and preserve in the section all the substance and tone of each of the contributor acknowledgements and/or dedications given therein.

L.   Preserve all the Invariant Sections of the Document, unaltered in their text and in their titles. Section numbers or the equivalent are not considered part of the section titles.

M.   Delete any section Entitled "Endorsements". Such a section may not be included in the Modified Version.

N.   Do not retitle any existing section to be Entitled "Endorsements" or to conflict in title with any Invariant Section.

O.   Preserve any Warranty Disclaimers.

If the Modified Version includes new front-matter sections or appendices that qualify as Secondary Sections and contain no material copied from the Document, you may at your option designate some or all of these sections as invariant. To do this, add their titles to the list of Invariant Sections in the Modified Version's license notice. These titles must be distinct from any other section titles.

You may add a section Entitled "Endorsements", provided it contains nothing but endorsements of your Modified Version by various parties—for example, statements of peer review or that the text has been approved by an organization as the authoritative definition of a standard.

You may add a passage of up to five words as a Front-Cover Text, and a passage of up to 25 words as a Back-Cover Text, to the end of the list of Cover Texts in the Modified Version. Only one passage of Front-Cover Text and one of Back-Cover Text may be added by (or through arrangements made by) any one entity. If the Document already includes a cover text for the same cover, previously added by you or by arrangement made by the same entity you are acting on behalf of, you may not add another; but you may replace the old one, on explicit permission from the previous publisher that added the old one.

The author(s) and publisher(s) of the Document do not by this License give permission to use their names for publicity for or to assert or imply endorsement of any Modified Version.

5. COMBINING DOCUMENTS

You may combine the Document with other documents released under this License, under the terms defined in section 4 above for modified versions, provided that you include in the combination all of the Invariant Sections of all of the original documents, unmodified, and list them all as Invariant Sections of your combined work in its license notice, and that you preserve all their Warranty Disclaimers.

The combined work need only contain one copy of this License, and multiple identical Invariant Sections may be replaced with a single copy. If there are multiple Invariant Sections with the same name but different contents, make the title of each such section unique by adding at the end of it, in parentheses, the name of the original author or publisher of that section if known, or else a unique number. Make the same adjustment to the section titles in the list of Invariant Sections in the license notice of the combined work.

In the combination, you must combine any sections Entitled "History" in the various original documents, forming one section Entitled "History"; likewise combine any sections Entitled "Acknowledgements", and any sections Entitled "Dedications". You must delete all sections Entitled "Endorsements."

6. COLLECTIONS OF DOCUMENTS

You may make a collection consisting of the Document and other documents released under this License, and replace the individual copies of this License in the various documents with a single copy that is included in the collection, provided that you follow the rules of this License for verbatim copying of each of the documents in all other respects.

You may extract a single document from such a collection, and distribute it individually under this License, provided you insert a copy of this License into the extracted document, and follow this License in all other respects regarding verbatim copying of that document.

7. AGGREGATION WITH INDEPENDENT WORKS

A compilation of the Document or its derivatives with other separate and independent documents or works, in or on a volume of a storage or distribution medium, is called an "aggregate" if the copyright resulting from the compilation is not used to limit the legal rights of the compilation's users beyond what the individual works permit. When the Document is included in an aggregate, this License does not apply to the other works in the aggregate which are not themselves derivative works of the Document.

If the Cover Text requirement of section 3 is applicable to these copies of the Document, then if the Document is less than one half of the entire aggregate, the Document's Cover Texts may be placed on covers that bracket the Document within the aggregate, or the electronic equivalent of covers if the Document is in electronic form. Otherwise they must appear on printed covers that bracket the whole aggregate.

8. TRANSLATION

Translation is considered a kind of modification, so you may distribute translations of the Document under the terms of section 4. Replacing Invariant Sections with translations requires special permission from their copyright holders, but you may include translations of some or all Invariant Sections in addition to the original versions of these Invariant Sections. You may include a translation of this License, and all the license notices in the Document, and any Warranty Disclaimers, provided that you also include the original English version of this License and the original versions of those notices and disclaimers. In case of a disagreement between the translation and the original version of this License or a notice or disclaimer, the original version will prevail.

If a section in the Document is Entitled "Acknowledgements", "Dedications", or "History", the requirement (section 4) to Preserve its Title (section 1) will typically require changing the actual title.

9. TERMINATION

You may not copy, modify, sublicense, or distribute the Document except as expressly provided for under this License. Any other attempt to copy, modify, sublicense or distribute the Document is void, and will automatically terminate your rights under this License. However, parties who have received copies, or rights, from you under this License will not have their licenses terminated so long as such parties remain in full compliance.

10. FUTURE REVISIONS OF THIS LICENSE

The Free Software Foundation may publish new, revised versions of the GNU Free Documentation License from time to time. Such new versions will be similar in spirit to the present version, but may differ in detail to address new problems or concerns. See http://www.gnu.org/copyleft/.

Each version of the License is given a distinguishing version number. If the Document specifies that a particular numbered version of this License "or any later version" applies to it, you have the option of following the terms and conditions either of that specified version or of any later version that has been published (not as a draft) by the Free Software Foundation. If the Document does not specify a version number of this License, you may choose any version ever published (not as a draft) by the Free Software Foundation.

INDEX

good articles, 120, 227–228
    candidates, 228
Google. *See* search engines
GPL (GNU General Public License), 40. *See also*
        free licenses
Graphics Lab WikiProject, 268
graphs. *See* images
Greek letters, displaying, 283
groupthink, 393
guidelines, 13. *See also* policies; *individual*
            guideline names
    development, 369
    list of, 378–379

H

harassment, guideline on, 304, 379
hatnotes, 102, 236–238, *237*
Heavy Metal Umlaut article, 352
help, getting, 343–344
Help desk, 343
help namespace, 29
{{helpme}} template, 318
hieroglyphics, displaying, 414
history
    article. *See* page history
    of Wikipedia, 46–47, *47*, 456–457
History tab, 101
HTML (HyperText Markup Language), 281–282
humor, 351–352
hypertext, 36, 157
HyperText Markup Language (HTML), 281–282

I

Ignore All Rules (IAR), 364–365, 377
image description pages, 266
images. *See also* Wikimedia Commons
    categories, 263
    featured, 286
    gallery of, 268, 425–426, *426*
    licensing, 263–264. *See also* fair use criteria
        on Commons, 424
    policy, 268, 376
    searching for, 262–263, 422–423
    syntax for, 267–268
    uploading, 264–266, *265*
immediatism, 349

In the news section, 70–71. *See also* current
        events
inclusionism, 349
incubator wiki, 411, 444
indented lines, 146, *146*. *See also* threaded
        discussion
infobox templates, 103, 178, *178*, 273–274, *274*
internal links. *See* links, internal
International Standard Book Number (ISBN)
        linking, 186
Internet, history of, 37–38
Internet Protocol (IP) addresses. *See* IP (Internet
        Protocol) addresses
Internet Relay Chat (IRC), 346–347, 455
interwiki links
    between language editions, 414–416
    between sister projects, 103, 439–442
    templates for, 441–442, *441*
{{inuse}} template, 139
IP (Internet Protocol) addresses, 107, 304–305.
            See also anonymous users
    blocked, 305
IRC (Internet Relay Chat), 346–347, 455
ISBN (International Standard Book Number)
        linking, 186
italic text, formatting, 145

J

janitors. *See* administrators
JavaScript, customizing, 313–314
jokes, 352

K

keyboard shortcuts, 136–137
Klingon Wikipedia, 411

L

languages
    constructed, 410
    dead, 410
    editing in other, 411–412
    links between. *See* interwiki links
    number of, with Wikimedia projects,
        408, 411
    portal to other, *409*

preservation of, 410–411
script support for, 412–414, *413*
sidebar section, 79–80, *79*
starting a new project, 411
templates, 154
translations between, 417
lead section, of articles, 173
legal threats, policy on, 374
libel, in articles
    policy on, 373
    reporting, 344
Library of Congress Classification, 86
library research. *See* research, techniques
licensing. *See* GNU Free Documentation
            License (GFDL)
links
    between projects. *See* interwiki links
    to category pages, 151
    external, 83
        attack site, 155
        dead, 193
        formatting, 152–153
        guidelines on, 153
        in other languages, 154
        searching for, 64
        spam, 153–154
    to image description pages, 266
    internal, 82
        between namespaces, 150
        formatting, 149–150
        guidelines on, 151–152
        redlinks. *See* redlinks
        self-link, 152
    to sections, 156–157
Linux, 39
lists, 9–10, 83–86, *84*
    bulleted, 147, *147*
    vs. categories, 86, 247
    numbered, 148, *148*
logging in, 308. *See also* accounts, creating
logos, history of, 47, *47*, 448

M

m. *See* minor edits
magic words (MediaWiki variables), 284–285

tables, 278–280
    sortable, 280
    syntax, 279–280
tabs, 100–101, *101*
    Discussion, 101. *See also* talk page
    Edit This Page, 101, 132. *See also* editing
    History, 101. *See also* page history
    Move, 101. *See also* moving articles
    Watch, 101, 319, *321*. *See also* watchlists
talk pages, 113–117, 337–339, *338*. *See also* user
        talk pages
    archiving, 113, 318
    guidelines for, 116, 337–341
    namespace, 29
    signing, 115–116, 341. *See also* signatures
    threaded discussion on, 113–115, *115*
taxobox templates, 273
teachers, Wikipedia and, 464–466
Telugu Wikipedia, *410*
templates, 145, 270–277
    color coding of, 102
    creating, 275–277
    hidden, 274
    inline, *206*, 273
    namespace, 29
    parameters, 271–272
    placing, 270–272
    substitution, 272
    syntax, 270–271, 276–277
    transclusion, *272*
    used on a page, *134*, 136, 271
    uses of
        citation, 192–193
        cleanup, 102, 201–202, *201*
        disambiguation, 239
        formatting pages, 275, 281
        helpme, 318
        infobox, 103, *178*, 273–274, *274*
        interwiki, 441–442, *441*
        inuse (for drafting), 139
        language icons, 154
        merging articles, 241–242, *241*
        navigation, 274
        stubs, 204
        succession boxes, 274–275, *275*
        taxobox, 273

unreferenced articles, 206, *206*
user warning, 401
userbox, 315, 317
warning, *14*, *15*, *18*, 102, 121
welcome, 275, 333
TeX markup, 283–284, *284*
There Is No Cabal (TINC), 351
thesaurus
    Roget's, 86
    Wiktionary, 428
threaded discussion. *See* talk page, threaded
        discussion
Three-Revert Rule (3RR), 142, 385. *See also* edit
        wars
    policy on, 375
time-sensitive topics, templates, 164
TINC (There Is No Cabal), 351
titles, of articles. *See* article titles
to-do lists, article, 203
TOC. *See* table of contents (TOC)
tone. *See* writing style, tone
toolbar. *See* editing toolbar
toolbox, 78–79, *78*
tools, for editing, 210
transclusion, of templates, 272
translations. *See* languages, translations
        between
transportation, articles about, 9
transwiki, 442
trivia sections, 125
trolls, 341
Troubleshooting page, 343
Truth in Numbers (film), 347

U

Uncyclopedia, 351
underlined text, formatting, 146
undo edit link, 142. *See also* reverting edits
unicode. *See* languages, script support
unified login, 412, 420. *See also* accounts,
        creating
universities. *See* schools, Wikipedia use in
Unix, 37, 39
unusual articles, 352–353
urban myths, 183
user namespace, 25–26

user pages, 25–26
    braglist, 166
    content of, 315–317
    guidelines, 23
user scripts, 313–314
user talk pages, 25, 116–117, 318–319
    evaluating editor contributions and, 110
    new messages alert, 116, *116*
    replying to messages on, 117
userboxes, 317
    for languages spoken, 315
usernames, 305–308. *See also* accounts
    changing, 306–307
    finding, 307–308
    global. *See* unified login
    guidelines, 305–306
    policy on, 377
    and real names, 315–316
    usurping, 306

V

vandalism, 209–210
    patrolling for, 210
    policy on, 375
    undoing, 142, 209–210. *See also* reverting
        edits
variables
    MediaWiki, 284–285
    in templates. *See* templates, parameters
Verifiability, 13–14, *14*, 206
    policy on, 374
version history. *See* page history
video. *See* media files
Village Pump, 342–343, 344
voting. *See also* polling
    in deletion debates, 342
    and discussion, 341–342
    guideline on. *See* polling, guideline on

W

Wales, Jimmy, 46, 347
    arbitration and, 399
    statement of principles, 334–335
    Wikia and, 443
    Wikimedia Foundation and, 448, 450

Y

Electronic Frontier Foundation
Defending Freedom in the Digital World

Free Speech. Privacy. Innovation. Fair Use. Reverse Engineering. If you care about these rights in the digital world, then you should join the Electronic Frontier Foundation (EFF). EFF was founded in 1990 to protect the rights of users and developers of technology. EFF is the first to identify threats to basic rights online and to advocate on behalf of free expression in the digital age.

The Electronic Frontier Foundation Defends Your Rights!
Become a Member Today!
http://www.eff.org/support/

Current EFF projects include:

Protecting your fundamental right to vote. Widely publicized security flaws in computerized voting machines show that, though filled with potential, this technology is far from perfect. EFF is defending the open discussion of e-voting problems and is coordinating a national litigation strategy addressing issues arising from use of poorly developed and tested computerized voting machines.

Ensuring that you are not traceable through your things. Libraries, schools, the government and private sector businesses are adopting radio frequency identification tags, or RFIDs – a technology capable of pinpointing the physical location of whatever item the tags are embedded in. While this may seem like a convenient way to track items, it's also a convenient way to do something less benign: track people and their activities through their belongings. EFF is working to ensure that embrace of this technology does not erode your right to privacy.

Stopping the FBI from creating surveillance backdoors on the Internet. EFF is part of a coalition opposing the FBI's expansion of the Communications Assistance for Law Enforcement Act (CALEA), which would require that the wiretap capabilities built into the phone system be extended to the Internet, forcing ISPs to build backdoors for law enforcement.

Providing you with a means by which you can contact key decision-makers on cyber-liberties issues. EFF maintains an action center that provides alerts on technology, civil liberties issues and pending legislation to more than 50,000 subscribers. EFF also generates a weekly online newsletter, EFFector, and a blog that provides up-to-the minute information and commentary.

Defending your right to listen to and copy digital music and movies. The entertainment industry has been overzealous in trying to protect its copyrights, often decimating fair use rights in the process. EFF is standing up to the movie and music industries on several fronts.

Check out all of the things we're working on at http://www.eff.org and join today or make a donation to support the fight to defend freedom online.

ELECTRONIC FRONTIER FOUNDATION · 454 SHOTWELL STREET · SAN FRANCISCO, CA 94110 · 415.436.9333

MY NEW MAC
52 Simple Projects to Get You Started

by WALLACE WANG

Mac OS is a beautiful and reliable operating system, but it can be confusing to brand-new Mac owners—especially if they come from Windows. Using 52 essential step-by-step projects every Mac owner should know, *My New Mac* encourages readers to treat their new computer as an opportunity for fun and exploration, not something serious and overwhelming. Rather than focus each chapter on a specific program or feature of Mac OS (as most beginner books do), Wallace Wang takes a project-oriented approach that mirrors the sorts of things people want to do with their Mac, such as surf the Internet, send email, listen to CDs, take notes, or play with digital photos.

APRIL 2008, 480 PP., $29.95
ISBN 978-1-59327-164-0

UBUNTU FOR NON-GEEKS, 3RD EDITION
A Pain-Free, Project-Based, Get-Things-Done Guidebook

by RICKFORD GRANT

The new edition of this best-selling guide to Ubuntu Linux for beginners covers Ubuntu 8.04, Hardy Heron. Step-by-step projects have readers interact with their system, rather than just read about it, as they build upon previously learned concepts. *Ubuntu for Non-Geeks* covers topics likely to be of interest to the average desktop user, such as installing new software via Synaptic; Internet connectivity; working with removable storage devices, printers, and scanners; burning DVDs, playing audio files, and even working with iPods. This edition features increased coverage of Bluetooth, wireless networking, modems, and, of course, coverage of the significant new features in the 8.04 release.

JUNE 2008, 360 PP. w/CD, $34.95
ISBN 978-1-59327-169-5

THE MANGA GUIDE TO STATISTICS
by SHIN TAKAHASHI

This unique guide to learning statistics combines the Japanese-style comics called *manga* with serious educational content, making the challenging discipline of statistics entertaining and less daunting. *The Manga Guide to Statistics* uses real-world examples like teen magazine quizzes, bowling games, test scores, and ramen noodle prices to teach statistics. Reluctant statistics students will enjoy learning along with the book's charming heroine Rui, who wants to learn statistics in order to impress the dreamy Mr. Igarashi. With the help of her tutor, Mr. Yamamoto, Rui learns statistics—but is it enough to impress Mr. Igarashi?

NOVEMBER 2008, 224 PP., $19.95
ISBN 978-1-59327-189-3

THE ESSENTIAL BLENDER
Guide to 3D Creation with the Open Source Suite Blender

edited by ROLAND HESS

Blender is the only free, fully integrated 3D graphics creation suite to allow modeling, animation, rendering, post-production, and real time interactive 3D with cross-platform compatibility. *The Essential Blender* covers modeling, materials and textures, lighting, particle systems, several kinds of animation, and rendering. It also contains chapters on the compositor and new mesh sculpting tools. For users familiar with other 3D packages, separate indices reference topics using the terminology in those applications. The book includes a CD with Blender for all platforms, as well as the files and demos from the book.

SEPTEMBER 2007, 376 PP. W/CD, $44.95
ISBN 978-1-59327-180-0

STEAL THIS COMPUTER BOOK 4.0
What They Won't Tell You About the Internet

by WALLACE WANG

This offbeat, non-technical book examines what hackers do, how they do it, and how readers can protect themselves. Informative, irreverent, and entertaining, the completely revised fourth edition of *Steal This Computer Book* contains new chapters that discuss the hacker mentality, lock picking, exploiting P2P filesharing networks, and how people manipulate search engines and pop-up ads. Includes a CD with hundreds of megabytes of hacking and security-related programs that tie in to each chapter of the book.

MAY 2006, 384 PP. W/CD, $29.95
ISBN 978-1-59327-105-3

PHONE:
800.420.7240 OR
415.863.9900
MONDAY THROUGH FRIDAY,
9 AM TO 5 PM (PST)

FAX:
415.863.9950
24 HOURS A DAY,
7 DAYS A WEEK

EMAIL:
SALES@NOSTARCH.COM

WEB:
WWW.NOSTARCH.COM

MAIL:
NO STARCH PRESS
555 DE HARO ST, SUITE 250
SAN FRANCISCO, CA 94107
USA

Colophon

How Wikipedia Works was written on a MediaWiki wiki. It was laid out in Adobe InDesign. The font is Avenir.

The book was printed and bound at Malloy Incorporated in Ann Arbor, Michigan. The paper is Glatfelter Spring Forge 60# Smooth Eggshell, which is certified by the Sustainable Forestry Initiative (SFI). The book uses a RepKover binding, which allows it to lay flat when open.

Updates

Visit *http://www.nostarch.com/wikipedia.htm* for updates, errata, and other information.